HANDBOOK OF PULP & PAPER TERMINOLOGY
A Guide To Industrial and Technological Usage

by Gary A. Smook

HANDBOOK OF PULP & PAPER TERMINOLOGY

A Guide To Industrial and Technological Usage

by Gary A. Smook

 ANGUS WILDE PUBLICATIONS

Vancouver 🐦 Bellingham

Published by: **Angus Wilde Publications**
#203 - 628 West 13th Avenue
Vancouver, B.C. V5Z 1N9

Available in   Angus Wilde Publications
the USA from: P.O. Box 1036
                          Bellingham, WA 98227-1036

Canadian Cataloguing in Publication Data

Smook, G.A. (Gary A.), 1934–
    Handbook of Pulp and Paper Terminology

ISBN 0–9694628–0–8

1. Paper making and trade—terminology.
2. Wood-pulp industry—terminology.   I. Title.

TS1085.S66 1990   676´.03   C90–091417–3

ABOUT THE AUTHOR

Gary A. Smook is an instructor in pulp and paper technology and unit operations at the British Columbia Institute of Technology in Burnaby, B.C., Canada.

Mr. Smook is prominent in the North American pulp and paper industry, principally as the author of the best-selling *"Handbook for Pulp and Paper Technologists"*, which has 30,000 copies in print along with French and Spanish translated editions. He is also the author of more than 30 papers on various aspects of kraft pulping, paper machine operation, technical management, and industrial training, and has contributed to two additional books. He has been awarded the Weldon Gold Medal (CPPA, 1974) and TAPPI Fellowship (1987). He is a past chairman of the CPPA Professional Development Committee and an active member of the Joint Textbook Committee of the Paper Industry.

Mr. Smook is a chemical engineering graduate from the University of California, Berkeley, and a registered professional engineer. He accepted his present teaching position in 1974 after a distinguished 18-year career in industry, and now divides his time between teaching, consulting and writing activities. His industrial consulting has focussed on the areas of kraft mill process optimization, paper drying, technical information systems, and training seminars.

To Hilda —
without your support
and encouragement,
this book would not
have been possible

CHAPTERS OF HANDBOOK

PREFACE

Chapter   **Raw Material Terminology**   *Page*
1   Wood Raw Material For Pulping 1
              (Includes: Forestry, Logging/Woodroom Operations,
                Chipping, Chip Quality, & Material Handling)
2   Wood & Fiber: Structure & Identification 23
3   Nonwood Fibers 31

              Chemical Terminology
4   Cellulose Chemistry 37
              (Includes: Basic Organic Chemistry & Analytical Techniques)
5   Papermaking Chemistry and Microbiology 51
6   Pulping By-Product Processing & Chemistry 65

              Pulping Terminology
7   Mechanical Pulping 71
8   Chemical Pulping 79
9   Chemical Recovery & Steam Plant 97
              (Includes: Black Liquor Handling/Evaporation, Boiler Equipment/Operation,
                Steam Handling, Recausticizing & Lime Kiln)
10   Pulp Bleaching & Brightening 119
11   Properties/Testing of Pulp and Fiber 129
              (Includes: Refining Actions on Fibers)
12   Pulp & Stock Handling 141
              (Includes: Washing, Screening, Cleaning, Refining,
                Secondary Fiber Processing, Deinking, etc.)

              Papermaking Terminology
13   Papermaking Processes & Equipment 159
14   Paper Product Properties 209
              (Includes Characteristics, Testing, Defects, etc.)
15   Papermachine Clothing 245
16   Paper and Paperboard Grades 251
17   Paper Coating 263
              (Includes: Pigmented and Functional Coating)

              Paper Finishing & Converting Terminology
18   Paper Finishing & Converting 279
              (Includes: Handling & Shipping)
19   Printing 293

              Utilities & Environmental Terminology
20   Water and Effluent Treatment 307
21   Air Pollution Abatement 325
22   Energy Conversion & Electrical Systems 333

              Industrial Terminology
23   General Industry Terminology 339
24   Maintenance, Mechanical & Corrosion 347
25   Quality Control and Statistics 361
26   Cost Accounting & Engineering Economics 367
27   Abbreviations and Acronyms 371

              Word Index 375

PREFACE

The typical person who goes to work within the producing sector of the pulp and paper industry or has dealings with the industry, whether in a technical capacity or other role, is immediately confronted by seemingly arcane terminology. Without reference to a suitable dictionary or glossary, the deciphering of the new lexicon represents a considerable impediment to precise and efficient communication.

The few obtainable "pulp and paper dictionaries" are limited in scope and tend to concentrate on paper grade definitions. These books are helpful to paper salespeople, but they do not adequately serve the needs of operations-oriented engineers and other mill personnel such as technicians, operators, accountants, statisticians, etc. Nor do they serve the needs of consultants or vendors who deal with the industry. This completely new Handbook of Pulp and Paper Terminology is the most comprehensive collection of technical and operational terms ever assembled with respect to pulping, papermaking and related operations.

Newcomers to the industry should be aware of the efforts made by the ISO (International Organization for Standardization) and other organizations to standardize industrial terminology. Thus far, definitions for only a small number of commonly encountered terms within the pulp and paper industry have been accepted as international standards, and compendiums of these terms are not widely distributed. Where applicable, definitions compatible with the standardized versions have been utilized in this handbook of terminology.

The ever-increasing complexity of pulp and paper technology is continually creating new terms, utilizing idioms from other occupational groups and reinterpreting old words. Because most industrial terms are not standardized, they may have different meanings in different regions, or in different sectors of the industry, or in different contexts. The listener or reader should generally be aware of the context within which a word is used. This handbook cannot serve as an arbiter of usage, but should help to promote an awareness of generally accepted usage and assist in stabilizing terminology.

Although the sources are not given, all terms are presented in the language of those who use them. The overriding objective has been to categorize and define those words and terms that are commonly used within the industry. Occasionally, the basic definition has been embellished with factual information to make the term more understandable, but encyclopedic treatment is not presented. Little consideration has been given to etymology. No attempt has been made to provide pronunciation and syllabication.

ORGANIZATION OF HANDBOOK

Chapters

This handbook of terminology is organized into twenty-six (26) chapters according to specific technology or area of operations. This format allows users the opportunity to become more intimately familiar with the particular terminololgy which is most relevant to their needs. Inevitably, some definitions overlap into more than one chapter; where this occurs, the choice of chapter for inclusion of a term has been arbitrary. An additional chapter (No. 27) has been provided for deciphering those abbreviations and acronyms which are commonly used within the industry.

The primary goal has been to produce a definitive compilation of pulp and paper industrial and scientific terminology to serve the needs of the operations-oriented engineer or technologist. Toward that end, selected terms have been included from such related areas as forestry, logging, material handling, fiber physics, general chemistry, organic chemistry, water treatment, steam systems, electrical systems, corrosion, statistics, cost accounting, etc. Entries of paper grades have been intentionally limited (all within Chapter 16) to the major classifications and categories of interest to mill people; more specialized products are already adequately defined in other volumes (e.g., *The Dictionary Of Paper*). Instrumentation and computer terms have been totally excluded because adequate dictionaries of terminology are available in each of these specific areas, and piecemeal compilations would not be helpful or appropriate. Likewise, tree species are identified and defined in a number of texts, and for that reason have been excluded as entries in this Handbook.

Presentation

Words and compound terms are presented alphabetically. Occasionally, additional reference entries for a term have been used where placement is not obvious. If a word or compound term cannot be located easily, referral to the Index is recommended.

Generally, words are given in the form of nouns and gerunds. Where adjectives are used, they are so identified as [adj].

Cross referencing generally follows the rule of going from the general to the specific. However, occasionally a "see also" reference is made from a specific term to a general term so that the reader is made aware of other related terminology. Cross-referencing is generally to other terms within the same chapter, but also occasionally to a term in a different chapter.

Synonyms (syn.) given after a definition are often used interchangeably with the principal entry, but in some cases may not be exact equivalents.

Index

All word and compound term entries are listed alphabetically in the index and referenced to the applicable chapter. Where more than one chapter is cited, the term is defined differently in each chapter. Most modified word entries (i.e., compound terms) are further listed according to the modified word. For example, the entries:

    squeeze rolls
    stretch roll
    suction roll

are also listed as:

    roll(s)
      squeeze
      stretch
      suction

ACKNOWLEDGMENT

As the sole author, I am responsible for all phases of this handbook including the organization, selection of terms, and for the definitions themselves. It is obvious, however, that a compilation of terminology cannot be the exclusive product of one person's effort. Indeed, a vast number of sources have been tapped, far too many to be named here. Generally, I relied on the definitions as provided by the authors of books, journal articles and reference materials. I have not knowingly quoted a definition from another copyrighted source. Any apparent similarity to other "protected definitions" is purely accidental and the result of limitations in language.

On a very personal level, I thank my wife, Hilda Wiebe, for her understanding of the long periods that I spent "holed up" in my basement office during preparation of this handbook and for her full support of the project.

FEEDBACK

Because of the vast amount of material surveyed while preparing this book, it is inevitable that differences in perspective, background and connotation will cause certain definitions to be imprecise or incorrect. Perhaps some relevant terms have been inadvertently omitted. I welcome the critical comments of readers and users of this book to bring errors and inadequacies to my attention, so that I can incorporate improvements and corrections in subsequent editions.

DISCLAIMER

While no effort has been spared to make this handbook as complete and accurate as possible, it may contain typographical errors or mistakes in content. This handbook should be used only as a general guideline, and not as the ultimate or authoritative source of technical information. The author and Angus Wilde Publications shall have neither liability nor responsibility to any person or entity with respect to any loss or damage caused, or alleged to be caused, directly or indirectly, by the information contained in this book.

Gary A. Smook
Vancouver, February, 1990

Chapter 1
Wood Raw Material for Pulping
(Includes Forestry, Logging, Woodroom Operations, Chipping,
Chip Quality & Material Handling)

A

ABRASION BARKER: Any debarking equipment in which single stems are rotated and brought into contact with an independently rotated abrasion wheel. The wheel surface may be toothed or spiked.

ACCEPTED CHIPS: (1) Chips which are within acceptable limits for length, thickness, cleanliness, etc. (2) Portion of the chips remaining after removal of oversize, overthick and fines fractions; portion which is utilized as pulping raw material.

ACCUMULATOR FELLING HEAD: Cutting head for felling trees with an attachment for holding several severed trees. The accumulator feature increases the productivity of the conventional feller-buncher.

AERIAL SURVEY: See CHIP INVENTORY.

AFFORESTATION: Establishment of a tree crop on land not previously or recently forested. See also FORESTATION, REFORESTATION.

A-FRAME: Support structure with the main members set on slopes suggesting the letter "A".

AGED CHIPS: Chips that have been stored in a pile for varying lengths of time before being utilized in a pulping process, as opposed to "fresh chips".

AGRIFORESTRY: Forest crops on agricultural land, typically featuring rows of trees with fertilization and short rotation.

AIR CANNONS: Air nozzles mounted around the sides of a bulk storage silo (e.g., for chips or hog fuel) to control bridging and assist evacuation. Typically, the cannons fire in pairs at preset intervals.

AIR CLASSIFICATION: Fractionation of a nonuniform bulk material (e.g., wood chips) on the basis of whether or not the discrete constituents are entrained in a rising air column, a function of their density and air resistance. Syn. Winnowing, Air Elutriation. See also AIR FLOTATION SEPARATOR.

AIR DENSITY SEPARATOR: See AIR FLOTATION SEPARATOR.

AIR-DRIED CHIPS: Chips that have been seasoned by exposure to air without artificial heat.

AIR FLOTATION SEPARATOR: Device used to separate heavy, dense pieces of material from wood chips. Syn. Air Density Separator.

AIRVEYING: See PNEUMATIC CONVEYING.

ALLOWABLE CUT: Volume of wood which may be harvested from a managed forest within a given period. This volume is offset by the estimated growth volume, thus providing perpetual yield.

ANGLE OF REPOSE: Angle formed between the horizontal plane and the side of a freely-formed conical pile when a solid bulk material falls evenly from a moderate height; taken as an indication of the flow characteristic of the material. See also FLOWABILITY.

ANNUAL CUT: Volume or number of trees felled or salvaged from a specified area during the year, whether removed from the forest or not.

ANNUAL INCREMENT: Annual growth rate of forest crops, usually in units of cubic meters of wood per hectare or metric tons of dry wood per hectare. (Reported increments range from 0.5 ton/ha for northern spruce to 50 ton/ha for experimental stands of bamboo.) Syn. Growth Rate, Annual Yield.

APPARENT DENSITY: See BULK DENSITY.

ARCH: (1) Supporting device mounted behind a skidder, which is used to lift one end of a log to reduce sliding resistance. (2) Bridge or dome structure formed by bulk solid material over the opening of a bin or hopper which causes the flow to stop.

ARTICULATED: [adj] Descriptive of a boom or other machine member that is hinged at the center.

ATTRITION MILL: Shredding machine used for reducing chips into pin chips or strands for certain grades of particleboard.

B

BACKCUT: Final cut in felling a tree; made on the side away and slightly above the undercut which governs the direction of fall.

BAND SAW: Saw consisting of a continuous piece of flexible steel, with teeth on one or both sides, used to cut logs into cants or to rip lumber.

BARK ADHESION: Degree to which bark adheres to wood, an indication of barking difficulty (or "barkability"). Bark adhesion is measured as the force required to pull the bark off when the force is applied perpendicular to the plane of the interface, usually in units of kg/cm². Syn. Bark-To-Wood Bonding Strength. See also CAMBIUM SHEAR.

BARK CONTENT (of chips): Percent by weight of bark in a chip sample.

BARK DRYING: See HOG FUEL DRYING.

BARKED WOOD: Logs which have been through a barker and are relatively free of bark. Syn. Debarked Wood.

BARKER (or DEBARKER): (1) Machine used to remove bark from logs. See also ABRASION BARKER, HYDRAULIC BARKER, ROTARY DRUM BARKER, RING SHEAR BARKER, CUTTERHEAD BARKER, and STATIONARY FRICTION BARKER. (2) One who removes bark from a bolt, log or tree.

BARKER LOSSES: Losses of usable pulpwood during barking operations, usually reported as a percentage of incoming wood. Barker losses typically range from 1 to 5% depending on the size and species of log and on the method of barking.

BARKING (or DEBARKING): Process of removing bark from the surface of logs.

BARKING CLEANLINESS (of logs): Percentage of surface area free of bark.

BARKING DRUM: See ROTARY DRUM BARKER.

BARKING EFFICIENCY: Efficiency of bark removal, usually indicated indirectly by the bark content of the resultant chips.

BARK POCKET: Bark that is embedded in wood and cannot be removed by conventional log barking methods.

BARK PRESS: Equipment that extracts free moisture from wet bark and other wood residues by application of pressure.

BARK RECLAIM: Recovery of bark and hog fuel from storage for subsequent utilization as fuel in the boiler.

BARK SHREDDER: See SHREDDER.

BASAL AREA: Cross sectional area of a tree at breast height (1.3m); usually measured as part of a method to estimate the volume of timber in a given stand.

BASIC WOOD INCREMENT: Measure of the rate of total wood production of trees or stands, based on the weight or volume of wood produced in a given period. See also ANNUAL INCREMENT.

BELT CONVEYOR: Heavy-duty conveyor for chips and other bulk materials consisting of an endless belt driven over a supporting system of carrying and returning idler-rollers.

BELT CONVEYOR SCALE: Device that measures the rate at which bulk material is being conveyed and delivered on a moving conveyor belt; commonly used to monitor the weight of chips transported to a digester. Syn. Totalizing Belt Scale, Weightometer.

BIG-STICK LOADER: Short, rotatable horizontal boom attached to a center post mounted on a pulpwood truck.

BILLET: Any short log. Syn. Bolt, Block.

BIN: See HOPPER.

BINDER: Any device for securing a load of logs on a vehicle or for bundling in water. Syn. Wrapper.

BIN DISCHARGER: Device attached to the bottom of a bin to assure a continuous outflow of bulk solid material without bridging, jamming, segregation or ratholing. Syn. Bin Activator. See also VIBRATOR, LIVE BOTTOM BIN.

BLAZING: Marking trees with a shallow axe cut to indicate a boundary or trail, or to identify trees for cutting.

BLOCK: (1) Any short log. Syn. Bolt, Billet. (2) A large pulley used in logging to change the direction of the haul or increase pulling power. (3) A designated area to be logged. Syn. Strip, Setting.

BLOWER: See EXHAUSTER.

BLOWING: Term applied to pneumatic conveying of chips.

BLOWING-DISCHARGE CHIPPER: Disc chipper with vanes fitted to the disc which blow the chips out the top of the casing, and can transport the chips to a cyclone up to 60 m away.

BOARDS: Lumber of less than 2 inches nominal thickness. (Categories of greater thickness are dimension lumber, studs, and timbers.)

BOARD FOOT: Unit of measure for standing timber, logs and lumber equal to a board 1 foot wide, 1 foot long, and 1 inch thick. The term, "foot board measure" (FBM), is sometimes used interchangeably.

BOLE: Trunk or stem of a merchantable tree.

BOLT: Any short log. Syn. Billet, Block.

BONE DRY UNIT: Measure of wood-chip volume equivalent to 2,400 pounds of moisture-free wood.

BOOM: (1) Floating logs encircled by a ring of logs fastened together to enclose the raft. Syn. Log Raft. (2) Long beam projecting from the mast of a derrick to support or guide an object to be lifted or swung. Syn. Crane Arm. (3) Derrick for handling logs, usually called a "log boom".

BOOM LOGS: Large logs chained together and encircling floating logs to control their movement.

BOREAL FOREST: Northern forest.

BORER HOLE: Void in the wood made by insects or marine borers.

BREAKAGE: Damage to logs during harvesting operations in the form of cracks, fractures, splits, separations, etc.

BREAKDOWN: Converting barked logs, particularly by sawing longitudinally into cants. Also applies to subsequent sawmilling operations.

BREAKDOWN DECK: Woodroom conveyor designed to break up a load of logs and align them perpendicularly to the direction of travel.

BREAST HEIGHT: 1.3 m above average ground level, used as a reference point for many tree measurements.

BRIDGE CRANE: Lifting machine with a power-operated hoist traveling on a trolley along overhead fixed runways. Syn. Overhead Traveling Crane.

BRIDGING: Formation of arched cavities in a mass of bulk material.

BRIDLE: Two connected chokers placed around a large log.

BROOMAGE: Splintering of logs at the ends creating a broom-like condition. Broomage commonly occurs during tumble debarking in a rotary drum debarker. Syn. Brooming.

BRUSH: Any kind of forest undergrowth. Syn. Underbrush.

BUCKET ELEVATOR: Conveyor for vertical movement of bulk material, consisting of buckets attached to multiple chains or belts.

BUCKING: Sawing felled trees into shorter lengths. The crew member who does this job is called a "bucker".

BULK DENSITY: Weight (or mass) per unit volume of bulk solid material inclusive of void spaces, usually in units of lb/ft³ or kg/m³. Syn. Apparent Density.

BULK HANDLING: Moving, transporting, and storage of bulk materials, such as chips and hog fuel.

BULKHEAD: Upright partition or structural wall (e.g., of wood, steel or concrete) which serves to control material at one end of a storage container or within a process vessel.

BULK SAMPLER: See THIEF.

BULK STORAGE: Storage of large masses or volumes of material.

BULK VOLUME: Volume occupied by a bulk material including both solid volume and void volume.

BULLBUCK: Foreman of a logging crew.

BULL CHAIN: Heavy endless chain used for hauling logs from the water.

BULL OF THE WOODS: Logging superintendent or manager.

BUNCHING: Gathering trees, logs or stems into piles for subsequent skidding by other equipment.

BUNCH-LOADING: Loading several logs at one time, usually bound together with a chain or cable.

BUNDLE BOOM: Log raft made up of strapped bundles of logs.

BUNDLE DECK: Fixed platform where bundles of logs are opened.

BUNDLED LOGS: Bunches or parcels of logs bound together with wire or steel strapping for ease of handling and transport.

BUNK: Heavy steel frame or cradle assembly on logging trucks on which the logs rest.

BUNKER: See HOPPER.

BURL (or BURR): Hard, woody outgrowth on a tree, more or less rounded in form, usually caused by abnormal growth due to injury to the tree.

BUTT: Base of a tree or the big end of a log.

BUTTING OFF: See LONG BUTTING.

BUTTING ROLLS: Fluted, spiral-type rollers, rotating perpendicular to the log flow in a woodroom which force the log against a base plate for proper alignment.

BUTT LOG: First log above the stump (i.e., lowest log from a bole).

BUTT RIGGING: Cable and swivels that connect the mainline and haulback line in a high-lead cable logging system. Logs are attached to the butt rigging with chokers for yarding.

BUTT SWELL: Increased diameter at the base of a tree.

C

CABLE LOGGING: System of log transport utilizing a cable suspended between elevated supports to constitute a track on which carriers can be be pulled, and employing winches in fixed position.

CAMBIUM SHEAR: Force required to remove bark from the surface of a log when the force is applied parallel to the interface. See also BARK ADHESION.

CANT: Partially sawn log ready for subsequent processing by other saws.

CARD: Chip in which the width exceeds the length.

CARRIAGE: In logging, the load-carrying device to which logs are attached that travels along and is suspended above the ground by the skyline.

CATFACES: Defects on tree or log surfaces due to fire or injury, including scars on the trunks of pine trees resulting from turpentine tapping.

CHAIN SAW: Power-driven saw, used to fell trees and buck logs. A toothed endless chain is fitted as the sawing element.

CHASING: Unhooking chokers from logs at the landing. The person who does this job is called the "chaser".

CHECK: Longitudinal fissure in wood resulting from stresses that caused the wood to separate along the grain.

CHEMICAL BARKING: See CHEMICAL PEELING.

CHEMICAL PEELING: Stripping bark from trees after it has been loosened as a result of chemical treatment. Syn. Chemical Barking, Chemibarking.

CHEMICAL TREATMENT (of chips): Chip application (typically by spraying) with any of a number of chemicals which are purported to prevent deterioration and loss of wood substance during storage.

CHIP ANGLE: Acute angle between the cut surface (end of chip) and the shear surface (side of chip).

CHIP BIN: See HOPPER.

CHIPBOARD: Type of panelboard made with relatively large, discrete chips as the basic raw material. Also, used loosely to describe all types of particleboard or fiberboard.

CHIP CLASSIFICATION: Separation and weighing of wood chips into several fractions according to length or thickness, and subsequent calculation of percent by weight for each fraction. Syn. Chip Size Analysis.

CHIP CLASSIFIER: See CHIP SCREEN.

CHIP CLEANING: Process of removing non-wood contaminants from chips, usually by taking advantage of differences in physical properties.

CHIP CLEANLINESS: Freedom from bark, char, rot, dirt and other contaminants.

CHIP CRUSHING: Compression treatment of over-thick chips to develop fissures and cracks in the wood structure, thus improving alkali penetration during subsequent kraft pulping. Syn. Chip Destructuring.

CHIP DAMAGE: Any mechanical or biological action which reduces the quality or value of wood chips as a pulping raw material.

CHIP DESTRUCTURING: See CHIP CRUSHING.

CHIP DIGGER: Device used in conjuction with a suction unloading system which breaks down compacted chips and feeds them into a conveying line.

CHIP DOZER: Bulldozer-type vehicle used for spreading chips on an outside chip storage pile and for reclaiming chips, usually a crawler tractor equipped with a reinforced steel plate mounted in front perpendicular to the ground.

CHIP FINES: See FINES.

CHIP FISSURES: Fractures in the grain direction of the chips which are accessible to liquor penetration during chemical pulping.

CHIP GRAIN LENGTH: Actual grain-direction chip dimension. The term "chip length" is ambiguous with respect to certain types of chips (e.g., headrig chips) where there is little relationship between the longest chip dimension (i.e., "length") and grain length.

CHIP INVENTORY: Measurement of chip storage volume. For large chip piles, a common technique is to utilize aerial photography at about 500 m elevation; overlapping photographs are viewed through a stereoplotter to produce a three-dimensional image from which a technician can determine the dimensions of the pile.

CHIP IRRADIATION: Treatment of chips with electron-beam (beta) irradiation prior to storage as a means of reducing wood substance losses by fungal degradation. (Some disputed studies in the early 1970's indicated increased kraft pulping yield from irradiated chips.)

CHIP LENGTH: Nominal grain-direction dimension of a chip. See also CHIP GRAIN LENGTH.

CHIPPER: Machine for converting pulplogs and/or sawmill residuals into chips for use in a pulping process. See also DISC CHIPPER, DRUM CHIPPER, V-DRUM CHIPPER.

CHIPPER ANGLE: Angle between disc and spout on a disc chipper, or the angle at which logs are fed into the rotating disc; the angle is usually between 30° and 40°.

CHIPPER-CANTER: Machine that makes cants from whole logs using only chipping heads and no saws.

CHIPPER INFEED: That part of the chipping system which delivers wood to the disc (or other chipping element) at the proper speed and orientation required by the cutting action. Syn. Feedworks.

CHIPPER KNIFE: Sharp-edged blade mounted on a disc or other rotating member which provides a cutting action to the infeeding wood. Typically, the wedge shape of the knife builds up a compressive stress in the wood which exceeds the shear strength parallel to the grain and causes chips to split off. Traditional knives are re-sharpened many times before being discarded, but disposable "knife inserts" are now becoming more popular.

CHIPPER SPOUT: See DROP FEED CHIPPER.

CHIP PILE: See OUTSIDE CHIP STORAGE.

CHIP PILE ROTATION: Systematic turnover of chip inventory. Syn. Chip Pile Management.

CHIPPING: Reducing stems, logs and log segments, wood product residuals, and other pulpable wood waste into small pieces of relatively uniform size called "chips".

CHIPPING HEADRIG: Machine equipped with "cutterheads" that processes logs simultaneously into cants and chips without producing sawdust.

CHIP QUALITY: Composite of desirable attributes including uniformity of size and thickness, and freedom from such contaminants as rotten wood, bark, charred wood, and wood fines.

CHIP QUALITY INDEX: Numerical description of chip quality level based on a weighted summation of various measured chip attributes or characteristics.

CHIP RECLAIM: Recovery of chips from storage for subsequent utilization as a pulping raw material.

CHIPS: Small wood sub-divisions produced in a chipper, used for pulp and chipboard manufacture or for fuel, usually 10 to 30 mm long and 3 to 7 mm thick.

CHIP SCREEN: Equipment for segregating wood chips according to length or thickness. Traditionally, this equipment has utilized screening media that is subjected to either a vibrating or shaking action. Syn. Chip Classifier. See also SCALPING SCREEN, ROTARY SCREEN, DISC SCREEN.

CHIP SHREDDING: Increasing the exposed surface of wood chips by splitting along the natural lines of cleavage with minimal breakage across the grain, and with little crushing, bruising, or other mechanical damage to the fiber.

CHIP SILO: Large concrete, tile-lined retention bin for chips being supplied to the digesters or steaming vessels. Typically, a number of silos are used to house different species or qualities of chips; these can discharge simultaneously onto a conveyor belt to provide a blended chip furnish.

CHIP SIZE ANALYSIS: See CHIP CLASSIFICATION.

CHIP SLICER: Machine for reducing the thickness of chips by slicing them into narrower cross-sections.

CHIP TESTER: Technician who monitors chip quality by taking appropriate samples and carrying out tests for chip density, size classification, moisture, bark content, etc.

CHIP THICKNESS: Smallest dimension perpendicular to the grain of a chip, an important parameter with respect to uniform cooking by the kraft process. See also EFFECTIVE CHIP THICKNESS.

CHIP WASHER: Equipment for removing sand, bark, fines and other extraneous material from wood chips.

CHIP WIDTH: Largest dimension perpendicular to the grain of a chip.

CHOKER: Short length of wire rope that forms a noose around the end of a log so that it can be skidded or yarded.

CHUTE: Inclined conduit, often trough-shaped, for conveying free-flowing materials.

CIRCULAR SAW: Round saw with cutting teeth on the perimeter; used in sawmills for trim and cut-off service.

CLAMBUNK: Heavy-duty skidder used to collect logs from a cutting area and convey them to the landing. A front-end rotating grapple picks up each stem and arranges it in the pincer arms located on the bunk assembly. Some clambunks are also equipped with fellers.

CLEARCUTTING: Harvesting all merchantable trees from an area of forest land.

CLEARED LAND: Land permanently cleared of trees, usually as a result of human activities.

COLD DECK: Pile of logs stored for future use; usually built during the summer and early fall to provide logs for winter and early spring mill operation.

COMMERCIAL CHIPS: Chips obtained as a byproduct from typical forest products manufacturing operations, as distinct from chips that are produced under more ideal conditions.

COMMERCIAL SPECIES: Tree species for which there is a current market.

COMMINUTION: Any process of reducing material to smaller pieces. For wood, specific processes include those capable of producing chips, flakes, strands or fibers.

COMPLETE-TREE UTILIZATION: Extraction and utilization of the entire tree, including crown and roots. See also WHOLE-TREE LOGGING.

COMPRESSION BARKING (of chips): Method of removing bark from chips in which a single layer of chips is fed into a nip formed by a pair of rolls. The compression/rolling action serves to break bark free from the wood. Some of the bark adheres to the roll and is doctored off as a reject stream. Compression barking is often employed following a presteaming stage (which serves to plasticize the bark) and prior to a screening stage.

COMPRESSION DAMAGE (to chips): Localized deformation of the wood structure which occurs during chipping with dull knives.

CONCENTRATION YARD: Area at a railroad siding where large quantities of logs are piled for subsequent loading onto rail cars.

CONICAL CHIPPER: See V-DRUM CHIPPER.

CONSERVATION: Ongoing management and protection of natural resources (e.g., forests, wildlife, water, etc.).

CONVERSION: Transformation of a log into any kind of product.

CONVEYING MEDIUM: Fluid which supports and conveys. In a pneumatic chip handling system, air is the conveying medium. In a hydraulic system, water is the conveying medium.

CONVEYOR: Class of equipment for moving material from one end or at some point along a route and discharging it at the other end or at another point along the route. Various types employ endless belts, buckets, chains, cables, screws, water (hydraulic conveying) or air (pneumatic conveying).

COPPICE: Forest growth originating mainly from sprouts or root suckers rather than seed. A eucalyptus tree will typically produce 4 separate crops with "coppice cutting" before a new planting is required.

CORD: Unit of gross volumetric wood measurement for stacked logs equal to 128 cubic feet of wood, bark and space. The standard cord is 4 by 4 by 8 feet.

CORDWOOD: Four-foot long logs that have been cut for forming into a cord.

COUNTERKNIFE: Replaceable metal plate that is bolted to the knife carrier on a disc chipper and provides the lower surface to which the knife is clamped. Most of the wear due to breaking away of chips occurs at this point. Typically, worn-out knives are recycled as counterknives.

CRANE: Lifting device utilizing a traveling hoist. Many different types of cranes are in use for logging and wood handling applications. See BRIDGE CRANE, GANTRY CRANE, JIB CRANE, MOBILE CRANE, DERRICK.

CRANE-WAY: Track on which a traveling crane moves.

CRAWLER: Any machine mounted on and propelled by tracks.

CROOK: Abrupt bend in a log or tree.

CROSS CUTTING: Sawing wood across the grain.

CROWDING ROLLS: Power-driven spiral rolls used in the woodroom to align or index the ends of logs.

CROWN: Upper part of tree, consisting of the main branch system and foliage.

CROWN CLOSURE: Percentage of ground area covered by the vertically projected tree crown areas. Used to characterize forest density and forest type.

CROWN FOREST: Government-owned forest of British Commonwealth countries. In other jurisdictions, publically-owned forest may be identified as "national forest", "state forest" or "provincial forest".

CRUISING: Surveying forest area to obtain general information on forest conditions and timber volumes. The estimate obtained from such a survey is called a "cruise".

CULL: Logs which are rejected, or parts of logs which are deducted in measurement because of defect.

CUNIT: Unit of wood measurement equal to 100 cubic feet of solid volume.

CUTOVER AREA: Forest land from which some or all timber has recently been cut. Syn. Logged Area.

CUTOFF SAW: Large saw, usually circular, used to trim logs to specific lengths before they enter a processing plant.

CUTTERHEAD: Part of a machine that carries the cutting tools for abrading, chipping, or milling.

CUTTERHEAD BARKER: Type of barker that employs a rapidly rotating head with many cutting tools to cut and abrade the bark from an independently-rotating log moving longitudinally. Syn. Rosserhead Barker.

CUTTING: Process of felling trees. Syn. Felling.

CUTTING RIGHTS: Contractual agreement to cut designated timber on a property over a lengthy period, usually exceeding 10 years.

CYCLONE SEPARATOR: Device designed to continuously separate material from conveying air, utilizing centrifugal force and gravity.

D _____

DEADHEAD: Saturated log that floats very low in the water and poses a hazard to small boats. See also SINKER LOG.

DEAD WOOD: Wood taken from standing or fallen trees that have been dead for a considerable period prior to harvest.

DEBARKER: See BARKER.

DEBARKING: See BARKING.

DEBARKABILITY: Relative ease or difficulty in removing bark. See also BARK ADHESION.

DECADENT WOOD: Logs with a high content of decayed wood.

DECAYED WOOD: Portion of a log which is visually stained, discolored or obviously defective in relation to sound wood. Syn. Log Rot.

DECK: Area or platform on which logs are placed. See also LANDING, YARD.

DECURRENT GROWTH: Tree growth that tends to develop a large spreading crown. Syn. Deliquescent Growth.

DEFECTIVE STAND: Timber stand with a high proportion of stump rot, dead trees and snags. (Defective stands are more difficult and costly to harvest, and recovery is low.)

DEFORESTING: Clearing an area of forest without provision for regeneration. Note that clearcutting followed by reforestation is not deforesting.

DE-ICING OF LOGS: Thawing through the cambium layer of frozen logs to loosen the bond between bark and log.

DELIMBER: Machine for delimbing trees consisting of a sliding boom moving inside a stationary boom. Syn. Limber.

DELIMBING: Removing limbs from a felled tree. Syn. Limbing, Lopping.

DENDROLOGY: Identification and systematic classification of trees.

DENSIFICATION: Settling, compaction, and removal of entrained air from a bulk solid material, thus ensuring a uniform and near-maximum bulk density.

DENSITY: Weight (or mass) per unit volume. When applied to bulk materials, such as chips, density must be specified as either bulk density or solid density.

DEPLETION: Decrease in merchantable volume of timber for a managed forest area, possibly due to logging, fire, insect damage, or other cause.

DERRICK: Type of crane often employed in log sorting operations. It consists of a long moving beam or boom (usually a trussed assembly), equipped with a grapple, and pivoted from a vertical, stationary beam. A derrick for handling logs is often called a "log boom".

DIMENSION LUMBER: Lumber that is from 2 inches up to, but not including, 5 inches in thickness and is at least 2 inches wide. Depending on end-use, it can be further classified as framing, joists, planks, rafters, etc.

DISC CHIPPER: Most common design of chipper consisting of a flywheel-type disc with a series of blades mounted radially along the face and projecting about 20 mm. The logs are fed into the rotating disc at an angle of 30° to 40° from the long axis of the log.

DISC SCREEN: Equipment that utilizes a series of vertical rotating discs to separate chips by thickness. The gap between the discs determines the maximum acceptable thickness.

DISEASED WOOD: Wood taken from trees that are harvested when severely infected with blight or infested with insects, etc.

DISTRIBUTION CONVEYOR: Equipment for transporting and allocating bulk solid material to several processing units and/or feed points.

DOG: Projecting steel tooth for biting in and holding a log firmly, as fitted to a log carriage or jack ladder.

DOMINANT TREES: Most numerous and vigorous species in a mixed forest.

DOWN-MILLING: Cutting mode of a peripheral milling cutterhead in which the path traced by the knife is in the same direction as that of the workpiece. A down-milling chipper headrig cuts thicker and more uniform chips than the up-milling counterpart.

DOZER: See CHIP DOZER.

DRAG: Load of logs or trees being skidded.

DRIFTWOOD: Logs lost from rafts or other water conveyance that have subsequently washed up on shore. Salvaged driftwood is typically of good quality, but "beachcombed logs" often retain sand and gravel in open splits and checks, causing subsequent processing problems in the woodroom.

DRIVING: Moving and guiding floating logs along water courses.

DROP FEED CHIPPER: Chipper into which logs are fed by gravity through a sloping chipper spout.

DRUM CHIPPER: Type of chipper in which the knives are mounted on the surface of a rotating cylindrical drum and the log bolt is fed parallel to the drum axis.

DRY BARKING: Any log barking operation that does not utilize water, either during actual barking or for removal and transport of the bark refuse.

DRY BULK DENSITY: Weight (or mass) of dry solid matter per unit volume. The dry bulk density of chips is used to calculate the amount of wood substance in a given volume of chips.

DUFF: Layer of partially decomposed vegetable matter on the forest floor.

DUMPER: Platform on which a trailer or freight car of chips is positioned and then tilted by hydraulic action to unload the chips into a receiving bin.

E _____

EDGER: Machine used for breaking down cants coming from the headrig, squaring the edges and ripping the large timbers into lumber by means of several circular saws.

EDGE TRIMMING: Removal of surface wood from a log or cant to square the edges and produce a block from which different sawn timber dimensions can be produced without resawing.

EFFECTIVE CHIP THICKNESS: Fractional thickness of an over-thick chip that is equivalent to a thinner chip because of longitudinal lamellations (i.e., laminar separations) and fractures which allow cooking liquor to readily penetrate.

ENERGY WOOD: Wood used as an "energy feedstock", i.e., as fuel. Syn. Fuel Wood. See also FUEL CHIPS.

EUCALYPTUS: Genus of evergreen hardwoods native to Australia comprising more than 600 species, of which 30 to 40 are of commercial importance. Interest in eucalyptus as a pulping raw material is growing in view of the tree's high annual growth rate and because the uniformly short and stiff pulp fibers produce a high-bulk sheet that is prized for certain papermaking applications.

EXCURRENT GROWTH: Tree growth that tends to form a well-defined central bole; this type of growth is typical for mature softwoods.

EXHAUSTER: Powerful fan, often of positive displacement design, utilized as an air mover in pneumatic conveying systems. Syn. Blower.

F

FALLER: Person who fells timber as part of a logging operation. Syn. Feller.

FARMER WOOD: Small pulp logs harvested by a farmer and sold to a pulp mill.

FEEDER: Apparatus to extract and control the flow rate of bulk materials from hoppers. The main classes of equipment are rotating feeders, screw feeders, vibratory feeders, and belt feeders. See also ROTARY FEEDERS.

FEEDWORKS: Mechanism on certain barkers, chippers and wood-working machines that moves the log or work piece against the cutters.

FELLER-BUNCHER: Mobile machine with a knuckle boom equipped with a cutting head to grasp, cut, lift, swing, and bunch trees.

FELLER-FORWARDER: Mobile log carrier with attached rotating feller system which is used to grasp a tree, cut it off next to the ground, and place the severed tree on the carrier bunk. When fully loaded, the carrier transports the logs to the landing.

FELLER-SKIDDER: Combination mobile machine for felling and skidding trees, typically only one tree per cycle.

FELLING: Severing a standing tree from its stump. Syn. Cutting, Falling.

FELLING HEAD: Cutting unit used with feller-bunchers, feller-forwarders and other harvesting equipment. The cutting tool can be a disk saw, chain saw, cone saw, or mechanical shear. The feller head may be equipped with accumulator arms that permit the cutting of many small trees in succession before bunching. An optional side tilt mechanism allows more efficient work on sloping or uneven terrain.

FIBERBOARD: General term that applies to various panel products manufactured under heat and pressure from refined wood particles, with the primary bond derived from the inherent adhesive properties of the fibers. Additional bonding or impregnating agents may be used during manufacture to increase strength or improve other properties.

FIBER SOURCE: Any raw material that can be utilized economically as a source of cellulosic fiber, including wood residuals, cereal straws, cotton and linen rags, recycled paper, etc.

FILER: Person responsible for the conditioning of saws and chipper knives.

FINES: Wood particles having very short or fragmented fibers, usually taken as those particles passing through 3 mm (1/8 inch) diameter holes in a classifier.

FLAIL BARKER: Barking equipment utilizing rapidly rotating chains impinging on the log surface.

FLAKEBOARD: Particleboard composed of flakes.

FLAKES: Very thin pieces of wood (usually less than 1 mm thick) used with adhesives to make a type of particleboard. Somewhat thicker flakes are called "wafers"; flakes reduced in width are called "strands".

FLAT CAR: Freight rail car with a flat bottom and without top or sides.

FLIGHT CONVEYOR: Conveyor in which paddles attached to a continuous moving chain push or drag bulk materials along a trough. Syn. Drag Conveyor.

FLOWABILITY: Handling characteristic of a bulk solid material. A free flowing material is characterized by an angle of repose up to 30°. Materials having an angle of repose between 30 and 45° have reasonable flowability. Angles above 45° indicate poor flowability.

FLUME: Trough for carrying water. See also LOG FLUME.

FOREST: (1) Large tract of land covered with a dense growth of trees and underbrush. (2) Dense growth of trees and underbrush covering a large tract of land.

FORESTATION: Establishment of forest on any land area whether or not previously forested. See also AFFORESTATION, REFORESTATION.

FOREST ECONOMICS: Management of forest resources considered from an economic perspective, and therefore principally concerned with the financial costs and returns as affected by the general business environment and other factors.

FOREST GENETICS: Applied science of systematic genetic improvement of a species of tree or a population of trees using such techniques as selection, mutation, and hybridization. Syn. Genetic Tree Improvement.

FOREST INVENTORY: Survey of a forest area to determine the age, condition, volume, species, etc. of standing timber for purposes of planning, management and harvesting.

FOREST LAND: Land primarily intended for growing, or currently supporting forest. "Productive forest land" is capable of producing a merchantable stand within a reasonable time. "Unproductive forest land" is incapable of producing merchantable timber and includes such areas as muskeg, rock, barrens, marshes and meadows. Syn. Timberland.

FOREST PRODUCTIVITY: See ANNUAL INCREMENT.

FOREST RESIDUALS: See SLASH.

FOREST TREE IMPROVEMENT: Practical extension of forest genetics with assistance from such supporting disciplines as ecology, cytology, physiology, morphology, silvics and soil science toward the objective of superior tree production.

FORESTRY: Systematic forest management for the production of timber, provision of wildlife habitat, etc.

FOREST TYPE: Category of forest differentiated by species composition, height and crown closure.

FORWARDER: Any of numerous machines used to forward logs.

FORWARDING: Moving logs off the ground from the felling area to the landing. Syn. Prehauling.

FRAME SAW: Power saw that utilizes one or more web saws in a reciprocating frame.

FREEZE CONDITIONING AGENT (for chips): Chemical applied to chips to reduce handling problems in freezing weather. The agent disrupts the crystal lattice on the wood chip surface and thus reduces the compressive and shear strength of the frozen material; the weakened structure more readily breaks apart, rendering wood chips which are easier to load and transport.

FRESH CHIPS: Chips that are utilized directly for pulping without storage, as distinct from "aged chips".

FRONT-END LOADER: Wheel or tractor loader with a bucket or lifting arms which loads entirely from the front end.

FUEL CHIPS: Low-grade chips produced by mobile chippers from scrub and slash.

FUEL WOOD: Standing trees or logs that are suitable only for firewood or fuel chips.

FULL-TREE LOGGING: See WHOLE-TREE LOGGING.

G

GAFF: Pole with an attached hook used in handling wood. See also PEAVEY, PICKAROON, PIKE POLE.

GANG SAWING: Use of multiple saws on a common shaft.

GANTRY CRANE: Lifting machine with a power-operated hoist that rides on a trolley between two wheeled support columns, each running along a ground-level track. See also PORTAL-TYPE GANTRY CRANE.

GENETIC TREE IMPROVEMENT: See FOREST GENETICS.

GIRDLING: Cutting a ring section of cambium from a tree in order to kill the tree prior to harvesting. This procedure facilitates subsequent bark removal from certain species.

GRADE (of log): Log classification by quality or end-use. Typical grades are peeler, sawlog, pulplog, etc. See also SORT.

GRAPPLE: Heavy set of hinged jaws at the working end of a boom, used to grip logs during yarding or loading.

GREEN: [adj] Term applied to freshly felled logs, or to timber which still contains free water in its cell cavities. Syn. Unseasoned.

GREENCHAIN: Moving chain or belt on which lumber is transported from the saws in a mill. The lumber is pulled from the chain by workers and stacked according to size, length, species or other criteria.

GROUND-LEAD LOGGING: Type of powered cable logging in which the pull of the hauling line is parallel to the ground.

GROUND SKIDDING: Pulling logs along the ground without raising the forward end.

GROUND SLASH: See SLASH.

GROWING STOCK: Sum of all trees (by number or volume) in a designated forest.

GROWTH RATE: See ANNUAL INCREMENT.

GROWTH-TO-REMOVAL RATIO: Ratio of the volume of wood grown to the volume harvested, an index of wood availability for a particular area. Generally, individual ratios are calculated for softwood and hardwood, and often the values are quite different for the same area.

GUYLINE: Cable or wire rope used to stabilize a tower (or spar) so that forces against the tower do not pull it over.

GYPO: Small contract logger. Syn. Jobber.

GYRATORY SCREEN: Type of chip screen having horizontal plane motion due to an eccentric mounting.

H _____

HAMMERMILL: Equipment for reducing the size of bulk solid materials (e.g., wood waste) using pivoted hammers revolving at high speed within a steel casing.

HARDBOARD: Fiberboard with a density of at least 30 lb/cu ft. Several grades are differentiated according to density up to above 60 lb/cu ft.

HARVESTER: Felling machine performing multiple operations on trees at a logging site including topping, slashing, delimbing, stacking, and sometimes forwarding. Syn. Tree Combine.

HARVESTING: Removal of trees from the forest for product utilization.

HATCH: Covered access opening to the top of a tower or bin.

HAUL: Transport distance for a log truck between loading and unloading points.

HAULBACK LINE: Cable used in a cable logging system to pull the butt rigging or carriage out to the operating area.

HAUL-UP: Reclaiming of pulpwood logs from a river or pond into the woodroom, typically by means of a jack ladder.

HEADRIG: Principal breakdown saw in a sawmill, where logs are first cut into cants before being sent to other saws for further processing.

HECTARE: Land area of 10,000 square meters, equivalent to 2.47 acres.

HEEL BOOM: Type of log boom that picks up a log near the end and braces it against the boom to control and carry it.

HIGH-FLOTATION TIRES: Over-size, low-pressure tires for logging vehicles that work effectively in soft, shallow, and erosion-sensitive areas.

HIGHGRADING: Harvesting only the best trees in a stand. Syn. Creaming.

HIGH-LEAD LOGGING: Method of powered cable logging in which the main line blocks are fastened high on a spar tree or portable steel tower to enable the front end of logs being skidded to be lifted clear of the ground.

HOG: Machine for grinding sawmill and woodmill refuse. Several types are in general use, the most common being the "swing hammer hog". See also SHREDDER.

HOG FUEL (or more correctly, "hogged fuel"): Hogged woodmill refuse used to fire boilers, often at the plant where the material was processed.

HOG FUEL DRYING: Reduction in the moisture content of hog fuel by evaporation in order to upgrade its value as fuel, most commonly by utilizing waste heat. The moisture reduction can be from a few percent up to bone dry depending on the particular requirements. Syn. Bark Drying, Biomass Drying. See also ROTARY HOG FUEL DRYER.

HOIST: Device for lifting, consisting of hook, block, lifting medium (e.g. rope or chain), and drum or container for unused rope or chain. Hoists may be manually operated or driven by electricity or air. See also TACKLE.

HOLDING GROUND: Site along a waterway for storage of log booms.

HOPPER: Vessel for temporary storage of bulk materials, such as wood chips. The material is fed into the top and is discharged by power or gravity through outlets at the bottom. Syn. Bin, Bunker, Silo.

HORIZONTAL FEED CHIPPER: Chipper that utilizes a horizontal infeed of logs or offcuts.

HOT LOGGING: Logging operation where the logs go directly from stump to mill without intermediate storage.

HOT POND: Holding flume or pond for de-icing of logs in northern climes utilizing hot wastewater streams from the pulp mill.

HYDRAULIC BARKER: Barker that employs a high-velocity jet of water to erode or blast the bark away from the wood.

HYDRAULIC CONVEYING: Movement of bulk material through a pipeline or channel using a liquid (usually water) as the conveying medium. See also LOG FLUME.

I _____

INDUSTRIAL FORESTRY: Practice of forestry in support of an industrial enterprise or complex, e.g., a saw mill, pulp mill, etc.

INTEGRATED FOREST PRODUCTS OPERATIONS: Coordinated logging, log sorting, sawmilling and woodroom operations that make the best use of timber resources.

INTERFACE OPENING: Spacing between disc faces on a chip thickness screen (typically 8 to 10 mm).

J _____

JACK LADDER: Endless power-driven cable, fitted with dogs, set into inclined trough for hauling logs to the mill deck. Syn. Log Haul-Up.

JACKSTRAWED: [adj] Refers to randomly piled logs as distinguished from logs piled in oriented tiers. See also RICKED.

JAMMER: Lightweight ground-lead yarder mounted on a truck with a spar and boom.

JIB CRANE: Lifting machine with a power-operated hoist traveling on a trolley along a horizontal beam that is cantilevered from a vertical mast and pivoted so that it works over a circular area.

JOBBER: Logging contractor or subcontractor. Syn. Gypo.

K _____

KERF: Width of cut made by a saw.

KICKER: Lever mechanism for pushing logs off the jack ladder onto the deck, or for moving logs from the deck onto the log carriage.

KNIFE: See CHIPPER KNIFE.

KNOT: In wood chipping operations, refers to irregularly shaped chips containing compression or tension wood.

KNUCKLE BOOM: Hydraulically operated loading boom which imitates the action of the human arm.

L _____

LANDING: Area where logs are assembled for subsequent transport. Syn. Yard.

LAP: Unmerchantable tree top left at the logging site. Syn. Lapwood.

LAY: (1) Position of a felled tree on the ground. (2) Position of a log in a pile or load.

LIGHTWOOD: Resin-soaked wood produced by judicial application of certain herbicides to the living tree stem which stimulate resin production in the immediate area of treatment. Syn. Candlewood, Lighter Wood.

LIGNIFICATION: Process whereby plant cells become woody by conversion of certain constituents in the cell wall into lignin.

LILY PAD: Flat disc of wood sawed off the end of a log.

LIMBING: See DELIMBING.

LIVE BOTTOM BIN: Bin equipped with one or more discharge devices that keep the solid bulk material in continuous motion in the bottom portion (i.e., directly over the discharge feeder) to avoid stagnant areas and excessive compaction.

LOADER: Any of a variety of track or wheel mounted machines designed primarily to lift and load.

LOADING BOOM: Structural member used to raise and position logs during loading.

LOG: Length of tree trunk. See also BOLE, BOLT, BUTT LOG, LONGWOOD, PEELER LOG, PULP LOG, ROUGHWOOD, ROUNDWOOD, SAWLOG, SHORTWOOD, STEM, TOP LOG.

LOG BOOM: See DERRICK.

LOG CARRIAGE: Track-mounted vehicle in the sawmill which holds and carries the log through the headrig during breakdown.

LOG FLUME: Long trough through which logs are floated on flowing water, typically used as a method of moving logs in a woodyard. Syn. Sluiceway. See also HYDRAULIC CONVEYING.

LOGGER: One who works at logging. Syn. Lumberjack.

LOGGING: Felling and extraction of logs. See also CABLE LOGGING, HOT LOGGING, SALVAGE LOGGING, SHORTWOOD LOGGING, SKY-LINE LOGGING, TREE-LENGTH LOGGING, WHOLE-TREE LOGGING.

LOGGING OPERATIONS: Includes all operations performed in harvesting and transporting logs from the standing tree to the final landing, which may be the mill site.

LOGGING RESIDUES: Parts of the tree (unmerchantable top and branches) left at the logging site. See also SLASH.

LOG MERCHANDISING: Slashing of logs into segments and segregating according to end-use, e.g., separating higher-quality log segments (for conversion into lumber and veneer) from lower-quality segments (for chips).

LOG PILE: See WOOD PILE.

LOG RAFT: See BOOM.

LOG RULE: Table showing the amounts of lumber which can be sawed from logs of different sizes under assumed conditions.

LOG SCALE: Any system for measuring the wood volume of logs. The collective record is called a "log tally".

LOG TALLY: See LOG SCALE.

LOG YARD: Area next to a pulp mill or saw mill for accumulating an inventory of logs and chips.

LONG BUTTING: Cutting a short log off the butt end of a felled tree to remove butt rot. Syn. Butting Off.

LONGWOOD: Pulpwood 120 inches or more in length.

LOOSE VOLUME: Total space occupied by any accumulation of wood elements, from logs to sawdust, as determined from the external dimensions of a pile or the average height within a storage bin. For logs, a more explicit term is "stacked volume".

LUFFING: Up and down motion of a boom (i.e., crane arm).

LUMBER: Product of a sawmilling operation. Many types and qualities of lumber are produced. See also BOARDS, DIMENSION LUMBER, ROUGH LUMBER, STUDS, TIMBERS.

LUMBER RECOVERY: Yield of lumber from a sawlog (or other grade of log), expressed as the actual volume of finished lumber produced as a percentage of the volume consumed.

M _____

MAIN LINE: In powered cable logging, the cable that does the actual hauling.

MARINE BORERS: Organisms which attack logs that are stored or transported in seawater. The principal boring species are the teredo or "shipworm" and the limnoria or "wood gribble".

MATERIAL HANDLING: Art and science of moving, packaging, and storing substances in any form.

MECHANICAL BARKER: Any machine that removes bark by mechanical methods, as opposed to hydraulic means.

MECHANICAL HARVESTING: Cutting and removing trees from the forest by means of mobile machines (where tree size, terrain, and ground conditions are favorable).

MENSURATION: In forestry, the measurement of timber, both standing and harvested.

MERCHANDIZER: Log handling equipment that sorts and slashes tree lengths into different grades of log segments.

MERCHANTABLE: [adj] Describes trees or stands of a size, quality, and condition suitable for marketing under given economic conditions.

MIDDLE CUT: Log cut from the middle of the bole. Depending on the length of the bole, there may be more that one middle cut, but only one top log or butt log.

MILL DECK: Platform in a sawmill or woodroom on which logs are placed just before processing.

MIXED STAND: See STAND.

MOBILE CRANE: Hoisting machine with a power-operated inclined or horizontal boom and lifting tackle for moving loads vertically and horizontally.

MOBILE TOWER YARDER: Type of powered cable yarding system employing a tower and yarder assembly mounted on a carrier. For easy transport, the tower is laid down over the carrier and is sometimes hinged to shorten its length. The larger towers are telescoping and usually stabilized with a number of guylines.

N

NATIONAL FOREST: In the United States, forest land owned and administered by the federal government. See also CROWN LAND.

NOTCH: See UNDERCUT.

O

OFFCUT: Any unmerchantable portions of a cut timber produced in sawing to a specified dimension, including slabs from the headrig and ends from cut-off saws. These are usually converted to chips.

OLD GROWTH: Standing or harvested timber from a mature, well-established forest (which may or may not be virgin forest).

OPERATING DRUM: Winch drum on a yarder that controls the movements of an operating line during a yarding cycle.

OUTSIDE CHIP STORAGE (OCS): Open-air storage of wood chips, utilizing various pile shapes (e.g., ring, conical, "windrow") and different methods of chip reclaim. Syn. Open-Air Chip Storage.

OVERHEAD TRAVELING CRANE: See BRIDGE CRANE.

OVERSIZE CHIPS: Chips that exceed maximum tolerances for length or thickness. Oversize chips are usually reprocessed into smaller subdivisions using either a rechipper or chip slicer.

OVER-THICK CHIPS: Chips that exceed maximum tolerance for thickness (or chips that will not pulp completely in a standard kraft cook). See also OVERSIZE CHIPS.

P

PANEL PRODUCT: Any of a variety of wood products such as plywood, fibreboard or particleboard, usually sold in 4x8 ft sheets.

PARALLEL BARKING: Debarking of long tree lengths within a rotary barking drum in which logs are aligned with the drum axis and roll on one another as the drum rotates.

PARTICLEBOARD: General term for panel products made from discrete wood particles which are bonded together using synthetic resins under heat and pressure.

PARTICLE SEGREGATION: Variation in the concentration of particles of differing size (e.g., chips, granules, etc.) within a solids handling system during handling and storage. A major cause of particle segregation in a chip handling system is the trajectory effect while building a chip pile; the pin chips and fines are more affected by air resistance and prevailing winds, thus causing nonuniform deposition onto the pile.

PEAVEY: Traditional tool for handling and turning logs, consisting of a stout lever up to 8 ft long equipped with a spike and curved hook to provide grip and leverage. See also GAFF, PICKAROON, PIKE POLE.

PEELER CORE: Slender cylinder of wood remaining when a rotary-cutting veneer operation has been completed. Syn. Veneer Core.

PEELER LOG: High grade log of suitable size and quality for producing rotary cut veneer.

PEEWEE: Small merchantable log.

PICKAROON: Short, pick-like tool used for moving timbers and lumber. See also GAFF, PEAVEY, PIKE POLE.

PIKE POLE: Long pole equipped with a spike and hook, used for handling floating logs. See also GAFF, PEAVEY, PICKAROON.

PIN CHIPS: Pieces of wood with normal chip length, but with width and thickness approximately 3 mm or less. Syn. Shoe Pegs.

PLANTATION FOREST: Forest crop or stand established artificially.

PLYWOOD: Panel product consisting of several layers of thin veneer bonded with resins under pressure. The grain direction usually alternates at right angles between plies.

PNEUMATIC HANDLING/CONVEYING: Movement of bulk solids through pipelines utilizing air (or other gas) as the conveying medium. Syn. Airveying, Blowing.

POLE: Young tree, more mature than a sapling, from the time its lower branches begin to die, up to the time when the rate of height growth begins to slow down and crown expansion becomes marked.

PORTAL-TYPE GANTRY CRANE: Versatile design of gantry crane. The term "portal" indicates that the crane girder (i.e., the cross member) may be extended beyond the end supports on one or both sides, permitting the grapple to work outside the tracks. With some designs, this extension is through the legs, thus the term "portal".

PRE-LOGGING: Removal of smaller trees or "understory" from a mature or over-mature stand of timber.

PRIME CUTTING: Clear cutting of an area that has been prelogged.

PROCESSOR: Portable machine which delimbs and bucks tree lengths into shortwood at the landing.

PRODUCER: Individual who manages a pulpwood harvesting crew and has access to timber resources; he sells his wood directly to the mill or to a pulpwood dealer.

PULP LOG: Log suitable in size and quality for the production of pulp. Pulp logs are usually too small, of inferior quality or the wrong species to be used in the manufacture of lumber or plywood.

PULPWOOD: Wood cut or prepared primarily for manufacture into wood pulp.

PULPWOOD DEALER: Intermediary agent who buys pulpwood from the producers and resells it to the pulpmill, or acts as a commission broker for the pulpmill in procuring wood.

PUSHER: Attachment at the front of a loader which clears the ground in front of the wheels, used to compress a roundwood storage pile.

Q ——————————————

QUARTER SECTION: In land surveying, a quarter of a section (160 acres or 64.75 hectares).

R ——————————————

RAIN FOREST: Evergreen forest associated with high rainfall, high humidity, and the absence of a dry season.

RATE OF TREE GROWTH: Rate at which a tree has laid on wood, measured radially in the trunk by the number of annual growth rings per inch.

RATHOLE: No-flow condition within a hopper characterized by the formation of a stable, hollow core within the bulk material directly above the outlet, typically caused by hopper walls that are not steep enough to cause the solids to flow down.

RECHIPPER: Any of several machines for reducing the thickness or length of over-size chips. See also CHIP SLICER.

RECIPROCATING SCREEN: Type of chip screen having the feed end gyrated and the discharge end vibrated. Additional vibration may be provided by balls bouncing against the underside of the screen surface.

RECLAIMING: Taking out of storage and feeding into the process, as applied to roundwood and chips.

RECOVERY: Net volume of merchantable timber from a logging operation.

REDUCER CHIPPER: Any chipper device which removes surface wood from a log to shape the cross section for subsequent division into lumber.

REFORESTATION: Re-establishment of a tree crop on forest land. See also FORESTATION, AFFORESTATION.

REGENERATION: Renewal of the forest crop by natural or artificial means. Syn. Restocking.

RELEASE: Marked increase in the growth of trees due to removal of competitive plant growth. See also SUPPRESSION.

RELOAD YARD: Landing at which the mode of log transport is changed and/or the size, content, or shape of the load is modified.

RESIDUAL CHIPS: Wood chips produced from the remaining portions of the log after extraction of lumber.

RESIDUAL STAND: Community of trees remaining in a forest area after completion of a logging operation.

RICK: Pile of bolts, usually piled 4 ft high and 8 ft long.

RICKED: [adj] Refers to logs stored in oriented tiers, as distinguished from randomly piled logs. See also JACKSTRAWED.

RIGGING: Cable, lines, blocks and hooks used in cable logging systems.

RING-SHAPED PILE: "Donut shaped" outside chip storage pile with one slice or sector missing. The two open faces form the beginning and end of the pile, the chips being fed to one face and removed from the other face. Syn. Circular Pile.

RING SHEAR BARKER: Type of barker consisting of a rotating ring carrying several arms with scraping tips that apply radial and tangential pressure against the log as it passes through the ring.

RIPPING: Sawing in line with the grain of the wood. Syn. Longitudinal Cutting.

ROSSERHEAD BARKER: See CUTTER-HEAD BARKER.

ROTARY-CUT: [adj] Refers to veneer cut or "peeled" on a lathe where the log is rotated against a fixed knife.

ROTARY DRUM BARKER: Large, angled, hollow cylinder rotating in a horizontal plane through which logs are tumbled and rolled. Bark is removed by the abrading action between logs. Syn. Barking Drum. See also TUMBLE BARKING, PARALLEL BARKING.

ROTARY FEEDER: Rotor with three or more vanes rotating in a housing, commonly installed at the outlet of a hopper or cyclone separator, allowing bulk material to flow out at a controlled rate without allowing gas to enter or leave. Syn. Rotary Air Lock.

ROTARY HOG FUEL DRYER: Tilted cylinder rotating in a horizontal plane which acts as a container for the transfer of thermal energy from a hot gas stream to moisture-laden hog fuel for the purpose of moisture reduction in the hog fuel.

ROTARY SCREEN: Equipment that utilizes a series of perforated plates for chip classification to which are imparted a circular motion.

ROTATION: Planned number of years between formation or regeneration of a forest stand and the final cutting at a specified stage of maturity.

ROUGH LUMBER: Undressed lumber as it comes from the saw.

ROUGHWOOD: Wood without bark removal.

ROUND REDUCER: Reducer chipper which shapes oversize sections of the log, most often the root swelling, into a cylindrical form matching the rest of the log.

ROUNDWOOD: Wood in the form of logs, with or without bark.

S _____

SALVAGE CUTTING: Exploitation of trees that are dead, dying or deteriorating due to overmaturity or damage by fire, fungi, insects, etc. before the timber becomes worthless.

SALVAGE LOGGING: Exploitation of trees that for one reason or other were not removed during the principal logging operation. If the trees were left because of smaller size, the equipment for salvage logging will be different.

SAMPLE PLOT: Section of forest chosen to represent a much larger area, used principally for yield studies; e.g., to determine the effect of different thinning strategies on the annual increment.

SAMPLER: Device for obtaining a representative sample of a bulk solid or liquid. Some automatic samplers operate continuously or intermittently to obtain small portions which are composited over a long period. See also SAMPLE THIEF.

SAMPLE THIEF: Probe for sampling bulk solid materials consisting of two close-fitting concentric tubes with open slots along the sides and ending with a cone. The tubes and openings are sized to accommodate the largest sizes in the material to be sampled. The sample is obtained by inserting the thief (with openings misaligned) vertically into the dry bulk material; the inner tube is then rotated until the openings are aligned, thus permitting the inner tube to fill up; the openings are then again misaligned to retain the sample when the probe is withdrawn. Syn. Bulk Sampler, Grain Sampler.

SAPLING: Young tree intermediate between a seedling and a pole, with specified diameter at breast height from ½ to 4 inches.

SAP PEELING: Stripping bark manually from logs (i.e., by axe or spud) when the cambium is actively growing. When forming new tissue, the cells of the cambium (from certain species) are relatively easy to tear under mechanical stress.

SATELLITE CHIP MILL: Assemblage of equipment for converting pulplogs into chips, located away from the pulpmill.

SAW: Cutting tool for wood consisting essentially of a thin blade of metal, the edge of which is a series of sharp teeth. Various shapes and sizes are used.

SAWDUST: Finely divided wood produced during sawing.

SAWING: Cutting with a saw. See also CROSS CUTTING, RIPPING.

SAWLOG: Log suitable in size and quality for producing lumber.

SAWMILL RESIDUALS: Salvageable materials from logs after lumber has been exacted, including slabs, edgings and trims, but excluding bark and sawdust. Residuals are usually chipped and used in pulp, fiberboard or particleboard manufacture. Syn. Industrial Wood Residuals.

SAWYER: Person in the sawmill who operates the headrig.

SCALER: One who determines the wood volume in a load of logs by applying appropriate formulas or "log rules".

SCALPING RINGS: Serrated rings around the inside of the entrance into a rotary barking drum.

SCALPING SCREEN: Coarse screen for removing overly large pieces of material from the chip flow.

SCARF: Sloping surface left on a butt log or stump as a result of the undercut.

SCARIFICATION: Breaking up the soil surface of a logged site in preparation for regeneration by seeding.

SCREW CONVEYOR: Conveyor for bulk solids consisting of a driven cylindrical shaped helicon within a trough or cylinder housing. Syn. Helix Conveyor.

SCREW FEEDER: Screw conveyor used to supply bulk material at a controlled rate into a process.

SCRUB: Inferior growth of small or stunted trees and shrubs, of no merchantable value.

SEASONING (of wood): Storage of wood on land to reduce pitch problems during subsequent sulfite pulping operations. The seasoning period allows for the escape of volatile compounds and the air oxidation of other wood extractives.

SECOND GROWTH: Forest growth that has come up naturally after the first-growth timber (virgin forest) has been cut or destroyed by fire.

SECTION: Land survey unit measuring 1 mile square (640 acres or 259 hectares).

SEEDLING: Young tree having a diameter at breast height of 1 cm or less. See also SAPLING.

SEED TREE CUTTING: Method of tree harvesting wherein all trees are removed from a large area except for 10 to 15 selected trees per hectare. These trees, isolated but relatively windfirm, act as seed sources and remain until the new seedlings are established.

SELECTIVE CUTTING: Tree harvest limited to certain species above a specified size or value.

SELF-LOADER: Truck equipped with a small boom and winch for loading logs onto its bunk.

SHAVING: Small, thin wood particle produced by cutting action during certain woodworking operations. It is usually feathered along one edge, thicker at another edge, and typically curled.

SHEAR: (1) Mechanized cutting head mounted on a boom for felling timber consisting of a hydraulically-operated scissors-like device; it is utilized on several designs of feller-bunchers and feller-forwarders. (2) Scissors-like device for slashing pulp logs.

SHEAVE: Wheel of a block with a grooved rim to fit over the cable.

SHIM: In chipping or wood handling operations, thin, irregular pieces of wood.

SHOE PEGS: See PIN CHIPS.

SHORT-ROTATION INTENSIVE CULTURE (SRIC): Silvicultural system that utilizes relatively closely-spaced, improved tree species, subjecting them to fertilization and intensive weed control. Variations in technique are utilized, but the objective is always high forest productivity at competitive cost.

SHORTWOOD: Logs less than 120 inches in length.

SHORTWOOD LOGGING: Felling and cross cutting on the spot, with transport of the shortwood. This is the traditional method of logging.

SHREDDER: Machine for converting logging and woodroom residue into boiler fuel. The refuse material is sheared between rotating blades and a set of fixed anvils. See also HOG.

SILO: See HOPPER, CHIP SILO.

SILVICULTURE: Theory and practice of forest cultivation based on scientific principles.

SINKER LOG: Saturated log that does not float in the water. See also DEADHEAD.

SITE PREPARATION: Treatment of a cutover area (e.g., scarification) to create favorable microsites for the establishment and growth of forest tree seedlings.

SKIDDER: Machine used to drag or skid logs from the cutting area to the landing. Several designs are commonly used including "grapple skidders", "chain skidders" and "clambunks".

SKIDDING: Act or process of dragging logs from the stump site to the landing, part of the tree being in contact with the ground. See also GROUND SKIDDING.

SKYLINE CARRIAGE: See CARRIAGE.

SKYLINE LOGGING: Method of powered cable logging used in very rough or broken terrain, in which a heavy cable (the skyline) is stretched tautly between two spar trees or towers, the whole functioning as an overhead track for suspending and transporting logs.

SLAB: Piece cut from the outside of the log, with one flat surface, the other being the natural curve of the log, with or without bark.

SLASH: Debris, such as limbs, tops, bark, knocked-down scrub, etc. left on the ground after a logging operation. Sometimes more precisely called "ground slash". Syn. Forest Residuals.

SLASH BURNING: Disposal of logging debris by controlled burning. The practice is controversial with respect to habitat management and because of pollution problems.

SLASHER: Portable or stationary sawbench having several circular saws mounted at intervals for cutting logs or slabs into suitable lengths.

SLASHING: Act or process of cross-cutting logs to standard lengths. Syn. Trimming.

SLEWING: Rotary or sideways motion of a crane about its vertical axis. Syn. Swinging.

SLIDER BED: Support configuration for a conveyor belt having no moving parts, consisting of low-friction, wear-resistant runners or tracks. A slider bed is typically installed in the impact area of a shortwood conveyer to eliminate damage to idlers and rollers.

SLIVER: Thin, narrow piece of wood split off of a larger piece.

SLOPE ANGLE: In hopper terminology, the angle of the wall from horizontal, generally 60° or more to help promote discharge.

SLUICEWAY: See FLUME.

SMALL LOG MILL: Sawmill designed specifically for efficient processing of logs 5 to 14 inches in diameter.

SNAG: Standing dead tree.

SOLID DENSITY: Term applied to bulk materials when specifying the density of the solid material itself exclusive of void volume.

SORTING: Segregating logs according to species, quality, size, end-use or destination. Logs may be sorted at the stump, at a landing or storage site, or as they enter the mill process. See also GRADE.

SORT YARD: Landing adjacent to the logging area where logs are sorted before transport to the mill.

SOUND WOOD: Wood free from any form of decay or insect damage.

SOUTHERN PINE: Collective term for softwood fiber sources in the Southeastern United States. The principal species included under this term are longleaf pine, shortleaf pine, slash pine, loblolly pine, pitch pine, and pond pine.

SPAR: Tall tree or tower used as a support for one of many cable hauling systems. If a tree is used, it must be stripped of top and branches and rigged with cables. More often, a man-made metal tower is used.

SPLITTER: Shearing device mounted behind a saw to prevent boards or cants from falling into the saw.

SPONTANEOUS COMBUSTION: Fire in a chip pile or hogged fuel pile due to heat buildup, caused by the natural processes of respiration, auto-oxidation and biological oxidation.

SPUD: Hand tool with a narrow, sharp, curved blade and wooden handle especially designed for removing bark from trees or logs.

STACKER: (1) Mobile machine for unloading and stacking or decking logs using the forklift principle and curved top clamps. (2) Equipment for transporting and placing chips onto a storage pile.

STAND: Community of trees similar in species, age, size and condition, clearly distinguishable from adjacent communities, and thereby constituting an identifiable section of timber occurring in a particular area. If both softwoods and hardwoods are present, the term "mixed stand" is applied.

STAND DENSITY: Number of merchantable stems per acre.

STATIONARY FRICTION BARKER: Trough-shaped pocket in which uniformly long and parallel lying logs are kept in a rolling motion against each other so that the rubbing action between logs promotes bark removal.

STEM: Principal axis of a plant. With woody species, the term is applied to all ages and thicknesses.

STICK: Piece of short pulpwood.

STOWAGE: Cargo properly stowed.

STOWAGE FACTOR: Index used to characterize the volume requirements of bulk materials (e.g., chips) for transocean shipment. For chips, the typical unit used is cubic meters per green tonne.

STRANDS: See FLAKES.

STUDS: Wood structural members used as supporting elements in walls and partitions, nominally 2x4, 2x6, or 2x8 (inches).

STUMP: That portion of the trunk of a tree left standing after the tree has been felled.

STUMPAGE: Value of timber as it stands uncut in the woods. In a more general sense, the term can also refer to standing timber itself.

SULKY: Towed logging arch mounted on wheels.

SUPPRESSION: Marked reduction in the growth of trees due to crowding or shading from neighboring trees. See also RELEASE.

SUSTAINED YIELD: System of forest management in which the volume of timber harvested is regulated so that the land will continue to yield indefinitely. See also ALLOWABLE CUT.

SWELL BUTTED TREE: Tree with a large flaring base.

SWINGING: Process of yarding logs from one landing to another.

T _____

TACKLE: Combination of blocks and ropes used for lifting or pulling. See also HOIST.

TALLY: See LOG TALLY.

THINNING: Cutting made in immature stands for the purpose of increasing the growth rate of the remaining trees.

TIMBER: Term loosely applied to forest stands (more specifically called "standing timber") and their products.

TIMBERLAND: See FOREST LAND.

TIMBER RIGHTS: Usually denotes ownership of standing timber without title to the land. Syn. Timber Title, Timber Contract.

TIMBERS: Heavy construction lumber nominally 5 inches or more in the least dimension.

TONGS: Implement used to pick up logs, consisting of a pair of curved arms pivoted like scissors so that a pull on the ring connecting the shorter segments will cause the points on longer segments to bite into the log.

TOP LOG: Uppermost merchantable log to be cut from the tree.

TOPPING: Severing the unmerchantable top portion of the tree.

TOTALIZING BELT SCALE: See BELT CONVEYOR SCALE.

TOWER: Steel mast or framework, generally portable, used instead of a spar tree for cable logging.

TOWING: Transporting a boom from one location to another by pulling from one end.

TRAMP METAL: Unwanted metal which finds its way into a mill chip supply or stock stream.

TREE: Woody, perennial plant generally with a single, well-defined stem and a more or less definitely formed crown.

TREE COMBINE: See HARVESTER.

TREE FARM: Privately owned parcel of land, dedicated to the production of forest crops.

TREE FARM LICENSE: In Canada, a means of assigning to a company the responsibility for management and protection of an area of crown land. It is essentially a lease, and the company must pay the going appraised stumpage value calculated by the government for timber taken out.

TREE HARVESTING MACHINE: See FELLER-BUNCHER, FELLER-FORWARDER, HARVESTER.

TREE-LENGTH LOGGING: Any system of logging that harvests the entire tree, with the exception of the unmerchantable top and limbs.

TRIM ALLOWANCE: Extra length allowed when bucking logs or estimating wood volume to compensate for end injury, uneven cut, etc.

TRIMMER: See SLASHER.

TROLLEY: Carriage mounted on wheels, used on cranes to support and move the hoist mechanism.

TROPICAL HARDWOODS: Mixture of hardwoods which comprises the bulk of the tropical rain forest.

TRUNK: Main stem of a tree. See also BOLE, STEM.

TUMBLE BARKING: Debarking of short tree lengths within a rotary barking drum wherein the logs are tumbled end over end.

TURN: Logs brought to the landing in any one yarding or skidding cycle.

TURN AROUND TIME: Required time for a logging truck upon arrival at the mill site to complete the scaling and unloading operations and start back to the woods.

U

UNDERCUT: Wedge-shaped piece cut in the base of a tree to govern the direction of fall and also to prevent the butt splitting. Syn. Notch.

UNDERSIZE CHIPS: Chips that are below the minimum size acceptable for cooking or refining; chips that pass the smallest accept screening perforation. Sometimes undersized chips are processed separately into pulp, e.g., in a sawdust digester. See also PIN CHIPS, FINES.

UNIT: Measurement of chip volume equivalent to 200 cubic feet of solid wood plus void volume.

UNSCRAMBLER: Usually a V-shaped trough in a wood processing system that takes in a group of logs and passes on single logs.

UP-MILLING: Cutting mode of a peripheral milling cutterhead in which the path traced by the knife is in the direction opposite to that of the workpiece. An up-milling headrig produces chips with a non-uniform thickness profile resembling a scimitar. See also DOWN-MILLING.

UTILIZER: Portable barking and chipping machine which works in the woods.

V

V-DRUM CHIPPER: Design of chipper in which two truncated cones are joined together at their small ends and chipper knives are mounted on the cone surfaces facing the V-shaped space. The log is fed endwise into this space at right angles to the axis of rotation of the chipper assembly. Syn. Conical Chipper.

VENEER: Thin sheet of wood of uniform thickness, usually produced by rotary cutting or slicing of a log.

VENEER CORE: See PEELER CORE.

VIBRATOR: Device that causes the walls of a hopper to quiver, to help move the contents toward the outlet.

VIRGIN FOREST: Natural forest essentially undisturbed by man; it may well be seconday forest.

VOID VOLUME: In log stacks or chip piles, the volume not occupied by wood or bark.

W

WAFERS: See FLAKES.

WEAR PLATE: Plate mounted on the spout side of a disc chipper which guides the logs into the chipper knives and prevents wear on the basic disc.

WEB SAW: Flat, straight strip of steel, toothed along one or both edges, used in reciprocating saws, in contrast to an endless band saw.

WEIGHTOMETER: See BELT CONVEYOR SCALE.

WET BARKING: Any barking operation that utilizes water during actual debarking and/or for removal and transport of the bark refuse.

WHOLE-TREE CHIPS: Product from chipping the whole unbarked tree, usually by means of a mobile chipper at the logging site. Often, chips are mechanically separated into two grades, for pulping and fuel. Syn. Full-Tree Chips.

WHOLE-TREE LOGGING: Felling and transporting the whole tree, complete with the crown, and sometimes even the roots. Syn. Whole-Bole Logging, Full-Tree Logging. See also COMPLETE TREE UTILIZATION.

WINCH: Steel spool connected with a source of power, used for reeling or unreeling cable.

WINNOWING: See AIR CLASSIFICATION.

WOOD: Raw material from the forest consisting mainly of tree boles, but also including branches, stumps and roots.

WOOD COMPOSITION BOARDS: Large grouping of sheet products composed of wooden elements of various sizes held together by adhesive bonds. Included under this heading are fiberboard, particleboard and flakeboard.

WOOD FLOUR: Very finely divided wood.

WOODLOT: Area of land covered with trees where the owner produces pulpwood for sale, generally to a pulp mill.

WOOD PILE: Woodyard storage of pulplogs, either in a parallel-piled stack (common for longwood) or in a random pile (more common for shortwood).

WOOD QUALITY: Arbitrary term used to describe the suitability of a particular wood source for a specific end-use. As applied to pulp and paper operations, the quality of wood tissue is determined by the nature of the various wood cells and their respective proportions in a given tree or tree type.

WOOD RESIDUES: See SAWMILL RESIDUALS.

WOODROOM: Area where logs are processed into chips for the pulp mill, usually including facilities for sorting, barking, and chipping the logs and for screening the chips. Some woodrooms are equipped to extract dimension lumber from the better quality logs.

WOOD SUBDIVISIONS: Grouping that includes chips, sawdust, flakes, wafers, strands, pin chips, and shavings, but excludes fines and wood flour.

WOOD SUBSTANCE: Basic material of which wood is composed (i.e., polysaccharides and lignin), as distinct from the extractives. Sometimes termed "lignocellulose".

WOOD YARD: Area of the pulp mill where logs are sorted, stored and transported to the wood room, and usually including the chip storage and hog fuel storage areas.

XYZ _____

YARD: Place where logs are accumulated. Syn. Landing, Log Dump.

YARDER: Machine equipped with power winches, used to haul logs to the landing.

YARDING: Moving logs from the stump to a landing area. Where the logs are dragged on one end, a more precise term is "skidding".

Chapter 2
Wood & Fiber: Structure & Identification

A

AGGREGATE RAY: Composite ray consisting of several small rays, fibers, and sometimes also vessel elements; it appears under low magnification as a single broad ray.

ALTERNATE PITTING: Refers to bordered pits that are offset in alternate rows across a fiber or vessel element.

AMORPHOUS REGION: Portion of the cell wall of plants in which the carbohydrate chains are not closely ordered.

ANGIOSPERM: Woody plant having true flowers and seeds enclosed in a fruit; this subdivision includes all hardwoods or broad-leaved trees.

ANISOTROPIC: [adj] Not isotropic; exhibiting different properties when tested along axes in different directions.

ANNUAL GROWTH RING: Layer of wood grown by a tree during a single growing season. Annual rings of many species are readily distinguished by the differences in cell growth during the early and late parts of the season. Syn. Annual Growth Layer.

ANNULAR VESSEL: Vessel with close-spaced, wide-spaced or irregular annular thickenings on the inner surface of any otherwise thin wall.

AXIAL: [adj] Oriented along the long axis of a plant stem or parallel to the grain of wood. Syn. Longitudinal.

AXIAL ELEMENT: Term of convenience for any vertical cell, i.e., an element oriented roughly parallel to the axis of the stem. Applies essentially to any cell except a ray. Syn. Longitudinal Element.

B

BALLOON SWELLING: Localized swelling of fibers caused by treatment with concentrated agents such as acids and bases. Balloons appear when the inner layers of the secondary wall burst through the outer layers at weak points.

BARK: Nontechnical term used to describe the rind or covering of stems, branches, and roots; that is, the tissue outside of the vascular cambium of trees and other plants. It consists of inner living bark (phloem) and outer dead bark (rhytidome).

BENDING FACTOR (of pulp fibers): Method of characterizing the shape of fibers which are bent or twisted, defined as the ratio of the fiber length to the distance of greatest fiber spread. Therefore, the value can never be less than 1. The larger the value, the greater is the deformation of the fiber.

BORDERED PIT: Pit with an overhanging margin, i.e., a pit in which the cavity, abruptly constricted during the thickening of the secondary wall, appears to have a border or circle around it when viewed radially with a microscope.

BORDERED PIT PAIR: Two complementary bordered pits in adjacent cells.

BOUND WATER: Water contained within the cell walls of wood and held by hygroscopic forces.

BROADLEAF TREE: See DECIDUOUS TREE, HARDWOOD.

BROWN ROT: Any type of wood rot where the fungal attack concentrates on the cellulose and the associated carbohydrates rather than on the lignin, leaving a light to dark brown friable residue.

BUTT ROT: Decay developing in and typically confined to the base portion of the bole.

C

CAMBIUM: Growing layer between the xylem and the phloem, i.e., between bark and wood; it can include the undifferentiated cells on either side.

CAPILLARY: Any tube or vessel with a fine bore.

CAPILLARY SYSTEM: Network of capillaries. Most woods have a capillary system containing 50–75% of void spaces, consisting mainly of the lumina of fibers, tracheids and vessels. These capillaries are filled with air and/or water.

CELL: General term for the basic structural unit of plant tissue, including wood fibers, vessel members, and other elements of diverse structure and function.

CELL WALL: Membrane that encloses the cell contents. In a mature cell, the cell wall is compound, i.e., it consists of several layers.

CELL WALL CHECK: Fissure in the secondary cell wall, as in the tracheids of compression wood.

CIRCULARITY: Method of characterizing the cross-sectional roundness of a fiber, defined as the ratio of the area of the cross section to the area of a circle having a circumference equal to the perimeter of the fiber. See also ROUNDNESS FACTOR.

COMPRESSION WOOD: Reaction wood in coniferous trees which forms on the lower side of branches and inclined stems, characterized anatomically by heavily lignified tracheids that are rounded in cross section. Zones of compression wood are typically denser and darker than surrounding tissue.

CONFLUENT PITTING: Bordered pit-apertures of adjacent pits coalescing in a spiral groove across a vessel element.

CONIFER: Tree of the gymnosperm group, so called because it is cone bearing. See also SOFTWOOD.

CORE WOOD: See JUVENILE WOOD.

CROSS FIELD: Common-wall contact area between a fiber or vessel element and a single ray cell (ray tracheid or ray parenchyma), usually applied to conifer tracheids.

CROSS-FIELD AREA: Region on a fiber or vessel element composed of one or more cross fields; signifies a ray-crossing area.

CROSS SECTION: Section cut at right angles to the grain; same as transverse section.

CRYSTALLITE: Region in the cell wall of plants in which the cellulose is arranged in a highly ordered, crystal lattice of parallel chains; these regions are of limited size and are separated by amorphous regions. Syn. Micelle.

CUPRESSOID PIT: Small, cross-field pit in earlywood of conifers, with an ovoid or elliptical included aperture that is narrower than the lateral space on either side between the aperture and the border.

D _____

DECAY: Decomposition of wood substance by fungi and other micro-organisms, resulting in softening, changes in color and texture, and loss of strength and weight. Decay is usually categorized into stages as incipient (early, initial), intermediate, or advanced. Syn. Rot.

DECIDUOUS TREE: Any tree shedding its leaves in the autumn, usually a broadleaf (i.e., hardwood) tree.

DENTATE: [adj] Having the appearance of being toothed or with tooth-like projections. Refers to dentate ray tracheids.

DIFFUSE-POROUS WOOD: Wood of certain hardwood species with pores of relatively uniform size and distribution throughout both earlywood and latewood. See also RING POROUS WOOD.

DRY ROT: Special type of brown rot in which a specific fungus transfers water to "dry" wood to facilitate attack.

E _____

EARLYWOOD: Wood produced in the annual ring during the early part of the growing season, usually characterized by large, thin-walled cells. Syn. Springwood.

ELEMENT: General term for a specific cell type, used particularly to distinguish between vessels and the individual cells of which they are composed.

ELEMENTARY FIBRIL: Small, filamentous molecular aggregate, suggested by researchers as the basic structural unit of cellulosic fibers. Syn. Protofibril, Crystallite.

END WALL: Wall at right angles to the long axis of the cell, e.g., the transverse walls of axial parenchyma cells.

EPIDERMAL CELL: Cell derived from the tissue which forms the outermost layer of a leaf or stem.

EPITHELIUM: Layer of parenchyma cells (epithelial cells) surrounding a resin duct.

EXTENDED PIT-APERTURE: Inner pit-aperture whose outline, in surface view, extends beyond the outline of the pit border. See also INCLUDED PIT-APERTURE.

EXTRACTIVE: Any substance in wood, not an integral part of the cellular structure, that can be dissolved out by a solvent that does not react chemically with wood components (e.g. hot or cold water, ether, alcohol, or benzene). See also EXTRANEOUS MATERIALS.

EXTRANEOUS MATERIALS: Non-cell wall constituents of wood which resist extraction by water, steam, or various organic solvents. Examples are starches, pectins, and certain inorganic salts.

EXTRAXYLARY FIBERS: Class of fibers found outside the xylem. Of this class, the bast fibers of certain plants are notably useful for textile and papermaking applications. See also BAST FIBERS.

F _____

FENESTRIFORM PIT: Large window-like pit between ray parenchyma and fibers in the soft pines, red pine, Scots pine and some exotic softwoods. A pit border is located on the fiber side, but is extremely narrow.

FIBER: Long, cylindrical cell, tapered and closed at both ends; includes fiber tracheids with bordered pits and libriform fibers with simple pits. See also CELL, TRACHEID.

FIBER ANATOMY: Branch of fiber morphology dealing with structure.

FIBER NODE: Weak point in a wood pulp fiber where a parenchyma cell crosses at right angles. Under electron microscopic examination of an unbeaten fiber, a node can be seen as a localized partial collapse of the cell wall into the lumen.

FIBER SATURATION POINT: Stage in the drying or wetting of wood when the cell cavities are free of water, but the cell walls are saturated with moisture.

FIBER STRUCTURE: See FIBER ANATOMY, MORPHOLOGY.

FIBER TRACHEID: See TRACHEID.

FIBRARY: Catalog or file of authentic specimens or samples of fibers which the fiber microscopist uses for reference purposes.

FIBRIL: Threadlike component of cell walls visible under an optical microscope. Note: Fibrils (or fibrillae) are composed of more elementary morphological units called microfibrils, which are only visible under an electron microscope. Without qualification, the term "fibril" is taken as equivalent to "macrofibril", as opposed to the ultrastructural microfibril. See also MICROFIBRIL.

FIBRIL ANGLE: Angle between the longitudinal axis of the cell and the direction of the fibrils in the secondary cell wall. Syn. Filament Winding Angle, S_2 Angle.

FIBRILLAR: [adj] Having a structure composed mainly of fibrils.

FREE WATER: Moisture contained in wood cell cavities and intercellular spaces, held by capillary forces only.

FUSIFORM RAY: Multiseriate ray containing a resin canal; it is spindle-shaped as viewed in the tangential section.

G _____

GELATINOUS FIBERS: Modified fibers that are associated with tension wood in hardwoods. They have a more or less unlignified inner layer in the secondary wall.

GROWTH RING: See ANNUAL GROWTH RING.

GUM: Non-volatile, viscous, plant exudate consisting mainly of carbohydrate material. Some substances commonly referred to as gums are actually oleoresins.

GYMNOSPERM: Woody plant that produces naked seeds, i.e., not enclosed in an ovary. The conifers are the only common trees of this group. See also SOFTWOOD.

H _____

HARD HARDWOOD: Designation for any of the harder and denser species of hardwood, including such pulpwood species as yellow birch, beech, the hard maples and the oaks. See also SOFT HARDWOOD.

HARDWOOD: Generally, wood produced by a broadleaf tree and containing pores. The term has no relation to the actual hardness of the wood.

HEARTWOOD: Dead central portion of the trunk of a tree or of a large branch; often, but not always, darker colored than the outer sapwood.

HELICAL THICKENING: See SPIRAL THICKENING.

HETEROCELLULAR RAY: Ray consisting of two different cell types. In hardwoods, upright and procumbent ray parenchyma; in softwoods, ray parenchyma and ray tracheid. Syn. Heterogeneous Ray.

HETEROGENEOUS: [adj] Consisting of parts or elements that are dissimilar. This term is often applied to native pulp fibers because of their large variability in length, diameter and wall thickness.

HOMOCELLULAR RAY: Ray consisting of only one cell type. Syn. Homogeneous Ray.

I _____

INCLUDED PIT-APERTURE: Inner pit-aperture whose outline, in surface view, is included within the outline of the pit border. See also EXTENDED PIT-APERTURE.

INNER BARK: See PHLOEM.

INNER PIT-APERTURE: Opening of the pit canal into the lumen.

INTERCELLULAR CANAL: Intercellular space generally serving as a repository for gum or resin; the orientation may be vertical or radial.

INTERCELLULAR LAYER: Layer of isotropic substance between cells composed mainly of lignin. See also MIDDLE LAMELLA.

INTERCELLULAR SPACE: Space between cells, including canals, cavities and actual openings between rounded corners of cells.

INTERMEDIATE WOOD: Inner layers of the sapwood that are transitional between sapwood and heartwood in color and general character.

INTERTRACHEID PIT: Pit of pit pair in the wall of a tracheid leading to a contiguous tracheid (before the wood is pulped).

INTERVESSEL PIT: Pit of pit pair in the wall of a vessel leading to a contiguous vessel (before the wood is pulped). Syn. Intervascular Pit.

ISOTROPIC: [adj] Having identical properties in all directions.

J _____

JUVENILE WOOD: Innermost layers of wood adjacent to the pith, formed during the "juvenile period" of the tree's growth. Typically, the cells are smaller and/or less structurally developed than in mature wood. Sometimes referred to as core wood.

K _____

KNOT: Branch base that is embedded in the wood of a tree trunk or of a larger branch.

L _____

LAMELLA: (Plural: LAMELLAE) Thin layer. See also MICROFIBRILLAR LAMELLA, MIDDLE LAMELLA.

LATEWOOD: Relatively more dense and smaller-celled wood produced in the annual ring during the later part of the growing season.

LIBRIFORM FIBER: Elongated, thick-walled cell in hardwoods having simple pits. The distinction is blurred as the pitting becomes more obviously bordered, and this fiber type merges imperceptibly into tracheids.

LINEAR PIT: Pit with an aperture that is long, narrow and of uniform breadth as seen in surface view.

LONGITUDINAL: See AXIAL.

LUMEN: (Plural: LUMINA) Cavity of a cell enclosed by its wall.

M _____

MACERATION: Process of separating small pieces of wood into constituent cell elements for morphological study. A classic method is to boil the wood pieces in a solution of acetic acid and hydrogen peroxide.

MACROFIBRIL: See FIBRIL.

MARGO: Thin, perforated outer portion of a pit membrane lying between the torus and pit border in softwood bordered pits.

MATRIX: Intercellular substance. The wood matrix is made up of lignin, hemicelluloses and extractives.

MATURE WOOD: Wood formed outside of the juvenile wood zone and away from the active tree crown, characterized by relatively constant cell size. Syn. Adult Wood.

MERISTEM: Region of a plant where cells are actively growing and dividing. The meristem that forms wood fibers and other wood cells in trees is the cambium layer.

MICROFIBRIL: Threadlike component of the cell wall structure composed of cellulose polymer chains and associated polysaccharides united through crystalline regions (crystallites) and amorphous regions. See also ELEMENTARY FIBRIL.

MICROFIBRILLAR ANGLE: Angle between the longitudinal axis of the cell and the direction of the microfibrils of the middle layer of the seconday wall.

MICROFIBRILLAR LAMELLA: Thin sheet of microfibrils with similar orientation which spiral about the fiber axis. Orientation can vary in adjacent lamellae.

MICROFIBRILLAR LAMINA: (Plural: LAMINAE) Single layer of microfibrils. The cell wall of a typical tracheid contains 40 to 160 laminae.

MICROFIBRILLAR STRUCTURE: Organization, orientation and structural connection between microfibrils in successive lamellae of a cellulose fiber.

MIDDLE LAMELLA: General term for the lignin-rich cementing layer between cell walls in plants, usually referring to the intercellular layer, but sometimes including the primary walls of adjacent cells and even the outer layers of the secondary wall. The term, "true middle lamella", can be used to specify the intercellular layer. The term, "compound middle lamella", is sometimes applied to the compound layer or "intercellular matrix" between the secondary walls of contiguous cells.

MORPHOLOGY: In general, the study of form and structure. Of particular interest is the morphology of various pulp fibers.

MULTISERIATE: [adj] Consisting of a number of contiguous rows.

MULTISERIATE RAY: Ray consisting of several to many rows of cells in width, as viewed in the tangential section.

N

NANOFIBRIL: Designation for a bundle of elementary fibrils up to about 30 nm in thickness, too small to be seen with an optical microscope.

NODE: See FIBER NODE.

NONPOROUS WOOD: Wood devoid of pores or vessels, from coniferous trees.

O

OPPOSITE PITTING: Multiseriate pitting in which bordered pits are arranged in transverse rows extending across the cell and in horizontal pairs or short horizontal rows. When crowded, the outlines of the pits become rectangular in surface view.

OUTER-PIT APERTURE: Opening of the pit canal into the pit chamber.

P

PARENCHYMA: Short, thin-walled cells having simple pits and functioning primarily in the metabolism and storage of plant food materials. They live longer than most cells, sometimes for many years. Two types of parenchyma cells are recognized: those in vertical strands known as axial parenchyma, and those in rays, called ray parenchyma.

PERFORATION: Opening (or openings) between two vertical vessel elements, most commonly located near the ends of the elements.

PERFORATION PLATE: Wall area involved in the vertical coalescence of two vessel elements.

PHENOLOGY: Science that correlates climatic conditions with periodic biological phenomena (e.g., annual ring formation).

PHLOEM: Inner bark; the principal food-conducting tissue in vascular plants; characterized by the presence of sieve tubes.

PICEOID PIT: Small, bordered, generally elliptical cross-field pit in earlywood of certain conifers; characterized by a narrow inner aperture that frequently extends slightly beyond the outline of the border.

PICIFORM PIT: Small pit in ray paryenchyma cells, as in spruce.

PINOID PIT: Term of convenience for the smaller types of earlywood cross-field pits found in several pine species. Characteristically, these are simple or with narrow borders and often variable in size and shape.

PIT: Recess in the secondary wall of a cell together with its external closing membrane (pit membrane). The recess is open to the lumen.

PIT-APERTURE: Opening of a pit into a cell lumen ("inner pit-aperture") or into a pit chamber ("outer pit-aperture").

PIT CANAL: Passage from the cell lumen to the chamber in bordered pits.

PIT CAVITY: Entire space within a pit from the membrane (middle lamella) to the lumen.

PIT CHAMBER: In a bordered pit, the space between the pit membrane (middle lamella) and the overhanging border.

PITCH POCKET: Lens-shaped opening extending parallel to the annual layers that contains or has contained liquid or solid pitch, found in certain coniferous woods.

PITH: Soft, thin-walled tissue at the center of plant stems, made up of parenchyma with unlignified cell walls.

PITH FLECKS: Dark areas in wood due to patches of wood parenchyma resulting from the healing of injuries, such as those made by certain insect larvae working in the cambium.

PIT MEMBRANE: That portion of the compound middle lamella which closes a pit cavity externally.

PIT PAIR: Two complementary pits of adjacent cells.

PORE: Cross section of a vessel as it appears in a transverse section of wood.

POROUS WOOD: Wood containing pores (vessels), i.e., a hardwood.

PRIMARY WALL: Outermost, very thin, highly lignified layer of the cell wall.

PROCUMBENT RAY CELL: Narrow cell elongated in the radial direction. It is the most common type of ray cell, and composes most homocellular rays and the body of heterocellular rays.

PROTOFIBRIL: See ELEMENTARY FIBRIL.

PROTOPLASM: Living matter of plant cells, a colloidal complex of protein.

PUNKY: [adj] Soft, weak, often spongy. Refers to a condition in wood caused by decay.

R _____

RADIAL: [adj] Extending from the center, coincident with the radius; from the pith to the circumference of a tree or log.

RADIAL SECTION: Longitudinal section of a stem (or branch) in the plane that passes through the center line.

RAY: Ribbon-like strand of cells extending radially within a tree and varying in height from a few cells to several centimeters depending on species. The face of the ribbon is exposed in a radial section. Rays serve to store food and transport it horizontally through the tree.

RAY CROSSING: Local weakening in the cell wall of tracheids where they have been intercepted by ray cells.

RAY MARGIN: Upper and lower edges or boundaries of a ray, as seen in a radial section.

RAY TRACHEID: Small cell with bordered pits and devoid of living contents, found in the ray tissue of most softwoods.

REACTION WOOD: Wood with abnormal structure and properties formed in parts of leaning or crooked stems and in branches. In hardwoods it is called "tension wood"; in softwoods, "compression wood".

RESIN: Secretions of certain trees, consisting of mixtures of aromatic acids and esters insoluble in water, but soluble in ether, alcohol, and other organic solvents. The designation "natural resin" is often used to distinguish it from synthetic organic products.

RESIN DUCTS: Intercellular canals or passages that contain and transmit resinous materials within the tree, either vertically or radially.

RESINOUS WOOD: Softwood species having a comparatively high content of resinous substances, e.g., southern pines.

RETICULATE: [adj] Net-like. Applied either to cell openings or to variations in wall thickness that have a net-like pattern.

RHYTIDOME: Technical term for the outer bark.

RING-POROUS WOOD: Porous wood in which the pores formed at the beginning of the growing season (in earlywood) are much larger than those farther out in the ring, and the transition from one type to the other is abrupt. If the change is gradual, the wood is decribed as either "semi-ring-porous wood" or "semi-diffuse-porous wood".

ROT: See DECAY.

ROUNDNESS FACTOR (of fibers): Characterization of a fiber cross-section to provide a relative measure of roundness. One method defines the roundness factor as the ratio of the cross-sectional area of the fiber to the area of a circumscribed circle. For example, a fiber in the form of a collapsed ribbon would have a low roundness factor. See also CIRCULARITY.

S _____

SAP: Liquid within unseasoned wood or the living tree containing the nutrients and other chemicals in solution which are required for growth.

SAPWOOD: Lighter-colored, water-conducting, outer portion of the tree stem with living ray tissue, as differentiated from the darker heartwood portion in the center of the stem.

SCALARIFORM: [adj] Ladder-like. Applied to pitting in some hardwoods where linear bordered pits are arranged in a ladder-like series; and to perforation plates with multiple, elongated and parallel perforations separated by bars of wall material.

SCLEREID: Strengthening element in wood characterized by a thick, lignified secondary wall, and variable shape from polyhedral to somewhat elongated and often branched, but usually one axis is not significantly longer than the other. The most common type is the "stone cell", roughly cylindrical in shape with a massive lignified secondary wall that is often conspicuously laminated and may contain simple pits.

SECONDARY WALL: Portion of the cell wall that contains most of the fiber substance, formed in three distinct layers characterized by different fibril alignments. See also S-LAYERS, PRIMARY WALL.

SEPTATE FIBER: Fiber divided into compartments along its length by the formation of walls (septa) consisting entirely of secondary wall material.

SIEVE TUBE: Food-conducting tube of the phloem made up of an axial series of long, conducting cells, called sieve-tube elements.

SIMPLE PERFORATION: Single, usually large, and more or less rounded opening in a perforation plate.

SIMPLE PIT: Pit that has no border, i.e., a pit in which the cavity becomes wider, remains of constant width, or only gradually narrows toward the cell lumen.

S-LAYERS: The three layers of the secondary cell wall, designated as S_1 for the outer layer, S_2 for the central layer, and S_3 for the inner layer. The last is sometimes called the tertiary wall.

SOFT HARDWOOD: Designation for any of the less hard and dense species of hardwood, such as certain poplars, gums, aspens, magnolias and soft maples. See also HARD HARDWOOD.

SOFT ROT: Special type of decay developing under wet conditions in the outer wood layers, caused by fungi that destroy the cellulose in the secondary cell walls. The surface of the affected wood is typically softened.

SOFTWOOD: Wood produced by coniferous trees, i.e., nonporous wood. The term has no reference to the actual hardness of the wood.

SPECIES: Category of tree, e.g., pine, spruce, hemlock, aspen. Also used to designate the wood, pulp, or fiber derived from a particular tree type. Syn. Tree Species, Wood Species.

SPIRAL THICKENING: Spiralled ridge-like thickening of the inner wall of a cell. Syn. Helical Thickening.

SPRINGWOOD: See EARLYWOOD.

STAIN: Discoloration in wood from whatever cause. For example, "blue stain" is a bluish or grayish discoloration of sapwood caused by fungi; "brown stain" is a dark brown discoloration of the sapwood of some pines during storage, also caused by fungi; "chemical brown stain" is a brownish discoloration that may occur during the seasoning of certain softwoods, apparently caused by the concentration and oxidation of extractive chemicals.

STAINING: Technique of applying stains or dyes to fibers mounted on microscope slides in order to provide maximum color differentiation of the morphological details of the various fibers.

STONE CELL: See SCLEREID.

STORIED: [adj] Term applied to either axial cells or rays when they are arranged in horizontal tiers. Best observed in tangential sections.

STRIATIONS: Fine striped or grooved linear markings, typical characteristics of certain cellulosic fibers as seen under the microscope. The presence or absence of such features can be used as the basis of fiber identification.

SUMMERWOOD: See LATEWOOD.

T _____

TANGENTIAL SECTION: Longitudinal section through a stem or limb perpendicular to a radius, as made by slicing off part of the trunk of a tree.

TAXODIOID PIT: Rather small, cross-field pit in earlywood of conifers, characterized by a large oval-to-circular aperture that is much wider than the fairly narrow and uniform border to either side.

TENSION WOOD: Reaction wood formed on the upper side of branches and inclined stems of hardwood trees, characterized anatomically by lack of cell wall lignification and often by the presence of a gelatinous layer in the fibers.

TERTIARY WALL: See S-LAYER.

TISSUE: Aggregation of cells having a common function.

TORUS: Central non-perforated, often thickened portion of a pit membrane in softwood bordered pits.

TRACHEA: Pore or vessel in hardwood.

TRACHEID: Elongated cell with bordered pits and imperforate ends. Relatively long tracheids (up to 7 mm) constitute the principal part of the cellular structure of softwoods, and shorter tracheids (seldom over 1.5 mm) are present in many hardwoods.

TRANSVERSE DIRECTION: Direction at right angles to the axis of the fiber.

TRANSVERSE SECTION: Section cut at right angles to the fiber direction, commonly used to illustrate growth increments. Syn. Cross Section.

TYLOSIS: (Plural: TYLOSES) Bubble-like or sac-like structure in the lumen of a vessel caused by ingrowths of parenchyma cells, occurring in the heartwood of certain hardwoods.

U _____

ULTRASTRUCTURE: Internal organization of the fiber wall, a realm of fiber anatomy that is beyond the resolving power of the optical microscope and where a clear separation between structure and chemistry becomes less distinct.

UNISERIATE RAY: Ray consisting of one row of cells, as viewed in the tangential section.

UPRIGHT RAY CELL: Ray parenchyma cell in hardwoods having its major axis perpendicular to the direction of the ray, occurring mainly in the upper and lower margins of heterocellular rays.

V _____

VASCULAR PLANT: Plant with a circulatory system composed of xylem and phloem, for conduction of water and foodstuffs, respectively.

VASCULAR TRACHEID: Specialized cell in certain hardwoods, similar in shape, size, and arrangement to a small vessel element, but imperforate at the ends.

VASICENTRIC TRACHEID: Short, irregularly shaped fibrous cell with conspicuous bordered pits, occurring in immediate proximity to earlywood vessels of certain ring-porous hardwoods.

VESSEL: Articulated, tube-like structure of indeterminate length in porous woods (hardwoods), formed through the vertical coalescence of individual vessel elements inter-connected at or near their ends by perforation plates.

VESSEL ELEMENT: One of the cellular components of a vessel. Syn. Vessel Member.

VESSEL ELEMENT EXTENSION: Tail-like extension at the end of a vessel element, of variable length and thickness.

VESTURED PIT: Bordered pit with its cavity wholly or partly lined with minute projections from the overhanging secondary wall.

W _____

WART: Microscopic drop-like or cone-like protuberance from the S_3 layer of a cell wall into the lumen.

WARTY LAYER: Isotropic layer of material on the inner surface of the secondary wall, consisting of a random pattern of warts, sometimes accompanied by an amorphous coating. The warty layer is a characteristic of most softwoods fibers. In hardwood fibers, both the presence and appearance of the warty layer is species-dependent.

WET ROT: Any wood rot characterized in its active state by a high moisture content, where the rotting mass readily exudes water under moderate pressure.

WHITE ROT: Type of wood-destroying fungus that attacks both cellulose and lignin, producing a generally whitish residue that may be spongy or stringy.

WOOD: Hard part of the stem of a plant lying between the pith and the bark. More specifically, the xylem tissue formed by the vascular cambium during the period in which the plant undergoes an increase in diameter; known technically as secondary phloem.

WOOD DENSITY: Weight of wood per unit volume. Since measurement is greatly affected by wood moisture content, relative wood density is frequently compared on a moisture-free basis (i.e., bone dry density).

WOOD ROT: See DECAY.

WOOD SPECIES: See SPECIES.

XYZ _____

XYLARY FIBERS: Fibers extracted from the xylem, consisting of tracheids, vessel members, libriform fibers, and parenchyma.

XYLEM: Wood portion of the tree stem, branches and roots lying between the pith and the cambium. The xylem is the principal water-conducting tissue in vascular plants and constitutes the mechanical structure of the tree.

Chapter 3
Nonwood Fibers

A

ABACA: Plant (Musa textiles), related to the banana, consisting of 12 to 30 stalks radiating from a central root system. The fiber (often called Manila hemp) is extracted from the stem of the leaf. It is used mainly for cordage, but sometimes for specialty papermaking applications where high strength is required.

ACRYLIC FIBER: Fibrillating, thermoplastic, water-dispersible, non-hygroscopic synthetic pulp fiber.

ADANSONIA FIBER: Bast fiber of the baobab or monkey's bread tree (Adansonia digitata), used as cordage in Africa.

AGAVE: See SISAL.

AGRICULTURAL RESIDUES: Source classification of vegetable fiber including sugar-cane bagasse, cereal straws, sorghum, rice straw, corn husks, and rice hulls.

ANIMAL FIBER: Fiber of animal origin (e.g., wool, silk, alpaca, mohair, leather, etc.).

ANNUAL CROP FIBER: Pulp fiber derived from plants that are cultivated and harvested on an annual cycle. Examples are kenaf and flax.

ARAMID FIBER: See POLYAMIDE FIBER.

ARUNDO: Giant cane (Arundo donax), a perennial grass growing up to 8 meters in height; cultivated and pulped to a limited extent in Italy.

ASBESTINE: Mineral fiber intermediate in physical properties between talc and asbestos.

ASBESTOS: Any of three naturally occurring fibrous crystalline silicates, at one time commonly used in heat-resistant and flame-retardant paper and board furnishes. Its use is now restricted because of health hazards associated with asbestos fibers in the environment.

B

BAGASSE: Sugar cane residue (crushed stalks) after extraction of sugar (sucrose), consisting of both fibrous and non-fibrous (pith) cells. Bagasse is a good raw material for the production of papermaking fiber, but must be depithed before it is pulped. The fibers are about 1.5 mm in length and have a favorable length-to-diameter ratio.

BAMBOO: Perennial grass, used extensively as a chemical pulping raw material in India, Taiwan, and other Asian countries. Over 1250 species of bamboo are recognized and a large number of these are utilized for pulping. Typically, the bamboo is run through a modified horizontal-feed slab chipper for subdivision, and then subjected to a conventional kraft cook. The resultant mixed-length, slender-fibered pulp is relatively soft and bulky, and used primarily in blended furnishes. All bamboos have pronounced node formations in the stem, which are hard and resistant to liquor penetration. The nodes are usually segregated and crushed prior to pulping.

BAST FIBER: Fiber obtained from the inner bark (phloem) of woody plants. Commercial bast fiber includes flax, hemp, ramie, jute, mitsumata and sunn fiber.

BHUTANG: Grass, related to sugar cane, pulped in India.

C

CANE: Any of various tall woody grasses and reeds.

CARBON FIBERS: Fibers of high strength made by heating precurser filaments, usually rayon or acrylic, to appropriate temperatures which convert the substances to essentially pure carbon.

CAROA: Cordage and papermaking fiber extracted from the leaves of Neoglazovia variegata, a Brazilian wild plant.

CERAMIC FIBER: Fiber made from refractory materials used in the ceramics industry, e.g., alumina, zirconia, fused silica, magnesia, hafnia, etc. This classification does not include glass fiber or graphite fiber. Ceramic fiber is used in paper products requiring stability at high temperatures along with good chemical and corrosion resistance.

CEREAL STRAW: Any of several cereal straws used as pulping raw materials, notably wheat, oat, rye, barley and rice straws. Rye straw is best because of somewhat longer fiber and higher cellulose content, with wheat straw a close second in preference. Barley straw is objectionable because of persistent "beards" (hair-like protuberances) which do not disappear in the pulping process. Rice straw is less desirable because of high silica content.

CHAFF: Portion of cereal straw consisting of small broken pieces of stem, leaf sheath and blade, along with various materials such as seed hulls and bristles.

CHAFFED FIBER: Also Fiber Chaff. Term used to designate raw vegetable fiber following removal of juice and pith, most commonly applied during the processing of leaf fibers.

COCONUT FIBER: See COIR.

COIR: Relatively short fiber obtained from the husk of the fruit of the coconut palm (Cocos nucifera), used mainly for cordage and for the manufacture of mats.

COMMA CELLS: See ESPARTO GRASS.

CORDAGE FIBER: Fiber which is extracted in the form of long strands, primarily used for the manufacture of ropes and cords. Manila hemp, sisal, istle, New Zealand hemp and Mauritius hemp are the primary sources. Plants that have been exploited on a more limited basis are zapupe, fique, cabuya, mescal, bowstring hemp, pita floja, and pineapple fiber. Cordage fiber usually comes to the paper mill in the form of old cordage and rough textiles (sacking and burlap), and must then be chemically pulped to free up the individual fibers for papermaking applications. Syn. Hard Fiber.

CORN HUSKS: Dry, outer covering of an ear of corn; agricultural by-product touted in the late 1920's as a pulping raw material. However, its bulkiness and relatively low cellulose content have precluded commercial development.

CORN STALKS: Similar to bagasse as a pulping raw material, with a high proportion of pith cells; used for the production of paper and paperboard on a limited scale.

COTTON: Long, soft, white or yellowish fiber of high cellulose content attached to the cottonseeds, removed from the seeds by the ginning process. Cotton is used in the manufacture of the highest quality papers, but is usually introduced into the papermaking process in the form of cuttings from the textile industry.

COTTON LINTERS: Short, fuzzy fibers that cling to the cottonseed after the long, spinnable staple fibers are removed by ginning. Linters are cut from the cottonseed by a second "saw gin" operation. If all linters are removed in the same operation, the product is called "mill run linters". If the linters are removed in two stages, the longer fibers are called "first-cut linters" and the remaining shorter fibers are called "second-cut linters". Most linters are used for the production of high alpha-cellulose dissolving pulps.

CULM: Jointed stem of grasses.

D

DECORTICATOR: Machine used to extract cordage or textile fiber strands from the raw plant parts and to clean the strands free of surrounding plant tissue; more commonly employed with leaf fiber, but in some cases also applied to the extraction of bast fiber. The mechanical (or manual) process of fiber separation is known as "decortication".

DEGUMMING: Chemical process of removing the mucilages or gums (mainly pectins and remnants of cells) from decorticated fiber bundles, applied during the extraction of ramie fiber.

DENIER: Mass-per-unit-length measurement applied to a fiber, thread or filament which is equal to 1 gram for 9000 meters.

DEPITHING: Separation of minute pith particles from good-quality fiber, most commonly applied to preparation of bagasse for pulping. Either wet or dry methods can be used to economically concentrate the "good fiber"; but complete pith removal is usually uneconomic. Typically, the waste pith is burned as an energy source, but sometimes it is converted to fodder.

DESILICATION: Removal of silica from the alkaline pulping chemical cycle. Because grasses and straws take up from the soil 10 to 100 times more silica than does pulp wood, the need to "bleed out" siliceous material from non-wood chemical systems is a serious impediment to greater utilization of non-wood pulping raw materials.

DICOTYLEDON: Class of angiosperms having net-veined leaves such as kenaf, okra, flax, hemp and the common broadleaf trees. In plants of this class, fibers are arranged in a definite ring of vascular tissue. Dicotyledonous phloem fibers are commonly designated as bast fibers.

DUSTING: See THRASHING.

E

ELEPHANT GRASS: (Pennisetum purpureum) Grass common in Mozambique and Ghana which is suitable as a pulping raw material, but which has not been utilized on a commercial basis.

ESPARTO GRASS: (Lygeum spartum and Stipa tenacissima) Coarse grass from Southern Spain and Northern Africa used as a source of papermaking fibers. After cutting and dusting, the grass is usually chemically pulped using either a soda or a modified kraft cooking process. The long, relatively small-diameter fiber is used in the manufacture of high-quality book and printing papers. A significant feature of esparto pulps is the presence of small seed hairs (trichomes), called "comma cells", that contribute to closeness of sheet formation and opacity. Syn. Spanish Grass.

F _____

FIBER CROP: Any plant, such as flax, hemp, jute or sisal, that is cultivated specifically for its content or yield of fibrous material.

FIBRIDS: Short synthetic pulp fibers (0.1 to 1.2 mm) with many branched and curled fibrils. Fibrids are produced from polymer solutions and are fibrillar when formed.

FIBROVASCULAR ELEMENTS: Filaments obtained from leaves and leaf stalks by means of scraping, beating, scutching, and combing. The product is usually valued for its strength and ability to be twisted into cords or coarse threads. The filaments have essentially the same chemical composition as the original plant. Among fibers of this class are abaca, sisal, New Zealand hemp, istle, and pineapple. When these materials are subjected to alkaline cooking treatments, the ultimate fibers are liberated and non-cellulosic constituents are dissolved. The lengths of the ultimate fibers bear no relation to the lengths of the filaments from which they were derived.

FLAX: (Linum usitatissimum) Annual plant cultivated for its seed and stalks, but not necessarily from the same crop. The bast fiber strands for linen are most easily obtained from immature plants, while the best oil comes from completely ripened plants (i.e., seed flax). The long strands of textile fiber (up to 1 m in length) are extracted by first retting and then scutching the stalks. Flax fiber enters the paper industry in two forms, as linen rags or directly as flax pulp. Pulp is often made from "flax straw" which is mechanically decorticated to produce "flax tow" and then pulped by a modified kraft process.

FLAX STRAW: That portion of the mature flax plant which is left after the seed has been removed; a by-product of seed flax. Flax straw consists of about 25% bast fiber and 75% of a short woody fiber, known in the industry as "shive". See also FLAX, FLAX TOW.

FLAX TOW: Decorticated flax straw, used as a raw material for alkaline pulping. The yield of flax tow from flax straw is in the 40 to 50% range. See also FLAX.

FRUIT FIBERS: Grouping of plant fibers that include seed hairs (e.g., cotton, milkweed), pod fibers (e.g., kapok) and hull fibers (e.g., coir).

G _____

GAMPI: Bast fiber from a wild shrub (Wikstroemia canescens). It is a traditional fibrous raw material for hand-made Japanese paper, especially suitable for making thin, tough sheets.

GIN: Machine used to separate cotton fibers from the seed and other waste components.

GLASS FIBER: Staple fiber prepared from small-diameter glass thread or filament, used as a reinforcing material in certain paper products.

H _____

HACKLING: Combing of flax, jute or other hard fiber to clean and straighten the fiber, usually carried out mechanically.

HARD FIBER: See CORDAGE FIBER.

HEMP: Annual plant (Cannabis sativa) long cultivated for its seed or stalks; but in recent years cultivated more for its leaves, flowers and juices which have potent narcotic properties (hashish and marijuana). The bast fibers are separated from the stalks in the same manner as for flax, and are of similar quality to flax fibers.

HENEQUEN: See SISAL.

HOP VINE: (Humulus lupulus) Sometime source of bast fiber for papermaking in Europe.

HULL FIBER: Pulp obtained by digesting the crushed hulls of cottonseeds or rice.

HURDS: Incompletely separated residues (of flax, hemp, kenaf, etc.) in bast fiber pulps. Hurds are sources of dirt which are analogous to shives in wood pulp.

I _____

INTERNODES: Sections of culm or stem between nodes.

ISTLE: Any of several species of plant of which leaf fiber is extracted for cordage and other uses. The major istle fiber of commerce is derived from the tula, juamave, palma, pita and zamandoque plants.

J

JUTE: Bast fiber from various species of the annual plant genus, Chorchurus, especially C. capsularis, used mainly for sacks and bags. The fiber is extracted after retting of the stems.

K

KAPOK: Very thin-walled fiber obtained from the pod of the kapok tree (Ceiba petandra), used mainly for stuffings and fillers.

KENAF: Annual plant (Hibiscus cannabinus) cultivated for its bast fiber, which is suitable for cordage and papermaking. Kenaf grows as a stalk with a woody core containing very short fiber and pithy material. To obtain fiber strands for cordage, the stalks are usually retted. Good quality chemical pulp can be made from either retted or unretted material. The cordage fiber is sometimes called "mesta fiber".

KOZO: Bast fiber of the paper mulberry (Broussonetia papyrifera), a traditional fibrous raw material for hand-made oriental papers.

L

LEAF FIBER: Fiber extracted from a leaf or leaf stalk. Commercial leaf fibers include abaca, sisal, istle, pineapple and New Zealand hemp. See also FIBROVASCULAR ELEMENTS.

LEATHER FIBER: Fiber originating from animal hides. When subjected to beating or other mechanical action, leather breaks down into fibrous bundles or individual fibers.

LEMON GRASS: Member of the genus, Cymbopogon, used as a pulping raw material in India after primary extraction of essential oils.

LINEN: Cloth made from flax bast fiber. In the paper industry, linen rags are used in the manufacture of high quality papers. The term "cotton fiber content" embraces both cotton and linen.

M

MANILA HEMP: See Abaca.

MAN-MADE FIBER: Fiber produced through chemical reactions controlled by man, as opposed to fiber occurring naturally.

MAURITIUS HEMP: Cordage fiber extracted from the leaves of genus, Furcraea, plants related to the agaves.

MERCERIZATION: Treatment of vegetable fiber with heated alkali solutions, either under tension or slack, so as to change the structural features of the fiber, by increasing its diameter, strength, and capacity for dyes.

METALLIC FIBER: Manufactured fiber composed of metal, plastic-coated metal or metal-coated plastic.

MINERAL FIBER: Synthetic inorganic fiber obtained from such sources as rock, ore, or glass by melting and fiberizing.

MITSUMATA: Bast fiber from a cultivated shrub (Edgeworthia papyrifera), a traditional fibrous raw material for hand-made Japanese paper. It is used in the manufacture of a special grade of paper called "imperial Japanese vellum".

MONOCOTYLEDON: Class of angiosperms having parallel veined leaves, such as grasses and palms. In plants of this class, the fibers are arranged in vascular bundles which are generally distributed at random throughout the greater part of the plant stem.

N

NATURAL FIBER: Fiber obtained in usable form directly from vegetable, animal or mineral origin.

NEW ZEALAND HEMP: The only cordage fiber of commercial importance produced outside the tropics. The fiber is extracted from the leaves of the Phormium tenax plant, which is not in any sense a true hemp or flax. Syn. New Zealand Flax.

NODE: Region of the stem where one or more leaves are attached. In the pulping of certain reeds and grasses (notably bamboo), the nodes which occur as vascular bundles crowded together are more difficult to delignify and are typically the source of most screen rejects.

NONWOOD FIBERS: Usually refers to papermaking fibers from fibrous plants other than trees.

O

OKRA: Bast fiber obtained from Hibiscus esculentus, used for bagging and cordage in India. This plant was given serious consideration as a commercial crop for American papermaking in the 1860's and 1870's.

P

PAPER MULBERRY: See KOZO.

PAPYRUS: Common reed of the sedge family, used by the ancient Egyptians to make a type of writing paper (made up of thin cross layers of pith pounded into a unified sheet). Actually, it is the rind of the plant which is rich in conventional papermaking fiber. Efforts have been made to develop a modern paper industry based on this raw material; however, technical problems combined with the uncertainty of papyrus supply on a sustained-yield basis make the prospects unfavorable.

PINEAPPLE: Leaf fibers of this cultivated fruit-bearing plant (Ananas comosus), noted for their extreme fineness, are utilized in special papermaking applications. The fibrovascular elements are also used for cordage.

PITA FLOJA: Cordage and papermaking fiber extracted from the leaves of Aechme magdalenae.

PITH: Non-fibrous cellulosic material which makes up much of the structure of such potential pulping raw materials as bagasse and corn stalks. See also DEPITHING.

POLYAMIDE FIBER: Strongest and stiffest synthetic fiber available with good high-temperature stability, often used as a replacement for asbestos in various products. It has the ability to fibrillate and has found application in some specialty paper products. Syn. Aramid Fiber.

POLYETHYLENE FIBER: Thermoplastic, water-dispersible, non-hygroscopic synthetic pulp that is produced with a shape and size distribution similar to different types of refined wood pulp.

POLYOLEFIN FIBER: Term applied to polyethylene and polypropylene fiber collectively.

POLYPROPYLENE FIBER: Water dispersible synthetic pulp fiber produced with a shape and size distribution similar to different types of refined wood pulp, notable for high opacity and high scattering coefficient.

R

RACHIS: Top portion of the culm to which the seed is attached.

RAGS: Discarded textile materials derived from vegetable fibers, such as clothing, curtains, linen, etc. and cuttings from factories manufacturing these products. Rags are the preferred raw material for the highest quality papers. The increased use of synthetics in textiles has caused a scarcity of good-quality rags.

RAMIE: Bast fiber obtained from the stem of a perennial plant (Boehmeria nivea) related to and resembling the common nettle. Two varieties of the plant are cultivated, "China grass" in temperate climates and "rhea" in tropical climates. The fiber cannot be extracted by a retting process; rather a severe decorticating treatment is required to remove the outer bark. The long-fiber tissue must then be degummed to leave the ramie in the form of single cells or small bundles of cells. The ultimate ramie cells are the longest and broadest of any vegetable fiber.

REEDS: Generally refers to the Phragmites Communis reeds, common river delta plants in Europe, Asia and the Middle East. These perennial plants with 4–5 m stems are utilized as a chemical pulping raw material in Rumania, Russia and Egypt. The reed is collected in bundles, and then processed through a chipper. The raw chips are screened to remove leafy and sheath material, and the clean chips are cooked either by the kraft process or by the neutral semi-chemical process.

RETTING (ROTTING): Bacterial or fungal action to separate the various layers of a plant stalk and allow the extraction of the bast fibers. The dissolution of the semi-ligneous layer (mainly pectins), which connects the woody core to the bast, is accomplished by fermentation or decomposition induced by microbial activity. The middle lamellas of the fiber bundles are not dissolved because they are more lignified. In practice, retting is carried out either by letting the stalks rot naturally or by artificially accelerating the process.

ROPE FIBER: Without further qualification, usually refers to Manila hemp; but the designation can be applied to any cordage fiber.

S

SABAI GRASS: (Eulaliopsis binata) Grass similar to esparto grass, used as a source of papermaking fiber in India and Pakistan.

SCUTCHING: Breakup and removal of the internal pith, or boon, from fiber-bearing stalks after retting and drying. The boon is initially crushed and broken, followed by a scraping process that removes the woody core from the fiber.

SEED FIBER: Fiber that grows attached to the seed coat or to the inner wall of the fruit or seed capsule. Cotton is the most important fiber of this type, which also includes kapok, coir, and vegetable silk.

SEED FLAX: See FLAX.

SHOCK: Conical pile of vertically oriented bundles (e.g., of reeds) stacked together to cure and dry.

SISAL: Any of several members of the Agave plant group from which leaf fiber is extracted for cordage and other uses. Three species are of commercial interest. Although the generic term, "sisal", is applied to all species, certain of these fibers are further differentiated as "henequen" or "cantala" to distinguish them from technically true sisal. A mature plant has a short trunk from which radiate as many as 150 stiff, fleshy leaves. From 180 to 240 leaves are harvested during the 4 to 6 year productive period of the plant. The strands of fiber are embedded longitudinally in the leaves, and are extracted by scraping away the surrounding pulpy flesh.

SOFT FIBER: Designation applied to fine and flexible bast fiber suitable for manufacturing into textile fabric.

SORGHUM: Any of various grasses, cultivated mainly for their sweet juices and as fodder, but sometimes used as pulping raw material. One variety (S. almum) merits special attention because of drought resistance, toleration of poor soil, and good crop yield.

STALK: Stem or axis of plant.

STEM FIBER: Fiber from the main stem or trunk of the plant. Examples are wood fiber, bast fiber and vascular bundles.

STRAW: See CEREAL STRAW.

SUGAR CANE: Grass (Saccharum officinarum) widely cultivated in tropical and sub-tropical areas, containing 15% sugar (sucrose) in the pith cells. The residue from extracted sugar cane, bagasse, is either utilized as a pulping raw material or burned as a valuable fuel. See also BAGASSE.

SUNN HEMP: Bast fiber extracted from the stem of Crotalaria juncea, an annual legume cultivated commercially mainly in India, where the fine strands of fiber are used for cordage, nets and sacking. In Western countries, sunn pulp fibers are used in specialty papermaking applications. Syn. Benares Hemp.

SYNTHESIZED FIBER: Fiber made from chemicals which were originally nonfibrous; more frequently referred to as man-made fiber.

SYNTHETIC PAPERMAKING FIBER: Broad classification of fiber which includes rayons, acrylics, polyamides, polyesters, glass fiber, ceramic fiber, metal fiber, and polyolefins, all of which are used in specialty or experimental papers.

SYNTHETIC PULP: In papermaking, any synthetic fiber that can be spun into fine microfibrils. Examples are polyethylene and polypropylene. Syn. Synpulp.

T _____

TENACITY: Tensile strength of a fiber, usually expressed as grams per denier. Typically, wood pulp fibers have a tenacity of 7 to 9 g/denier.

TEXTILE PLANT FIBER: Fiber of sufficient fineness to be spun into thread and manufactured into fabric. This category can be further differentiated into fine textile fiber used for wearing fabrics, and rough textile fiber used mainly for sacks and bags. The principal fine textile fiber is cotton; other examples are flax, hemp and ramie. Rough textile fiber includes jute, coir, and sunn hemp.

THRASHING: Processing operation for rags prior to their disintegration into fibers. The rags are passed through a revolving cylindrical drum which opens up the rags and removes loose dirt and dust. Syn. Dusting.

TOW: Short fibers removed by hackling.

TRICHOMES: Certain epidermal cells with altered shapes such as spur-like projections or long tubular hairs. Identification of a nonwood fiber sample may depend on the presence or absence of a particular trichome.

TUXY: Outer portion of the leaf sheath on such plants as abaca and banana. The tuxy contains most of the desirable fiber strands of the abaca plant.

TUXYING PROCESS: Peeling or stripping of the tuxy from the undesirable portion of the leaf sheath, followed by scraping of the fiber strands to remove pulp and extraneous matter.

U _____

URENA FIBER: Jute-like fiber from a plant (Urena lobata) cultivated in sections of Africa.

V _____

VASCULAR BUNDLE: Strandlike part of a plant's vascular system composed of xylem and phloem.

VEGETABLE FIBER: Nonwood, natural cellulosic fiber that originates from four principal sources: (1) seed hairs; (2) bast fiber derived from herbaceous plants, shrubs and trees; (3) leaf fiber; and (4) grass and cereal fiber.

VEGETABLE HAIRS: Fiber that grows in the form of hairs on some part of the plant, usually on the seeds.

VISCOSE RAYON FIBER: Most popular fiber used in wet-lay nonwoven manufacture, generally in lengths of 3 to 30 mm and deniers of 1 to 22.

Chapter 4

Cellulose Chemistry

(Includes basic organic chemistry and analytical techniques)

A _____

ACCESSIBILITY: See CHEMICAL ACCESSIBILITY.

ACETATE: (1) Chemical compound containing the acetyl group, CH_3CO. (2) Common commercial name for cellulose acetate fiber or plastic.

ACETATE PULP: Dissolving pulp tailor-made for conversion into cellulose acetate or other esters. Syn. Acetylation Pulp.

ACETIC ACID: (CH_3COOH) Clear, colorless liquid with sharp, pungent taste and odor, the acid found in vinegar and the source of acetyl radical, CH_3CO in chemical reactions. Obtained commercially by the destructive distillation of wood and by synthetic manufacture. The concentrated product is called "glacial acetic acid".

ACETIC ANHYDRIDE: [$(CH_3CO)_2O$] Colorless liquid with pungent odor, used as the acetylating agent for cellulose in the manufacture of cellulose acetate.

ACETONE: (CH_3COCH_3) Colorless, flammable liquid of characteristic odor, obtained commercially by the destructive distillation of wood and by fermentation of starch; also produced synthetically. An important commercial solvent for cellulose nitrates, cellulose acetate, and laquers.

ACETYL RADICAL: See ACETIC ACID.

ACETYLATING AGENT: Chemical used to produce acetyl radical for reaction with cellulose; usually a mixture of acetic anhydride, glacial acetic acid and concentrated sulfuric acid.

ACID: Large group of inorganic and organic chemical compounds containing one or more active hydrogen atoms (or ions) which can be replaced by metal atoms (or ions) forming a salt.

ACID GROUPS: Functional groups having the properties of acids. In cellulose and its derivatives, these are usually carboxyl groups.

ACID HYDROLYSIS: Hydrolysis under acid conditions. See also HYDROLYSIS, PREHYDROLYSIS.

ACIDIFICATION: Transformation into acid conditions, e.g., making a solution acidic by the addition of a strong acid.

ACIDULATING: Converting a salt to an acid by replacing the metal atom with a hydrogen atom.

ACIDULATING AGENT: Reagent used to convert a metal salt into an acid.

ACTIVATION: Treatment by heat, radiation, chemicals, etc. in order to make a substance (e.g., lignin) more reactive in a subsequent chemical conversion.

ADDITION REACTION: Chemical reaction in which there is an increase in the number of groups attached to carbon atoms so that the molecule becomes more saturated.

AFFINITY: (1) Attractive force which causes substances to combine chemically. (2) Ability of a paper dye to become bound to a cellulose fiber. See also SUBSTANTIVITY.

ALCOHOL: Any of a family of organic compounds containing one or more OH (hydroxyl) groups. The most common are: ethanol or ethyl alcohol (C_2H_5OH); and methanol or methyl alcohol (CH_3OH), also known as wood alcohol.

ALDEHYDE: Any of a family of organic compounds containing the CHO group. They are oxidized to acids and reduced to alcohols. The simplest are formaldehyde (HCOH) and acetaldehyde (CH_3CHO).

ALIPHATIC: [adj] Designation for any organic compound composed of chains of carbon atoms without carbon rings.

ALIQUOT: Volume of liquid which is a fractional part of a larger volume.

ALKALI: Any of a group of inorganic compounds containing a reactive OH (hydroxyl) group. They neutralize acids to form salts. Syn. Base.

ALKALI CELLULOSE: Compound resulting from the treatment of cellulose with sodium hydroxide. Conversion to alkali cellulose constitutes the first step in the viscose process.

ALKALIZATION: Transformation into alkaline conditions, e.g., making a solution alkaline by addition of a strong alkali.

ALKANE: Any saturated aliphatic hydrocarbon compound. The simplest are methane and ethane.

ALKYL: [adj] Compound containing a univalent hydrocarbon radical such as $-(CH_3)$ or $-(C_2H_5)$.

ALKYLATION: Introduction of an alkyl radical onto an organic compound by substitution or addition. An example is the methylation or ethylation of pulps, i.e., the attachment of methyl or ethyl groups to the hydroxyl groups of the cellulose molecules.

ALPHA-CELLULOSE: Portion of a pulp or other cellulosic material that is defined chemically as being insoluble in 17.5% caustic soda under specified conditions. Alpha-cellulose consists chiefly of long-chain cellulose, but the test does not discriminate from other components of the sample that are also insoluble in caustic. See also BETA-CELLULOSE, CELLULOSE, GAMMA-CELLULOSE.

AMORPHOUS CELLULOSE: Portion of the cell structure in which the adjacent chains of cellulose are not well ordered, i.e., noncrystalline.

ANALYTICAL METHOD: Method of finding the nature and/or the amounts of ingredients in a particular substance. See also QUALITATIVE ANALYSIS, QUANTITATIVE ANALYSIS, CHEMICAL ANALYSIS.

ANHYDRO: Prefix applied to certain polymeric units, suggesting that the linkage occurs because of the absence of a water (i.e., by a condensation reaction), and will be broken by hydrolysis. Cellulose, for example, can be said to be made up of a number of polymerized anhydroglucose units.

ARABINAN: Pentosan from which the sugar, arabinose, is derived by hydrolysis.

ARABINOSE: Pentose which is polymerized in wood (arabinan), and is liberated by hydrolysis of the hemicelluloses.

AROMATIC: [adj] Designates a compound containing one or more benzene rings.

ARRHENIUS ACTIVATION ENERGY: Temperature coefficient in the Arrhenius expression for the rate constant. See also RATE CONSTANT, REACTION RATE EXPRESSION.

ATOM: Smallest particle of an element retaining the properties of that element.

B _____

BASE: See ALKALI.

BENZENE: (C_6H_6) Colorless, flammable liquid used as a solvent and as an intermediate in the manufacture of other chemicals. It has a six-carbon ring structure with alternating single and double bonds, a simple cyclic compound.

BETA-CELLULOSE: Portion of a pulp or other cellulosic material that dissolves in 17.5% caustic soda under standard conditions, but is reprecipitated on acidification. This portion is composed principally of short-chain cellulose having a DP between 15 and 90. See also ALPHA-CELLULOSE, CELLULOSE, GAMMA-CELLULOSE.

BIOCHEMISTRY: Chemistry of living organisms. Included within the wide scope of biochemistry are certain aspects of cellulose chemistry, in particular the biosynthesis of the cellulose polymer.

BIOSYNTHESIS: Formation of complex organic compounds within the living cells of plants and animals. For plants, this includes photosynthesis and protein synthesis by means of nitrogen fixation.

BLANK: Analysis run without a sample. The blank provides a value for the experimental conditions of a given test procedure, which is subtracted from the value obtained for each sample analysis in order to calculate the net analytical result.

BOND: Chemical linkage between two atoms, groups of atoms, ions, molecules, or between combinations of these. The most common chemical bond in organic compounds is the type called "covalent".

BONE FIBER: See VULCANIZED FIBER.

BUFFER: Chemical solution that resists change in pH when acids or alkalis are added.

BUFFERING ACTION: Ability to neutralize acids and bases as they are formed during a chemical reaction and thus resist a change in pH.

C _____

CAPILLARY VISCOMETER: Glass tube with a calibrated capillary section and enlarged sections on either side of the capillary. Viscosity is measured by the time required for a specified volume of solution to flow by gravity through the capillary section (i.e., efflux time). The capillary viscometer is commonly used to measure the viscosity of cellulose solutions.

CARBOHYDRATE: Large group of compounds synthesized by plants, containing carbon, hydrogen and oxygen, in which the latter two elements are usually in the two-to-one proportion of water. Cellulose, sugars and starches are all carbohydrates. The chemistry of carbohydrates is essentially the chemistry of two functional groups, the hydroxyl group and the carbonyl group. Syn. Saccharide.

CARBON DISULFIDE: (CS_2) Colorless, volatile liquid with a characteristic odor, used as a solvent in the viscose process. Syn. Carbon Bisulfide.

CARBONYL GROUP: Divalent organic radical $C=O$, characteristic of aldehydes, ketones and carboxylic acids. Carbonyl groups are formed on the cellulose molecule during bleaching.

CARBOXYL GROUP: Radical $-COOH$ of an organic acid. Carboxyl groups are formed on cellulose fibers by oxidation during pulping and bleaching processes. In paper pulps, the carboxyl groups contribute to the bonding of fibers and to the retention of rosin size; but they also represent ion exchange capacity, and absorbed cations contribute to discoloration during drying.

CARBOXYMETHYLCELLULOSE (CMC): Cellulose in which CH_2COOH groups are substituted on the glucose units of the cellulose chain through an ether linkage. Since the reaction takes place in alkaline media, the usual product is the sodium salt. It is a hydrophilic colloid, with physical properties that depend on the extent of etherification. CMC has found application as a pigment coating binder.

CATALYST: Substance that promotes or accelerates a chemical reaction without being consumed by it. A catalyst may either be uneffected by the reaction or enter into the reaction and then be reformed.

CELLOBIOSE: Alternating arrangement of two glucose residues. Cellobiose units are joined together to form molecular chains of cellulose. See also MALTOSE.

CELLOPHANE: Generic name for transparent film of regenerated cellulose used for wrapping.

CELLULASE: Extracellular enzyme produced during the growth of fungi, bacteria, insects and other lower animals that hydrolyzes cellulose.

CELLULOLYTIC: [adj] Term used to describe organisms that have the ability to hydrolyze cellulose.

CELLULOSE: ($C_6H_{10}O_5)_n$ Material that forms the solid framework or cell walls of all plants; the most abundant organic compound in nature. It is a straight-chain (linear) polysaccharide composed of repeating glucose residues (or more precisely, cellobiose units), the number of which can vary over a wide range.

CELLULOSE ACETATE: White, flaky material produced by acetylation of cellulose, of which two forms are commercially important. A modified, partially hydrolized form (DS of 2.2 to 2.5) is used in the production of fibers, films and plastics. The "triacetate" (DS of at least 2.8) is used in the production of fibers. Most cellulose acetate products are made by solvent evaporation methods. See also DEGREE OF SUBSTITUTION.

CELLULOSE ACETATE BUTYRATE: White flaky material produced according to butyrol content by reacting cellulose with various mixtures of acetic and butyric anhydrides, used for molding compositions.

CELLULOSE ESTER: Cellulose in which the free hydroxyl groups have been replaced wholly or in part by acidic groups, e.g., cellulose acetate, cellulose propionate.

CELLULOSE ETHER: Cellulose in which the free hydroxyl groups have been wholly or partially converted to ethers by reaction with alcohols, e.g., methyl cellulose, ethyl cellulose.

CELLULOSE FIBER: Natural cellulosic material derived from wood or other plant materials by pulping and bleaching operations.

CELLULOSE FILM: See CELLOPHANE.

CELLULOSE NITRATE: Product obtained by treating cellulose with a mixture of concentrated nitric and sulfuric acids, used as explosive and propellent. Syn. Nitrocellulose.

CELLULOSE PROPIONATE: White flaky material produced by reacting cellulose with propionic anhydride, used for molding compositions.

CELLULOSE TRIACETATE: See CELLULOSE ACETATE.

CELLULOSE VISCOSITY: Property of a pulp or other cellulosic material which is expressed by the viscosity of a dilute solution of the material in a suitable solvent under specified conditions. The viscosity is related to the molecular DP, and thus to the strength and other properties of the fibers. See also CUENE.

CELLULOSIC: Collective term referring to any of the numerous compounds and products made by reacting cellulose with various chemicals, usually involving substitution of the hydroxyl groups of the cellulose. The products include regenerated cellulose (e.g., rayon or cellophane), cellulose acetate, nitrocellulose, and methylcellulose.

CHEMICAL ACCESSIBILITY: Extent to which cellulose and other carbohydrates are available for chemical reactions, a function of the index of order.

CHEMICAL ANALYSIS: Analytical method using chemical techniques.

CHEMICAL CELLULOSE: Highly processed pulp with high alpha cellulose content, used for chemical conversion into such products as viscose rayon and cellulose acetate. Syn. Dissolving Pulp.

CHEMICAL COTTON: Chemical cellulose prepared from cotton, usually from cotton linters.

CHEMICAL EQUATION: Shorthand to summarize the results of a chemical reaction, for example:
$$HCl + NaOH = NaCl + H_2O$$
The number of atoms must be accounted for in the result.

CHEMICAL EQUIVALENT: Weight in grams of a chemical compound that combines with or displaces one gram of hydrogen, calculated by dividing the molecular weight by the valence.

CHEMICAL FORMULA: Representation of a chemical compound using symbols for the elements and subscript numbers to indicate the relative number of atoms of each element present. For example, the formula for water, H_2O, shows that two atoms of hydrogen have combined with one of oxygen.

CHEMICAL REACTION: See REACTION.

CHEMICAL SHORTHAND: Representation of chemical elements and compounds by symbols, for example C for carbon, Fe for iron, H_2O for water. See also CHEMICAL FORMULA.

CHEMICAL STRUCTURE: Arrangement, orientation and interrelationships of the atoms making up a molecule.

CHEMICAL SYNTHESIS: See SYNTHESIS.

CHITIN: Polysaccharide chemically similar to cellulose, but containing about 7% nitrogen within the structure. It is the principal constituent in the shells of lobsters, crabs and beetles.

CLEAVAGE REACTION: Reaction in which a chain molecule is divided into two or more segments. An example in cellulose chemistry is the hydrolysis of the glycosidic linkage between anhydroglucose units.

COMPOUND: Chemical combination of two or more elements. (The smallest amount of a compound that can exist is a molecule.)

CONCENTRATION: Amount of a given substance in a solution or mixture, usually expressed as a percent by weight or volume, normality, molarity, or weight per unit volume.

CONDENSATION REACTION: Reaction in which a solvent, usually water, is released. The foremost example is the polymerization of cellulose, during which one unit of water is given off as each glucose unit is incorporated into the polymer. The units (less the water) are then termed "glucose residues". A condensation reaction is the reverse of a hydrolysis reaction.

CONTROL: Procedure carried out under established conditions which gives a standard of comparison in an experiment.

COPOLYMER: Polymer made by polymerization of two or more monomers at the same time.

CROSS LINKAGE: Chemical bonds between adjacent molecular chains of polymers.

CRYSTALLINE CELLULOSE: Part of the molecular structure in which the individual chain molecules have a regular and repeating arrangement in three dimensions as in a crystalline lattice. See also INDEX OF ORDER, MICELLES.

CUENE: Abbreviated form for cupriethylenediamine hydroxide, the cellulose solvent most often utilized in the viscosity test for measuring DP. The test itself is called either "cuene viscosity" or "CED viscosity". See also CELLULOSE VISCOSITY.

CUPRAMMONIUM HYDROXIDE: $[Cu(NH_3)_4(OH)_2]$ Solvent for cellulose.

CUPRAMMONIUM RAYON: Rayon fibers formed by precipitating cellulose dissolved in cuprammonium hydroxide.

CUPRIETHYLENEDIAMINE HYDROXIDE: $[Cu(en)_2(OH)_2]$ Solvent for cellulose obtained by mixing together cupric hydroxide $[Cu(OH)_2]$ with ethylenediamine. (Note that "en" is used in the chemical formula as an abbreviation for the diamine complex.) See also CUENE.

CUPRIETHYLENEDIAMINE VISCOSITY: See CUENE, CELLULOSE VISCOSITY.

CYCLIC COMPOUND: Organic compound having a ring structure.

D _____

DEGRADATION: With respect to cellulose, refers to excessive shortening of the long-chain molecular structure by either chemical or physical action.

DEGREE OF CRYSTALLINITY: See INDEX OF ORDER.

DEGREE OF POLYMERIZATION (DP): In general, the number of monomer units in an average polymer molecule in a given sample. The weight-average number of glucose units in a sample of cellulose is usually inferred by measuring the viscosity of a dilute solution of cellulose in cuene.

DEGREE OF SUBSTITUTION (DS): Average number of hydroxyl groups that have been replaced per monomer unit of a polymer. For cellulose, the maximum DS is three. Cellulose acetate is normally produced with a DS between 2.2 and 2.5. Cellulose ethers are produced over a wide range of DS.

DEHYDRATING AGENT: Substance that removes water from a reaction mixture or from a process system. The agent may be an absorbent or adsorbent.

DERIVATIVE: Compound derived from a "parent compound" by replacement of one atom or group of atoms with another atom or group of atoms.

DIFFUSION: Net movement of molecules or ions of a given substance from a region of relatively high concentration to a region of relatively low concentration.

DIMER: Polymeric compound formed by the union of two molecules of a compound (i.e., of a monomer).

DIPOLAR MOLECULE: Molecule in which the electrons forming the valency bond are not symmetrically arranged, thus giving it a positive charge on one end and a negative charge on the other end. The foremost example of a divalent molecule is water. When wet cellulosic fibers are brought together during the sheet-forming operation, bonding is promoted by the polar attraction of the water molecules for each other and for the hydroxyl groups covering the cellulose surface. Syn. Polar Molecule.

DISSOLUTION: Molecular dispersion of a material into a solvent, i.e., passing into solution. Syn. Dissolving.

DISSOLVING PULP: See CHEMICAL CELLULOSE.

DOPE: Solution of cellulose ester (e.g., cellulose acetate, cellulose nitrate,) or cellulose ether (e.g., ethyl cellulose) in a suitable solvent.

DP DISTRIBUTION: Characterization of the molecular makeup of a sample of cellulose by fractional separation into increments of dp. Typically, the results of this tedious laboratory procedure are shown graphically (called the "dp distribution curve") with increments of dp on the horizontal scale and mass percentage on the vertical scale.

DP NUMBER: See DEGREE OF POLYMERIZATION.

E _____

EFFLUX: Generally, something that flows out. Specifically, the volume of flow through a capillary viscometer during a cuene pulp viscosity test.

ELECTROLYTE: Compound which conducts electrical current when dissolved in water (or other suitable solvent).

ELEMENT: Matter, all of whose atoms are alike, which thus cannot be further decomposed by chemical action.

EMPIRICAL FORMULA: Simplest formula for a chemical compound, indicating only the numerical ratio of atoms present in a molecule, and not their actual number. For example, the empirical formula for cellulose is $(C_6H_{10}O_5)_n$; the empirical formula for all carbohydrates is $C_x(H_2O)_y$

END GROUPS: Functional groups at either end of a cellulose molecule which are distinguished from those in the body of the chain, one by the presence of a reducing hemiacetyl group, the other by the presence of an extra hydroxyl group.

END POINT: Final stage in a titration as indicated by a color change or potentiometric inflection point.

EQUILIBRIUM: State of balance.

ESTER: Product of the reaction of an alcohol and an acid with elimination of water.

ESTERIFICATION: Reaction in which the replaceable H of an acid is exchanged for an organic radical; comparable to "salts" in inorganic chemistry.

ETHER: Organic compound derived from alcohols with elimination of water, characterized by the grouping R-O-R. The term "ether" is often used as a synonym for ethyl ether.

ETHERIFICATION: Process of making an ether.

ETHYL CELLULOSE: Ethyl ether of cellulose, prepared from cellulose and ethyl alcohol in the presence of a dehydrating agent.

F _____

FORMALDEHYDE: (CH_2O) Simplest aldehyde, a colorless, acrid-smelling gas; commonly handled in a water solution, called formalin.

FORMIC ACID: (HCOOH) Simplest and strongest organic acid, formed by oxidation of methanol and formaldehyde or by destructive distillation of wood.

FUNCTIONAL GROUPS: Certain groups of atoms having the same reactive properties when appearing in various molecules.

G _____

GALACTAN: Hexosan from which the sugar, galactose, is derived by hydrolysis.

GALACTOMANNON: See GUM.

GALACTOSE: Hexose which is polymerized in wood (galactan), and is liberated by hydrolysis of the hemicelluloses.

GAMMA-CELLULOSE: Portion of a pulp or other cellulosic material that dissolves in 17.5% caustic soda under standard conditions, and is not re-precipitated on acidification. This portion is actually hemicellulose and is composed of non-glucose polymers having a DP of 15 or less.

GELATINIZED FIBER: Partially solubilized cellulose fiber, such as the intermediate product during vulcanizing or parchmentizing.

GLUCAN: Hexosan from which the sugar, glucose, is derived by hydrolysis. Syn. Anhydroglucose.

GLUCOMANNAN: Polysaccharide composed of repeating glucan and mannan units (i.e., glucose and mannose residues).

GLUCOSE: Hexose which is polymerized in wood (glucan) and other vascular plants, to form cellulose. Glucose is liberated by hydrolysis of cellulose. Syn. Dextrose.

GLUCOSIDE: See GLYCOSIDE.

GLUCURONIC ACID: Glucose molecule that contains a carboxyl (acid) group (COOH) in place of a primary hydroxyl group. Generally, carboxyl groups in the sugar units are referred to as "uronic acid". Uronic acids are present in the wood structure, mainly in the hemicelluloses.

GLYCOSIDE: Any of a group of organic compounds, abundant in plants, which can be hydrolyzed into sugars. They are designated individually as glucosides, galactosides, mannosides, etc. Glycosides were formerly called glucosides, but the latter term now refers only to the glycoside having glucose as its sugar derivative.

GLYCOSIDIC BOND: Specifically, the C-O-C bond between the pentosan and hexosan units in cellulose and hemicellulose. It is similar to an ether linkage; but one of the carbons in the glycosidic bond is also linked with oxygen which makes it more susceptible to hydrolysis by the action of acids. Syn. Glycosidic Linkage.

GRAFTING: Attachment of polymer branches to the cellulose chain. The chemical product is called a "graft polymer" or "graft co-polymer". A large number of synthetic polymers have been successfully grafted to the cellulose molecule and the resulting products (called "graft pulps") show some interesting properties for papermaking and other applications.

GRAFT PULPS: See GRAFTING.

H _____

HARD FIBER: General term usually applied to vulcanized fiber or other very stiff, dense boards. See also VULCANIZED FIBER.

HEMIACETAL GROUPS: Functional groups derived from carbonyl groups by addition of one molecule of an alcohol.

HEMICELLULOSE: Short-chain polysaccharides having a DP of 15 or less, mainly polymers of sugars other than glucose; any of the non-cellulosic cell-wall polysaccharides. Principal hemicelluloses are xylan in hardwoods and glucomannon in softwoods.

HERMETIC FIBER: See VULCANIZED FIBER.

HEXOSAN: ($C_6H_{10}O_5$) Resultant dehydrated, polymeric unit when two or more hexose molecules are joined together and water is eliminated as occurs in the synthesis of cellulose and hemicelluloses.

HEXOSE: ($C_6H_{12}O_6$) Any six-carbon sugar, of which glucose, mannose, and galactose are the prime examples in cellulose and hemicellulose chemistry.

HIGH POLYMER: Long-chain polymer, typically with a molecular weight above 10,000.

HOLOCELLULOSE: Total carbohydrate content of fibers, i.e., cellulose plus hemicellulose.

HOMOPOLYSACCHARIDE: Polysaccharide composed of only one type of monomer.

HYDRATE: Substance that has had water added to its molecule.

HYDRATE CELLULOSE: Cellulose with a "hydrate crystalline structure", typical of regenerated cellulose and mercerized fiber. Following the removal of a swelling agent (e.g., caustic), the cellulose structure differs crystallographically from the native form. It has the same chemical structure, but is more reactive and is able to form additional interchain bonds. The increased chemical reactivity is explained partly by an altered geometrical arrangement of glucose units and partly by the greater proportion of amorphous areas. (Note that the term "hydrate cellulose" harks back to a period when it was assumed that mercerized cellulose retained water in its structure. The name persists even though it is now well known that this form is also free from water.) See also SWELLING AGENT.

HYDROCARBON: Organic compound consisting only of carbon and hydrogen.

HYDROCELLULOSE: Water insoluble product of the hydrolysis of cellulose with acids, usually in the form of a gelatinous mass. The product is typically heterogeneous with respect to DP.

HYDROGENATION: Chemical process of adding hydrogen to a compound.

HYDROGEN BOND: Attraction occurring between a covalently linked hydrogen atom and a neighboring atom or group of atoms. The attraction between bound hydrogen atoms and adjacent bonded atoms is especially strong with respect to nitrogen, oxygen, and fluorine atoms, increasing in that order. Hydrogen bonds are responsible for holding cellulose molecules together in the fiber structure and for bonding fibers together in a sheet of paper. See also DIPOLAR MOLECULE.

HYDROLYSIS: (1) Chemical decomposition or conversion of a complex molecule (e.g. a polymer) into two or more smaller molecules by reaction with water. A good example is the conversion of cellulose into glucose; one molecule of water is absorbed for each molecule of glucose formed. (2) Chemical reaction of a dissolved substance with water to produce either a weak acid or weak base.

HYDROLYZATES: Products of hydrolysis.

HYDROLYZING: Carrying out a hydrolysis reaction.

HYDROXY ACID: Organic acid that contains both alcoholic and carboxyl radicals and shows properties of both groups. Hydroxy acids are a significant carbohydrate degradation product during kraft pulping.

HYDROXYL GROUP: Monovalent radical, -OH. In organic chemistry, alcohols are characterized by a hydroxyl group attached to an aliphatic carbon chain, while phenols are compounds that contain a hydroxyl group on a benzene ring. All carbohydrates contain multiple hydroxyl groups. The hydroxyl group is responsible for many of the unique properties of cellulosic fibers.

I _____

INDEX OF ORDER: Measure of the relative amount of crystalline cellulose in wood cellulose; it is an important parameter for characterizing the physical and chemical properties of the derivative pulp fibers. Syn. Degree Of Crystallinity.

INHIBITOR: Substance which slows chemical reactions such as oxidation, corrosion, adhesive deterioration, etc.

INORGANIC: [adj] Pertaining to chemical compounds which do not contain carbon (carbonates and cyanides excepted).

INTERMEDIATE: Synthesized or recovered organic compound whose main use is as a raw material for further synthesis or processing into a final product.

INTRINSIC VISCOSITY: Intercept found by extrapolation of the viscosity vs. concentration relationship for cellulose solutions to zero concentration. The extrapolation is made from a linear section of the viscosity vs. concentration function at low concentrations. Intrinsic viscosity is the viscosity function used for relating viscosity measurements to molecular weight for the dissolved cellulose.

IRREVERSIBLE REACTION: Chemical reaction that can proceed in one direction only.

ISOMER: One of two or more compounds having the same molecular composition, but differing in structure. One example is provided by the hexoses found in wood: glucose, galactose and mannose.

ISOMERIZATION: Process whereby a compound is changed partly or wholly into an isomer.

K

KETONE: Organic compound containing the carbonyl group attached to two carbons. The simplest ketone is acetone, CH_3COCH_3.

KINETICS: Study of the rates at which changes occur in chemical, physical, or biological processes. Chemical kinetics is concerned with the measurement and interpretation of reaction rates.

L

LIGNIN: Natural binding constituent of the cells of wood and plant stalks, a complex three-dimensional polymer of phenylpropane or propylbenzene structure. The chemistry of lignin is characterized by having hydroxyl or methoxyl groups attached to the benzene carbon atoms. Lignin as it occurs in the plant is called "native lignin" or "protolignin" to distinguish it from the modified forms isolated by chemical means, e.g., Klason lignin or alkali lignin.

LIGNOCELLULOSE: General term for wood substance, the basic material of which wood is composed (i.e. carbohydrates and lignin), excluding extractives and extraneous substances.

LINEAR POLYMER: Polymer composed of open, unbranched chains, e.g., cellulose.

LONG-CHAIN MOLECULE: Molecule made up of many chemical units linked together in a continuous, chainlike structure. Syn. Linear Polymer.

M

MACROMOLECULE: Large molecule formed by polymerization of small molecules.

MANNAN: Dehydrated, polymerized form of manose. See HEXOSAN.

MANNOGALACTAN: See GUM.

MANNOSE: Hexose which is polymerized in wood (mannan), and is liberated by hydrolysis of the hemicelluloses.

MER: Shorthand term for the repeating structural unit of a high polymer. See also MONOMER.

MERCERIZED CELLULOSE: See HYDRATE CELLULOSE, SWELLING AGENT.

MESOMORPHOUS CELLULOSE: Those regions of the cellulose structure that are ordered to a degree, but not enough to be crystalline; structurally in between crystalline cellulose and amorphous cellulose.

METHOXYL GROUP: Oxygen-containing methane radical CH_3O-. The combining form is called "methoxy". Methoxyl groups are prominent in the chemistry of lignin.

METHYL CELLULOSE: Methyl ether of cellulose, prepared from alkali cellulose and methyl alcohol in the presence of a dehydrating agent.

MICELLES: Long chains of individual structural units (molecules) chemically joined together side-by-side to form bundles, as for example crystalline cellulose.

MICROBIAL CELLULOSE: Cellulose microfibrils biosynthesized by a micro-organism (acetobacter xylinum) from starch. The cellulose obtained is substantially pure, of high molecular weight and highly crystalline.

MINERAL ACID: Common inorganic acid, such as hydrochloric acid, sulfuric acid, or nitric acid.

MOIETY: Indefinite portion of a complex molecule having a characteristic chemical property.

MOLARITY: Unit of chemical solution concentration which is defined as the number of gram moles per liter of solution.

MOLE: Weight or mass of a chemical compound corresponding to its molecular weight. For example, a kilogram mole of water has a mass of 18 kilograms.

MOLECULAR CHAIN: Sequence of carbon atoms in an organic molecule. A straight chain is one in which the carbons extend in a linear sequence. A branched chain has one or more branches. A closed chain, in which the carbon atoms form a ring (e.g. benzene), is called a cyclic compound. A ring in which one or more of the atoms is not carbon is called heterocyclic.

MOLECULAR MORPHOLOGY: Form and structure at the molecular level. For cellulose and other polysaccharides, there are three levels of structure that are relevant: chemical, conformation (i.e., attractive and repulsive forces), and crystal.

MOLECULAR WEIGHT: Sum of all the atomic weights of the elements in a compound, arrived at by multiplying each atomic weight by the number of atoms and adding all together.

MOLECULE: Smallest amount of a compound that can exist as an entity

MONOMER: Simple compound that is capable of being polymerized or copolymerized; the repeating unit structure in polymeric compounds.

MONOSACCHARIDE: Simple sugar with the general formula $C_nH_{2n}O_n$, where n varies from three to eight. In cellulose chemistry, the monosaccharides of interest are pentoses and hexoses; these are the monomeric units of which the polymeric carbohydrates are composed.

N _____

NATIVE CELLULOSE: Cellulose with the crystalline structure found in native fibers. See also HYDRATE CELLULOSE.

NATIVE LIGNIN: See LIGNIN.

NEAT LIQUIDS: Pure liquids, as opposed to solutions.

NEUTRALIZATION: Chemical reaction between acid and alkali such that the resultant solution contains neither an excess of hydrogen ions (H^+) nor hydroxyl ions (OH^-).

NITROCELLULOSE: See CELLULOSE NITRATE.

NORMALITY: Unit of chemical solution concentration which is defined as the number of gram equivalent weights per liter of solution.

O _____

OLIGOMER: Polymer molecule consisting of only a few monomer units.

OLIGOSACCHARIDE: Carbohydrate consisting of from two up to about eight monosaccharide units joined by means of glycosidic bonds. Beyond eight sugar units, the compound is called a polysaccharide. See also POLYSACCHAROSE.

ORGANIC: [adj] Pertaining to chemical compounds containing carbon.

ORGANIC CHEMISTRY: Chemistry of compounds containing carbon, in particular hydrocarbons and their derivatives, but including compounds containing oxygen, nitrogen, sulfur and other inorganic elements. Developments in modern chemistry have tended to obscure the division between organic and inorganic chemistry. See also BIOCHEMISTRY, TOPOCHEMISTRY, STEREOCHEMISTRY.

OXYCELLULOSE: Structureless substance formed by the drastic action of oxidizing agents on cellulose. The chemical nature of oxycellulose depends on the particular oxidizing agent used and the degree of treatment. Syn. Oxidized Cellulose.

P _____

PARCHMENTIZING: Process in which waterleaf is passed through a sulfuric acid bath to partially solubilize or gelatinize the cellulose. Upon leaching out the residual acid, a coherent fibrous/amorphous mass remains which is permanently fused together.

PARTS PER MILLION (ppm): Unit of concentration; one part of a substance per million total parts. Usually refers to weight concentration, but is also used for volume concentration when specified.

PECTIN: Water-soluble polymer of galacturonic acid, closely related to the polysaccharide group. Pectins occur in fruits and in plant structures, notably between the bast fiber and the surrounding tissue of woody stalks.

PEELING REACTION: Polymeric degradation reaction which mainly involves the more reactive end groups, causing reduction in chain length one unit at a time.

PENTOSAN: ($C_5H_8O_4$) Resultant deydrated, polymeric unit when two or more pentose molecules are joined together and water is eliminated as occurs in the synthesis of hemicelluloses.

PENTOSE: ($C_5H_{10}O_5$) Any five-carbon sugar, of which arabinose and xylose are the prime examples in hemicellulose chemistry.

pH: Logarithm of the reciprocal of the hydrogen ion concentration of a solution. It is indicative of the acidity or alkalinity of an aqueous solution.

PHOTOCHEMISTRY: Branch of chemistry that deals with the effect of light in causing or modifying chemical changes. Important examples are in natural photosynthesis, in the production of photographic images, in polymerization and cross-linking reactions, in various degradation processes, and in the generation of secondary air pollutants.

PLASTIC: Amorphous material capable of being formed into definite shapes, which after setting, are retained more or less exactly. In modern usage, the term is mainly applied to synthetic organic polymers with these properties.

POLYDISPERSITY: See POLYMOLECULARITY.

POLYMER: High molecular weight compound consisting of long chains that may be open, closed, linear, branched, or cross-linked. The chains are composed of repeating units, called monomers, which may be either identical or different.

POLYMERIC: [adj] Consisting of repeating units. See also POLYMER.

POLYMERIZATION: Chemical reaction by which single molecules are linked together (e.g., condensed) to form large molecules without change in their fundamental chemical composition.

POLYMOLECULARITY: Distribution of molecular weights of a polymer within a sample. For cellulose, a full appreciation of its physical and chemical properties requires consideration of the fact that any given sample consists of a mixture of molecules of widely differing chain lengths. Syn. Polydispersity.

POLYMORPH: Chemical substance that either occurs in different structural forms or alternates between forms. Cellulose, having at least four recognized crystalline structures, is an example of a polymorphic compound.

POLYSACCHARIDE: Linear or branched polymer of more than ten monosaccharides that are linked by means of glycosidic bonds. A polymer of ten or less monosaccharides is called an oligosaccharide.

POLYSACCHAROSE: Sugar of high molecular weight. Syn. Polyose. See also OLIGOSACCHARIDE.

POTENTIOMETRIC TITRATION: Titration in which the end point is determined by observing the change in electric potential of an electrode immersed in the solution titrated. Syn. Electrometric Titration.

PRECURSOR: Any biochemical intermediate, either a compound or molecular complex, present in living organisms.

PREHYDROLYSIS: Relatively mild, selective hydrolysis treatment. In the chemical pulping of wood, prehydrolysis refers to a specific cooking treatment used in the manufacture of dissolving pulps, designed to remove hemicelluloses by hydrolysis.

PRIMARY HYDROXYL GROUP: In a complex organic molecule, the hydroxyl attached to a carbon which in turn is linked to only one other carbon (i.e., singly linked). Primary hydroxyl groups are generally more reactive than secondary hydroxyl groups. Both kinds of hydroxyls are found on cellulose.

PROTOLIGNIN: See LIGNIN.

PYRANOSE: Monosaccharide having a six-membered ring.

PYRANOSE RING: Closed ring in glucose and similar molecules consisting of five carbons and one oxygen atom.

Q

QUALITATIVE ANALYSIS: Chemical analysis of a sample to identify the constituent elements or compounds.

QUANTITATIVE ANALYSIS: Chemical analysis of a sample to determine the exact percentage composition of elements or compounds.

R

RADICAL: Group of atoms in a molecule that behaves in chemical reactions as a unit. Examples are ammonium (NH_4), sulfate (SO_4), hydroxyl (OH), and methyl (CH_3).

RATE CONSTANT: Term in the "reaction rate expression" which generally depends on absolute temperature (T) following the form proposed by Arrhenius:
$$k = Ae^{(-E/RT)}$$
where k is the rate constant, A is a constant for a given reaction, E is the "activation energy", and R is the gas constant.

RAYON: Generic name for man-made fibers of regenerated cellulose.

RAYON PULP: Dissolving pulp tailor-made for conversion into rayon. Specifications for rayon pulps include viscosity, moisture content, sheet properties, and freedom from certain chemical impurities.

REACTION: Any chemical change regardless of the amount of product formed or whether it is slow or rapid. Among the important types of reactions are decomposition, replacement, condensation, neutralization, oxidation-reduction, rearrangement, saponification, polymerization, and cross-linking.

REACTION KINETICS: Study of the rates at which chemical reactions occur and the resistances that must be overcome to allow the reactions to occur. The latter is indicated by the activation energy needed to initiate the reaction.

REACTION MECHANISM: Vague term used to loosely describe a chemical reaction network, reaction sequence, or the stereochemistry of an elementary step. Syn. Reaction Model.

REACTION NETWORK: Parallel and consecutive chemical reactions occurring within a single reactor.

REACTION ORDER: Method of expressing the effect of reactant concentration on reaction rate. A reaction is of the *n*th order with respect to a given component if its rate is proportional to the concentration of that component to the *n*th power.

REACTION RATE: Rate at which products are formed from reactants, which generally depends on the composition and temperature, and possibly other factors. See also REACTION RATE EXPRESSION.

REACTION RATE EXPRESSION: Usually written in the form: $r = kF(C_i)$ where $F(C_i)$ is a function that depends on the composition of the system as expressed by C_i. The coefficient k does not depend on the composition of the system and is therefore independent of time; for this reason, k is called the "rate constant".

REACTION THERMODYNAMICS: Study of chemical reactions concerned with the initial and final chemical states and the energy liberated or absorbed during the transition from the initial to the final states.

REACTIVITY: Relative ability of an atom, molecule or radical to react chemically with another atom, molecule or radical.

REAGENT: (1) Chemical used in the laboratory for detecting, measuring, or analyzing other substances. (2) Compound that supplies the attacking species in a chemical reaction.

REGENERATED CELLULOSE: Cellulose that has been dissolved, with or without chemical modification, and re-precipitated as cellulose.

RESIDUE: That portion of a monomer that is present in a polymer, i.e., the monomer minus the atoms removed from it in the process of polymerization. In cellulose, the glucose residues are the glucan units.

REVERSIBLE REACTION: Chemical reaction that can proceed to either direction depending on conditions.

S _____

SACCHARIDE: See CARBOHYDRATE.

SACCHARIFICATION: Hydrolysis of cellulose and other polysaccharides into simple sugars.

SACCHARINIC ACIDS: Hydroxy acids of simple sugars, formed by reaction of alkali with simple sugar molecules that are "peeled" from the cellulose molecule during kraft pulping.

SALT: (1) Reaction product between an acid and a base. (2) Commonly applied to sodium chloride (NaCl).

SAPONINS: Group of glucosidal compounds associated with some tree species that form foaming solutions and emulsions.

SATURATED COMPOUND: Compound without double bonds, in which all valences are satisfied. See also UNSATURATED COMPOUND.

SATURATED SOLUTION: Solution having a maximum solute concentration (at a given temperature), i.e., having the extreme degree of concentration beyond which additional solute can no longer be dissolved into it.

SECONDARY HYDROXYL GROUP: In a complex organic molecule, the hydroxyl attached to a carbon which in turn is attached to two other carbon atoms (i.e., doubly linked). See also PRIMARY HYDROXYL GROUP.

SELECTIVE ION ELECTRODE: Glass electrode filled with an ion solution of fixed activity and equipped with an internal silver-silver salt junction. When the electrode is immersed in a solution containing the particular ion, an electric potential is generated which provides a measure of ion concentration. The selective ion technique has been applied to measurements of sulfide and sodium in black liquors.

SOLUBILITY: Ability of one substance (solute) to blend uniformly with another substance (solvent). For example, the solubility of a dye in water is usually measured in terms of the highest concentration (g/liter) at which the material is totally dissolved at a prescribed temperature.

SOLUTE: Substance which is dissolved in another substance (called the "solvent"). Generally, the solute is uniformly dispersed in the solvent either as molecules or ions.

SOLUTION: Homogeneous liquid resulting from the mixing of a solid, liquid or gas (the "solute") into a liquid (the "solvent"), from which the dissolved matter can be recovered by evaporation, crystallization or distillation.

STANDARDIZATION (of chemical solutions): Procedure used to verify or adjust a chemical solution to conform to an established standard of concentration and purity.

STANDARD SOLUTION: Reference chemical solution which is certified to contain a specified concentration of the correct chemical substance within very close tolerance.

STEREOCHEMISTRY: Study of the spatial arrangement of three-dimensional chemical structures, especially with respect to isomerism. Of particular interest is the stereochemistry/topochemistry (i.e., "stereotopochemistry") of cellulose.

STOPPING REACTION: Reaction with the cellulose molecule which provides an end unit with a configuration that is stable to alkali. The stopping reaction occurs during kraft cooking following a certain amount of "peeling".

SUBSTANTIVITY: Property of a paper dye which makes it capable of being adsorbed by cellulose fibers from an aqueous medium. See also AFFINITY.

SUBSTITUTION REACTION: Chemical reaction in which an atom or radical attached to a carbon atom is removed and replaced by another atom or radical.

SUGAR: Any of the monosaccharides and oligosaccharides of comparatively low molecular weight; they have a characteristic sweet taste.

SWELLING AGENT: In cellulose chemistry, a liquid which is capable of breaking and supplanting the secondary valence bonds between the molecular chains. The swelling action may result from chemical combination with the glucose units, or may be due only to secondary valence forces between the hydroxyl groups of the glucose units and the swelling agent. The action of swelling agents is usually easily reversed by water, while the crystalline structure reverts to hydrate cellulose. The best known swelling agent is caustic solution, and the action of sodium hydroxide on cellulose is known as mercerization.

SYNTHESIS: Creation of a substance by means of one or more chemical reactions which either matches a natural substance or constitutes a unique material not found in nature. See also BIOSYNTHESIS.

T

THERMAL DECOMPOSITION: Series of physical and chemical changes which occur to cellulosic structures (or other materials) when they are heated. At lower temperatures, thermal decomposition involves reduction in dp or molecular weight by bond scission, appearance of free radicals, elimination of water, formation of carbonyl and carboxyl groups, and evolution of carbon monoxide and carbon dioxide. No clear line of demarcation exists between normal aging and low-temperature decomposition, which accelerates by heating. Syn. Thermal Degradation.

THERMOPLASTIC: Solid that becomes soft or plastic when heated, such as glass, nylon, or wax.

THERMOSETTING: [adj] Term describing a solid that changes from plastic to a rigid form when heated. Phenolics and ureas are themosetting resins.

TITRATION: Laboratory technique of quantitative analysis whereby measured amounts of a standard solution are successively added and reacted with a sample substance in solution until a desired end point is reached as shown by a color change, potentiometric inflection point, or other indicator.

TOPOCHEMICAL REACTION: Any of those site-specific chemical reactions, which are characteristic of cellulose. They can take place only at certain sites on the molecule where reactive groups are available (e.g., in amorphous areas or on the surfaces of crystalline areas).

TOPOCHEMISTRY: Chemistry in a definite area of a system. The topochemistry of cellulosic fibers is concerned with the distribution of chemical components and their site-specific reactions.

TRACE: Very small amount or concentration of a constituent.

U

UNSATURATED COMPOUND: Compound in which all the available valence bonds are not satisfied. The extra bonds are usually held as double bonds, chiefly by carbon. Unsaturated compounds are more reactive than saturated compounds because other elements readily add to the unsaturated linkage.

URONIC ACID: See GLUCURONIC ACID.

V

VALENCE: Bonding power of an element or radical to combine with other atoms in definite proportions.

VISCOMETRY: Utilization of viscosity measurements for determining average molecular weight. Syn. Viscometric Methods. See also CELLULOSE VISCOSITY.

VISCOSE SOLUTION: Solution of sodium cellulose xanthate in dilute caustic soda; the viscid, orange spinning solution from which cellulose is regenerated in an acid bath.

VISCOSITY OF CELLULOSE SOLUTIONS: See CELLULOSE VISCOSITY.

VOLATILE: [adj] Easily vaporized at normal temperature.

VOLATILITY: Relative ability of a liquid or solid material to pass into the vapor state at ordinary temperature.

VULCANIZED FIBER: Cellulose fiber sheet that has been partially solubilized by zinc chloride solution (to form "gelatinized paper"); the chemical is subsequently leached out leaving a residue of partially regenerated cellulose in which the fibrous structure is retained to a degree depending on the particular treatment. The resultant vulcanized fiber is a dense material that can be machined, formed, embossed or combined with other materials for a variety of end-uses. Various grades are called electrical insulation fiber, hard fiber, hermetic fiber, bone fiber, railroad fiber, shuttle fiber and white fiber. See also HARD FIBER.

W _____

WATER CELLULOSE: Form of cellulose that retains water in its structure. The term "water cellulose" is applied since the preferable term "hydrate cellulose" already has a well established meaning. Water cellulose is formed when alkali cellulose is washed free of alkali. It is stable indefinitely if kept in water at room temperature, and is more reactive than hydrate cellulose. See also HYDRATE CELLULOSE.

X _____

XANTHATE: See VISCOSE SOLUTION.

XYLAN: Pentosan from which the sugar, xylose, is derived by hydrolysis.

XYLOSE: Pentose which is polymerized in wood (xylan), and is liberated by hydrolysis of the hemicelluloses.

Chapter 5
Papermaking Chemistry and Microbiology

ABSORPTION: Taking up of a liquid or gas on or into a solid (without concern for the mechanism).

ACCELERATOR: Substance that hastens a reaction or curing process caused by a catalyst. Syn. Activator. See also PROMOTER.

ACETYLATED STARCH: Starch for surface sizing which has been chemically modified by partial or superficial acetylation. Syn. Feculose Starch.

ACID DYE: Class of analine dye; any of a group of sodium salts of colored acids which are not readily absorbed by cellulosic fibers, but are retained by adding rosin size and alum.

ACIDITY: State of being acid; the condition in aqueous solution wherein the concentration of hydrogen ions exceeds that of hydroxyl ions.

ACID SIZE: Rosin size which contains a substantial portion of unsaponified, but emulsified free rosin.

ACID-STABLE SIZE: See WAX SIZE.

ACRYLAMIDE RESINS: SEE DRY STRENGTH RESINS.

ACTIVATOR: See ACCELERATOR.

ADAPTATION: Advantageous variation which enables an organism to live successfully in a specific environment, e.g., in paper mill systems.

ADSORPTION: Physical or chemical phenomenon, consisting of the adhesion of molecules or colloids to solid surfaces with which they are in contact. In papermaking, adsorption usually refers to the adhesion of additive particles to fiber surfaces during papermaking. Adsorption is the primary mechanism for retention of many papermaking additives.

AGALITE: Mineral with the same chemical composition as talc (hydrated magnesium silicate), but with a less soapy feel; used as a filler in certain grades of writing paper.

AGAR: Substance derived from marine algae or seaweeds which is used to solidify microbiological culture media.

ALDEHYDE STARCH: Cationic starch to which aldehyde groups have been added. A unique property of this material is its ability to impart transient wet strength to paper.

ALKALINE FILLER: Mineral filler that causes an alkaline reaction in the presence of water or reacts with acid. Calcium carbonate is the most important alkaline filler.

ALKALINE PAPERMAKING: Papermaking system that is maintained above 7 pH. Alkaline papermaking is essential for products requiring a high degree of permanence, but usually involves more sophisticated and costlier wet end chemistry.

ALKALINE SIZE: See SYNTHETIC SIZE.

ALKALINITY: State of being alkaline; the condition in aqueous solution wherein the concentration of hydroxyl ions exceeds that of hydrogen ions.

ALKENYL SUCCINIC ANHYDRIDE (ASA): Water insoluble synthetic sizing agent, usually added to the stock in the form of a cationic starch-stabilized emulsion. Since this agent has limited stability in water, the ASA must be emulsified in the mill just prior to use.

ALKYLKETENE DIMERS (AKD): Water insoluble fatty acid derivatives used as internal sizing agents, usually in the form of cationic starch-stabilized emulsions.

ALUM: Term applied by papermakers to aluminum sulfate, $Al_2(SO_4)_3$, which is widely used in papermaking systems for pH control, as an acidic source of alumina to precipitate rosin size, as a retention aid, and as a mordant for dyes. (More correctly, alum is the general name for a group of double sulfates, most commonly aluminum potassium sulfate.) Syn. Papermakers Alum.

ALUMINA: Aluminum oxide (Al_2O_3) or hydrated aluminum oxide. See also ALUMINUM TRIHYDRATE, BAUXITE.

ALUMINATES: Sources of alumina for papermaking systems which do not lower the stock pH. For example, sodium aluminate ($NaAlO_2$) is alkaline rather than acidic.

ALUMINA TRIHYDRATE (ATH): ($Al_2O_3 \cdot H_2O$) Precipitated pigment used as a papermaking filler and in coating formulations. The principal source is bauxite ore. Syn. Aluminum Hydroxide, Hydrated Alumina, Hydrated Aluminum Oxide.

ALUMINO-SILICATE: Crystalline combination of silicate and aluminate.

ALUMINUM CHLORIDE: ($AlCl_3$) Chemical used in papermaking systems as a source of alumina, which performs in a similar manner to alum. Since it is far more expensive than alum, its use is limited to those applications where other additives in the stock are sensitive to sulfate ion concentration.

ALUMINUM RESINATE: Precipitate formed from soap sizes by the action of alum which has great affinity for cellulose fibers.

ALUMINUM SULFATE: See ALUM.

AMINO RESINS: Condensation products of formaldehyde with reactive amino groups, used as internal strength additives at the wet end and in functional coatings.

AMORPHOUS SILICAS/SILICATES: Synthetic white pigments prepared by precipitation of soluble silicates by the use of acids, alkaline earth metal salts, or aluminum salts. The products can be hydrated silica or silicic acid, a simple alkaline earth silicate, or a complex aluminosilicate.

AMPHIPATHIC MOLECULE: Molecule having both hydrophilic and hydrophobic parts. The foremost example in papermaking systems is rosin, which is precipitated onto fibers with the hydrophobic parts oriented outward.

AMPHOLYTIC STARCH: Any of a group of modified starches containing both cationic and anionic groups which are purported to perform well as wet end additives under variable conditions of pH, water hardness and alum concentration.

AMPHOTERIC: [adj] Capable of reacting in water either as a weak acid or as a weak base. For example, aluminum salts hydrolyze in water to form a compound that may be considered a weak base [$Al(OH)_3$] or a weak acid [H_3AlO_3].

AMYLACEOUS: [adj] Pertaining to starch. Syn. Starchy.

AMYLASE: Any of several varieties of an enzyme which catalyzes the hydrolysis of starch. Thinning of starches at the mill is commonly carried out by enzyme conversion.

AMYLOPECTIN: In natural starches, the form of starch composed of branched chains of maltose. This so-called "waxy starch" forms clear pastes and is non-gelling.

AMYLOSE: In natural starches, the form of starch composed of continuous chains of maltose.

ANATASE: Crystal form of titanium dioxide, used to make the white papermaking filler. See also TITANIUM DIOXIDE.

ANHYDROUS: [adj] Describes the chemical form that does not have water attached to the molecule.

ANILINE DYE: Dye derived from aniline, a coal tar derivative. Aniline is the most important dye intermediate, being readily converted under carefully controlled conditions into a wide range of specific dyes.

ANIMAL SIZE: Gelatinous material extracted by hot water cooking of hides, and utilized as size in papermaking.

ANION: Negatively charged ion. So-called because these ions collect at the anode when current is passed through an ionized solution.

ANIONIC STARCH: Any of a group of modified starches which ionize with a negative charge, including starch phosphates, starches with carboxyl and sulfonic acid groups, and starch xanthates. Starch phosphate is the principal anionic starch used as a wet end additive.

ANTIFOAM: See DEFOAMER.

ASH: Inorganic residue from burning a sample of paper. The weight of ash is used to determine the percentage of mineral filler in the sheet.

ASPENWAX: Benzene-extractable sterols (complex cyclical compounds) and related compounds (components of aspen and other hardwoods) which provide a significant self-sizing effect when retained in the pulp.

ASPHALT: Dark solid or semisolid material which is a complex mixture of high-molecular weight hydrocarbons obtained by refining petroleum. It is used for internal sizing of certain light to dark brown paperboards such as those used for beverage cases and similar products designed for water-abuse conditions. It is often used as a barrier material in laminates.

B

BACTERIA: Single-celled microorganisms that reproduce by binary fission (splitting). They occur in many shapes, e.g., round (coccus, cocci), rods (bacillus, bacilli) and spiral (sprillum, sprilli).

BACTERIA COUNT: Analytical procedure for determining bacterial growth (amount of slime) in papermill process waters, measured in number of organisms per mililiter.

BACTERICIDE: See BIOCIDE.

BARIUM SULFATE: ($BaSO_4$) White pigment, used mainly as a coating pigment for photographic papers. Its high specific gravity and relative high price have limited its use in other papermaking applications. See also BARYTE, BLANC FIXE.

BARYTE: Mineral consisting of almost pure barium sulfate, prepared for papermaking applications by grinding to a fine powder.

BASIC DYE: Any dye which is the salt of a colored organic base combined with a colorless acid, such as hydrochloric or sulfuric. Basic dyes as a class are the most important for coloring paper, combining the advantages of low cost, high tinctorial strength and great brilliance. Syn. Cationic Dye.

BENEFICIATION: Improving the physical properties of an ore; commonly applied to the processing of raw clay.

BENTONITE: Naturally occurring clay mineral containing smectite, a hydrous aluminum silicate containing small amounts of alkali and alkaline earth metals. Because of its fine particle size and high sorptivity, smectite is used in deinking processes to adsorb ink particles and in papermaking systems to absorb pitch.

BEWOID SIZE: Rosin emulsion containing about 90% unsaponified rosin dispersed in a small amount of rosin soap and stabilized by about 2% casein.

BIOCATALYST: Biochemical catalyst, usually an enzyme.

BIOCIDE: Class of chemical utilized in the papermaking system to control slime formation by killing microorganisms. A bactericide or germicide is an agent that kills bacteria (but not necessarily bacterial spores), while a fungicide or myocide is a chemical agent that kills fungi or molds. Syn. Slimicide, Microbiocide. See also BIOSTAT.

BIOSTAT: Class of chemical utilized in the papermaking system to control slime formation by inhibiting the growth of microorganisms, thereby preventing them from producing adverse effects. A bacteriostat is a chemical agent that inhibits bacteriological growth, while a fungistat or mycostat is a chemical agent that inhibits the growth of fungi or molds. Syn. Microbiostat.

BIREFRINGENCE: Difference between maximum and minimum refractive indices of anisotropic materials such as cellulose fibers and starch granules.

BITUMINOUS EMULSIONS: Specially prepared sizes normally used for producing certain board grades. The base material is petroleum asphalt, and the application has a light-to-dark brown color which restricts utilization.

BLANC FIXE: Commercial name for precipitated barium sulfate, used mainly in photographic paper coatings.

BLEEDING: Giving up of color in water or other solvent.

BLUNGER: Mixing unit used to disperse clay with water and a chemical dispersing agent into a fluid slurry (slip).

BONDING AGENT: See DRY STRENGTH ADHESIVE.

BORAX: See SODIUM BORATE.

BOTTOM COLORS: Dyes which have a distinct affinity for cellulose fibers, as opposed to top colors which have a greater affinity for clay.

C

CALCINED CLAY: See CALCINED KAOLIN, DEHYDROXYLATED KAOLIN.

CALCINED KAOLIN: Kaolin which has been thermally treated (at 1000–1050°C) to increase its brightness and light-scattering properties. (The treatment also increases its abrasiveness.) Syn. Calcined Clay. See also DEHYDROXYLATED KAOLIN.

CALCIUM CARBONATE: ($CaCO_3$) White pigment used as a filler in alkaline papermaking furnishes. Although available in several forms, the trend is toward precipitated calcium carbonate, which is produced in high purity, high brightness and controlled particle size and shape.

CALCIUM SULFATE: ($CaSO_4$) White pigment occasionally used as a filler in papermaking. Relatively high water solubility has limited its use.

CATIONIC DYE: See BASIC DYE.

CATIONIC DIRECT DYES: Newest class of dyes which behave as direct dyes, but are cationic rather than anionic in nature. Many of these dyes have excellent affinity for cellulose fibers.

CATIONIC STARCH: Any of a group of chemically modified starches which ionize with a positive charge. The electrochemical affinity of cationic starch with negatively charged cellulose fibers results in excellent wet-end retention.

CHALK: Natural, relatively pure form of calcium carbonate with a fine, soft structure consisting of fragments of tiny marine organisms.

CHEMICAL CONVERSION (of starch): See STARCH CONVERSION.

CHINA CLAY: Fine grade of clay used in fillers and coatings.

CLAY: Natural, fine-grained pigment with a plate-like morphology, composed primarily of silica and alumina, widely used as a papermaking filler. A number of grades are available depending on particle size and shape, as well as brightness. See also KAOLIN, DELAMINATED CLAY.

CLEAVAGE: Ability of minerals to break along certain crystallographic planes, e.g., clay delamination.

COFLOCCULATION: Term used to describe the attachment of filler or polymeric particles to fibers because of interfacial forces (i.e., by adsorption), analogous to fiber flocculation.

COLLOID: Substance present in extremely small particles.

COLLOIDAL SYSTEM: Intimate mixture of two substances, one of which (called the dispersed phase, or colloid) is uniformly distributed in a finely divided state through the second substance (called the dispersing medium). Several types of colloidal systems are possible, but only two are of interest in papermaking: solid-in-liquid (called a "sol") and liquid-in-liquid (called an "emulsion"). Colloidal systems have properties distinct from true solutions because of the larger size of the particles. The molecular groups (i.e., colloidal particles) carry a resultant electric charge, generally the same for all particles.

COLORANT: Agent added to papermaking furnish to impart color; e.g., dye, color lake, pigment.

COLORED PIGMENTS: Grouping that includes minerals (e.g., iron oxides, ultramarines, umbers, sienna and chrome yellows), lampblack, and both organic and inorganic synthetic pigments. The principal organic synthetic pigments are color lakes.

COLORIMETER: Reflectometer for measuring concentrations of colored materials for analytical purposes.

COLOR LAKE: Artificial pigment prepared by precipitating an organic dye onto inorganic base particles of alumina, barium sulfate or clay. Syn. Lake.

CONVERTER: See COOKER.

COOKER: Device wherein mechanical, thermal or thermal-chemical energy is used to produce low-viscosity solutions from unmodified starch. Syn. Converter. See also JET COOKING.

CULTURE: Active growth of microorganisms in or on nutrient media.

D _____

DEFLOCCULANTS: Class of chemicals that can be added to the papermaking stock to reduce the flocculating tendency of the fibers.

DEFOAMER: Class of surfactant chemical that inhibits foam formation and/or reduces foam stability. Often the terms "defoamer" and "antifoam" are used interchangably. Where applied differentially, an antifoam is used to prevent foam formation, and a defoamer is used to knock down foam that has already formed.

DEHYDROGENASE: Key enzyme in the biological oxidation of organic compounds. Measurement of dehydrogenase in pulp and paper mill water systems can be used to estimate the microbial content within the system.

DEHYDROXYLATED KAOLIN: Kaolin which has been thermally treated (at 650–700°C) to the point where the hydroxyl groups in the chemical structure are driven off as water. This produces a form with greater bulk and improved optical properties. Syn. Partially Calcined Kaolin.

DELAMINATED CLAY: Grade of filler clay produced by splitting apart the larger particles of kaolin (called "books" or "stacks"), yielding particles (called "platelets") which tend to be thinner and wider than the normal clay particles. See also CLAY, KAOLIN.

DELAMINATION: Process of breaking down kaolin stacks into thin plates. See also CLEAVAGE.

DETERGENT: Class of surfactant chemical utilized as a cleaning agent. It resembles soap in its ability to emulsify oil and hold dirt in suspension.

DEWATERING AGENT: Polymeric flocculant which, when added to stock, accelerates drainage. Syn. Drainage Aid.

DEXTRINIZING: Modifying starch by reducing its polymer chain length by partial hydrolysis with acids, enzymes and/or heat. The shorter chain forms, called "dextrins", are used as adhesives. Syn. Starch Depolymerization.

DEXTRINIZING VALUE (of enzymes) (DV): Measure of dextrinizing enzyme activity by test.

DIATOMACEOUS EARTH: Natural silica, consisting of the skeletons of various minute marine organisms, occasionally used as a papermaking filler. Abrasiveness is a problem with diatomite fillers.

DIPSLIDE TEST TECHNIQUE: Method of monitoring microbiological activity within a papermaking system. A sample of headbox stock or wire pit water is placed in a clear plastic container along with a plastic slide covered with agar and incubated at the normal temperature of the particular fluid. After the incubation period (usually from 24 to 72 hours), any colonies of organisms present in the water can easily be seen and quantified.

DIRECT DYE: Class of analine dye; any of a group of sodium salts of colored acids which act on cellulosic fibers without a mordant. As a class, direct dyes are less soluble than acid dyes, tending to form colloidal systems. Syn. Substantive Dye.

DIRECT SIZING: Internal sizing with rosin where the rosin is added to the stock first, followed by addition of alum.

DISPERSANT: Class of surfactant chemical utilized in papermaking systems to reduce deposits of pitch and slime, in de-inking systems to disperse the ink particles, and in coating formulations to keep the clay particles in suspension. Syn. Dispersing Agent, Emulsifier.

DISPERSE DYE: Nonionic organic colorant with extremely low water solubility. These colorants are ground to a specific particle size range and combined with a dispersing agent to make them compatible with water systems.

DISPROPORTIONATION: Method to stabilize rosin size against oxidation by converting one portion into a more reduced form and another portion into a more oxidized form.

DRAINAGE AID: Chemical substance that can be added to the papermaking furnish to increase the water removal on the wire. Syn. Dewatering Agent.

DRY-STRENGTH ADHESIVE: Any of a wide class of substances which is added to the papermaking furnish to strengthen fiber bonding and improve paper stiffness and pick resistance. Examples are starches, gums, latices, cellulose derivatives and resins. Syn. Bonding Agents.

DRY-STRENGTH RESINS: Type of dry-strength adhesive; primarily water soluble acrylamide based polymers and copolymers which are effective at low concentration in developing fiber-to-fiber bonds.

DYE: Colored soluble substance which is used to impart a more or less permanent color to another material. Syn. Dyestuff. See also ACID DYE, ANALINE DYE, BASIC DYE, CATIONIC DIRECT DYE, DIRECT DYE.

E _____

ELECTRICAL DOUBLE LAYER: Electrically-charged surface of a colloidal particle together with a diffuse surrounding layer of counter ions.

ELECTROKINETIC CHARGE: See ZETA POTENTIAL.

ELECTROPHORESIS: Migration of charged colloidal particles in a solution under the influence of an external potential gradient.

ELECTROPHORETIC MOBILITY: Relative ability of charged colloidal particles to migrate in a solution under the influence of an external potential gradient.

ELECTROSTATIC INTERACTIONS: Actions or effects that charged particles exert on one another due to the forces of attraction and repulsion.

EMULSIFIER: (1) Dispersing agent or emulsifying agent. (2) Mixing system for preparing a stable dispersion from two or more nonmiscible liquids, usually with addition of a chemical additive such as a detergent or other surfactant.

EMULSION: Colloidal dispersion of a liquid in another liquid with which it is not normally miscible. The dispersion is stabilized by the addition of a surfactant (e.g., soap, detergent) which acts as an emulsifying agent.

ENZYME: Class of complex organic substances that accelerate or catalyze specific chemical transformations, such as the modification of native starches for size press applications.

ENZYME CONVERSION (of starch): See STARCH CONVERSION.

EXTENDER: Inexpensive mineral filler which is normally used in conjunction with an expensive filler (e.g., titanium dioxide) to space the particles and thus increase the effectiveness.

F

FECULOSE: See ACETYLATED STARCH.

FILAMENTOUS BACTERIA: See FIMBRIATED BACTERIA.

FIMBRIATED BACTERIA: Numerous species of bacteria that are characterized by attached filamentous appendages or organs (called fimbriae). The fimbriae impart adhesive properties to the bacterial cells, enabling them to fasten to a variety of surfaces within a papermaking system. Syn. Filamentous Bacteria.

FIXING AGENT: Type of retention aid chemical that causes soluble materials (e.g., anionic trash) to become adsorbed or precipitated onto the fibers.

FLUORESCENT BRIGHTENING AGENT: See OPTICAL BRIGHTENER.

FLUORESCENT WHITENING: See OPTICAL WHITENING.

FLUOROCARBON SIZE: Any of a family of water soluble, synthetic fluorocarbon compounds used as internal or surface sizing agents. When used as an internal sizing agent, retention is dependent on the use of a strongly cationic retention aid which serves as a bonding agent between the anionic fiber and the anionic fluorocarbon.

FLUOROCHEMICALS: Long-chain molecular compounds containing fluorine, used as wet-end additives in the manufacture of oil-proofing papers.

FOAMING AGENT: Surfactant which reduces the surface tension of water and promotes foam formation, used in the flotation deinking process. Syn. Frothing Agent, Frother.

FORTIFIED ROSIN: Chemically modified form of rosin (e.g., with maleic anhydride) used as internal sizing, either alone or in combination with unmodified rosin. Less fortified rosin is required for a given sizing effect as compared to normal rosin size. Syn. Fortified Size.

FREE: [adj] Present in a chemically uncombined state, e.g., free rosin.

FREE MOISTURE: Moisture associated with fibers, fillers, chemicals. etc. in excess of that chemically held. Syn. Free Water, Hygroscopic Moisture.

FREE ROSIN: Unsaponified rosin, used in combination with rosin size in colloidal suspension for internal sizing. Under some conditions, high free-rosin size is more efficient than other types of size.

FUNGICIDE: See BIOCIDE.

G

GEL: Molecular structure formed in aqueous media by hydrophilic colloidal polymeric substances such as hemicellulose, pectin and starch. Gels absorb many times their own weight of water with consequent swelling and can set to a viscous or semisolid jelly (gel) when cool.

GELATIN: Albuminous material extracted from animal bones, ligaments and skins, utilized in tub sizing and other surface applications. It differs from animal glue in its purity.

GELATINIZATION: Absorption of water with profound irreversible swelling, as occurs when starch granules are cooked in an aqueous suspension to form a viscous solution for papermaking applications. Syn. Solvation. See also HYDRATION.

GELATINOUS: [adj] Viscous; having the consistency of gelatin.

GELATION: Formation of a gel.

GLUE: Adhesive of animal origin, composed of complex protein structures. In modern usage, the terms, ''glue'' and ''adhesive'', are used interchangably.

GRANULE: Small discrete mass of a solid substance. For example, starch is naturally obtained in granules which range in size from 2 to 100 μm.

GUM: Water soluble mannogalactan mucilage derived from the locust bean or the seed of the guar plant, used as an internal strength additive in papermaking furnishes. The term "mannogalactan" (or "galactomannan") refers to a complex polysaccharide composed of mannose and galactose units.

GYPSUM: Naturally occurring hydrate of calcium sulfate ($CaSO_4 \cdot 2H_2O$), used as a paper filler.

H

HOLLOW-SPHERE PIGMENT: Aqueous styrene/acrylic polymer dispersion, used mainly as a coating pigment. The particles are hollow spheres, shells of hard polymer surrounding a core of water. During drying of the coating, water diffuses out of the particles leaving air-filled voids.

HYDRATION: Incorporation of water into a complex molecule, as occurs with the gelatinization of starch.

HYDROGEN-FORMING BACTERIA: Clostridia-type bacteria which produce hydrogen during anaerobic incubation. These thermophilic acid-forming bacteria have been responsible for explosive buildups of hydrogen in white water storage tanks.

HYDROLYZED: [adj] Applied to chemical compounds that have incorporated water into their chemical structures, forming either weak acids or weak bases.

HYDROPHILIC: [adj] Having a strong affinity for binding or absorbing water, which results in swelling and formation of gels. All carbohydrates are hydrophilic, especially starches and gums.

HYDROPHOBIC: [adj] Having no affinity for water, resistant to wetting and penetration by water. This property is characteristic of fats, oils and waxes.

HYDROUS: [adj] Describes chemical form having water attached to its molecules.

HYGROSCOPIC: [adj] Having the ability to absorb water vapor from the surrounding atmosphere.

HYGROSCOPIC MOISTURE: See FREE MOISTURE.

I

INCRUSTATION: Process whereby depositions become infiltrated, coated or covered with naturally occurring fatty, waxy, resinous, nitrogenous or ligneous compounds that render them more resistant to chemical and/or physical agents.

INERT: [adj] Not capable of reaction under prevailing conditions.

ION: Electrically charged atom or group of atoms. Ions in solution are due to ionization of a dissolved substance, and may be either positively of negatively charged.

IONIC COMPOUND: Compound that ionizes or dissociates into ions in water solution.

IONIZATION: Any process by which a neutral atom or molecule gains or losses electrons, thereby acquiring a net charge. Ionization occurs by dissociation in water solution (e.g., $NaCl = Na^+ + Cl^-$).

IRON BACTERIA: Bacteria that metabolize reduced iron and deposit ferric oxides with secretions.

ISOELECTRIC POINT: pH value of the dispersion medium of a colloidal system at which the particles do not move in an electric field; i.e., the pH at which the charge on the particles is neutralized.

J

JET COOKING: Continuous starch cooking system in which a starch slurry is mixed with high-pressure steam in a chamber where intense shear is developed. Starches processed in this way are referred to as "thermomechanical starches".

K

KAOLIN: Any of several clay minerals with a two-layer crystal in which silica and alumina sheets alternate. See also CLAY, DELAMINATED CLAY.

KAOLINITE: [$Al_2Si_2O_5(OH)_4$] Main mineral constituent of kaolin clay.

KARAYA GUM: Polysaccharide used as a deflocculating agent for long-fibered stock dispersions.

L

LAKE: See COLOR LAKE.

LATEX: Colloidal suspension or emulsion of natural or synthetic rubber or plastic in water.

LATICES: Plural of latex. See also SYNTHETIC LATICES.

LEVAN: Gooey polysaccharide generated by various forms of bacteria, most of which are attached to solid surfaces. These "colonizing bacteria" create a biofilm of levan that eventually grows into large, complex slime deposits.

LIQUID DYE: Dye in concentrated liquid form. Liquid dyes are not simply powder dyes dissolved in water, since most powder dyes have limited water solubility, within the range of one to ten percent.

LIQUIFIER: Substance used to reduce the gel point and viscosity of starch and gum solutions.

LITHOPONE: Mixture of zinc sulfide and barium sulfate, used as a paper filler.

M

MALTOSE: Non-alternating arrangement of two glucose residues. Maltose units are joined together either in a continuous molecular arrangement (amylose) or a branched arrangement (amylopectin) to form starch.

MELAMINE-FORMALDEHYDE RESIN: Wet strength resin produced by copolymerization of melamine and formaldehyde.

MICELLES: Molecular aggregates of soaps and surfactants in colloidal solutions at concentrations above a well-defined concentration, called the critical micelle concentration.

MICROBIOLOGICAL ANALYSIS: Approximate measurement of the number and types of microorganisms in a given amount of sample.

MICROBIOLOGICAL SURVEY: Systematic sampling and biological analysis of selected flows within the papermaking system so that a complete microbiological picture is obtained.

MICROBIOLOGY: Study of microorganisms which include bacteria, algae, yeast-type fungi and mold-type fungi which grow in paper mill systems.

MICROCRYSTALLINE WAX: Petroleum derivative distinguished from paraffin by smaller crystal size and more branched chemical structure; used as a component in paper surface coatings.

MICROORGANISM: Microscopic or sub-microscopic organism. In papermaking systems, the microorganisms that cause problems are certain bacteria and molds.

MILDEW: Surface growth of mold.

MINERAL: Naturally occurring solid inorganic substance with a crystalline structure and a characteristic chemical composition expressed by a chemical formula.

MINERALOGY: Study and classification of minerals by source, chemical composition, crystalline structure and properties.

MISCIBILITY: Ability of two or more liquids to mix together without separating, i.e., to dissolve in each other.

MODIFIED STARCH: See STARCH CONVERSION.

MOLD: Filamentous fungus composed of many cells in thread-like formations (called hyphae) that form a network (called a mycelium).

MORDANT: Substance that has the ability to fix or bind dye molecules to cellulosic fibers. Syn. Coupling Agent.

MUCILAGE: Polysaccharide or carbohydrate polymer extracted from the roots, seeds or twigs of certain trees and plants, in particular from the seeds of the guar plant and locust beans. Mucilages do not produce gels (as does starch), but form thick, slippery dispersions in water. No clear distinction exists between gums and mucilages.

MUCOID: Microbiological growths which are characteristically plastic and possess a slimy or gelatinous covering layer which imparts a sticky consistency to the growth.

N

NEUTRAL SIZE: Rosin size (saponified rosin) which contains no free rosin.

NON-FIBROUS ADDITIVE: Any component of the papermaking furnish that is non-fibrous in structure. See ADDITIVE.

NONIONIC COMPOUND: Hydrophilic compound that does not ionize in water.

NONOXIDIZING BIOCIDE: Biocide whose effectiveness does not depend on its ability to oxidize organic material, e.g., systemic poisons or surface active agents.

O

OLEOPHILIC: [adj] Descriptive of substances that are readily wetted by oil.

OPTICAL BRIGHTENER: Chemical additive to a papermaking furnish that improves the apparent brightness of the product by the introduction of fluorescence. The action of an optical brightener is based on the ability of the molecule to absorb ultraviolet light and re-emit as visible blue light. Syn. Fluorescent Brightening Agent.

OPTICAL WHITENING: Process of adding an optical brightening agent to paper stock in order to achieve a specified improvement in apparent brightness. Syn. Fluorescent Whitening.

OXIDIZED STARCH: See STARCH CONVERSION.

OXIDIZING BIOCIDE: Biocide whose action depends on its ability to oxidize and thus destroy material, e.g., chlorine, chlorine dioxide, ozone.

P

PARAFFIN: Wax obtained from petroleum by distillation, used in the manufacture of waxed paper and in other paper sealing applications.

PASTE SIZE: Most widely used form of rosin size, containing up to 30% of free- acid rosin at a solids content of 70–80%. Mill preparation requires two stages of dilution in a suitable "emulsification unit"; hot-water dilution down to 10–20% solids followed by cold-water dilution to a working concentration of 2 to 6%.

PEARL FILLER: Anhydrous calcium sulfate ($CaSO_4$), used as a paper filler. It occurs naturally or can be prepared by dehydrating gypsum.

PEARL STARCH: See STARCH.

PEPTIZATION: Stabilization (i.e., prevention of aggregation) of hydrophobic colloidal particles within a water system by addition of a suitable electrolyte, called a "peptizing agent", which is adsorbed on to the particle surfaces.

PEPTIZING AGENT: Substance which promotes colloidal dispersion. See also PEPTIZATION.

PETROLEUM WAXES: Waxes produced as byproducts during refining of crude petroleum. See PARAFFIN, MICROCRYSTALLINE WAX.

PHYSICO-CHEMICAL MECHANISM: Chemical reaction or interaction manifested by physical change. Examples in papermaking are flocculation, dispersion, solids retention, and sizing.

PIGMENT: Finely divided solid organic or inorganic coloring material that is insoluble in the medium in which it is applied (as contrasted to a dye which is soluble). White pigments are commonly employed as fillers in papermaking furnishes and they constitute the principal ingredient in coating mixtures. See also FILLER.

PITCH: Oleophilic resinous material released from wood by mechanical and/or chemical processing. Pitch includes fatty acids, resin acids, their insoluble salts, and esters of fatty acids with glycerol and sterols, as well as other fats and waxes.

PITCH CONTROL: Prevention of the formation of pitch deposits and agglomerates within the papermaking system. The usual control strategy is either to keep the material dispersed or add a high-specific-surface substance like talc, which has an affinity for pitch particles.

PITCH DEPOSITS: Complex resinous hydrophobic agglomerates containing organic and inorganic portions.

PLASTIC PIGMENTS: Bulky organic pigment-like particles manufactured by an emulsion polymerization process, used mainly in coating formulations. A number of different polymers and copolymers can be used, but polystyrene is the usual choice from a cost/performance standpoint. See also HOLLOW-SPHERE PIGMENT.

PLATE COUNT: Determination of the number of colonies of bacteria that develop after plating appropriate dilutions of a sample under specified conditions.

POLYACRYLAMIDES: High molecular weight compounds utilized as bridging flocculants and retention aids in papermaking suspensions. They become adsorbed on several particles at once, forming three-dimensional matrixes.

POLYALUMINUM HYDROXY CHLORIDE: Form of aluminum used to precipitate rosin size in neutral papermaking systems around pH 7.0.

POLYDISPERSE SYSTEM: System containing particles of different sizes or in which polymer molecules vary widely in molecular weight.

POLYELECTROLYTE: Long-chain polymer that when dissociated in solution does not give uniform distribution of positive and negative ions. The ions of one sign are bound to the polymer chain, while the ions of the other sign diffuse through the solution. Natural and synthetic polyelectrolytes are utilized in papermaking systems as either cationic or anionic retention aids, and for optimizing the zeta potential.

POLYSTYRENE: Polymer of styrene, a cyclic monomer. See PLASTIC PIGMENT.

POLYVINYL ALCOHOL (PVOH): Polymer used in papermaking systems as a wet-end additive for internal strength, and as a sizing agent and coating binder. It is available in a number of grades varying in viscosity and degree of hydrolysis.

PRECIPITATE: Solid substance formed from solution, usually by chemical action.

PRECIPITATING AGENT: Usually refers to the chemical added to papermaking stock which precipitates rosin (or other internal sizing agent) onto the fibers. Typically, alum is used. Syn. Precipitant.

PRECONVERTED STARCH: See STARCH CONVERSION.

PREGELATINIZED STARCH: Starch which has been precooked and dried, and has the ability to hydrate and swell in cold water.

PROMOTER: Substance which when added to a catalyst increases its activity. See also ACCELERATOR.

PROTECTIVE COLLOID: Material that surrounds colloidal particles and prevents coagulation or agglomeration. In papermaking, the presence of oxidized starch, carboxymethylcellulose, or gelatine can improve internal sizing results by keeping the rosin size precipitate well dispersed.

PROTEINACEOUS: [adj] Of protein base; refers to substances such as animal glue, casein, soya, etc. which are protein materials.

PUTREFACTION: Spoilage or degradation due to bacterial or fungal action. Starch and animal size solutions are susceptible to putrefaction, and it customary to add a preservative such as formaldehyde if they are stored for any significant length of time.

R _____

REACTIVE DYE: Dye of high substantivity which is capable of chemical bonding to cellulose.

REACTIVE SIZE: See SYNTHETIC SIZE.

RESIN: Generically, any polymer that is a basic material for plastics; often designated as "synthetic resin" to differentiate from natural resin.

RESIN EMULSIONS: Non-elastomeric polymers used as stock additives to improve sheet strength, provide specific sizing effects, and improve other sheet properties. Examples are polystyrenes, polyalkylacrylate, and polyvinyl acetate.

RETENTION AID: Chemical added to the papermaking furnish to increase the retention of fiber fines, mineral fillers, or other additives. See also FIXING AGENT.

RETROGRADATION: Formation of an insoluble precititate during solubilization of starch.

REVERSE SIZING: Internal sizing with rosin in which the order of adding rosin and alum is reversed, i.e., alum is added to the papermaking stock before the rosin.

ROSIN DISPERSIONS: See FREE ROSIN.

ROSIN EMULSIONS: Very high free-acid-content rosin dispersions, with free-rosin acid contents in the 75 to 100% range. Some types are stabilized with a protective colloid such as casein or soy protein.

ROSIN SIZE: Saponified rosin (i.e., alkali metal salts of rosin) used as a wet-end additive. It is added as a solution and is precipitated onto the fibers by the action of alum.

RUTILE: Crystal form of titanium dioxide, used to make the papermaking filler. See also TITANIUM DIOXIDE.

S _____

SATIN WHITE: Bulky white pigment made from the interaction of slaked lime and aluminum sulfate. It can be described chemically as a calcium sulfo-aluminate complex.

SILICA: Silicon dioxide (SiO_2), occurring naturally in many forms. A sythetically-prepared amorphous form is used as a papermaking filler.

SILICATE: Any of a number of compounds containing silicon, oxygen, and one or more metals, with or without hydrogen. Certain synthetically-prepared amorphous silicates are used as papermaking fillers. See also SODIUM SILICATE.

SINTERING: (1) Forming a coherent bonded mass by heating. (2) Conversion of the rosin-alum precipitate, which is retained within the paper sheet during internal sizing, into an efficient hydrophobic material in the dryer section.

SIZE: Any material used for sizing (i.e., reducing liquid penetration), for example rosin with alum, starch, animal glue, gelatin, latex, etc. Syn. Sizing Agent.

SIZE PRECIPITANT: Chemical in the papermaking system which serves to precipitate rosin out of solution onto the fibers. Alum is commonly used for this purpose, but other aluminum and copper compounds are also suitable.

SLIME: Gelatinous, stringy, viscous, pasty or leathery masses of bacteria (aerobic and anaerobic) and fungi (yeasts and molds), often in symbiotic associations. See also SLIME DEPOSITS.

SLIME CONTROL: Inhibition or elimination of slime formation.

SLIME DEPOSITS: Deposits in the papermaking system characterized by some degree of microorganism activity, but also consisting of various combinations of organic and inorganic material. See also LEVAN.

SLIMICIDE: See BIOCIDE.

SMECTITE: See BENTONITE.

SODIUM ALUMINATE: ($Na_2Al_2O_4$) Chemical used in the sizing process as a source of alumina. Unlike alum solutions which are acidic, sodium aluminate solutions are alkaline. In most papermill applications, sodium aluminate is used in combination with alum to achieve both the desired pH and alumina content.

SODIUM BORATE: ($Na_2B_4O_7 \cdot 10H_2O$) Additive for starch adhesive solutions which improves the water-holding capability of the starch and provides increased viscosity stability. Syn. Borax.

SODIUM SILICATE: ($Na_2O \cdot 3SiO_3$ or $Na_2O \cdot 4SiO_3$) Soluble chemical used as a wet-end additive, usually in combination with other chemicals, for pitch control, internal strength, and optimization of other paper properties. It is also used as a buffer and stabilizer in peroxide bleaching. Syn. Water Glass.

SOFTENING AGENT: Surfactant-type chemical which is added to papermaking stock to impart a softer feel to the paper product. Syn. Softener.

SOL: Colloidal dispersion of solid particles in a liquid. The particles may be macromolecules or clusters of small molecules. "Lyophobic sols" are those in which there is no affinity between the dispersed particles and the liquid. "Lyophilic sols" are those in which the solute molecules are large and have an affinity for the solvent. Starch in water is an example of a lyophilic sol.

SOLVATION: See GELATINIZATION.

SPORE: (1) Minute, thick-walled body forming within the cells of certain bacteria, considered a resting stage for the micro-organism. (2) Differentiated cell for dissemination or reproduction of fungi.

STABILIZATION: Prevention or control of scale, corrosion and microbiological fouling in water systems.

STABILIZER: (1) Substance added to an emulsion to prevent coagulation and separation. (2) Substance added to a formulation to protect against degradation during processing. Syn. Stabilizing Agent.

STARCH: Polymer of glucose derived from various plants, principally corn, tapioca, potato, and wheat. It is widely used in papermaking as an internal strength wet-end additive, as the major component in surface sizing solutions and as an adhesive in coating formulations. Many types and forms are available including the native product (called "pearl starch"), fractionated starches, and starches modified by chemical and thermal action. (Structurally, starch is characterized by a nonalternating arrangement of repeating glucose units, called "maltose units" as opposed to cellulose which is formed of alternating glucose molecules called "cellobiose units". In contrast to cellulose molecules which are straight and of indefinite length, starch molecules have a helical or spiral construction. Thus, starch molecules cannot join laterally by hydrogen bonds to adjacent starch molecules as can linear cellulose molecules.) See also STARCH CONVERSION.

STARCH CONVERSION: Modification of starch. Because of the high viscosity and poor flow characteristics of naturally occurring starch solutions, some modification is usually required to facilitate use as a sizing agent or in coating formulations. Chemical modifications by the manufacturers include dextrinization (heating in powder form with acid or salt), acid thinning (treatment with mineral acid in aqueous slurry), oxidation (e.g., reaction with hypochlorite in suspension), etherification, esterification, and cross-linking with reagents. Mill treatments of native starch include enzyme conversion (heating a solution with alpha amylase), thermal conversion (starch slurry subjected to high-temperature steam and shear mixing in a pressurized heater), and thermochemical conversion (pressurized oxidation of starch solution at high temperature).

STARCH DERIVATIVES: Chemically modified starch products, including those which involve oxidation, esterification and etherification.

STREAMING POTENTIAL: Difference in electric potential between the liquid leaving a constricted opening and the surface of the opening. For example, if water is forced through cellulose fibers, the surfaces of the fibers become negatively charged by the loss of hydrogen ions, while the water becomes positively charged by virtue of carrying these hydrogen ions.

SULFUR BACTERIA: Aerobic bacteria which are able to oxidize reduced forms of sulfur to sulfate and sulfuric acid. These bacteria can cause corrosion where oxidizable forms of sulfur are present and a thin film of slime serves as a substrate.

SULFUR-REDUCING BACTERIA: Colonies of anaerobic bacteria that utilize a food supply (e.g., wood sugars in white water) to reduce sulfate ions to sulfide and generate electrical energy. In effect, the colony acts as an electric cell. The steel surface on which the colony is attached functions as the anode and is eaten away to form iron sulfide and iron oxide.

SUPERABSORBENTS: Chemicals (e.g., cross-linked carboxymethylcellulose and crosslinked vinyl-grafted starches) having the ability to absorb water in quantities hundreds of times their own weight. Dry blends of superabsorbents with fluff pulps are being used for diapers and other non-woven products.

SURFACE ACTIVE AGENT: Any chemical which migrates to an interface (liquid/liquid, liquid/solid or liquid/gas) is said to be "surface active". Surface active agents usually comprise an organic molecule containing both a hydrocarbon portion (oil-soluble) and a polar portion (water-soluble). These chemicals can be further delineated according to application into detergents, dispersants, foaming agents, defoamers, etc. Syn. Surfactant.

SURFACE ACTIVITY: Change in the surface energy and surface tension of a liquid, caused either by changes in the liquid's physical or chemical conditions or by the addition of a surface active agent to the liquid.

SURFACE CHARGE: Charge arising on the surfaces of particles from the ionization of constituent molecules or by the capture or adsorption of positive ions (cations) or negative ions (anions) from the surrounding liquid. Pulp fibers, filler colloids, and size particles in a papermaking system usually carry a negative charge. See also ZETA POTENTIAL.

SURFACE TENSION: Stress in a liquid surface due to lateral attraction of molecules for each other. Surface tension causes drops of liquid to try to assume a spherical shape.

SURFACTANT: See SURFACE ACTIVE AGENT.

SWELLING: See GELATINIZATION.

SYNTHETIC: [adj] Man-made, as opposed to naturally occurring. The term usually implies a product made by chemical synthesis.

SYNTHETIC DRY-STRENGTH RESINS: See DRY-STRENGTH RESINS.

SYNTHETIC FILLER: Under this heading are amorphous silicas and silicates, as well as organic pigments such as polystyrene latex particles.

SYNTHETIC LATICES: Colloidal dispersions of synthetic polymers or copolymers of such monomers as styrene, butadiene, vinyl chloride, vinyl acetate, and acrylates, used as coating binders and as stock additives for internal bond strength and internal sizing. The dispersions became known as synthetic latices because of their resemblance to natural rubber latex.

SYNTHETIC SIZE: Sizing agent that has been developed as a wet-end additive in a neutral/alkaline system where rosin cannot be used. Among the chemicals used for this purpose are alkyl ketone dimers, dicarboxylic acid anhydrides, maleic anhydride co-polymers, and cationic acrylic co-polymers. Syn. Reactive Sizes.

T _____

TALC: White pigment with a plate-like morphology, composed mainly of hydrated magnesium silicate [$Mg_3Si_4O_{10}(OH)_2$], occasionally used as a papermaking filler. Certain grades of talc with high specific surface can selectively absorb pitch particles and are used to prevent their deposition within pulp and papermaking process equipment.

THERMAL CONVERSION (of starch): See STARCH CONVERSION.

THERMOPHILIC BACTERIA: Bacteria which thrive at temperatures between 50 and 65°C, and higher.

THICK-BOILING STARCH: Starch which forms high-viscosity solutions.

THIN-BOILING STARCH: Starch which forms low-viscosity solutions.

TITANIUM DIOXIDE: (TiO_2) White pigment widely used as a papermaking filler. It is the prime filler for optical effects and probably the most expensive. Two molecular forms are available, derived from anatase and rutile. Syn. Titania.

TOP COLORS: Dyes that have greater affinity for clay, as opposed to bottom colors that have greater affinity for cellulose fibers.

U _____

UREA-FORMALDEHYDE RESIN: Wet-strength resin produced by copolymerization of urea and formaldehyde.

V _____

VERMICULITE: Complex hydrated aluminum iron magnesium silicate mineral with a platelet structure, sometimes used as a filler or coating pigment for specialty products.

W _____

WATER GLASS: See SODIUM SILICATE.

WATER OF HYDRATION: Envelope comprising layers of water that surround hydrophilic colloids in an aqueous suspension.

WAX: Class of high-molecular-weight substances with thermoplastic properties, derived from a number of sources. Their chemical structures are similar to fats and oils. Since they are not high polymers, they are not considered to be true plastics. See PARAFFIN WAX, MICROCRYSTALLINE WAX.

WAX EMULSION: Aqueous emulsion of wax (usually paraffin) prepared in a high-energy dispersion mill with a suitable emulsifying agent, such as ammonium oleate.

WAX SIZE: Wax emulsion used for internal sizing, usually in combination with rosin size. There are two main types: acid-stable sizes and non-acid-stable sizes (or alum-sensitive sizes). Acid-stable types do not react with alum; the wax particles are probably attracted to the fibers by electrostatic forces and may be entrapped by rosin-alum floc. Non-acid-stable sizes react with alum in the same way as rosin size.

WET-END CHEMISTRY: Physical and surface chemistry of fines and additives and their interactions with fibers.

WET-STRENGTH RESINS: Chemicals added to the papermaking stock that serve to reinforce normal fiber-to-fiber bonds and provide strength retention in aqueous media. Common agents are urea-formaldehyde, melamine-formaldehyde, and polyamide resins; these are applied at an intermediate degree of polymerization, so that the final "cure" is obtained during drying of the paper.

WETTING AGENT: Material capable of lowering the surface tension of water solutions, and thus increasing their wetting powers.

WHITE PIGMENTS: Category of pigments which includes all the common pigments used as fillers or in coatings (e.g., clay, calcium carbonate, titanium dioxide, talc, etc.). See also COLORED PIGMENTS.

WHITING: Precipitated calcium carbonate pigment.

WITHERITE: Naturally occurring barium carbonate ($BaCO_3$), sometimes used as a coating pigment.

Z

ZETA POTENTIAL: Difference in electrical charge between the dense layer of ions surrounding a colloidal particle and the bulk of the surrounding fluid. The zeta potential is sometimes erroneously interpreted as a measure of the surface charge on fibers and particles. Syn. Electrokinetic Charge.

ZINC SULFIDE: (ZnS) Yellowish chemical precipitate used as a filler or coating pigment, and as a component in lithopone.

ZINC WHITE: Zinc oxide (ZnO) obtained as a fume following high-temperature oxidation of the zinc metal, used as a filler or coating pigment.

Chapter 6
Pulping By-Product Processing & Chemistry

A

ABIETIC ACID: Most common resin acid, a major constituent of tall oil. See RESIN ACIDS, ROSIN.

ACID NUMBER: Test to measure the quality of crude tall oil and tall oil derivatives. The test is conducted by dissolving a sample in alcohol and titrating the acidity with standard alkali. A high value is desirable since it indicates a high proportion of fatty acids and free resin acids which are the recoverable constituents in refined tall oil.

ACID-PRECIPITATED LIGNIN: See ALKALI LIGNIN.

ACID-REFINED TALL OIL: Product obtained by treating crude tall oil in solvent solution with sulfuric acid under controlled conditions to remove dark color bodies and odoriferous materials. Removal of the solvent yields a product with lighter color and higher viscosity than crude tall oil with approximately the same ratio of fatty acids to resin acids. See also TALL OIL.

ACIDULATION: Process for converting tall oil soap into raw tall oil. The metallic atom of the soap is replaced by a hydrogen atom by the action of strong sulfuric acid.

ALKALI LIGNIN: Product obtained by acidification of soda black liquor. Sulfonation of this lignin yields products which are competitive with lignosulfonates from sulfite waste liquor. See also THIOLIGNIN.

B

BALSAM: Comprehensive term applied to the resinous substances exuded or extracted from certain trees or other plants, consisting of oleoresin and essential oils.

BY-PRODUCT: Product of lesser value (or negligible value) which is produced as a direct consequence of producing a primary product.

C

COLOPHONY: Term denoting medium and high grades of rosin.

CONIFERIN: Glycoside contained in pine bark and other conifers having the chemical formula $C_{16}H_{22}O_8$, used as an intermediate in the manufacture of vanillin. When decomposed, it yields coniferyl alcohol which can be oxidized to vanillin.

CRUDE SOAP WASHING: Removal of black liquor from crude tall oil soap, usually based on mixing with a suitable water solution followed by gravity or centrifugal separation.

CRUDE SULFATE TURPENTINE (CST): Unrefined sulfate turpentine as it is recovered in the kraft mill.

CRUDE TALL OIL (CTO): Dark brown mixture of fatty acids, resin acids, and neutral materials (unsaponifiables) liberated by the acidulation of tall oil soap. The fatty acids are a mixture of oleic and linoleic acids with lesser amounts of saturated and other unsaturated fatty acids. The resin acids are similar to those found in gum and wood rosin. The neutral materials consist mainly of polycyclic hydrocarbons, sterols and other high molecular weight alcohols.

CYMENE: Cyclic terpene compound, of which several isomers are known, obtained from turpentine or from sulfite digester relief gases, used as solvent, catalyst and intermediate.

D

DECANTER: Tank or vessel in which two immiscible liquids separate. The lighter liquid overflows (decants) from the top, and the heavier liquid is removed from the bottom. Decanters are commonly used to separate the turpentine phase from the aqueous phase following condensation of digester relief gases.

DESTRUCTIVE DISTILLATION: Decomposition of a material by heat in the absence of air (a form of pyrolysis) and simultaneous distillation of the volatile products.

DESTRUCTIVELY DISTILLED TURPENTINE: Product obtained by fractionation of certain oils recovered from the destructive distillation of pine wood, consisting of a wide variety of aromatic hydrocarbons with only moderate amounts of terpenes. See TURPENTINE.

DIMETHYL SULFIDE: [(CH$_3$)$_2$S] Silvichemical produced by treating black liquor with sulfur at high temperature and pressure, used industrially as an intermediate.

DIMETHYL SULFOXIDE (DMSO): [(CH$_3$)$_2$SO] Industrial solvent with many applications, obtained by oxidation of dimethyl sulfide.

DIPENTENE: Monocyclic terpene hydrocarbon having the chemical formula C$_{10}$H$_{16}$, also known as limonene. Being unsaturated, it oxidizes readily. Commercial dipentenes are usually obtained by fractional distillation of turpentine and contain substantial portions of other monocyclic and bicyclic terpenes as well as oxygenated terpenes having similar boiling ranges.

DISTILLATION: Unit operation or process for separating one or more liquid components from a liquid mixture by exploiting their differences in volatility.

DISTILLED TALL OIL: Class of products obtained by fractional distillation of crude tall oil. These products are composed mainly of fatty acids, but contain at least 10 percent of other constituents.

E ————————————————

ESSENTIAL OIL: Generic term for the volatile liquids obtained from various plant parts, often consisting mainly of terpenes, but other types also exist. Usually, resinous products are admixed with them. Turpentine is an example of a resinous essential oil.

ETHYL ALCOHOL: (C$_2$H$_5$OH) Grain alcohol, manufactured from starchy or sugary materials by fermentation. Syn. Ethanol. See also FERMENTATION.

F ————————————————

FACE: See TURPENTINE TAPPING.

FATTY ACID: Carboxylic acid usually derived from animal fat or vegetable oil, composed of a chain of alkyl groups containing from 4 to 22 carbon atoms and terminating with the characterizing carboxyl radical. Tall oil contains more than ten fatty acids of variable molecular size, mostly unsaturated with some saturated. The most common are oleic and linoleic which are unsaturated, and palmitic and stearic which are saturated.

FATTY ACID SOAP: Salt or soap obtained by neutralization of a fatty acid with a base. The fatty acid soaps of sodium, potassium and ammonia are water soluble while those of calcium and magnesium are water insoluble. The multivalent salts are commonlly called metallic soaps.

FERMENTATION: Gradual decomposition of certain organic compounds by the action of enzymes, yeast or bacteria; specifically, the conversion of glucose into ethyl alcohol and carbon dioxide.

FLAVONOIDS: Class of polyphenolic constituents in plants consisting of a C$_6$C$_3$C$_6$ carbon skeleton. Their polymers are called condensed tannins.

FURFURAL: Monocyclic organic compound with the chemical formula C$_5$H$_4$O$_2$ of which four carbon atoms and one oxygen atom form a ring, to which is attached an aldehyde group. It is an important solvent as well as the source for many derivatives. Significant quantities of furfural are typically formed in kraft production during the presteaming of chips, but commercial recovery is generally not attractive. The chemical is more cheaply obtained by distillation of bran, corn cobs and similar agricultural waste products containing pentosans in the presence of sulfuric acid.

G ————————————————

GUM ROSIN: Rosin obtained from the oleoresin collected from living trees.

GUM TURPENTINE: Product obtained by distilling the crude exuded gum (oleoresin) collected from living pine trees, containing mostly alphapinene, with a lesser substantial amount of betapinene and a small quantity of other terpene hydrocarbons. See also TURPENTINE.

H ————————————————

HEAVIES: Term for high-boiling components found in raw sulfate turpentine.

K ————————————————

KRAFT LIGNIN: See THIOLIGNIN.

L ————————————————

LIGNAN: Class of polyphenolic extractive compounds formed by the oxidative coupling of phenylpropane (C$_6$C$_3$) units. Lignans have little commercial importance except as food preservatives.

LIGNOSULFONATE PRODUCTS: Main chemical byproducts of the sulfite pulping process, obtained by precipitation from waste liquor; used in the petroleum industry to reduce the viscosity of oil well muds and slurries, and as extenders in glues, synthetic resins and cements.

LIMONENE: See DIPENTENE.

LINOLEIC ACID: Common fatty acid constituent of tall oil, typically composing 40–45 percent by weight of the total fatty acids.

M

METALLIC RESINATE: See RESIN ACID SOAP.

MONOCYCLIC COMPOUND: Compound containing a single ring of atoms.

MUKA: Animal feed supplements made from tree foliage. Tests have shown that feeds made from both softwood and hardwood foliage are nutritionally comparable to other feeds, but cannot be cost competitive at the present time.

N

NAVAL STORES: General term applied to the oils, resins, tars, and pitches derived from the oleoresin contained in, exuded by, or extracted from trees, chiefly of the pine species, or from the wood of such trees. The three present sources of naval stores are the gum exudate from living trees, wood and the kraft pulping process. The major products are turpentine, rosin and other tall oil derivatives. The term has historical roots from the days when wooden vessels were calked with pine tar and pitch.

O

OLEIC ACID: Most prevalent fatty acid constituent of tall oil, typically composing about 50 percent by weight of the total fatty acids. See also FATTY ACID.

OLEORESIN: Pine gum; more specifically, resin acids dissolved in a terpene hydrocarbon as produced in the intercellular resin ducts of trees. Oleoresin can be collected as an exudate from living trees or extracted from the dead wood of stumps or limbs.

OVERFLOW: Flow from the upper phase of a two-phase liquid system. In a turpentine decanter, the overflow is the lighter turpentine phase.

P

PHENOL: Versatile and industrially useful aromatic alcohol derived from benzene. A number of polyphenols and polyphenolic polymers can be extracted from the wood and bark of various tree species.

PINENE: Bicyclic terpene hydrocarbon, the principal constituent of turpentine. It exists in two isomeric forms, alpha- and beta-pinene, with alpha-pinene being the more common form. If not qualified, the term pinene usually refers to the alpha form.

PINE NEEDLE OIL: Essential oil of characteristic fragrance obtained by steam distillation of pine needles.

PINE OIL: Colorless to amber-colored volatile oil with characteristic pinaceous odor, consisting principally of cyclic terpene alcohols with variable quantities of terpene hydrocarbons, ethers, ketones, phenols, and phenolic ethers. The chemical composition depends on the method of extraction and/or chemical treatment.

PINE PITCH: Dark-colored, somewhat pliant, solidified residue obtained by distilling off practically all the volatile oil from a pine tar. Several grades of pitch are manufactured by blending pine pitch with rosin and/or various oils.

PINE TAR: Tar usually produced by partial removal of volatile oils from pine tar oil by steam distillation; several grades of variable viscosity are produced depending upon the degree of volatile oil removal. Pine tar can also be produced by controlled "slow burning" (carbonization) of pine stumpwood and knots.

PINE TAR OIL: Oil obtained by condensing the vapors emitted during the destructive distillation (carbonization) of resinous pine wood. Steam distillation of pine tar oil provides a separation into pine oil and pine tar.

POLYPHENOL: Compound formed by the coupling of two or more phenol or phenol-like structures by various linkages.

R

REFINED SULFATE TURPENTINE: Sulfate turpentine that has been treated and distilled to remove sulfur bodies and residues to give a clear product.

RESENES: Organic constituents of tall oil that cannot be saponified with alkali, but contain carbon, hydrogen and oxygen in the molecule. These include higher fatty alcohols, esters, plant sterols, and some hydrocarbons. Syn. Unsaponifiables.

RESIN ACID: Component of softwood resin, occurring in several isomeric forms. Nearly all the resin acids have a three-ring fused structure with the molecular formula $C_{20}H_{30}O_2$. Two functional groups are present, the carboxyl group and the double bonds, enabling a number of reactions with

RESIN ACID (cont):
these activity centers. The most common resin acids are abietic, levopimaric, palustric, and neoabietic (classified as abietic types of resin acids) and pimaric and isopimaric (classified as pimaric types). Syn. Rosin Acids.

RESIN ACID SOAP: Metallic resinate or soap obtained by neutralization of a resin acid with a base. Limed rosin, zinc-treated rosin, and the resinates of lead, cobalt, copper, and manganese have found industrial importance.

RESIN TAPPING: See TURPENTINE TAPPING.

ROSIN: Specific type of natural resin obtained as a vitreous, water insoluble material either from pine oleoresin by removal of the volatile oils or from tall oil by removal of the fatty acid components. It consists primarily of abietic acid and other tricyclic monocarboxylic acids having the general empirical formula $C_{20}H_{30}O_2$ with small quantities of saponifiable and unsaponifiable compounds. Three classifications of rosin products are recognized depending on the method of collection: gum rosin, wood rosin, and tall oil rosin. A number of commercial rosin products have been modified by chemical and/or physical treatments, e.g., dehydrogenated rosin, heat-treated rosin, hydrogenated rosin, and polymerized rosin. See also RESIN ACID.

ROSIN OIL: Relatively viscous, oily portion of the condensate obtained when rosin is subjected to dry destructive distillation. The term is also applied to certain compounded oils having a rosin oil base.

ROSIN SPIRITS: Relatively light, volatile portion of the condensate obtained in the first stages when rosin is subjected to dry destructive distillation.

S _____

SAPONIFICATION: Generally, the hydrolysis of fat with an alkali to form soap. Specifically, the formation of sodium salts from fatty and resin acids during kraft pulping.

SAPONIFICATION NUMBER: Test to measure the reactivity of tall oil and tall oil derivatives with potassium hydroxide under specified conditions, defined by the milligrams of KOH reacting with 1 gram of sample.

SEAL LEG: Line carrying the underflow liquid from a vessel (e.g., a decanter), constructed to maintain a liquid trap that will not empty upon nominal pressure changes in the vessel.

SESQUITERPENE: Class of unsaturated organic compounds having the empirical formula $C_{15}H_{24}$, occurring in small concentrations in oleoresinous plants. Turpentine generally contains less than 1% sesquiterpenes.

SILVICHEMICALS: General term applied to all chemical and nonfibrous products derived from tree components and spent pulping liquors. This class of materials includes such diverse products as wood charcoal, naval stores, lignin derivatives, vanillin, essential oils, maple syrup, resins, muka, yeast, alkaloids, tannins, natural rubber, true gums, ethanol, and acetic acid. Those products under the classification of naval stores have the largest aggregate volume and value.

STEAM-DISTILLED TURPENTINE: Product obtained either by direct steaming of mechanically disintegrated resinous wood or by steam distillation of the extracted oleoresin. Steam-distilled turpentine consists mostly of alpha-pinene with small quantities of camphene, dipentene, menthenes, and other terpene hydrocarbons. See also TURPENTINE.

STILBENE: Class of polyphenolic constituents in plants related to flavonoids. Stilbene derivatives are characterized by a conjugated double bond system and are, therefore, extremely reactive compounds.

SULFATE TURPENTINE: Product recovered during kraft pulping of resinous wood, consisting mostly of a mixture of alpha-and-beta pinenes with small quantities of other terpene hydrocarbons. See also TURPENTINE.

T _____

TALL OIL: Generic name for a number of products derived from the resinous mixture of saponified fatty and resin acids, sterols, high-molecular-weight alcohols and other materials skimmed from kraft pulping waste liquors. A number of qualifying designations are used in accordance with the process state or composition.

TALL OIL FATTY ACIDS: Class of products obtained by fractional distillation of crude tall oil containing at least 90 percent fatty acids.

TALL OIL HEADS: Low boiling fractions obtained by the fractional distillation of crude tall oil under reduced pressure. The composition of these products varies over a wide range but contains palmitic, oleic, linoleic, and stearic acids and normally has a high neutrals content.

TALL OIL PITCH: Undistilled residue from the distillation of crude tall oil.

TALL OIL PRECURSORS: Chemical constituents in the wood (extractives) that provide the basis of tall oil recovery. Qualitative and quantitative changes occur in these precursors during kraft pulping. Typically, isomerization of both fatty and resin acids takes place, and significant losses of resin acids are sustained.

TALL OIL ROSIN: Rosin remaining after the removal of most of the fatty acids from tall oil by fractional distillation or other suitable means. The fatty acid content is less than 5 percent.

TALL OIL SKIMMINGS: See TALL OIL SOAP.

TALL OIL SOAP: (1) Raw material for conversion into tall oil; the sodium soap which is skimmed from the surface of black liquor. (2) Product formed by the saponification or neutralization of tall oil with an inorganic base.

TANNINS: Polymeric polyphenols extracted from the wood and bark of various tree species. Natural tannins are classified chemically as either condensed or hydrolyzable tannins. Condensed tannins are polymeric derivatives of flavonoids; they are used for leather tanning and as ingredients in preservative and medicinal products. Hydrolyzable tannins are esters of a sugar with one or more polyphenolic carboxylic acids.

TERPENE ALCOHOL: Any alcohol directly related to or derived from a terpene hydrocarbon. Syn. Terpinol.

TERPENES: Class of unsaturated organic compounds having the empirical formula $C_{12}H_{16}$ occurring in most essential oils and oleoresinous plants. The most important terpenes and their derivatives are classifed by structure as monocyclic (e.g., dipentene), bicyclic (e.g., pinene) and acyclic (e.g., myrcene).

THIOLIGNIN: Product obtained by acidification of kraft black liquor. Sulfonation of this lignin yields products which are competitive with lignosulfates from sulfite waste liquor. Syn. Kraft lignin, Sulfate Lignin.

TORULA YEAST: High-protein food yeast which can be produced from the pentose and hexose sugars in spent sulfite liquor.

TROPOLONES: Class of phenolic extractive compounds characterized by an unsaturated seven-membered carbon ring. These compounds are usually associated with decay-resistant conifers, principally the cedars.

TURPENTINE: Light-colored, volatile essential oil obtained from resinous exudates or resinous wood associated with living or dead coniferous trees, particularly pines. Turpentine usually consists of 90–95% terpenes, 4–7% terpene alcohols, and less than 1% sesquiterpenes. Four distinct turpentine products are recognized. See also GUM TURPENTINE, STEAM-DISTILLED TURPENTINE, SULFATE TURPENTINE, DESTRUCTIVELY DISTILLED TURPENTINE.

TURPENTINE TAPPING: Operation to harvest oleoresin from living pine trees. Typically, a longitudinal strip on the bole (called a "face") is cut and regularly chipped to stimulate exudation of the resin which is collected in an attached cup. Syn. Turpentining, Resin Tapping.

U _____

UNDERFLOW: Flow from the lower phase in a two-phase liquid system. In a turpentine decanter, the underflow is the higher-density water phase.

UNSAPONIFIABLE MATTER: Percentage of tall oil or tall oil derivatives which are not reactive with strong alkali.

UNSAPONIFIABLES: See RESENES.

V _____

VANILLIN: Flavoring agent and chemical intermediate, formed by the alkaline oxidation of lignosulfonates in desugared spent sulfite liquor. Chemically, vanillin is a cyclic aldehyde (3-methoxy-4-hydroxy benzaldehyde).

W _____

WOOD ROSIN: Rosin obtained from the oleoresin contained in dead wood, such as stumps and knots.

Chapter 7
Mechanical Pulping

A _____

ABRASIVE: Hard substance comprising the grit component in a pulpstone. The most commonly used substances are aluminum oxide (alumina) and silicon carbide.

ABRASIVE SEGMENT: See PULPSTONE SEGMENT

ALKALINE PEROXIDE MECHANICAL PULPING (APMP): Mechanical pulping process for softwoods and hardwoods that utilizes a multi-stage impregnation of chips with alkaline peroxide bleaching liquor, followed by refining and conventional processing steps.

ALPHABET PULPS: Refers to all mechanical and high-yield pulps with abbreviated letter designations, such as RMP, TMP, CTMP, etc.

ALUMINUM OXIDE: Abrasive material used in the construction of manufactured pulpstones. Syn. Alumina.

B _____

BACKFLOW STEAM: Steam generated in a chip refiner which flows back through the feeder, counterflow to the chip mass.

BAUXITE: Mineral deposit consisting of impure alumina. Can be converted to extremely hard crystalline aluminum oxide abrasive of high purity by fusing in an electric furnace.

BEVEL: See PULPSTONE BEVEL.

BEVELING TOOL: Tool used for impressing a bevel to the edge of a pulpstone, usually a burr mounted at a 45° angle.

BLOW BACK: Sudden release of steam in a chip refiner back through the feeder.

BLOW OUT: Sudden release of steam in a chip refiner at the periphery of the plates.

BLOW-THROUGH STEAM: Steam generated in a chip refiner which flows with the pulp mass into the cyclone steam separator.

BLUE GLASS: Piece of dark blue glass set in a frame, used to visually examine a dilute slurry of groundwood fibers and assess pulp quality.

BOND: Material that holds the abrasive grits together in a pulpstone. The relative weight of grits to bonding material and the kind of vitrified bond determines the stone hardness and density. Typically, a vitrified bond is created by the glass-like fusion of ceramic materials, principally clays and feldspar.

BREAKER BAR SECTION: Section of a disc refiner plate (for refining chips) that is closest to the eye of the refiner and is equipped with a pattern of coarse, widely-spaced bars with relatively large clearance. These bars shred the chips and promote the development of centrifugal forces which move and align the wood particles for optimum results in the adjacent refining sections.

BRICK: Abrasive block used to dull a pulpstone face.

BRICKING: Act or process of applying a brick to the face of a revolving pulpstone to dull the grinding surface. See also DULLING.

BRIDGE TREE: Heavy cast iron or steel bar separating and holding the side frames of a grinder to which the holding bolts are attached.

BRUSHING: Application of a wire brush to a revolving pulpstone surface to clean the stone; sometimes used in lieu of a burr to extend the sharpening cycle.

BULL SCREEN: Coarse screen that separates gross reject material (e.g., splinters or pieces of wood) from low-consistency groundwood pulp.

BULL SCREEN RAKERS: Moving scraper device employed on bull screens to facilitate discharge of rejects.

BURN: Area on pulpstone face with embedded charred wood or other charred material. Can be due either to lack of shower water and insufficient cooling or to the localized presence of a difficult-to-grind material that raises the temperature in the area above the charring point.

BURR: Small seamless steel cylinder with a raised pattern of "teeth" cut on the outside surface and heat-treated for wear resistance; used for renewing the surface of a pulpstone. A variety of surface patterns are used, the most common being spiral

BURR (cont):
grooves and diamond points. Diamond burrs have a pattern of straight grooves and crossing circular grooves resulting in rows of pyramidal points. Spiral burrs are characterized by various groove angles and groove spacings.

BURR HOLDER: Device upon which the burr is mounted, containing the bearings and spindle.

BURR IMPRESSION: Pattern of grooves impressed into the pulpstone face by the application of the burr.

BURRING: Act or process of applying a burr to the face of a pulpstone. The burr impinges at high pressure against the revolving pulpstone face, thus causing the pattern to be impressed into the surface. Syn. Dressing, Jigging. See also PULPSTONE SHARPENING.

BURRING INTERVAL: Operating time between routine pulpstone sharpenings. See also SHARPENING SCHEDULE.

BURR LEAD: For a spiral burr, the angle formed by the axis of the burr and the teeth. Syn. Burr Tooth Angle.

C _____

CANAL: Receiving ditch underneath grinders through which the groundwood suspension flows to the bull screen. Syn. Ditch, Trough.

CASING: Outer shell of the grinder which encloses the pulpstone.

CERAMIC PULPSTONE: Pulpstone in which the abrasive segments are made from grits of aluminum oxide or silicon carbide held together by bonding material that has been vitrified. Syn. Vitrified Bond Pulpstone.

CERAMICS: Science and art of clay working and various related industries. The use of vitrified bonds brings pulpstone manufacture under this classification.

CHAIN GRINDER: Design of continuous loading grinder with a single pocket placed vertically above the grindstone. Grinding pressure is achieved by pairs of endless chains on either side of the pocket with attached points or dogs which engage the column of wood and pull it down against the revolving pulpstone.

CHEMICALLY MODIFIED MECHANICAL PULPING: Designation for any mechanical pulping process in which the pulp is first produced in a pressurized refiner and then given a chemical treatment. Examples are the OPCO and CTLF processes.

CHEMICALLY TREATED LONG FIBER (CTLF): Process to augment the quality of thermomechanical pulp by sulfonating the long fiber fraction (i.e., the screen reject fraction).

CHEMIGROUNDWOOD: Mechanical pulping process (probably no longer used commercially) in which pulpwood blocks are cooked with chemicals and steam prior to grinding at atmospheric pressure. Also refers to the product of this process.

CHEMI-MECHANICAL PULPING (CMP): Any mechanical pulping process in which chips are given a relatively severe chemical pretreatment followed by atmospheric refining into pulp. A process with this designation produces a pulp in the 80 to 90% yield range.

CHEMI-REFINER MECHANICAL PULPING (CRMP): Any mechanical pulping process in which chips are given a chemical pretreatment followed by atmospheric refining into pulp. A process with this designation produces a pulp above 90% yield.

CHEMI-THERMOMECHANICAL PULPING (CTMP): Any mechanical pulping process in which chips are given a chemical pretreatment either prior to or during a presteaming treatment of the chips, followed by first-stage refining at a temperature above 100°C and any subsequent refining at atmospheric pressure. Conditions are usually controlled to produce a pulp above 90% yield.

CHIP GRINDING: Little-used groundwood process utilizing wood chips as the raw material. The chips are fed against the rotating stone surface using screw conveyers.

CHOP: Cubical particles of wood found in groundwood pulps which generally consist of shive fragments.

CLASH: Direct physical contact (i.e., metal-to-metal contact) between opposing plates in a disc refiner.

COLD GRINDING: Stone grinding with sufficient shower water flow on the stone to maintain the pit temperature below 50°C.

COLD SODA PROCESS: Type of chemimechanical pulping in which caustic soda at room temperature is used to soften the chips prior to refining.

COMPRESSION RATIO: Volume ratio of the chip mass before and after compression dewatering (e.g., prior to entering the chemical impregnation vessel for the CTMP process where the compressed chips absord liquid like a sponge).

which there is no interruption in the feed of wood to the stone. Representative designs are the chain grinder and the ring grinder.

CROSS HEAD: Portion of the burring lathe on a grinder which holds the burr assembly and traverses across the face of the pulpstone on the lathe rods.

CURL SETTING: High-consistency treatment of already-curled mechanical or high-yield pulp (e.g., before latency removal) for up to an hour in a steam environment that provides a temperature in the 130 to 170°C range. The resultant permanent curly condition of the fibers enhances certain pulp properties (notably wet-web strength) while adversely affecting other properties.

CYCLONE QUENCH FLOW: Dilution/cooling water flow into the cyclone steam separator.

CYCLONE STEAM SEPARATOR: Device for separating steam from thermo-refiner pulp utilizing centrifugal force.

CYLINDER: Circular body placed over the grinder pocket containing the hydraulic piston which forces the pressure foot against the wood and thus against the pulpstone.

CYLINDER PRESSURE: Hydraulic pressure times the cross sectional area of the cylinder which gives the total force applied.

D _____

DAM: (1) Adjustable baffle board extending across the full width of a grinder pit, over which pulp flows into a common channel, used to control pulpstone immersion. Syn. Weir. (2) Projection within the groove of a refiner plate which blocks the groove and forces pulp fibers to move over bars during the refining process.

DEFIBRATION: Separation of wood (or other plant material) into fibers or fiber bundles by mechanical means, sometimes assisted by prior chemical action. Syn. Fiberization.

DEGREE OF SULFONATION: Amount of sulfur bound to a unit mass of pulp, usually taken as the prime measure of pulp sulfonation. Syn. Level Of Sulfonation. See also SULFONATE CONTENT.

DISC OSCILLATION: Oscillating change in plate clearance in an operating chip refiner due to cyclic deflection of the shafts which causes their ends to orbit at their natural frequency of lateral deflection. Syn. Dynamic Out-Of-Tram.

of disc alignment, usually with respect to a vertical axis. Disc runout measurements on opposing discs are used to check the tram condition.

DITCH: See CANAL.

DULLING: Process of applying a brick or blank burr against the rotating surface of a pulpstone to reduce the sharpness of the pattern. Syn. Knocking Back.

E _____

ENERGY SPLIT: Partitition of energy input during mechanical pulping to different stages of refining (e.g., between the primary and secondary stages).

EXTRUDER: Device used experimentally for chip refining consisting of two parallel intermeshing horizontal screws rotating in the same direction within a common casing. The pitch of the screws can be changed along the length to define successive zones of high compression with combined shear forces.

EYE (of a refiner): Centermost area between refiner plates wherein the chip mass is introduced and from which the material travels radially between the plates.

F _____

FACE: That part of a pulpstone which does the grinding, the peripheral surface.

FEED RING: Large ring that surrounds the pulpstone in a ring type grinder that feeds or forces the wood against the revolving pulpstone. See RING GRINDER.

FIBERIZATION: See DEFIBRATION.

FILLING STATE CURVE: Plot of the void space between refiner plates when just touching as a function of the plate radius. A design objective is to achieve a smooth curve which does not open up too much at the outer periphery. See also SPECIFIC VOLUME CURVE.

FINGER BARS: Steel plate from which fingers protrude, located in the grinder pocket on the down running side of the stone. The finger bars are adjusted to hold shims and large slivers in the pocket while allowing free passage of pulp and water.

FLANGES: Large steel or cast iron circular plates attached to the grinder shaft on either side of the pulpstone that hold the pulpstone in position.

FLINGERS: Pieces of steel attached radially and projecting on the outside of the grinder flanges, used to propel the stock forward in the grinder pit and break up accumulations of stock and/or debris between the flanges and side frames of the grinder.

G

GLASS TRANSITION: Change in an amorphous polymer from a hard, brittle condition to a visco-elastic or viscous condition. During mechanical pulping, if fibers are separated above the glass transition temperature for lignin, the fibers are easily separated at low energy consumption; but the fibers are then coated with soft lignin which reverts on cooling to the hard glassy state, a serious impediment to further fibrillation and development of the fibers.

GOVERNOR: Device for regulating the power usage of grinders by controlling the grinding pressure, either directly or indirectly.

GRINDER: Machine for grinding wood bolts into pulp. Typically, the wood is pressed against a rotating pulpstone while being sprayed with water. See also CHAIN GRINDER, HYDRAULIC POCKET GRINDER, MAGAZINE GRINDER, RING GRINDER.

GRINDER PIT: Shallow trough beneath the pulpstone in which groundwood pulp and shower water are collected.

GRINDER POCKET: Part of the grinder into which wood is placed for grinding.

GRINDER ROOM: Department in a pulp mill where wood blocks are ground into pulp. Syn. Groundwood Plant.

GRINDING OF WOOD: Fiberization of wood by pressing blocks against a rotating synthetic stone. The dominant action is the high-frequency compression and decompression at the interface which loosens fibers by fatigue and failure. At the same time, tremendous heat is generated which softens the lignin binding the fibers together and assists in separating fibers from the wood mass.

GRINDING PRESSURE: Typically, taken as the gauge pressure on the cylinder for pocket-type grinders. The actual grinding pressure is higher because the total force of the cylinder is distributed over the smaller area of the grinding surface.

GRINDING SURFACE: Area of pulpstone surface that is instantaneously in contact with the wood in a grinder.

GRINDSTONE: See PULPSTONE.

GRIT: (1) Particles of abrasive material, which when bonded together form the grinding surface of a pulpstone. (2) Any mineral particles in the groundwood whether derived from the wood, the water supply, or disintegration of the stone.

GROUNDWOOD: See STONE GROUNDWOOD.

GROUNDWOOD PLANT: See GRINDER ROOM.

H

HIGH-SULPHONATION MECHANICAL PULPING: Designation for any chemimechanical pulping process in which the level of sodium sulfite application is in the range 4 to 14% on oven-dry wood and the pulp yield is above 80%. Examples are the UHYS and SCMP processes.

HOT GRINDING: Stone grinding with shower water flow controlled to ensure a pit temperature in the 70° to 95°C range.

HYDRAULIC POCKET GRINDER: Design of grinder with two or more pockets, each of which is defined by the stroke of a hydraulic cylinder. Grinding pressure is achieved by the hydraulic cylinder pushing against a "pressure foot" which, in turn, forces the wood against the revolving pulpstone. The hydraulic cylinder is retracted at the end of the stroke to allow an empty pocket to be refilled by gravity from the pre-loaded magazine located above the pocket.

HYDRAULIC THRUST: Force exerted by hydraulic fluid against a refiner plate to control refiner loading and plate clearance. (Note: Not used on modern chip refiners.)

I

INTERMITTENT GRINDER: Any design of grinder in which the applied load must be periodically reduced to allow for recharging of wood blocks.

J

JIGGING: See BURRING.

K

KNOCKING BACK: See DULLING.

L

LATENCY: Refers to the "unravelled" appearance of fresh refiner pulp. It is necessary to disintegrate the fibers in hot water to remove this latency. The term evolved from the fact that freeness decreases as latency is removed, i.e., develops latent freeness.

LATENCY REMOVAL: See LATENCY.

LATENT MECHANICAL PULP: Refiner pulp that has not been subjected to a hot disintegration treatment to remove latency.

LATHE: Hydraulically or mechanically-operated device on a pulp grinder that traverses across the face of the pulpstone in the burring operation. It consists of a cross head, lathe rods and traversing mechanism. Some lathes are equipped with a micrometer adjustment for controlling the depth of the "bite" on the stone surface by the burr.

LONG-FIBER FRACTION: Term used for the quantitative characterization of mechanical pulps, usually referring to the percentage of fibers retained on the 14 and 24-mesh screens of the Bauer-McNett fiber classifier. Sometimes, this designation also includes the fibers retained on the 48-mesh screen. In a mill situation, the term often refers to screen rejects, especially when the screen is operated as a fiber fractionation device.

LOW-SULFONATION MECHANICAL PULPING: Designation for any chemimechanical pulping process in which the level of sodium sulfite application is less than 4% on oven-dry wood. Examples are the CTMP and CRMP processes.

M

MAGAZINE: Storage hopper for wood blocks that is an integral part of the grinder, used for continuous feed to the pulpstone or for rapid recharging to a pocket.

MAGAZINE GRINDER: Design of grinder similar to the hydraulic two-pocket grinder, but with two high magazines, one over each pocket.

MANDREL: Part of the burr holder assembly; it is the shaft or spindle that holds the burr.

MECHANICAL PULP: Any pulp obtained from wood (or other plant material) principally by mechanical means, including stone groundwood, refiner mechanical pulp, thermomechanical pulp and chemi-mechanical pulps above 85% yield.

MECHANICAL PULPING: Any pulping process relying primarily on mechanical energy and/or mechanical methods to separate the fibers. Generally, any pulping process that produces pulp with a yield above 85% is grouped under this heading, notwithstanding any chemical treatments that may be used as part of the process.

MULTISTAGE REFINING: Utilization of two or three refiners in series to produce pulp. Chips are shredded and partially defibered in the first refiner; the second and third refiners further develop the fibers.

N

NUBBIN: Unground chunk of wood resulting when a wood block projects over the side of the pulpstone as it is being ground.

O

OPCO PROCESS: Proprietary high-yield pulping process (Ontario Paper Co.) in which RMP or TMP fibers are cooked at high consistency to 90% yield using sulfite liquor.

OPEN-DISCHARGE REFINING: Refining carried out at atmospheric pressure. Syn. Atmospheric Refining.

P

PERIPHERAL SPEED: Speed at which any point on the face of a rotating pulpstone is traveling, expressed in feet per minute (or meters per minute). Product of the circumference in feet (or meters) and the revolutions per minute. Syn. Surface Speed.

PIT: Space underneath the grinder which receives the stock discharged by the grinder. The level of stock in the pit is controlled by the position of the dam which, in turn, controls the stone immersion.

PITCH: Number of teeth per inch (or per cm) on a burr; this corresponds to the number of grooves per inch on a stone face. Syn. Groove Spacing.

PITLESS GRINDING: Method of grinding with the dam dropped or removed so there is no pond underneath the grinder and no stone immersion. Proper showering of the stone is critical with this method of operation to keep the stone cool and clean.

PLASTIC PLATE: Disc refiner plate constructed of a thermoplastic material having a modulus of elasticity close to that of cellulose. Extensive trials in the late 1970's on both chips and pulp appeared promising, but the concept has not been applied commercially.

PLATE CLASH: See CLASH.

PLOW: (1) Device to deflect or facilitate removal of wood blocks from a conveyor. (2) Device used on some grinders to remove shim accumulations at the top of the rotating pulpstone.

PLUG SCREW FEEDER: Device for feeding and dewatering chips consisting of a rotating screw within a tapered perforated enclosure. When used as a feeder to the steaming vessel, it will remove a significant portion of the color-forming materials in the chips (i.e., resins and fatty acids) and also much of the air trapped between chips.

PLUG WIPER FLOW: Dilution flow of white or fresh water into the center of a chip refiner. The objective is usually to maintain as high a consistency as possible without causing feed problems or burning of the pulp.

POCKET: See GRINDER POCKET.

POCKET COUNTER: Device that records and totalizes the number of times a pocket is charged with wood, thus providing an approximation of the grinder output.

POCKET FEEDER: See HYDRAULIC POCKET GRINDER.

POCKET GRINDER: See HYDRAULIC POCKET GRINDER.

POST REFINING: Refining of mechanical pulp to reduce its shive content and/or to control freeness within a specified range (i.e., for drainage control).

POST TREATMENT: Treatment to increase the strength of a mechanical pulp by alkaline swelling or lignin sulfonation.

PREHEATING: See PRESTEAMING.

PRESSURE FOOT: Ram or plunger which transmits pressure through a piston from a hydraulic cylinder to the wood in a grinder pocket.

PRESSURE/PRESSURE THERMOMECHANICAL PULPING (PTMP): Any mechanical pulping process in which chips are steamed and refined, all steps being carried out under pressurized conditions at a temperature above 100°C. Syn. Tandem Thermomechanical Pulping.

PRESSURE REFINED MECHANICAL PULPING (PRMP): Any mechanical pulping process in which no presteaming stage is used at elevated pressure, but chips are refined under pressure in both the primary and secondary stages.

PRESSURIZED REFINING: Refining carried out in a steam pressurized environment (i.e., above atmospheric pressure). Syn. Elevated-Temperature Refining.

PRESSURIZED STONE GROUNDWOOD (PGW): Mechanical pulping process in which pulpwood blocks are ground within a pressurized atmosphere at temperatures over 100°C. Also refers to the product of this process.

PRESTEAMING: In thermomechanical pulping, contacting of chips with steam at elevated pressure within a horizontal or vertical tube (or special digester) prior to refining. Syn. Preheating.

PRIMARY REFINING: Initial refining stage in refiner mechanical pulping systems in which wood chips are progressively shredded and separated into fibers, and fibers are partially developed.

PULPSTONE: Grinding wheel of a size to fit the grinder, usually of manufactured construction, consisting of a ring of abrasive segments assembled on a reinforced concrete core. Syn. Stone, Grindstone. See also CERAMIC PULPSTONE.

PULPSTONE BEVEL: Angled flat area at edge of pulpstone face. The bevel assists the burring process by giving the burr a smooth start.

PULPSTONE GRADE: Indication of the hardness of the abrasive segments, from A (soft) to Z (hard). Syn. Pulpstone Hardness.

PULPSTONE IMMERSION: Depth that the pulpstone projects into the pond of dilute stock in the grinder pit.

PULPSTONE JOINTING MATERIAL: Compressible material placed between the abrasive segments of a pulpstone to absorb expansion and contraction of the segments and to support the burr in the burring operation.

PULPSTONE POROSITY: Measure of the void volume in a pulpstone segment. Open pores are produced during the vitrification process.

PULPSTONE SEGMENT: Grinding surface segment of a pulpstone manufactured from fractionated abrasive grits held together by vitrified bonding material. Segments are bolted to a reinforced concrete core to form the abrasive layer on the face of the stone. Syn. Abrasive Segment.

PULPSTONE SHARPENING: Process of renewing the grinding surface on a pulpstone by removing dull and ineffective abrasive grains. The method used is burring. The objective is to increase the groundwood production rate and/or raise stock freeness. Stones are generally sharpened on a staggered cycle so that overall blended pulp quality will not change abruptly. See also BURRING.

PULPSTONE STRUCTURE: General term referring to the size of the abrasive grits used as well as the relative proportion and arrangement of grits and bond in the pulpstone segments. Also refers to the grit spacing within the structure.

R

REFINER BLEACHING: Addition of bleaching chemical to the chip mass as it is being converted into pulp in a disc refiner.

REFINER CYCLING: Pulsation of material coming into a refiner (e.g., because of a slow-turning feed conveyor) which causes cycling of the motor load between higher and lower levels.

REFINER GROUNDWOOD: Obsolete designation formerly applied to refiner mechanical pulp.

REFINER MECHANICAL PULPING (RMP): Any mechanical pulping process in which chips or other wood subdivisions are refined into pulp at atmospheric pressure with no pretreatment.

REFINER PULP: Generic term referring to any mechanical pulp produced in open-discharge or pressurized refiners.

REFINING ENERGY SPLIT: Ratio of primary refiner load to secondary refiner load.

REFINING FREQUENCY: Characterization of the chip refining process as a sequence of powerful pressure pulses of rapidly increasing frequency as the wood material passes radially out from the center toward the periphery between two grooved refiner discs. The pulse frequency has been calculated at a few hundred hertz near the center and up to 15,000 to 25,000 Hz at the periphery.

REGRINDING: Secondary mechanical treatment of those groundwood fibers that either adhere to the stone surface or are picked up from the pit during submersion of the stone and are carried back into the grinding zone.

REGULATOR LOAD: Controlled load on a grinder motor, usually by varying the grinding pressure.

REJECT REFINING: Refining of the coarse fiber fraction which does not pass through screen perforations. Refining of any reject stream from screening or cleaning operations.

REJECT SULFONATION PROCESS: Treatment of the coarse mechanical pulp fraction (typically 30% of the total production) with alkaline sodium sulfite at elevated temperature before it is processed through the reject refiners.

RING GRINDER: Design of grinder wherein the standard pulpstone is positioned eccentrically within a large-diameter ring. The wood is placed parallel to the axis in the "horn" created by the positions of the ring and stone. The stone rotates at con-ventional speed and the ring turns slowly in the same direction, thus wedging the wood against the stone and grinding it. The rotational speed of the ring is regulated to control the power consumption.

ROLL BACK: Operation where a blank burr or worn diamond burr is rolled across the stone face to knock off high points.

ROTATIONAL SPEED: Measure of how rapidly a rotating member is turning, usually in units of rotations per minute (rpm). See also PERIPHERAL SPEED.

S

SAWDUST REFINER PULP: Refiner pulp manufactured from sawdust or pin chips.

SELF-PRESSURIZATION: Generation of steam pressure between the plates of a chip refiner due to high energy dissipation.

SEMICHEMICAL MECHANICAL PULPING (SCMP): Semichemical pulping process in which the pulp yield is at least 80% on oven-dry wood.

SEQUENTIAL VELOCITY REFINER: Experimental chip refiner having two counter-rotating surfaces, each composed of four concentric rings driven at sequentially increasing speeds.

SHARPENING: See PULPSTONE SHARPENING.

SHARPENING SCHEDULE: Staggered cycle for sharpening individual pulpstones so that overall blended groundwood quality will not change abruptly. See also BURRING INTERVAL.

SIDE FRAME: Vertical housing plate at each end of the pulpstone forming part of the ginder. The stone shaft extends through the side frames to the bearing brackets.

SILICON CARBIDE: (SiC) Abrasive made from coke and silica in an electric furnace; used in the construction of manufactured pulpstones.

SLIVER: Small, narrow splinter of wood which forms the bulk of the screen rejects from stone groundwood and causes problems in paper products if allowed to remain in the pulp.

SPECIFIC ENERGY: Energy consumed per unit weight of pulp production, usually in units of mega joules per kilogram or horsepower days per ton.

SPECIFIC VOLUME CURVE: Similar to the "filling state curve", but also takes into account the actual gap between refiner plates.

STEAMING TUBE: Tubular steaming vessel utilized in thermomechanical pulp refining and digesting systems to subject chips to a controlled vapor environment (and possible chemical treatment) for a specified time period. Material is transported through the unit by means of a screw conveyor.

STONE: Abbreviated designation for a pulpstone.

STONE GROUNDWOOD: (GW) Mechanical pulping process in which pulpwood blocks are ground into pulp at atmospheric pressure. Also refers to the product of this process.

STONE SHARPENING: See PULPSTONE SHARPENING.

STONE SUBMERGENCE: Percentage of the stone diameter (or amount of the stone diameter) that is immersed in the pit.

SULFONATE CONTENT: Measure of the degree of pulp sulfonation. Pulp samples may be either analyzed for sulfite ion directly, or analyzed for sulfur content which is then (assuming that all sulfur is present as sulfonate) multiplied by 2.5 to convert to sulfonate content.

SULFONATED CHEMI-MECHANICAL PULPING (SCMP): Proprietary high-yield pulping process (CIP) in which wood chips are first subjected to a sodium sulfite cook and then defibered in two stages of atmospheric refining.

T _____

TANDEM THERMOMECHANICAL PULPING: See PRESSURE/PRESSURE THERMOMECHANICAL PULPING.

THERMAL SOFTENING: Transition of lignin from a hard, brittle condition into a soft, plastic condition by heating.

THERMOGRINDING (TGW): Groundwood process in which the temperature in the grinding zone is increased (as compared to conventional grinding), but is controlled below 100°C (i.e., below the temperature of pressurized groundwood).

THERMOMECHANICAL CHEMI-PULPING (TMCP): Any mechanical pulping process in which the chips are initially refined under pressure at a temperature above 100°C with chemical treatment of fibers before or after the subsequent refining stages.

THERMOMECHANICAL PULPING (TMP): Any mechanical pulping process in which the chips are steamed and initially refined under pressure at a temperature above 100°C, followed by secondary atmospheric refining.

THERMO-REFINER MECHANICAL PULPING (TRMP): Any mechanical pulping process in which chips are steamed under pressure at a temperature above 100°C, followed by atmospheric refining.

TRAM CONDITION: Degree of parallelism between refiner plates. An "out-of-tram" condition can cause substantial variation in refiner load and contribute to the production of a high-shive-content pulp. Syn. Disc Parallelism.

TRAMMING: Aligning refiner discs to achieve parallelism.

TRUING: Removal of outside layer of abrasive grits on a pulpstone for the purpose of restoring the face to running truth. Truing is usually required for a newly installed pulpstone to put it in perfect concentricity, and is accomplished by burring with a diamond point burr until the stone runs in truth.

TURNING: Procedure where the pulpstone face is lightly burred with a diamond point burr to remove resinous deposits in the pores.

TURNING POINT OF STEAM: See ZERO STEAM VELOCITY POINT.

V _____

VITRIFIED BOND: See BOND.

XYZ _____

ZERO STEAM VELOCITY POINT: Radial distance along a refiner plate at which the gap between plates is at a minimum. This narrowest point is where the generated steam flows either backward toward the inlet or forward toward the periphery. In practice, most of the steam must flow out with the pulp mass to ensure uniform refiner feed. Syn. Turning Point Of Steam.

Chapter 8
Chemical Pulping

ACCUMULATOR: (1) Pressure vessel used in sulfite mills to hold raw acid during fortification with digester relief. (2) Storage tank for contaminated condensate in blow heat recovery systems that provides surge capacity by means of a moving interface between the hot (top) and cold (bottom) sections. Syn. Heat Accumulator.

ACCUMULATOR ACID: Usually denotes sulfurous acid held in pressure vessels (accumulators) while being fortified with sulfur dioxide from sulfite digester relief gases.

ACID: General term used in sulfite mills to denote sulfurous acid at different stages in the process. See also ACCUMULATOR ACID, COOKING ACID, DIGESTER ACID, RAW ACID, STORAGE ACID.

ACID-ALKALI COOKING PROCESS: Term descriptive of several two-stage cooking processes including prehydrolysis/kraft, sulfite/kraft and sulfite/carbonate (known as the Sivola Process), all of which are used for production of high-alpha dissolving pulps.

ACID CLEANING: Circulation of an acid solution through an alkaline digester and/or its ancillary equipment for the purpose of removing scale and other acid-soluble deposits.

ACID-INSOLUBLE LIGNIN: See KLASON LIGNIN.

ACID MAKING: Term used in sulfite mills which refers collectively to all operations associated with the preparation and fortification of cooking acid.

ACID PLANT: Area in a sulfite mill devoted to the production of sulfurous acid, including the controlled burning of sulfur into sulfur dioxide and the absorption of the gas in water to form the raw acid.

ACIDPROOF BRICK: Ceramic brick of suitable composition used for the inner linings of sulfite digesters. Due to several inherent disadvantages of brick linings, they are gradually being replaced by stainless steel linings.

ACID PULPING: General term usually denoting the sulfite process. However, the term could apply to any low pH chemical pulping process such as (the experimental) nitric acid pulping.

ACID SULFITE PROCESS: Sulfite pulping process in which the cooking acid used contains a high percentage of free sulfur dioxide (SO_2) relative to combined SO_2 and therefore has a very low pH. The base may be calcium, sodium, magnesium or ammonium.

ACID TOWER: Packed tower in which sulfur dioxide (SO_2) gas is absorbed by a base liquor to form sulfite cooking liquor. Syn. Absorption Tower.

ACTIVATION ENERGY: Energy that must be added to a system to allow a particular chemical process to be carried out. In chemical pulping, the "apparent activation energy" is the empirical value that fits the Arrhenius equation for the cooking reaction rate constant; also called the "Arrhenius activation energy".

ACTIVE ALKALI (AA): With respect to kraft white liquor, the amount or concentration of sodium hydroxide (NaOH) plus sodium sulfide (Na_2S), expressed as sodium oxide (Na_2O).

ACTIVE ALKALI-TO-WOOD RATIO: Weight ratio of active alkali (expressed as equivalent sodium oxide) to bone dry wood, an important control parameter in kraft pulping.

ACTIVITY: Measure of white liquor potency, calculated as the ratio of active alkali to total titratable alkali, usually expressed as a percentage.

AIR LOCK: Rotary valve which minimizes air or gas flow between places of unequal pressure, while allowing the continuous passage of flowable dry solids.

ALKAFIDE PROCESS: Proprietary modified kraft pulping process employing very high sulfidity liquor in a two-stage impregnation/vapor phase cooking sequence.

ALKALI ANALYZER: Automatically controlled titrator for batch-wise sampling and analysis of circulating kraft cooking liquor. The alkali content is usually determined by conductometric titration (i.e., by adding acid until the conductivity falls to a predetermined minimum value).

ALKALINE PULPING: General term usually denoting the kraft process. However, the term is also applied to other high pH chemical pulping processes such as soda pulping or soda-oxygen pulping.

ALKALINE SULFITE PROCESS: Sulfite pulping process in which the cooking liquor contains sulfite plus an alkaline agent at a pH of 10 or higher. This process is not used commercially.

ALKALI PURIFICATION: See COLD ALKALI PURIFICATION, HOT ALKALI PURIFICATION.

AMMONIA: (NH_3) Gas which is reacted in solution with sulfur dioxide to form ammonium base liquor.

AMMONIUM BASE LIQUOR: Bisulfite cooking liquor containing ammonium bisulfite (NH_4HSO_3) as the principal active cooking chemical.

ANTHRAQUINONE (AQ): Unsaturated tricyclic compound used as an additive in alkaline cooking processes to accelerate cooking rates and/or stabilize the carbohydrate fraction, i.e., increase the retention of hemicellulose.

AQUEOUS SO_2: See SULFUROUS ACID.

ARBISO PROCESS: Proprietary sodium bisulfite pulping process.

ASTHMA FEEDER: Rotating pocket device used for transferring small wood subdivisions (pin chips and fines) from a steaming vessel into a continuous digester vessel. As the feeder rotates, bursts of live steam (sounding like a person with asthma) blow the feed material into the vessel.

AUTOHYDROLYSIS: See PREHYDROLYSIS.

AUTOMATIC TITRATION: See ALKALI ANALYZER.

B _____

BASE: Cation which combines with sulfurous acid to form sulfite cooking liquor. The bases used are calcium, magnesium, sodium and ammonium.

BASKET COOKING: Hanging of baskets within a batch digester to isolate small unit volumes of chips during the cooking process.

BATCH COOKING: Chemical pulping operation in which a discrete quantity or batch of chips is individually processed . The total pulp production depends on the number of batches (i.e., cooks) that are processed. Syn. Batch Digesting. See also CONTINUOUS COOKING.

BATCH DIGESTER: Process vessel (up to a volume of 9,400 cubic feet or 266 cubic meters) for producing chemical pulp batchwise.

BATCH DIGESTER SCHEDULING: Specifying when batch digesters are to be charged, heated and blown. The objectives are to smooth the load on steam generation and associated processing equipment, meet a production target for number of cooks, minimize the need for holding digesters, and maintain a supply of pulp in the blow tank.

BIOPULPING: Partial delignification of wood chips using selective fungal species or mutants. Biopulping is the focus of much scientific interest, but it is still at an early stage of development and far from commercial application.

BISULFITE PROCESS: Sulfite pulping process in which the cooking liquor is in the pH range from 2 to 6 and contains a predominance of bisulfite ion (HSO_3^-) with little or no true free SO_2. Bases used are magnesium, sodium and ammonium.

BISULFITE PULP: Pulp prepared by the bisulfite process.

BLACK COOK: See BURNT COOK.

BLACK LIQUOR: Residual liquor from the kraft cooking process containing spent chemicals and wood residues (i.e., modified lignin and carbohydrates); it is usually concentrated by evaporation and then burned to recover the pulping chemicals.

BLEACHABLE GRADE PULP: Pulp which has been sufficiently cooked so that on discharge from the digester the mechanical action involved in discharging is sufficient to break the chips apart into discrete fibers. Syn. Fully-Cooked Pulp, Low-Yield Pulp.

BLOW: Discharge of digester contents under the action of digester pressure. If complete discharge is achieved, the term "clean blow" is applied. If some of the pulp mass is retained in the digester, the term "dirty blow" or "hangup" is applied.

BLOW BACK: Back flow of steam or vapors when feeding material from a low-pressure compartment into a high-pressure compartment.

BLOWDOWN: Relief of gas and steam at the end of a sulfite cook to lower the digester pressure from the maximum to the blow pressure, and for recovery of SO_2.

BLOW GAS: SO_2 gas which is released during the blow of a sulfite or bisulfite cook. It is generally recovered by absorption and re-used for liquor makeup or fortification.

BLOW-HEAT RECOVERY: Recovery of heat from the flash steam that is generated during a typical batch digester blow. A number of systems are used, most of which utilize direct contact condensation with cold contaminated condensate, followed by indirect transfer of heat from the hot contaminated condensate into fresh process water.

BLOW LINE: Pipeline which transports stock from the digester to the blow tank. A common line may be used for a number of batch digesters.

BLOW PIT: Large vessel into which pulp is blown at the end of a sulfite cook, containing a perforated bottom through which the waste liquor and successive washings are drained. Blow pits were once commonly used in sulfite mills, but are being replaced with blow tanks.

BLOW PRESSURE: Digester pressure at which the blow valve is opened.

BLOW SAMPLE: (1) Sample of pulp obtained during a blow. (2) Sample of pulp taken from the blow tank or blow pit.

BLOW TANK: Large vessel into which pulp is blown at the end of a cook, and from which the pulp is pumped to the next processing step, usually a washing stage. It serves as a surge chest to level out pulp flow variations.

BLOW TIME: Elapsed time between the start and completion of a blow; i.e., from opening the blow valve to emptying the digester.

BLOW UNIT: Device on the blow line from a Kamyr digester which controls stock flow while reducing the pressure from about 200 psig down to atmospheric. It usually consists of a small pressure vessel equipped with a variable orifice along with a control valve on either side to provide three stages of pressure drop.

BLOW VALVE: Valve at the bottom of the batch digester that is opened to initiate a blow.

BORATE-BASED KRAFT PROCESS: Experimental method of kraft pulping in which sodium borate (Na_2HBO_3) replaces NaOH as an active cooking chemical. This salt has the advantage of being sufficiently alkaline to digest wood and is able to regenerate itself in the combustion of black liquor, thus eliminating causticizing and the lime kiln.

BROWN FIBER: Unbleached kraft pulp. Syn. Brown Stock.

BROWN STOCK: Unbleached pulp from an alkaline pulping process. The term is derived from the dark brown color of the pulp. Syn. Brown Fiber.

BUFFERING AGENT: Chemical added to regulate the pH of sulfite cooking liquor. A common buffering agent is sodium carbonate (Na_2CO_3).

BUFFERING RATIO: In sulfite pulping, the ratio of chemical equivalents of buffering agent to sulfite.

BULK DELIGNIFICATION: Phase of kraft cooking in which the major portion of the delignification occurs as a first order reaction and with a selectivity that is high compared to the initial delignification.

BUMPING: See DIGESTER BUMPING.

BURNT COOK: Sulfite cook containing dark-colored, insoluble compounds (actually, the polycondensation of lignin) that give a burnt appearance, usually caused either by extreme cooking temperature or excessive acid concentration. Syn. Black Cook.

C

CAPPING: Sealing off the top of a batch digester after addition of chips and liquor preparatory to starting a cook. Capping may be accomplished by bolting the head, but is more often carried out in modern mills by remote closure of a large ball valve or other device.

CAPPING VALVE: Valve used to seal the top of a batch digester after it has been charged with chips, most commonly a remote operated ball valve.

CAPTIVE PULP: Pulp that is produced for immediate conversion into paper or paperboard at the same plant site.

CARRYOVER: Entrainment of liquor droplets in the gas-off vapors from the digester.

CAUSTICITY: Measure of white liquor potency, measured as the ratio of sodium hydroxide (NaOH) concentration to the concentration of sodium hydroxide plus sodium carbonate (Na_2CO_3), both in terms of equivalent sodium oxide (Na_2O), expressed as a percentage.

CAUSTIC SODA: See SODIUM HYDROXIDE.

CHARGING: Filling a batch digester with chips and adding the requisite amounts of cooking liquor and dilution liquor.

CHARGING FLOOR: Floor level in a digester house which is built around the top necks of the batch digesters and where chips are fed into these vessels. Often, the batch digesters are also operated from the charging floor.

CHEMICAL BALANCE: Accounting of the distribution of chemical input and output. The elements, sodium and sulfur, are the focus of most kraft mill chemical balances.

CHEMICAL CHARGE: Amount of active chemical added to a batch digester for a cook.

CHEMICAL CONSUMPTION: General term for the net amount of chemical consumed or lost within a pulping process per unit of pulp production. For the kraft pulping process, the chemical consumption is usually calculated in terms of equivalent sodium oxide (Na_2O). The chemical makeup rate is commonly adjusted to equal the rate of chemical consumption.

CHEMICAL DIFFUSION: Transport of cooking chemicals from the cooking liquor into the water inside the chip.

CHEMICAL PULP: Any pulp obtained from wood (or other plant raw material) principally by chemical means. The two major types of chemical pulp are kraft pulp and sulfite pulp.

CHEMICAL PULPING: Any pulping process relying primarily on chemical methods to separate the fibers. The separation is accomplished by dissolving away the lignin to release the intact fibers.

CHEMICAL-TO-WOOD RATIO: Ratio of the weight of active chemicals charged to the weight of o.d. wood charged, an important control parameter in any chemical pulping process.

CHIP CHARGE: Weight of bone dry chips added to a batch digester for a cook.

CHIP CHUTE: Vertical conduit through which chips fall from the steaming vessel into the high-pressure feeder, a component of Kamyr continuous digester systems.

CHIP COLUMN: Chip mass within a vertical continuous digester that moves downward in plug flow. The liquid associated with the chips can either move downward with the chips or upward in countercurrent flow depending on the operating mode or position within the digester.

CHIP FILLING: Operation in which chips are loaded into a batch digester, typically from an overhead conveyor.

CHIP METER: Device used with the Kamyr continuous digester to control the chip feed rate, consisting of a rotating star feeder with seven pockets having a measured volume of chips per revolution.

CHIP PACKING: Any method utilized to achieve increased chip fill in a batch digester, including mechanical and/or steam chip spreaders to distribute chips uniformly within the cross section of the digester.

CHIP PACKING EFFECTIVENESS: Percentage increase in chip fill (in a batch digester) due to packing. See also DEGREE OF PACKING.

CHIP ROT INDEX: Measure of rot severity in pulpwood as it affects kraft cooking, usually defined as the weight of bone dry screened pulp at 22 permanganate number per unit green volume. The chip rot index can be predicted from the 1% NaOH solubility test carried out on the chips.

CHIP SPREADER: Device inserted into a batch digester during chip filling operations which serves to fling or deflect the entering chips toward the periphery wall of the vessel. See also CHIP PACKING.

CIRCULATION: Movement of cooking liquor within a batch digester during a cook which may be natural or forced. Natural circulation occurs with direct steaming. See also FORCED CIRCULATION.

COLD ALKALI PURIFICATION: Treatment of dissolving pulp with 10% sodium hydroxide (NaOH) at room temperature to remove short-chain material (hemicelluloses and degraded cellulose) and thereby increase the alpha cellulose content. Syn. Cold Caustic Extraction. See also HOT ALKALI PURIFICATION.

COLD BLOW: Pressure ejection of cooked pulp from a batch or continuous digester after the pulp has been cooled, normally to between 80 and 100°C. The cooling step reduces damage to the fiber.

COLD SODA PULPING: Semi-chemical pulping process in which the fibrous raw material is treated with sodium hydroxide (NaOH) solution below 100°C followed by mechanical treatment to separate the fibers.

COMBINED SO_2: SO_2 in the form of bisulfite or sulfite ion as applied to sulfite cooking liquor. With respect to cooking acid analysis, the combined SO_2 is measured by the difference between the total SO_2 and the free SO_2.

COMPACTION FACTOR: Measure of chip column compaction within a Kamyr digester, defined as the ratio of the bulk density of compacted bone dry chips at any position within the chip column to the bulk density of bone dry chips entering the digester. The compaction factor increases during downward movement due to the increasing height of the chip column and the softening of the chips during cooking.

CONDENSIBLE VAPORS: Organic vapors generated during a chemical pulping cook which will condense at normal temperatures. Examples are methanol and terpene compounds.

CONDITIONING (of chips): Presteaming of chips entering the continuous digester to remove air and other gases, raise the temperature to approximately 120°C and bring the chips to a more uniform moisture content.

CONDUCTIVITY (of solutions): Measure of the active ions present in water solution. Conductivity measurements of alkaline liquor samples extracted from a digester are sometimes used for delignification control. See also ALKALI ANALYZER.

CONTAMINATED CONDENSATE: Usually refers to the condensed steam from digester relief which contains various organic compounds as well as carry-over of cooking liquor. Can also apply to the condensate from certain evaporator effects, or to any other condensate stream that contains odoriferous components, color bodies or substantial levels of BOD.

CONTINUOUS COOKING: Chemical pulping operation in which wood chips (or other plant material) and cooking liquor are fed at a constant rate into the digester and move in continuous fashion through successive zones or stages of equipment. See also BATCH COOKING.

CONTINUOUS DIGESTER: Process vessel for producing chemical or semichemical pulp in a continuous mode.

COOK: (1) Product of a chemical digestion. (2) Operator who carries out a chemical digestion.

COOKING: Carrying out a chemical digestion of wood chips or other plant material to produce pulp.

COOKING ACID: Fortified sulfurous acid with bisulfite ions (HSO_3^-) and base ions, used as sulfite cooking liquor in the digesters. Syn. Strong Acid.

COOKING CURVE: Plot of digester temperature as a function of time during the course of a cook. Sometimes pressure is plotted in addition to or instead of temperature.

COOKING CYCLE: Elapsed time from the start of one cook to the start of the next cook in the same batch digester, often referred to as "cover-to-cover time".

COOKING DEGREE: See DEGREE OF COOKING.

COOKING LIQUOR: Any chemical solution used to delignify wood (or other plant material) and convert it into pulp.

COOKING PRESSURE: Essentially the equivalent steam pressure corresponding to the digester temperature, except in the case of acid sulfite cooks where sulfur dioxide gas exerts a significant partial pressure. See also FALSE PRESSURE.

COOKING TIME: Time from initial steaming in a batch digester to start of the blow.

COOKING ZONE: Section within a continuous digester in which the major portion of the cooking reactions occur; the section in which the chip mass is at or near the maximum cooking temperature.

COUNTERCURRENT COOKING: Cooking technique for a kraft continuous digester wherein cooking liquor and heat are introduced at the point where pulp is removed; the liquor then moves countercurrent to the chip mass flow until it is extracted as black liquor at the point where the chips are introduced.

D _____

DEGREE OF COOKING: Amount of delignification as measured by the kappa number test or other comparable method of determining residual lignin. If the degree of delignification is significantly greater or less than the target level, the pulp is described as "overcooked" or "undercooked". Syn. Degree of Delignification.

DEGREE OF PACKING: Average dry bulk density of chips in a batch digester, a measure of the extent to which the volume of the digester is utilized during cooking. Syn. Packing Density. See also CHIP PACKING EFFECTIVENESS.

DELIGNIFICATION: Removal of all or part of the lignin from wood or plant material by chemical treatment. Chemical pulping and the initial stages of bleaching are examples of delignification.

DELIGNIFICATION INDEX: Measurement of the degree of delignification. The most commonly used delignification index is the kappa number test.

DERESINATION: Actions taken to remove or neutralize resinous substances (pitch) during wood storage or in the pulping process.

DIFFUSER: Obsolete equipment for draining and washing freshly cooked pulp, consisting of a false bottom tank with overhead nozzles. The false bottom is a screen-covered perforated plate through which liquor and wash water can drain.

DIGESTER: Pressure vessel used to treat cellulosic raw material with chemical to produce pulp. See also BATCH DIGESTER, CONTINUOUS DIGESTER.

DIGESTER ACID: Cooking liquor as it exists in the digester at any stage of the sulfite cooking process. Syn. Digester Liquor.

DIGESTER BUMPING: Sudden, violent infusion of steam into a digester to activate and realign the chip mass. The steam for this purpose is sometimes referred to as "shakeup steam".

DIGESTER BURPING: Rapid reduction of pressure in the vapor space of a kraft batch digester, thus causing a boiling action which agitates the chip mass. The pressure reduction can be achieved either by spraying cold black liquor into the top or opening the top relief valve for a specified period.

DIGESTER CHARGE: Amount of wood chips (or other cellulosic raw material) and cooking chemicals in the digester.

DIGESTER HEAD: See HEAD.

DIGESTER HOUSE: Building in which the digesters are housed.

DIGESTER LIQUOR: Cooking liquor as it exists in the digester during the cooking operation.

DIGESTER NECK: See NECK.

DIGESTER PERFORMANCE EFFICIENCY: Ratio of a specific strength value of mill pulp to that of a corresponding reference laboratory pulp. For normal papermaking pulps, the ratio of values of the tear index at 9 km breaking length is suggested. Other strength properties could alternately be used depending on the pulp end use. (Concept proposed by A.J. Horng.)

DIGESTER RELIEF: Venting of steam and noncondensibles from the digester during the cook to prevent hot spots and buildup of excessive pressure. In sulfite cooking, the term "top relief" is used to distinguish from side relief.

DIGESTER SCREENED YIELD: Bone dry screened pulp from the digester expressed as a percentage of the bone dry weight of chips charged to the digester.

DIGESTER VENT GASES: Vapors and noncondensible gases removed during a digester cook, consisting mainly of steam, air, and volatile organic constituents, the makeup of which is dependent on the pulping raw material and the type of chemical pulping process employed.

DIGESTER YIELD: Bone dry pulp from the digester expressed as a percentage of the bone dry weight of chips charged to the digester.

DIGESTION: With respect to chemical pulping, the process carried out at high temperature and pressure whereby wood chips are chemically attacked to solubilize the lignin and release the intact cellulosic fibers.

DIRECT-CONTACT CONDENSER: Device which mixes cold water with steam, thus condensing the steam and raising the temperature of the water.

DIRECT STEAMING: Method of batch cooking whereby the cooking temperature is attained and controlled by introducing steam directly into the digester. Syn. Direct Cooking.

DISPLACEMENT HEATING: Operational technique for kraft batch digesters which recovers a large portion of the digester heat from one cook and utilizes it in the next cook. Hot spent liquor is displaced from the digester at the end of a cook with brown stock washer filtrate; this hot liquor is then used to preheat the white liquor charge for a subsequent cook and also provides the black liquor makeup for that cook.

DMSO PULPING: See SOLVENT PULPING.

DRAW-DOWN TANKS: See MEASURING TANKS.

DRIVING FORCE: Factor which compels a change of state or causes a move in a desired direction. The driving forces in kraft pulping are temperature and effective alkali concentration. In sulfite pulping, the driving forces are temperature, pH, and free sulfur dioxide concentration.

DUMPING: Emptying a sulfite digester at atmospheric pressure, usually with the assistance of a flushing system.

DUMP TANK: Storage tank into which a sulfite cook is discharged at atmospheric pressure.

E

EFFECTIVE ALKALI (EA): With respect to white liquor, the amount or concentration of sodium hydroxide (NaOH) plus one-half of the sodium sulfide (Na_2S), both expressed as sodium oxide (Na_2O).

EFFECTIVE CAPILLARY CROSS-SECTIONAL AREA: Ratio of the rate of sodium ion diffusion through the wood structure (e.g., during chip impregnation) to that through pure water at the same concentration gradient and temperature. It may be visualized as the area of unobstructed capillary equivalent to that of one unit area of wood.

EFFECTIVITY: Measure of white liquor chemical potency, calculated as the ratio of effective alkali to total titratable alkali, usually expressed as a percentage.

EXPLOSION PULPING: Experimental pulping method in which chips (or other plant materials) are partially delignified with chemical at high temperature and pressure and then discharged rapidly through a special nozzle to atmospheric pressure. Two mechanisms are responsible for defibration: the "popcorn effect" of superheated steam trapped within the structure of the furnish and the work done by the pressurized gas on the cellulosic material as it passes through the discharge nozzle.

EXTENDED COOKING: Modification of the conventional batch kraft cooking process which utilizes a two-stage cook to achieve greater overall delignification of the pulp. See also EXTENDED DELIGNIFICATION.

EXTENDED DELIGNIFICATION: Kraft pulping modification within a Kamyr continuous digester which utilizes a two-stage, partially counter-current cooking sequence to achieve lower kappa number and improved overall washing efficiency. See also EXTENDED COOKING.

EXTRACTION: Removal of spent liquor from the Kamyr continuous digester.

F

FALSE PRESSURE: Digester pressure in excess of the equilibrium steam pressure corresponding to the digester temperature, which is due to the presence of air and other noncondensibles. The pressure approaches that which corresponds to steam alone as noncondensibles are vented during a cook.

FIBER LIBERATION: Disintegration of the pulping raw material into discrete fibers on blowing or discharging from the cooking vessel without sup-plementary defibering action. Bleachable grade pulps are generally cooked beyond the "point of fiber liberation".

FLUFF PULP: Bleached pulp suitable for dry fiberization into the soft, bulky product called fluff, the principal constituent in disposable diapers, feminine care products, hospital wads, and various types of disposable tissues and towels.

FLUSH DUMPING: Emptying of a digester through the bottom opening using flushing liquor, but without the help of internal digester pressure.

FODDER PULP: Chemical pulp used as auxiliary fodder for animals.

FORCED CIRCULATION: In batch cooking, extracting liquor from one or more points in the digester and returning it by means of a pump to another point or points in the digester. Forced circulation is usually combined with indirect heating.

FORTIFYING TOWER: Absorber used in sulfite mills to increase the free SO_2 level in the accumulator acid through contact with the digester relief gas.

FREE LIQUOR: (1) Liquor outside the chips in a digester. (2) Weight or volume of liquor added to the wet chips in a batch digester. See also LIQUOR CHARGE.

FREE SO_2: SO_2 in the form of sulfurous acid as applied to sulfite cooking acid. With respect to chemical analysis, the free SO_2 is determined by titration with NaOH, which actually measures all the sulfurous acid plus one-half of the bisulfite. The "true free SO_2" is equal to the free SO_2 minus the combined SO_2.

FREE SPACE: Unoccupied volume in a batch digester above the chips and cooking liquor.

FULLY COOKED PULP: Pulp which has been cooked sufficiently in the digester so that mechanical action incurred during the blow will disintegrate the chips into fibers and fiber bundles. Syn. Bleachable Grade Pulp.

G

GAS COOLER: Banks of water-cooled tubes which cool the hot gases from the sulfur burner before these gases are introduced into the absorption towers for sulfite cooking acid makeup.

GAS-OFF: Venting of a digester to release trapped air and noncondensible gases along with steam and volatile organic compounds.

G-FACTOR: Combination of time and temperature during kraft cooking which relates to pulp viscosity (in the same manner that H-factor relates to kappa number). See also H-FACTOR.

GREEN LIQUOR PULPING: Semi-chemical pulping process in which the chips, usually hardwood, are treated with cooking liquor made up of a mixture of sodium carbonate and sodium sulfide, followed by mechanical defiberizing. The process is used primarily to make pulp for corrugated medium stock.

H _____

HANGUP: (1) Interruption to the free downward movement of the chip mass within a continuous digester. (2) Incomplete blow from a batch digester.

HARD COOK: General term for a cook that is insufficiently delignified.

HARD PULP: Pulp that has not been sufficiently delignified for the intended usage.

HEAD: Bolted cover to the top opening in a batch digester through which chips are charged.

HEAT ACCUMULATOR: See ACCUMULATOR.

HEATING ZONE: Section within a continuous digester where liquor is extracted, heated indirectly with steam, and returned to the digester in order to heat up the contents to the cooking temperature. Typically, there are two distinct heating zones.

HEAT-UP RATE: Rate at which a batch digester is brought up to cooking temperature, typically in degrees of temperature increase per hour. The heatup rate depends on the type of cook and the equipment used. See also TIME TO TEMPERATURE.

H-FACTOR: Method of expressing cooking time and temperature as a single variable for kraft delignification. "Relative reaction rates" have been calculated for all normal temperatures starting with an arbitrary value of 1 at 100°C; and a complete table of values is provided in all reference textbooks on kraft pulping. When the relative reaction rate is plotted against the cooking time in hours, the area under the curve is the H factor. The concept of the H-factor (introduced by K.E. Vroom) is widely applied to kraft cooking control, especially where temperature variations are experienced during the cooking period.

H-FACTOR CONTROLLER: Device that continuously calculates H-factor during a kraft cook and can be used for automatic cooking control.

HIGH-ALPHA PULP: Dissolving pulp which consists mainly of alpha cellulose.

HIGH-PRESSURE FEEDER: Key component of the Kamyr continuous digester system, consisting of a plug revolving in a casing, similar in appearance to a revolving plug cock. The plug is equipped with four through pockets, so spaced on the plug that as one pocket is being discharged by high-pressure sluicing liquor, another pocket is filling with chips from the chip chute.

HIGH-YIELD: [adj] Term descriptive of semichemical pulps up to 80% yield. For pulps above 80% yield, the term "ultra-high-yield" is applied.

HIGH-YIELD PULPING: Kraft or sulfite pulping process where the cooking treatment is less severe than the conventional chemical pulping process and some mechanical fiberizing is required to separate the fibers. The resultant semichemical pulp retains a higher proportion of lignin and hemicellulose than the full chemical pulp.

HOLOPULPING: Experimental high-yield pulping process (Institute of Paper Science and Technology) in which small wood subdivisions are treated with a mild oxidizing agent to modify the lignin, followed by an extraction step to remove the lignin, and finally, a bleaching stage to brighten the pulp.

HORIZONTAL-TUBE DIGESTER: Design of continuous digester used primarily for sawdust and nonwood pulping, consisting essentially of a series of horizontal or inclined pressure tubes equipped with screw conveying elements. The pulping raw materials, chemicals and steam are fed continuously into one end, and the cooked mass is discharged at the other end.

HOT ALKALI PURIFICATION: Treatment of sulfite dissolving pulp with up to 3% caustic at temperatures between 70 and 120°C to remove shortchain material (hemicelluloses and degraded cellulose) and thereby increase the alpha cellulose content. See also COLD ALKALI PURIFICATION.

HYDRAULIC DIGESTER: Digester that operates completely filled with cooking liquor, without gas space.

HYDRAULIC MASS: Chips and liquor in a hydraulic digester.

HYDROGENATION PULPING: Noncommercial chemical pulping process in which lignin is made soluble by treatment with hydrogen over a suitable catalyst in aqueous solvent at elevated temperature and pressure.

HYDROLYSATE: Liquor resulting from a prehydrolysis of wood chips (or other cellulosic raw material) with water and steam.

HYDROSULFIDE: Ionic species derived from sodium hydrosulfide (NaSH), a hydrolysis product of sodium sulfide (Na_2S) in alkaline solution. Hydrosulfide is the active species of sulfur in kraft pulping. Syn. Sulfhydrate.

HYDROTHERMAL INJECTION COOKING: Variation of kraft cooking for hardwoods wherein the chips after charging are brought into immediate contact with an excess of white liquor that has been preheated to maximum temperature in a separate pressure vessel.

HYDROTROPE: Compound having the ability to increase the solubility of certain slightly soluble organic compounds.

HYDROTROPIC PULPING: Delignification with concentrated aqueous solutions of a hydrotrope, usually sodium xylenesulfonate. This experimental process appears most suitable for hardwoods, grasses and cereal straws.

I
_____

IMPREGNATION: Process of distributing cooking chemicals through the wood chips by the mechanisms of penetration and diffusion. This usually occurs at a temperature significantly lower than the maximum cooking temperature.

IMPREGNATION VESSEL: Component part of some continuous cooking systems (usually called "two vessel systems") in which the chips (or other fibrous raw material) are impregnated with cooking liquor at a temperature significantly below the maximum cooking temperature.

IMPREGNATION ZONE: Section within a continuous digester in which impregnation occurs.

INCLINED SEPARATOR: See MUMIN TUBE.

INCLINED TUBE DIGESTER: See M & D DIGESTER.

INDIRECT CONDENSER: Condenser in which latent heat is removed from condensing vapor through heat conducting surfaces (i.e., in a heat exchanger) into a cooling fluid. See also SURFACE CONDENSER.

INDIRECT STEAMING: Method of batch cooking whereby the cooking temperature is attained and controlled by circulating the cooking liquor through an external heat exchanger.

INITIAL DELIGNIFICATION: Earliest stage of a kraft cook characterized by rapid delignifica-tion, significant hemicellulose degradation, and high alkali consumption. See also BULK DELIGNIFICATION.

INJECTION COOKING: Modified kraft process using continuous injection of white liquor during the cook to maintain alkali concentration at a constant level, lower than at the beginning of a conventional cook.

IN-LINE DRAINER: Device in a Kamyr continuous digester system which allows separation of liquor from the carryover chip fines and maintains a constant liquid level in the chute feeding the high-pressure feeder.

K
_____

KAMYR CONTINUOUS DIGESTER: Downward-flow continuous digester manufactured by Kamyr, Inc. The basic design includes a chip bin feeding through a metering valve and low-pressure feeder into a presteaming vessel which, in turn, discharges into a chute where liquor is added; a high-pressure feeder then sluices the chips up to a separator which discharges the chips with some liquor into the top of the tall, cylindrical cooking vessel.

KAPPA NUMBER: Modified permanganate test value on pulp which has been corrected to 50 percent consumption of the chemical. Kappa number has the advantage of a linear relationship with lignin content over a wide range. For pulp samples under 70% yield, the percent Klason lignin is approximately equal to the kappa number times a factor of 0.15.

KLASON LIGNIN: Lignin content of pulp as determined by the Klason Procedure. Syn. Acid-Insoluble Lignin.

KLASON PROCEDURE: Classical gravimetric laboratory procedure for determining the lignin content of pulp in which a solvent-extracted pulp is treated with concentrated sulfuric acid to dissolve the carbohydrate fraction, thus leaving the lignin as a residue to be weighed. Delignification indices such as kappa number are usually correlated against Klason lignin to calculate conversion factors for different pulps.

K NUMBER: See PERMANGANATE NUMBER.

KRAFT COOKING LIQUOR: See WHITE LIQUOR.

KRAFT HIGH-YIELD PULP: Semichemical pulp manufactured by the kraft process. Syn. Kraft Semichemical Pulp. See also HIGH-YIELD PULPING.

KRAFT PROCESS: Alkaline chemical pulping process using sodium hydroxide (NaOH) and sodium sulfide (Na_2S) as the active cooking chemicals. The process is noted for producing the strongest pulps. The word kraft means strength in both German and Swedish. Syn. Sulfate Process.

KRAFT PULP: Pulp manufactured by the kraft process. Syn. Sulfate Pulp.

L _____

LEACH CASTER: Wooden tank with a perforated bottom into which is dumped the high-yield cook from a spherical digester. Excess liquor is drained away and the cooked chips are then plowed by means of revolving sweep arms toward an opening, from which the chips are conveyed to refiners for defiberization.

LEVEL TANK: Surge tank within the Kamyr continuous digester system between the chip chute circulation and the makeup liquor pump.

LIGNOSULFONATES: Compounds formed during sulfite cooking by the reaction of sulfurous acid or bisulfite ion with the lignin in the wood. These compounds are soluble in the cooking liquor.

LIGNOSULFONIC ACID: Organic sulfonic acid formed during sulfite pulping by reaction between lignin and sulfite or bisulfite ions.

LIMING UP: Precipitation and deposition of calcium compounds in a digester due to carrying out calcium acid sulfite cooks at too high pH.

LIQUOR: Term used to designate the liquid phase when other phases are present.

LIQUOR CHARGE: Weight (or volume) of white liquor and/or black liquor added to a batch digester for a cook. See also FREE LIQUOR.

LIQUOR CIRCULATION: Movement of cooking liquor through the chip mass during a cook, either by convection or pumping. When a pump is employed, the liquor is usually extracted through strainer plates, pumped through a heat exchanger and returned to different points in the digester.

LIQUOR FILLING: Operation in which white and black liquors are added to a batch digester, usually from measuring tanks.

LIQUOR PENETRATION: See IMPREGNATION.

LIQUOR-TO-WOOD RATIO: Ratio of the weight of cooking liquor charged (including moisture in the wood) to the weight of oven dry chips charged, an important control parameter in any chemical cooking process. Syn. Liquid-To-Wood Ratio.

LIQUOR TRAP: Type of entrainment separator, usually of cyclonic design, which removes liquid droplets and/or solid particles from a gas stream, e.g., from digester relief gases.

LOW-LIGNIN PULPING: Proposed modification of kraft pulping to produce softwood pulp of 20 kappa number by supplementing kraft liquor with anthraquinone and increasing effective alkali charge and sulfidity.

LOW-PRESSURE FEEDER: Tapered star feeder with six pockets that feeds chips from atmospheric pressure to approximately 20 psig as they enter the steaming vessel of a Kamyr digester system.

M _____

MAGNEFITE PROCESS: Proprietary magnesium bisulfite pulping and recovery process.

MAGNESIA: Magnesium oxide.

MAGNESIUM BASE LIQUOR: Bisulfite cooking liquor containing magnesium bisulfite $[Mg(SO_3)_2]$ as the principal active cooking chemical.

MAGNESIUM OXIDE: (MgO) Entrained inorganic residue formed during the combustion of magnesium bisulfite waste liquor which is recovered and reacted with sulfur dioxide to reconstitute the magnesium base cooking liquor. Syn. Magnesia.

MAKEUP CHEMICAL: Chemical which is added to a chemical pulping system in order to replace losses, e.g., saltcake in the kraft system, to compensate for soda and sulfur losses.

MASONITE PULPING PROCESS: Pulping process to convert wood chips into a fibrous raw material for fiberboard. The chips are first softened by relatively low-pressure steam (350 psig, 430°F) and then elevated to high pressure (about 1000 psig, 540°F) before being discharged through a slot (down to atmospheric pressure) where the chips are exploded and shredded into a mass of fiber bundles.

M & D DIGESTER: Continuous digester designed by Messing and Durkee and manufactured by C.E. Bauer. It consists essentially of an inclined tube with a length-wise midfeather around which conveyor flights are carried. Retention time of the pulping raw material can be precisely controlled by the speed of the conveyor.

MEASURING TANKS: Tanks that are filled to a prescribed level and then dumped into a batch digester. Typically, measuring tanks are used for adding the required amounts of white and black liquors into a kraft batch digester. Syn. Draw-Down Tanks.

MICRODIGESTER ASSEMBLY: Configuration of small-scale laboratory digesters (most commonly six units) utilizing a common circulating medium, which serves either as a pulping liquor for wire mesh containers or as a precisely controlled temperature bath for stainless-steel bombs.

MITSCHERLICH PULP: Sulfite pulp prepared by a low-temperature, slow-cooking process, used in the manufacture of glassine and greaseproof papers.

MODIFIED KRAFT PROCESS: Kraft pulping process that has been augmented with one or more modifications, usually with the objective to stabilize the end groups of the cellulose and hemicellulose polymer chains against peeling reactions during cooking, and thereby increase the pulp yield. Examples of modified kraft pulping are by addition of anthraquinones or polysulfides.

MONOSULFITE PROCESS: Any sulfite pulping process in which the dominant form of sulfite chemical is monosulfite, i.e., there is an absence of free acid and bisulfite. Both neutral sulfite and alkaline sulfite are essentially monosulfite pulping processes.

MOXY PROCESS: Proprietary process (Mead Corp.) for converting a portion of the sodium sulfide present in kraft white liquor to sodium polysulfide and sodium hydroxide. The conversion is carried out as a single-step oxidation using compressed air in a reactor containing a fixed bed of treated activated carbon catalyst. See also POLYSULFIDE.

MULTISTAGE SULFITE PROCESS: Any sulfite pulping process in which two or more cooking liquors of different pH and/or composition or concentration are applied successively to wood chips during the impregnation or cooking processes. A number of two-stage sulfite processes are used commercially.

MUMIN TUBE: On some Kamyr continuous digesters, the outside inclined top separator which retains chips received from the high-pressure feeder while returning liquor.

N_____

NAOH SOLUBILITY TEST: Degree of solubility of a wood sample in 1% NaOH under specified conditions, a measure of rot content. The test value is used to predict the chip rot index.

NECK (of a digester): Large nozzle which is connected to the upper dished head of a stationary vertical batch digester and to which is connected the capping valve or flanged capping head.

NEUTRAL SULFITE PROCESS: Any sulfite pulping process that is carried out in the pH range from 7 to 9. See also NSSC PROCESS.

NITRIC ACID PULPING: Experimental chemical pulping method which utilizes a nitric acid cook followed by alkaline extraction.

NITROGEN DIOXIDE DELIGNIFICATION: Experimental chemical pulping method which utilizes a cook with NO_2 in coal oil or carbon tetrachloride, followed by alkaline extraction.

NONCONDENSIBLES: Gases and vapors which collect at the top of a batch digester during the cook. If not properly removed or "relieved", these gaseous constituents will cause a "false pressure", i.e., a pressure higher than that which corresponds to steam at the same temperature.

NON-WOOD PULP: Pulp derived from plant sources other than wood.

NO-SULFUR PULPING: Usually refers to a semichemical pulping process which utilizes mixtures of sodium carbonate (soda ash) and sodium hydroxide (caustic soda) as the active chemicals in the cooking liquor. See also SODA ASH COOKING.

NSSC PROCESS: (Neutral Sulfite Semi-Chemical) Sulfite cooking process in which chips, usually hardwood, are treated with a cooking liquor made up of a mixture of sulfite and carbonate (or other alkali), at pH 7 to 9, followed by mechanical defiberizing. The base used can be either sodium or ammonium. The process is used primarily to make pulp for corrugated medium stock.

O_____

ORGANOSOLV PULPING: See SOLVENT PULPING.

OUTLET DEVICE: Rotating scraper assembly at the bottom of a continuous digester which conveys the chips from the column into the blow line.

OVERCOOKED: See DEGREE OF DELIGNIFICATION.

OXYGEN DELIGNIFICATION: Any alkaline treatment of pulp with oxygen. If used as the primary delignification step, this treatment is usually

OXYGEN DELIGNIFICATION (cont): referred to as "oxygen pulping". If used as a secondary delignification step, it is often referred to as "oxygen bleaching".

OXYGEN PULPING: See SODA-OXYGEN PULPING.

P

PACKING: See CHIP PACKING, TOWER PACKING.

PACKING DENSITY: See DEGREE OF PACKING.

PAPERMAKING PULP: Pulp manufactured for use in papermaking. Syn. Paper Pulp.

PARTIAL PRESSURE: Pressure exerted by one component of a multi-component liquid or gaseous mixture.

PENETRABILITY: Ability of wood subdivisions to become impregnated with cooking chemicals through direct liquid intrusion. See also PENETRATION FACTOR.

PENETRATION: Direct liquid intrusion into the wood structure through lumina and interconnecting capillaries. See also IMPREGNATION.

PENETRATION FACTOR: Measure of air penetrability of chips, defined as the fourth power of the radius of a glass capillary which will permit the same rate of air flow as one square centimeter of a particular wood.

PERMANGANATE NUMBER: Test result which indicates the lignin content of a pulp sample based on its consumption of permanganate (a powerful oxidizing agent). Syn. P Number, K Number.

PEROXIDE DELIGNIFICATION: Experimental non-sulfur chemical pulping process in which high-yield soda pulps are delignified under atmospheric conditions with mixtures of caustic soda and hydrogen peroxide.

PIGGYBACK DIGESTERS: Arrangement of two M & D digesters in series, one placed above the other. The top impregnation vessel discharges by gravity into the bottom vessel where bulk delignification is carried out.

POLYCONDENSATION (of lignin): Undesirable reaction that occurs during sulfite cooking under conditions of high acid concentration and/or high temperature. The dark-colored and insoluble compounds formed give rise to the apt description of "burnt cook".

POLYSULFIDE: Sodium polysulfide (Na_2S_n) in kraft pulping liquors, generated by reacting elemental sulfur with the sulfide in solution or by air oxidation of the sulfide. During alkaline cooking, the polysulfide serves to stabilize the hemicelluloses against peeling reactions, and therefore, provides an increase in yield as compared to normal kraft pulping.

POLYSULFIDE PULP: Pulp obtained by a modified kraft cooking process in which sodium polysulfide is added to the cooking liquor. Polysulfide pulp has a higher yield than kraft pulp at the same kappa number due to better retention of hemicelluloses during cooking; it is, therefore, easier to beat than kraft pulp, has a lower tear strength, but higher burst and tensile strengths.

PRECIRCULATION: Pumping sulfite cooking liquor continuously for a period of time from the accumulator to the digester and back again, either with or without steaming.

PREHYDROLYSIS: Treatment of wood chips (or other cellulosic raw material) with dilute acid or alkali to hydrolyze the hemicelluloses, used prior to the conventional cook in the production of dissolving pulps. The most common method of prehydrolysis utilizes direct steaming; the action of the steam (sometimes known as autohydrolysis) liberates organic acids from the wood which at elevated temperature hydrolyze hemicellulose to soluble sugar.

PREHYDROLYZED KRAFT PULP: High-alpha dissolving pulp.

PRE-STEAMING: (1) Injection of steam into a batch digester during or after charging with chips, but before the cooking liquor is added. (2) Introduction of steam at atmospheric pressure into the chip bin just before the chips are metered into a steam pressurized environment. In both cases, the objective is to pre-heat the chips and remove a portion of the air from the chip mass. See also STEAMING.

PULP: Fibrous material produced either chemically or mechanically (or by some combination of chemical and mechanical means) from wood or other cellulosic raw material. Pulp is the principal raw material for papermaking.

PULPABILITY: Combination of properties that determines the resistance of wood chips to being reduced to pulp by a chemical pulping process. Relevant factors are lignin content and those structural characteristics that affect penetration and diffusion.

PULPING PROCESS: Any process for converting fibrous raw material into pulp. Pulping processes are usually classified into mechanical, chemical and semichemical methods.

PULPING REACTION: Any of the chemical reactions between active cooking chemicals and the pulping raw material during cooking which accomplish delignification and liberation of the cellulosic fibers, but which also cause a certain amount of dissolution and modification of the carbohydrate fraction. See also SELECTIVITY.

PYRITE: Iron Pyrite (FeS_2) a brass-yellow mineral used as raw material in the production of sulfur dioxide. Syn. Fool's Gold.

Q

QUENCHING: Slowing down the cooking reaction in the Kamyr continuous digester at the end of the cooking zone by displacing the hot residual liquor with ascending wash liquor and extracting it to the flash tank.

R

RAW ACID: Sulfurous acid made in the acid plant before fortification.

REACTOR: Vessel in which a chemical reaction is carried out. Examples of reactors in a kraft mill are digesters, bleaching towers, slakers, lime kilns and causticizers.

RED LIQUOR: Residual liquor from sulfite and semichemical pulping processes containing spent chemicals and wood residuals.

REDUCTIVE ALKALINE DELIGNIFICATION: Alkaline pulping process utilizing a chemical additive (e.g., sodium sulfide, reduced quinone) which serves as a "reservoir of reducing power" to accelerate delignification.

RELATIVE REACTION RATE: See H FACTOR.

RELIEF: Venting of a digester in the early stages of a batch cook to remove noncondensible gases that can cause excessive pressure buildup.

RESIDUAL ALKALI: With respect to black liquor, the amount or concentration of active alkali that was not consumed during the kraft digestion.

RESIDUAL DELIGNIFICATION: Final stage of a kraft cook corresponding to "overcooking". It is characterized by very slow delignification, significant carbohydrate degradation, and significant alkali consumption.

RESIDUAL LIGNIN: Lignin remaining with the pulp after chemical digestion.

RESIDUAL PULPING LIQUOR: See SPENT PULPING LIQUOR.

ROSS DIAGRAM: Plot of lignin-to-carbohydrate ratio vs. pulp yield during the course of chemical pulping, usually employed for the comparison of different pulping processes. The plot is often augmented with a skew grid representing the coordinates for the quantity of lignin and carbohydrate remaining in the pulp. (After J.H. Ross)

ROTARY DIGESTERS: Pressure vessels used for chemical pulping of straw and other non-wood fiber sources. They are commonly of spherical construction and revolve on trunnions at a speed of 10 to 20 revolutions per hour. Steam is introduced into the digester through a pipe in one of the trunnions. "Rotaries" are often equipped on the inside surface with pins or baffles to reduce the tendency of the fibrous material to form a ball or to slide during a cook.

ROTARY POCKET FEEDER: Rotary device containing radial pockets used to continuously convey bulk solid material (e.g., chips) from one atmospheric state to another, e.g., from ambient to digester pressure or vice versa. Syn. Rotary Valve, Star Valve. See also AIR LOCK.

S

SAND SEPARATOR: Device used within a Kamyr continuous digester system to remove sand. Liquor pumped from the chip chute enters the separator tangentially and centrifugal forces carry the sand to the periphery. Sand accumulates and settles to the bottom where it is periodically removed.

SAWDUST DIGESTER: Pressure vessel used for the continuous cooking of sawdust or other small wood subdivisions. A sawdust digester is simpler in design than a continuous digester for chips because it is assumed that liquor impregnation occurs almost instantaneously and therefore, a specific impregnation zone is not included.

SAWDUST PULPING: General term for the mechanical or chemical pulping of small wood subdivisions. These small wood subdivisions may be actual sawdust, chip screen fines, or pin chips.

SCALING: Formation of scale due to precipitation, principally of inorganic compounds, on the inside surfaces of digesters and other equipment.

SELECTIVITY: Relative extent to which active pulping chemicals attack the lignin and preserve the carbohydrates, i.e., better selectivity is synonymous with higher yield at a given kappa number. Selective removal of lignin with "protection" of the holocellulose fraction is an ultimate goal of chemical pulping research.

SEMICHEMICAL PULP: Any pulp obtained from wood (or other plant material) using a balanced combination of chemical and mechanical means. Among pulps of this classification are high-yield kraft, high-yield sulfite and NSSC pulps. Generally, semichemical pulps fall into the yield range from 60 to 80% on b.d. wood.

SEMICHEMICAL PULPING: Any pulping process relying on a balanced combination of chemical and mechanical means to separate the fibers. A portion of the lignin is first removed by chemical treatment, and then the softened chips are refined into pulp.

SHAKEUP STEAM: Steam injected into a batch cook to activate or re-align the chip mass. See also DIGESTER BUMPING.

SHUT-IN: Shutdown of a continuous cooking operation while maintaining a full digester.

SIDE RELIEF: Withdrawal of cooking liquor from a sulfite digester during the early stages of digestion when impregnation is known to be complete. This is done to provide a gas space at the top of the digester and permit top relief with minimum entrainment of liquor.

SLUICING LIQUOR: Excess cooking liquor which is recirculated between the high-pressure feeder and the top separator in order to transport chips into a Kamyr digester.

SODA ASH: Soda makeup chemical for the kraft process; and also a buffer chemical for the sulfite process. Chemically, it is sodium carbonate (Na_2CO_3).

SODA ASH PULPING: Method of semichemical pulping utilizing sodium carbonate (soda ash) as the principal active chemical in the pulping liquor, supplemented with small amounts of caustic soda. See also NO-SULFUR PULPING.

SODA-OXYGEN PULPING: Chemical pulping process using oxygen and sodium hydroxide as the active chemicals. It is not used commercially.

SODA PULPING: Alkaline chemical pulping process similar to the kraft process, except that sodium hydroxide (NaOH) is used alone as the active chemical. The commercial application is primarily for hardwoods and some nonwood cellulosic raw materials.

SODIUM BASE LIQUOR: Bisulfite cooking liquor containing sodium bisulfite ($NaHSO_3$) as the principal active cooking chemical.

SODIUM CARBONATE: See SODA ASH.

SODIUM HYDROSULFIDE: See HYDROSULFIDE.

SODIUM HYDROXIDE: (NaOH) Active chemical in all conventional alkaline pulping processes. Syn. Caustic Soda.

SODIUM OXIDE: (Na_2O) Anhydrous sodium hydroxide. This form of sodium is typically used as the basis for calculating equivalent weights of all soda chemicals encountered in the kraft mill.

SODIUM SULFATE: See SALTCAKE.

SODIUM SULFIDE: (Na_2S) Active chemical in the kraft pulping process. Sodium sulfide in solution hydrolyzes into sodium hydrosulfide and sodium hydroxide.

SOFT COOK: General term for a cook that has been over-delignified.

SOLUBLE BASE: Base which is soluble over the full range of pH encountered in sulfite pulping. Of the four bases used, sodium and ammonium are soluble; magnesium is an intermediate and calcium is insoluble except at very low pH.

SOLVENT PULPING: Chemical pulping process in which wood chips (or other cellulosic raw materials) are treated with an organic solvent at high temperature and pressure to liberate cellulosic fiber and lignin. Numerous methods have been investigated, using e.g., ethanol, methanol (with and without alkali), butanol, phenol, acetic acid, formic acid, formaldehyde, glycerol, glycol, dioxane, and dimethylsulfoxide (DMSO). No solvent pulping process is presently being used on a full commercial scale, but feasibility has been demonstrated at the pilot plant level.

SORPTION COOKING: Proposed scheme to increase the yield of brown kraft pulps by reducing the pH at the end of the cook in order to redeposit lignin onto the fibers.

SPENT PULPING LIQUOR: Liquor separated from the pulp following a chemical cook, containing the residual cooking chemicals and the dissolved constituents of the wood. Syn. Residual Pulping Liquor, Waste Pulping Liquor.

SPENT SULFITE LIQUOR: Liquor separated from the pulp following a sulfite cook, containing the residual cooking chemicals and the dissolved constituents of the wood. Syn. Red Liquor.

SPHERICAL DIGESTER: Rotary digester of spherical construction. Syn. Globe Digester.

SPRAY COOLING: Method of cooling and absorbing SO_2 gas during preparation of cooking acid in which water in finely divided form is contacted with the sulfur burner gas in two stages. In the first stage, the hot gas is saturated with water vapor to drop the temperature; in the second stage, water vapor is condensed and SO_2 gas is absorbed.

STEAMING: Treatment of chips with steam in a separate vessel before they enter a continuous digester. The objective is to pre-heat the chips and remove air from the chip mass. See also PRE-STEAMING.

STEAMING VESSEL: Vessel in a continuous cooking system through which chips are conveyed and exposed to a displacement flow of steam which heats the chips and flushes out air and other non-condensibles.

STEAM-PHASE DIGESTER: Cooking vessel in which impregnated chips are heated with direct steam to bring them up to the cooking temperature.

STORAGE ACID: Raw acid held in reserve for later transfer to the sulfite mill accumulators.

STRAINER: Perforated ring on the inside surface near the midpoint of a batch digester through which liquor is extracted and circulated during a cook.

SULFATE PROCESS: See KRAFT PROCESS.

SULFATE PULP: See KRAFT PULP.

SULFIDATION: Chemical substitution of sulfide ions for hydrogen atoms. Sulfidation of lignin is a minor reaction during alkaline pulping processes.

SULFIDE: See SODIUM SULFIDE.

SULFIDITY: With respect to white liquor or green liquor, the ratio of sodium sulfide (Na_2S) concentration to either active alkali concentration or to total titratable alkali concentration, all in terms of equivalent sodium oxide (Na_2O), usually expressed as a percentage. The basis of white liquor sulfidity must be specified.

SULFITATION: Reaction of SO_2 gas with a base chemical to produce sulfite or bisulfite cooking liquor.

SULFITE PROCESS: Generic term for any chemical pulping process employing sulfurous acid and/or bisulfite or sulfite ions as the primary or secondary delignification chemicals. Generally a qualifying term is prefixed. See also ACID SULFITE PROCESS, BISULFITE PROCESS, NSSC PROCESS, ALKALINE SULFITE PROCESS, MULTI-STAGE SULFITE PROCESS.

SULFITE PULP: Pulp manufactured by any sulfite process.

SULFONATION: Chemical substitution of SO_3H groups for hydrogen atoms. The sulfonation of lignin is a major mechanism for lignin dissolution during sulfite pulping.

SULFUR: (S) Yellow nonmetallic element, used as raw material for makeup of sulfur dioxide. It is also used as a makeup chemical in the kraft recovery cycle and for polysulfide formation.

SULFUR BURNER: Furnace used for the controlled burning (oxidation) of elemental sulfur into sulfur dioxide.

SULFUR DIOXIDE: (SO_2) Toxic gas formed readily by burning sulfur in air or by roasting pyrite. Aqueous sulfur dioxide (solution of sulfur dioxide in water) and the metallic salts are used extensively in acidic and high-yield pulping processes. Aqueous sulfur dioxide is also used in pulp bleaching.

SULFUROUS ACID: Solution of sulfur dioxide (SO_2) in water. Since the actual compound, "sulfurous acid" (H_2SO_3), has been shown not to exist, the term "aqueous SO_2" has been suggested as a better descriptive term.

SULFUR TRIOXIDE: (SO_3) Toxic gas formed by further oxidation of sulfur dioxide (under certain conditions) which forms sulfuric acid (H_2SO_4) when dissolved in water. Sulfur trioxide is an undesirable byproduct when burning sulfur for sulfite cooking liquor preparation. In sulfuric acid plants, a heated catalyst is used to promote oxidation to the trioxide form.

SURGING: Sudden changes in process inputs during batch cooking to promote circulation and improve temperature uniformity. Examples of surging techniques are digester "bumping" and "burping".

T _____

TARGET PLATE: Surface within a blow tank where the discharging pulp/liquor/steam mixture from a batch digester first impinges.

TEMPERATURE CYCLE: Programmed temperature during a batch cook, typically consisting of an initial gradual rise to a maximum value, followed by a holding time at the maximum temperature.

THIOSULFATE: ($S_2O_3^=$) Species of oxidized sulfur which forms in both the sulfite and kraft chemical systems. Its formation is generally considered undesirable, and the chemical is known to be corrosive in the alkaline kraft system.

TIME AT TEMPERATURE: Total elapsed time after the batch digester has reached maximum cooking temperature until the blow or blowdown.

TIME TO TEMPERATURE: Period of controlled heating in which a batch digester is brought up to the cooking temperature. Syn. Heat-Up Time. See also HEAT-UP RATE.

TOP CIRCULATION SYSTEM: Pumping circuit on a Kamyr continuous digester that transports chips in sluicing liquor from the high-pressure feeder to the top separator and returns the sluicing liquor to the high-pressure feeder.

TOP SEPARATOR: Equipment at the top of the Kamyr continuous digester used for separation of chips and liquor from excess transport (sluicing) liquor. The standard top separator, used for hydraulic digesters, employs a top entry for liquor and chips. The inverted top separator, used for gas phase digesters, is characterized by a bottom entry for liquor and chips.

TOTAL ALKALI: With respect to white liquor or green liquor, the total amount or concentration of all sodium alkali compounds in terms of equivalent sodium oxide (Na_2O). The figure does not include NaCl.

TOTAL SO$_2$: Sum of the free and combined SO_2 as applied to sulfite cooking liquor. With respect to sulfite liquor analysis, the total SO_2 is determined by straight iodometric titration.

TOTAL TITRATABLE ALKALI (TTA): With respect to white liquor and green liquor, the amount or concentration of sodium hydroxide (NaOH) plus sodium carbonate ($NaCO_3$) plus sodium sulfide (Na_2S), all in terms of equivalent sodium oxide (Na_2O).

TOWER: See ACID TOWER.

TOWER PACKING: Inert material used within an acid absorption tower to provide contact surface between the base liquor and SO_2 gas to facilitate absorption. Typical packing materials are perforated cylinders, cylindrical rings and curved saddles.

TWO-STAGE STEAMING: Utilization of two pressure levels for indirect steaming of batch digesters in order to optimize electrical output from the steam turbine. The digester is initially heated and pressurized to an intermediate level using relatively low-pressure steam (e.g., 60 psig), and then the cooking is completed utilizing higher-pressure steam (e.g., 150 psig).

TWO-STAGE SULFITE PROCESS: See MULTI-STAGE SULFITE PROCESS.

TWO-TEMPERATURE COOKING: Technique for cooking linerboard pulp in a Kamyr digester utilizing an initial short-duration cooking period at high temperature (i.e., about 180°C) followed by a more extended cooking period at lower temperature (i.e., about 160°C). The ability to produce pulps at higher kappa number without adverse effects on quality are claimed.

TWO-VESSEL DIGESTER: Usually refers to a modified Kamyr continuous digester system where one vessel is used for impregnation in series with a second vessel for cooking. The first vessel is a hydraulic digester; the second vessel can be either hydraulic or gas-phase.

U _____

ULTRA HIGH-YIELD SULFITE PROCESS: Sulfite pulping process in which the chips are lightly sulfonated and then defibrated by mechanical action. The pulp yield is near to that for purely mechanical pulps, in the 80 to 92% range. Syn. Very High-Yield Sulfite Pulping.

UNDERCOOKED: See DEGREE OF COOKING.

V _____

VAPOR PHASE PULPING: Any chemical or semichemical pulping process in which fully impregnated chips are separated from the excess impregnation liquor and cooking subsequently takes place predominantly in a steam (water vapor) atmosphere.

VIRGIN PULP: Manufactured pulp that has never been converted into paper or other end product.

VOMIT STACK: Stack through which large volumes of steam are vented from a sulfite blowpit.

W _____

WATER COOK: Trial cook with only water in the digester to check out a system for leaks and malfunctions, used for new installations and retrofits.

WHITE LIQUOR: Kraft cooking liquor containing the active alkali components of sodium hydroxide (NaOH) and sodium sulfide (Na_2S).

WHITE LIQUOR STRENGTH: Concentration of active alkali (or effective alkali), usually in units of grams NaO_2 per liter.

WHOLE TREE PULPING: Kraft pulping utilizing a chip furnish made up principally of whole tree chips (i.e., chips from the branches and top of the tree, as well as from the bole).

WOOD PULP: Pulp derived from a wood furnish.

WOOD RESIDUE: Portion of the original wood substance remaining with the cooking liquor after the cellulosic pulp has been separated.

XYZ _____

YIELD: In pulping, the ratio of oven dry output pulp to oven dry input wood, expressed as a percent. (Sometimes, the ratio of air dry pulp to oven dry wood is used.) Syn. Pulp Yield.

Chapter 9

Chemical Recovery & Steam Plant

(Includes: Black Liquor Handling & Evaporation, Boiler Equipment/Operation, Steam Handling, Recausticizing & Lime Kiln)

A

ACID DEW POINT: Flue gas temperature at which sulfuric acid first condenses, usually considered to be the minimum operational gas temperature following the economizer section. The acid dew point is principally a function of the sulfur trioxide (SO_3) concentration and is typically below 140°C for kraft recovery boilers.

ACOUSTIC LEAK DETECTOR: Sensing equipment for recovery boilers which detects the sound generated by water or steam escaping from a hole in a tube and alerts the operator to the possibility or likelihood of a leak.

ACTIVATABLE CHEMICAL: Any chemical in the kraft recovery cycle such as sodium carbonate (Na_2CO_3) and sodium sulfate (Na_2SO_4) that is capable of being transformed into an active form (i.e., NaOH and Na_2S) for cooking.

AGGLOMERATION: Process in which small particles adhere to one another and grow into a larger mass, as for example with sticky particulates.

AGGREGATE: Mass of consolidated particles that is likely to break apart during subsequent operations.

AIR BOX: See WINDBOX.

AIR DEFICIENCY: Insufficient air in an air-fuel mixture to supply the oxygen theoretically needed for complete combustion of the fuel.

AIR-FUEL RATIO: Weight ratio (or volume ratio) of air to fuel in the combustion mixture at the burner of the furnace.

AIR HEATER: Heat transfer apparatus through which air passes and is heated prior to entry into the furnace or boiler. See also REGENERATIVE AIR HEATER, RECUPERATIVE AIR HEATER.

AIR INFILTRATION: Leakage of air into the furnace from the surrounding environment. A certain amount of air infiltration is expected because the furnace is always operated under draft.

AIR PORTS: Entry points provided in the water walls of the furnace for combustion air. On recovery furnaces, the primary ports are located on all four walls just above the floor; secondary and sometimes tertiary ports are located higher up on the furnace. For furnaces using conventional fuels, the primary air is introduced with the fuel at the burners.

ALLOWABLE WORKING PRESSURE: Maximum pressure for which a boiler is designed and constructed.

ALUMINATE RECOVERY PROCESS: Proprietary sulfite recovery process (Sonoco) in which concentrated spent liquor is mixed with alumina and processed through a rotary kiln where sodium is converted to sodium aluminate, organics are destroyed, and sulfur is converted to sulfur dioxide. The sodium aluminate is solubilized and used in an absorber to react with sulfur dioxide in the flue gases. Sodium sulfite is recovered from the absorber and is used again in the pulping system, while the re-formed alumina is returned to the recovery cycle.

AMINES: Class of ammonia derivatives in which one or more hydrogen atoms have been replaced by an organic radical. See also FILMING AMINES, NEUTRALIZING AMINES.

ASH: Incombustible solid matter; the residue after burning.

ASH CONTENT: Weight ratio of ash to fuel, usually expressed as a percentage.

ASH FUSION CHARACTERISTICS: Temperature range over which both solid and liquid phases are present for a particular recovery furnace ash, a function of its chemical composition. See also EUTECTIC POINT, LIQUIDUS TEMPERATURE.

ASH HOPPER: Receptacle below the furnace where ash and other furnace debris is collected and from which it is periodically removed. Syn. Ash Pit.

ASH SLUICE: Trench or channel used for transporting the ash from the ash hoppers to a disposal point by means of sluicing water.

ASPIRATING BURNER: Burner which utilizes the energy in the jet of gaseous fuel to draw in air and create a uniform combustion mixture, which is then burned in suspension.

ATOMIZATION: Process of dividing a liquid into minute, air-borne droplets either by impact with a jet of steam or compressed air or by passage through a mechanical device.

ATOMIZER: Device used to convert a liquid flow into a fine spray.

ATOMIZING MEDIUM: Supplementary fluid, such as steam or air, applied to an oil burner to assist the atomization of oil.

ATTEMPERATION: Controlled cooling of steam at the superheater outlet (or at some intermediate point within the superheater) to regulate the final steam temperature.

AUTOCAUSTICIZING: System to convert sodium carbonate to sodium hydroxide within the kraft chemical recovery cycle without addition of lime.

AUXILIARY FUEL: Gas or oil fuel which supplement black liquor in a recovery furnace.

AVAILABLE LIME INDEX: See LIME AVAILABILITY.

AXIAL FAN: Fan which produces pressure from the change in axial and tangential velocity components through the impeller. (No pressure is produced by centrifugal force, as in a centrifugal fan.)

B _____

BALLS: Large aggregates which sometimes form in the lime kiln.

BARK BOILER: Boiler which is designed to burn bark and other hogged wood waste materials with variable moisture content either as the sole fuel or in mixtures with coal, oil and other fuels. Syn. Wood Waste Boiler, Biomass Boiler, Multifuel Boiler.

BAROMETRIC CONDENSER: Direct contact condenser often used with black liquor evaporators that utilizes a condensate or wastewater stream flowing down a long vertical pipe to draw in vapors through an eductor opening by virtue of the pressure created at the low end of the pipe (i.e., the barometric leg).

BASE LOAD: Term applied to the portion of a boiler load that is essentially constant for long periods.

BAUMÉ HYDROMETER SCALE: Sensitive scale for liquor density that is easily converted to specific gravity or to percent solids according to individual mill calibration.

BELT FILTER: Modified drum filter sometimes employed to separate fibers from black liquor or to remove lime mud and dregs from white or green liquors. The distinguishing characteristic is the takeoff run of the filter cloth from the drum over a discharge roll and around aligning and takeup rolls and back to the filter drum. Often water sprays are applied to both sides of the cloth during passage around the rolls.

BIOFUEL: Any fuel derived from biological materials.

BIOGASIFICATION: Process of gasifying a biological product such as wood waste by thermal treatment.

BIOMASS FUEL: Fuel consisting of wood waste, peat, municipal/industrial refuse or other biological material.

BLACK LIQUOR BURNING: Incineration of concentrated black liquor in the recovery furnace with the objectives of chemical recovery and production of steam.

BLACK LIQUOR EVAPORATION: Process of concentrating black liquor from 12–18% solids to 65–80% solids through a series of multi-effect evaporators.

BLACK LIQUOR FIRING SYSTEM: System within the recovery unit itself that provides for black liquor handling, conditioning and firing.

BLACK LIQUOR OXIDATION (BLO): Reaction of black liquor with air or oxygen to oxidize sulfide to thiosulfate, carried out in kraft mills to "stabilize" the sulfur and prevent stripping out of hydrogen sulfide gas at the direct contact evaporator. Oxidation is carried out on either weak black liquor or strong black liquor.

BLACK LIQUOR PROPERTIES: Usually refers to those thermal and transport properties of black liquor that directly affect evaporator and recovery boiler design, operation, and optimization. The properties of interest include viscosity, heating value, boiling point rise, heat capacity, surface tension, inorganic solubility, density, and thermal conductivity.

BLACK OUT: Marked reduction in the rate of burnup of the organic material in the black liquor so that autogenous (self-generating) burning is lost, either occurring locally or generally in the recovery furnace.

BLOWDOWN: Removal of a portion of the boiler water for the purpose of removing sedimental sludge; it can be either continuous or intermittent. The rate of blowdown is usually expressed as a percentage of the water feed rate.

BLOW HEAT EVAPORATOR: Evaporator system that utilizes batch digester blow steam condensate at 96–99°C as the heating medium in a two or three effect configuration to partially evaporate weak black liquor. With this arrangement, the first effect of the blow heat evaporator becomes a secondary condenser for the accumulator system, thus facilitating segregation of volatiles into one condensate stream.

BOILER: Closed pressure vessel in which a liquid, usually water, is vaporized by the application of heat. It should be noted that a furnace is usually integral with the boiler, and the term, boiler, is commonly applied to the integrated equipment. See also FIRETUBE BOILER, WATERTUBE BOILER.

BOILER CODE: Usually refers to standard specifications by the American Society of Mechanical Engineers (ASME) for the construction of boilers.

BOILER EFFICIENCY: See STEAM-GENERATING EFFICIENCY.

BOILER FEED PUMP: High-pressure, heavy-duty pump that introduces feedwater into the boiler circuit, typically driven by a steam turbine.

BOILER FEEDWATER: Water introduced into the boiler during operation, including both freshly treated water and return condensate.

BOILER FEEDWATER TREATMENT: Specifically, the addition of chemicals to prevent formation of scale and eliminate other objectionable characteristics. (It is usually assumed that the basic water supply has already been given external treatment for removal of suspended solids and color.)

BOILER HOUSE: Building in which the boiler is situated.

BOILER TUBES: Steel or composite tubes carrying water, steam, or water/steam mixtures which constitute the major heat transfer surfaces within a boiler.

BOILER WATER: Circulating boiler water after separation of steam and before the addition of boiler feedwater or chemicals.

BOILING: Conversion of liquid into vapor.

BOILING POINT (BP): Temperature at which water is converted to saturated steam for the prevailing pressure.

BOILING POINT RISE (BPR): Difference between the temperature of a boiling liquid and the saturation temperature of its equilibrium vapor.

The boiling point rise increases with the solids content of a solution and acts as a restraint on the number of evaporation effects that are possible between two operating pressures.

BOILOUT: (1) Running water through evaporator sets, essentially a washing process to remove build-up of deposits on tubes. (2) Boiling of highly alkaline water in boiler pressure parts for the removal of oils and greases.

BREECHING: Duct for transport of combustion gases to the stack or between parts of a steam generating unit.

BRIDGING: Accumulation of slag partially or completely blocking spaces between heat absorbing surfaces of a boiler.

BULL NOSE: See FURNACE NOSE BAFFLE.

BUNKER C OIL: Residual oil of high viscosity, commonly used as boiler fuel.

BURKEITE: Double salt of sodium carbonate and sodium sulfate ($2Na_2SO_4 \cdot Na_2CO_3$) which crystallizes out from kraft liquors when they are concentrated by evaporation.

BURNABILITY: Properties of a black liquor that influence its drying rate and combustible gas formation during pyrolysis in a recovery furnace. Combustion can be maintained when firing a liquor with good burnability without supplemental use of fossil fuel.

BURNER: Device for the introduction of fuel and air, properly mixed in correct proportions, into the combustion zone of the boiler.

BURNING: See COMBUSTION.

BURNT LIME: Lime that has been converted from lime mud or limestone in a kiln or fluid-bed calciner. Syn. Reburnt Lime.

C

CAKING: Buildup of material on the outside or inside surfaces of an orifice or flow passage, e.g., as typically occurs for a recovery boiler spray nozzle.

CALCINATION: Burning of lime mud ($CaCO_3$) to produce quick lime (CaO). Syn. Reburning.

CALCINER: Apparatus in which calcination takes place; usually a kiln, but could also be a fluid-bed reactor. See LIME KILN, FLUID-BED CALCINER.

CALCITE LIMESTONE: Limestone high in calcium content.

CALCIUM HYDROXIDE: See HYDRATED LIME.

CALCIUM OXIDE: (CaO) Chemical description of lime.

CALORIFIC VALUE: Quantity of heat produced by a unit mass of fuel on complete combustion. The SI unit is joules per kilogram (J/kg). Syn. Heating Value, Fuel Value.

CARBON: (C) Principal combustible constituent of all fossil fuels.

CARBONACEOUS: [adj] Term descriptive of materials that are rich in carbon.

CARBONATION: Conversion of sodium carbonate (Na_2CO_3) and sodium sulfide (Na_2S) in green liquor to sodium bicarbonate ($NaHCO_3$) and sodium hydrosulfide (NaSH) by saturating the liquor with carbon dioxide (CO_2).

CARBON DIOXIDE: (CO_2) Principal combustion product of all fossil fuels when sufficient air or oxygen is provided for complete combustion. An air deficiency causes the formation of soot or carbon monoxide (CO), and therefore, the loss of a portion of the fuel's heating value.

CARBON MONOXIDE: (CO) Poisonous, colorless gas which is the product of incomplete combustion.

CARRYOVER: General term applied to all contaminants entrained with the steam leaving the boiler.

CASCADE EVAPORATOR: Type of direct-contact evaporator consisting of a rotating assembly of tubes that alternately are submerged in liquor and exposed to hot gases. See also DIRECT CONTACT EVAPORATOR.

CASTABLE: Refractory material which is supplied as a dry powder and is mixed with water before use; it is installed by pouring, trowelling, and gunning. Since castables are not fired before installation, prolonged exposure to heat is required before they take on the reversible expansion and contraction characteristics found in fixed ceramics. Syn. Refractory Cement.

CAUSTIC: [adj] Descriptive term for strongly alkaline substances which are corrosive or have an irritating effect on living tissue.

CAUSTIC EMBRITTLEMENT: Stress corrosion cracking of steel exposed to alkaline solutions. It occurs in boiler tube joints and ends due to excessively high pH in the boiler water.

CAUSTICIZER: Small, agitated tank used to allow calcium hydroxide [$Ca(OH)_2$] and sodium carbonate (Na_2CO_3) to react and form sodium hydroxide (NaOH) and calcium carbonate ($CaCO_3$). Two or more causticizers are used in a series arrangement to minimize short-circuiting of the mixture and assure high reaction efficiency.

CAUSTICIZING: Conversion of green liquor into white liquor by reaction with quick lime. Syn. Recausticizing, Caustification.

CAUSTICIZING EFFICIENCY: Measure of the completeness of the causticizing reaction, calculated as the ratio of sodium hydroxide (NaOH) formed in the white liquor to the sodium carbonate (Na_2CO_3) present in the green liquor, both in terms of equivalent sodium oxide (Na_2O), and expressed as a percentage. It can be calculated from white liquor analysis as the ratio of NaOH to NaOH plus Na_2CO_3; however, the concentration of NaOH in the original green liquor should be subtracted so that the value of NaOH represents only the portion produced by the causticizing reaction.

CAUSTICIZING PLANT: Section of the pulp mill where green liquor is converted into white liquor, usually in a series of sedimentation and reaction vessels. Syn. Causticizing Department.

CAUSTICIZING POWER (of lime): See LIME REACTIVITY.

CENTRIFUGAL FAN: Fan which creates pressure from two sources: the centrifugal force created by rotating the air column between the blades of the impeller, and the kinetic energy imparted to the air by virtue of its increased velocity leaving the impeller.

CHAIN SECTION: Steel chains attached to the shell of a lime kiln and hanging in the hot gases, which provide extended heat transfer surface. Chains may be hung as "garlands" where the individual chains are suspended from two points, or as "curtains" with each chain hanging vertically from one point only.

CHANGE OF STATE: Transformation of a substance from one state (i.e., solid, liquid, or gaseous) into another, accompanied by dramatic changes in physical properties.

CHAR: Carbonaceous material formed by incomplete combustion of an organic material.

CHAR BED: Heap of burning solids on the hearth of the recovery furnace. The char bed provides a reservoir of combustible material within the furnace.

CHEMICAL ASH: Carbon and chemical dust entrained with the gases from the burning zone of the recovery furnace. The chemical ash settles out at various points in the boiler and is recovered in the chemical ash hoppers.

CHEMICAL CYCLE: Recirculation of inorganic chemicals within the cooking and recovery areas, being transformed in the process from active cooking agents to residual reactants and back to active cooking agents.

CHEMICAL LOSS: Cooking chemicals which are not recovered for various reasons, usually reported in units of kilograms per metric ton of production. The chemicals of interest for the kraft process are soda and sulfur.

CHEMICAL RECOVERY: Process encompassing the burning of waste liquor to recover inorganic chemicals and subsequent conversion of these chemicals into the active form for cooking.

CHIMNEY: See STACK.

CHLORIDE: Elemental contaminant in the chemical recovery system, especially in those coastal kraft mills that transport logs in salt water. The chloride, combined with soda, constitutes a dead chemical load to the system and lowers the melting point of the chemical ash.

CHLORIDE ENRICHMENT: Increased concentration of chloride compounds in the fume from a recovery furnace as compared to the black liquor or smelt, due to the greater volatility of chlorides.

CHLORIDE ENRICHMENT FACTOR: Ratio of Cl/Na in the precipitator dust to that in the white liquor or smelt. Chloride enrichment factors observed in mill operation range from 1.5 to 4.0.

CHLORIDE REMOVAL: See SALT REMOVAL.

CINDERS: Particles of incombustible matter remaining after a burning process.

CIRCULATION: Movement of water and steam within a boiler. See also NATURAL CIRCULATION.

CIRCULATION RATIO: Weight ratio of water feed rate to rate of steam generation in a boiler.

CLARIFIED WHITE LIQUOR: White liquor from which most of the lime mud particles have been removed by sedimentation.

CLASSIFIER: Section of the lime slaker where unslaked lime (grits) and other solid debris are removed.

CLEANABILITY: Ability to maintain recovery boiler tubes free of fouling and plugging.

CLINKER: Hard, congealed mass of fused furnace refuse, usually slag.

COAL-FIRED BOILER: Any of various boilers which is designed to use coal as the primary fuel.

COLLECTING PLATES: Grounded plates in the electrostatic precipitator, the collecting surface for dust.

COMBUSTIBILITY: Relative measurement of the rate of fuel combustion, most commonly applied to coal, but more recently used to characterize spent liquor solids. Of the main organic components of spent liquor, degraded carbohydrates are more combustible than kraft lignin. Certain types of wood resins have a pronounced detrimental effect on liquor combustibility.

COMBUSTIBLE: (1) Substance or group of substances capable of combustion; the heat producing constituents of fuel. (2) [adj] Term applied to a liquid if its flash point is above 100°F (37.8°C). If the flashpoint is below 100°F, the liquid is described as "flammable".

COMBUSTIBLE LOSS: Energy loss from unburned combustible matter, i.e., the unliberated thermal energy.

COMBUSTION: Production of heat through the rapid chemical combination of oxygen with the combustible elements of a fuel.

COMBUSTION AIR: Primary air introduced into the furnace through the fuel bed by induced or forced draft. See also OVERFIRE AIR.

COMBUSTION CHAMBER: That part of a furnace or boiler in which combustible solids, vapors and gases are burned and settling of fly ash takes place.

COMBUSTION GASES: Gases, vapors and entrained materials resulting from the combustion of fuel. Syn. Flue Gas.

COMBUSTION RATE: Quantity of fuel fired per unit time.

COMPLETE COMBUSTION: Fuel burning where all combustible is burned. See also PERFECT COMBUSTION.

COMPOSITE TUBES: Boiler tubes constructed of two different materials, used in cases when the corrosion conditions at the inner and outer surfaces differ greatly.

CONCENTRATOR: Indirectly heated evaporator effect (or effects) of special design to handle liquor of high solids content. Syn. Finisher.

CONDENSATE: (1) Any liquid formed by condensation of vapor. (2) Condensed water resulting from the removal of latent heat from steam.

CONDENSATE RECEIVER: Holding tank which receives condensate from diverse process sources, and from which the condensate is returned to the boiler. Most condensate receivers are part of a condensate return system.

CONDENSATE RETURN SYSTEM: Usually, a closed pressurized system for collecting condensate from diverse process sources and returning the condensate to the boiler, consisting of a condensate receiver, pump, piping, and various controls.

CONDENSATION: Process of forming a liquid from a vapor.

CONDENSER: Device that removes heat from a vapor and causes it to condense into liquid. See also BAROMETRIC CONDENSER, JET CONDENSER, SURFACE CONDENSER.

CROSSFLOW HEAT EXCHANGER: Heat exchanger in which one fluid flows perpendicular to the other. A typical configuration has one fluid flowing across a bank of finned tubes or finned channels containing a second fluid.

CROSS RECOVERY: Combination of processes in which spent sodium-base sulfite liquor is evaporated and burned together with kraft black liquor, after which the raw green liquor from the dissolving tank is processed into both white liquor and sulfite cooking liquor.

CURTAIN CHAINS: See CHAIN SECTION.

CYCLONE EVAPORATOR: Type of direct-contact evaporator consisting of a vertical cylindrical vessel with a conical bottom into which flue gas enters tangentially and contacts liquor which has been sprayed across the flue gas opening. See also DIRECT CONTACT EVAPORATOR.

CYCLONE FURNACE: Relatively small water-cooled horizontal cylindrical chamber in which fuel (e.g., pulverized coal, oil, gas) is fired, heat is released at extremely high rates, and combustion is completed. The gaseous products of combustion are discharged into the main gas-cooling boiler furnace.

D

DAMPER: Device for regulating the flow of air or other gas by introducing a variable resistance across the flow path. Many designs are used.

DEADBURNED LIME: Calcium oxide formed at excessively high kiln temperature. It has a dense physical structure which does not allow it to hydrate readily under normal conditions. See also HARD-BURNED LIME.

DEADLOAD: Unreactive chemicals, principally sodium carbonate and sodium sulfate, that are recycled in the kraft recovery system. These compounds are present due to the incompleteness of the causticizing and furnace reduction reactions. (Sodium chloride can also be a significant deadload chemical in coastal kraft mills.) Syn. Ballast.

DEAERATION: Removal of air and gases from boiler feedwater prior to its introduction to a boiler. Syn. Degasification.

DEALKALIZATION: Any process for reducing the alkalinity of water. The term often refers to the removal of carbonates and bicarbonates from boiler feedwater.

DECANTING HEARTH: Level recovery boiler hearth where heat transfer into the floor solidifies the smelt to form a protective layer and no hearth refractory is used. Molten smelt flows over the frozen smelt and discharges (decants) from multiple spouts which are provided on one or two sides of the boiler.

DECREPITATION: Collapse of a lump by sudden and general cracking during calcination, usually accompanied by a cracking noise.

DEHYDRATION: Generally synonymous with drying. It refers to that stage of the black liquor incineration process where water and volatile organic compounds are driven off prior to pyrolysis.

DEPOSIT CONTROL: Maintaining the cleanliness of heat transfer surfaces in a boiler. Soot blowers are commonly used for fireside deposit control.

DEPOSIT CONTROL AGENT: Proprietary chemical which is intermittently added to black liquor prior to its combustion in the recovery furnace. After combustion, the agent purportedly becomes a component in fireside deposits and renders the deposits dry and friable so they can be easily removed. Syn. Black Liquor Additive.

DESIGN LOAD: Steam generating rate for which a boiler is designed, usually considered the maximum rate that can be maintained for a sustained period.

DESIGN PRESSURE: Maximum allowable working pressure permitted under the rules of the ASME Boiler Code.

DESIGN STEAM TEMPERATURE: Temperature of steam for which a superheater is designed.

DESLAGGING: Removal of slag from heat absorbing surfaces.

DESUPERHEATER: Apparatus for reducing and controlling the temperature of a superheated vapor. A heat exchanger can be used; but more commonly the temperature is reduced by direct contact with an atomized fluid that is injected into the vapor.

DILUTION: Increased ratio of solvent to solute. Most commonly, the addition of water to reduce the solids content.

DIRECT ALKALI RECOVERY SYSTEM (DARS): Proprietary recovery process for sulfur-free alkaline liquors in which the spent liquor is evaporated and burned with ferric oxide (Fe_2O_3) in a suitable furnace to form a product of sodium ferrite ($Na_2Fe_2O_4$). The product is then treated with water to generate sodium hydroxide solution leaving a solid residue of ferric oxide which is separated out and used repeatedly.

DIRECT-CONTACT EVAPORATOR: Equipment for increasing liquor solids level by contacting the liquor with the hot exhaust gases from the recovery furnace. Two types of direct-contact evaporators are in common use: the cascade evaporator and the cyclone evaporator.

DISINTEGRATOR PUMP: Special type of radial-discharge centrifugal pump having teeth in the rotor shaft which mesh with teeth in the peripheral stator bars to provide a mechanical action on the liquid passing through the machine. This device is used to disintegrate solid lumps in heavy black liquor as it is pumped to the recovery boiler liquor nozzles. Syn. Disperser.

DISPERSER: See DISINTEGRATOR PUMP.

DISSOCIATION: Reversible decomposition of the molecules of a compound. An example is the separation of carbon dioxide from calcium carbonate to form lime.

DISSOLVING TANK: See SMELT DISSOLVING TANK.

DISTRIBUTOR: Device for dividing a fluid flow between two or more parallel paths, as in an evaporator body.

DOGHOUSE: Area underneath the recovery furnace floor which is accessible for inspection.

DOLOMITE LIMESTONE: Limestone containing a large proportion of magnesium carbonate.

DOWNCOMER: Any vertical conduit through which fluid flows downward, especially in a natural-circulation system such as a boiler.

DRAFT: Difference in pressure between the ambient atmosphere and some lower pressure existing in the furnace or gas passages of a steam generating unit. Note that draft by definition is a vacuum value.

DRAFT LOSS: Difference in static pressure of a gas between two points in a system, caused by resistances to flow. If both points are below atmospheric pressure as measured by draft, then the difference in draft is equal to the difference in static pressure. Syn. Draft Differential.

DREGS: Insoluble debris (carbon and inorganic solids) that settles out of the green liquor during the clarification process.

DREGS WASHER: Vessel in which dregs are contacted with fresh water to wash out and recover alkali chemicals.

DRUM: Cylindrical shell closed at both ends, designed to withstand internal pressure. Two types of drums are commonly employed in boilers, the steam drum and the mud drum.

DRUM INTERNALS: All aparatus within a drum.

DRY PYROLYSIS PROCESS: Experimental kraft chemical recovery method involving the production of dry liquor solids which are then pyrolyzed and gasified to produce oils, fuel gas and inorganic salts.

DRY STEAM: Saturated steam containing no entrained moisture.

DUCT: Conduit used for conveying air at low pressure.

DUSTING: Refers to the propensity of the lime kiln product to be formed or abraded into fine powder which is then entrained by the high-velocity gases at the hot end of the kiln. Typically, dust recycle amounts to 5% of the feed on a modern kiln, but can be much higher on an older or over-loaded kiln.

E

ECONOMIZER: Heat recovery device designed to transfer low level heat from the combustion gases to a fluid, usually feedwater. An economizer can be considered as a secondary heat absorbing surface.

EFFECT: Evaporation taking place at a certain steam pressure, typically corresponding to what occurs in a single evaporator body. For a multiple-effect evaporation process, effects are numbered from the high-pressure side.

EMBRITTLEMENT: Intercrystalline corrosion common to boiler heat transfer surfaces, occurring in highly stressed areas and adversely affecting the ductility or toughness of the metal.

EMERGENCY SHUTDOWN: Immediate shutdown of the recovery boiler as dictated by safety requirements; in particular, whenever water in any amount is known to be entering the furnace and cannot be immediately stopped, or whenever a leak develops in any pressure part.

ENCRUSTATION: Scale buildup on the inside of heat exchanger tubes or hard slag buildup on the outside of boiler tubes. See also FOULING.

ENDOTHERMIC REACTION: Reaction that occurs with the absorption of heat. An example is the reduction of higher oxidation states of sulfur to sulfide.

EQUALIZING TUBE: Boiler tube used to connect the steam spaces of two steam drums or other pressure parts of a boiler.

EROSION: Wearing away of exposed surfaces by the physical action of swirling gases and entrained dust particles.

EUTECTIC POINT: Temperature at which first melting occurs for a specified solid mixture, an important property of recovery furnace ash. For example, the eutectic point for a fireside deposit of sodium sulfate and sodium carbonate is about 620°C; but if the deposit contains significant proportions of sodium chloride, potassium and sulfide, the eutectic point decreases markedly.

EVAPORATOR: Equipment to remove water from an aqueous solution (e.g. black liquor), thereby producing a solution of higher concentration. See also MULTIPLE-EFFECT EVAPORATOR, DIRECT-CONTACT EVAPORATOR, FALLING-FILM EVAPORATOR, RISING-FILM EVAPORATOR, CONCENTRATOR.

EXCESS AIR: Air supplied for combustion in excess of the theoretical requirement, usually quantified as a percentage of the theoretical amount.

EXCESS LIME: Lime remaining after the causticizing reaction has come to equilibrium conditions.

EXCESS LIME FACTOR: Excess lime expressed as a percentage of the lime reacting in the causticizing system.

EXHAUST GASES: Gases leaving a boiler or lime kiln. These contain the products of combustion (and in the case of the lime kiln, the products of dissociation), water vapor, excess air and entrained particulates. Syn. Exit Gases.

EXOTHERMIC REACTION: Reaction that occurs with the release of heat. All combustion reactions are exothermic.

EXTENDED ECONOMIZER RECOVERY BOILER: Low-odor design of recovery boiler which utilizes an extended economizer section to extract residual heat from the flue gases.

EXTENDED HEAT TRANSFER SURFACES: Augmented surfaces in the form of fins, rings or studs added to such conventional heat absorbing elements as tubes or plates.

F

FACTOR OF SAFETY: Ratio between the stress that will cause failure and the working stress, applied to pressure vessels. The ratio of the pressures may also be used to calculate a factor of safety.

FALLING-FILM EVAPORATOR: Evaporator in which liquor is collected in the sump beneath the heat transfer surfaces and is circulated to the top of the evaporator. A distribution system evenly divides the flow across the heat transfer surface which may be either tubes or plates. The liquor then falls by gravity as a thin film over the heat transfer surface.

FAN: Device used to move gas from one point to another. The pressure rise across a fan (as distinct from a blower or compressor) is generally so small that the volume rate of the gas across the fan can be considered constant. See also AXIAL FLOW FAN, CENTRIFUGAL FAN.

FATIGUE LIMIT: Measure of the ability of a material to withstand multiple stress reversals without fracture or damage to its crystalline structure. This property is important in steam boiler construction.

FEEDWATER: See BOILER FEEDWATER.

FEEDWELL: Central feed point for slurry (or influent) into a sedimentation clarifier. From the feedwell, the liquid moves radially toward the periphery where the clarified liquid is discharged.

straight molecular chains which function as corrosion control agents in steam systems. They form an adherent, nonwettable film on metal surfaces which protects the surface from corrosive condensate.

FIN: Extended surface on a tube which serves to increase the heat transfer surface.

FIN TUBE: Heat transfer tube with one or more fins.

FIRE BOX: Flame containment area of a boiler.

FIRESIDE DEPOSITS: Deposits on the outside surfaces of boiler tubes (for watertube boilers).

FIRETUBE BOILER: Boiler which carries the products of combustion inside the tubes and transfers heat to water and steam which are outside the tubes.

FIRING HOOD: See KILN HOOD.

FIRING RATE: Weight of solids burned in a recovery boiler in a 24-hour period. See also LIQUOR SOLIDS LOADING.

FIXED FIRING: See STATIONARY FIRING.

FLAME: Rapid, gas-phase exothermic combustion process, characterized by self-propagation.

FLAME DETECTOR: Device which indicates if a particular fuel is burning.

FLAME OUT: Condition in a recovery furnace when only auxiliary fuel is being fired and loss of fire takes place.

FLAME PATTERN: Visual appearance of burning gas or vapor. For a lime kiln, the desired flame is long, soft and feathery, indicating an even distribution of heat through the calcining zone.

FLAREBACK: Burst of flame from a furnace in a direction opposite to the normal flow, usually caused by ignition of an accumulation of combustible gas.

FLASH CALCINER: Compact, static lime mud reburning system consisting of a swirl-type furnace in which the material being calcined is in intimate contact with the combustion of fuel. The turbulent swirling mixture of preheated air, fuel, combustion gases and predryed feed material is said to produce a uniform temperature profile throughout the furnace. Syn. Swirl-Type Calciner.

FLASHING: Producing steam by discharging water (or a water solution) at or near its saturation temperature into a region of lower pressure.

substance, such as fuel oil, gives off a vapor that will burn when ignited.

FLASH STEAM: Steam produced by flashing.

FLASH STEAM EVAPORATOR: Evaporator system that utilizes flash steam from extraction liquor (from a continuous cooking system) as the heating medium in a two or three stage configuration to partially evaporate weak black liquor.

FLASH TANK: Vessel which facilitates the separation of steam from liquor during flashing.

FLUE: Any conduit for combustion gases, e.g., duct, breeching, stack, or other passageway.

FLUE GAS: See COMBUSTION GASES.

FLUID-BED CALCINER: Lime mud reburning system in which the hot combustion gases are used to fluidize dried lime mud particles while rapidly converting them into lime pellets. The heavier pellets then fall out of the fluidized stream into a cooling compartment.

FLUIDIZATION: Flow-like properties assumed by a bed of particulate solids when gases passing upward through the bed experience a loss in static pressure equal to the weight of the bed. The fluidized particles are highly mobile in the bed and are circulated through the bed by the rising gas. The bed itself has the appearance of boiling liquid and has properties similar in certain respects to liquids.

FLUIDIZED BED COMBUSTION: Combustion of ground fuel such as coal in a bed of inert particles such as sand, ash and limestone. Combustion air is blown into the bed from below causing the bed to behave like boiling liquid and providing very thorough combustion.

FLUIDIZED BED RECOVERY: Burning of concentrated spent liquor in suspension in such a way that inorganic ash forms pellets to help sustain the fluidized bed. As the pellets become more dense, they fall into a lower zone of the bed and are subsequently removed. Regeneration of kraft chemical requires that the pellets be added to the bed of a conventional recovery furnace for reduction.

FLUIDIZING: Causing a mass of particulate solids to assume some of the properties of a fluid.

FLY ASH: Particles of ash carried by the combustion gases. See also CINDERS.

FORCED CIRCULATION: Circulation of water in a boiler by mechanical means external to the boiler.

FORCED DRAFT: Air supplied under pressure to fuel burning equipment.

FORCED-DRAFT FAN (FD Fan): Fan supplying air under pressure to the fuel burning equipment.

FOSSIL FUEL: Fuel consisting of coal, oil, natural gas or other material developed from plants and animals that became embodied in the earth and changed their form over extended periods of time.

FOULING: (1) Deposition of materials normally found in suspension (as opposed to scaling which is deposition of materials normally found in solution). (2) Any accumulation of dust, scale or other refuse in gas passages or on heat absorbing surfaces that results in reduced flow of gas or heat. See also ENCRUSTATION, SCALING.

FOULING FACTOR: Allowance or measure of the thermal resistance due to fouling or scaling in a heat exchanger.

FREEBOARD BURNING: Combustion that takes place above the fuel bed involving liquor solids or gases which are produced as a result of incomplete combustion of the bed.

FUEL: Substance containing combustibles, used for generating heat.

FUEL ADDITIVES: Chemicals which are added to fuels for any combination of the following purposes: improved combustion control, lower exit-gas temperature, reduced emissions, reduced fouling, reduced corrosion.

FUEL BED: Layer of burning fuel on a furnace grate.

FUEL ECONOMY: See HEAT ECONOMY.

FUEL VALUE: See CALORIFIC VALUE, HEATING VALUE.

FUME: Minute suspended particles in gas, usually formed by the sublimation of vaporized salts.

FURNACE: Enclosed space provided for the combustion of fuel.

FURNACE ARCH: Substantially horizontal structure extending into the furnace to deflect the combustion gases. See also FURNACE NOSE BAFFLE.

FURNACE EXPLOSION: Violent combustion of dust or gas accumulation, or violent reaction between water and smelt within the furnace. See also SMELT/WATER EXPLOSION.

FURNACE FOULING: Usually refers to slag buildups on tube surfaces in the upper furnace areas.

FURNACE NOSE BAFFLE: Furnace arch with a rounded angle. On the recovery furnace, it serves to shield the superheater section from the radiant heat of the burning zone and distributes the gas as it enters the slag screen and superheater sections. Syn. Bull Nose.

FURNACE SCREEN: See SLAG SCREEN.

G _____

GARLAND CHAINS: See CHAIN SECTION.

GAS ANALYSIS: Determination of the constituents of flue gas.

GASIFICATION: Process of converting solid or liquid fuels into gaseous fuel.

GAS TEMPERING: Method of cooling hot furnace gas above the combustion zone of the boiler by addition of relatively cool gas from the economizer outlet.

GENERATING TUBE: Boiler tube in which steam is generated.

GRATE: Surface on which fuel is supported and burned, and through which air is passed for combustion.

GREEN LIQUOR: Liquor obtained by dissolving kraft recovery smelt in weak wash. The solute consists mainly of sodium carbonate ($NaCO_3$) and sodium sulfide (NaS_2).

GRIT: Unreactive and insoluble material that is removed from the lime slaker.

GRIZZLY: Classification device for separating large lumps, consisting of several inclined metal bars with spaces between them. It is sometimes used at the discharge end of the lime kiln.

H _____

HAMMER: Violent reaction in a pipeline that carries both liquid and vapor phases (e.g. steam and condensate), caused by the sudden flashing of liquid or sudden collapse of vapor.

HARDBURNED LIME: Quicklime that has been calcined at high temperature and is slow to hydrate. See also DEADBURNED LIME.

HEADER: Pipe which supplies or receives fluid through a series of connected smaller lines; for example a steam header or water header. See also DISTRIBUTOR.

HEARTH: Bottom of the recovery furnace where burning and smelting of the liquor solids takes place. Either level (decanting) or sloping designs are used.

HEAT BALANCE: Accounting of the distribution of heat inputs and outputs.

HEAT CAPACITY: Relative measure of a material's ability to absorb heat energy; defined as the amount of heat energy required to raise the temperature of one unit mass by 1 degree. Syn. Thermal Capacity, Specific Heat.

HEAT ECONOMY (of a lime kiln): Measure of the heat energy expended for lime production, most commonly in units of millions of BTU's per ton of product (at 86% to 92% CaO). Syn. Heat Consumption, Fuel Economy, Fuel Efficiency.

HEAT EXCHANGER: Device for transferring heat from one medium to another, e.g., from one liquid to another through a heat-conducting solid partition. See also CROSSFLOW HEAT EXCHANGER, PLATE HEAT EXCHANGER, SPIRAL HEAT EXCHANGER, TUBE-IN-SHELL HEAT EXCHANGER.

HEAT FLUX: Rate of heat transfer across a unit area surface. Syn. Thermal Flux.

HEATING SURFACE: Surface that is exposed to the heating medium for absorption and transfer to the heated medium.

HEATING VALUE: Quantity of heat obtained from the complete combustion of a specified amount of fuel. Syn. Calorific Value.

HEAT OF COMBUSTION: Quantity of heat released when a substance is completely burned.

HEAT OF CONDENSATION: See HEAT OF VAPORIZATION.

HEAT OF DISSOCIATION: Heat consumed in breaking chemical bonds. In the lime kiln calcination reaction, approximately 5200 kJ of heat are consumed for every tonne of kiln product to dissociate $CaCO_3$ into CaO and CO_2.

HEAT OF REACTION: Quantity of heat consumed or liberated in a chemical reaction, e.g., heat of combustion.

HEAT OF VAPORIZATION: Amount of heat energy required to vaporize a certain amount of liquid at constant pressure; also equal to the heat given up when the vapor condenses to liquid, called "heat of condensation". See also LATENT HEAT.

HEAT RECOVERY: Utilization of heat energy contained in effluent streams (i.e., waste heat) to generate steam or preheat selected input streams.

HEAT RECUPERATION: Recovery of heat from a waste stream by direct heat transfer across a solid interface into a feed stream. See also RECUPERATIVE AIR HEATER.

HEAT REGENERATION: Recovery of heat by a feed stream from a waste stream by alternating contact with a solid surface. The most common design is by means of a rotating solid, which is continuously heated by the hot stream and cooled by the cold stream.

HEAT TRANSFER: Energy transfer process that occurs as a result of a temperature difference. Heat moves from one body to another by means of conduction, convection or radiation.

HEAT TRANSFER COEFFICIENT: Proportionality constant in the heat transfer equation, equal to the amount of heat which passes through a unit area (of a medium or system) in a unit time when the temperature difference between the boundaries of the system is one degree.

HEAVY BLACK LIQUOR: Black liquor as fed to the recovery furnace nozzles after all evaporation stages and after admixture with chemical ash and/or salt cake, usually at 65–70% solids.

HEEL: Layer of cake remaining on the drum of a precoat filter after the discharge point.

HIGHER HEATING VALUE (HHV): Heating value of black liquor solids as measured by an oxygen bomb calorimeter, which measures the energy released after all combustion products are brought to a temperature of 25°C. This is not the energy available in the recovery furnace where the water produced leaves in the vapor state and where the sulfur compounds are not oxidized. See also NET HEATING VALUE, LOWER HEATING VALUE.

HOLDING TANK: Large storage tank not part of a normal process flow sequence, used to hold the contents of any other tank that is taken out of service for cleanout or repair.

HOT-KILN ALIGNMENT: Alignment measurements taken on a lime kiln when it is in full production.

HYDRATED LIME: Calcium hydroxide [$Ca(OH)_2$], the reaction product of quicklime and water. Syn. Slaked Lime. See also MILK OF LIME.

HYDROMETER: Direct-reading device for measuring liquid density which floats in the liquid exposing a hollow rod with a sensitive calibration, usually in degrees Baumé.

HYDROPYROLYSIS: Experimental kraft chemical recovery method in which black liquor at 25% solids is heated under pressure to a temperature sufficient to decompose the organic compounds into a char, and simultaneously reduce the oxidized sulfur to sulfide. The supernatant liquid is removed as green liquor, while the char is filtered, washed, and burned in a conventional boiler.

HYDROSTATIC TEST: Test of a closed pressure vessel by application of water pressure to ensure strength and water-tight integrity.

I _____

IGNITION: Initiation of combustion.

IGNITION TEMPERATURE: Lowest fuel temperature at which combustion is self-sustaining.

INCOMBUSTIBLE: [adj] Not capable of combustion. Syn. Non-Combustible.

INDUCED DRAFT: Draft produced by a fan (or fans) at the point where gases are exhausted from the boiler or kiln.

INDUCED-DRAFT FAN (ID Fan): Fan exhausting hot gases from heat absorbing equipment.

INSULATION: Material of low thermal conductivity, used to cover hot surfaces and reduce heat losses.

INTERMEDIATE: Relatively short-lived chemical product that is presumed to be created and then consumed in a combustion process.

INTERMEDIATE BLACK LIQUOR: Black liquor taken to the soap skimmer after 3 or 4 stages (or effects) of evaporation.

J _____

JET CONDENSER: Direct contact condenser that utilizes the aspirating effect of a jet of water for the removal of steam and noncondensibles.

K _____

KILN: See LIME KILN.

KILN CYCLING: Usually refers to an erratic feed rate or intermittent retardation of flow within the lime kiln which results in lime product which is alternately underburned and overburned. Syn. Kiln Flushing.

KILN DAM: Series of small step reductions in kiln diameter at the hot end of the kiln, which increases the retention time of the product in the burning zone. Purported benefits include higher heat absorption by the product and improved burning zone refractory life.

KILN HOOD: Retractable firebrick-lined steel covering for the firing end of the lime kiln, equipped with a seal assembly at the point where the rotating kiln and stationary hood join. Syn. Firing Hood.

KRAFT RECOVERY PROCESS: Series of unit operations (e.g., washing, evaporation, burning, causticizing, settling, etc.) in which the spent kraft cooking liquor (i.e., black liquor) is separated from the pulp and reconstituted into white liquor.

L _____

LAGGING: Covering of insulating material on pipes, ducts, etc.

LANCE: Manually manipulated length of pipe carrying air or steam for blowing ash and slag accumulations from heat absorbing surfaces. Syn. Hand Lance.

LIFTERS: See TUMBLERS.

LIME: Calcium oxide (CaO), more specifically called QUICK LIME. See also BURNT LIME, SLAKED LIME, LIME MUD, LIMESTONE.

LIME AVAILABILITY: Weight percent of calcium oxide (CaO) in the calciner product as determined by chemical analysis, a measure of calciner efficiency. Syn. Available Lime Index.

LIME KILN: Furnace-type apparatus used to heat lime mud or other form of calcium carbonate ($CaCO_3$) above 900°C to produce lime (CaO). Typically, a rotary kiln is a long, tilted cylinder that is slowly rotated so that the material fed into the high end flows down to the fire at the low end.

LIME KILN CAPACITY: Daily tonnage of lime product at a specified CaO content (usually between 86% to 92%).

LIME MUD: Calcium carbonate ($CaCO_3$) precipitated in the causticizing reaction. Syn. Lime Sludge.

LIME MUD FILTER: Rotary vacuum filter, used to thicken lime mud to 70–75% solids for feed to the lime kiln.

LIME MUD WASHER: Vessel in which lime mud is contacted with fresh water to wash out and recover alkali chemicals.

LIME REACTIVITY: Measure of the extent to which a given sample of burnt lime will react with green liquor. (Some burnt lime with high measured availability may have poor reactivity with green liquor because of fusing with silicates and other impurities.) Syn. Causticizing Power.

LIME RECOVERY CYCLE: Chemical cycle within the kraft recausticizing area in which quicklime (CaO) is reacted with green liquor to form white liquor and lime mud ($CaCO_3$); the lime mud is then washed and thickened, and is subsequently calcined in the lime kiln to regenerate the quicklime.

LIME SLAKER: Apparatus in which lime (CaO) is reacted with green liquor or water to form calcium hydroxide [$Ca(OH)_2$].

LIMESTONE: Naturally occurring calcium carbonate ($CaCO_3$) containing various amounts of impurities, often used as makeup to the lime kiln. See also CALCITE LIMESTONE, DOLOMITE LIMESTONE.

LINING: Refractory layer on the inner face of the shell of the lime kiln.

LIQUIDUS TEMPERATURE: Temperature at which crystallization just begins for a liquid salt mixture (smelt) as the temperature is lowered (or the temperature at which fusion is completed as the temperature is raised), a function of composition. The liquidus temperature is an important property affecting recovery furnace ash behavior. See also STICKY ASH.

LIQUOR DENSITY: Weight of liquor per unit volume. A liquor density reading, when corrected for temperature, is a good indication of solids content. Liquor density is usually measured with a hydrometer in degrees Baumé (written °Baumé).

LIQUOR GUN: See LIQUOR NOZZLE.

LIQUOR INVENTORY (in a kraft mill): Total quantity of liquor (white liquor, green liquor, black liquor, etc.) expressed in terms of active or activatable cooking chemicals, usually either as NaOH or Na_2O. Syn. Soda Inventory.

LIQUOR NOZZLE: Specially designed assembly through which heavy liquor is pumped to produce a conical or flat spray into the recovery furnace. Syn. Liquor Gun.

LIQUOR SOLIDS: Dissolved organic and inorganic solids in spent liquor.

LIQUOR SOLIDS LOADING: Capacity rating of a recovery boiler in terms of weight of solids burned in a 24-hour period. See also FIRING RATE.

LIVE STEAM: Steam, direct from the boiler, which has not performed any of the work for which it was generated; distinguished from exhaust steam which has been dispossessed of its available energy.

LOWER HEATING VALUE (LHV): Term applied to the net heating value of black liquor as fired in the recovery furnace.

LOW-LEVEL HEAT: Heat which exists at a low temperature, and is normally unattractive for recovery.

LOW-ODOR RECOVERY BOILER: Recovery boiler which does not utilize a direct-contact evaporator and in which there is no significant exposure of black liquor to the gas stream, thereby keeping reduced sulfur emissions at a low level. See also EXTENDED ECONOMIZER RECOVERY BOILER.

LUMP CRUSHER: Device for breaking down oversize reburnt lime aggregates, typically consisting of a shallow trough grate with a rotating shaft; the shaft is studded with curved blades which break up the aggregates as the shaft turns until the particles are small enough to pass through the grate openings.

M _____

MAKEUP WATER: Raw water added to the boiler feedwater supply to compensate for condensate losses from the system.

MANHOLE: Access opening to the interior of a boiler or furnace.

MECHANICAL VAPOR COMPRESSION EVAPORATOR (VCE): Single-effect evaporator in which the vapor produced by the boiling liquid passes through a compressor to increase its pressure and temperature and is returned to the heating element of the evaporator.

MECHANICAL VAPOR RECOMPRESSION (MVR): Method of increasing steam pressure and temperature by mechanical compression.

MEMBRANE WALL: Water tube wall in which adjacent tubes are joined together by means of narrow welded bars. See also TUBE PLATEN.

MILK OF LIME: White, milk-like suspension of hydrated lime in water.

MUD DRUM: Drum located at the lower extremity of a water tube boiler convection bank which is normally provided with a special valve for periodic blowdown. Syn. Water Drum.

MUD WASHER: See LIME MUD WASHER.

MULTIFUEL BOILER: Boiler which is capable of firing wood waste, pulverized coal, heavy oil and various combinations of these fuels.

MULTIPLE-EFFECT EVAPORATOR: Series of evaporators operated at different pressures so that the vapor from one evaporator body becomes the steam supply to the next evaporator. The main advantage of the multi-effect system is the high steam economy which can reach 7.4 kg of water evaporated per kg of supply steam for eight effects.

N _____

NATURAL CIRCULATION: Circulation of water and steam/water mixtures in a boiler due to differences in density.

NATURAL DRAFT: See STACK EFFECT.

NET HEATING VALUE (NHV): Calculated value for the actual heat available in a "wet fuel", equal to the heating value of the moisture-free components minus the heat required to evaporate the water. To calculate the NHV of black liquor solids in a recovery furnace, the endothermic reduction of sulfur must also be considered.

NEUTRALIZING AMINES: Class of amines used as corrosion control agents in steam systems because of their ability to neutralize acidity and raise the condensate pH.

NONCONDENSIBLES: Small concentrations of gases and non-condensible vapors released from black liquor during evaporation that are carried with the steam into the next effect. If not removed, noncondensibles build up in the system and adversely affect condensing rates and heat transfer.

NOSE BAFFLE: See FURNACE NOSE BAFFLE.

NOZZLE: See LIQUOR NOZZLE.

NOZZLE PORTS: Openings provided in the water walls of the furnace to allow entry of the liquor nozzles.

NOZZLE PUMP: Pump that delivers heavy liquor to the furnace guns or nozzles.

O _____

ONCE-THROUGH BOILER: Boiler in which water flows sequentially and without recirculation through the economizer, furnace wall, and generating/superheating tubes.

ORGANIC-TO-INORGANIC RATIO: Characterization of spent pulping liquor with respect to its general chemical makeup. Several analytical methods are used, the most expedient being the ashing of a dried sample and then assuming that the weight of the ash is equal to the inorganic portion.

ORSAT ANALYSIS: Traditional gas analysis method in which certain gaseous constituents of a sample (oxygen, carbon dioxide, carbon monoxide) are measured by absorption in separate chemical solutions.

OVALITY: Measure of deflection for a rotary kiln; the difference between the horizontal and vertical measurements on the inside of the kiln shell. The "relative ovality" is this difference divided by the nominal internal diameter, expressed as a percentage.

OVERBURNT LIME: See HARDBURNED LIME, DEADBURNED LIME.

OVERFIRE AIR: Air for combustion introduced into the furnace at a point above the fuel bed.

OXIDIZED BLACK LIQUOR: See BLACK LIQUOR OXIDATION.

OXIDIZED WHITE LIQUOR: White liquor in which the sulfide has been oxidized to thiosulfate by contacting with oxygen or air. Oxidized white liquor can be used in place of caustic soda for various application in the kraft mill.

OXIDIZING ATMOSPHERE: Atmosphere which tends to promote oxidation reactions (e.g., combustion).

OXYGEN ENRICHMENT: Addition of pure oxygen at the burner of a boiler or lime kiln, sometimes used to increase unit productivity without high capital cost.

P _____

PACKAGED BOILER: Shop-fabricated boiler equipped and shipped with all ancillary equipment, accessories and controls.

PELLETIZATION: Formation of product into pellets, as occurs during fluidized bed calcination or fluid bed recovery.

PENDANT-TUBE SUPERHEATER: Suspended assembly of heat-absorbing elements in a boiler, usually with vertical orientation.

PENT HOUSE: Compartment enclosing the superheater headers and other tubes above the furnace roof.

PERFECT COMBUSTION: Fuel burning where all combustible is burned with no excess air, so that only the theoretical amount of oxygen is used.

PIRSSONITE: Double salt of sodium carbonate and calcium carbonate which can precipitate from green liquor as a scale deposit when the sodium carbonate concentration exceeds a certain level, depending on the temperature and the total concentration of other sodium salts.

PLATE HEAT EXCHANGER: Pack of corrugated metal plates provided with ports for the passage of hot and cold fluids between which heat is transferred. Adjoining plates are spaced by gaskets to form a narrow uninterrupted passage through which a liquid flows in contact with the corrugated surfaces of the two plates. Hot and cold streams flow in alternate spaces between the plates.

PLATEN: See TUBE PLATEN.

PLENUM: Enclosure through which gas or air passes at relatively low velocity. It is usually connected to one or more ducts for distribution.

POLISHED WHITE LIQUOR: White liquor from which virtually all suspended solids have been removed by pressure filtration.

POTASSIUM: Metallic element which is introduced into the kraft recovery cycle with the chips. Although it serves a useful chemical role in the same manner as sodium, it is generally regarded as a contaminant because it lowers the melting point of the chemical ash.

PRECOAT FILTER: Filter which employs a buildup of solid material on the filter screen to assist in the filtering action. In the pulp mill, precoating with lime mud is commonly utilized in the dregs filtering operation to provide a more porous and efficient filter medium.

PREHEATING ZONE: Section of the lime kiln in which the feed material is heated up to just below its dissociation temperature.

PRESSURE FILTER: Pressure vessel containing rigid filter elements into which a feed slurry is pumped. Solid particles collect as a cake on the filter elements while the filtrate passes through. Pressure filters are often used for white liquor clarification or "polishing".

PRIMARY AIR: See AIR PORTS.

PRIMARY AIR PORT BLACK-OUT: Condition when gummy black ash blocks off the passage of air through the primary ports of a recovery furnace. This may take place at one or more ports.

PROCESS STEAM: Steam used for industrial processes, as distinct from steam used for space heating.

PROCESS STEAM LOAD: Amount of steam per unit time required for a specified industrial process.

PRODUCTS OF COMBUSTION: Gases, vapors, and solids resulting from the combustion of fuel.

PUFF: Minor combustion explosion within a boiler furnace. All furnaces are subject to occasional pressurizations which usually occur without warning. Puffs are more severe in a recovery furnace as they cause flame and char to spew out of the furnace openings.

PULVERIZING: Reduction of coal (or other solid material) to fine particle size. Pulverizing equipment can achieve size reduction by the mechanism of impact, attrition, compression or various combinations of these.

PURGING: Flushing of air through a furnace and its associated passages to remove combustible gases.

PURGING STEAM: Steam used to back-flush heavy black liquor lines, valves and pumps in order to prevent the liquor solidifying in these components.

PYROLYSIS: Chemical decomposition by the action of heat.

PYROLYSIS RECOVERY PROCESS: Recovery process for soda-based pulping liquors developed by SCA-Billerud, in which the liquor is heated in a reducing atmosphere at 600°C. The organic components are pyrolyzed into gases that are carried into a conventional boiler for burning; the inorganic residue containing sodium carbonate and sodium sulfide is dissolved to form green liquor.

PYROMETER: Any of a broad class of temperature measuring devices, principally used for measuring high temperature.

PYROSONICS: Technique for determining furnace gas temperatures by measuring the speed of sound across fixed dimensions of the furnace.

Q ───────────────────────────

QUICK LIME: See LIME.

R _____

RADIANT-DESIGN BOILER: Boiler design in which the heat-absorbing surfaces are substantially "in the light" of the fire and can absorb radiant energy.

RADIANT ENERGY: Energy of electromagnetic waves.

RADIATION LOSS: Comprehensive term in boiler heat balances to account for all heat losses into the ambient atmosphere by conduction, convection and radiation.

RADICAL DEFORMATION POINT: Temperature between the eutectic and liquidus temperatures at which a specified solid mixture becomes fluid enough to flow. The radical deformation point usually occurs at about 70% liquid for recovery flue gas particles.

RAPID DRAIN: Prompt drainage of the recovery boiler under emergency conditions according to procedures recommended by the boiler manufacturer.

RATED CAPACITY: Manufacturer's stated capacity rating for a given system or piece of equipment. For example, the continuous capacity of a recovery boiler in tonnes of liquor solids per day.

RATHOLE: Clear gas flow channel through the center of a garland chain section within a lime kiln.

RAW GREEN LIQUOR: Unclarified green liquor, i.e., green liquor containing unsettled dregs.

RAW WHITE LIQUOR: Unclarified white liquor, i.e., white liquor containing unsettled lime mud solids.

REBOILER: Heat exchanger which utilizes heat from condensing vapor (e.g., contaminated steam) to vaporize another stream (e.g., clean steam at lower pressure).

REBURNING: See CALCINATION.

REBURNT LIME: See BURNT LIME.

RECOVERY AREA: Area within the mill devoted to the concentration and burning of waste liquors and the subsequent recovery of chemicals in a form suitable for use in cooking.

RECOVERY BOILER: Water tube boiler which utilizes concentrated black liquor or other chemical pulping waste liquor as the principal fuel. See also RECOVERY FURNACE.

RECOVERY BOILER AUDIT: Review of overall recovery boiler operations with respect to safety.

RECOVERY CYCLE EFFICIENCY: Percentage of chemical utilized in cooking that is recovered through washing and the subsequent recovery area operations. In a modern kraft mill, a typical recovery cycle efficiency is 98% for sodium and 94% for sulfur.

RECOVERY FURNACE: Furnace specifically designed to burn concentrated waste pulping liquor to recover heat and chemicals. The prototype of the modern recovery furnace dates from 1934, a design generally credited to G. H. Tomlinson of Howard Smith Paper.

RECUPERATIVE AIR HEATER: Air heater in which the heating medium is the combustion gas from the furnace and heat transfer takes place through the partition wall separating the two gases. See AIR HEATER.

REDUCING ATMOSPHERE: Atmosphere which promotes the removal of oxygen from a chemical compound. A reducing atmosphere is maintained in the area of the char bed in kraft recovery furnaces to encourage formation of sulfide from the higher oxidation states of sulfur.

REDUCTION EFFICIENCY: Conversion efficiency with respect to the chemical reduction of higher oxidation states of sulfur to sulfide in the kraft recovery furnace; calculated as the ratio of sodium sulfide (Na_2S) to the sum of all soda sulfur chemicals in the green liquor, all in terms of sodium oxide (Na_2O) and expressed as a percentage.

REFRACTOMETER: Device used for in-line monitoring of the solids content of heavy black liquor by measuring its refractive index.

REFRACTORINESS: Ability to resist heat and the normal effects of heat.

REFRACTORY: Any substance or mixture that withstands extremely high temperature without softening or degradation. The term is applied to the fire brick lining in the lime kiln and to furnace linings.

REGENERATIVE AIR HEATER: Air heater in which the heating medium is the combustion gas from the furnace, but the heat is first taken up and stored in the structure itself before it is transferred from the structure into the air.

REGISTER: Apparatus used in a burner to regulate the direction of combustion air flow.

REHEATER: Group of steam tubes in a boiler which absorb heat from the combustion gases to re-superheat steam that has partly expanded through a turbine.

REINJECTION: Method of handling combustible fly ash by reinjecting it into the furnace for further burning.

RESIDUAL FUEL OIL: Heavy fuel oil remaining from crude petroleum after the lighter fractions, lubricants, waxes and asphalt have been removed.

RIDING RING: One of a series of projecting rings on the periphery of the kiln which rest upon a roller assembly through which the kiln is driven.

RINGS: Buildups of material on the inside surface of the lime kiln.

RISER: Any vertical conduit through which fluid flows upward, especially in a natural circulation system such as a boiler.

RISING FILM EVAPORATOR: Evaporator in which the liquor is introduced at the bottom sump beneath the tube sheet and the liquor travels up the heat transfer tube.

RODDING: Removal of solid buildups from recovery furnace air ports by manual thrusting with a metal rod.

S _____

SALTCAKE: Anhydrous sodium sulfate (Na_2SO_4) containing varying amounts of impurities, usually obtained from mineral deposits. It is used as a soda and sulfur makeup chemical for the kraft process, and is commonly added to the heavy black liquor just prior to the recovery furnace.

SALTCAKE-FREE: [adj] Term applied to black liquor as fed to the recovery furnace, but exclusive of the saltcake makeup, chemical ash and precipitator catch. The saltcake-free basis is normally used by boiler manufacturers to specify the design solids loading and the design heat load.

SALT REMOVAL: Process to remove sodium chloride (NaCl) from the kraft recovery cycle, usually involving concentration of white liquor and selective crystallization and separation of the sodium chloride and other inert chemicals. Syn. Chloride Removal.

SATURATED STEAM: Steam at its condensing temperature (for the prevailing pressure).

SCALE: See SCALING.

SCALING: Deposition of crystals from solution caused by changes in the chemical composition of water resulting in supersaturation of the particular deposit-forming mineral. Scale usually consists of a dense, adherent deposition of minerals, tightly bound to each other and to the metal suface. Common examples are calcium carbonate, silica, and iron and magnesium compounds. See also FOULING, ENCRUSTATION.

SCALING TENDENCY (of black liquor): Characterization of black liquor with respect to the likelihood of calcium carbonate ($CaCO_3$) scale formation during evaporation.

SHATTER STEAM: Jets of steam used below the smelt spout to break up the smelt stream into smaller particles before it reaches the liquor surface in the dissolving tank. Syn. Shatter Spray.

SHELL: Outer wall of a vessel or tank, e.g., the cylindrical wall forming the structural enclosure of a lime kiln or dryer cylinder.

SHELLSIDE: [adj] Outside the tubes, but within the shell, of a tube-in-shell heat exchanger.

SHOOTING: Firing of shotgun shells into a lime kiln to break apart ball or ring formations, thus permitting normal movement of material down through the kiln. Syn. Shotgunning.

SINGLE-DRUM BOILER: Boiler which utilizes a single drum for separation of steam from water and for removal of sludge (blowdown). The drum is usually located outside of the furnace.

SLAG: Molten or fused ash which is entrained with the furnace gas and builds up on tube surfaces. In recovery furnaces, it is particularly important that the entrained chemical ash is below the fusion point before contact with the superheater tubes to prevent troublesome slag buildup.

SLAGGING PROPERTIES: Those properties of entrained ash which enable it to stick to tube surfaces and build up into troublesome deposits. See also ASH FUSION CHARACTERISTICS.

SLAG SCREEN: One or more rows of widely spaced tubes constituting part of the superheater section or water tube convection bank which function to lower the temperature of the combustion products before they reach the more closely spaced superheater tube section. Syn. Furnace Screen.

SLAKED LIME: Calcium hydroxide [$Ca(OH)_2$], the reaction product of reburned lime with water or green liquor. Syn. Hydrated Lime. See also MILK OF LIME.

SLAKER: See LIME SLAKER.

SLAKING: Addition of water to quick lime to form calcium hydroxide. Slaking is an exothermic chemical reaction.

SLOPE: Measure of lime kiln tilt, usually expressed in degrees of angle from the horizontal.

SLUDGE: In boilers, the mineral precipitate that builds up in the mud drum and is removed by blowdown.

SLUG: Intermittent large dose of chemical additive.

SMELT: Molten chemical ash which flows from the floor of the recovery furnace. In a kraft mill, the smelt is composed principally of sodium carbonate ($NaCO_3$) and sodium sulfide (Na_2S).

SMELT BED: Accumulation of smelt in the bottom of the recovery furnace. The layer of smelt next to the floor solidifies to form an insulating layer between the hot smelt and the water tube floor.

SMELT DISSOLVING TANK: Tank in which smelt from the recovery furnace is dissolved in weak wash to form green liquor.

SMELT SPOUT: Water-cooled trough through which smelt flows from the recovery furnace into a dissolving tank.

SMELT/WATER EXPLOSION: Physical explosion caused by extremely rapid generation of steam when hot smelt and liquid water contact each other. Smelt/water explosions have caused devastating damage to recovery boilers on a number of occasions when a severe tube leak has allowed significant quantities of water to contact a smelt bed.

SMOKE: Micron-size, gas-borne particles of carbon or soot, of sufficient number to be observable, resulting from incomplete combustion of carbonaceous materials.

SODA INVENTORY: See LIQUOR INVENTORY.

SODA MAKEUP: Chemical added to the kraft liquor recovery cycle to compensate for losses of soda from the process. Common chemicals utilized for this purpose are saltcake, caustic soda, and soda ash.

SOLIDS: See LIQUOR SOLIDS.

SOLUBLE SCALE: Generic name for any water soluble scale deposited in black liquor evaporators, of which sodium carbonate-sulfate scales are the most common. The scale usually precipitates as burkeite or as a coprecipitate of burkeite and sodium carbonate.

SOOT: Unburned particles of carbon derived from hydrocarbons.

SOOT BLOWER: Device employing superheated steam through a retractable nozzle for removing soot, chemical ash and other deposits from the outside surface of tubes in the superheater, steam-generating, and economizer banks of a boiler. The nozzles are mounted on a track arrangement, and when in operation, are automatically rotated and moved forward under sequential control.

SPALLING: Breaking off of surface refractory material as a result of internal stresses.

SPECIFIC ENERGY (for calcination): Energy consumption per unit weight of calciner product.

SPIRAL HEAT EXCHANGER: Essentially, an assembly of two long strips of metal plate wrapped to form a pair of concentric spiral passages through which the hot and cold liquids flow. True counter-current flow can be achieved when one fluid flows from the center outward and the other fluid enters at the periphery and flows toward the center.

SPLASH PLATE: (1) Impingement plate utilized on some designs of liquor nozzles which provides a relatively flat formation of coarser droplets. (2) Impingement surface for the liquid and vapor emerging from rising film evaporator tubes which deflects most of the liquor into an annular sump. Syn. Deflector, Splash Umbrella.

STABILIZATION TANK: Agitated holding tank for raw green liquor prior to clarification, used in some causticizing systems to reduce density and temperature swings and enhance clarifier performance.

STACK: Tall, vertical conduit for venting of combustion gases or gaseous process waste products. Syn. Chimney.

STACK EFFECT: Natural draft created at the base of a stack due to the difference between internal and external gas density.

STATIONARY FIRING: Liquor burning utilizing fixed-position, multiple nozzles to inject the liquor into the furnace. With this method, the nozzles should be positioned so that the liquor spray covers the entire furnace cross section symmetrically. Syn. Fixed Firing.

STEAM: Vapor phase of water, essentially free of contaminants.
> **DRY STEAM** is free of suspended liquid water.
> **WET STEAM** contains suspended liquid droplets.
> **SATURATED STEAM** is at its condensing temperature (for the prevailing pressure).
> **SUPERHEATED STEAM** is at a temperature above the condensing temperature.

STEAM ACCUMULATOR: Pressure vessel partially full of water into which steam is either charged during periods of low demand or discharged during periods of high demand. When charging, the water is heated and the temperature increases; when discharging, the accumulator pressure is allowed to drop and some of the water flashes into steam.

STEAM BALANCE: Accounting of the generation and distribution of steam throughout the mill and the return or disposition of the condensate.

STEAM BINDING: Restriction in circulation due to rapid steam formation or the presence of a steam pocket.

STEAM DEMAND: Requirement for steam from each of the major process areas of the mill and for the turbine generators. Sometimes, "total steam demand" is subdivided into "process steam demand" and "power generation steam demand".

STEAM DISTRIBUTION: Delivery of requisite quality steam to all thermal and mechanical customers at the required temperature, pressure, and flows.

STEAM DRUM: Drum, located at the upper extremity of a boiler circulatory system, in which the generated steam is separated from the water. The drum is level-controlled and equipped with steam separators, scrubbers and washers.

STEAM ECONOMY: Measure of steam utilization. For evaporators, it is measured in kg of water evaporated per kg of steam used.

STEAM GENERATING EFFICIENCY: Ratio of the heat absorbed by the water and steam to the heat value in the fuel fired, expressed as a percentage. Syn. Thermal Efficiency, Boiler Efficiency.

STEAM GENERATING UNIT: See BOILER.

STEAM HAMMER: See HAMMER.

STEAMING RATE: Rate at which steam of a specified pressure is produced from a boiler.

STEAM SCRUBBER: Device in a steam drum consisting of a series of screens, wires, or plates (baffles) through which steam is passed to remove moisture.

STEAM SEPARATOR: Device in a steam drum for removing entrained water from steam.

STEAM TRAP: Separation device on a steam header or heating coil, etc. that allows condensate to flow out, but prevents the escape of steam.

STEAM TUBES: Boiler tubes that carry steam.

STEAM WASHER: Device in a steam drum in which steam is contacted with water having a lower solids content than boiler water, to reduce the solids concentration in the entrained moisture.

STICKINESS (of fireside deposits): Tendency of flue gas particles to remain attached to an impacted surface. The stickiness of fireside deposits is related to the liquid phase content of the particles.

STICKY ASH: Ash which is above the temperature of total fusion (i.e., total solidification). Sticky ash, if present in the combustion gases contacting superheater tubes, rapidly builds up on heating surfaces. See also EUTECTIC POINT, LIQUIDUS TEMPERATURE.

STOICHIOMETRIC MIXTURE: Mixture of fuel and oxygen (or air) which is in exactly the right proportions for combining into the products of combustion, leaving no surplus of either. (The term can be applied generically to any exact combination of chemical reactants.)

STOKER: Mechanical means of feeding coal or hog fuel into a furnace and providing a structure for burning.

STRAIGHTENING VANES: Vanes inserted into gas ducts to direct the flow of gas parallel to the walls.

STRONG BLACK LIQUOR: Black liquor in storage following conventional multi-effect evaporation, usually at 50–55% solids content. Syn. Concentrated Black Liquor, Thick Black Liquor.

SUBLIMATION: Conversion from a gaseous state to a solid state (or vise versa) without passing through a liquid phase. (Soda fume is formed by this mechanism in the recovery furnace gases.)

SUPERHEATED STEAM: Steam at a temperature above its condensing temperature (for the prevailing pressure).

SUPERHEATER: Group of steam tubes in the boiler which absorb heat from the combustion gases to raise the steam temperature above the saturation temperature.

SURFACE BLOWOFF: Removal of foam and other contaminants from the water surface in a boiler drum.

SURFACE CONDENSER: Heat exchanger used to condense vapor (e.g., steam under vacuum) by absorbing its latent heat into a cooling fluid, usually water.

SUSPENSION FIRING: Burning of finely divided combustibles which are carried to the burner suspended in air. The air from the conveying system generally provides the primary air for the burner.

SWINGING LOAD: Any type of load (e.g., steam, electrical, etc.) that changes at relatively short intervals.

T _____

TANGENTIAL FIRING: Traditional method of firing in a recovery furnace with the burners located so that their center lines are tangential to an imaginary circle. Tangential firing promotes turbulent mixing with the incoming air. However, recent findings indicate that this method also promotes the formation of a cone-shaped body of combustibles at the core of the furnace and also enhances entrainment of liquor particles.

THEORETICAL AIR: Quantity of air calculated as being just sufficient for complete combustion.

THERMAL CYCLE: Total energy circuit in the pulp and paper mill, including conversion of fuel into steam, steam pressure reduction for electric power generation, utilization of steam for process heating, and return of condensate to the boiler house.

THERMAL CYCLING: Temperature variations within the recovery furnace and the resulting thermal expansions and contractions.

THERMAL DEACTIVATION: Process for reducing or eliminating the calcium scaling tendency of a black liquor by heating the liquor to about 150°C and holding it at this temperature for about 15 minutes.

THERMAL EFFICIENCY: See STEAM GENERATING EFFICIENCY.

THERMAL LOADING (of a boiler): Heat released in the furnace.

THERMAL VAPOR RECOMPRESSION: Method of increasing steam pressure by eduction of the low-pressure steam into a thermocompressor and mixing with higher pressure steam.

THICK BLACK LIQUOR: See STRONG BLACK LIQUOR.

TOMLINSON FURNACE: Recovery furnace design developed by G.H. Tomlinson of Howard Smith Paper in Ontario in the 1930's, the precurser of the modern recovery furnace.

TRAVELING GRATE STOKER: Stoker with a chain-driven grate onto which solid fuel is fed from a hopper.

TUBE COOLER: Tubes assembled on the outside periphery of a lime kiln (integral with the kiln) through which the reburned lime product is discharged and through which air enters and travels countercurrent to the lime. The lime product is cooled and the heat is recovered in the air which is then used for kiln fuel combustion. Syn. Integral Cooler, Orbital Cooler.

TUBE-IN-SHELL HEAT EXCHANGER: Common type of heat exchanger consisting of a bundle of parallel tubes, through which one fluid flows, enclosed in a container through which another fluid flows in the same or opposite direction. Many design variations are utilized. Syn. Shell And Tube Heat Exchanger.

TUBE PLATEN: Tubes fabricated in the form of a panel. The tubes may be arranged tangentially or connected by membrane.

TUBESIDE: [adj] Within the tubes of a heat exchanger or boiler.

TUBE-TO-TUBE WALL: Water tube wall in which the tubes are substantially tangent to each other, with practically no space between the tubes. Syn. Tangent Tube Wall.

TUMBLERS: Radial projections within the inner periphery of the lime kiln (usually prefabricated blocks welded to the shell) which are designed to prevent the formation of a "sliding bed" in the drying zone. The tumblers also increase the surface for thermal transmission to the sludge. Syn. Lifters.

TURNING VANES: Sheet metal strips mounted inside ducting in contoured layers which are parallel to the bend of the ducting; they reduce frictional losses in ducting having a bend of 45° or more.

U _____

UNACCOUNTED FOR LOSS: That portion of a boiler heat balance which represents the difference between 100% and the sum of the heat absorbed by the unit and all classified losses.

UNBURNED COMBUSTIBLE: Combustible portion of the fuel which is not completely oxidized.

UNDERBURNED LIME: Feed material which has passed through the lime kiln without dissociating completely, thus leaving a core of calcium carbonate with the quicklime.

UNDERFIRE AIR: Air introduced into the furnace beneath the grate holding solid fuel.

UNOXIDIZED BLACK LIQUOR: Black liquor that has not yet been subjected to an oxidation process. The term is used in mills utilizing an oxidation process to distinguish from oxidized black liquor.

V

VAPOR RECOMPRESSION: See MECHANICAL VAPOR RECOMPRESSION, THERMAL VAPOR RECOMPRESSION.

VENT STACK: Over-sized stack on the dissolving tank designed to relieve pressure in the event of an explosion.

W

WATER DRUM: See MUD DRUM.

WATER TUBE: Boiler tube containing water, usually along with some steam.

WATER TUBE BOILER: Boiler in which the tubes contain water and steam; heat is applied to the outside surfaces of the tubes.

WATER TUBE WALL: Furnace wall composed of heat absorbing water tubes. Syn. Water Wall, Water-Cooled Wall.

WATER WALL: See WATER TUBE WALL.

WATER WASHING: Common "off-line" method of removing fireside deposits within a recovery furnace, often by means of high-pressure water applied through soot blowers.

WEAK BLACK LIQUOR: Black liquor in storage after it has been separated from the pulp, usually at 12–16% solids content.

WEAK WASH: Weak alkali solution, resulting from water washing the lime mud and green liquor dregs to recover residual alkali. Weak wash is used to dissolve smelt in the dissolving tanks.

WET COMBUSTION: Heating waste liquor under pressure to reaction temperature at which air or oxygen is introduced. The resulting oxidation can be complete or leave a carbonaceous residue that can be burned separately. Syn. Wet Oxidation.

WET CRACKING: Heating of black liquor in the absence of oxygen to a sufficiently high temperature (about 360°C) to cause decomposition of the organic constituents into char, tar oil and gases.

WET OXIDATION: See WET COMBUSTION.

WET STEAM: Steam containing entrained liquid water droplets.

WINDBOX: Chamber surrounding a burner or below a grate that supplies pressurized air for combustion of fuel. Syn. Air Box.

WOOD WASTE BOILER: See BARK BOILER.

Chapter 10
Pulp Bleaching & Brightening

ACID PRETREATMENT: Treatment of unbleached pulp with acid, usually to remove heavy metal ions that may interfere with a subsequent bleaching or brightening stage.

ACID TREATMENT: See SULFUROUS ACID TREATMENT.

AIR DRYER: Flow-through chamber containing a regenerative-type dessicant which is capable of removing moisture from air down to a dew point of at least -30°C, measured at atmospheric pressure.

AIR PAD: High-pressure air in the upper volume of a chlorine tank car which acts to push the liquid chlorine out through a bottom opening.

ALKALINE EXTRACTION STAGE (E-Stage): Essential stage in any multistage bleaching sequence; it solubilizes the dark-colored chlorinated and oxidized lignin compounds formed in the initial acid bleaching stages (e.g., chlorination). When used prior to the final bleaching stage, an E-stage also serves to "activate" the pulp for more effective brightening. Syn. Caustic Extraction. See also OXIDATIVE EXTRACTION STAGE.

ANTICHLOR: Reducing chemical used to remove residual chlorine, hypochlorite or chlorine dioxide from pulp or white water. The most common antichlor is sulfite ion.

AVAILABLE CHLORINE: Measurement of oxidative chemical strength or concentration in terms of chemically equivalent chlorine.

BATCH BLEACHING PROCESS: Operation in which pulp and the requisite amount of bleaching agent are introduced into a reaction vessel, mixed together and retained until the bleaching reaction is essentially complete. The batch of pulp is then completely transfered to a subsequent washing operation, and the vessel is refilled for another batch bleaching. See also CONTINUOUS BLEACHING.

BLEACHABILITY: Qualitative term describing the relative ease with which pulp can be bleached. Sometimes the term is erroneously used to describe the amount of bleaching agent needed (i.e., the bleach requirement).

BLEACH CHEMICAL: See BLEACHING AGENT.

BLEACH DEMAND: Amount of bleach chemical required for delignification of a specific pulp, as indicated by any of several tests. Most of the tests currently used are based on the reaction of lignin with acidic permanganate (e.g., Kappa Number, Permanganate Number). Syn. Bleach Chemical Requirement.

BLEACHED PULP: Pulp that has been subjected to a bleaching sequence or bleach treatment. See also FULLY BLEACHED PULP, SEMI-BLEACHED PULP.

BLEACH EFFLUENT: Overflow stream of process water from any bleach stage.

BLEACHERY: See BLEACH PLANT.

BLEACHING: Whitening process carried out on pulps by selective chemical removal of residual lignin and other colored materials, and with minimal degradation of the cellulosic constituents. See also BRIGHTENING.

BLEACHING AGENT: Active chemical in a bleach stage or bleach treatment. The term is more appropriately applied to a chemical agent that causes a specific brightening effect, as distinct from one that provides a predominant delignifying effect. Syn. Bleach Chemical.

BLEACHING EFFECT: Change in brightness as a result of a specific bleaching treatment. Syn. Bleaching Response.

BLEACHING INDEX: Measurement of bleach chemical requirement for a pulp. The most commonly used bleaching indices are permanganate number tests. See also BLEACH DEMAND.

BLEACHING POWER: Ambiguous term referring to the ability of a bleaching agent to react with lignin on a weight-per-unit-weight basis, usually in comparison to chlorine. For example, chlorine dioxide may be considered to have 2.6 times the bleaching power of chlorine on a pound-per-pound basis.

BLEACHING SEQUENCE: Series of stages, each with specific objectives (e.g., delignification, solubilization, destruction of chromophoric groups), that contribute to an overall whitening effect. Typically, the pulp is washed between stages. Syn. Multistage Bleaching.

BLEACHING STAGE: Single discrete chemical treatment that typically includes a subsequent washing step; usually carried out as part of a multistage sequence. See also BLEACHING SEQUENCE.

BLEACHING TIME: Retention time of pulp in a bleaching stage or the elapsed time that pulp is subjected to an active bleaching chemical.

BLEACHING TOWER: Vertical retention vessel for pulp bleaching. See also UPFLOW TOWER, DOWNFLOW TOWER, UPFLOW/DOWNFLOW TOWER.

BLEACHING YIELD: Weight percent of pulp retained after a bleaching process. See also SHRINKAGE.

BLEACH LIQUOR: Bleaching chemical solution that is applied to the pulp.

BLEACH LIQUOR STRENGTH: Concentration of active chemical in a bleach liquor, usually in units of grams per liter.

BLEACH PLANT: Mill department where bleaching operations are carried out. Syn. Bleachery, Bleaching Department.

BLEACH REQUIREMENT: Amount of bleach chemical application required to reach a given objective (which may be in terms of delignification or brightness).

BLEACH RESPONSE CURVE: Curve showing the increase in pulp brightness (or decrease in lignin content) with increasing chemical application. Generally, the response to treatment is nearly linear up to a point, after which the increment of response per unit of chemical applied decreases as a hyperbolic curve.

BLEACH SLUDGE: Sediment formed during preparation of calcium hypochlorite solution due to excess hydrated lime and the insoluble components of the lime.

BLEACH WASHER: Equipment for washing the pulp free of residual chemicals and reaction products following a bleaching stage.

BOROHYDRIDE: Usually in the form of sodium borohydride ($NaBH_4$), a powerful reductant pulp brightener. Its high cost makes direct commercial application as a pulp brightener impractical; however, it is widely used (as part of a proprietary mixture) for on-site manufacture of sodium hydrosulfite.

BRIGHTENER: Chemical agent that decolorizes or brightens the lignin and other colored components, without dissolving them. The two basic types of brightening agents are oxidants (e.g., peroxide, peracetic acid) and reductants (e.g., hydrosulfite, borohydride).

BRIGHTENING: (1) Any chemical treatment to pulp that increases its brightness. (2) Chemical modification of colored elements in high-yield pulps to render them colorless without removing them, thus retaining the yield advantage of these pulps. Syn. Lignin-Preserving Bleaching.

BRIGHTNESS REVERSION: Loss of brightness with aging. All bleached or brightened pulps yellow with age to a greater or lesser degree. Pulps of high lignin content that have been whitened only by reductive treatment are particularly sensitive to brightness reversion. Syn. Color Reversion.

BRIGHTNESS STABILITY: Qualitative term for the ability of a pulp to retain brightness under a range of conditions.

C

CALCIUM HYPOCHLORITE: [$Ca(OCl)_2$] Oxidative bleaching chemical produced by reacting chlorine with slaked lime. In dry form, it is called "bleaching powder". See also HYPOCHLORITE.

CHELATING AGENT: Organic compound which encloses a multivalent cation within its molecular ring structure, thus preventing its normal chemical activity.

CHELATION VALUE: Value which signifies the strength of the chelate reaction between a particular chelating agent and a specific metal ion, usually expressed as the amount of calcium (as calcium carbonate) chelated by a given amount of chelating agent in units of mg/g.

CHEMICAL APPLICATION: Amount of bleaching chemical mixed into a given amount of pulp during a bleaching treatment, usually expressed as the weight percent on oven dry pulp.

CHEMICAL CONSUMPTION: Amount of bleaching chemical consumed by a given weight of pulp during a bleaching treatment, usually expressed as the weight percent on oven dry pulp.

CHEMICAL RESIDUAL: See RESIDUAL CHEMICAL.

CHLOR-ALKALI PROCESS: Process for production of chlorine and sodium hydroxide (or sodium chlorate) by electrolysis of brine.

CHLORATE: Sodium chlorate ($NaClO_3$), the principal compound used in the manufacture of chlorine dioxide. Sodium chlorate is produced by electrolysis of brine.

CHLORATE CELL LIQUOR: Chlorate-rich liquor (containing NaCl) taken directly from electrolytic cells without further purification or crystallization; used partly or wholly as feed to a chlorine dioxide generator when NaCl is used as a reducing agent for the chlorate.

CHLORINATION RATIO: Available chlorine application in the chlorination stage as a ratio (or percent) of the chlorine demand, as indicated by any of the standard indices (e.g., roe number, kappa number, etc.). Syn. Chlorine Level, Chlorine Dosage, Charge-To-Demand Ratio, Chlorination Factor. See also KAPPA FACTOR.

CHLORINATION STAGE (C-Stage): Initial stage of most bleaching sequences wherein chlorine reacts with lignin to form orange-colored chlorolignins which are partly removed in the washing step and more completely removed in the subsequent alkaline extraction stage. The chlorination and extraction stages serve mainly to remove lignin rather than to brighten the pulp, and therefore, are sometimes considered an extension of the delignification process.

CHLORINATION STAGE, MODIFIED: Any modification of the traditional ambient-temperature, low-consistency chlorination stage, including the supplemental application of chlorine dioxide either in admixture with chlorine (C/D Stage) or in sequential applications (D-C Stage), raising of the reaction temperature (called "hot chlorination"), and raising of the consistency.

CHLORINE: Major bleaching chemical used both in its elemental form (Cl_2) and as alkaline hypochlorite (NaOCl). Chlorine is produced by electrolysis of brine and usually arrives at the mill site as a dry liquid. It is vaporized and usually dispersed in water before being mixed with the pulp slurry.

CHLORINE DIOXIDE: (ClO_2) Valuable bleaching chemical, especially suitable for softwood kraft pulps. Under controlled conditions, it selectively oxidizes lignin with minimal effect on the carbohydrate components. Chlorine dioxide is produced at the mill site by chemical reduction of sodium chlorate; the generated gas is absorbed in chilled water to form a dilute solution at about 7 grams per liter. It is commonly used as the sole oxidizing agent in the later stages of a bleaching sequence and acts synergistically with chlorine in the chlorination stage. See also CHLORINE DIOXIDE BLEACHING STAGE, CHLORINATION STAGE MODIFIED.

CHLORINE DIOXIDE BLEACHING STAGE (D-Stage): Oxidative stage in a bleaching sequence, used to achieve high brightness on extracted pulp. It is almost always preceded by chlorination/extraction, and sometimes by a hypochlorite stage. To produce the highest and most stable brightness (especially for softwood kraft pulps), two chlorine dioxide stages are used with an alkaline extraction in between.

CHLORINE DIOXIDE GENERATION: Chemical reduction of sodium chlorate under controlled conditions to generate gaseous chlorine dioxide.

CHLORINE DIOXIDE GENERATOR: See REACTION VESSEL.

CHLORINE DIOXIDE PLANT: Area of the pulp mill where chlorine dioxide gas is generated and absorbed in cold water.

CHLORINE DIOXIDE PLANT EFFICIENCY: Moles of chlorine dioxide produced per mole of sodium chlorate reacted, expressed as a percent.

CHLORINE DIOXIDE SOLUTION: Final product from the chlorine dioxide plant, obtained by contacting chlorine dioxide gas from the reaction vessel with chilled water in an absorption tower.

CHLORINE DOSAGE: See CHLORINATION RATIO.

CHLORINE EVAPORATOR: Heat exchanger which uses steam or hot water to vaporize liquid chlorine as it is transferred from tank cars to the bleaching process. Syn. Chlorine Vaporizer.

CHLORINE-FREE BLEACHING: Chemical pulp bleaching sequence that excludes use of chlorine or chlorine-containing agents.

CHLORINE HYDRATE: ($Cl_2 \cdot 8H_2O$) Greenish yellow crystals which form in chlorine water when the temperature falls below 10°C.

CHLORINE MIXER: Equipment which vigorously mixes gaseous chlorine or chlorine water with unbleached stock wherein any minute bubbles of chlorine gas become attached to the fibers. (The gas bubbles are subsequently dissolved; all reactions with pulp occur when the chlorine is in solution.)

CHLORINE MONOXIDE: (Cl_2O) Reddish-yellow gas, the anhydride of hypochlorous acid, used as an experimental bleaching agent. See also HYPOCHLOROUS ACID.

CHLORINE NUMBER: Test on a pulp sample to determine its lignin content or its bleach chemical demand, based on consumption of chlorine under standardized conditions. This test is not routinely used in the mill environment because of potential hazards in handling the chlorine. Syn. Roe Number.

CHLORINE WATER: Clear yellowish liquid obtained by dissolving gaseous chlorine in water. At 20°C, a saturated chlorine water solution contains about 7.3 grams of chlorine per liter (or 0.73% by weight).

CHLORITE BLEACHING: Bleaching with sodium chlorite ($NaClO_2$), whose chemical action is similar to chlorine dioxide. This agent is commonly used for laboratory work, but is too expensive for mill bleaching.

CHLOROLIGNIN: Highly-colored, alkali-soluble and partially water-soluble chlorinated phenolic material formed from the reaction of chlorine and the ligneous components of chemical pulp.

CHROMATIC SENSOR: See OPTICAL SENSOR.

CHROMOPHORES: Colored compounds or chemical groups in pulp which absorb radiation in the ultra-violet and visible region, mainly ligneous materials. The objective in brightening mechanical pulps is to modify the chromophoric groups to eliminate their absorption in the visible range, thus increasing the whiteness of the pulp.

CLOSED CYCLE BLEACH PLANT: Process concept developed (by H. Rapson) to utilize bleach plant effluents in the kraft recovery system, thus eliminating or reducing the discharge of effluent streams into the environment.

COLOR REVERSION: See BRIGHTNESS REVERSION.

COMBINATION STAGE: Bleaching stage that utilizes a second bleaching agent at some point in the process to obtain special effects or to intensify the bleaching reaction.

COMPLEXING AGENT: Any compound that will inactivate a metallic ion. Syn. Ligand. See also CHELATING AGENT, SEQUESTERING AGENT.

CONTINUOUS BLEACHING: Bleaching process in which pulp and chemicals are fed at a constant rate and move in continuous fashion through the various processing steps (e.g. pumping, heating, mixing, retention, washing). Virtually all modern bleach plants utilize a continuous process.

CONTINUOUS STIRRED TANK (CST): Flow-through vessel containing one or more impellers which produce bulk movement within the fluid by the pumping action and turbulence of the rotating blades. CST's are typically utilized for mixing chlorine gas with stock in the chlorination stage.

COUNTERCURRENT BLEACH PLANT WASHING: Water-saving system of washing pulp in a multistage bleachery, wherein filtrate from a later stage is used for dilution and shower water on a preceding stage. Some mills utilize a system of partial recycle, where alkaline and acidic filtrates are used repectively only for preceding alkaline and acidic stages; however, a few bleach plants with suitable metallurgy are using full countercurrent washing.

CRYSTALLIZATION: Process by which dissolved solids in a supersaturated solution are forced out of solution by cooling or evaporation, and then recovered as solid crystals.

D

DEGRADATION INHIBITOR: Chemical agent added to a bleaching stage to reduce undesirable degradation of cellulose. Magnesium compounds are commonly used as protective additives during oxygen bleaching. Other chemicals used are sodium silicate, sulfamic acid and glucitol. Syn. Protective Additive. See also VISCOSITY PRESERVER.

DEHUMIDIFYING: Removing moisture from air by means of air conditioning (i.e., cooling the air and condensing water from the saturated vapor) or by using a dessicant.

DESICCANT: Material with high affinity for moisture which absorbs it by physical or chemical action. Syn. Dehydrating Agent, Drying Agent.

DIAPHRAGM CELL: Type of electrolytic cell used to produce chlorine and sodium hydroxide from brine, characterized by a porous asbestos diaphragm that separates the anode and cathode compartments.

DIFFUSION STAGE: Soaking stage which occasionally follows the alkaline extraction stage in older bleacheries. The objective is to allow time for organic and inorganic constituents to diffuse from the interior of the fibers, so they can be more easily removed in the subsequent washing step.

DILUTION ZONE: Bottom section of a downflow bleaching tower or pulp storage chest where the consistency is controlled at a level suitable for pumping. Dilution water is added continually and the zone is kept fluid by agitation.

DISPLACEMENT BLEACHING: Multistage bleaching process utilizing the displacement principle, wherein chemicals are continuously displaced transversely through a pulp mat rather than mixing into the pulp in the conventional manner. Bleaching is very rapid due to the high concentration gradients that are maintained throughout the displacement operation, and the entire process can be carried out in one or two reaction vessels. Syn. Dynamic Bleaching.

DITHIONITE: See HYDROSULFITE.

DOWNFLOW TOWER: Bleaching tower in which the treated pulp enters the top of the vessel and moves in plug flow down through the tower. An advantage of the downflow tower is that retention time can be varied by changing the level of pulp in the tower.

DYNAMIC BLEACHING: See DISPLACEMENT BLEACHING.

DYNAMIC MIXER: In-line mixing device for pulp stock utilizing one or more rotating elements to impart turbulence to the fiber suspension. Syn. Active Mixer, Mechanical Mixer.

E _____

EASY BLEACHING PULP: Imprecise term denoting a low-yield pulp that can be readily bleached with a minimum of chemical agent.

ELECTROCHEMICAL BLEACHING: Novel single-stage bleaching process for producing semibleach chemical pulp by electrolysis of a fiber suspension in aqueous sodium chloride solution.

ELECTROLYSIS: Decomposition of an inorganic compound by means of an electric current; the compound is split into positive and negative ions which migrate to and collect at the electrodes. A typical industrial application is the production of chlorine and sodium hydroxide from sodium chloride.

EXCESS ALKALI: Alkali added to a bleaching solution or bleaching stage to maintain pH above a specified level. For example, sufficient excess alkali must be added to a hypochlorite stage to neutralize acidic reaction products and maintain the terminal pH above 9.0.

EXCESS CHEMICAL: Amount of active bleaching agent remaining at the completion of a bleaching stage. A measurable concentration is usually required at the end to ensure that a reactive driving force is operative during the entire retention period.

EXTRACTED PERMANGANATE NUMBER: Permanganate number test performed on pulp following the chlorination and extraction stages of bleaching.

EXTRACTION STAGE: See ALKALINE EXTRACTION STAGE.

F _____

FILTRATE: Liquid which separates from a solid/liquid mixture by being passed through a porous medium that retains the solid fraction. Filtrates are obtained from each washing stage in the bleachery.

FORMAMIDINE SULFINIC ACID (FAS): Alkaline reductive brightening agent, presently utilized on an experimental basis.

FULLY BLEACHED PULP: Pulp that has been bleached to a high level of brightness.

G _____

GAS-OFF: Release of chlorine or chlorine dioxide gas from solution into the surrounding atmosphere.

GAS-PHASE BLEACHING: Bleaching of high-consistency, fluffed pulp with a gaseous reagent at high pressure. High specific surface is required to achieve adequate mass transfer from the gas phase to the pulp. Gas-phase bleaching has been the subject of intense laboratory study with a variety of reagents, but the only commercial process thus far utilizes oxygen.

GRINDER BLEACHING: Addition of alkali/peroxide to the shower water in a pressurized grinder. In this system, the dilute stock from the grinder pit is subsequently thickened to recover the hot water, which is returned to the grinder showers in a closed loop.

H _____

HARD BLEACHING PULP: Imprecise term denoting a pulp that is difficult to bleach because of dark color and/or high lignin content.

HEAVY METAL IONS: Metal ions such as iron, copper, aluminum, chromium and manganese that have a detrimental effect on brightness development and brightness stability. The adverse effects of heavy metal ions during brightening are mitigated through use of a chelating or sequestering agent. Syn. Transition Metal Ions.

HIGH-INTENSITY MIXER: Active mixer producing a fluidized fiber suspension, specifically designed for mixing liquids and gases with medium consistency stock.

HIGH-YIELD BLEACHING: See BRIGHTENING.

HOT CHLORINATION: See CHLORINATION STAGE, MODIFIED.

HYDROSULFITE: Common reductive brightening agent for mechanical pulps, usually in the form of sodium hydrosulfite ($Na_2S_2O_4$). It is relatively unstable and is usually shipped as a dry powder or may be generated on site. Syn. Dithionite. See also REDUCTANT.

HYDROSULFITE BRIGHTENING STAGE: Lignin-preserving reductive brightening stage for mechanical pulps, used either as a single-stage treatment or in sequence with peroxide. As a single stage, it typically provides a brightness increase of 10–12 points. For best results, the pulp is pretreated with sequesterants to minimize adverse effects from heavy metal ions. The stage is controlled under mildly acidic conditions, and air is excluded to minimize decomposition of the chemical.

HYPOCHLORITE: Oxidative bleaching or brightening agent prepared by reacting chlorine with either sodium hydroxide (NaOH) or calcium hydroxide [$Ca(OH)_2$]. Calcium hypochlorite [$Ca(OCl)_2$] was the original bleaching agent used for wood pulps, but is little used today because of greater handling and scaling problems relative to sodium hypochlorite (NaOCl). Hypochlorite solutions are prepared with an excess of hydroxide to prevent decomposition.

HYPOCHLORITE BLEACHING STAGE (H-Stage): Oxidative bleaching stage, often used as the last stage in a short bleaching sequence (e.g., CEH) or as an intermediate stage in a longer sequence (e.g., CEHDED). The bleaching action is achieved by destructive oxidation of lignin, but because the action is not entirely lignin-specific, only a limited brightness gain can be achieved without substantial cellulose degradation. A relatively high-temperature hypochlorite treatment is used in dissolving pulp mills as a controlled viscosity-reducing stage.

HYPOCHLORITE BRIGHTENING STAGE: Mild hypochlorite treatment, used occasionally for hardwood mechanical pulps where a significant brightness gain can be made with minimal loss of pulp yield and strength.

HYPOCHLOROUS ACID: (HOCl) pH-dependent chlorine species which is present as an equilibrium product in chlorine water or hypochlorite solution, and is the dominant species in the pH range from 4 to 6. It is a strong bleaching agent in its own right, but is not lignin-specific and therefore potentially detrimental to pulp strength. In a conventional bleaching sequence the effect of hypochlorous acid is minimized by operating the chlorination stage at a pH well below 2, while the pH of the hypochlorite stage is around 10. A proprietary bleaching agent consisting mainly of hypochlorous acid is now being promoted commercially.

HYPO NUMBER: Result of a bleach demand test in which a pulp sample is reacted with acidified sodium hypochlorite under controlled conditions. Once commonly used, it is now superceded by those test methods utilizing permanganate solution.

HYPO REACTOR: Apparatus in which chlorine is reacted with either sodium hydroxide (NaOH) or calcium hydroxide [$Ca(OH)_2$] to form hypochlorite solution.

I _____

IN-LINE INJECTOR: Any device for injecting chemicals into a stock line under pressure.

IN-LINE MIXER: Device mounted within a process line for mixing chemicals into stock. The energy for mixing can either be supplied by the stock pump (in the case of a static mixer), or an external motor can supply power to a rotating impeller (in which case, it is called an "active mixer" or a "dynamic mixer").

K _____

KAPPA FACTOR: Ratio of the available chlorine application (percent on oven dry pulp) to the kappa number of the pulp for the chlorination stage, a measure of the dosage. See also CHLORINATION RATIO.

L _____

LAUNDER RING: Peripheral trough at the top of an upflow tower into which the stock "overflows" and channels to a common outlet. More precisely, the stock is "laundered" into the launder ring by rotating rakes as it wells up at the top of the tower. Usually, dilution water is added at the launder ring to assist the outflow of stock.

LIGNIN-PRESERVING BLEACHING: See BRIGHTENING.

M _____

MEMBRANE CELL: Type of electrolytic cell used to produce chlorine and sodium hydroxide; it utilizes a cation exchange membrane that is impervious to chloride ion flow and produces a pure NaOH product.

MERCURY CELL: Type of electrolytic cell used to produce chlorine and sodium hydroxide, in which metallic sodium forms an amalgam with mercury at the cathode; it is then removed from the cell before the sodium reacts with water. Therefore, the mercury cell produces essentially pure caustic soda.

MULTISTAGE BLEACHING: See BLEACHING SEQUENCE.

N _____

NEUTRALIZATION STAGE (N-Stage): Mild alkaline extraction, mitigated with respect to either pH or temperature, occasionally used in selective bleaching situations to achieve higher retention of hemicelluloses.

NITROGEN DIOXIDE BLEACHING: Experimental method of bleaching in which NO_2 is used in combination with oxygen.

O _____

OPTICAL SENSOR: Device that measures the color or brightness of pulp following a specific bleaching treatment and is used either for feedback control of the preceeding chemical addition or for feed-forward control of the subsequent bleaching stage. Optical sensors are commonly used for control of the chlorination and hypochlorite stages. Syn. Chromatic Sensor.

OXIDANT: In general, any material that can gain electrons. In pulp brightening, the term refers to an oxidative brightening agent such as peroxide or peracetic acid.

OXIDATION: Chemical process of combining with oxygen. The term is often used in a generic sense to indicate the chemical process of combining with any strong oxidizing agent.

OXIDATION-REDUCTION POTENTIAL (ORP or Redox): Electrical potential generated between two dissimilar electrodes. In the chlorination stage, an ORP is generated proportional to the ratio of unreacted chlorine to chloride ion. If this potential can be accurately measured at the optimal point in the process (i.e., following the initial rapid reaction), it can be used to control the addition rate of chlorine, resulting in more uniform chlorination.

OXIDATIVE BLEACHING AGENT: Any chemical which develops brightness in pulps by oxidizing the lignin. Common oxidative bleaching agents are chlorine dioxide, hypochlorite, oxygen and peroxide.

OXIDATIVE EXTRACTION STAGE: Alkaline extraction stage supplemented with an oxidizing agent, most commonly oxygen. Peroxide or hypochlorite may also be used as supplemental chemicals to provide a brightening effect and/or to reduce effluent color.

OXIDIZING AGENT: Chemical compound that gives up oxygen easily, removes hydrogen from another compound, or attracts electrons (i.e., becomes reduced).

OXIDIZING POWER: See BLEACHING POWER.

OXYGEN: (O_2) Common constituent of air, produced in large industrial tonnages by first liquifying air under pressure, and then fractionally distilling the liquid air to obtain pure liquid oxygen. The utilization of oxygen as a bleaching/delignifying agent for chemical wood pulps is expanding as ways are found to minimize its adverse effects on cellulose degradation.

OXYGEN BLEACHING STAGE (O-Stage): Treatment of pulp in alkaline medium with oxygen to degrade and solubilize lignin, typically employed for partial delignification prior to conventional chlorination. Existing systems utilize a wide range of consistencies, but in all cases the oxygen is added as a gas and the reaction mixture is maintained at high pressure to allow the oxygen to diffuse into the liquid phase and react with the pulp. Magnesium salts are usually employed as an additive to "protect" the cellulose from degradation.

OXYGEN-ENRICHED EXTRACTION STAGE (E/O-Stage): Modification of the alkaline extraction stage wherein gaseous oxygen is added to the stock at the beginning of the stage and maintained under pressure for a sufficient period of time to allow the oxygen to dissolve into the liquid phase and react with the pulp. This mild oxidative treatment improves the overall delignification of the extraction stage. See also OXIDATIVE EXTRACTION STAGE.

OZONATION STAGE (Z Stage): Experimental delignification or bleaching treatment of pulp with ozone, carried out under acidic conditions. This stage has not been applied commercially.

OZONATOR: Device for converting oxygen into ozone, usually by passing air through an electric discharge (corona). Syn. Ozonizer.

OZONE: Unstable triatomic form of oxygen (O_3), formed by passing an electric current through oxygen. It is an effective delignifying and brightening agent for wood pulps, but not lignin-specific; therefore, process conditions must be carefully controlled to minimize cellulose degradation.

P _____

PEG MIXER: Traditional design of mixer for distributing bleach chemicals into medium and high-consistency pulp, consisting of a tubular vessel having one or two shafts with pegs that rotate between stationary elements attached to the mixer casing.

PERACETIC ACID: (CH_3CO_3H) Effective oxidative brightening agent for mechanical pulps that destroys chromophores without dissolving lignin. It is too costly for commercial application.

PERHYDROXYL ION: (OOH⁻) Active species in peroxide bleaching.

PEROXIDE: Oxidative brightening or bleaching agent, available either as hydrogen peroxide (H_2O_2) or sodium peroxide (Na_2O_2).

PEROXIDE BLEACHING STAGE (P-Stage): Usually used as the last stage in a multistage bleaching process to gain a few points of extra brightness. Can also be used in place of the extraction stage between two chlorine dioxide stages. Peroxide bleaching is carried out under alkaline conditions, and in admixture with supplemental chemicals. Magnesium sulfate is added to prevent decomposition of the active perhydroxyl ion during bleaching, and sodium silicate is used because of its buffering and stabilizing capabilities.

PEROXIDE BRIGHTENING STAGE: Single-stage oxidative process for the brightening of mechanical pulps or can be used in sequence with a hydrosulfite stage. The temperature for lignin-preserving brightening is controlled at a lower level than for bleaching; but otherwise conditions are similar. It is also common practice to pretreat mechanical pulps with sequestering agents to remove metallic ions that could promote decomposition of the peroxide.

PLUG FLOW: Idealized flow in which fluid or stock is discharged from a pipe or vessel in the same order in which it entered. In plug flow, there is no intermixing and no channeling of flow.

POLARGRAPHIC CHEMICAL SENSOR: Electrochemical instrument for determining the concentration of certain chemicals used in pulp bleaching, typically applied to the measurement of residual chlorine.

PREBLEACHING: Term sometimes applied to those initial treatments in the bleaching sequence that delignify the pulp, but which do not materially improve the color (e.g., chlorination, alkaline extraction, oxygen stage).

PRERETENTION TUBE: Upflow tube which provides a short retention period under pressure at the beginning of an oxygen-enriched extraction stage to allow sufficient time for the oxygen to dissolve into the liquid phase and react with the pulp.

PROTECTIVE ADDITIVE: See DEGRADATION INHIBITOR.

PUFF: Decomposition of chlorine dioxide during generation resulting in an abrupt increase in gas evolution from the reaction vessel. In severe cases, puffs become violent and even explosive.

R _____

REACTION VESSEL: Glass-lined vessel in which chlorine dioxide is generated by chemical reduction of sodium chlorate in a sulfuric acid medium. Syn. Reactor, Generator.

REACTIVATION (of desiccant): Driving off of absorbed water by heat and/or vacuum, thereby restoring the original capacity of the desiccant to absorb water. Syn. Regeneration.

REDOX POTENTIAL: See OXIDATION-REDUCTION POTENTIAL.

REDUCING AGENT: Chemical compound that loses hydrogen to another compound or loses electrons to another compound (i.e., becomes oxidized).

REDUCTANT: In general, any material which can lose electrons. In pulp brightening, the term refers to a reductive brightening agent such as hydrosulfite or borohydride.

RESIDUAL BLEACH DEMAND: Bleach demand of a pulp following a specified bleaching treatment, most commonly after chlorination and extraction as measured by the extracted permanganate number.

RESIDUAL CHEMICAL: Active bleaching chemical remaining in contact with pulp. If no residual chemical is present at the end of a retention period, it means that the reaction has stopped at some prior point.

RESIDUAL LIGNIN: Lignin remaining in pulp following a specified bleaching treatment.

RETENTION TIME: (1) Contact period of pulp with a bleaching chemical; usually measured from the point of chemical addition to the point where residual chemical is washed out or displaced by another chemical. (2) Period of retention in a flow-through reaction vessel. Unless the vessel contains stagnant zones, the retention time is equal to the volume of the vessel divided by the flowrate through the vessel. Syn. Displacement Time.

REVERSION: See BRIGHTNESS REVERSION.

ROE NUMBER: See CHLORINE NUMBER.

S _____

SEMI-BLEACH PULP: Pulp that has been bleached to an intermediate level of brightness, i.e., between that of unbleached pulp and fully bleached pulp.

SEQUENTIAL CHLORINATION: See CHLORINATION STAGE, MODIFIED.

SEQUESTERING AGENT: Substance that inactivates a metallic ion within a solution system by forming an unreactive complex ion. It can be a chelating agent or a complexing agent.

SHORT-SEQUENCE BLEACHING: Technique of bleaching in which 3 or 4 stages are more fully exploited to achieve fully bleached brightness levels for softwood kraft pulp.

SHRINKAGE: Weight loss of pulp substance resulting from bleaching treatments, usually expressed as a percentage of the unbleached weight.

SILICA GEL: Highly absorbent colloidal silica, often employed as a dehumidifying agent for air systems used to unload liquid chlorine.

SODIUM CHLORATE: See CHLORATE.

SODIUM CHLORITE: See CHLORITE BLEACHING.

STAGE: Part of a process that is isolated for independent optimization. Pulp bleaching is usually carried out in a multistage sequence.

STATIC MIXER: Intricately baffled conduit which causes violent direction changes in any fluid flowing through it. The flow is divided many times in transit which ensures efficient blending. Static mixers are often used to disperse chlorine gas into stock.

STEAM-JET REFRIGERATION: Method of producing chilled water for chlorine dioxide absorption in which a vacuum is created above the water by a steam eductor, thus causing the water to boil at a lower pressure and give up heat. This method is capable of cooling water to a temperature as low as 2°C.

STEEP BRIGHTENING: Addition of brightening chemical to wet lap or other high density stock which is then stored at ambient temperature for a period of days. It is usually assumed that the chemical is totally consumed at the end of the storage period, and the typical subsequent washing stage is omitted.

SULFAMIC ACID: (NH_2SO_3H) Chemical used as a "protector" to prevent or minimize cellulose degradation in the chlorination and hypochlorite bleaching stages.

SULFURIC ACID: (H_2SO_4) Strong mineral acid used as a raw material in all chlorine dioxide generating processes and for the acidulation of tall oil.

SULFUROUS ACID TREATMENT: Application of H_2SO_3 (i.e., aqueous solution of sulfur dioxide) to the pulp following the last oxidative bleaching stage. It serves to destroy residual bleaching chemical, removes metal ions that could contribute to brightness reversion and creates a more favorable pH for brightness stability.

T

TAIL GAS: Exit gas stream from the chlorine dioxide absorption tower.

TAIL GAS SCRUBBER: Backup absorption tower to remove residual chlorine and chlorine dioxide gases from the tail gas.

TERMINAL CONDITIONS: Conditions (e.g., pH, temperature, residual chemical, etc.) prevailing at the completion of a bleaching stage.

TOWER: See BLEACHING TOWER.

U

UNBLEACHED PULP: Pulp that has not been subjected to any type of bleaching or brightening treatment.

UPFLOW-DOWNFLOW TOWER: Retention vessel for pulp bleaching in which the pulp first flows upwards (through an "upflow leg" or "updraft tube") under hydrostatic pressure and overflows into a conventional downflow tower. This type of tower is commonly used for chlorine dioxide bleaching.

UPFLOW TOWER: Retention vessel for pulp bleaching in which the stock mixture enters at the bottom and moves upward in plug flow. At the top of the tower the stock is laundered into a peripheral trough through which the stock overflows by gravity.

V

VISCOSITY PRESERVATIVE: Chemical utilized in a bleaching stage which serves to prevent pulp viscosity loss. See also DEGRADATION INHIBITOR.

VISCOSITY-REDUCING BLEACHING: Bleaching of pulp with hypochlorite at relatively high temperatures, used in dissolving pulp mills to reduce pulp viscosity to a controlled level.

W

WASTE ACID: Spent sulfuric acid from the chlorine dioxide generator, usually containing sodium sulfate and other reaction products.

Chapter 11

Properties/Testing of Pulp and Fiber

(Includes: Refining Actions on Fibers)

A ————————————————————

ABSORBENCY: Property of pulp (or other material) to entrain and hold liquids with which it comes in contact. The rate and capacity of liquid absorbency are important for certain commercial products containing fluffed pulp fibers. See also RELATIVE ABSORBENCY.

ABSORBENT CAPACITY: Amount of absorbed substance retained by a pulp pad under specified conditions. Syn. Absorptive Capacity.

ACID-INSOLUBLE ASH (of pulp): Quantity determined by analysis which is usually taken as the silica content of the pulp.

AIR DRY CONTENT: According to trade convention, air dry pulp is assumed to contain 90% oven-dry pulp and 10% moisture. The air-dry content of a pulp sample is therefore equal to the oven-dry content divided by 0.9.

AIR DRY PULP: (1) Pulp in equilibrium with the surrounding air. (2) Pulp having a theoretical commercial dryness (usually 90% oven-dry content by trade convention).

AIR DRY WEIGHT: Weight of pulp containing 10% moisture. The oven-dry weight divided by 0.9 equals the air-dry weight.

ALKALI SOLUBILITY: See CAUSTIC SOLUBILITY.

ALPHA PULPS: Bleached wood pulps that have an alpha-cellulose content above 88%. Most alpha pulps are dissolving grades. Syn. High-Alpha Pulps.

ASPECT RATIO (of fibers): Ratio of the major to the minor axis of a fiber within a paper sheet. The aspect ratio provides information on the relative flexibility and collapse of fibers, and therefore, on their bonding ability. (The major axis is taken as the maximum distance between any two points on the perimeter of the fiber, the minor axis is taken as the distance across the fiber normal to the major axis.)

AVERAGE FIBER LENGTH: Fundamental property or characteristic of papermaking pulps indicative of their suitability for different applications. The weight average fiber length is the relevant measurement of this property, as distinct from the numerical average fiber length. The average fiber length can be measured or estimated by fiber classification methods, by microscopic visual analysis, or by fiber length grid methods.

B ————————————————————

BALL MILL: Laboratory beating device in which a pulp sample is placed inside a rotating cylinder and subjected to the mechanical action of falling pebbles or porcelain balls. Syn. Pebble Mill.

BAUER-McNETT CLASSIFIER: Laboratory device for carrying out a fiber length classification. See also FIBER CLASSIFICATION.

BEATABILITY: Pulp property indicative of the mechanical treatment that must be administered to achieve a specific objective, usually expressed in terms of the time or number of revolutions required to beat a specified weight of pulp under carefully controlled conditions in a standard laboratory device to reach a given freeness value.

BEATER EVALUATION: Method of evaluating the papermaking attributes of a pulp by beating or refining a sample in the laboratory under controlled and reproducible conditions, then forming the pulp into standardized handsheets, and finally performing suitable physical tests on the conditioned handsheets. These tests show the relative rate of response of a pulp to the beating process, the maximum strength that is developed, and the relationships that prevail between the various physical parameters. See also BEATING CURVE.

BEATING CURVE: Common method of presenting beater evaluation results in which various sheet physical properties are plotted as a function of beating time, beating energy, or freeness.

BONDED FIBER SURFACE AREA: Sum of the bonded areas on the fiber surfaces as a percentage of the total surface area of all fibers within a fiber assemblage.

BONDING POTENTIAL: Contact area between fibers in a sheet as a percentage of total fiber surface area. The bonding potential is related to fiber flexibility. Syn. Contact Ratio.

BONDING STRENGTH: Measure of the tenacity with which fibers adhere to each other within a paper sheet structure. Syn. Cohesiveness.

BONE-DRY: [adj] Used interchangably with oven-dry. Oven-dry is the preferred term.

BORING METHOD (for pulp bale moisture): See DISC MOISTURE.

BOUND WATER: Water held by pulp fibers which exerts a vapor pressure less than that of the pure liquid at the same temperature. The amount of bound water under equilibrium conditions is highly dependent on the temperature and humidity of the surrounding environment and varies with the type of pulp. In a "standard environment" (i.e., 21°C, 50% relative humidity), the equilibrium moisture content ranges between 6 and 9%. Syn. Water of Constitution.

BOUND WATER LAYER: Adsorbed water molecules on the surface of a cellulosic fiber. The first molecular layer is so rigidly oriented and tightly packed that the density appears to be about 2.5 g/cm³. Subsequent layers are successively less orderly, less strongly bound and less dense. For conditioned fibers, the number of molecular layers is calculated to be about six.

BRITISH SHEET MACHINE: Standard laboratory apparatus employing a 15.9-cm diameter column and mold for forming test handsheets. It utilizes a stock consistency of 0.15% to make a 60 g/m³ handsheet.

BRITT JAR: Design of dynamic drainage jar. (After the inventor, K.W. Britt)

BRUISING: See INTERNAL FIBRILLATION.

BRUSHING: See EXTERNAL FIBRILLATION.

C _____

CALIBRATION PULP: See STANDARD PULP.

CANADIAN STANDARD FREENESS: See FREENESS.

CAUSTIC SOLUBILITY: Test to measure the "purity" of chemical cellulose, in which pulp samples are exposed to 10% and 18% solutions of sodium hydroxide (NaOH) to preferentially dissolve the lower molecular weight cellulosic compounds. The amounts dissolved are expressed as the percent S10 and S18 respectively, and these values are used to calculate a relative index of the alpha cellulose content.

CLEARING: Disentangling fibers or breaking down fiber networks within a fiber suspension, usually by disintegration. See also DISINTEGRATION.

COARSENESS: See FIBER COARSENESS.

COHESION: Fundamental property of papermaking fibers which enables them to form strong fiber-to-fiber bonds. The manifestation of this property in a sheet of paper depends not only on the intrinsic cohesiveness of the individual pulp fibers but also on the effective contact area between adjacent fibers, which is a function of fiber flexibility.

COHESIVENESS: See BONDING STRENGTH.

COLLAPSED FIBER: Ribbon-like element formed when the cell wall collapses into the lumen. Generally, fibers of relatively small cell wall thickness collapse readily while those with thicker cell walls resist collapse. The percent of collapsed fibers in a pulp sample correlates well with relative bonded area, tensile breaking length and sheet density.

COMBINED STRENGTH PARAMETER (CSP): Index of pulp strength that incorporates measurements of both fiber strength and bonding strength. In practice, the CSP is a combination of tear and burst or tear and tensile measurements. Syn. Pulp Strength Index.

COMMERCIAL DRYNESS (of pulp): See THEORETICAL COMMERCIAL DRYNESS.

COMPACTABILITY: See WET COMPACTABILITY.

COMPOSITE SAMPLE: Aggregate sample of pulp, paper, or other material that is made up of a mixture of individual samples taken at specific time intervals or at different positions.

COMPRESSIBILITY: Characterization of the degree to which pulp fibers can be compressed together to form a more or less coherent sheet.

COMPRESSIBILITY CURVE: Plot of pulp pad thickness against compression pressure, under specified conditions.

COMPRESSING: Densification of pulp fibers due to refining action.

CONDITIONING: Exposure of pulp or paper test specimens to a standard environment for a sufficient time for them to come to equilibrium with the environment. In North America, the standard conditioning environment is 50% relative humidity and 21°C. Syn. Seasoning.

CONFORMABILITY: Ability of pulp fibers to be formed, matted and compressed into a uniform sheet.

CONSISTENCY: Mass or weight percentage of bone dry fiber in a stock. Consistency is often described qualitatively as low, medium, or high without reference to a standard nomenclature. The following ranges are given as a general guide:

very low consistency	0–1%
low consistency (LC)	1–8%
medium consistency (MC)	8–16%
high consistency (HC)	16–40%

Syn. Mass Concentration, Solids Concentration, Solids Content.

CONSTANT TEMPERATURE/HUMIDITY ROOM (CTH Room): Room used for physical testing of pulp and paper products, which is maintained at the standard environment.

CONTACT RATIO: See BONDING POTENTIAL.

COUCH BLOTTER: Special blotter paper for removing pulp handsheets from the wire mold after forming. Standard specifications in North America require that the blotter sheets be 20 cm square, with a grammage of 250 g/m³, a caliper of 0.51 mm, an absorbency of 15 seconds for 0.1 ml of water, and a cross sectional expansion of less than 2.5% when wetted with water (all within prescribed tolerances).

COUCHING: Action of picking off a newly formed paper web from a forming medium. The couching of pulp handsheets is usually carried out by placing dry blotters and a brass plate on top of the wet sheet and then applying rolling pressure to cause the assembly to stick together so it can be lifted off.

CRILL: Extremely fine particles abraded from the surface of cellulose fibers by the action of a refiner. See also FIBER DEBRIS, FINES.

CRIMP: Waviness or curl of a fiber. Syn. Curl.

CRIMP RATIO: Percentage change in the linear measurement of a fiber as it undergoes change from a crimped configuration to a fully straightened configuration without extending it. Syn. Curl Index, Curl Value.

CRITICAL PAIR OF PROPERTIES: Comparison of pulps with respect to a hypothetical change in the process that causes an advantageous change to one key property and a disadvantageous change to another key property. This concept is commonly applied to the relationship between tear strength and tensile breaking length at different levels of refining.

CRITICAL POINT DRYING: Laboratory technique for drying pulp fiber samples which virtually eliminates the surface distortions associated with conventional air drying. The technique consists of dehydrating the fiber sample with a solvent (e.g., ethanol) followed by replacing the dehydrating solvent with a transitional fluid (e.g., liquid carbon dioxide). Subsequently, the transitional fluid is brought to its critical point (i.e., the temperature and pressure at which densities of the gas and liquid phases are identical), and as a result, the liquid in the cell wall passes from the liquid phase to the gaseous phase without exerting surface tension on the fibers. See also FREEZE DRYING.

CRUSHING (of fibers): Extreme state of fiber compaction evidenced by plastic deformation and mechanical disruption of the fiber wall layers and the microfibrillar structure.

CURL INDEX: SEE CRIMP RATIO.

CURLING: Permanent reduction in the radius of curvature of pulp fibers due to refining action. See also KINKING.

CUT: See SLIT WIDTH.

CUTTING: See SHORTENING.

D _____

DEBRIS: (1) Specifically, nondisintegrated woody materials associated with mechanical pulps which are detrimental to pulp quality. These are in the form of shives and minishives. (2) Generally, any type of wood or fibrous particle which would normally be retained on a 6- or 8-cut screen plate.

DEGREE OF COHESION: Characterization of overall fiber cohesion in a standard handsheet, indicated by the ratio of the tensile breaking load to the zero-span tensile breaking load. Syn Bonding Index.

DEGREE OF DISINTEGRATION: Relative extent of fiber separation for a pulp sample (or sample of paper stock) following a standard laboratory disintegration, which is quantified by making handsheets and comparing them under transmitted light to a series of reference sheets. See also DISPERSABILITY, RESISTANCE TO DISINTEGRATION.

DEGREE OF SWELLING: Amount of water entering the cell wall, and hence a measure of water absorptivity and/or accessibility by aqueous reagents. It is also taken as an indication of fiber conformability.

DELAMINATION: Separation of layers of the fiber wall due to mechanical action such as beating or refining.

DENSITY: Mass or weight per unit volume. The true density of cellulose fibrous material (also called "packing density") is the mass divided by the volume of solid material, excluding the volume of open or closed voids or pores.

DIMENSIONAL PROPERTIES (of fibers): Grouping of fiber parameters that includes length, width, cross-sectional area, surface area, degree of flattening (collapse), aspect ratio and Runkel ratio; as well as characterizations of crimping, twisting, kinking, and other deformations.

DIRT: Any foreign particulate material embedded within a pulp sheet that has a marked contrasting color to the rest of the material.

DISC MOISTURE: Characterization of pulp bale moisture content by boring into a bale at specified locations with a special tool to obtain discs of pulp and then determining the moisture content of these discs.

DISINTEGRATION: Dispersing a pulp or stock sample to obtain a suspension of free fibers. (The term "disintegration" is usually applied to laboratory work; the comparable mill operation is more commonly referred to as "pulping" or "repulping".) See also DEGREE OF DISINTEGRATION, RESISTANCE TO DISINTEGRATION, CLEARING.

DISINTEGRATOR: Laboratory apparatus for pulp disintegration.

DISLOCATION: Region of a fiber where microfibrils are misaligned from the original to a more transverse direction due to compressive stress, usually caused by refining at high consistency. Syn. Slip Plane.

DISPERSIBILITY: Ability of a pulp to succumb to disintegration action relative to the resistance or compliance of other pulps. See also RESISTANCE TO DISINTEGRATION, DEGREE OF DISINTEGRATION.

DRAINABILITY: Relative resistance of a forming fiber mat to the drainage or passage of water, an important property with respect to pulp processing and papermaking. Measurements of this property are referred to as freeness, slowness, wetness, or drain time, according to the instrument or method used. See also DYNAMIC DRAINABILITY.

DRAINAGE FACTOR: Slope of the lineal graph obtained from plotting the mass of moisture-free pulp in a sheet machine against drainage time, expressed as seconds per gram; used to characterize the drainage behavior of free stock.

DRAINAGE RESISTANCE: Tendency of a stock to retain water on the forming medium.

DRAINAGE TIME: Time for a specified volume of water to drain through the forming medium during sheet formation, under carefully controlled conditions. This measurement is used as a relative indication of drainability. See also FREENESS, SLOWNESS, and WETNESS.

DRIED PULP: Pulp which has been dried in the pulp mill, as distinct from never-dried pulp. Pulp fibers undergo irreversible structural changes during drying which affect their subsequent utilization in papermaking.

DRYING PLATE: Mirror-polished plate (commonly 158 mm diameter) made of stainless steel or chrome-plated brass, used as a support and finishing surface for a laboratory pulp handsheet during pressing and drying.

DRYING RINGS: Hard plastic or brass rings for holding and stacking drying plates while allowing free circulation of air around them. The rings are designed to fit into each other while clamping one or two plates around the edges.

DRY REFINING: Experimental refining of pulp at dryness levels above 85%.

DRY SOLIDS CONTENT: See DRYNESS.

DYNAMIC DRAINABILITY: Measure of drainage resistance in which the range of conditions used in the test more nearly corresponds to conditions on a paper machine than do those of commonly used laboratory tests.

DYNAMIC DRAINAGE JAR: Sheet forming apparatus which imparts shear to the fiber suspension during formation.

E _____

EASY BEATING: [adj] Descriptive term for a pulp that reaches target strength levels with a relatively small input of refining energy.

EQUIVALENT BLACK AREA: Area of a black spot on a standard dirt estimation chart that gives the same visual impression as a particular dirt speck in a pulp sheet.

EXTERNAL FIBRILLATION: Changes in the external structure of the fiber due to beating or refining, seen as the unraveling of microfibrils which make the fiber surface look "hairy". Syn. Brushing.

EXTRACTION: Method of determining the resin content of pulp by extracting a sample with an appropriate organic solvent, usually either ethyl ether or ethanol or an ethanol/benzene mixture. Typically the solvent is refluxed and the pulp sample is always in contact with condensate as it returns to the boiling flask. After a standardized refluxing period, the solvent is evaporated and the resin residue is weighed.

F

FAST BEATING: [adj] Refers to a pulp that develops strength properties during beating or refining with relatively small input of mechanical energy. See also BEATABILITY.

FAST PULP: See FREE PULP.

FIBER ANALYSIS: Microscopic differentiation and counting of fibers to determine the approximate percentages by species or type in a given sample of pulp or paper.

FIBER AXIS RATIO: Ratio of width to thickness for a collapsed fiber, sometimes used as a rough indication of fiber coarseness.

FIBER BONDING INDEX: Measure of the bonding ability of a mechanical pulp, defined (by U.B. Mohlin) as the tensile index of handsheets produced under standard conditions from the 16–30 mesh fraction (i.e., passing 16 mesh, but retained on 30 mesh).

FIBER CLASSIFICATION: Separation of pulp into fractions of different fiber length, usually by utilizing a specific apparatus. Conceptually, a dilute suspension of fibers is made to flow at high velocity parallel to screen slots, while a much slower velocity passes through the slots. In this way, the fibers are presented lengthwise to a series of screens with successively smaller mesh openings, and only the fibers short enough not to bridge the opening pass to the next chamber. See also FIBER FRACTIONATION.

FIBER COARSENESS: Weight of fiber wall material per unit length of fiber, usually measured in mg per 100 m. Fiber coarseness is a fundamental property of papermaking pulps and is used as a relative indicator of the fineness or slenderness of the fibers and, therefore, their flexibility. Syn. Fiber Linear Density.

FIBER COMPOSITION: Percentages of different fibers present in a particular sample of stock, as determined by fiber analysis.

FIBER COUNT: Number of fibers present in a unit mass of pulp. Counts are carried out by pipetting known amounts of fiber suspensions onto slides where dyed fibers are counted under the microscope. See also FIBER NUMBER.

FIBER CURL: Fiber curvature, also including bends and kinks. Within a sheet structure, fiber curl can be observed in the plane of the sheet or out-of-plane as the fiber passes over and under crossing fibers. See also CRIMP.

FIBER DEBRIS: Pieces of primary wall which have been separated from chemical pulp fibers by refining action. See also CRILL and FINES.

FIBER FLEXIBILITY: Ability of a fiber to bend or deform. See also WET FIBER FLEXIBILITY.

FIBER FLOCCULATION: Aggregation of fibers in suspension.

FIBER FRACTIONATION: Separation of a pulp sample into one or more fractions on the basis of fiber length, fiber stiffness or other property. See also FIBER CLASSIFICATION.

FIBER LENGTH: See AVERAGE FIBER LENGTH.

FIBER LENGTH ANALYZER: Automated device for scanning a pulp suspension which utilizes the ability of cellulose to depolarize a polarized light beam in order to measure the number of fibers sequentially in each of 35 separate length categories.

FIBER LENGTH DISTRIBUTION: Representation of data from microscopic or optical fiber length measurements or fiber classifications. In the former case, the data are usually displayed in a diagram with the horizontal scale showing fiber length increments (in mm) and the vertical scale showing the number of fibers in each range of length. In the latter case, the data are usually displayed in a diagram showing the weight percentage retained as a function of screen slot opening.

FIBER LENGTH GRID: Bronze ring equipped with a number of equally spaced blades fixed with their narrow edge upwards, used in place of the screen in a Standard British Sheet Machine. A specified stock suspension is allowed to flow past the grid, and the weight of fibers which are retained on the grid is measured and reported as the "fiber weight length", an indication of the average fiber length in the sample.

FIBER LINEAR DENSITY: See FIBER COARSENESS.

FIBER NETWORK STRENGTH: Measure of the stress that must be applied to a fiber network (as well as the flocs within it) in order to produce flow in the pulp suspension or to expose fibers to a chemical at the point of addition. This strength has a marked dependency on consistency, represented by aC^b where C is the consistency in % and a and b are fitted constants that depend on the fiber type.

FIBER NUMBER: Number of fibers per gram (or number of fibers per cubic centimeter), a basic morphological measurement used to characterize a pulp. See also FIBER COUNT.

FIBER SATURATION POINT (FSP): Moisture content of the water-saturated cell walls of cellulosic fibers (usually expressed as grams water per gram dry fiber) as determined by the solute exclusion technique. See also WATER RETENTION VALUE.

FIBER SHEARING: Sliding of two contiguous parts of a fiber relative to each other in a direction parallel to their plane of contact, due to refining action.

FIBER STIFFNESS: See WET FIBER FLEXIBILITY.

FIBER STRENGTH: See INTRINSIC FIBER STRENGTH.

FIBER SURFACE: See SPECIFIC EXTERNAL SURFACE, SPECIFIC SURFACE.

FIBER TWIST: Rotation of a fiber about a fixed end to provide a spiral form. Freely dried pulp fibers exhibit considerable twist. Bond formation in typical paper sheets effectively prevents twist; but a degree of twist can be observed in bulky thin sheets.

FIBER WEIGHT LENGTH: See FIBER LENGTH GRID.

FIBRILLATION: Refining action which disrupts lateral bonds between adjacent microfibrillar layers of pulp fibers. "External fibrillation" refers to the loosening of fibrils and raising or partial detachment of microfibrils on the surface of fibers. "Internal fibrillation" refers to the less visible disruption of bonds within the fiber.

FIBRILPLASMA FINES: Groundwood fines produced by conditioned grits which contribute significantly to the burst and tensile strength of the pulp, as differentiated from "flour fines". Syn. Slimestuff.

FILTRATION RESISTANCE: Measure of drainage resistance through a pulp mat during sheet formation. See also SPECIFIC FILTRATION RESISTANCE.

FINES: Very short fibers, fiber fragments, ray cells or debris from mechanical treatment. Typically, all material that passes through the final screening element of a fiber classifier (usually a 200-mesh screen) is collectively referred to as fines. See also CRILL, DEBRIS, FIBRILPLASMA FINES, FLOUR FINES.

FLOUR FINES: Groundwood fines produced by sharp grits which contribute little to the strength properties of the pulp, as differentiated from the more desirable "fibrilplasma fines".

FLUFFABILITY: Ability of a pulp to be dry disintegrated with minimum energy and produce a uniform fluff with minimum fiber damage.

FORMABILITY: Ability of a pulp to form a uniform sheet under standard conditions, usually assessed on a qualitative basis. Formability can be inferred from a knowledge of fiber characteristics. A relative assessment can be made by comparing handsheets formed from different pulps. A quantitative value can be obtained from the "wildness test".

FREE FIBER SURFACE AREA: Percentage of the total surface area of fibers within an assemblage that is not bonded to any other fiber; equal to 100% less the bonded surface area.

FREENESS: Measurement of pulp drainability, usually by means of the Canadian Standard Freeness (CSF) test. The CSF is defined as the number of ml of water collected from the side orifice of the standard tester when a dilute stock drains through a perforated plate under carefully controlled conditions. The higher the number, the freer is the pulp. See also SLOWNESS, DRAIN TIME, WETNESS.

FREENESS TESTER: See FREENESS.

FREE PULP: Rapidly draining pulp. Syn. Fast Pulp, Free Stock.

FREE SHRINKAGE: Change in dimensions of a test handsheet due to drying without restraint, expressed as a percentage.

FREE WATER: Moisture taken up by cellulose fibers past the fiber saturation point.

FREEZE DRYING: Laboratory technique for drying pulp fiber samples. Water in the fibers is frozen and then sublimed (i.e., evaporated directly from the solid phase into the gaseous phase without passing through the liquid phase) into a vacuum. Freeze drying reduces the distortion of the fiber surface associated with conventional air drying because no liquid/vapor interface passes through the fibers. See also CRITICAL POINT DRYING.

G _____

GRAB SAMPLE: Any sample (e.g., wood chips, pulp, paper) that is taken at random for testing or analysis. Syn. Random Sample.

H

HANDSHEET: Sheet made from a suspension of fiber and water on a laboratory sheet mold, followed by pressing and drying, all operations being carried out under carefully controlled conditions. Typically, replicate handsheets are subjected to a series of standard tests to evaluate pulp quality. See also BEATER EVALUATION.

HANDSHEET DRYER: Laboratory equipment for drying and simultaneously conditioning pressed handsheets. The sheets are air-dried by circulation of conditioned air.

HANDSHEET MACHINE: Laboratory equipment for making wet handsheets The British apparatus (with associated methodology) is widely accepted as the standard for making test sheets. Syn. Laboratory Sheet Mold.

HANDSHEET PRESS: Laboratory equipment for mechanically dewatering and consolidating wet handsheets.

HARD BEATING: [adj] Descriptive term for any pulp that requires a relatively large input of refining energy to reach target strength levels.

HARDNESS INDEX (of sheet pulp): Measurement that indicates the relative ease or difficulty by which a pulp sheet may be ground or shredded. It is calculated as the ratio between the bursting strength and the thickness of the sheet.

HERZBERG STAIN: Solution of zinc chloride, potassium iodide and iodine, used in the microscopic identification and quantitative estimation of the types of fibers present in a sample of pulp or paper. (Kraft and sulfite fibers take on a dark blue color; linen and cotton fibers appear purplish pink; and groundwood fibers are stained intense yellow.)

HOLOPULPS: Bleached wood pulps which retain a large portion of the wood hemicellulose; as differentiated from alpha pulps.

HORNIFICATION: Descriptive term for the physical and chemical changes that occur to pulp fibers during drying, principally shrinkage and formation of internal hydrogen bonds. Some of these effects are irreversible. Hornification takes place mainly within the hemicellulose material of the fibers, and the effects are more pronounced with hemicellulose-rich pulps.

HYDRATED FIBER: Fiber that has soaked in water to the extent that water has penetrated the interior, thus allowing the fiber structure to swell.

HYDRATING: Imprecise term used to denote increasing capacity of pulp fibers for water retention due to refining action. The term "wetting" is preferred.

HYDRODYNAMIC SPECIFIC VOLUME: Swollen volume of wet fibers per unit dry weight of pulp, usually reported in cm^3/g. This property is inferred by measuring the water permeability of a mat of fibers under different degrees of compressibility.

HYGROSCOPICITY: Property of a substance to absorb water vapor and attain moisture equilibrium with the ambient air condition. Cellulosic materials are distinctly hygroscopic.

HYSTERESIS: See MOISTURE HYSTERESIS.

I

IMAGE ANALYSIS: Measurement by electronic scanning methods of the size, shape, and distributional parameters of an image (e.g., produced by orienting a sample in a viewing field). This technique has been successfully applied toward the characterization of pulp fibers.

IMBIBED WATER: Water held by cellulose fibers within the fiber walls. The transition between imbibed water and free water is generally taken to be the fiber saturation point.

IMBIBITION: Sorption of water by pulp fiber without increase in volume. See also SWELLING.

INTERNAL FIBRILLATION: Loosening of the internal structure of the fiber due to beating or refining, which enables the fiber to swell and makes the fiber soft and flexible. Syn. Bruising.

INTERNAL SPECIFIC SURFACE: All fiber surfaces within a unit mass of pulp, both external and internal, that are not joined together in complete contact or through short water linkages. (J.d'A. Clark suggests "total specific unconnected surface" as a more descriptive term for this property.)

INTRINSIC FIBER STRENGTH: Usually refers to the tensile strength of individual pulp fibers. Several methods have been investigated to measure the strength of individual fibers; however, more commonly the average fiber strength of a pulp sample is inferred from a zero-span tensile test of a representative handsheet.

K

KINK INDEX: Number of kinks along a fiber multiplied by the severity of the angle of kinking selected from four ranges (conceptualized by Kibblewhite).

KINKING: Abrupt change in the radius of curvature of pulp fibers due to refining action. See also CURLING.

L

LABORATORY BEATER: Device for mechanical treatment of small pulp batches under controlled conditions. Many different devices employing various combinations of mechanical actions have been developed and applied by different sectors of the industry. In North America, the two devices most commonly used are the PFI mill and the Valley beater. See also BEATER EVALUATION.

LABORATORY SHEET MOLD: See HANDSHEET MACHINE.

LENGTH FACTOR (L-FACTOR): Empirical number (conceptualized by Forgacs) that is intended to characterize the average fiber length of mechanical pulps, usually taken as the weight percentage of fibers retained on a 48-mesh screen. The length factor generally correlates well with tear resistance. See also SHAPE FACTOR.

LENGTH/THICKNESS RATIO: Ratio of pulp fiber length to cell wall thickness, sometimes used as an index to assess the papermaking potential of a pulp, especially with regard to strength.

M

MICROCOMPRESSIONS: Series of closely spaced kinks in cellulose pulp fibers due to high-consistency refining action. Both microcompressions and dislocations are associated with axial compression of the fibers, but they differ in their morphological manifestations. See also DISLOCATION.

MICROCREPING: Reduction in length of fibers due to corrugating of the fiber wall on a microscopic scale, caused principally by the compressive forces acting on the fibers during beating or refining.

MILL: Term applied to any of a number of laboratory beating devices, all of which utilize the continuous repetition of some simple mechanical action.

MOISTURE CONTENT: Percentage of water in a material, determined by completely drying a representative sample to constant weight at 105°C. This procedure yields an oven dry (o.d.) moisture content. Because of its hygroscopicity, cellulosic materials may not attain a true moisture-free state unless care is taken to dry the air which is introduced into the oven.

MOISTURE HYSTERESIS: Refers to the difference in equilibrium moisture content of conditioned pulp and paper products depending on whether they had previously been wetter or drier than the equilibrium value. This difference is caused by the more expanded structure of a wet sheet, providing additional internal surface to accept water. When the fibers are dried, many of these surfaces are "locked together" by hydrogen bonding and are no longer available. Syn. Humidity Hysteresis.

MOISTURE RATIO: Ratio of the weight of water in a moist material to the weight of dry material. Syn. Moisture Content (Dry Basis).

MORPHOLOGICAL PROPERTIES: Pulp properties or characteristics that are dependent on the form and structure of the fibers. Basic morphological properties include average fiber length, cell wall thickness, cross sectional area, fibril angle, fiber coarseness, and specific surface.

MUHLSTEPH RATIO: Ratio of the net cross-sectional area of a fiber (i.e. area of cell wall material) to the gross cross-sectional area (i.e. area of cell wall plus lumen). This measurement is used primarily to evaluate the suitability of fibers as they exist in wood for technical uses such as papermaking.

N

NEPS: Tightly bonded fiber aggregates. Neps are sometimes a problem in chemical pulp that has been flash-dried and baled for fluffing.

NEVER-DRIED PULP: Cellulose pulp fibers that have not been dried since their liberation from wood or other plant source.

O

OVEN-DRY: [adj] Condition of cellulosic material that has been dried to constant mass (or weight) at a temperature of about 105°C. Syn. Bone-Dry.

OVEN-DRY WEIGHT: Taken as the moisture-free weight of cellulosic material. (Note: An oven-dry material will be completely moisture-free only if the air supplied to the drying oven has been previously dessicated.) Syn. Bone-Dry Weight.

P

PACKING DENSITY: See DENSITY.

PEBBLE MILL: See BALL MILL.

pH (of pulp): pH measured on an aqueous extract of a pulp sample that is obtained by standard procedure.

POST COLOR VALUE (P.C. Value): Change in the ratio of absorption coefficient to scattering coefficient for a sheet of paper upon aging under standard conditions. The post color value is related to the change in brightness before and after aging (or accelerated aging).

PROJECTED AREA: Total area occupied by all the fibers contained in a known mass of pulp if they are laid out singly in a field of view, a measure of maximum surface coverage for a given fiber stock.

PULP EVALUATION: Term applied either to measurement of basic fiber properties (length distribution, coarseness, fiber strength, fiber bonding, etc.) or to a beater evaluation.

PULP QUALITY INDEX: Attempt to characterize pulp quality by a single number. Several approaches have been used, one of which is based on a weighted average of a number of strength and optical properties. The concept of a quality index is generally discredited.

PULP STRENGTH INDEX: See COMBINED STRENGTH PARAMETER.

PULP WEIGHT FACTOR: Correction factor applied to microscopic fiber counts to calculate the weight proportions of two fiber types.

R

RANDOM SAMPLE: See GRAB SAMPLE.

REFERENCE PULP: See STANDARD PULP.

RELATIVE ABSORBENCY: Comparative absorbency test for fluffed pulp, usually evaluated by means of a "sinking time test", e.g., the time required for a wire basket containing 5 g of fluffed pulp to completely submerge after it is dropped onto a water surface.

RELATIVE BONDED AREA: Ratio of the total bonded area of fibers within an assemblage to one-half of the total external surface area of component fibers.

RESISTANCE TO DISINTEGRATION (of pulp): Relative ease or difficulty in disintegrating a sample of pulp, usually measured by the time required for complete disintegration of the sample under specified conditions. See also DISPERSI-BILITY.

RUNKEL RATIO: Method of characterizing the cross section of pulp fibers, expressed as the ratio of twice the wall thickness to the lumen width.

S

SCATTERING POWER: Ability of fibers in a sheet to scatter incident light.

SCHOPPER-RIEGLER SLOWNESS: See SLOWNESS.

SEASONING: See CONDITIONING.

SELF-SIZING (of pulp): Redistribution of dispersed resin particles over the fiber surface during storage. This phenomenon can be troublesome in the manufacture of absorptive tissues where the wettability of pulp fibers is lost during storage.

SHAPE FACTOR (S-FACTOR): Empirical number (conceptualized by Forgacs) that is intended to characterize a mechanical pulp sample with respect to the shape of the fibers, usually taken as the CSF of the 48/100-mesh fraction. The shape factor correlates with some handsheet properties. See also LENGTH FACTOR.

SHINER: Intact fiber bundle whose color is the same as the pulp fibers under reflected light.

SHIVE: Intact fiber bundle or fibrous mass having a contrasting color to the pulp fibers and having dimensions greater than some arbitrarily set minimum. In chemical pulp, a shive is usually defined as a fiber bundle that is at least 1 mm long and cannot pass through a 0.15 mm slit. See also SHINER.

SHIVE CONTENT (of pulp): Percentage of o.d. pulp retained on a standard slotted fractionating plate, usually with slit width of 0.15 mm.

SHIVE COUNT: Quantitative measurement of shive concentration based on counting the number of shives present in a pulp sheet or handsheet of known mass.

SHIVY PULP: Mill jargon for bleachable grade chemical pulp containing an inordinant concentration of shives.

SHORTENING (of fiber): Cleavage across the axis of a fiber into one or more pieces due to refining action. Syn. Cutting.

SIGMOID ADSORPTION CURVES: S-shaped adsorption and desorption curves for pulps as a function of increasing and decreasing relative humidity; they show the characteristic hysteresis effect.

SINKING TIME TEST: See RELATIVE ABSORBENCY.

SLIP PLANE: See DISLOCATION.

SLIT WIDTH: Width of slit openings in a laboratory flat screen, usually measured in thousandths of an inch, e.g., a "6-cut screen" has slit opening that are 0.006 inches (0.15 mm) wide. The slit width determines what portion of a pulp sample is classified as "screen rejects" or "debris".

SLOW: [adj] Descriptive term for a pulp that drains slowly.

SLOW BEATING: [adj] Refers to a pulp that requires a relatively high input of mechanical energy during beating or refining to develop the required strength properties. See also BEATABILITY.

SLOWNESS: Measure of pulp drainability, usually by means of the Schopper-Riegler instrument. Slowness and freeness scales have an inverse relationship. Slowness is defined as 1000 minus the number of ml of water collected from the side orifice of a standard tester when a dilute stock drains through a perforated plate under carefully controlled conditions. See also FREENESS, DRAIN TIME, and WETNESS.

SOFTNESS (of pulp): Subjective property of pulp not readily measurable; long, unbonded fibers have the best "feel".

SOLUTE EXCLUSION TECHNIQUE: Procedure for determining the fiber saturation point of a pulp sample. The sample at 25% consistency is placed in a known weight of dilute solution of a polymer with molecules of such size that they are too large to enter the cell wall pores. From the resultant change in concentration of the polymer solution once equilibrium is established, the amount of water that is associated with the fibers but does not contribute to the dilution of the polymer can be calculated.

SOMERVILLE SCREEN: Laboratory apparatus used for quantitative fractionation of debris from a pulp sample, consisting of a screen box fitted with a plate having narrow slits (usually 0.15 mm wide). Screening action on a dilute suspension is provided by means of a rubber diaphragm under the plate which is actuated by an eccentric mechanism.

SORBED WATER: See IMBIBED WATER.

SPECIFIC EXTERNAL SURFACE: External surface area of dry fibers per unit mass of pulp, usually reported in cm²/g; taken as a measure of the average fineness of the material.

SPECIFIC FILTRATION RESISTANCE: Measure of drainage resistance through a pulp pad during mat formation exclusive of the resistance due to the forming media itself or to any interaction between the forming media and the mat. Specific filtration resistance is a fundamental property that is independent of any particular instrument geometry.

SPECIFIC SURFACE: External surface area of wet fibers per unit dry mass of pulp, usually reported in cm²/g. Several methods of measurement have been used. Most commonly, the specific surface is inferred by measuring the water permeability of a mat of fibers under different degrees of compressibility.

SPECIFIC VOLUME: Volume of fibers per unit dry weight in cc/g.

SPLITTING: Physical separation of a fiber parallel to its axis due to refining action.

SPRINGBACK: Amount of expansion of a pulp mat following compression under specified conditions, a measure of resilience.

STANDARD CONDITIONS: Those conditions specified by standardized test procedures.

STANDARD ENVIRONMENT: Conditions of temperature and humidity agreed by convention as reference conditions for testing. In North America, the standard environment is 21°C and 50% relative humidity.

STANDARD PULP: Pulp that is used to calibrate or rationalize the results of diverse laboratory beater evaluations. It is a large, aged, uniform sample, similar to pulps that are normally tested. After accepted values for the standard pulp have been established, it can then be used as a basis of comparison between different sets of testing equipment or the same equipment over a span of time. Typically, routine test results are corrected by a factor relating the current value of the standard pulp to the accepted value. Syn. Reference Pulp, Calibration Pulp.

STEREOSCOPY: Science and art that deals with the use of binocular vision for the observation of a pair of perspective views, and with the methods for such viewing.

SURFACE ACTIVATION: Creation during refining of fresh surface area on pulp fibers which is available for water adsorption.

SWELLING: Sorption of water by fiber causing an increase in volume. See also DEGREE OF SWELLING.

SYNERGISM: Cooperative action between two agents which is greater than the sum of the individual contributions. Syn. Potentiation. (The opposite effect is termed "antagonism" or "antienergism".)

T _____

THEORETICAL COMMERCIAL DRYNESS (of pulp): Value used by trade custom for the equilibrium dry solids content of market pulp, normally taken as 90% by weight.

TWISTING: Producing fibers in spiral form due to torsional refining action.

U _____

UNIFORMITY: Consistent level of quality without large deviations from the norm. Uniformity is highly regarded for market pulps.

W _____

WALL FRACTION: Percent of the cross section occupied by the various wall layers, a means of characterizing pulp fibers. The wall fraction varies from 7% in thin-walled extremes to 95% in thick-walled extremes. The wall fraction is also sometimes expressed in terms of the ratio of the lumen width to the overall fiber diameter. See also RUNKEL RATIO.

WATER ABSORBENCY: See ABSORBENCY.

WATER RETENTION VALUE (WRV): Ratio of water to dry fiber after centrifuging a wet pulp sample for a specified time at a specified g-force (usually 30 minutes at 900g). The WRV is used as an indication of how tightly free moisture is held within the fiber structure, and is a good approximation of the fiber saturation point. Syn. Water Retention Ratio.

WEDGE SAMPLING: Method of sampling baled pulp to obtain a representative moisture sample. Bales are opened is successive lots of six, and in each bale a 12° wedge is cut from sheets in a specified way in each of five successively lower strata. (If the wedges from all six bales were then rearranged and placed above each other in space, they would form a circular staircase with 30 12° steps.)

WET FIBER COMPACTABILITY: Property of wet fibers that permits them to collapse into a compact mass, and thus make a more dense sheet. Relative wet compactability is measured by the density (or specific volume) of a standardized handsheet, and is dependent mainly on the thickness and nature of the fiber walls. (Wet fiber compactability is probably a manifestation of the same basic property as wet fiber flexibility.)

WET FIBER FLEXIBILITY: Property of fibers that affects their response to hydrodynamic forces during drainage and to mechanical forces during pressing, and is strongly related to such pulp properties as drainage, wet web strength and dry sheet strength. Several methods to measure wet fiber flexibility have been proposed including the use of mat compressibility, beam-type tests, and differentiation during screening. See also WET FIBER COMPACTABILITY.

WETNESS: Indication of pulp drainability obtained by measuring the thickness of the sedimentation layer after allowing a dilute stock to drain through a screen for a specified time. See also FREENESS, SLOWNESS, and DRAIN TIME.

WET STOCK: Stock with a low drainability.

WETTABILITY: Ability of pulp fibers to absorb water.

WETTING: Increasing capacity of pulp fibers to absorb water due to refining action.

WETTING TIME: See RELATIVE ABSORBENCY.

WET WEB STRENGTH (WWS): Tensile strength or tensile energy absorption measurement on a wet sheet, used as an indication of how well the wet web resists fracture as it passes through the various sections of the paper machine. Since wet web strength depends strongly on the solids content of the sheet, it is important that comparative measurements are carried out at (or can be corrected to) the same solids level.

WILDNESS TEST: Measure of pulp formability in which standardized handsheets are made and inspected under transmitted light to identify areas of low and high fiber concentration. These areas are punched out and weighed to measure in a relative way contrasting extremes of localized formation, and to calculate a "wildness index".

Chapter 12

Pulp and Stock Handling

(Includes: Washing, Screening, Cleaning, Refining,
Secondary Fiber Processing, Deinking, etc.)

A

ACCEPTED STOCK: Usable fiber that has passed through the screening and/or cleaning operations.

ACCEPT NOZZLE: See VORTEX FINDER.

ACCEPTS: That portion of material (e.g., chips, pulp) which passes through a separation process (e.g., screening, cleaning, classification) and is thereby upgraded sufficiently for continuation into the next stage of operations. (The portion which is not accepted must be further treated or eliminated from the process.)

AGITATOR EFFICIENCY (for a blending chest): Ratio of the actual mixing efficiency in a blending chest to the theoretical efficiency obtained with perfect mixing. (Theoretical efficiency can be calculated if the period and amplitude of the disturbance is known.)

AIR-FLOAT DRYING: Type of air-impingement drying utilized for pulp and paper webs in which the web is carried in a number of passes through a chamber where heated air is used both for drying and for supporting the sheet.

ASH CONTROL: Control of secondary stock ash content during deinking operations.

B

BACKFALL: Raised section of channel over which stock circulates in a beater just downstream of the beater roll which gives the stock a hydrostatic head for the return travel to the beater roll.

BAFFLE: Plate that regulates or directionalizes the flow of a fluid, as in a mixing tank or reaction vessel.

BALE: Solid, pressed packaging unit for pulp made up of sheets or slabs.

BALING: Forming a bale by compressing. (Note that a "bundle" is formed without compression.)

BALING OPERATION: Conversion of piles of pulp sheets or slabs coming from the pulp machine into ready-for-shipment bales. Discrete processing

steps carried out on each pile include weighing, compressing, wrapping, folding of wrapper, binding and printing. In many cases, these operations are fully automated.

BALING PRESS: Press in which a stack of pulp sheets or slabs is compressed into a more compact package.

BAR ANGLE: Angle between bars of opposing elements in a conical refiner (i.e., stator vs. rotor) or beater (i.e., beater roll vs. bedplate).

BAROMETRIC LEG: Strictly speaking, a downcomer from a vacuum compartment which handles liquid flow and is sealed at the bottom by a reservoir of liquid equal to the volume of the downcomer. In practice, the terms "barometric leg" and "drop leg" are often used interchangeably. See also DROP LEG.

BARRIER SCREENING: Stock screening process utilizing apertures that are sufficiently small (e.g., 0.2 mm slots) to block contaminant passage regardless of particle orientation. See also PROBABILITY SCREENING.

BARS: Projecting metal pieces on rotating beater rolls and refiner tackle which impart mechanical treatment to pulp fibers during beating and refining. Syn. Knives, Flybars.

BAR SCREEN: Set of closely spaced stationary bars set in the flume carrying groundwood pulp from the grinders, used to screen out coarse material. A scraper continuously removes pieces of wood and other large debris caught in the bars.

BAR WIDTH: Distance across the working face of a conical refiner bar or beater bar.

BASKET SCREEN: Centrifugal or pressure screen utilizing a screen basket.

BEATER: Batch equipment for mechanically treating pulp fibers, consisting of a heavy roll revolving against a bedplate set into a partitioned tub around which the stock is channeled. Beaters are traditional pieces of papermaking equipment, but have now been largely superceded by refiners. Industrial application is now limited to handling difficult furnishes such as jute, hemp, flax and cotton.

BEATER ROLL: Heavy, loaded rotating cylinder with axial bars along its circumferential surface which bring to bear significant contact presure against a bedplate in a conventional beater.

BEATER ROOM: Area in the paper mill where refining and other stock preparation operations are carried out. Syn. Stock Prep Area.

BEATING: Mechanical treatment of papermaking fibers to develop their optimum properties. Often the terms "beating" and "refining" are used interchangeably. More precisely, beating refers to a specific refining action where rotating bars opposite a stationary bedplate act on fibers flowing past perpendicular to the bars. In current usage, beating can refer to any laboratory pulp refining or milling process. See also REFINING.

BEATING SCHEDULE: (1) Nature and degree of beating or refining treatment specified for a particular stock. (2) Specific conditions for a beater treatment including spacing between roll and bedplate, loading of the roll, and time of beating.

BEATING TIME: Relative measure of the amount of mechanical energy imparted to a batch of pulp in the beater.

BED LOAD: Weight applied to the bedplate of a beater to obtain a specified contact pressure between the working surfaces of the beater roll and bedplate.

BEDPLATE: Fixed plate in the floor of a Hollander-type beater with bars or knives, situated directly under the beater roll.

BELT THICKENER: Equipment for dewatering a pulp mat up to 35–40% consistency on which the pulp moves between two wires over a series of rollers and press nips.

BLACK STOCK SCREENING: See HOT STOCK SCREENING.

BLANK NEWS: Grade of waste paper consisting of unprinted waste newsprint.

BLEND: Uniform mixture obtained by combining various stocks and additive streams.

BLENDING: Mixing of stock in a batch vessel or large surge vessel equipped with continuous infeed and outfeed streams, to produce some degree of uniformity. See also COMPLETE BLENDING.

BLENDING CHEST: Large tank equipped with adequate agitation to ensure complete mixing of its contents.

BLEND TIME: Method of characterizing the blending effect in an agitated vessel, defined as the time to achieve some specified degree of uniformity after introduction of a tracer.

BLINDING: (1) Blocking of the openings on a screen plate. (2) Filling in or blockage of open areas on a filter cloth to reduce filtrate flow capacity.

BLOW BOXES: Pressurized air ducts equipped with a series of openings which discharge the air for specified purposes, e.g., for air impingement or ventilation.

BLOWLINE REFINING: See HOT STOCK REFINING.

BOX CLIPPINGS: Grade of waste paper consisting of paperboard cuttings and trimmings from box manufacturing operations. Syn. Box Cuttings.

BREAKER: See PULPER. See also PRE-BREAKER.

BREAKER BEATER: Batch equipment for repulping, similar in appearance to a Hollander beater. The stock is channeled past a large rotating beater roll with cross bars set at a close clearance between a contoured cover plate and contoured floor.

BROWN STOCK WASHING: Processing step to remove residual liquor from brown stock. A number of methods are used commercially including rotary vacuum washers, rotary pressure washers, diffusion washers, horizontal belt filter, wash presses and dilution/extraction stages. Each method employs a series of stages with a countercurrent flow sequence.

BRUSHING OUT: Light refining action on pulp fibers, designed to achieve external fibrillation.

BUFFER STORAGE: Large-volume, high-density storage of unbleached or bleached pulp to provide surge capacity between the pulp and paper mills or between sections of the pulp mill, and thus allow for interruptions in either supply or demand.

C

CANISTER ASSEMBLY: Radial arrangement of a large number of small-diameter centrifugal cleaners in a circular housing, connected to common feed, accept and reject compartments.

CASCADE SEQUENCE: Refers to typical arrangement of screens and centrifugal cleaners where the function of secondary, tertiary, and subsequent stages is to concentrate the reject material and return usable fiber to the system. The reject stream from the primary stage constitutes the main feed to the secondary stage; the reject stream from the secondary stage constitutes the main feed to the tertiary stage; etc.

CENTRIFUGAL CLEANER: Cyclone device which removes unwanted particles from fiber suspensions by a combination of centrifugal force and fluid shear. The power source is the stock pump which generates a free vortex in the cleaner at the expense of a pressure drop. Syn. Centricleaner, Vortex Cleaner, Liquid Cyclone, Hydrocyclone, Cyclone Cleaner.

CENTRIFUGAL SCREEN: See GRAVITY CENTRIFUGAL SCREEN, PRESSURE SCREEN.

CHANNELING: Disproportionate rates of material mass flow through a reaction tower or storage tank due to wall effects or other causes, which result in nonuniform retention time of material within the vessel.

CHEST: Storage vessel or tank.

CIRCUMFERENTIAL VALVE: Stationary timing valve for rotary vacuum washers which is located on the periphery between the two segments of a two-piece drum.

CLAFLIN REFINER: See CONICAL REFINER.

CLEANER: See CENTRIFUGAL CLEANER.

CLEANER HEAD ASSEMBLY: Upper section of a centrifugal cleaner including the inlet nozzle and vortex finder.

CLEANING: See STOCK CLEANING.

CLEANING EFFICIENCY: For chemical pulps, percent removal of particle dirt. For other stocks, efficiency measurements are based on percent removal of the specific type of contaminants within the system.

CLEANLINESS RATIO: Ratio of the debris content (e.g., shives) in the screen accepts to the debris content in the feed.

CLEARANCE: Distance between projecting plate surfaces of a disc refiner.

CLOSED SCREENING: Chemical pulp mill screening operation in which no filtrate from the screened pulp is sewered, but is returned as wash water to the pulp washing operation. Syn. Inter-Stage Screening.

COARSE SCREENING: Screening operation to remove gross debris such as knots or uncooked chips from chemical pulps, and splinters or pieces of wood from groundwood pulps. See also DEKNOTTER, BULL SCREEN.

COLD PULPING: Generally refers to all repulping operations carried out at temperatures under 60°C.

COMPACTION BAFFLE: Stationary surface which is loaded against a rotating wire mold carrying a wet pulp mat; it serves to compress the pulp mat and thereby increase its consistency.

COMPLETE BLENDING: For a chest with continuous flow in and out, complete blending is achieved when the outlet composition is equal to the average tank composition and a sample taken at any point is within 2.5% of the average composition.

CONCENTRATION QUOTIENT: Concentration ratio of the liquor recovered to the liquor from the digester, used in sulfite mills as a measure of dilution effects during pulp washing.

CONICAL DISC REFINER: Refiner having sequential planar and conical refining zones, with the peripheral section being oriented through an angle of some 75° in relation to the planar section.

CONICAL REFINER: Equipment for mechanical treatment of pulp fibers consisting of a rotating conical plug (rotor) and a stationary conical housing (stator), each fitted with metal bars oriented lengthwise. The fibers flow parallel to the bars. The relative position of the plug determines the clearance of the bars and controls the amount of work done on the fibers. Conical refiners can be differentiated into low-angle types (Jordans) and high-angle types (Claflins).

CONTAMINANT CONCENTRATOR: Modification to an in-line pulper which removes lightweight contaminants from the pulper vortex before they are broken down by the action of the rotor into smaller pieces. Syn. Pulper Sweetener.

CONTAMINANTS: See CONTRARIES.

CONTINUOUS DIFFUSION WASHER: Vertical cylindrical vessel in which medium-consistency stock moves upwards between concentric perforated suction surfaces at the same time that wash liquid is introduced by rotating jets in the space between the suction surfaces. Syn. Continuous Diffuser.

CONTOURED PLATE: Screen plate having a contoured or profiled surface on the feed side which affects the hydrodynamic condition of the incoming stock, and is claimed to improve the efficiency of contaminant removal.

CONTRARIES: Term applied to all contaminant substances introduced into a secondary fiber system with waste papers. Syn. Contaminants.

CORE BLEED CLEANER: Centrifugal cleaner in which high-density contaminants are removed from the under flow tip while the overflow stream is split into two fractions by the use of two coaxial tubes. Lower-density contaminants migrate toward the center of the core and are removed via the central "core bleed" tube while the clean stock is recovered from the annulus.

COUCH ROLL: Soft rubber-covered roll used to transfer the sheet from a gravity decker. The couch roll applies gentle pressure to the sheet on the mold causing the sheet to adhere to the couch roll from which it is removed by a doctor.

COUNTERCURRENT FLOW: Relative movement of two streams of material in opposite directions so as to effect chemical, physical or thermal changes between the two streams. This type of flow is most frequently applied to multistage unit operations such as pulp washing and black liquor evaporation.

COUNTERCURRENT WASHING: Pulp washing in which pulp flow and wash water flow are in opposite directions. The term is applied both to true countercurrent washing (as occurs in the bottom of a Kamyr continuous digester) and to multistage washing that employs a countercurrent flow sequence between stages.

CRUMB PULP: Pulp that has been pressed to high consistency (45–55%) and then crumbled or separated into small wads to facilitate handling as a bulk solid for storage or shipment.

CURLATOR: Equipment for processing screen rejects, designed to rub and curl fiber bundles at high consistency to liberate fibers with minimum damage.

CURVED SCREEN: Thickening and fractionating device utilizing a vertical, curved screen plate. The fiber suspension is injected at a small angle against the upper part of the plate and then slides down the plate. The coarse fraction retained on the plate undergoes continuous thickening while the fine fraction is removed with the bulk of the water.

CURVILINEAR SURFACE: Term denoting the continuous surface of a rotating cylinder, e.g., the area of mat formation on a decker or rotary vacuum washer.

CUTTER-LAYBOY: Equipment at the end of the pulp machine for cutting and collecting pulp sheets into bales. The full-width sheet from the dryer is typically conveyed to a set of slitters which cut to width, then to a rotating fly knife which cuts to length. The cut sheets are then conveyed on tapes to the layboy boxes where they are stacked on the layboy table. A hydraulic system lowers the table as the stacks get higher. When the stacks have reached a predetermined height, layboy "fingers" come out to support oncoming sheets while the table lowers and discharges to a conveyor. The emptied table is then raised and assumes the load from the fingers to begin another cycle of accumulating sheets for bales.

D

DANCER ROLL: Free-moving turning roll which changes its position (e.g., vertically) in response to varying sheet tension, used in conjunction with nip roll to take up slack and control sheet tension into and out of an airborne pulp dryer. See also NIP ROLL.

DEAD BEATEN: [adj] Term descriptive of pulp that has been heavily refined to a low freeness. See also GREASY.

DEASHING: Removal of mineral fillers from recycled paper stock.

DEBONDING AGENT: Chemical which can be added to kraft fluff pulp to aid in the fluffing operation. (Although a debonding agent significantly reduces the power requirement for fluffing, it also makes the fibers more hydrophobic, and thus adversely affects absorption properties).

DECKER: See GRAVITY THICKENER.

DEFIBERING: Separation of fiber bundles into constituent fibers by mechanical action. The operation of defibering is most commonly applied during processing of semichemical or high-yield pulps where the initial chemical digestion is insufficient to release discrete fibers. Syn. Defiberization, Defibration.

DEFILLERS: Chemical additives used during waste paper processing to facilitate removal of filler material. These special polymers cause the filler material to float so that it can be removed and dumped.

DEFLAKER: In-line equipment for separating and dispersing pulp fibers by producing zones of intense hydraulic shear, utilized primarily in the processing of secondary fiber.

DEGREE OF REFINING: Extent of mechanical action on pulp fibers as measured by changes in pulp properties, most commonly by changes in pulp drainage or freeness.

DEINKABILITY: Ability of printed waste papers to be deinked and produce an acceptable papermaking material.

DE-INKING or DEINKING: Removal of ink and other extraneous materials (contraries) from printed, reclaimed papers by mechanical disintegration and chemical treatment, with subsequent washing or flotation separation. See also WASH DEINKING, FLOTATION DEINKING.

DEKNOTTING: Coarse screening operation to remove gross reject material from chemical pulp brown stock, usually performed prior to washing. The reject material, which is composed mainly of compression wood, is either discarded as waste or returned to the digester infeed. Syn. Knotting.

DENSITY: Percentage of fibrous material by weight in a stock, normally applied when the percentage is above 10%. See also CONSISTENCY, DRYNESS.

DESHIVE REFINING: Low-energy refining of high yield stock with the objective of defibering the incorporated shive material and producing an essentially shive-free stock without significantly reducing freeness. Syn. Deshiving.

DEVIL-TOOTH PLATES: Intermeshing disc refiner plates with teeth that are coarse, unconnected individual units arranged in concentric rings, used principally for breakdown of kraft knots and other gross reject material.

DEWATERING: Process of partially removing water. When applied to pulp stock, the preferred term is "thickening".

DIFFUSION WASHING: Method of pulp washing where the wash liquor is passed through a mass of pulp stock (or cooked chips) at a slow rate, thus allowing time for diffusion of dissolved liquor solids from the interior of fibers. See also CONTINUOUS DIFFUSION WASHER, PRESSURE DIFFUSION WASHER.

DILUTION/EXTRACTION WASHING: See EXTRACTION WASHING.

DILUTION FACTOR (DF): Weight of water or wash liquor per unit weight of oven-dry pulp added to the liquor system during washing. The dilution factor is a measure of the amount of wash water applied which is in excess of that required for theoretical displacement. Syn. Excess Wash Liquor.

DILUTION RING: High-pressure water header equipped with a number of equally-spaced nozzles, located within the bottom circumference of a high-density storage tank or bleach tower; used to dilute the stock down to a consistency suitable for pumping.

DILUTION WATER: Water added to stock to reduce its consistency.

DISC FILTER: Rotating suction filter consisting of a number of closely spaced, coaxial ring-shaped discs with screen surfaces on both sides, typically used to recover fine fibers from white water. Syn. Disc Save-All.

DISC KNOTTER: Design of pressure knotter utilizing two discs with cam-shaped projections rotating between two fixed rings, thus forming four slots for accepting stock. The discs create a pulsating movement in the pulp suspension, keeping the slots clear of knots and preventing plugging.

DISC PRESS: Thickening device in which pulp is pressed between conical screen surfaces on two adjacent rotating discs.

DISC REFINER: Equipment utilizing two opposing discs for continuous defiberization of chips and screenings or for mechanical treatment of papermaking fibers. The following configurations are used: rotating disc opposite stationary disc; two opposing rotating discs; rotating double-sided disc between two stationary discs.

DISINTEGRATION: See REPULPING.

DISPLACEMENT RATIO (DR): Measure of displacement washing efficiency. For brown stock washing, it is calculated by determining the actual reduction in black liquor solids and dividing this number by the maximum possible reduction.

DISPLACEMENT WASHING: Basic method of pulp washing which involves formation of a pulp mat followed by application of wash liquid to the mat. In principle, the wash liquid (e.g. water) displaces the liquid associated with the pulp (e.g. black liquor). The displacement principle in utilized in most pulp washing systems.

DOUBLE-DISC REFINER: Disc refiner utilizing two opposed independently rotating discs.

DOUBLE DILUTION: Lowering the consistency of high density stock in two stages. Typically, the bulk of the water is added in the dilution zone of the storage tank and the balance is added to the pump suction.

DOUBLE SCREENING: Pulp screening operations utilizing two stages of primary screens, either in series or at different points in the process, e.g., screening of both unbleached and bleached pulp.

DOUBLE-WIRE PRESS: Forming/pressing equipment for pulp machines, consisting of two endless wire belts converging to form a long decreasing wedge. Stock is distributed from a closed headbox into the wedge where initial dewatering and sheet formation take place. Dewatering continues in an "S" section followed by an integral inclined press nip.

DRAINER: See ROTARY DRAINER.

DROP LEG: Long downcomer from a vacuum washer which discharges filtrate and air (usually through a seal chamber), and creates the vacuum for washer operation by a syphon effect. The drop leg does not have to be sealed to operate, but is normally sealed to prevent more air from being drawn into the liquid. Syn. Seal Leg. See also BAROMETRIC LEG.

DRUM: Cylindrical rotating filter element, the major component of all drum filters.

DRUM DISPLACER WASHER: Novel, multistage washing apparatus consisting of a perforated drum which is divided into several sectors by steel separators. Nonrotating sealing bars, in contact with the rotating separators, separate the drum into as many as four discrete washing stages. Surrounding the drum is a casing which forms the liquid inlet chambers for the washing stages and to which are attached the sealing bars. All washing takes place near the boiling point under pressurized, submerged conditions excluding any air entrainment.

DRUM FILTER: Any equipment employing a rotating screen drum. This class of process equipment includes rotary vacuum filters, rotary pressure filters, and gravity thickeners.

DRUM SUBMERGENCE: Percent of the drum diameter which is submerged in the slurry. Drum submergence typically varies from 25 to 55%. Syn. Diametrical Submergence.

DRY SHREDDING: See FLUFFING.

E _____

EFFECTIVE POWER: As applied to refiners, refers to the power actually consumed by mechanical treatment of fiber; calculated as the total power minus the no-load power. Syn. Net Power.

EFFECTIVE REFINING AREA: As applied to refiners, bar-to-bar contact area between refining surfaces for a specified time or stock throughput.

ELUTRIATOR: Attachment below the cone on some designs of centrifugal cleaners where elutriation (i.e. dilution water) is added to refloat acceptable fiber into the apex of the cone.

ENGINE: Term applied in the papermill to the Hollander beater or other production-size beater.

EXCESS WASH LIQUOR (EW): See DILUTION FACTOR.

EXTRACTION WASHING: System of pulp washing utilizing a series of dilution and thickening steps. The efficiency of an extraction washing stage is dependent on the ratio of the discharge to the incoming consistency and the amount of dilution water added to the system. Syn. Dilution Washing, Dilution/Extraction Washing.

F _____

FACE: Filtration (sur)face on a rotary vacuum washer or decker.

FACE LENGTH: Axial dimension of the filtration surface on a rotary washer or decker. Drum Length.

FACE WIRE: See FILTRATION MEDIA.

FAN NOZZLE: Spray nozzle which produces a relatively flat, fan-shaped liquid distribution. See also WHISTLE SHOWER.

FEED BOX: Entry point of stock into the vat of a rotary washer or decker, which serves to distribute the stock uniformly across the face of the rotating mold.

FIBER BUNDLE: Cluster of parallel fibers which are bonded together.

FIBERIZER: In-line equipment for separating and dispersing pulp fibers.

FIBER RECOVERY: Salvage of fiber from overflow white water by screening, filtration, sedimentation or flotation. Equipment for fiber recovery is often called a "saveall".

FIBRILIZER: See PRE-BREAKER.

FILLER PIECES: Wooden blocks inserted between the bars in a conical refiner or beater.

FILLET: Concave junction between two intersecting surfaces, e.g., between the vertical walls and the bottom surface of a storage tank.

FILLING: Arrangement of bars and filler pieces in a beater or refiner.

FILTER: Class of equipment used to remove solids from liquids by causing the liquid to flow through a filtration medium with openings too fine to permit the particles to pass. See also ROTARY VACUUM FILTER.

FILTER CLOTH: Outer mesh covering of a rotary washer or decker through which the filtrate passes and on which stock is retained. It covers the entire drum surface except for the drum ends. Various weaves and materials are used depending on the application. Syn. Face Wire.

FILTER TANK: See FILTER VAT.

FILTER VAT: Housing surrounding the lower portion of a filter drum and holding the slurry to be filtered. Filter vats may have a rounded or V-bottom shape depending on the type of agitator required. Syn. Filter Tank.

FILTER VAT AGITATOR: Mechanism located in the bottom of a filter vat for the purpose of keeping the solids uniformly suspended in the slurry to be filtered. Syn. Filter Tank Agitator.

FILTRATION MEDIUM: Any material through which liquid passes for the purpose of intercepting fibers or other solid particles. Syn. Filter Medium.

FINE SCREENING: Screening with relatively small perforations; the definitive screening operation as distinct from coarse screening.

FLASH DRYING: Process where pulp is first pressed and fluffed, then injected into a stream of hot gases where the high-temperature heat of the gas stream causes the moisture to flash into vapor.

FLAT BAND WASHER: Design of pulp washer on which the pulp is first dewatered and then subjected to a series of countercurrent washes while transported from the inlet to the discharge on an endless steel band filter medium.

FLAT SCREEN: Stock screen consisting of a sloped flume-like box with a slotted plate forming the bottom. As dilute stock flows over the vibrating plate, accepted fiber passes through the narrow slots while rejects flow over the end of the plate.

FLAT WIRE WASHER: See HORIZONTAL BELT WASHER.

FLOTATION CELL: Process vessel in which grey stock is mixed with air in such a way that ink and dirt particles become attached to small air bubbles. The mixture is retained for sufficient time to allow the dirt-encrusted bubbles to rise to the surface, where they are skimmed off as a dirty froth.

FLOTATION DEINKING: Deinking process for secondary fiber in which the dispersed ink particles are removed by aerating the stock in a series of flotation cells, causing the light flocs of ink particles to rise to the surface where they are skimmed off.

FLOTATION PURGE: Adjunct equipment on continuous waste paper pulper to remove lightweight contaminants.

FLOWING FULL: Situation in a drop leg when air and filtrate are throughly mixed and effective leg length for generating vacuum is at a maximum. When air separates from the filtrate, the situation is described as "pipe not flowing full".

FLOW RATE: Amount of material that moves past a reference point (e.g., entering or leaving a process) per unit time.

FLOW RESISTANCE: Any impediment to free flow within a pipe or other pressurized conduit or within an open channel, such as contractions, bends and blockages.

FLOWTHROUGH CLEANER: Type of reverse flow cleaner in which both the accept and reject exits are placed at the opposite end from the feed inlet.

FLUFFER: Device to separate pressed or dried pulp into individual fibers. Hammermills and tooth-roll devices have traditionally been used as fluffers, but rotating-disc devices are now generally preferred.

FLUFFING: (1) Operation on pressed pulp to dissociate and disperse the compressed fiber and thereby expose a large amount of surface area. (2) Defibration of dry pulp. Syn. Dry Shredding.

FLUIDIZATION POINT: Minimum amount of shear stress applied to a fiber suspension at which the suspension assumes liquid-like flow characteristics.

FLUID MOBILITY: See MOBILITY.

FLYBARS: See BARS.

FOAM: Gas dispersed in a liquid in a ratio such that the bulk density of the mixture approaches that of a gas rather than a liquid. When foam collects at the air/liquid interface, it is called "surface foam". When foam is mixed into liquid and is only slightly visible on the surface, it is called "entrained foam". See also STATIC FOAM.

FOAM BREAKER: Device for breaking down foam into its constituent parts of liquid and air, typically installed on black liquor seal tank vent lines. Mechanical devices are commonly used, but steam-powered sonic devices have also been applied for this service.

FOAM INHIBITION: Ability of a defoamer to sustain foamless conditions for a sustained period.

FOAM STABILITY: Relative persistance of a foam as measured by the time dependent changes in such foam properties as bulk density, rheology and structure.

FOAM TANK: Tank which receives foam from black liquor oxidation or brown stock washer seal tanks and houses foam breaking equipment.

FRACTIONATOR: Device used to separate stock into two or more fractions on the basis of fiber length, fiber stiffness, or other property.

FREEBOARD: Space or height in a storage tank or chip bin above the level of stored material.

FREE DISCHARGE: Atmospheric discharge, e.g., into an open channel.

FROTATION: Unique mechanical action achieved by two intermeshing screws working on high-consistency stock. The frotation action implies a combination of compression, shearing and twisting causing separation and curling of fibers.

FROTH FLOTATION: Process of removing dispersed ink particles from deinked stock in which the ink particles adhere to bubbles and are removed as part of the froth.

FURNISH: Fibrous materials and additives in correct proportion being prepared for conversion into paper or paperboard.

FURNISHING: Process of charging a beater with pulp and nonfibrous additives.

G

GO-DEVIL: Stiff piece of cardboard used to thread the sheet through a vacuum dryer.

GRADES OF PULP: See PULP GRADES.

GRAVITY CENTRIFUGAL SCREEN: Gravity-fed screening device utilizing a horizontal cylindrical screen with round holes up to 3 mm in diameter and with an internal "paddle-wheel" type rotor to impart centrifugal force to the stock mass and keep the screen plate clean.

GRAVITY FLOW: Flow of material from higher to lower elevation due to the force of gravity alone.

GRAVITY THICKENER: Device for increasing the consistency of dilute fiber suspensions to 2–8 percent, consisting of a rotating screen drum which is wholly or partially submerged in an open vat containing the fiber suspension. Water flows into the cylinder by virtue of the difference in liquid level between the vat and cylinder. In one type of design (commonly called a "slusher" or "slush thickener"), the stock moves from the inlet side of the vat through the dewatering zone to the other side of the vat where the stock is discharged. In another design (sometimes called a "roll-type thickener"), pulp is retained on the cylinder and is couched off by a rubber roll. Syn. Decker.

GREASY: [adj] Term used to describe the feel of a well beaten or well refined stock. See also DEAD BEATEN.

GREY STOCK: Secondary fiber stock containing dispersed ink and dirt particles.

GRINDING IN: Procedure for new or refilled conical refiners allowing for soaking and swelling of the wood separators and smoothing of the bars by pumping through a slurry of fine, screened sand.

GUNK: Colloquialism for unidentified deposits in the secondary pulp or papermaking system.

H

HALFSTUFF: Rag pulp that is ready to be charged to the beater. After beating, rag pulp is called "stuff".

HANGING BAFFLE: Baffle suspended from above to regulate a flow opening in the bottom of a channel or tank.

HARD BEATING: [adj] Describes pulps produced from rags, rope or jute that require large inputs of mechanical energy to condition the fibers for papermaking.

HARD STOCK: Papermaking stock containing a significant proportion of jute, rag or rope fibers.

HARDWOOD PULP: Pulp produced from hardwood.

HELICAL: [adj] Having the shape or appearance of a helix or screw.

HELICAL PULPER: Mixing chamber with a helical-shaped rotor, used to repulp and prescreen waste paper, broke and pulp bales.

HIGH CONSISTENCY REFINING (HCR): Vague terminology which usually refers to the refining of stock or screen rejects within the 20 to 30% range of consistency.

HIGH-DENSITY STOCK: Imprecise designation for stock of medium-to-high consistency; typically refers to stock in the 8–15% range of consistency. Syn. Thick Stock.

HIGH-DENSITY STORAGE: Storage of pulp within the 8 to 15% range of consistency. See also BUFFER STORAGE.

HIGH-HEAT WASHING: Name given (by Kamyr) to the countercurrent diffusion washing which takes place at 130–140° in the bottom of the Kamyr continuous digester.

HOLDBACK: Reverse pumping effect of a low-consistency disc refiner when the plates are run in the opposite direction of their normal rotation. Holdback is not energy-efficient, but is utilized in some instances to avoid overpressurization of the refiner.

HOLLANDER: Type of production-size beater.

HORIZONTAL BELT WASHER: Equipment for thickening and washing brownstock employing a horizontally moving filter fabric on which a fibrous mat is continuously formed and carried through a series of wash displacements.

HOT DISPERSION: Process of dispersing hot melt contaminants in a waste paper furnish by defibering action at high consistency and high temperature.

HOT-STOCK REFINING: Fiberizing of high-yield kraft pulp in the presence of hot residual liquor. Syn. Blow Line Refining, Black Stock Refining.

HOT-STOCK SCREENING: Screening of high-yield kraft pulp following cooking and refining, and prior to washing. Syn. Black Stock Screening.

HYBRID DEINKING: Deinking system utilizing both flotation and washing techniques. Typically, the majority of ink particles are removed by initial flotation treatment, and a subsequent washing stage is employed for further removal of ink particles and for ash control.

HYDRATED STOCK: Well refined or well beaten stock which has enhanced ability to hold water.

HYDRAULIC CAPACITY: Maximum liquid throughput rate. For pressure screens, the hydraulic capacity is equal to the stock feed rate plus the dilution water rate and is dependent on stock consistency.

HYDROCYCLONE: See CENTRIFUGAL CLEANER.

HYDROFOIL: Unit within a pressure screen which rotates with a slinging motion creating a series of pressure and vacuum pulses on the screen surface which serve to drive fibers through the screen basket and prevent plugging of the holes.

I_____

INCLINED SCREW DRAINER: Medium consistency thickening device in which a screw moves stock upwards in a perforated inclined cylinder. Water drains through the perforations and the thickened stock is discharged at the top at 8 to 15% consistency.

INTENSITY FACTOR (for a refiner): Net energy applied per unit effective refining area. This parameter provides a means of comparing refiners and/or tackle independent of stock throughput.

INTERNAL VALVE: Timing valve for a vacuum washer that is located at a point close to the center of the axis. This location has the advantage (compared to the more conventional trunnion area) of shorter pipe lengths and utilizes radial ducts between the channels and the valve.

INTER-STAGE SCREENING: See CLOSED SCREENING.

J_____

JOG: Horizontal offset in a vertical pipe, for example in a drop leg.

JORDAN REFINER: See CONICAL REFINER.

JUNKER: Adjunct equipment on a continuous waste paper pulper that separates, collects and removes heavy contaminants. The material is thrown into a recess at the side of the pulper by centrifigal force and is usually removed through a "junking tower". Syn. Junk Remover.

K_____

KITE: Large piece of fabric with pockets to pick up air, used with some designs of air impingement dryer to carry the tail (narrow strip of pulp sheet) through the dryer section during startup.

KNEADER PULPER: Equipment consisting of a single-shaft disintegrator for the defibering of high consistency stock (about 30%) by generating intense stock friction in the kneading zone. The operation is often carried out at high temperature in a pressurized environment.

KNOTS: That fraction of pulp which is retained on a 3/8-inch perforated plate. These rejects may be "true knots" (i.e., compression wood) or uncooked chips, often referred to as "false knots".

KNOTTER: Coarse screening device for removing gross oversize material from unwashed brown stock. Pressure centrifugal-type screens are most commonly used for this application. See also DISC KNOTTER.

KNOTTER REJECTS: That portion of the pulp which is retained on the knotter screen and is separated from the deknotted stock.

KOLLERGANG: Obsolete type of beater utilizing two heavy stone rolls rotating around an annular trough containing the stock, causing the fibers to become crushed and abraded. A miniature version has been used as a laboratory beater.

L

LAP PULP: See WETLAP PULP.

LAY-BOY: Receiving table with partitions for collecting and accumulating piles of sheets from the slitter cutter.

LEACHING: Desorption and diffusion of solute from within pulp fibers (e.g., as occurs during pulp washing).

LIQUID CYCLONE: See CENTRIFUGAL CLEANER.

LONG FIBER: Softwood chemical pulp.

LONG PULP: Refined stock that retains a predominance of longer fibers, i.e., stock that has been given a refining treatment that preserves fiber length.

M

MARKET PULP: Pulp of any type that is produced for sale on the open market or on contract to specific customers. It is then used as raw material for paper and other products.

MARKET PULP MILL: Pulp mill that produces finished pulp for sale under contract or in the open market.

MECHANICAL TREATMENT: Abrading, bruising, kneading, shearing, twisting, crushing, bending, etc. of pulp fibers by machine action; typically as carried out in a refiner or beater with the objective to develop certain desirable characteristics.

MEDIUM-CONSISTENCY SCREENING: Screening of stock at consistencies as high as 13% by applying shear forces of sufficient intensity for complete fluidization of the fiber suspension at the face of the separating screen.

MIDFEATHER: Center partition in a beater or stock chest which provides a flow channel and facilitates dispersion and mixing.

MINTON DRYER: See VACUUM DRYER.

MIXED PAPERS: Waste paper collected from sources such as schools and offices, which contain a high percentage of better grades, but is unsorted.

MIXING EFFICIENCY (ME): Measure of blending chest effectiveness, usually defined as ME = 1—DF where DF is the dampening factor, i.e., the ratio of the amplitude of the output to the input fluctuations. See also AGITATOR EFFICIENCY.

MOBILITY (of a fluid): Ratio of the permeability of a filter medium (e.g., a pulp mat) to the viscosity of the fluid flowing through it (e.g., wash liquor), a parameter that characterizes the resistance to flow for a particular displacement washing system.

MOBILITY RATIO: Ratio of the mobility of the displaced liquid (e.g., black liquor) to the mobility of the displacing liquid (e.g., wash liquor), a parameter of displacement washing systems. At mobility ratios above one, microchanneling occurs due to the greater mobility of the displacing liquid.

MOLD or MOULD: Any support structure that is an integral part of a sheet forming apparatus, e.g., the cylindrical skeleton on which a woven wire is attached, as for a vacuum washer.

MORDEN: Type of production-size beater.

MUCILAGE: Small gelatinous particles formed on the fibers during refining due to partial solubilization of hemicelluloses. Syn. Gels.

MULTIDISC REFINER: Refiner for low-consistency stock having a series of alternately rotating and stationary discs mounted within a conventional-type housing. Stock enters the refiner from both ends.

N

NET POWER: See EFFECTIVE POWER.

NET SPECIFIC ENERGY: As applied to refiners, the net energy applied per unit weight of pulp throughput.

NIP ROLLS: Two-roll unit used in conjunction with a dance roll to control sheet speed in and out of an air-borne pulp dryer. Syn. Nipping Section. See also DANCE ROLL.

N-NUMBER: See NORDEN EFFICIENCY FACTOR.

NODULE: Small case-hardened particles of pulp that are sometimes formed during flash drying operations. They are difficult to disperse during subsequent pulping operations. Syn. Pill, Fish Eye.

NO-LOAD POWER: As applied to refiners, refers to the power required to rotate the unit against the stock flow without performing work on the fibers. Syn. Idling Power. See also EFFECTIVE POWER.

NORDEN EFFICIENCY FACTOR: (N-Number) Number of mixing stages required to achieve a given washing result at a specified dilution factor (after H.V. Norden). The Norden efficiency factor allows direct comparison of different washing methods, and the total Norden efficiency for a system made up of different types of washing equipment in series may be found by adding the N numbers for the various components.

O

OVERISSUE NEWS: Grade of reclaimed waste paper consisting of newspapers that were issued, but not sold. Syn. Unsold News.

P

PAPER STOCK: Reclaimed waste papers that have been sorted into different grades.

PARCHMENTIZING: Beating or refining pulp with sufficient energy input to produce a stock suitable for greaseproof paper.

PELLETIZATION: Forming of high-consistency pulp into worm-shaped particles for bulk handling.

PERFORATED PLATE: Screen plate with straight-through holes, usually made by a punch. Syn. Punched Plate.

PERNICIOUS CONTRARIES: Contaminant materials in the paper recycling system that cannot be removed by conventional methods.

PLATE CLEARANCE: See CLEARANCE.

PLATES: See REFINER PLATES.

PLUG: Cone or rotor of a conical refiner.

POST-CONSUMER WASTE PAPER: Paper discarded from residences, institutions (e.g., schools, hospitals), and businesses (e.g., offices, stores).

PRE-BREAKER: In-line equipment that utilizes hydraulic shear and attrition to reduce the size of high-yield stock bundles prior to refining, thus allowing the refiner plates to be set closer together and still accept the mass flow. Syn. Fibrilizer.

PRE-REFINING: Refining carried out in the pulp mill for the purpose of defibering knots and other fiber bundles, usually limited to the handling of high-yield chemical stocks and reject streams. Syn. Prefining. See also HOT STOCK REFINING.

PRESSATE: Liquid which separates from solid/liquid mixture on being passed through a pressing operation.

PRESSURE DIFFUSION WASHER: Vertical, tapered, cylindrical vessel containing an annular space through which blow stock moves at full digester pressure in a downward direction. Wash liquor is pumped into a central core, then flows from outlets through the pulp mat, and finally through a screen plate into an annular channel formed by the screen plate and the outer wall of the vessel. Syn. Pressure Diffuser.

PRESSURE SCREEN: Pulp screening equipment with tangential entry at full line pressure and passage of accepted stock through a perforated plate, which is kept clean by means of a rotating hydrofoil or other rotating element designed to provide alternating pressure and vacuum pulses.

PRESSURE WASHER: See ROTARY PRESSURE WASHER.

PRIMARY CLEANERS: Centrifugal cleaners which handle the entire stock flow as well as certain recycle streams (e.g., secondary cleaner accepts). Generally, all accepted stock must pass through the primary cleaners.

PRIMARY SCREENS: Screens which handle the entire stock flow as well as certain recycle streams (e.g., secondary screen accepts). Generally, all accepted stock must pass through the perforations of the primary screens.

PROBABILITY SCREENING: Stock screening process utilizing relatively large apertures (e.g., round holes) through which undesirable particles can pass on their minimum dimensions, but passage is restricted by other factors such as particle orientation or particle interaction.

PULPABILITY: Relative ability of dry pulp sheets or pulp slabs to be dispersed in water to form slush.

PULPER: Batch or continuous equipment for dispersing dry pulp or waste paper in water to prepare papermaking stock. Syn. Breaker, Repulper.

PULPER STOCK: Stock prepared from dry broke, purchased pulp, waste paper, etc. in the pulper.

PULPER SWEETENER: See CONTAMINANT CONCENTRATOR.

PULP GRADES: Various types and qualities of pulp for different end uses, including chemical, semi-chemical and mechanical pulps made from various sources.

PULPING: See REPULPING.

PULP MACHINE: Equipment for preparing pulp for shipment, usually consisting of a forming section, pressing section, drying section and cutter-layboy. In a wet-lap pulp machine the drying step is omitted.

PULP MILL: Factory or plant where fibrous raw materials are processed into pulp.

PULP PROCESSABILITY: All-encompassing term referring to a pulp's relative performance with respect to disintegration, refining, draining, forming, pressing, drying, etc.

PULP ROLL: Web of pulp wound up in a roll. Syn. Roll Pulp.

PULP STORAGE: See HIGH-DENSITY STORAGE, BUFFER STORAGE.

PULP SUBSTITUTE: High quality grade of waste paper consisting of unprinted wood-free paper sheets, cuttings and trimmings.

PULP TRANSPORT: Movement of pulp from one processing stage to another by pumping, conveying, or other method.

PURGING: Term used to describe the continuous or periodic ejection of reject material from certain types of pressure screens or centrifugal cleaners.

Q ⎯⎯⎯⎯⎯⎯⎯⎯⎯⎯⎯⎯⎯⎯

QUATERNARY: [adj] Term denoting the fourth stage of such multi-stage processes as screening or centrifugal cleaning.

R ⎯⎯⎯⎯⎯⎯⎯⎯⎯⎯⎯⎯⎯⎯

RAG BOILER: Cylindrical or spherical rotating drum in which rags are cooked at elevated temperature and pressure with caustic soda or other alkali agents.

RAGGER: Adjunct equipment on a continuous waste paper pulper that removes the "rag rope", made up of non-fibrous contaminants introduced with the waste paper bales.

RAG PULP: Pulp produced from cotton, flax, hemp, or ramie in the form of textile waste or textile returns.

RAG ROPE: Intertwinement of wires, strings, rags, plastic material and other contaminants which is removed continuously from a ragger as an elongated twisted body resembling a rope (up to 30 cm in diameter). Syn. Debris Rope.

RAYON REJECTS: Dissolving pulps that are off-specification for chemical conversion. They are used in papermaking applications where softness and absorbency are the prime requisites.

RECLAIMED WASTE PAPER: See SECONDARY FIBER.

RECYCLED FIBER: See SECONDARY FIBER.

REFINER: Equipment for continuous mechanical conditioning of papermaking fiber, of which there are two major designs. See CONICAL REFINER, DISC REFINER.

REFINER CHEST: Tank which holds the stock being pumped to the refiners.

REFINER PLATES: Segmented castings which are mounted on the stationary and rotating disks of a refiner to provide the working surfaces. These surfaces consist of various patterns of bars, grooves and dams, and are tapered radially from the center.

REFINING: Mechanical treatment of papermaking fibers to develop their optimum properties. More precisely, refining refers to the action carried out in conical or disc-type refiners where the fibers flow parallel to the bar crossings. See also BEATING, REFINER.

REFINING DEGREE: See DEGREE OF REFINING.

REFINING EFFICIENCY: Effective power divided by total power to the refiner, expressed as a percent, a measure of energy efficiency.

REFINING INTENSITY: Measure of relative severity of refining, calculated as the ratio of net energy input to effective refining area, both calculated on the same basis. See also SPECIFIC EDGE LOADING.

REGULATOR BOX: Device for maintaining a fixed level in a continuous pulper, consisting of a small-diameter cylindrical tank (the same height as the pulper) with a fixed dam dividing the "box" into two vertical compartments. A movable weir, raised and lowered by a handwheel, adjusts the stock level.

REJECT RATE: Percent of fiber entering a screen or centrifugal cleaner that is discharged with the reject flow.

REPULPABILITY: Relative ability of waste paper to be converted into good quality secondary fiber. Repulpability infers that adhesives, tapes and additives are water-dispersible. Syn. Recyclability.

REPULPING: Operation of dispersing dry pulp or high-density pulp in water to form a slush or stock. In practice, this operation can be either batch or continuous. Syn. Pulping, Disintegration, Slushing, Breaking.

REVERSE FLOW: Flow in a direction opposite to normal flow.

REVERSE FLOW CLEANER: Centrifugal cleaner that has been modified to remove lightweight contaminants. The underflow nozzle is enlarged to become the accept discharge, while the overflow nozzle is reduced in diameter to become the lightweight reject discharge. See also FLOW-THROUGH CLEANER.

RIFFLER: Modified settling trough through which low-consistency stock is channeled at low velocity, allowing relatively heavy particles to settle out.

ROD MILL: Equipment used for pulp beating and defibering consisting of a hollow, rotating cylinder filled with hardened steel rods approximately 8 cm in diameter. As stock moves through the cylinder, the rotating action causes the rods to roll downhill over one another with a crushing and rubbing effect on the fibers.

ROLL PULP: Web of pulp wound up in a roll.

ROLL-TYPE THICKENER: See GRAVITY THICKENER.

ROTARY DRAINER: Equipment to free water from easily drained materials such as knots, secondary screen rejects or chips, consisting of a rotating perforated drum with an internal scroll to carry the draining material from the inlet end to the discharge.

ROTARY PRESSURE WASHER: Equipment for thickening and washing brownstock, similar in principle and application to the rotary vacuum washer except that positive external pressure (rather than internal vacuum) is used for mat formation, dewatering and liquor displacement.

ROTARY SCREEN: Coarse stock screen consisting of a large rotary shell fitted with perforated screen plates and having an internal spiral arrangement. Stock enters at one end and the accepted fiber is washed through the screen plates by high-volume showers. The reject material travels to the opposite end of the cylinder (assisted by the spiral) where it is discharged.

ROTARY VACUUM FILTER: Equipment for thickening stock, similar in design to a rotary vacuum washer, but without provision for wash water application. Some filters are equipped only with internal droplegs and operate with somewhat lower pressure differential for sheet forming and dewatering.

ROTARY VACUUM WASHER: Equipment for thickening and washing stock consisting of a wire- or cloth-covered cylinder rotating about its main axis in a vat containing the unwashed dilute stock. The outer periphery of the drum is divided into a number of shallow sections or compartments equipped with drainage grids that support the cloth filter medium. Individual pipe outlets connect each section with an annular stationary timing valve, supported in different ways depending on design (e.g. by a drum journal or center shaft). Separation of stock and liquor is accomplished through a pres-sure differential created by a vacuum on the underside of the filter cloth, normally produced by a sealed drop leg on the discharge line. As the cylinder rotates through the vat, a thick layer of unwashed pulp builds up and adheres to the wire face. The sheet emerges from the vat and wash water is applied to displace the associated liquor. Finally, the vacuum is cut off and washed stock is removed from the mold. Rotary vacuum washers for brown stock are typically operated in a multistage countercurrent arrangement.

S

SALEABLE MASS (of pulp)**:** Actual mass of pulp multiplied by the dry solids content and divided by the theoretical commercial dryness (usually 90%).

SAVEALL: Any piece of equipment whose function is to clarify white water and recover usable fiber for return to the papermaking system. Types of equipment in common use are drum filters, flotation saveall, disc saveall and scalping screens.

SCALPING SCREEN: Inclined, fine-mesh screen used to recover usable fiber from white water. Typically it has no moving parts, but may be equipped with an oscillating shower to prevent blinding.

SCRAPER SCREEN: Type of coarse screen used for groundwood consisting of an inclined plate with large holes through which pulp passes. Chunks of wood remaining on the plate are removed by a continuous scraper.

SCREEN: Separation device utilizing some type of perforated barrier for removing unwanted material from a stock stream. See also GRAVITY CENTRIFUGAL SCREEN, PRESSURE SCREEN, VIBRATORY SCREEN, ETC.

SCREEN ACCEPTS: Material passing through the screen perforations during a single stage of screening.

SCREEN BASKET: Integral component of many screen designs, consisting of a cylindrical screen plate with top and bottom retainer rings.

SCREENING: Processing step involving passage of stock through some form of perforated barrier to remove oversize, troublesome and unwanted particles from good fiber. See also BARRIER SCREENING, PROBABILITY SCREENING.

SCREENING EFFICIENCY: Percent removal of debris. For chemical pulps, efficiency is based on shive removal. Because efficiency for probability screening devices is greatly influenced by the fraction of material rejected, a plot of efficiency versus percent reject material is required for a complete picture. See also SCREENING QUOTIENT.

SCREENING QUOTIENT: Single-number index for screening efficiency which takes into account both debris removal and fraction of material rejected (proposed by G.L. Nelson).

SCREENINGS: See SCREEN REJECTS.

SCREEN PLATE: Perforated metal plate utilized on many designs of pulp screening equipment that impedes bulk flow and is instrumental in causing a separation between suspended particles on the basis of their size, shape, and/or flexibility. The open area varies from 5–8% for slotted plates to 12–33% for plates with holes.

SCREEN REJECTS: Material retained by the screen perforations during a single stage of screening. Syn. Screenings.

SCREEN ROOM: Department of the pulp mill in which screening and other pulp cleaning operations are carried out.

SCREEN TAILINGS: Discarded reject material from the screen room.

SCREW EXTRACTOR: Device for thickening stock in which vertically arranged conical screws continually feed stock through a conical perforated enclosure causing the stock to dewater before it is discharged at the small-diameter end. Syn. Screw Press.

SEAL BOX: Small receiving vessel for vacuum washer filtrate with sufficient storage capacity to maintain a seal on the drop leg.

SEAL CHAMBER: Small chamber within a seal tank which serves to keep the drop leg submerged and is usually designed to help separate air from the filtrate. Syn. Seal Pot.

SEAL TANK: Receiving and storage vessel for vacuum washer filtrate which also serves to keep the drop leg submerged and thus preserve the vacuum on the washer.

SECONDARY CLEANERS: Centrifugal cleaners which handle stock rejected by the primary cleaners.

SECONDARY FIBER: Pulp fiber with a previous history of incorporation in paper or paperboard products. Syn. Recycled Fiber, Reclaimed Waste Paper. See also PAPER STOCK.

SECONDARY SCREENS: Screens which handle stock rejected by the primary screens.

SEMI-CLOSED SCREENING: Chemical pulp mill screening operation in which only a small portion of the filtrate from the screened stock thickener is sewered, the major portion being utilized as wash water in the pulp washing system.

SHAVINGS: Class of reclaimed paper stock consisting principally of unprinted trimmings from converting operations.

SHEET COOLER: Equipment to cool the sheet as it emerges from the pulp drying machine. Cooling the sheet to below 40°C prevents deterioration of certain pulp grades during storage. Syn. Web Cooler.

SHEET TAKEOFF: Removal of the fibrous mat from the mold of a decker or rotary vacuum washer. A couch roll or takeoff roll may be used, or the mechanism of removal may be by means of a steam or air shower.

SHIVE DETECTOR: Any device to indicate equipment malfunction and/or poor operation of the fine screens. A simple device is a coarse screen or wire mesh which receives a side stream flow; a sudden increase of shives will result in an accumulation of trapped particles and cause an overflow which actuates an alarm. Syn. Sliver Detector.

SHORT FIBER: Hardwood chemical pulp.

SHORT STOCK: Short-fibered chemical pulp, either hardwood fibers or softwood fibers that have been shortened due to refining action.

SHREDDER: Machine for fluffing of dry pulp.

SHRINKAGE: Fiber and pigment loss during processing of waste paper into secondary fiber, expressed as a percent. Shrinkage occurs during sorting, screening, fines carryover with wash water, spills and because some material is solubilized.

SIDEHILL SCREEN: Thickening equipment in which stock rolls down an inclined screen without mat formation. Since this equipment dewaters stock with very little filtering action, it is commonly used in de-inking processes for separating the ink dispersion from the clean fiber. Syn. Slide-Wire Washer.

SLAB: Compressed rectangular block of flash-dried pulp.

SLAB PRESS: Press that compresses flash-dried pulp into rectangular slabs. Typically, 3 to 7 slabs stacked together form the contents of a bale of flash-dried pulp.

SLIPPING: Backward movement of upturning stock on a rotating cylinder mold.

SLOTTED PLATE: Screen plate equipped with narrow slots. Slot widths for pulp screening vary from 0.2 to 0.8 mm.

SLURRY: Any dispersion of insoluble matter in water.

SLUSH: Imprecise term for a pulp slurry or paper stock, usually referring to stocks in the 1–4% range of consistency.

SLUSHER: See GRAVITY THICKENER.

SLUSHING: See REPULPING.

SOFTWOOD PULP: Pulp produced from softwood.

SOLVENT EXTRACTION PROCESS: Fiber recovery process that utilizes hot sequential extractions with perchloroethylene to remove plastic and wax contaminants from certain waste paper feed stocks.

SORBED SODA: Sodium ions that are absorbed and adsorbed onto the pulp fibers during kraft pulping and cannot be washed out using conventional brown stock washing methods. The amount of sorbed soda is generally deducted from the total soda carryover with the washed pulp for purposes of calculating washing efficiency.

SORTING: Separation of waste paper into different grades or quality categories.

SPECIFIC EDGE LOADING: Measurement of refining intensity, defined as effective power input (watts) per total edge crossing rate (km/s).

SPECIFIC LOADING: Measure of stock loading on a vacuum drum filter or decker. The traditional unit of measurement is oven dry (or air dry) tons per day of pulp per square foot of drum surface. Syn. Unit Loading Rate.

STATIC FOAM: Old surface foam that has dried out, leaving fiber fines and stabilizers to hold the bubble shape.

STEAM DRYING: Novel method for flash drying of pulp utilizing a medium of slightly superheated low-pressure steam rather than air.

STICKIES: Sticking conditions in secondary fiber or papermaking systems created by such contraries as ink residuals, tars, latexes, and heat-melt materials. The term "tackies" refers to the same type of problem, perhaps less severe.

STOCK: Any mixture of pulp and water with or without non-fibrous additives. See also FURNISH.

STOCK BLENDING: See BLENDING.

STOCK CLEANING: Removal of undesirable particles from stock by such mechanical means as sedimentation, centrifugation and screening.

STOCK PREPARATION or STOCK PREP: That part of the papermaking process in which pulp is treated mechanically, and sometimes chemically by use of additives, to prepare it for forming into a sheet of paper or paperboard.

STOCK PREPARATION AREA or STOCK PREP AREA: See BEATER ROOM.

STOCK PUMP: Equipment to transport stock through a pipeline or process vessel. The centrifugal pump design can be adapted for stock consistencies up to 6%. For higher consistencies, special pump designs are used.

STORAGE CAPACITY: Amount of pulp that can be contained in the high-density storage chest, measured either in terms of oven dry tons or hours of operation.

STRAINER: Coarse filter, usually an in-line device with provision for backflushing.

STRAINING: Depletion of the loose rotating mat within a centrifugal screen, thus allowing shives to be accepted. This condition can occur from over-dilution or by impinging the dilution into the mat with excessive force.

SUBSTANCE YIELD FACTOR: Measure of solids recovery in pulp washing expressed as weight percent inorganic solids reclaimed as compared with the total inorganic solids applied to the cook.

SUPERFICIAL FLOW: Volumetric flow of filtrate only in the drop leg of a pulp vacuum washer, ignoring the flow of air accompanying the filtrate. Superficial flow is used in design calculations because the airflow is a large variable dependent on the characteristics of the pulp and the operation of the filter.

T _____

TACKIES: See STICKIES.

TACKLE: Working surfaces in refiners and beaters. A description of the tackle might include the materials of construction, the width, number, and spacing of bars, and the edge sharpness.

TAILINGS: See SCREEN TAILINGS.

TAKEOFF ROLL: Small roll with axially ridged or fluted surface, used on some rotary vacuum washers to remove the sheet from the mold. It is placed in close proximity to the face and rotates in the direction opposite to the mold.

TANK: Vessel used for storage and blending of chemical solutions, stock suspensions, and other liquids.

TERTIARY: [adj] Term denoting the third stage of such multi-stage operations as screening or centrifugal cleaning.

THICKENER: Name given to various designs of equipment for pulp thickening. See GRAVITY THICKENER, VALVELESS FILTER, ROTARY VACUUM FILTER, DISC FILTER, SIDEHILL SCREEN, SCREW EXTRACTOR, DISC PRESS.

THICKENING: Increasing consistency of stock by removal of liquid or water.

THICKENING FACTOR (TF)**:** Measure of thickening effectiveness, defined as the weight of liquid removed divided by the weight of liquid entering, both calculated per unit weight of oven dry pulp basis.

THICKENING RATIO: Operational parameter for screens and centrifugal cleaners, defined as the ratio of reject consistency to feed consistency.

THICK STOCK PUMP: Special design of pump for handling high-consistency stock, most commonly utilizing double-meshing rotors.

TICKLER REFINER: Refiner used to impart a light mechanical treatment (i.e., a "touch-up treatment") to the stock furnish, usually just prior to the paper machine.

TIMING VALVE: Interconnecting member on a rotary vacuum filter/washer between the drainage compartments and the lower-pressure filtrate outlet. The stationary annular valve is supported by wear plates and sealed against leakage. As the cylinder turns, the valve's fixed position cuts off vacuum just before the sheet takeoff point and restores vacuum just after submergence of the filter medium into the vat. See also CIRCUMFERENTIAL VALVE, INTERNAL VALVE.

TRAMP MATERIALS: Unwanted foreign materials in the pulp, either originating with the chip supply or from subsequent contamination within the process. Typical tramp materials are rocks, nails, nuts, bolts, tools and parts of chipper knives.

TRASH EXTRACTOR: Combination of large hydrocyclone and sieve, used to remove oversize debris from stock or water streams.

U ———————————————————

UNBEATEN PULP: Pulp which has not been subjected to any mechanical treatment. Syn. Unrefined Pulp.

UNIT LOADING RATE: See SPECIFIC LOADING.

V ———————————————————

VACUUM DRYER: Usually refers to the Minton dryer, employed for the continuous drying of a pulp or paperboard web. This design utilizes conventional steam cylinders and ancillaries, but the entire drying unit is enclosed in a vacuum chamber or vacuum hood which is equipped with seals at the point where the sheet enters and leaves the dryer section.

VACUUM WASHER: See ROTARY VACUUM WASHER.

VALVE: See TIMING VALVE.

VALVELESS FILTER: Equipment for thickening stock similar to a rotary vacuum thickener except that an external drop leg is not employed. A modest pressure differential is developed by means of internal droplegs connected to each suction compartment.

VIBRATORY SCREEN: Any pulp screen depending on a vibratory mechanism to keep screen perforations clean.

VORTEX CLEANER: See CENTRIFUGAL CLEANER.

VORTEX FINDER: Modification on some designs of centrifugal cleaner consisting of an extension of the accept orifice pipe into the body of the cleaner. This modification is designed to reduce the tendency for some of the flow to short-circuit directly from the inlet to the accept. Syn. Accept Nozzle.

W ———————————————————

WASH DEINKING: Deinking process for secondary fiber in which the dispersed ink particles are removed in a series of dilution/thickening operations.

WASHER: Equipment for removing soluble material from pulp. A number of designs are utilized.

WASHER FILTRATE: Weak residual liquor produced by shower displacement (or diffusion flow, or press extraction, etc.) of residual liquor from the pulp. The liquor solids content is related to the washing stage of the filtrate.

WASHER ROOM: Department in a pulp mill where pulp washing operations are carried out.

WASHER SHOWER: See WHISTLE SHOWER, WEIR SHOWER.

WASHING: Displacement and leaching of soluble material from pulp using fresh water or recycle liquor. The soluble material normally consists of residual chemicals and reaction products from cooking and bleaching operations.

WASHING AID: Chemical added to the stock during brown stock washing to improve washing efficiency.

WASHING EFFICIENCY: Measure of dissolved solids removal from the pulp. With respect to rotary vacuum washing, efficiency of solids removal is a function of both displacement ratio and thickening factor.

WASH LIQUOR: Dilute liquor (often washer filtrate from the previous stage) which is used to displace more concentrated liquor in a pulp washing stage.

WASH PRESS: Equipment for thickening and washing brownstock consisting of a cloth-covered cylinder rotating within a pressurized vat containing the unwashed dilute stock. The overpressure and geometric configuration between the cylinder and vat cause the stock to dewater. During passage through a "wash flap", wash liquid is distributed into the web to displace residual liquor. Finally, the sheet passes through a press nip where the pulp consistency is increased to 30–40% before discharge.

WASTE PAPER: See SECONDARY FIBER.

WASTE PAPER GRADES: Categories of waste paper depending on furnish, source, color, and whether printed or unprinted.

WASTE PAPER RECOVERY RATE: Index of national or regional waste paper recovery efficiency, defined as the amount of waste paper recovered and utilized as a percentage of paper and board consumption. See also WASTE PAPER UTILIZATION RATE.

WASTE PAPER UTILIZATION RATE: Index of national or regional waste paper utilization efficiency, defined as the amount of waste paper recovered and utilized as a percentage of paper and board production. See also WASTE PAPER RECOVERY RATE.

WATER BALANCE: Accounting of all water flows into and out of a process or segment of a process.

WAVELINE PLATES: Matching disc refiner plates with surfaces that form a series of hills and valleys in the radial direction, thus causing material to be thrown from one plate to the other while moving toward the periphery. These plates are used principally in low-energy input applications where the main objective is to disperse fiber bundles.

WAVE PLATE: See CONTOURED PLATE.

WEB COOLER: See SHEET COOLER.

WEIR SHOWER: Shower for rotary vacuum washers consisting of an open trough containing a pressurized pipe. The wash liquor is distributed into the trough through a series of submerged holes, and then transferred without turbulence over a bent plate onto the pulp mat.

WET BEATEN: [adj] Term applied to well beaten, thoroughly hydrated stock. See also DEAD BEATEN.

WETLAP MACHINE: Pulp machine designed to produce wetlap pulp.

WETLAP PULP: Pulp prepared for storage or shipment by pressing to high consistency (45–55%), in the form of a continuous folded web or cut sheets.

WET MACHINE: Pulp or paperboard machine with a single cylinder mold former, used to produce wetlap pulp or such paperboard products as matrix board and acoustical board.

WET SHREDDING: Mechanical disintegration of a wet pulp sheet by the tearing action of a toothed roll.

WHISTLE SHOWER: Common type of washer shower for rotary vacuum washers employing a distribution pipe equipped at intervals with fan nozzles.

WHITE FIBER: Bleached chemical pulp.

WHITE PITCH: Term used to describe agglomerated white stickies in repulped stock which are derived from the synthetic binders in coated broke.

WHITE WASTE: Unprinted waste paper salvaged from printing operations, consisting principally of core waste, trim waste and outside waste.

WIRE CLOTH: Fine mesh wire screen used as the filtration element on certain washers, filters, deckers, and similar equipment. See also FILTRATION MEDIA.

WOVE MOLD: Cover of a mold made from wire or plastic filaments woven like a piece of cloth.

WRAPPER STOCK: Large sheets of pulp used to wrap pulp bales.

XYZ

YELLOW PULP: Unbleached straw pulp.

ZONE AGITATION: (1) Mixing of stock with dilution water in the bottom of a high-density storage tank. (2) Any situation within a stock tank in which stock mixing is limited to the "active volume" surrounding the agitator. Syn. Controlled Volume Blending.

Chapter 13
Papermaking Processes and Equipment

ABRASIVITY (of mineral fillers): Relative ability of filler substances such as clay or talc to cause abrasion, generally measured in terms of weight loss per unit area of forming fabric using the Valley Abrasion Tester.

ACCELERATION RATIO: Ratio of the fluid velocity in the laterals to the fluid velocity in the cross header, a basic design parameter of tapered inlet flow spreaders. In most designs, a ratio of about 1.5 is used.

ACTIVE SURFACE AREA (of a furnish): Actual surface area divided by some factor of hydrophobicity to account for sizing effects.

ACTIVITY: Stock turbulence on the forming wire generated by drainage elements.

AC VARIABLE-FREQUENCY DRIVE: Type of paper machine sectional drive system utilizing the induction motor principle that speed is proportional to frequency. A static inverter is used to provide a varying frequency supply, thus controlling speed.

ADDITIVES: See PAPERMAKING ADDITIVES.

ADDITIVE SYSTEM: System consisting of mixing and blending tanks, pumps, flowmeters, and flow control valves for accurate metering of nonfibrous additives to the stock. The control valves are operated automatically and the amount of addition is proportional to the machine stock flow.

ADJUSTING COLOR: Colorant that is used in combination with other dyes and pigments to achieve a desired color for a paper product.

ADJUSTING RODS: Rods connected to the slice lip or top nozzle blade of a headbox with which the operator makes micro adjustments to the slice opening.

ADMIXTURE: Modified blend after addition of one or more ingredients. The term is sometimes applied to machine chest stock after addition of additives.

AIR BALANCE: (1) Ratio of supply air to exhaust air for a paper machine hood or for any other ventilation system. (2) Accounting of all air flows into and out of a process. Air balances are typically carried out on paper machine hoods and machine rooms as part of a paper machine dryer audit.

AIRBORNE WEB DRYING: Air impingement drying of a web supported primarily by the drying air.

AIR BUBBLES: Minute gas bubbles entrained in stock or in coating color. See also AIR CONTENT (in stock).

AIR CHANGE: Rate of ventilation in terms of the number of complete air replacements in a building per hour. For paper machine rooms, typical air change rates vary from 5 to 12 per hour depending on climatic and operating conditions.

AIR CLEANER: Device for cleaning ventilation and recirculation air, most commonly consisting of replaceable or renewable filter media (e.g., moving curtain or roll filters) within the duct cross section.

AIR CONTENT (of stock): Percentage by volume of air (including other gases) in papermaking stock, consisting of free gas bubbles and tiny bubbles either trapped in the fiber lumina or firmly attached to the fiber surfaces.

AIR COOLING: Cooling of a surface by means of cold air impingement, or by other means of contact between a surface and cool air.

AIR CURTAIN: High-velocity stream of temperature-controlled air which is directed downward across an opening to seal it against outside currents, thus permitting air conditioning of a space with an open entrance.

AIR-CUSHIONED HEADBOX: Pressurized, closed headbox with a controlled liquid level. The air cushion above the liquid level serves to dampen out small pressure fluctuations in the approach flow.

AIR DECKLE: Deckle edge fashioned on a fourdrinier or cylinder mold by means of a jet of air. See also JET DECKLE.

AIR DOCTOR: Deflector which is positioned against a moving dryer fabric to control the amount of air carried by the fabric.

AIR DRYING: Drying by means of freely circulating air, typically with hot air within a chamber or tunnel.

AIR ENTRAINMENT: Trapping and holding of free air in stock or white water, mainly by means of agitation and cascading.

AIR EXHAUST: Moisture-laden air discharged into the atmosphere from paper machine hoods, machine rooms, vacuum pumps, etc.

AIR FOIL THREADING: Method of threading the tail at the dry end of the paper machine utilizing a layer of air from one point to another. The tail is conveyed over a series of foils following a proven aerodynamic propulsion phenomenon and into the in-running nip.

AIR FORMING: Forming technique in which the individual fibers (at high dryness levels) are transported and uniformly distributed onto the forming medium in an air stream. Syn. Aerodynamic Forming.

AIR-IMPINGEMENT DRYING: Any drying process in which evaporation is achieved primarily by means of heated air impinging on the surface of the wet sheet. See also FAN DRYING.

AIR-LAID SHEET: Sheet made by any of several dry forming methods. See also DRY FORMING, DRY-LAY NONWOVENS.

AIR PAD: Volume of air above the stock in an air-cushioned headbox which acts as a pulsation damper.

AIR PUMPING: Refers to the ability of a dryer fabric to carry along air and pump it into and out of a dryer pocket, thus ventilating the pocket and removing humid air. The rate of air exchange is mainly a function of the fabric permeability and the machine speed.

AIR SHOWERS: (1) Manifold of individually-controlled, cool-air jets across the machine, commonly used on calender rolls to selectively dissipate frictional heat and modify localized calendering effects. (2) Array of air jets on the return run of a dryer fabric, used for maintaining the cleanliness of high-permeability fabrics.

AIR SUPPLY: Fresh air supplied by fans to paper machine hoods, machine rooms, and for other ventilation purposes. See also INFILTRATION AIR, MAKEUP AIR.

ALIGNMENT: See PAPER MACHINE ALIGNMENT.

ALIGNMENT ROLL: See GUIDE ROLL.

ANEMOMETER: Sensitive air flow measuring device, often used to measure air velocities within a paper machine hood and to obtain those measurements required for an air balance.

ANGLE OF OUTFLOW: Angle of the headbox jet with the horizontal.

ANGLE OF WRAP: See WRAP.

ANIONIC TRASH: Anionic oligomers and polymers that accumulate in the paper machine white water system and are detrimental to the papermaking process. The accumulation depends on the degree to which these materials are adsorbed onto the fibers, fines and fillers, by their solubility, and the degree of closure of the white water system. In practice, the terms "anionic trash" and "detrimental substances" are used interchangably.

ANTIDEFLECTION ROLL: See SWIMMING ROLL.

APPROACH FLOW: Dilute combined stock flow to the headbox, i.e., the fan pump flow. Syn. Thin Stock.

APPROACH SYSTEM: Fan pump loop wherein the paper stock is measured, diluted, mixed with any necessary non-fibrous additives and finally screened and cleaned before being discharged onto the paper machine forming medium. The approach system extends from the machine chest to the headbox slice lip; occasionally, certain stock chests and refiners may also be considered part of the approach system.

APRON: Structural component of the headbox which forms the lower part of the slice opening. (On some very slow machines, a flexible rubber or plastic "apron" projects from the bottom of the slice onto the forming wire.) Syn. Stationary Lip, Lower Lip, Apron Lip. See also SLICE.

APRON BOARD: Rigid metal plate which forms the bottom structural member in some headbox designs and from which the apron is attached.

ASH RETENTION: Ratio of the amount of ash in the paper to the total amount of ash in the papermaking system, expressed as a percentage. The ash retention is used as a measure of mineral filler retention.

ASPIRATOR HOLE: Small-diameter bleed hole drilled either in the dryer syphon shoe or in the syphon pipe itself, the purpose of which is to assist a dryer to recover from a flooded condition and return to an unflooded state. The aspirator hole assures a small continuous flow of bleed-through steam to carry away condensate even when the minimal opening into the syphon shoe becomes completely submerged.

ASSIST DRIVE: See HELPER DRIVE.

ATTRITION-TYPE REPULPER: Repulper having an impeller running in close proximity to a perforated extraction plate, thus providing a high shear component to the recirculation flow.

AUTO SLICE: Device on a top former employing inertial forces to remove water in an upward direction.

AUXILIARY EQUIPMENT: Accessory equipment on the paper machine which serves a useful, but subordinate function. Examples are doctors, cleaning showers, and threading devices.

AVERAGE SPECIFIC NIP PRESSURE: Average pressure applied in a press nip, calculated by dividing the so-called lineal pressure by the nip width (or by dividing the total force applied by the area of contact).

B _____

BABY DRYER: Single, small-diameter dryer cylinder preceding the main dryer section of a paper machine. Syn. Lead Dryer.

BABY PRESSES: See PRIMARY PRESSES.

BACKING WIRE (on a twin-wire former): Forming fabric that does not retain the sheet when the two fabrics separate. See also CONVEYING WIRE.

BACKLASH: Offsetting distortion of the slice lip profile that tends to negate the effect of microslice adjustments.

BACK SIDE: Drive side of the papermachine. The side away from the operating side. See also FRONT SIDE.

BACK STAND: See UNWIND STAND.

BACK TENDER: Papermachine operator who is next in authority to the machine tender. His routine areas of concern are moisture control and reel building.

BACK WATER: See WHITE WATER.

BAG: Slack area in the paper which has been stressed beyond its elastic limit and retains a deformation, often due to excessive nip pressure in a localized area.

BAGGALLAY BOX: Device similar to a flat box, used at the takeoff position on the fourdrinier underneath the forming fabric. It consists of a two-part box, the first part being a conventional suction box while the second part is pressurized and blows the sheet off the wire. It is typically utilized on slower machines producing specialty grades.

BAGGINESS: Slackness or drooping of the paper between draws of the paper machine. Syn. Baggying.

BALANCED LOOP FORMER: Drainage device consisting of a jet impinging upon a forming fabric running through an open suction box, which allows the fabric to form a shape defined by the expression $T = PR$, where T is the tension of the fabric, P is the pressure drop across the fabric, and R is the radius of curvature of the fabric.

BARRELLING: Separation of the mass of filler material from the shaft of a filled supercalender roll.

BASIS WEIGHT VALVE: Valve controlling the flow of stock into the paper machine system. Syn. Stuff Gate, Stuff Cock.

BATCH COLORING: Term generally applied to any method involving addition of dye or pigment to a batch pulper or beater.

BEATER ADDITIVES: Papermaking additives which are added to the stock at the beater or just prior to the refiners. See also PAPERMAKING ADDITIVES.

BEDROLL-TYPE WINDER: See TWO-DRUM WINDER.

BED ROLLS: See WINDING DRUMS.

BILGE: Outer surface of a paper roll; that part of a roll that is in contact with the ground when the axis of the roll is horizontal to the ground. (The term is a misnomer when applied to paper rolls; it correctly refers to the bulge of a barrel.)

BILLY STICK: Wooden stick used by the back tender to "sound" a reel. He monitors the hardness uniformity of the reel by listening to the sound produced when he hits the reel at a number of positions across the machine.

BLADE GAP FORMER: See CONVERGING WEDGE FORMER.

BLEED-THROUGH: Loss of fibers and fines from the sheet while dewatering through the forming fabric.

BLIND-DRILLED PRESS: Two-roll wet press in which one roll contains many shallow, closely-spaced holes which provide easily accessible receptacles for the expelled water.

BLISTERING: Drying problem on a Yankee cylinder manifested by small sheet areas breaking away from intimate contact with the dryer surface. The underlying cause may be the formation of steam pockets due to over-heating or simply dirty areas on the dryer surface.

BLOW: Separation between two adjacent plies of a wet sheet of multiply board caused by air entrained in the wet sheet.

BLOWDOWN VALVE: Valve used to create the required differential pressure across a dryer section during certain periods of operation, usually by allowing steam to pass to a lower-pressure heat exchanger.

BLOWING: Localized accumulation of air between felt and sheet at the ingoing side of a press nip.

BLOWING ROLL: See FELT ROLL.

BLOW PIPE: Device for obtaining a sample of the wet stock traveling on top of the fourdrinier. It typically consists of a length of pipe sealed at one end with a slit or series of holes parallel to the centerline, while the other end is equipped with a quick-opening valve and attached to the mill compressed air supply. Syn. Blow Gun, Sample Pipe.

BLOW ROLL: (1) Roll over which the wet paper web runs between the fourdrinier and the felt on open-draw machines. (2) Any of the free-running rolls around which the sheet runs between nips on a supercalender. They provide for sheet cooling and prevent wrinkling into the next nip. Syn. Air Roll.

BLOW SAMPLE: Sample of the wet stock traveling on top of a fourdrinier forming fabric, obtained by blowing the stock upward by compressed air and catching it in a suitable container, usually for purposes of consistency determination.

BLOW-THROUGH STEAM: Steam leaving the dryer along with condensate through the syphon. This steam entrains the condensate, thus reducing its effective density and lowering the required pressure differential.

BOARD: See PAPERBOARD.

BOARD MACHINE: Machine for the manufacture of paperboard, which may be a fourdrinier, multiply machine or wet machine.

BOARD MILL: (1) Independent paperboard plant. (2) Section of a paper and board manufacturing complex where paperboard is produced.

BODY WRAP: Wrapper for the cylindrical surface of a finished paper roll. The number of turns (or wraps) are usually specified depending on the type of paper product and whether for domestic or export shipment.

BOILOUT: Movement of a hot cleaning solution (about 65°C) stepwise through the entire papermaking system, allowing the solution to remain in contact with the walls of all stock and white water chests and with the inside of all connecting pipelines for about 2 hours. Immediately following circulation, these surfaces and the system should be washed or flushed thoroughly to remove the cleaning solution, pitch, scale, slime, pulp, dirt, etc.

BONE HARD: Rock hard. The term is commonly applied to non-deformable roll covering materials such as granite.

BOTTOM FELT: (1) Felt which contacts the bottom side of the web. (2) Felt that picks up each ply on a typical multiply machine and carries the wet multiply web through a series of water removal and sheet consolidation steps. Syn. Carrying Felt, Long Felt.

BOTTOM LINER: Inside liner of multiply paperboard; the side of lesser quality.

BOTTOM ROLL: Press roll, usually rubber covered, which is in contact with the felt. The design of this roll depends on the type of press, e.g., the surface may be plain, grooved or blind drilled.

BOUNDARY LAYER: Stationary film of liquid that forms adjacent to the wall of the conduit during laminar flow.

BOWED ROLL (or BOWD ROLL): Web control roll consisting of a stationary, curved axle around which a rubber sleeve rotates, typically supported by a series of ballbearing assemblies mounted on the axle. In operation, the rubber sleeve expands and contracts as it rotates around the stationary axle. Bowed rolls are available with fixed or adjustable bows. Syn. Expander Roll, Spreader Roll, Curved Roll, Rotating Spreader.

BOWL: See FILLED ROLL.

BRAKING: Controlling the speed of the roll on the unwind stand during winding operations. See also FRICTION BRAKING, REGENERATIVE BRAKING.

BRANCH TUBES: See LATERALS.

BREAK: Total rupture of the paper web during manufacture, printing or converting, which results in a tear from edge to edge.

BREAK DETECTOR: Optical and/or mechanical device to record the time and location of a break on the paper machine and log the downtime associated with the break.

BREAK END: Part of the paper sheet in which a sheet break was initiated.

BREAKER STACK: Single-nip calender placed between dryer sections of the paper machine. Typically, one or both of the metal rolls are steam heated.

BREAKING BACK: Condition in a thermocompressor when high-pressure motive steam discharges to suction, usually caused by overloaded conditions. Typically, this condition occurs when the high-pressure steam valve is wide open trying to create high pressure differentials across the dryers. See also CHOKING.

BREAST ROLL: Large-diameter roll around which the fourdrinier forming wire passes at the end where the stock is discharged onto the wire. The breast roll serves only to support the wire in the typical fourdrinier situation, but is sometimes used as a suction former in other applications.

BREAST ROLL DISCHARGE: Dewatering of fourdrinier stock as it impinges on the wire immediately divergent from the breast roll, generally considered undesirable because of the strong suction forces operative at this earliest stage of formation.

BRIDLE: Piece of small-diameter pipe equal in length to a dryer fabric width which connects to the tail of a new dryer fabric to lead it through the dryer section.

BROKE: Paper discarded from any point in the manufacturing or finishing process, which is generally repulped and reprocessed. "Wet broke" is taken from the wire or presses, while "dry broke" emanates from the dryers, reel, winder, and finishing.

BROKE BOX: Large container used to collect broke in the finishing department. When full, it is transported to the broke pit and dumped.

BROKE CHIPS: Small undefibered pieces of waste paper or broke in the papermaking stock. Syn. Paper Specks.

BROKE PIT: Large floor opening at the dry end of the paper machine where broke is dumped. It is located above a dry broke repulper or broke conveyor.

BROKER: See DRY BROKE REPULPER, COUCH PIT.

BROKE RECOVERY SYSTEM: System consisting of repulpers, storage tanks, thickeners, deflakers, etc. which is designed to recover broke and re-process it for use in the papermaking furnish.

BRUSH CALENDERING: Surface treatment in which coated paper is pressed against one or more rotating cylindrical brushes. The circumferential speed of the brushes is several times higher than the web velocity. Syn. Brush Polishing, Brush Glazing.

BUILDUP: Accumulation of stock on rolls, doctor blades, headbox surfaces or other places within the paper machine system.

BULL'S EYE: Splice-free roll of paper.

BURNISHING: Smoothing of a paper surface by rubbing, as for example to achieve a burnished finish.

BURNING OUT: Losing color or whiteness during drying.

C

CALENDER: Assembly of rolls used to impart a finish to paper. See also CALENDERING.

CALENDER BARRING: Periodic variation in machine-direction sheet caliper or finish due to systematic vibration of the calender rolls as the paper passes from nip to nip. The vertical vibration (typically at frequencies in the range of 70 to 800 Hz) may be caused by corrugations on roll faces, or by a regenerative phenomenon in which the caliper variations impressed in the web provide a feedback loop.

CALENDER COLORING: Application of a dye solution by means of a water box at the calender stack, either to one or both sides of the sheet; used principally to color paperboard and heavier weight paper. Syn. Calender Dyeing, Calender Staining.

CALENDER COOLING: Impingement of cool air against a calender roll to selectively remove heat and thus produce micro-contraction of the high spots. See also AIR COOLING.

CALENDER CRUSHING: Disturbance of paper sheet formation (e.g. fibers pushed out of position) due to excessive pressure applied during calendering.

CALENDERING: General term meaning pressing with a roll. Several types of calendering operations are carried out by paper and paperboard manufacturers depending on product demands. The most common operation, machine calendering (usually called simply 'calendering'), is the passage of paper through one or more nips formed by a set of iron rolls, and is the principal on-machine calendering operation.

CALENDER NIP: See NIP.

CALENDER ROLL: Any roll used in a calendering operation. See also KING ROLL, QUEEN ROLL, INTERMEDIATE ROLL, FILLED ROLL.

CALENDER ROLL BLOCKING: Paper adhering to calender or supercalender rolls.

CALENDER ROLL OFFSETTING: Repositioning of certain rolls in a calender stack (i.e., slight movement in a horizontal direction) so that the axes of these rolls are no longer in vertical alignment with the rest of the stack. Syn. Calender Roll Staggering.

CALENDER SIZING: Application of sizing solution by means of a water box at the calender stack, either to one or both sides of the sheet.

CALENDER STACK: Vertical arrangement of calender rolls. On paper machines having two sequential calender stacks, the stack immediately following the dryers is called the "wet stack" and the second is called the "dry stack".

CAMBER: See CROWN.

CAN: Mill jargon for a dryer cylinder.

CANOPY HOOD: See OPEN HOOD.

CANTILEVERED FOURDRINIER: Fourdrinier wire part that is temporarily cantilever-supported from the drive side to permit installation of a wire from the tending side. Syn. Cantilevered Wire Part.

CANTILEVERING: Method of construction in which one end of a horizontal member is so securely anchored that the other end (which is otherwise not supported) may bear a load.

CAPILLARY ABSORPTION: Mechanism of sheet rewetting on the outgoing side of a press nip, due to the fact that water moves spontaneously from a material having a rough structure (i.e., the felt) to one whose pore structure is finer (i.e., the paper).

CAPSTAN WRAP: Sheet wrap on the drum roll before the ingoing nip on a reel or winder.

CARRYING FELT: See BOTTOM FELT.

CARRYING ROLL: Any non-driven roll on the paper machine that supports the sheet, forming fabric, press felt, or dryer fabric and has no other specific function.

CASCADE STEAM SYSTEM: Method of re-using blow-through steam and flash steam from one dryer section in an adjoining section which operates at slightly lower pressure. Typically, highest-pressure steam is used in the section nearest to the reel and steam pressure is reduced in steps toward the wet end.

CASCADING: (1) Condition within a dryer cylinder when condensate tends to be carried up the walls of the cylinder, but mostly falls back into the bottom puddle. A cascading condition is intermediate between "puddling" and "rimming" and usually occurs at paper machine speeds of 350 to 400 m/min. (2) Tumbling liquid flow within an open channel which promotes entrainment of air.

CASE HARDENING: Surface hardening due to high temperature, which can act as a barrier to heat transfer or evaporation.

CENTERLINE: See PAPER MACHINE CENTERLINE, OFFSET PARALLEL CENTERLINE.

CENTER STOCK: Low-grade secondary fiber that is used to form the filler plies for many grades of multiply board.

CENTERWIND REEL: Reel having the drive or torque provided to the center of the reel, as opposed to a conventional drum reel where the drive is applied to the outside surface. A centerwind is used where the material being reeled is sensitive to the nip.

CHECKING: Marking of the sheet with small cross direction creases, caused by application of excessive nip pressure to the wet sheet during pressing. Checking is a mild manifestation of crushing. See also CRUSHING.

CHEEKING PIECE: Removable dam within a headbox which forms part of the side of the box and seals the end of the slice opening.

CHEMICAL BONDING: Process of achieving bonding within a wet- or dry-lay nonwoven structure by deposition of a polymer latex or polymer solution in and around the fibrous structure.

CHEMICAL PULP DEMAND: Percentage of chemical pulp required in a mixed pulp furnish to achieve a target strength value in the resultant paper product.

CHILL HARDENING: Metallurgical treatment during manufacture of calender rolls to ensure high surface hardness. With rapid cooling of the surface layer of molten metal, the carbon is held in solution forming iron carbide which is extremely resistant to abrasion.

CHOKING: Condition in a thermocompressor when the amount of motive steam and suction steam is greater than can be pushed through the diffuser. See also BREAKING BACK.

CHOPPER-FAN: Suction fan that draws in trim from the winder, shreds it, and conducts it into a settling chamber or separating cyclone above the broke repulper.

CHUCK: Gripping device for the end of a shaft to ensure concentric running on the spindle, used for holding a reel during winding.

CIRCULATION SYSTEM: System for recycle and re-use of white waters on the paper machine. The utilization of wire pit water and rich white water from the flat box seal tanks within the approach system is termed "short circulation". The utilization of leaner white water for dilution of pulp and broke streams within the stock preparation area is termed "long circulation",

CLOGGING: Blockage of an orifice or flow passage by solid material, e.g., as can occur with a spray nozzle where recyled white water is used.

CLOSED DRAW: See CLOSED TRANSFER.

CLOSED-FRAME SUPERCALENDER: Supercalender with a frame consisting of two vertical columns, between which the bearings are housed. (Note: The open-frame design is used for all modern supercalenders.) Syn. A-Frame Supercalender, Closed-Face Supercalender.

CLOSED HOOD: Fully enclosed hood around the paper machine dryer section.

CLOSED TRANSFER: Fully-supported sheet transfer from the forming wire to the press section or between other sections of the paper machine. Syn. Closed Draw. See also SUCTION PICKUP, LICK-UP.

CLOSED TRANSFER PRESS: See NO-DRAW PRESS.

CLOSURE: In papermaking, refers to reductions in fresh water usage at the wet-end through improved recycle and utilization of white waters. See also WHITE WATER SYSTEM, DEGREE OF CLOSURE.

CLOTHING: Term applied collectively to all paper machine forming fabrics, press felts, dryer screens, and ropes.

CLOTHING LOST TIME: Lost production on the paper machine due to downtime for changing clothing, expressed as a percent of total available time (or a percent of theoretical production).

CLOVERLEAF PRESS: Three-roll press arrangement consisting of a single hard roll forming nips with felted vented rolls located 45° below the horizontal center line on both sides of the hard roll.

COLLAPSING SPEED: Paper machine speed at which condensate rimming (within a dryer) breaks down into a cascading condition. Collapsing speed is lower than rimming speed.

COLORED BROKE: Broke obtained from the paper machine during a run of colored paper. Colored broke cannot be utilized during production of white paper, and care must be exercised to ensure compatibility with other colored grades.

COLOR EQUILIBRATION: Adding of dye to the saveall and seal pit at the start of a color run in order to reduce the time required to reach wet-end equilibrium (i.e., the point where the stock system and white water system are in balance).

COLORING STRENGTH: Relative measurement of the amount of dye required to obtain a specified color change in the paper product. Syn. Coloring Power.

COLOR MATCHING: Procedure for achieving a particular color and shade with respect to a current run of paper to match a previous order or sample provided.

COLOR YIELD: Tinctorial value obtained on a paper product from a given application of dye under specified conditions. See also COLORING STRENGTH.

COMBINATION BOARD: See MULTIPLY BOARD.

COMBINATION VAT: Cylinder former which can be operated alternatively as a uniflow vat or as a counterflow vat. Flow direction is governed by manipulation of stock and overflow valves.

COMBINATION YANKEE MACHINE: Paper machine that utilizes both a Yankee cylinder and conventional steam cylinders for paper drying. Syn. Combined Machine.

COMBINED MACHINE: See COMBINATION YANKEE MACHINE.

COMMERCIAL MATCH: Paper product that meets the customer's specifications and/or is a close facsimilie of the sample of paper provided by the customer.

COMPACTION: Forced shrinkage of the paper sheet as occurs through a compactor. See also FELT COMPACTION.

COMPACTOR: Equipment used on sack paper machines to provide forced machine direction shrinkage of the sheet. In one design, the sheet is passed into a nip formed by independently driven rolls of hard steel and soft rubber; the hard roll rotates with a peripheral velocity matching the velocity of the incoming paper web, while the soft roll is driven at slower speed; the rubber is stretched in front of the nip and the paper adheres to the rubber and is forced to contract with it in the nip.

COMPRESSION MODULUS: Measurement taken from the stress/strain curve of a press roll cover material which indicates the amount that the cover will deform under load to produce the nip or pressure area. The higher the compression modulus, the less will be the deformation under a given load, with resulting smaller nip width and higher unit pressure in the press.

CONCENTRICITY: Important tolerance measurement with respect to paper machine press and calender rolls, defined as the distance between the centers of rotation of the bearing seat and the roll face, respectively.

CONDENSATE REMOVAL SYSTEM: Syphons, rotary joints, and accessories for evacuating condensate from paper machine dryers.

CONDENSATION: Transformation of water vapor into liquid droplets, commonly brought about by cooling air to its dew point.

CONDITIONING SHOE: Oscillating mechanical cleaning device used to condition press felts, having both a water applicator and a suction box, and often fed with a chemical cleaning solution.

CONDUCTIVE HEAT TRANSFER: Transfer of heat within a mass or contiguous series of masses which does not involve molecular movement.

CONSOLIDATION: See SHEET CONSOLIDATION.

CONSTANT-RATE DRYING: Refers to paper drying when evaporation is occurring from the surface of fibers or from large capillaries. See also FALLING-RATE DRYING.

CONTACT DRYING: Any drying method in which the heat for evaporation is supplied by conduction from a heated contact surface. Conventional steam cylinder drying is a prime example of contact drying.

CONTINUOUS COLORING: Metered addition of dye solution or pigment dispersion to the papermaking stock at the fan pump or at the headbox so that the dyed stock goes directly to the machine.

CONTRACTION: See SHEET SHRINKAGE.

CONTRACTION COEFFICIENT: Ratio of the minimum cross-sectional area of a liquid jet discharging from an orifice to the area of the orifice.

CONTROLLED CROWN ROLL: See VARIABLE CROWN ROLL.

CONTROLLED DEFORMATION ROLL: Press or calender roll with crown control combined with selective nip pressure adjustment across the machine, used for profile correction of the web. Syn. Zone-Controlled Roll.

CONVECTIVE DRYING: Paper drying system wherein the heat required is introduced by means of air and transferred from the air to the wet paper. Specific types of convective drying equipment include high-velocity hoods, float dryers, and through dryers.

CONVECTIVE HEAT TRANSFER: Transfer of heat within a gas or liquid by bulk transport and mixing of warmer portions with cooler portions. This mode of heat transfer typically involves an energy exchange between a solid surface and a fluid.

CONVERGING WEDGE FORMER: Type of twin wire former in which the headbox slice jet impinges into the converging gap between two wires that are then guided over stationary elements that exert increasing pressure between the wires. Syn. Blade Gap Former.

CONVEYING WIRE (on some twin-wire formers)**:** Forming fabric which retains the sheet when the two fabrics separate. See also BACKING WIRE.

CORE: Rigid tube onto which paper is wound for shipment, typically made by spirally winding several plies of heavy coarse paper onto a mandrel using suitable adhesive.

CORE PLUG: Conical piece, usually of wood, driven into the end of a core (after the paper has been wound) to prevent crushing or other damage to the core.

CORE SHAFT: Metal shaft inserted through cores for alignment and guidance during the winding operation.

CORE SHAFT SLIDE: Device which secures the core and/or core shaft and roll in the winding process, thus preventing sideways motion and roll offsets. Syn. Core Box.

CORE SLIPPAGE: See OFFSET CORE.

COUCH DRAW ROLL: Small-diameter transfer roll between the couch roll and press section on open-draw machines, used to control the wrap over the suction area of the couch roll.

COUCHER: One of the operators in the manufacture of handmade paper; the individual who transfers the sheet from the mould to the dampened felt for pressing.

COUCHING: Taking the sheet from the forming wire to the press felt. Originally, when paper was made by hand, this term was applied to the act of transferring a sheet from the mould to the felt.

COUCH MARKING: See SHADOW MARKING.

COUCH PIT: Wet-end pulper, usually located underneath the couch roll and presses, which takes broke from the wire and presses. Syn. Wet End Broker.

COUCH PRESS: Inverted felt run around the lumpbreaker roll to provide for higher loading and two-sided dewatering.

COUCH ROLL: Any roll used to separate the wet paper from the forming wire. See also SUCTION COUCH.

COUCH TRIM: Narrow strip of wet paper cut from each edge as the sheet leaves the couch.

COUNTERFLOW VAT: Cylinder former in which the incoming dilute stock flows opposite to the direction of cylinder rotation, causing sheet formation to begin at the point of highest consistency. Syn. Contra-Flow Vat.

COVER: (1) Wire mesh surface of a hand mould through which water drains, leaving the fibers behind to form a sheet of paper. (2) Surface of a dandy roll.

COVERED ROLL: Metal body with a polymeric surface covering. Coverings on press and pressure rolls serve to distribute the pressure in the nip over a wide area and cause the application and release of pressure to occur more gradually. In other applications, the covering protects rolls against corrosive attack and provides a smooth surface against the paper web or machine clothing. Any roll in direct contact with the wet web must be covered with compositions that release the sheet and minimize fiber picking.

CRAWL SPEED: Very slow speed for a paper machine section, usually employed for purposes of clothing changes, maintenance, or inspection. See also JOGGING.

CREEP: Time-dependent strain following imposition of a stress, typical behavior for a viscoelastic material such as wet paper.

CREPE PULLOUT: Amount of reduction in the original crepe which occurs during subsequent processing of the creped web.

CREPING: Formation of micro-corrugations in the cross-direction of paper imposed by a doctor blade as the paper is peeled off a steam cylinder. Creping renders paper softer and more extensible. See also SEMI CREPING, DRY CREPING, SECONDARY CREPING, CROSS CREPING.

CRIMPING: In roll finishing, refers to the operation of folding the wrapper overlap down over the ends of the roll so that a circular piece can be glued on top.

CRINKLE CREPING: See SECONDARY CREPING.

CRITICAL DRYNESS: Dryness at the point on the drying curve where the slope changes rapidly, i.e., the dryness level at which the evaporation rate begins to drop.

CRITICAL SPEED (of rolls): Rotational speed at which a rotating tube or shaft tends to vibrate excessively in a transverse (crosswise) direction. The phenomenon results from the imbalance of the rotating system; the critical speed can be shown to coincide with the natural frequencies of lateral vibration and is, therefore, a characteristic of a particular shaft or tube.

CRITICAL VELOCITY: Rate of straining of paper at which stresses and strains cannot propagate and failure occurs immediately at the impact point.

CROSS-AXIS CROWN COMPENSATION: Method of producing uniform nip pressure under varying loads (for calenders, presses, etc.) by means of cross axis misalignment of the rolls. This was one of the first methods used to effect variable crown, and is still being used in some applications.

CROSS CREPING: Process in which paper that has already been creped in the machine direction is wetted and pressed against another revolving dryer which crepes it in the cross direction, thus producing a sheet with stretch in all directions. The product is called "all-direction stretch paper".

CROSS DIRECTION (CD): Direction perpendicular to web travel on the paper machine. Syn. Cross-Machine Direction, Cross The Grain.

CROSS FLOW: Lateral flow of stock or water occurring on the fourdrinier wire, usually originating from the headbox.

CROSS HEADER: Usually refers to the large tapered conduit which carries the stock flow across the width of the paper machine and which forms an integral part of a tapered inlet flowspreader. Syn. Spreader Pipe.

CROSS-MACHINE DIRECTION: See CROSS DIRECTION.

CROSS SHAFT AGITATOR: Rotating shaft extending across the full width of a chest with propellor blades attached at various intervals. This type of agitator is used on some designs of broke repulper, usually accompanied by a perforated plate pump suction with a wiper blade at one end of the shaft.

CROWN: Gradual, minute increase in diameter of a roll from each end toward the center. Certain rolls in the presses, calenders, and other paper machine sections require a crown to compensate for deflection due to roll weight and/or external loading. Syn. Camber.

CROWN, AMOUNT OF: Difference in roll diameter between any intermediate point along the crowned face and the ends, traditionally measured in mils (thousandths of an inch). Normally, measurement is made only at the midpoint of the crowned face and is referred to as the "total amount of crown".

CROWN CURVE: Setting on the grinder cam to achieve a specified crown shape. For example, a setting of 70° means that the cam rotates 70° when traveling from the center of the roll face to the roll end.

CROWN FACE: Axial distance along the roll which has been ground with the crown curve.

CROWNING: Grinding of a roll according to a specified crown curve.

CROWN SHAPE: Plot of the amount of crown from one end of the crown face to the other.

CRUMB: Accumulations of fiber which are doctored off press rolls or other rolls in direct contact with the paper web.

CRUSHING: Displacement of fiber clusters in the paper sheet during wet pressing due to application of excessive nip pressure. See also FLOW-LIMITED PRESSING.

CULLED PAPER: Paper rejected as inferior. See also OFF-GRADE PAPER.

CULL ROLL: Rejected roll of paper.

CURVED ROLL: See BOWED ROLL.

CUTPOINT: Point of contact between the top and bottom components of a slitter, i.e., the vertex of the two scissors-like rotating cutting elements.

CYLINDER DRYING: Method of paper drying employing a number of conventional steam cylinders to transfer heat to the moist web.

CYLINDER FORMER: Sheet forming equipment utilized primarily for multiply paperboard production in which a screen drum rotates in a vat of dilute paper stock. Water associated with the stock drains through the mold by virtue of the differential head between the vat level and the white water level inside the cylinder, and a layer of fibers is deposited on the cylinder mold. The fiber layer is continuously transferred to a moving felt by means of a soft rubber couch roll. Syn. Vat Former. See also COUNTERFLOW VAT, UNIFLOW VAT, DRY VAT.

CYLINDER MACHINE: Any paper or board machine that utilizes cylinder formers. Syn. Mold Machine.

CYLINDER-ON-TOP FORMER: Cylinder mold former where the sheet is formed and dewatered on the top portion and then travels downward to be transferred to the top of a carrier felt or fabric.

CYLINDER WRAP: Failure of the sheet to couch off the forming cylinder face onto the underside of the carrying felt, with the result that the stock continues around the cylinder in a tightly formed sheet.

D _____

DAMPENER: Equipment for dampening paper preparatory to supercalendering, often as part of a rewinding operation. Typically, a cylindrical brush rotating at high speed transforms water from a pickup roll into a spray directed toward one side of the travelling web. The paper is rewound following dampening to allow transfer of moisture to the side not exposed to the spray.

DAMPENING: Usually refers to the application of moisture to the paper or paperboard surface prior to or during calendering.

DAMPENING FACTOR: See MIXING EFFICIENCY.

DAMPING: Reducing variations in magnitude or amplitude.

DAMPING ROLL: Chilled roll, situated just ahead of the calender stack, which condenses steam onto its surface and transfers this moisture to the paper web as it passes to the calenders. See also SWEAT DRYER.

DAMPING STRETCH: Increased extensibility of the paper web caused by moisture pickup, as from a damping roll.

DANDY MARK: (1) Watermark impressed from a dandy roll. (2) Synonym for Dandy Pick.

DANDY ROLL: Skeletal roll with a wire cloth covering which is mounted above the fourdrinier and rides on the stock in the suction box area. The dandy roll serves to compact the sheet and improve formation in the top portion. Some dandy rolls carry a pattern in the wire facing that is transferred to the sheet to provide watermarking or other special effects. See also LAID DANDY ROLL, WOVE DANDY ROLL.

DANDY ROLL FORMER: Top-wire former that combines the dandy roll effect (i.e., improvement of sheet formation) with upward water removal.

DC VARIABLE-VOLTAGE DRIVE: Type of paper machine sectional drive system utilizing direct-current motors controlled by thyristors. Speed is proportional to voltage and torque is proportional to current, both of which are controlled by the thyristor controller over the operating speed range.

DEAERATION: Removal of entrained air from papermaking stock, usually accomplished by spraying dilute stock (usually centrifugal cleaner accepts) into a vacuum compartment where the air is boiled off.

DECKLE: Vertical rubber strip placed at each edge of the fourdrinier near the forming board to contain stock during the initial formation stage, but required only on relatively slow-speed paper machines. Syn. Deckle Board.

DECKLE EDGE: Feather edge on untrimmed paper. A carefully formed deckle edge enhances the aesthetic appeal of certain text and writing papers.

DECKLE FRAME: Loose wooden frame on a hand mould which holds the correct quantity of stock to form a sheet of paper.

DECKLE POSITION: Relative position of a paper roll in a set taken from the reel, numbered from front to back on the paper machine. Syn. Roll Position.

DECKLE STAIN: Decorative coloring or tint given to the deckle edge of some papers.

DECKLE STRAP: Endless belt, typically having a rectangular cross section, that travels with the fourdrinier fabric and has the same function as the deckle.

DECKLING: Forming a deckle edge, or trimming the edges of the sheet on the wire.

DECKLING CALENDER: Calender arrangement which is capable of producing and controlling a uniform caliper for a wide range of loads and sheet widths.

DEFLECTION: Bending of a machine roll due to its own weight and/or applied loading in a particular application.

DEFLECTOR: Stationary blade placed before a table roll on the fourdrinier drainage table to deflect drained water and prevent disruption of formation. Syn. Baffle.

DEFLOCCULATION (of stock): Removal of fiber flocs from a papermaking stock either by mechanical or chemical action.

DEGREE OF CLOSURE: Measure of the white water recirculation in a paper mill, most commonly indicated by the percentage of total flow through the headbox slice that is sewered.

DELUGE SHOWERS: High-volume showers used to dilute stock in the couch pit and dry-end broke pulper, which generally turn on automatically in the event of a machine break.

DENSIFICATION: Increasing the density of paper. Typical densification operations are pressing and calendering.

DEPOSIT: Any solid material that is gradually laid down on a surface by a natural process. Typical papermill deposits include scale, pitch, slime, and various combinations of materials with fibers.

DETRIMENTAL SUBSTANCES: All dissolved and colloidal materials in paper stock that interfere with papermaking and process chemicals. See also ANIONIC TRASH.

DEW POINT: Temperature at which a gas/vapor mixture will begin to condense when cooled. Normally refers to a mixture of air and water vapor.

DIAGNOSTICS: Techniques to diagnose problems, but more specifically the interpretation and analysis of dynamic measurements to define problems and formulate recommendations. Typical paper machine measurements are machine-direction and cross-direction pressure variations and mechanical vibrations. Analysis techniques may include spectral analysis, triggered time averaging, and multichannel autoregression modelling.

DIELECTRIC DRYING: Technique for drying paper utilizing a high-frequency electromagnetic field to produce a useful current flow and rapid heating of polar materials such as water. Microwave drying is a special case of dielectric drying. Syn. Radio Frequency Drying.

DIFFERENTIAL DRIVE: Paper machine drive arrangement consisting of individual gear units for each machine section located on the drive side of the machine and connected together by a single line shaft driven by a prime mover. The differential unit is integral with the line shaft and forms a geared connection through which draw adjustments are made.

DIFFERENTIAL NIP: Variation in nip pressure for a nip-type winder because of variable paper profile or roll weight across the reel.

DIFFERENTIAL PRESSURE: See PRESSURE DIFFERENTIAL.

DIFFERENTIAL TORQUE: Difference in torque between the two drums of a two-drum winder during the winding process.

DIFFUSER TUBES: See LATERALS.

DIFFUSION AIR: Paper drying ventilation air that is not specifically supplied by fans, but rather enters the hood in random fashion from the machine room.

DIRECT-HEATED HOOD: Paper drying hood supplied by hot gases from an oil or gas burner, often the exhaust from a turbine. (As distinct from an "indirect-heated hood" where the supply air has been heated through a heat exchanger, usually from condensing steam.)

DISCHARGE OPENING: Slice opening. See also SLICE.

DISCHARGE RATIO: See JET-TO-WIRE SPEED RATIO.

DISPLACEMENT PRESSING: Air displacement of water from a wet web of paper, an experimental method of low-compression mechanical water removal that offers the potential for controlling the relationship between sheet density and water removal.

DISTRIBUTOR: See FLOWSPREADER.

DISTRIBUTOR ROLL: See RECTIFIER ROLL.

DIVERTED ROLLS: Paper rolls which are diverted from the normal flow at any point in the handling process for whatever reason. These rolls are typically reprocessed either by refinishing, rewinding or by addition to the broke system.

DOCTOR: Stationary device or assembly utilizing a scraper mechanism for removing or assisting take-off of a paper web or other material from a rotating machine roll.

DOCTOR BACK: Supporting member for a doctor blade assembly which also provides a machined surface for the mounting of the doctor blade holder.

DOCTOR BLADE: Thin metal plate or scraper in direct contact with a machine roll along its length to keep it free from deposits of pulp, pigment, dirt, etc. Also used in performing creping. On paper machines, the doctor blades are virtually always set in a "cleaning attitude", i.e., directed opposite to the direction of roll rotation.

DOCTOR BLADE HOLDER: That portion of a doctor which holds the blade and provides flexibility between the doctor back and the blade.

DOCTORING (the shade): Making a slight change in the formulation of dyestuffs being added to a papermaking stock in order to more precisely reproduce or match a desired shade for the paper product.

DOUBLE DILUTION: Paper machine approach system flow sequence with two fan pumps, used when the headbox consistency is very low. In the primary fan pump circuit, sufficient flow is maintained through the cleaners for efficient operation. This flow then goes to the secondary fan pump where additional dilution water is admixed to feed the headbox via the pressure screens.

DOUBLE FELTING: Press configuration in which the sheet is carried between two felts into the nip.

DOUBLE-FINISHING SUPERCALENDER: Supercalender stack with a reversing nip, so that a similar finish is given to both sides of the sheet.

DOUBLE SIZING: On-machine surface sizing followed by off-machine tub sizing.

DOUBLE-TIER DRYERS: Common arrangement of dryer steam cylinders in two horizontal rows, one above the other. The paper web travels between the top and bottom cylinders, picking up sensible heat while in contact with the dryer surface and flashing off steam in the open draw between cylinders.

DOVETAIL SUPPORT: Method of foil blade support where a projecting wedge-shaped part on the underside length of the foil blade fits into a corresponding indentation on the length of the support structure. (The projecting wedge-shaped part is called a "tenon" and the corresponding indentation is called a "mortise").

DOWNTIME: Any time that the paper machine is inoperative. See also LOST TIME, OUTAGE.

DRAGGED: [adj] Term applied to a paper sheet formed while the jet speed is less than the forming wire speed.

DRAG LOAD: Power required to pull the forming fabric over the flatbox area of the fourdrinier.

DRAG REDUCTION: Phenomenon of fluid mechanics when the friction loss for a fiber suspension in a piping system is less than for water alone.

DRAINAGE: Drawing off of water from a forming fiber suspension.

DRAINAGE CONTROL: Regulation of the rate of water drainage along the length of the forming fabric, usually toward the objective of an ideal drainage profile.

DRAINAGE PROFILE: Graph showing water removal rate as a function of position along the fourdrinier or distance from the headbox. The ideal profile shows a gradual reduction in drainage rate as the sheet is formed with no abrupt increases or decreases. See also WHITE WATER CONSISTENCY PROFILE.

DRAINAGE RATE: Rate at which the papermaking stock dewaters at each element on the forming wire, typically in units of kg/s per meter of machine width or kg water per kg b.d. stock.

DRAINAGE SYMMETRY RATIO (for twin-wire formers)**:** Ratio of the amount of water drained through the conveying wire (or inward wire for a Webster-type former) to the amount drained through the backing wire. For fully symmetrical drainage, the ratio is 1.0.

DRAINAGE TABLE: Arrangement of table rolls, deflectors, foils, suction boxes and flat boxes underneath the fourdrinier wire, which assist in water removal.

DRAW: Difference in speed between two adjacent sections of the paper machine. The term is also applied to the tension in the sheet caused by the speed differential or to the condition or appearance of the web between sections, whether tight or slack.

DRILLING PATTERN: Arrangement of holes for a suction press roll.

DRIVE ROLL: Roll that is driven (i.e., by a motor or prime mover) and transmits power to a fabric or felt to drive a section or assembly of other rolls.

DROP OFF: Separation of the wet sheet from the underside of a carrying felt.

DRUM: Any rotating metal cylinder. In the paper mill, the term is most often applied either to a dryer cylinder or winding drum.

DRUM DIFFERENTIAL CONTROL: Amount of overspeed between drum rolls on a winder.

DRUM GROOVING: Usually refers to the grooving configuration utilized on the drum or drums of a nip-type winder.

DRUM PRESS: Cylinder machine press located at the first suction turning roll after the last cylinder former.

DRUM REEL: Typical equipment for reeling the product at the end of the paper machine in which the web wraps around a motor-driven drum and feeds into the nip formed by a spool contacting the drum and driven by the drum. The paper wraps the spool and builds up into a reel. Syn. Pope Reel.

DRYABILITY: Relative ease or difficulty in evaporating water from a paper web in the dryer section. Differences in dryability between paper grades can be inferred by comparing their evaporation drying rates (e.g., as provided by TAPPI TIS sheets) at a specified weighted average steam pressure.

DRY BOX: Any vacuum-assisted drainage element on the fourdrinier that utilizes an exterior air/water separator discharging through a barometric leg to a seal tank. The most common example of this high-vacuum element is the flat box. Syn. Dry Suction Box.

DRY BROKE: See BROKE.

DRY BROKE REPULPER: Repulping tank located underneath the dry end of the paper machine which processes dry end broke. Syn. Dry End Broker.

DRY CREPING: Creping of the paper sheet as it is removed dry from the Yankee dryer.

DRY END: That part of the paper machine where the paper is dried, calendered, and reeled.

DRYER: When used without qualification, refers to a conventional steam dryer cylinder. See DRYER CYLINDER.

DRYER BARS: Axial bars attached to the interior surface of high-speed dryer cylinders which produce a wave action within the rimming condensate. This wave action (called "sloshing") greatly decreases the thermal resistance of the rimming condensate and thus allows an increased rate of heat transfer. Syn. Thermal Bars, Spoiler Bars.

DRYER CYLINDER: Hollow, steam-filled, rotating metal cylinder from which heat is transferred to the paper web in contact with the shell surface. Syn. Dryer, Dryer Can, Dryer Drum.

DRYER FABRIC: Endless belt of woven monofilament cloth used to hold the paper web firmly against the dryer cylinder surface. Syn. Dryer Felt, Dryer Screen.

DRYER HEAD: Flanged and dished removable capping piece at each end of a pressurized dryer cylinder. (The dryer cylinder is a pressure vessel and must conform to safety code requirements.)

DRYER HOOD: See HOOD.

DRYER PART: That part of the paper machine in which the wet pressed paper web is dried. It is the most massive part of the machine and usually takes up as much space as the other parts combined.

DRYER PERFORMANCE: Inclusive term referring to evaporation rate, uniformity of evaporation and steam economy.

DRYER POCKET: Volume bounded by open-draws on both sides as the sheet moves up and down between top and bottom cylinders in a conventional steam cylinder drying section.

DRYER SCREEN: See DRYER FABRIC.

DRYER SECTION: Grouping of contiguous dryer cylinders sharing the same dryer fabric or operating at the same steam pressure.

DRYER WRINKLE: Sheet defect caused by a lightweight sheet folding over on itself in the dryer section in reaction to a cross-machine disturbance. The amount of foldover is generally very small, of the magnitude of one sheet thickness, but the wrinkle can be several centimeters to several meters long. Most dryer wrinkles occur within 20 centimeters of the sheet edge.

DRY FINISHING: Calendering without dampening.

DRY FORMING: Paper forming process using little if any water. Most dry forming methods rely on air forming of dry fiber with spray application of binder followed by sheet consolidation. Syn. Air Felting.

DRYING CURVE: Graph showing the moisture ratio as a function of time in the dryers. The drying curve illustrates the change from constant-rate drying to falling-rate drying as the moisture ratio decreases.

DRYING INTENSITY: See HIGH-INTENSITY DRYING.

DRYING RATE: Traditional index of paper dryer productivity, in units of pounds of paper dried per hour per square foot of dryer surface contacted. This index is too dependent on press performance to be a useful gauge of dryer performance. See also EVAPORATIVE DRYING RATE.

DRYING RESTRAINT: Immobilization of paper during drying to inhibit free sheet shrinkage. In general, the less shrinkage that is allowed to occur during drying, the better will be the dimensional stability of the paper.

DRYING SYSTEM SURVEY: Investigation carried out to determine the existing evaporative performance of a dryer section for comparison with an industry average, to define the current operation of a dryer hood in order to pinpoint deficiencies in maintenance and operation, and to identify any factors which are limiting productivity and uniformity of paper product. Syn. Drying System Audit.

DRY LINE: Visible line of demarcation on the fourdrinier wire corresponding to the point where a glassy layer of water on top of the stock suddenly fades away. The machine tender interprets the position of the dry line as an indication of stock drainage behavior. Syn. Wet Line, Water Line.

DRYNESS: Weight percent of bone dry fiber in a sample of pulp, paper, or wet web. (Note that dryness and consistency are defined the same way. By convention, consistency applies to stocks, while dryness applies to sheets above 20% dryness.) Syn. Dry Solids Content.

DRY NIP OPERATION: Pressing operation where no water leaves the nip. This occurs when the water expressed from the paper web is totally contained in the void structure of the felt. (The felt is then dewatered by suction before re-entering the nip.)

DRY ROLLING: Any calendering or other roll finishing operation carried out on the dry web. See also DRY FINISHING.

DRY SUCTION BOX: See DRY BOX.

DRY VAT: Cylinder former in which the vat encloses only a small portion of the circumference of the cylinder mold. Syn. Restricted Flow Vat.

DUAL PRESS: Press composed of three rolls set in approximately the same horizontal plane, having two pressing nips. The hard center roll rotates on a fixed center line, while the two felted rolls on either side are pivoted and held in position by pneumatic or hydraulic loading. The wet web passes through one nip, adheres to the bare center roll and passes on through the second nip, after which it is stripped off the bare roll.

DUB: End relief ground on paper machine rolls which may be in the form of a taper, step or a combination of both.

DUCTORS: Bent steel fingers which guide the paper sheet into the nips on some calender stacks.

DUPLEX SHEET: Paper or paperboard sheet composed of two plies, traditionally manufactured on a conventional fourdrinier augmented with a secondary headbox located above the suction box area of the forming table.

DUPLEX WINDER: Winder in which the rolls are partially or fully supported on their cores (rather than on the outsides of the rolls) during the winding process. This method necessitates that the rolls be wound alternately on either side of a central drum to allow for support chucks on the end of each individual roll.

DYEING: Adding liquid or soluble powder dyes to papermaking stock in order to produce paper of a specified color. See also INTERNAL COLORING, CONTINUOUS COLORING.

DYNAMIC MODULUS: Property of a press roll cover material which determines the actual nip width and pressure distribution in an operating press. This property can be measured directly with suitable laboratory equipment. (Roll hardness measurements are not sufficient to fully predict dynamic operating characteristics.)

E

ECONOMIZER: Equipment for recovering heat from the paper machine dryer exhaust air. The key element is the air-to-air heat exchanger for transferring heat from the hot, humid exhaust air to the fresh, ambient supply air.

EDDY: Vortexlike motion of a fluid running contrary to the main flow stream.

EDGE: Terminating margin for a sheet or web.

EDGE CUTTERS: See SQUIRTS.

EDGE RELIEF: Tapering thickness of roll cover material at the edge of a covered press roll, designed to prevent cover damage caused by the polymeric cover material flowing out the edge of the nip.

EDGE TRIMMINGS: Narrow strips removed from the outer edges of the web during winding or sheeting operations. Typically, these strips are pneumatically conveyed directly into the dry broke repulper. Syn. Shavings.

EFFLUX RATIO: See JET-TO-WIRE SPEED RATIO.

ELASTOMER: Synthetic rubber-like polymer. Elastomers such as neoprene and polyurethane are often used as paper machine roll covering materials (i.e., as the main constituent in a formulation). See also ROLL COVER.

ELECTRO-ASSIST DRYING: Drying of paper in the presence of an electrostatic field; an experimental technique that is reported to increase drying rates by 10 to 30%.

EMITTER: Energy source for infra-red drying.

ENGINE SIZING: Addition of sizing materials to the paper stock during beating or refining.

ENTRAINED AIR: Usually refers to small bubbles of air, captured by cascading white water, that ultimately become attached to pulp fibers in the approach system. A high level of entrained air can cause instability in the approach system, reduced drainage on the forming wire, and blemishes in the sheet due to holes or thin spots. See also DEAERATION.

EVAPORATION DRYING RATE: Measure of drying rate for conventional steam cylinder drying, usually calculated as pounds of water evaporated per hour, per square foot of dryer surface contacted.

EXHAUST AIR: See AIR EXHAUST.

EXPANDER ROLL: See BOWED ROLL.

EXTERNAL ADDITIVES: Papermaking additives applied to the surface of the paper web or sheet. See also PAPERMAKING ADDITIVES.

EXTRACTOR PRESS: Cylinder machine press located immediately after the last cylinder former.

F

FABRIC PRESS: Plain press which has been augmented with a non-compressible fabric belt that passes through the nip between the felt and the rubber-covered roll to provide void volume to receive the expressed water.

FACE LENGTH: Length measurement that characterizes the working surface of a paper machine roll. Dubbed end sections are excluded from this dimension.

FACE-SIDE SHOWERING: Cleaning of fabrics and felts with high-pressure jet showers directed against the side carrying or contacting the paper web. Syn. Face-Side Cleaning.

FAIL-SAFE OPERATION: Control condition such that any alarm signal from the machine will shut down the operation to minimize damage or injury.

FALL DOWN: Percentage of stock that passes through the forming fabric of a paper machine while the web of paper is being formed.

FALLING-RATE DRYING: Refers to paper drying when the free moisture is concentrated in smaller capillaries. See also CONSTANT-RATE DRYING.

FAN DRYING: Paper drying process that utilizes fans to circulate air through heaters and into direct contact with the wet paper. See also AIR-IMPINGEMENT DRYING, HIGH-VELOCITY AIR HOOD.

FAN PUMP: Large centrifugal pump that mixes stock furnish with wire pit white water and delivers this dilute fibrous dispersion to the headbox. Syn. Mixing Pump.

FAN-TYPE SPREADER: Device (e.g., bowed roll, spreader bar) which spreads the web in the cross direction in the manner of a fan, so that parallel webs (e.g., after slitting) diverge from a central location.

FEENEY DRYER: See FELT DRYER.

FELT: Continuous belt of various constructions, used to mechanically convey the wet sheet and provide a cushion for the sheet between press rolls, and serve as a medium through which water is removed. In addition, it provides power transmission to various rolls in the press section. See also PRESS FELT, WET FELT.

FELT AIR: Heated supply air which is specifically directed against a dryer fabric to dry or condition the fabric.

FELT CLEANING: See FELT CONDITIONING.

FELT COMPACTION: Reduction in the bulk of a pressing felt due to the compressive action of the press nip, abetted by materials accumulating within the felt structure which act as adhesives to stick the felt together.

FELT CONDITIONING: Some combination of traversing high-pressure shower, detergent shower and flooding shower along with a suction box or wringer press. Syn. Felt Cleaning.

FELT DRYER: Dryer cylinder wrapped by a dryer fabric on its return run. A dryer wrapped by a fabric during its machine-direction travel is called a "Feeney Dryer".

FELTED STRUCTURE: Paper sheet structure with a predominance of three-dimensional entangled fibers. A felted structure is typical of paper sheets formed by the mechanism of thickening, i.e., where fibers in suspension are originally entangled in a coherent network and react as a compressible structure during drainage.

FELT FILLING: Accumulation of materials (e.g., fiber fines, fillers, rosin, pitch, etc.) within the wet felt structure which reduces the ability of the felt to handle water and to drain properly. Syn. Felt Blinding.

FELT HAIRS: Small woolen or synthetic strands that become separated from press and dryer clothing and sometimes appear on the surface of paper. See also FIBER SHEDDING.

FELTING: Settling and interweaving of fibers to form a mat or sheet. See also MATTING.

FELT MONITORING: Measuring selected properties of an operating felt on a regular basis in order to assess water removal performance and conditioning procedures and to identify the optimum time for replacement. Among the properties measured are felt substance (weight per unit area), thickness, moisture content, and permeability.

FELT PICKING: Adherence of fibers to the wet felt after sheet separation.

FELT ROLL: Usually refers to any of the carrying rolls which support a dryer fabric between dryer cylinders of a typical double-tier dryer section. Some felt rolls (called "blowing rolls") utilize a perforated shell through which ventilating air can be injected through the dryer fabric into the dryer pocket.

FELT RUN: Path and direction followed by a felt (or fabric) as it travels over transfer, tensioning and guide rolls; through nips and cleaning sprays; over suction boxes, etc.

FELT SEAM: Guideline imprinted across the felt to indicate straightness during operation. (Since most felts are woven in the form of an endless belt, there is usually no actual felt seam.) Syn. Tradeline.

FELT STRETCHER: Equipment for moving the stretch roll to automatically compensate for changes in felt length and maintain uniform running tension.

FESTOON DRYING: Method of air drying in which the paper is hung in a series of loops or festoons as it travels through a drying chamber. Syn. Loop Drying.

FESTOONING: Accumulating on the surface, as for example a floating mass of dry-end broke building up in the repulper chest.

FIBER BONDING: Development of hydrogen bonds between adjacent fibers in a paper sheet during the papermaking process. Syn Interfiber Bonding.

FIBER NETWORK: Entanglement of fibers. See also FLOC.

FIBER SHEDDING: Adhesion of loose felt fibers to the paper sheet.

FIBER SUSPENSION: Dilute stock.

FILL: Maximum width of trimmed sheet that can be made on a particular paper machine. Syn. Machine Fill, Maximum Fill.

FILLED IN: [adj] Refers to felts or fabrics that are embedded with an accumulation of foreign material (deposits) which markedly reduces their permeability and compressibility.

FILLED ROLL: Calender roll with elastic or plastic properties, typically used in an alternating arrangement with metal rolls on a supercalender. It is manufactured by cutting sheets of composition material (typically a mixture of cotton and other cellulosic fibers) into donut-shaped discs which are assembled and compressed onto a shaft. The shaft is then fitted onto a lathe and ground to a polish. Syn. Bowl.

FILLED ROLL BURNOUT: Surface damage to a filled roll caused by local temperature peaks due to either excessive profile variation or roll markings.

FILLER: Inert finely divided material added to a papermaking furnish to modify the sheet properties by filling in the void spaces between fibers, most commonly a mineral filler.

FILLER PLY: Any of the inner plies of a multiply board product, composed of the cheapest furnish. Syn. Core Ply, Middle Ply, Center Stock.

FILLING: Compressed fibrous material used to make a bowl.

FILTRATION: Designation for a dilute stock dewatering or forming process characterized by a clear separating surface between the fiber suspension not yet drained and the fibers already forming the fiber mat. Filtration produces a fiber mat with a clearly layered structure. See also THICKENING.

FINISHING: Imparting a finish to paper or paperboard, usually expressed in terms of the actual operation used for this purpose, including coating, cast coating, calendering, supercalendering, friction calendering, brush calendering, etc.

FIRST-PASS RETENTION: See SINGLE-PASS RETENTION.

FLAG: Marker inserted within a reel and extending beyond the edge to identify the location of a break or other defect.

FLAT BOX: High-vacuum drainage element consisting of a rectangular channel with a thick, slotted cover over which the wire passes. See also DRY BOX.

FLEX FATIGUE RESISTANCE: Measure of the ability of a roll cover material to withstand repeated nip displacements without developing surface cracks.

FLEXFORMING: Proprietary paper forming process in which the sheet is formed in a closed space between an extended flexible overlip and the unsupported wire. The flexible overlip is attached at its upper end to the ordinary rigid overlip of the headbox.

FLOATING DRYER: Dryer roll immediately following the doctor on some creping tissue machines. It runs at slightly lower speed than the subsequent rolls, thus enhancing the creping effect.

FLOC (of fibers): Discrete entanglement of fibers in papermaking stock.

FLOCCULATION: Process of forming flocs.

FLOCCULATION INDEX: Quantitative measurement of the degree of flocculation within a fiber suspension, usually by light transmission methods. Syn. Degree Of Flocculation, Flocculation Number.

FLOODED CONDITION: Situation in a dryer cylinder when the rimming thickness of condensate is sufficient to submerge the syphon pickup fitting. In this condition, only condensate can move into the fitting rather than the normal two-phase mixture of steam and condensate. Since a higher pressure differential is required to move pure condensate, a flooded condition once reached will tend to worsen. Syn. Water-Logged Condition, Water-Filled Condition. See also ASPIRATOR HOLE.

FLOODED NIP SHOWER: Water spray directed into the ingoing nip between the turning roll and the forming fabric, used for fabric cleaning or as a knock-off shower.

FLOODING SHOWER: High-volume, low-pressure shower used to supply water which flushes dirt particles from a felt.

FLOWBOX: See HEADBOX.

FLOW EVENER ROLL: See RECTIFIER ROLL.

FLOW EVENERS: Assemblies of fins set in the stock stream to break up eddies and produce a smooth flow. Syn. Rectifiers.

FLOW EVENING: Merging of individual streams from the flowspreader inlets or leveling of the velocity profile from the flowspreader.

FLOW-LIMITED PRESSING: Refers to any press nip in which the flow resistance within the fiber structure restricts the level of pressure that can be applied. If excessive pressure is applied in a flow-limited situation, sheet crushing will result.

FLOW RESISTANCE (within a press nip): Any impediment to water movement due to the characteristics of the wet sheet and the surrounding surfaces.

FLOWSPREADER: Headbox inlet assembly which receives a pipeline flow of dilute stock and distributes this fiber dispersion uniformly across the width of the headbox. The most common type of flowspreader in current use may be described as a multi-tube, tapered inlet manifold with recirculation. Syn. Distributor, Manifold, Manifold Distributor.

FLUID MECHANICS: Science of fluids in motion based on physical analysis and experimental verification. Syn. Fluid Dynamics, Hydraulics. See also HYDRODYNAMICS.

FOAM FORMING: Papermaking process in which the sheet is formed from a fiber furnish suspended in a thick creamy foam. The foam serves to dampen the relative movement of fibers and reduce their flocculating tendency.

FOIL: Static drainage element consisting of an angled stationary surface, which supports the wire and assists drainage by virtue of hydrodynamic suction forces created as the wire moves across the divergent angle. Syn. Hydrofoil, Foil Blade.

FOIL ANGLE: Divergent angle on the trailing edge of a foil.

FOIL UNIT: Assemblage of two or more parallel foil blades within a support structure that fits on the drainage table. Syn. Foil Assembly, Foil Box.

FOOTAGE: Length of paper, expressed in lineal feet.

FORMATION AID: Wet end additive which helps to keep the fibers dispersed in the headbox and prevent the formation of flocs; typically, a hydrophilic colloid such as a gum or other polysaccharide is used for this purpose.

FORMATION SHOWER: Perforated pipe mounted in the cross direction above a fourdrinier, usually just ahead of the headbox. The pipe has small-diameter holes (1 to 3 mm) at closely spaced intervals (2 to 3 mm) which discharge needle jets of water down onto the stock, thus creating machine-direction ridges and inducing "inversion" on the fourdrinier. See also INVERSION.

FORMER: Device which converts the slice discharge into a continuous fibrous mat. Syn. Sheet Former.

FORMING: Systematic deposition and dewatering of a fibrous suspension to form a coherent mat.

FORMING BOARD: Static drainage element under the fourdrinier wire located adjacent to the breast roll. The forming board supports the wire at the point of jet impingement and generally serves to retard the rate of initial drainage.

FORMING ELEMENTS: Support and drainage devices under the fourdrinier forming fabric, principally forming boards, foils and table rolls with deflectors.

FORMING FABRIC: Endless belt of woven synthetic monofilament cloth for the drainage of stock and forming of the fiber web. Syn. Plastic Wire.

FORMING ROLL: Designation for the screen drum of a cylinder former.

FORMING SECTION: That part of a former in which the fibrous web is produced. On a fourdrinier, the process of sheet forming is usually considered to occur between the breast roll and the first dry box; beyond this point, further dewatering action has a negligible effect on sheet formation.

FORMING SHOE: Long-radius stationary forming element over which dewatering takes place on some twin-wire former designs. The dewatering may be one-sided (e.g., a solid shoe surface) or in both directions (e.g., a shoe equipped with suction slots or foils).

FORMING STATION: Position where one layer of a multiply paperboard web is formed.

FORMING WIRE: Endless belt of woven wire cloth for drainage of stock and formation of the fibrous web. Forming wires are almost obsolete because of the development of forming fabrics.

FORWARD DRIVE ROLL: See WIRE TURNING ROLL.

FOURDRINIER: Horizontal forming device consisting of an endless fabric (onto which the the fiber suspension impinges) travelling between the breast roll and the couch roll and supported by various elements which dewater the fiber suspension. (Originally, it referred to the wet end of the earliest commercial paper machine invented by Louis Robert and first constructed in 1803 by Henry and Sealy Fourdrinier.) Syn. Wire Part.

FOURDRINIER BOARD: Paperboard which is specifically manufactured on a fourdrinier machine.

FOURDRINIER MACHINE: Conventional papermachine with horizontal forming wire. See also FOURDRINIER.

FREE SURFACE: Boundary between two homogeneous fluids. In papermaking, the free surface of interest is usually between water and air.

FRESH WATER: Treated or untreated water introduced into a process for the first time, as distinct from white water or other recycle water streams.

FRICTION BRAKING: Mechanical braking system for unwind stands, used to control web tension, in which air pressure applies a force between a brake lining and a drum or disc. The power supplied to the winder drive, less the friction and windage requirements, must be absorbed by this brake, which is typically dissipated by water cooling.

FRICTION CALENDERING: Calendering operation in which the paper passes through either a single nip formed by two different sized iron rolls or a double nip formed by two iron rolls separated by a large fiber roll, and in which the rolls are driven separately at speeds which differ by 10 to 30%. Syn. Friction Glazing.

FRONT SIDE: Operating or working side of the machine. Syn. Tending Side.

FURNISH LAYER: In multiply forming, either a single ply or two or more plies of the same furnish that have been couched together.

G

GAP FORMER: See CONVERGING WEDGE FORMER, ROLL FORMER.

GEARING: Layer-to-layer slipping of paper near the core of a paper roll during unwinding due to insufficient wound-in tension.

GILLING: Applying a gloss finish to the paper web by means of a Gill glazing machine.

GLAZING: Operation which imparts increased gloss and surface smoothness to the paper product, applied during manufacture or subsequently.

GLOSS CALENDERING: Calendering operation in which the paper passes through one or more nips formed by a relatively soft roll (e.g., rubber) and a very smooth, mirror-like steel or plated roll at high temperature. Syn. Thermoplanishing.

GLOSSING: Operation carried out on supercalendered paper in which the paper surface is remoistened and pressed against a highly polished Yankee dryer.

GOOSENECK: Air vent line connected to the Hornbostel hole of an air-padded headbox.

GRANITE ROLL: Press roll made from a large block of solid granite which is either fitted over a steel shaft or supported between two shaft flanges by means of steel rods located in holes drilled lengthwise through the granite shell.

GRANITING: Selectively dyeing certain fibers in the paper sheet to a deeper shade than the base shade, either deliberately to create special effects or unintentionally when trying to produce a uniform shade.

GREWIN NOZZLE: Nozzle which injects a small jet of high-velocity air into one end of a dryer pocket to induce a larger flow of air across the pocket to flush out the humid air. (Named for Swedish inventor.)

GROOVED-ROLL PRESS: Two-roll press in which one roll is equipped with concentric grooves in the roll cover to provide easily accessible receptacles for the expelled water. Syn. Vented Nip Press.

GROOVE MARKING: Marking of a sheet caused by uneven removal of water between the grooved areas and land areas of a grooved-roll press and the resultant nonuniform fines distribution.

GUIDE ROLL: Roll incorporated into every forming wire run, press felt run or dryer fabric run, which has a positioning adjustment at one end and serves to keep the fabric or wire running without lateral movement. Syn. Alignment Roll.

GUIDING: Continuous tendency of paper machine clothing to move to one side of the machine.

GUILLOTINE ROLL CUTTER: See ROLL SPLITTER.

H

HANDED: Term describing the orientation of a paper machine or converting machine. Looking toward the wet end (or feed end) from the dry end (or product end), a machine is described as "right-handed" when the drive is on the right side. When viewed from the tending side, the flow of material is from left to right on a right-handed machine. The opposite orientation is described as "left-handed".

HAND MOLD (or **HAND MOULD**): Principal device for forming handmade paper consisting of a rectangular wooden frame across which is stretched a covering of wire cloth to act as a sieve or strainer. The mold is manipulated to filter an even layer of fibers from a dilute fiber suspension in a vat.

HARDNESS TESTER: See PLASTOMETER.

HARD-NIP PRESS: Press nip formed by two hard rolls.

HARD ROLLS: Those rolls having direct contact with wet paper in press nips. Two basic types of hard rolls are used: granite rolls and metal rolls covered with a hard synthetic material, the composition of which sometimes includes stone particles.

HARPER MACHINE: Tissue machine that utilizes a couch press to transfer the sheet from the forming fabric to the felt. The relative positions of the wire part and press part are reversed to keep the paper web on top of the felt as it enters the first press nip.

HAYOUT: Colloquialism for a break on the machine that produces large quantities of dry-end broke.

HEAD: (1) Height of fluid (and hence, pressure) above a reference point. In papermaking, the term usually refers to the equivalent height of stock above the slice lip, which determines the jet velocity. Syn. Hydrostatic Head. (2) Circular piece of paper used to protect the end of a paper roll for shipment.

HEADBOX: That part of the papermachine which receives the stock delivered by the fan pump and transforms the pipeline flow into a uniform rectangular flow equal in width to the paper machine and at uniform velocity in the machine direction. Syn. Flowbox. See also OPEN HEADBOX, AIR-CUSHIONED HEADBOX, HYDRAULIC HEADBOX.

HEADBOX PROPER: Portion of the headbox that is exclusive of the flowspreader.

HEADING: In roll finishing, the operation of placing and glueing circular pieces of wrapper (the heads) over the ends of the roll.

HEAD LOSS: Loss of pressure (in terms of fluid height) in a fluid system due to hydraulic friction.

HELPER DRIVE: Auxiliary drive on a paper machine, in addition to the main drive. Syn. Assist Drive.

HETEROCOAGULATION: Hypothesized mechanism of filler retention according to which deposition of fine particles onto fibers results from mutual attraction. The forces involved originate on the surfaces, and consequently the surface potential (or zeta potential) is a decisive factor.

HETEROFLOCCULATION: Hypothesized "bridging" mechanism of filler retention according to which a long-chain polymer acting as a retention aid provides a connection between particles and fibers by simultaneously adsorbing onto both components.

HIGH-CONSISTENCY FORMING: Method of forming paper from 3–6% consistency stock which has been dispersed by intense micro-turbulence. High-consistency forming has been successfully demonstrated on a pilot plant scale, but has not been applied on a commercial basis.

HIGH-HUMIDITY HOOD: Closed dryer hood which is specifically designed to operate with an exhaust humidity as high as 0.17 kg of water vapor per kg of dry air.

HIGH-IMPULSE PRESS: Any two-roll wet press able to apply very high linear loadings, typically 1100 to 2000 pounds per lineal inch or higher.

HIGH-INTENSITY DRYING: Any drying process where the heated surface of the wet web is maintained at or above the saturation temperature corresponding to the ambient pressure. See also IMPULSE DRYING, PRESS DRYING.

HIGH-VELOCITY AIR HOOD: Compact, enclosed hood delivering high-velocity hot air and removing moisture-laden air, used for drying wet webs that are supported by a rotating surface (e.g., a Yankee dryer).

HITCH ROLL: Used synonymously with "stretch roll" when applied to a dryer felt run.

HIVACS: Generic term for flat boxes and other high-vacuum drainage elements on the fourdrinier.

HOLEY ROLL: See RECTIFIER ROLL.

HONEYCOMB ROLL: Roll with radially-oriented cell structure providing up to 90% open area, used for through-drying, pocket ventilation and other papermaking applications.

HOOD: Enclosure, most commonly placed around the dryer section of the paper machine to control ventilation and carry away moisture-laden air. Hoods are also available for the wire part. See also CLOSED HOOD, OPEN HOOD.

HOOD VENTILATION: Integral part of the paper drying process consisting of supplying adequate amounts of heated dry air and exhausting the moisture-laden air. The incoming air must be strategically distributed to flush out and carry away the evaporated moisture. The amount of this air must be sufficient to avoid condensation anywhere within the hood and thus prevent drips, buildups and corrosion.

HOOD ZERO-PRESSURE LEVEL: Height within the dryer hood at which the pressure difference between the hood and the machine room is zero. The zero-pressure level is typically at the height of the ingoing/outgoing sheet.

HORIZONTAL PRESS: Press arrangement of two rolls side by side.

HORNBOSTEL HOLE: Opening on the side of an air-padded, pressurized headbox, used to control liquid level. The hole is placed at the desired liquid level, and under normal operation a mixture of stock and air is continuously ejected.

HOT PRESSING: Wet-web pressing at elevated temperatures from 60 to 80°C. Pressing of the wet web up to 95°C is usually called "ultra hot pressing".

HOT ROLLING: Calendering or supercalendering by means of steam-heated rolls.

HOT WELL: Collecting tank for steam condensate or other hot water streams.

HUMIDIFICATION: Addition of moisture to the air.

HUMIDITY: General term for the concentration of water vapor in air. "Absolute humidity" is the mass of water vapor per unit mass of dry air. "Relative humidity" is the concentration as a percentage of the saturation concentration for the same temperature.

HYBRID FORMER: Paper forming unit in which the sheet is first formed on a conventional fourdrinier-style table, and then a top wire is applied in some manner.

HYDRAULIC ENTANGLEMENT: Technique to enhance the level of bonding in wet-laid or dry-laid nonwoven webs by directing fine jets of water at one or both sides of a web that is supported by a conveyor belt.

HYDRAULIC FORMER: Forming device in which hydraulic pressure is contained in a restricted forming zone and acts as the primary impetus for dewatering. Syn. Pressure Former, Short Former.

HYDRAULIC HEADBOX: Pressurized, filled headbox. Although, this design does not utilize an integral air chamber, some method of surge suppression is usually incorporated within the approach system.

HYDRAULIC PRESSURE: Fluid pressure created by compression of a liquid in a closed or constricted structure.

HYDRODYNAMICS: Study of fluid motion and interaction within a pressurized system, especially with respect to nonviscous, incompressible liquids. See also FLUID MECHANICS.

HYDRODYNAMIC SUCTION FORCES: Suction forces causing drainage on the fourdrinier, produced by the motion of the forming fabric over contoured supporting elements such as foils and table rolls. This mechanism accounts for 60 to 75% of the drainage on most paper machines.

HYDROSTATIC PRESSURE: Hydraulic pressure gradient causing drainage on the fourdrinier due to the weight of stock on the forming fabric. This factor is of practical importance only on very slow machines.

HYSTERESIS: Energy lost during each loading/unloading cycle as a covered press roll rotates into and out of a nip. This energy loss accounts for the heat build-up in the covering and influences the operating temperature of the roll.

I

IDLER ROLL: Paper machine roll which guides and supports the paper web or clothing. It may be driven or undriven, but does not transmit power.

IMPACT ANGLE: Angle created between the machined top surface of a creping doctor blade and the dryer surface.

IMPINGEMENT DRYING: See AIR-IMPINGEMENT DRYING.

IMPRESS WATERMARKING: Type of watermarking carried out in the press section by using a marking roll to press a pattern into the moist sheet as it passes over a press or smoothing roll.

IMPULSE: See PRESS IMPULSE.

IMPULSE DRYING: Experimental technique for evaporating and displacing water from a wet sheet. The sheet is pressed against a very hot surface which generates steam at the interface and blows out free water located between fibers in the fiber mat.

INCLINED PRESS: Press arrangement of two rolls contacting at an angle close to 45° from the horizontal.

INCLINED WIRE MACHINE: Machine designed for board production having a short fourdrinier equipped with suction boxes and inclined at approximately 30°. Essentially, the short fourdrinier takes the place of a cylinder former.

INERTIAL PRESSURE: Hydraulic pressure gradient causing drainage on the fourdrinier, produced by the impingement of the slice jet onto the wire at a large angle. Inertial pressure is utilized for initial drainage on some tissue machines.

INFILTRATION AIR: Air which enters the paper machine hood through openings from the machine room and makes up for the deficiency between supply and exhaust air.

INFRA-RED DRYING: Technique for evaporating water from a wet sheet. An emitter of infra-red radiation (usually a gas-fired heater) provides a compact, high-intensity heat source which transfers its energy to the sheet without physical contact, ideal for the drying of coatings. Syn. Radiant Drying.

INITIAL RETENTION: Retention on the open fabric before a layer of fibers are deposited.

INSIDE SHOWERING: High-pressure jet showers impinging on that surface of a felt or fabric which is not in contact with the sheet, i.e., from the inside of the felt or fabric run. Syn. Inside Cleaning.

INTEGRATED PAPER MILL: Mill that produces enough pulp to satisfy its own papermaking requirements.

INTENSITY OF TURBULENCE: One measure of stock turbulence on the fourdrinier, usually defined as the height of peaks. The scale of relative intensity proposed by Schmidt and Brabetz ranges from zero for no turbulence (glassy sheet) up to ten where spout separation (stock jump) occurs; this ranking method is subjective, but can be reproduced by trained observers. See also SCALE OF TURBULENCE.

INTERCALENDER DRYERS: Dryer cylinders located between two calender stacks, used for drying sizing applications or other surface coatings applied to the web at the first calender stack.

INTERMEDIATE CHAMBER: See MIXING CHAMBER.

INTERMEDIATE ROLLS: Those rolls positioned above the king and queen rolls on a conventional machine calender stack.

INTERMITTENT BOARD MACHINE: Wet lap machine for board grades that are cut into sheets before drying. The wet web is wound on a drum forming a continuous mat of several layers. When the required thickness is obtained, the sheet is cut and stripped from the drum.

INTERNAL ADDITIVES: Papermaking additives which are added to the machine furnish primarily for retention within the sheet. See also PAPERMAKING ADDITIVES.

INTERNAL COLORING: Addition of dye to the pulper so that the fibers are dyed before the sheet is made. Syn. Stock Dyeing.

INTERNAL SIZING: Sizing of the paper sheet achieved by application of wet-end additives, most commonly rosin and alum. Syn. Stock Sizing. See also ENGINE SIZING.

INTERWEAVING: Running together of two webs during winding resulting in rolls that are "locked together" and difficult to separate; usually caused by insufficient spreading of the web after slitting and/or alignment problems. Syn. Lacing.

INVERSION: Desirable phenomenon occurring on the fourdrinier during early forming of the sheet, in which longitudinal ridges of dilute stock invert to troughs while troughs invert to ridges, thus maintaining turbulence in the fiber suspension. Syn. Phase Shift, Repetitive Ridging.

J

JACKET: Fabric tube that is fitted over a press roll. See SHRINK-SLEEVE PRESS.

JACKING (of calender rolls): Adjusting threaded connecting rods between bearing housings on the sides of a calender stack in order to remove some of the weight of the upper rolls from the lower rolls. This technique may also be used to "cock" rolls to some extent to compensate for non-uniform roll taper.

JET: Discharge from headbox slice opening.

JET COMPRESSOR: See THERMOCOMPRESSOR.

JET DECKLE: Deckle edge set on a fourdrinier wire or cylinder mold by means of a jet of water or air.

JET IMPINGEMENT: Dynamic impact of the slice jet onto the forming fabric. The impingement angle, point of impingement and relative speed between jet and fabric all have a significant effect on subsequent sheet formation and wire mark.

JET IMPINGEMENT ANGLE: Angle between the jet and forming fabric at the point of impingement.

JET-TO-WIRE SPEED RATIO: Speed of the jet in relation to the speed of the forming fabric on a papermachine. Syn. Efflux Ratio, Discharge Ratio.

JET VELOCITY: Velocity of the jet as it discharges from the headbox. In practice, the velocity is not measured directly, but is calculated from the total head at the slice lip according to Bernoulli's equation (i.e., $v^2 = 2gh$ where g is the acceleration due to gravity). Syn. Jet Speed.

JOGGING: Running equipment very slowly (often using a helper drive) or in short bursts for purposes of maintenance or inspection. Syn. Inching.

JOINTLESS: [adj] Term applied to felts or forming fabrics indicating that they have been woven in the form of a continuous belt. Syn. Endless.

JOURNAL: Supporting shaft of a paper machine roll; that part which rotates in a bearing.

JUMBO ROLL: (1) Intact, wound reel of full-width, finished paper or paperboard removed from the papermachine. Syn. Reel, Jumbo Reel, Parent Roll, Mill Roll. (2) Any large roll of paper product that is to be used for converting purposes. Syn. Mill Roll.

K _____

KING ROLL: Bottom roll of a calender stack which is usually of larger diameter than the other rolls and is crowned. Often, it is the only driven roll in the stack; the other rolls are turned by friction.

KNOCK-OFF SHOWER: Shower which is designed to remove the sheet from the forming fabric as it comes around the couch roll and flush it into the couch pit.

L _____

LACING: See INTERWEAVING.

LAID DANDY ROLL: Dandy roll with a surface structure made up primarily of wires oriented either parallel or perpendicular to the axis of the roll. In the former case, the roll is known as a "parallel laid dandy roll", and in the latter case as a "circular laid dandy roll".

LAMINAR FLOW: Flow occurring in a conduit or channel with absence of eddies.

LASER SLITTER: Slitter which utilizes a laser beam to sever the web. This concept has not been commercially applied because of excessive energy requirements.

LATENT HEAT: Heat which when added or subracted results in a phase change at constant temperature and pressure (e.g., liquid water vaporizing at 100°C and 1 atmosphere). See also SENSIBLE HEAT.

LATERAL MOVEMENT: Movement from or to the side of the paper machine.

LATERALS: Small-diameter tubes which form an integral part of a tapered inlet flowspreader, connecting the cross header with the headbox proper. Syn. Branch Tubes, Diffuser Tubes, Multitube Section, Manifold Pipes, Manifold Tube Bundle.

LATH HEADBOX: Open headbox with two or more vertically adjustable plates (laths); the one nearest the slice determines the liquid flow.

LAYER: (1) One of the operators in the manufacture of handmade paper; the individual who removes the pressed sheets from the felt and stacks them for finishing. (2) Web which occupies a certain position or a certain application within a multilayered web.

LAYERED STRUCTURE: Paper sheet structure in which most fibrous components are oriented parallel to the plane of the sheet with a minimum of over-and-under crossovers. A layered structure is characteristic of sheets formed predominantly by the mechanism of filtration, the foremost example being a laboratory handsheet.

L/b RATIO: Papermakers' designation for the slice geometry that determines the jet impingement angle. (Sometimes the designation d/b is used.) See also SLICE GEOMETRY.

LEAD DRYER: See BABY DRYER.

LEADER: See TAIL.

LEADING EDGE: That edge of a foil, suction box, etc. that is first to be contacted by a section of moving web on the paper machine, i.e., that edge nearest to the headbox.

LEAN WHITE WATER: See WHITE WATER.

LEFT-HANDED PAPER MACHINE: See HANDED.

LICK-UP: Type of sheet transfer for picking lightweight sheets off the forming wire in which a special felt "kisses" the wire and the sheet preferentially adheres to the felt. The lick-up felt must be relatively non-permeable and is run moist.

LINEAL PRESSURE: Applied force per unit length of contacting face. For a press nip, lineal pressure is equal to the sum of the mechanical loading and the weight of the top roll, divided by the total length of roll contact. Syn. Linear Load.

LINER: External ply on one or both sides of a multiply board. The liner is typically formed from a higher quality furnish than the other plies. Syn. Outer Ply.

LINESHAFT DRIVE: Drive with one main driving shaft, whether driven electrically or by steam turbine.

LIP PROJECTION: Small vertical projection into the flow at the tip of the slice lip, used to provide a fine-scale turbulence to the jet at the point of discharge.

LIQUID-RING VACUUM PUMP: Vacuum pump in which a multibladed impeller mounted off center rotates without contact in a closed cylindrical casing. Rotation of the impeller causes liquid in the casing to form a ring. Because of the changing position of the liquid ring relative to the impeller hub, the water acts like a piston to create vacuum to draw air in and to compress the air before discharging.

LOADING: See FILLER.

LOFT DRYING: Any unrestrained, natural air-drying process for paper.

LONG CIRCULATION: See CIRCULATION SYSTEM.

LOST TIME: Interval of time that papermaking equipment is inoperative or product is not being manufactured for whatever reason (except when a paper machine is scheduled to be inoperative because of holidays or lack of orders). Lost time is usually categorized by cause under the headings of operating, mechanical, clothing and services. Syn. Downtime.

LOST TIME ANALYSIS: Systematic documentation and analysis of paper machine lost time to pinpoint specific areas of low efficiency and identify problems as they arise.

LOVACS: Generic term for vacuum-assisted foils and other low-vacuum (up to 20 inches of water) drainage elements.

LUBRICATING SHOWER: Low-volume, low-pressure shower used to lubricate and seal a felt as it passes over a dewatering suction box.

LUKENWALD DRYER: Steam dryer cylinder in which the steam is confined within a narrow, annular jacket formed by an outer and inner shell. The construction allows the use of relatively thin steel for high steam pressure.

LUMEN LOADING: Experimental technique to incorporate filler material within the lumina of fibers, so that the filler particles will not interfere with fiber-to-fiber bonding.

LUMP BREAKER ROLL: Plain covered roll riding on top of the couch roll, used to consolidate the web and aid in water removal.

M _____

MACHINE CALENDERING: See CALENDERING.

MACHINE CHEST: Chest that supplies the papermaking furnish through the basis weight valve to the paper machine approach system.

MACHINE CLOTHING: See CLOTHING.

MACHINE DECKLE: Total width of the wet web as it leaves the forming zone of the paper machine.

MACHINE DIRECTION: Direction of web travel on the paper machine.

MACHINE DRYING: Process of drying paper on the paper machine, most commonly by passing the damp sheet over a series of steam-heated cylinders.

MACHINE EFFICIENCY: Fraction or percentage of total time in which the paper machine is producing on-grade product. Daily machine efficiency is calculated by taking the figure for scaled, on-grade production over 24 hours and dividing by the theoretical production (i.e., the maximum tonnage that could be produced at the same speed, trim and grammage for a 24-hour period).

MACHINE FILL: See FILL.

MACHINE LOADING: Application of a mineral or synthetic filler to the paper at the size press. This infrequently-used process differs from pigment coating by the physical characteristics of the applied material.

MACHINE-MADE BOARD: Board made on a paper machine as a continuous web, as distinct from millboard which is made on an intermittent board machine.

MACHINE ROOM: Area that houses the paper or paperboard machine(s).

MACHINE ROOM VENTILATION: Replacement of hot, humid air with fresh air in the machine room at a sufficient rate to ensure a good working environment. A well-designed ventilation system provides a good balance between supply and exhaust flows (i.e., small proportion of infiltration air) with an adequate flow to the ceiling areas (i.e., "roof air") to avoid condensation. See also AIR CHANGE.

MACHINE SPEED: Speed at which paper is being reeled, in meters per minute or feet per minute. The operating speeds of other sections of the paper machine are always slightly lower than the reeling speed because of the draw imposed between sections.

MACHINE TENDER: Head papermachine operator, who normally concentrates on operations at the wet end of the machine.

MACHINE WINDING: Process by which a reel of paper from the paper machine, coater or super-calender is converted into shipping rolls of various widths and diameters. Included in this operation are trimming, slitting, splicing and web inspection.

MAIN PRESS: First large-diameter, high-pressure nip on a multiply machine wet end. On older cylinder machines, the main press drives all the cylinders, couch rolls, extractor rolls, and felt rolls utilizing the bottom felt as an endless belt for power transmission.

MAINTENANCE LOST TIME: Lost production on the paper machine due to downtime from planned or breakdown maintenance of equipment, expressed as a percent of theoretical production.

MAKEUP AIR: Air introduced into an area, either by supply fans or infiltration, to replace air that is being exhausted.

MAKEUP WATER: Fresh water added to the process system to compensate for water that is removed from the process for various reasons.

MAKING ORDER: Order of paper that cannot be filled from stock but must be run on the paper machine, often to the purchaser's own specifications. A making order must be of sufficient tonnage to meet the minimum requirement for a mill run.

MAKING ROLL: Upper roll of the wet press on an intermittent board machine containing a surface groove which steers the knife to cut off the built-up fiber mat as a wet sheet of board.

MANCOOLER: Localized ventilator to provide cool air and air movement in a work area of the machine room. Syn. Spot Cooler.

MANDREL: Central shaft of a roll or bowl.

MANIFOLD: See FLOWSPREADER.

MARKING FELT: Felt designed to impress a pattern into the moist paper as it passes through the felted press nip.

MARKING ROLL: Rubber-covered roll with raised or indented patterns which are impressed on the wet sheet surface as the sheet passes through a press nip.

MAT: General term applied to a thickened layer of fibers at any point in the pulp or paper manufacturing process.

MATTE CALENDERING: Any calendering technique used to produce a smooth surface without a considerable increase in gloss.

MATTING: Formation of a mat of fibers, sometimes used interchangably with "felting".

MAXIMUM DECKLE: Maximum practical width of wet web that can be produced in the forming zone of the paper machine.

MAXIMUM TRIM: Maximum practical width of trimmed sheet that can be utilized from a given reel.

MAXIMUM TRIMMED MACHINE WIDTH: Maximum width of paper or board that can be made on a given machine, the width being determined after the removal of the minimum amount of trimmings to eliminate the rough edges formed during manufacture.

MAXIMUM UNTRIMMED MACHINE WIDTH: Maximum width of paper or board that can be made on a given machine.

MECHANICAL ABSORPTION: Mechanism of sheet rewetting on the outgoing side of a press nip, caused by expansion of the sheet structure (when released from compressive load) which sucks fluid into its pores by purely mechanical action.

MECHANICAL ALIGNMENT: Application of such mechanical devices as plumbbobs, straight edges, machinist's levels, trammels and measuring tapes to the measurement and maintenance of paper machine alignment.

MECHANICAL DRIVE SYSTEM: Drive system for a paper machine in which a single motor or steam turbine supplies power to the entire machine by means of a line shaft running parallel to the machine. The indrive for each section can be transmitted mechanically by various means to provide speed adjustment.

MECHANICAL VENTILATION: Air movement caused by a fan or other air moving device, as distinct from natural ventilation (i.e., air movement caused by wind, temperature differences, stack effect or other nonmechanical factors).

MICRO-CREPING: See COMPACTING.

MICROENCAPSULATION: Chemical or mechanical process in which liquids or solids are encased within a membrane or film in the form of microscopic capsules. The process has many applications, the most common being the production of carbonless paper.

MICROSLICE: See SLICE.

MICROSLICE ADJUSTMENT: See SLICE.

MICRO-TURBULENCE: Small-scale, high-intensity turbulence. See also TURBULENCE.

MICROWAVE DRYING: Drying of paper utilizing microwave energy. This technique is said to have application for moisture profile leveling because the absorption of energy is proportional to the amount of free moisture present.

MIDDLE PLY: See FILLER PLY.

MILEAGE: Length of paper expressed in miles.

MILL ROLL: See JUMBO ROLL.

MINERAL FILLER: Finely divided mineral substance used as a papermaking additive to improve sheet opacity and smoothness. The most commonly used mineral filler is clay.

MINIFOURDRINIER: Short-length fourdrinier employed to form a single ply for a multiply board machine. This type of former is used either on the bottom side of a pickup felt or as an on-top former (in which case it may be called an "on-top fourdrinier").

MIXING CHAMBER: Term sometimes applied to the section of a hydraulic headbox which provides for proper blending of the individual jets issuing from the laterals. Syn. Intermediate Chamber, Stilling Chamber, Equalizing Chamber.

MIXING PUMP: See FAN PUMP.

MOISTURE-GRADIENT CALENDERING: Technique of calendering wherein the paper web is given a surface application of moisture on one or both sides just before it enters the calender nip.

MOISTURE PICKUP: Increase in paper sheet moisture content due to dampening, surface treatment, or environmental handling. See also WETTING.

MOLD MACHINE: See CYLINDER MACHINE.

MONUMENT: Reference point or reference plane for optical alignment measurements of the paper machine.

MOTIVE STEAM: Higher-pressure steam used in a thermocompressor to supply the energy to entrain low-pressure steam for re-use at an intermediate pressure.

MULTICHANNEL HEADBOX: Headbox in which two or more stock flows are delivered independently to the slice, and the slice discharge is made up of discrete layers of these different stocks. The development of multi-channel headboxes has made possible the production of multiply sheets utilizing only one or two forming units. Syn. Multi-Layer Headbox. See also STRATIFIED JET.

MULTICOMPONENT WET-END SYSTEM: Systems approach toward optimizing the balance between wet-end retention, stock dewatering, and product strength. A number of proprietary two-component systems are being offered by chemical companies.

MULTICYLINDER MACHINE: Multiply board machine utilizing cylinder formers.

MULTIFOURDRINIER MACHINE: Type of multiply board machine utilizing two or more fourdrinier forming units, the webs from which are couched together to form the multiply web.

MULTILAYER HEADBOX: See MULTI-CHANNEL HEADBOX.

MULTIPLY BOARD: Any paperboard product made up of two or more plies. Syn. Combination Board, Multi-Layer Board. See also FILLED BOARD.

MULTIPLY FORMER: Device that forms one layer of a multiply paperboard sheet. See also COUNTERFLOW VAT, UNIFLOW VAT, DRY VAT, SUCTION FORMER, HYDRAULIC FORMER.

MULTIPLY FORMING: Method of paperboard manufacture in which two or more layers or plies are formed separately and subsequently bonded together to constitute the sheet.

MULTIPLY MACHINE: Paperboard machine which utilizes two or more formers at the wet end to produce a number of plies. These plies are brought together on a carrying felt and plybonding takes place during pressing and drying.

MULTITUBE SECTION: See LATERALS.

N _____

NEEDLE SHOWER: High-pressure shower producing unbroken needle-like jets, used for oscillating, traversing or intermittent cleaning of fabrics and felts.

NEGATIVE CROWN: Gradual, minute decrease in roll diameter from each end toward the center. See also CROWN.

NIP: (1) Line of contact or force between two contiguous rotating rolls, such as press or calender rolls. The "line" is actually a narrow band (especially in press nips) owing to the compressibility of the web, felt and/or roll covers. Syn. Roll Nip. (2) Contacting force between a roll of paper and a drum, or between any two components.

NIP ACTION: Specific combination of pressure and friction which impart properties to the web during a calendering operation.

NIP IMPRESSION: Graphic representation of the nip width across the face of a press, used primarily to check for satisfactory roll crowning. A nip impression is obtained by placing a pressure sensitive material (e.g., embossed foil, carbon paper) across the face of an open, stationary press, then placing the two rolls in contact and loading the press to the operating pressure.

NIP LOAD: Total force applied to the paper web as it passes through a press or calender stack. See also LINEAL PRESSURE.

NIP MECHANICS: Process of creating tension in a moving web of paper by applying nip pressure between a roll of paper and a driving drum.

NIP-OUT ROLL: Free-running roll mounted along side a calender stack over which the sheet travels from one calender nip to another. If the nip-out roll position is horizontally adjustable, the travel time between nips can be varied.

NIP PRESSURE: See AVERAGE SPECIFIC NIP PRESSURE, LINEAL PRESSURE.

NIP RELIEVING: Providing an upward force on each end of a roll to compensate for the weight of bearings and journals. This technique is commonly applied to calender rolls to eliminate sheet edge pinching and produce a more level nip profile.

NIP-TYPE REEL: Winder with a single, large-diameter drum that winds paper on a reel spool or large-diameter core, typically utilized for a continuous process that cannot be readily stopped and started.

NIP-TYPE WINDER: Winder in which roll weight and other mechanical equipment provide nip pressure between the winding roll and some reference surface such as a winder drum.

NIP WIDTH: Circumferential distance over which pressure is applied in a press nip; i.e., the span of pressure distribution.

NO-DRAW PRESS: Press arrangement in which the sheet is fully supported during transfer between nips. Syn. Closed Transfer Press.

NONCONDENSIBLE GAS: Refers to the small concentration of gases contained in mill steam supplies. When steam condenses in the dryer cylinders, non-condensible gases can accumulate and adversely affect heat transfer unless provision is made to periodically or continuously evacuate these gases.

NON-INTEGRATED PAPER MILL: Mill which utilizes pulp produced at a different site.

NOZZLE: Converging and accelerating section of a headbox slice.

NOZZLE SLICE: Slice design in which the apron and slice lip protrude together with a downward slope.

O _____

OFF-GRADE PAPER: Paper that does not meet the minimum specifications established for the particular grade, often expressed as a percent of theoretical production. Syn. Off-Specification Paper. See also CULLED PAPER.

OFF-MACHINE: [adj] Applied to any processing, treatment or testing carried out on the paper product that is independent of the paper machine.

OFFSET PARALLEL CENTERLINE: Line or plane exactly parallel to the paper machine centerline, which can be used as a datum for 90° alignment measurements. Syn. Offset Line.

ON-LINE: [adj] Denoting active participation during operation or production, such as on-machine instrumentation or computers which are monitoring or controlling an on-going process.

ON-MACHINE: [adj] Applied to any treatment or monitoring of the paper product that is carried out on the paper machine.

ON-STREAM: [adj] Jargon meaning that operation of the paper machine or other designated equipment has been initiated.

ON-TOP FORMER: Forming unit for multiply board located above a felt or fabric onto which the formed ply is transferred by means of an extended wire or fabric.

OPACIFIER: Substance, typically a mineral filler, added to the papermaking furnish (or to coating color) to make a more opaque paper product.

OPEN DRAW: Unsupported paper web moving between rolls or supporting sections. Syn. Open Transfer.

OPEN-DRAW MACHINE: Paper machine with an open draw between the fourdrinier and press sections.

OPEN-FRAME SUPERCALENDER: Supercalender having two massive steel support columns on which the bearing housings are overhung by rugged suspension arms so that the roll ends are visible from the operating side and rolls may be removed endwise. Syn. C-Frame Supercalender, Open-Face Supercalender.

OPEN HEADBOX: Headbox open to the atmosphere. In this design, the discharge head is provided solely by a gravity head of stock.

OPEN HOOD: Enclosure for the dryer section to provide vapor confinement utilizing side curtains close to the machine frame which extend to within seven feet of the machine room floor. Syn. Canopy Hood.

185

OPERATING LIFE: Monitored service life of certain paper machine ancillaries such as forming fabrics, press felts, dryer fabrics, and press roll covers.

OPERATING LOST TIME: Lost production on the paper machine due to downtime from operational constraints and problems, such as startups, grade changes, reeling and stacking problems, sheet breaks, etc., expressed as a percent of theoretical production.

OPTICAL ALIGNMENT: Application of optical instruments to the measurement and maintenance of paper machine alignment.

OSCILLATOR: Device which provides a back and forth movement across the paper machine; used for example with a high-pressure shower or felt conditioner. Modern oscillators are usually electromechanical units.

OUTAGE: Downtime on the paper machine, usually of short duration.

OUTER PLY: See LINER.

OVERALL RETENTION: Percentage of stock (or of any particular papermaking component) flowing into the paper machine system that is retained on the forming fabric.

OVER-DRYING: Drying of paper below its equilibrium moisture content (about 8–10% moisture). It is necessary to over-dry on some machines in order to compensate for poor drying uniformity; a natural leveling effect occurs in the moisture profile at lower moisture content levels because the remaining water is progressively more difficult to remove.

OVERHUNG LOAD: Force applied to a machine roll at the journal.

OVERRUN: Amount of paper produced on the paper machine in excess of that required to fill existing orders.

OVERS: Mill jargon referring to an amount of overrun.

P_____

PADS: Usually refers to friction pads applied to calender rolls to expand the low spots on the rolls and improve the caliper profile of the sheet leaving the calender stack. Syn. Wrappers.

PAPER: Uniform, felted sheet composed of fibers and non-fibrous additives that has been formed on a fine screen from a water suspension and subsequently pressed, dried and calendered. The sheet may also be sized and/or coated depending on its intended end-use.

PAPERBOARD: Fundamentally, any thick, heavyweight papermaking product. The distinction between paper and paperboard is based on product thickness. Nominally, all sheets above 0.3 mm are classed as paperboard, but enough exceptions are applied to blur the exact line of demarcation. Paperboard made on a multiply machine may be described as combination board or multiply board. Also commonly referred to simply as "board".

PAPER MACHINE: Large-scale, multicomponent, integrated equipment for the continuous manufacture of paper or paperboard from fibrous and non-fibrous raw materials. A typical paper machine includes a headbox to distribute the stock dispersion onto the fabric, followed by the forming section, press section, dryer part, calender stack and reel.

PAPER MACHINE ALIGNMENT: Measurement and maintenance of tolerances with respect to the four basic "laws" of machinery installation: it must be straight; it must be square; it must be plumb; it must be level.

PAPER MACHINE CAPACITY: Actual amount of paper or paperboard produced on a paper machine over a prolonged period of time, expressed as tons per day or tons per year (or metric equivalents).

PAPER MACHINE CENTERLINE: Imaginary line or plane in the machine direction that bisects the web and the paper machine (from the headbox to the reel) into two equal sections.

PAPER MACHINE CLOTHING: See CLOTHING.

PAPER MACHINE DRIVE: Electrical or steam powered equipment to move the various sections of the paper machine. See also DIFFERENTIAL DRIVE, LINESHAFT DRIVE, SECTIONAL DRIVE, DC VARIABLE-VOLTAGE DRIVE, AC VARIABLE-FREQUENCY DRIVE, MECHANICAL DRIVE SYSTEM.

PAPER MACHINE FURNISH: See FURNISH.

PAPER MACHINE PRODUCTION: Output of the paper machine, usually on a daily basis. "Gross production" is the total amount of paper made; "net production" is the amount of salable paper.

PAPER MACHINE PRODUCTION RATE: Typical per day tonnage of on-grade product.

PAPER MACHINE PRODUCTIVITY: Measure of paper machine production relative to other machines or to some arbitrary standard. In order to compare paper machines of different widths manufacturing the same grade, the parameter, tons per day per inch of trim, is commonly used. In terms of an arbitrary standard, productivity may be expressed as a percentage. Syn. Paper Machine Rate Efficiency.

PAPER MACHINE RUNNABILITY: Ability to run the paper web through the various sections of the machine with minimum breaks.

PAPER MACHINE SECTIONS: Independently driven parts of the paper machine which generally include the wire part, press part, dryer section, calenders and reel-up. Many paper machines also have a size press and/or coating station.

PAPER MACHINE SPEED: See MACHINE SPEED.

PAPERMAKER: General term applied to paper machine operators, paper machine supervisors and paper mill managers.

PAPERMAKING: Art and/or science of converting pulp and additives into satisfactory paper products, whether using ancient handmade methods or modern high-speed machines.

PAPERMAKING ADDITIVES: Materials added to paper or to the papermaking furnish to modify or improve certain paper properties or to facilitate the papermaking process. This classification encompasses all materials that enter the system except fiber and water. Common additives are alum, fillers, sizing agents, dyestuffs, wet strength resins, biocides, defoamers, retention aids, etc. Syn. Papermaking Adjuvants, Stock Additives. See also INTERNAL ADDITIVES, BEATER ADDITIVES, WET-END ADDITIVES, EXTERNAL ADDITIVES.

PAPERMAKING MATERIALS: Fibrous and nonfibrous components used in a paper machine furnish.

PAPER MILL: Factory or plant where fibrous and non-fibrous raw materials are manufactured into paper or paperboard. Some paper mills are horizontally integrated to include pulp making and/or converting operations for further processing of the paper products.

PAPER STRUCTURE: See SHEET STRUCTURE.

PARENT ROLL: Intact wound reel of full-width, finished paper or paperboard removed from the paper machine. Syn. Reel, Jumbo Reel, Jumbo Roll, Mill Roll, Log.

PEELER ROLL: Unfelted top press roll with a very soft rubber cover, sometimes used on kraft paper and pulp machines. It provides a long nip at a low specific nip pressure.

PEELING: Pulling the wet web from an adhering surface. Syn. Stripping, Skinning.

PEELING ANGLE: Angle at which a wet web is pulled from an adhering surface such as a forming fabric or press roll. The adhesive resistance varies with the peeling angle. Syn. Stripping Angle. See also RELEASE PROPERTIES, WET WEB ADHESION.

PEELING FORCE: Tension required per unit width to peel a wet web from an adhering surface. The peeling angle and rate of peeling must be specified for comparative purposes. Syn. Stripping Force.

PENETRATION: Amount of overlap between the top and bottom cutting components in a shear-type slitter.

PERFORATED ROLL: See RECTIFIER ROLL.

PERIODIC: [adj] Recurring in a definite sequence, as for example certain headbox flow disturbances or web defects.

PERMANENT SET: Amount of displacement due to creep that remains in a press roll cover after loading is removed. (Note: Loading on press rolls must be removed as soon as the rolls are stopped; otherwise, a flat area will form where the rolls are in contact due to creep and permanent set.)

PERTURBATION: Induction of fine-scale turbulence to a flow stream, as occurs in a headbox, to prevent flocculation of fibers.

PHASE-CHANGING FORMING BOARD: Nondewatering forming board consisting of a number of foil blades butting up to one another so that the angles form v-shaped cavities. This type of forming board can be used to amplify the inversion effects from a serrated slice.

PHASE SHIFT: See INVERSION.

PHOTOGRAPHIC SURVEY: Utilization of high-speed photography for systematic analysis of flow conditions on the fourdrinier forming fabric.

PICKING: Leaving behind small sheet fragments when the wet sheet is peeled off the press roll surface. Picking can be caused by generally strong adherence of the wet pressed sheet to the press roll surface or to localized deposits.

PICKUP: Amount of uptake by the paper sheet of such applied liquids as water, sizing solution, or coating color. Pickup is a function of the liquid properties and the method of application; it also depends on such paper properties as moisture content, sheet roughness, and porous structure.

PICKUP FELT: Felt used with a suction pickup. In addition to those properties required by all wet felts, the pickup felt must have adequate surface fineness to promote a water film between the wet sheet and the felt which, in turn, provides surface tension to prevent drop-offs. Syn. Transfer Felt.

PIGTAIL: Accumulation on the surface of a felt caused by the twisting together of the fibrous cover material with entangled stock. Syn. Shanker.

PILOT DRYER: Conventional dryer cylinder located in the falling-rate zone to which steam is supplied at constant pressure. Measurement of steam flow to this dryer is used as an indication of changing moisture level in the sheet, e.g., an increase in steam flow would indicate an upward shift in moisture level. (A pilot dryer can also be supplied with a constant flow of steam. In this case, the variable pressure in the cylinder becomes the indication of sheet moisture level.)

PINCHING: Localized over-calendering of the paper sheet.

PIT: Receiving vessel or tank for stock or white water, e.g., broke pit, wire pit.

PITCH: Angle of inclination (or degree of slope) for a structure or assembly, as for example, the fourdrinier wire in the machine direction or a flow channel.

PLAIN PRESS: Basic wet press design utilizing two solid rolls. This type of press is often flow-limited because the water can leave only on the entering side of the nip by lateral movement.

PLAIN ROLL: Paper machine roll without an internal suction box for supporting and leading the web.

PLASTOMETER: Instrument for measuring the hardness of roll covers. For example, readings taken by the Pusey and Jones plastometer range from 0 P&J for rock hard materials up to 200–300 P&J for very soft compositions.

PLATEN DRYER: Equipment for drying paper or board in which the wet web is dried as it passes through the narrow space between two parallel heated surfaces.

PLUG: See CORE PLUG.

PLY: Independently formed fibrous web which is joined with other plies to form a multiply paperboard product.

POCKET VENTILATION: Continuous displacement of humid air in the dryer pocket with dry heated air.

POCKET VENTILATOR: Equipment for supplying hot dry air into a dryer pocket. Two general designs are used: the dual-purpose perforated felt roll (i.e., blow roll) which also serves as the air conduit and the separate cross-machine duct or air box with full-width nozzle, both of which blow air through the permeable fabric into the pocket.

POLYURETHANE: Generic term for a group of synthetic elastomers used for press roll covers and other applications. Polyurethane is characterized by a homogeneous structure and, in contrast to rubber, contains no fillers, softeners, or other additives.

POND: Volume of liquid held within the air-padded section of a headbox. That part of the headbox housing the pond is sometimes referred to as the "pond section".

POOR MAN'S PICKUP: Short open-draw arrangement off a fourdrinier that is equipped with a wire turning roll, in which the sheet is peeled off the inclined segment (between the couch roll and wire turning roll) and immediately supported by a felt.

POPE REEL: see DRUM REEL.

PORT EFFECT: Hydraulic friction loss in the laterals from a tapered inlet flowspreader.

POST: Pile of handmade paper sheets fresh from the mold interleaved with felts prior to pressing.

POWER TRANSMISSION: On the paper machine, the term often refers to torque transmitted through nips or to tension in clothing loops that drive parts of sections.

PRECONDITIONED PAPER: Paper manufactured to precise relative humidity specifications.

PREDRYERS: Steam cylinders used on pulp and board machines to heat the sheet between the 2nd and 3rd press nips and thereby increase water removal. (The value of predryers is often questionable, and many mills have discontinued using them.)

PREFLOCCULATION: Treatment of filler particles with a chemical modifier which causes them to flocculate prior to their addition to the paper stock.

PRESS: Water-removal device in which the wet paper sheet and carrying felt are pressed between two rotating rolls. Many different designs are used. See also PLAIN PRESS, SUCTION PRESS, GROOVED PRESS, BLIND-DRILLED PRESS, FABRIC PRESS, SHRINK-SLEEVE PRESS, WIDE-NIP PRESS.

PRESSABILITY: Capability of a fibrous web to give up water in the press section. Other than direct laboratory measurement of water removal to determine a comparative "pressability index", the best indication of pressability for a given furnish is provided by its water retention value.

PRESS FELT: Designation correctly applied to any felt, but more often applied to felts after the 1st press nip. See also FELT, WET FELT.

PRESS IMPULSE: Area under the curve of nip pressure vs. time for a press nip, a measure of the effectiveness of a press nip. See also PRESS IMPULSE CONCEPT, HIGH IMPULSE PRESS.

PRESS IMPULSE CONCEPT: Concept of wet pressing which holds that the duration of nip pressure is of equal importance to the magnitude of nip pressure.

PRESSING: Mechanically squeezing water out of a fiber mat by applying pressure. Syn. Wet Pressing.

PRESS MARK: Mark or design impressed into the wet paper web, usually at the 2nd or 3rd press.

PRESS NIP: See NIP.

PRESS PART: That part of the paper machine in which the formed sheet is pressed and consolidated. Syn. Press Section.

PRESS ROLL: Either roll used in a two-roll press. Typically, the plain roll is hard, either steel or granite. The other roll, which may be grooved, blind drilled, or equipped with suction holes, usually is covered with an elastomeric polymer to "soften the nip".

PRESS ROLL BOUNCE: Press roll vibrations that are actuated whenever an irregularity passes through the nip. Syn. Nip Bounce.

PRESSURE DIFFERENTIAL: Difference between pressures existing at two points in a system which act as the driving force for mass flow between those two points, such as condensate removal from a dryer cylinder.

PRESSURE FORMER: See HYDRAULIC FORMER.

PRESSURE FORMING: Type of sheet forming in which the initial dewatering occurs under pressure from the headbox.

PRESSURE-LIMITED PRESSING: Refers to any press nip in which the level of applied pressure is the only limitation to better water removal.

PRESSURE PROFILE: Graphical representation in the machine direction of the amount and shape of pressure and vacuum forces exerted by a single drainage device or series of drainage devices on the fourdrinier.

PRESSURE ROLL: Felted roll which presses the sheet against the Yankee cylinder on a tissue machine. The relatively high pressure used, augmented by the heat from the Yankee cylinder, provides an efficient water removal operation. Syn. Press Roll.

PRESS VIBRATIONS: Vibrations of press rolls, usually in the frequency range 15 to 100 Hz, commonly caused by corrugations that develop spontaneously either on the roll faces or in the press felts. See also PRESS ROLL BOUNCE.

PRESSURIZED HEADBOX: See AIR-CUSHIONED HEADBOX, HYDRAULIC HEADBOX.

PRIMARY ARMS: Arms which hold the empty spool on a drum reel. Once paper is established on the new spool, the primary arms are rotated downward so that the spool rests on the reel rails. As soon as the reel becomes large enough for the spool bearings to clear the arm ends, the primary arms are disengaged and returned to the upright position to receive a new spool.

PRIMARY CREPING: See SEMI CREPING.

PRIMARY HEADBOX: Designation for the conventional principal headbox on a fourdrinier that is also equipped with a secondary headbox for manufacturing two-ply sheets.

PRIMARY PRESSES: Series of small-diameter roll presses located before the first main press, used on multiply machines for gradual removal of water and consolidation of the multiple webs into a wet sheet of board. Syn. Baby Presses, Helper Presses.

PRIMARY WINDER: Apparatus for winding up a web as it emerges from a piece of production equipment. On a paper machine, the primary winder is a reel or drum reel.

PRODUCTION PLANNING: Scheduling of orders on the paper machine to facilitate grade changes and minimize off-grade production.

PRODUCTION RATE: Amount of paper produced in a given time frame by a paper machine or by a paper mill, usually expressed in tonnes per day.

PRODUCTION RATE CURVE: Curve showing paper machine production rate as a function of grammage and/or machine speed.

PRODUCTION RATE EFFICIENCY: See PAPER MACHINE PRODUCTIVITY.

PRODUCTIVITY: See PAPER MACHINE PRODUCTIVITY.

PROFILE ADJUSTING SCREW: Micro adjusting screw for making small, localized changes in the headbox slice opening.

PROFILING SPRAYS: Spray modules mounted across the paper machine which apply a fine exact water spray to the low-moisture areas of the paper sheet.

PROPORTIONER: Device for stock proportioning, most commonly a multicomponent regulating box provided with suitable inlet, outlet, and overflow ports and adjustable dams which permit manual adjustment of the amount of each of the separate stocks which make up the furnish. On modern paper machines, the proportioner has been displaced by a proportioning system, utilizing flow control and ratio control loops on each line.

PROPORTIONING: See STOCK PROPORTIONING.

PSYCHROMETER: Instrument for determining the humidity of air.

PSYCHROMETRIC PROPERTIES (of air): Properties of air/water vapor mixtures.

PUDDLING: Condition within a dryer cylinder when condensate forms as a puddle at the bottom of the cylinder. Puddling is typical for slow-speed paper machines (up to about 300 m/min).

PULSATION DAMPER: Device within the approach system to reduce the magnitude of pressure pulsations or disturbances at the headbox. Syn. Pulsation Attenuator, Pulse Attenuator.

PULSE ATTENUATOR: See PULSATION DAMPER.

PURGEABLE SHOWER: Shower equipped with self-cleaning (purgeable) nozzles. In most designs, the nozzle orifice is relatively open at low pressures, so that water flows freely while pressure is building up or when shower water pressure is momentarily reduced. Syn. Self-Cleaning Shower.

Q

QUARTER POINT PROBLEM: Problem in obtaining a uniform nip profile from a variable crown roll. The crown compensates in the center area for different nip loads at the edges of the sheet, but cannot adequately influence nip load at the points which are about one quarter of the face length of the rolls from the edge.

QUEEN ROLL: Usually refers to the roll next to the king roll in a conventional calender stack. The queen roll is typically of intermediate diameter between the king roll and the remaining rolls. It may be crowned; and sometimes it is the driven roll for the stack.

R

RADFOAM PROCESS: Proprietary foam forming process for paper manufacture. See also FOAM FORMING.

RADIANT DRYING: See INFRA-RED DRYING.

RADIANT HEAT TRANSFER: Transfer of heat energy by means of electromagnetic radiation from a high-temperature source to a low-temperature receptor.

RAKE ANGLE: Angle of displacement of the top cutting component with respect to the bottom cutting component in a shear slitter system.

RATED CAPACITY: Amount of paper or paperboard that a particular paper machine was designed to produce.

RECEPTION CHAMBER: That part of a headbox into which stock is discharged from the small distributor tubes of the flowspreader. Syn. Swirl Chamber, Explosion Chamber.

RECEPTOR ROLL: Press roll which is equipped with void areas to receive expressed water. Examples of receptor rolls are suction rolls, grooved rolls, and blind-drilled rolls.

RECTIFICATION: Re-alignment of flow to reduce or minimize cross flows and other flow disturbances.

RECTIFIER ROLL: Rotating, perforated roll within the headbox through which stock must pass on its way to the slice. The rectifier roll serves to even out flow irregularities and create microturbulence to keep fibers deflocculated. Typically, an air-cushioned box may contain between 3 and 5 rectifier rolls. The roll nearest the slice is referred to as the "slice rectifier roll". Syn. Perforated Roll, Holey Roll, Evener Roll, Distributor Roll.

RECTIFIERS: See FLOW EVENERS.

REEF ROLL: Fixed-position roll with 180° wrap which is utilized in a felt tensioning or guiding sequence in series with a stretch roll.

REEL: (1) Equipment for reeling the finished paper following the last calender nip. See also DRUM REEL, REELING. (2) Full-diameter roll from the reeling operation. Syn. Jumbo Roll, Parent Roll, Mill Roll, Machine Roll, Log.

REEL BUILDING: Synonymous with reeling. However, reel building often implies more operator involvement in the production of a uniformly hard reel.

REEL DRUM: Rotating metal roll in contact with the building reel which drives it by surface pressure. See also DRUM REEL.

REELING: Paper machine operation of collecting the finished paper on a rotating spool until it reaches a diameter that has been specified for subsequent breakdown. Syn. Primary Winding. See also REEL BUILDING.

REEL RAIL: Level rails on a drum reel on which the spool rests in the secondary winding position and over which the wound roll moves when it is pushed away from the drum to the end of the rails. Syn. Secondary Ways.

REEL SPOOL: Shaft on which paper is wound during the reeling operation.

REEL-UP: Last section of the paper machine where reeling takes place.

REFORMING: Altering the structure of a previously formed wet sheet. Reforming on a fourdrinier is accomplished by application of a dandy roll or top former.

REGENERATIVE BRAKING: Electrical braking system for unwind stands, used to control web tension, in which a direct-current motor acts as a generator to produce an opposing torque. The power thus generated is converted from direct current to alternating current and transferred back into the mill's power supply. Constant web tension is maintained through solid state logic used in conjunction with the winder's drive system.

REGULATING BOX: Constant-level, baffled flow box equipped with a consistency sensing element through which a small stock flow, representative of a larger stock flow, is recirculated. The sensor is part of a control loop to maintain consistency within a narrow range. Regulating boxes are found on stock feed lines to older-generation paper machines.

REGULATING LIP: Adjustable part of a headbox slice. On fourdrinier headboxes, the regulating lip is typically the upper lip of the slice.

REHUMIDIFYING: Adding moisture to an overdried sheet in order to reach the desired moisture content or the equilibrium moisture content. Syn. Remoisturizing. See also WETTING.

REINFORCEMENT PULP: Term sometimes used (especially in Europe) to denote the long-fibered component in a stock furnish, i.e., the fiber component primarily added to provide sheet strength.

RELEASE AID: Blend of oils, solvents and/or surfactants that is sprayed onto the paper surface or Yankee dryer surface to facilitate sheet release from the dryer surface.

RELEASE PROPERTIES: With respect to the characteristics of a press roll cover or forming fabric, the relative ease or difficulty in peeling the adhering sheet from the surface. See also WET WEB ADHESION, PEELING ANGLE.

RESIDUAL CONDENSATE: Amount of condensate contained within a dryer cylinder during normal operation.

RESILIENCY: Ability of a press roll cover to recover from a high-speed impact, defined as the ratio of energy given up on recovery from deformation to the energy required to produce the deformation. Resilience is related to hysteresis.

RESTRAINT: Usually refers to tension or pressure applied to the paper web during the drying process which does not allow the sheet to shrink freely.

RETENTION: Amount of any papermaking material which is retained in the paper forming process, usually expressed as a percentage of what was initially added. Exact percentages are often difficult to establish because of changes in the materials during the papermaking process or during analysis. Syn. System Retention. See also SINGLE-PASS RETENTION.

REVERSE PRESS: Either the second or third press in a straight-through configuration, in which the relative positions of the two press rolls are inverted. This arrangement allows the wire side of the sheet to come in contact with the bare roll and reduces the two-sided effect in certain grades of paper.

REVERSING NIP: Two adjoining steel rolls or bowls in the middle of a supercalender stack which have the effect of reversing the nips and giving equal finish to both sides of the sheet.

REWETTING: Reabsorption of water by the pressed sheet from the felt on the outgoing side of the press nip. The mechanisms of rewetting include capillary absorption, mechanical absorption and film splitting.

RHEOLOGY: Study of the deformation and flow of viscoelastic materials; of particular interest is the stress-strain behavior of wet webs.

RICEING: Special case of fiber flocculation involving well-digested esparto pulp in which tiny balls of fiber aggregates occur in the stock chest when the agitator exceeds a certain speed.

RICH WHITE WATER: See WHITE WATER.

RIDER ROLL: Weighted roller that sits atop the paper rolls in the initial forming stage on the winder to provide drive friction against the rewind roll. The rider roll is lifted off when the roll weight is sufficient to maintain friction.

RIGHT-HANDED PAPER MACHINE: See HANDED.

RIMMING: Condensate forming a continuous layer over the inside surface of the dryer cylinder due to centrifugal force. The transition between cascading puddle and rimming conditions usually occurs at a machine speed between 1200 and 1400 ft/min.

RIMMING SPEED: Speed of the paper machine at which a rimming condition is achieved. See also COLLAPSING SPEED.

RIMMING THICKNESS: Average thickness of the condensate layer in the dryer cylinder under rimming conditions.

ROLL: (1) Any material rolled up in cylindrical form, such as paper or paperboard. (2) Any rotating cylindrical body utilized as a paper machine element to support, drive or lead a web, fabric or felt, etc. and for such applications as pressing and coating. (Note that "roller" is a more precise term, but "roll" is almost universally applied in paper mills.)

ROLL BALANCING: Adding of weight, as required, circumferentially to each end of a paper machine roll to ensure a balanced condition in two planes. Roll balancing is necessary because of the dangerous centrifugal forces occurring with unbalanced rotators which lead to high dynamic stresses on bearings and possible production shutdowns.

ROLL COVER: Covering applied to a roll surface to control roll hardness and release properties. Cover materials include a wide range of elastomeric and plastic polymers combined with reinforcing fillers and other additives.

ROLL DENSITY: See ROLL HARDNESS.

ROLL EDGES: Ends of a cylinder-shaped paper roll. The roll edge corresponds to the sheet edge. Syn. Roll Ends, Roll Sides.

ROLL EJECTOR: Apparatus on a winder consisting of a movable plate or roll which serves to push a set of rolls out of the windup stand.

ROLLER: Any of various rotating cylindrical devices. See also ROLL.

ROLL FINISHING: Preparing paper rolls for shipment, including the operations of scaling, wrapping, crimping, heading, and labelling. In the modern paper mill, these operations are carried out automatically or semi-automatically.

ROLL FORMER: Type of twin-wire former in which the headbox slice jet impinges into the converging gap between two wires that are immediately carried around a roll (or rolls). The roll may be solid, in which case the initial drainage is one-sided; or, depending on design, a suction roll may be employed. Syn. Roll Gap Former.

ROLL GRINDING: Regenerating a roll surface. When the surface of a paper machine roll (e.g., press roll, calender roll) shows cracks or crazing, the roll must be removed from service and ground well below the affected depth. Surface finish is important for both satisfactory paper machine operation and wearability of the roll cover material. A more durable surface is obtained by grinding with successively finer grit wheels.

ROLL GRINDING MACHINE: Machine used to refinish the surfaces and provide the correct crown to press rolls, calender rolls, and other rolls that have become worn in service.

ROLL HANDLING: Movement of paper rolls from one location to another in the paper mill or warehouse.

ROLL HARDNESS: (1) Property of a press roll cover which is a measure of its resistance to deformation in the nip. (2) Measure of paper roll structure; the roll hardness is the density of the paper in the individual areas of the paper roll caused by radial and tangential stresses during winding. Syn. Roll Density.

ROLL HARDNESS MEASUREMENTS: See PLASTOMETER.

ROLLING FRICTION: Mechanism for sheet smoothing in supercalenders and other soft calendering operations caused by relative movement between adjoining soft roll and metal roll surfaces.

ROLL KICKER: Component of an automated roll handling system which pushes or rolls a paper roll on the bilge for transfer from one device to another.

ROLL NUMBER: Identifying number inscribed by the paper mill on the roll label or stencilled on the roll wrapper. The roll number may indicate only the chronological order of production, or it may convey additional information to the purchaser.

ROLL-OUT FOURDRINIER: Fourdrinier former that must be rolled out laterally to facilitate a wire change.

ROLL PAPER: Paper that is finished in rolls of any required width and diameter.

ROLL POSITION: See DECKLE POSITION.

ROLL SPECIFICATIONS: Information required when ordering paper rolls. In addition to specifying the width and diameter of the rolls, instructions must be given on core requirements, allowable number of splices, and any special packaging requirements.

ROLL SPLITTER: Wide knife actuated by one or two hydraulic cylinders, used to cut off-specification rolls across the diameter. The cut sheets are much easier to repulp than the whole roll. Syn. Guillotine Roll Cutter.

ROLL STRUCTURE (of a paper roll): Winding stress as a function of roll diameter, which may be characterized by roll hardness, wound-in tension and/or interlayer (radial) pressure. See also ROLL STRUCTURE PROFILE.

ROLL STRUCTURE CONTROL: Control of tension, torque and nip during winding in order to build and structure paper rolls in accordance with accepted standards of roll quality.

ROLL STRUCTURE PROFILE (of a paper roll): Profile of wound-in tension (hardness) from the core to the outside of a roll. An optimum structure would have a smooth diminution of hardness from the core to the outside; and the wound-in tension at the core would be great enough to prevent such structural defects as dishing, telescoping and bursting.

ROLL WRAPPING: See ROLL FINISHING.

ROOF AIR: Fresh, warm air directed into the ceiling areas of the machine room to flush out pockets of humid air and prevent condensation on ceiling surfaces. Roof air is an important component of an overall machine room ventilation system.

ROOSTER TAILS: Colloquialism for the ridges in and following the slice jet flow.

ROPE CARRIER: Principal method of sheet threading for the dryer section of a paper machine by means of two ropes that run in grooves on the front side of the dryer cylinders. The tail is placed between the ropes, which carry it through the dryer. Sometimes referred to as the "Sheehan carrier" after the inventor. A rope system can also be used for carrying the tail into the calender stack and reel.

ROPINESS: Gelatinous or stringy character, reminiscent of soured milk. The term can be descriptive of various dispersions including sizing solutions, coatings and adhesives.

ROPING (of a felt): Forming longitudinal wrinkles in the felt. Conventional felts are sometimes intentionally "roped up" during off-line cleaning operations.

ROTARY PRESSURE JOINT: Connection between a stationary flexible pipe (carrying steam, condensate, water, air, etc.) and a rotating dryer cylinder, calender roll, press roll, etc.

ROTARY SLITTER: See SLITTER.

ROTARY SUCTION BOX: Arrangement of dry boxes covered by an independently-driven endless belt which runs between rolls at each end of the assembly and moves with the forming fabric. The rotary suction box is designed to reduce frictional drag on the forming fabric and, therefore, reduce wear and tension.

ROTATING SYPHON: See SYPHON.

ROUNDNESS: Measurement of how a roll surface compares to a perfect circle, an important tolerance measurement for paper machine press and calender rolls.

RUN: See FELT RUN.

RUSHED: [adj] Term applied to a paper sheet formed while the jet speed exceeds the forming wire speed.

S

SADDLE: Any contoured support, but especially the reel spool support at the unwind stand of a winder.

SANKEY BALANCE: Graphical depiction of a material balance in which the width of each material stream is shown proportional to its flow rate. This method is often applied to illustrate wet end balances. Syn. Sankey Diagram.

SATURATED AIR: Air that is saturated with water vapor at the prevailing temperature, i.e., air at its dew point temperature. Any cooling of saturated air will result in condensation of moisture.

SAVEALL TRAY: Tray under the free-draining section of the fourdrinier which collects the drainage water.

SAW-BLADE FLOW CHANNEL: Parallel flow channel formed by combining straight or curved surfaces with sections of sharp expansion and gradual contraction, utilized as a headbox turbulence generator.

SCAB: Foreign material adhering to the surface of a calender roll.

SCALE OF TURBULENCE: One measure of stock turbulence on the fourdrinier defined as the number of peaks per unit area. See also INTENSITY OF TURBULENCE.

SCALING: Operation of weighing and labelling finished rolls, bales or packages.

SCANNING GAUGE: Sensing element (e.g., for moisture, grammage, caliper, etc.) which traverses the moving web on a paper machine to provide a cross-direction profile of a particular sheet property. Syn. Traversing Gauge.

SCHIEL PLOT: Graphical depiction of wet press performance in which the average pressure in the nip is displayed on the vertical axis; and the dwell time in the press nip is displayed on the horizontal axis. Equal pressed sheet moisture curves derived experimentally on the paper machine are the parameters. (after C. Schiel)

SCISSORED ROLLS: Two or more rolls on a web path whose axes are not parallel, but are crossed in a manner that is difficult to detect.

SCOOPING: Removal of fibers from suspension and their accumulation on the trailing edges of the holes of a perforated roll in a headbox, thus causing fiber flocs in the downstream flow. Scooping is usually associated with excessive rotational speed of the perforated roll. See also STAPLING.

SCORING: Surface markings on calender rolls caused by doctor blade defects or excessive pressure by the doctor.

SCUFFING: Raising of fibers on the surface of paper by rubbing against another surface.

SECONDARY ARMS: Pivoting arms which control the secondary winding position (i.e., along a level rail) during reeling.

SECONDARY CREPING: Creping that is carried out as a converting operation on the finished sheet. The paper is re-wetted and passed over a dryer roll equipped with a doctor. High crepe ratios may be achieved, but the stretch "pulls out" more easily than on semi creped and dry creped papers. Syn. Crinkle Creping, Water Creping, Off-Machine Creping.

SECONDARY HEADBOX: Headbox which is suspended above the drybox area of the fourdrinier and is used to apply a top layer of stock onto the primary paper web, commonly used in the manufacture of linerboard.

SECONDARY WINDER: Machine for rewinding a web that has already been wound up at the end of a processing machine. The equipment for rewinding a paper reel is called simply a "winder".

SECTIONAL DRIVE: Individual electrical drives for the different sections of the paper machine with no mechanical interconnections. Several methods are used to coordinate the speeds of the various sections. See also AC VARIABLE-FREQUENCY DRIVE, DC VARIABLE-VOLTAGE DRIVE.

SELF-SKINNING ROLL: Paper machine roll (e.g., press roll) that has good release properties and characteristically resists picking.

SEMI-CREPING: Creping carried out on the paper machine while the paper is still wet. The crepe ratio is low. Syn. Primary Creping, Machine Creping.

SENSIBLE HEAT: Heat which when added or subtracted results in a change of temperature. See also LATENT HEAT.

SEPARATOR: See STEAM SEPARATOR.

SERPENTINE FABRIC: Dryer fabric applied to a conventional double-tier steam cylinder section in which the bottom fabric is eliminated and the top fabric follows the sheet between the top and bottom dryers. This scheme is used in the first dryer section on light-weight paper machines to stabilize the sheet against flutter and wrinkling. Syn. Single Felting.

SERRATED SLICE: Slice having a serrated top lip which produces regular deep machine-direction ridges in the headbox discharge, thus causing "inversion" on the fourdrinier. See also INVERSION.

SERVICES LOST TIME: Lost production on the paper machine due to downtime caused by lack of services such as electrical power and steam, expressed as a percent of theoretical production. Sometimes lack of pulp furnish is grouped within this category of lost time.

SET OF ROLLS: Single run of rolls from the winder.

SHADED WATERMARK: Watermark in which the image is visible when viewed by transmitted light because it is more opaque than the rest of the sheet, as distinct from a conventional watermark which is visible because it is more transparent.

SHADOW MARKING: Marking of a sheet caused by uneven removal of water between the drilled areas and land areas of a suction press or suction couch roll and the resultant uneven fines distribution. Syn. Shell Marking.

SHAFTLESS WINDING: Winding a web material onto cores without the use of a winder shaft.

SHAKE: (1) Mechanism which imparts a cross-oscillation motion to the forming wire, used on slower-speed paper machines to improve sheet formation. (2) Vatman's stroke in forming handmade paper.

SHANKER: See PIGTAIL.

SHAPE TOLERANCE: Specification for a straight or crowned roll, defined as the deviation from a specified shape as measured by the distance between two parallel lines which envelop the actual shape of the roll. Shape variations for calender rolls cause nip variations and resulting hard spots, uncalendered areas and caliper variations.

SHEAR WRINKLES: Web wrinkles caused by lateral deformations of the sheet in directions other than the machine direction.

SHEET: Continuous web of paper at various stages of manufacture. Syn. Web.

SHEET CONSOLIDATION: Compaction of the wet sheet to improve contact between fibers and ensure the development of strong fiber-to-fiber bonds during drying. Sheet consolidation takes place during wet pressing.

SHEET FLUTTER: Flapping and billowing of the paper sheet in the open draws of the press and dryer sections caused by cross flows, uneven sheet tension, or mechanical disturbances. The flutter at the sheet edges leads to creases and breaks on lightweight paper machines. Syn. Sheet Blowing.

SHEET FOLLOWING: Tendency for the wet sheet to follow the felt on the outgoing side of a press nip. See also SHEET STEALING.

SHEET RELEASE: Relative ease or difficulty in removing the wet paper sheet from a forming fabric or press roll. See also RELEASE PROPERTIES.

SHEET SEALING: Abrupt reduction in stock drainage on the forming fabric due to severe penetration and compaction of fiber into the fabric openings, usually caused by excessive early drainage.

SHEET SEPARATION: Usually refers to the continuous removal of the wet paper web from the forming fabric during startups or wet-end breaks.

SHEET SHRINKAGE: Change in dimensions of the paper web due to drying, usually expressed as a percentage. On the paper machine, sheet shrinkage occurs in the cross-machine direction. Syn. Sheet Contraction.

SHEET STABILITY: Generally refers to efficient high-speed web transfer from the press section and web travel throughout the dryer section; stability infers freedom from sheet flutter, floppy edges, bagging and blowing, but without the need for high sheet tension. Syn. Web Control. See also WEB HANDLING, WEB INSTABILITY.

SHEET STEALING: Refers specifically to the situation on a conventional Yankee fourdrinier tissue machine when the wet sheet tends to follow the bottom wet felt rather than the pickup felt on the outgoing side of the suction press nip. See also SHEET FOLLOWING.

SHEET STRATIFICATION: Change in the vertical distribution of fiber and filler in the sheet caused by fluid shear forces during pressing.

SHEET STRUCTURE: Arrangement, orientation and closeness of fibers and non-fibrous components in a paper sheet. See also LAYERED STRUCTURE, FELTED STRUCTURE.

SHEET TENSION: Stress or tightness caused by pulling.

SHEET TRANSFER: Movement of the paper sheet from one supporting medium to another or from one section of the paper machine to another, e.g., from forming fabric to press felt or from press felt to dryer section. An unsupported sheet transfer is referred to as an "open draw". Syn. Web Transfer.

SHEET WETTING SHOWER: Fourdrinier shower positioned just before the knock-off shower which serves to thoroughly wet the sheet and loosen it from the forming fabric, thus facilitating the action of the subsequent knock-off shower.

SHELL MARKING: See SHADOW MARKING.

SHERATON ROLL: Table roll with a gear-like surface (i.e., a series of axial grooves) which induces intense fine-scale turbulence into the stock carried over the roll by the forming fabric.

SHORT CIRCULATION: See CIRCULATION SYSTEM.

SHORT FORMER: See HYDRAULIC FORMER.

SHOWERING: Application of water for puposes of wire, fabric, roll and felt cleaning, roll lubrication, sheet spraying, deckling, foam killing, etc. See also INSIDE SHOWERING, FACE-SIDE SHOWERING.

SHRINKAGE: See SHEET SHRINKAGE.

SHRINK-SLEEVE PRESS: Plain press in which a non-compressible fabric jacket or sleeve is shrunk over the rubber-covered roll to provide void volume.

SHUTDOWN: Cessation of operations.

SIDE RUN: Narrow roll of paper created during slitting-winding that is not part of an order, but is wide enough to be used for some purpose other than repulping.

SIDE LOADING: Pressure between top and bottom cutting components in a shear-type slitter to keep the two cutting elements in contact.

SILURIAN EFFECT: Preferential dyeing of certain fibers in a paper sheet. See also GRANITING.

SIMPLEX SHEET: Single-ply sheet. The term is usually applied to certain paperboard grades that are also manufactured as duplex or multiply sheets.

SINGLE FINISHING STACK: Supercalender with alternate rolls all the way down the stack, so that a higher finish is imparted to the surface in contact with the steel rolls.

SINGLE-PASS RETENTION: Percentage of the stock issuing from the headbox that is retained on the forming fabric during paper manufacture. Syn. First-Pass Retention, Wire Retention.

SINGLE-TIER DRYERS: Arrangement of dryer cylinders in a single horizontal row. The paper web is carried outside the dryer fabric around the felt rolls (or transfer rolls), but held to the fabric by means of suction boxes.

SIZE PRESS: Roll press (either horizontal, vertical or inclined) located between dryer sections in which the paper is given a one or two-sided application of sizing or other liquid coating. See also GATE ROLL SIZE PRESS.

SIZING: Treatment of paper to resist liquid penetration, either by means of wet-end additives (e.g., rosin and alum) or surface application (e.g., starch solution).

SKATING: Irregular flow streaking across the wire on a diagonal to the machine direction, caused by slice defects and instabilities in the headbox flow.

SKINNING: See PEELING.

SLABBING OFF: Cutting several hundred plies of paper simultaneously off the reel, usually for the purpose of discarding the paper into the dry-end broke pulper.

SLAB-OFF LOSSES: Lost production on the paper machine due to discarding paper into the dry-end broker, expressed as a percentage of theoretical production. Since slab-off losses are rarely measured, they must be estimated by the operators.

SLACK AREA: Section of fabric or felt having less tension than the rest. Syn. Baggy Area.

SLACK DRAW: Sheet transfer with low web tension. See also DRAW.

SLICE: Rectangular full-width nozzle with completely adjustable opening through which the headbox delivers the stock jet to the forming zone. The top and bottom of the slice opening are formed by the top lip and apron respectively. The top lip is adjustable up and down as a unit (main slice) and in localized areas (microslice adjustment). Either the top lip or apron extension is adjustable in the horizontal direction in order to change the impingement angle of the stock jet onto the forming wire. The apron is usually slightly sloped toward the opening.

SLICE COEFFICIENT: Ratio of the theoretical slice opening required for a given flow to the actual slice opening. The liquid stream contracts as it passes through the slice, necessitating that the slice opening be wider than calculated. Depending on slice design, the coefficient ranges between 0.62 and 0.95.

SLICE EDGE BLEED: Small, controlled flow of stock taken from the side of the headbox near the slice to offset the natural tendency of the jet to "fan out" at the extreme edge.

SLICE GAP: Distance between the lip and apron of the slice, i.e., the vertical slice opening.

SLICE GEOMETRY: Relative position of the top lip and apron of the headbox in relation to the breast roll, with respect to a conventional fourdrinier. The slice geometry determines the angle of impingement for the jet and the point of impingement on the wire.

SLICE LIP: See SLICE.

SLICE NOZZLE: Converging section of the slice. Syn. Slice Channel, Converging Channel.

SLICE OPENING: Partition between slice lip and apron through which the slice jet discharges.

SLIDING SPREADER: Non-moving surface with a bowed shape over which the web slides to induce spreading. See also SPREADER BAR.

SLING PSYCHROMETER: Device having wet and dry bulb thermometers that is whirled in the atmosphere to provide readings. The relative humidity or other psychrometric properties can then be obtained from a graph or table.

SLIP: Difference in velocity between two roll surfaces forming a nip. Whether slip actually occurs during conventional pressing and calendering operations is a matter of conjecture.

SLITTER: Cutting device used to slit a machine-direction paper web into specified widths or to trim the outside edge of a web. Two main types of slitters are used: in the "shear-type" slitter, the web is cut between two edge-contacting circular knives; in the "score-cut" design, a circular knife cuts against a hardened backing plate or roll. Syn. Rotary Slitter.

SLITTER BAND: Bottom cutting component of a shear-type slitter system.

SLITTER BLADE: Top cutting component of a shear-type slitter system.

SLITTER CUTS: Ragged sheet edge appearing nicked or torn, produced by dull slitter knives and generally accompanied by excessive slitter dust.

SLITTER DUST: Dust generated by the slitter, probably as a result of a dull blade or improper setting of the disc.

SLITTER JUMP: Up and down motion of the top cutting component (due to vibration) relative to the bottom cutting component for a shear-type slitter system.

SLITTER RINGS: Distinct rings visible on the ends of paper rolls; these are actually offsets or protrusions of a specific shape which are due to slitter band wobble. See also SLITTER RUNOUT.

SLITTER RUNOUT: Radial or axial wobble of the bottom cutting component on a shear-type slitter system which results in cutting a scalloped edge, visible as "slitter rings".

SLITTER TABLE: Area of a winder encompassing the web path through the slitter. The slitter table may be vertical, horizontal, or inclined with respect to the supporting floor.

SLITTING: Process of cutting the web of paper along the machine direction in order to obtain narrower widths. Slitting is an integral component of winding, and is also carried out as part of various finishing and converting operations. Syn. Slit Cutting.

SLOSHING: See DRYER BARS.

SLOWDOWN: Reduction in paper machine speed.

SMOOTHING PRESS: Feltless press placed either at the final press position or before a size press or coating unit in which the primary objective is to achieve surface smoothness rather than water removal.

SNAKING: Streaks of higher moisture which meander back and forth in the sheet, indicative of some instability in the forming fabric.

SNAPOFF: Sheet break sustained during calendering, reeling, winding, etc. due to excess tension. The term may be applied to all dry-end breaks.

SOFT CALENDERING: Any on-machine calendering process in which the nips are formed between compliant and non-compliant rolls. Gloss calendering is an example of soft calendering. Syn. Soft-Nip Calendering, Elastic-Nip Calendering.

SOFT PROCESS: Papermaking concept associated with the production of "soft tissues" which concentrates on avoiding compaction of the web. The fundamental characteristic is the absence of pressing.

SOLEPLATE: Supporting base of a paper machine.

SOLID ROLL: Press roll with a smooth surface without holes or grooves.

SOLVENT BONDING: Method for bonding non-woven fabrics where a solvent or swelling agent is added to the dry formed sheet to gelatinize the fibers, which are then bonded under pressure.

SPEAR: Long, light pole with a sharp steel head that is sometimes curved, used as a cutting tool to dislodge paper that has wrapped a dryer during a break.

SPECIFICATIONS: In papermaking, a set of prescribed properties or characteristics that must be matched for a particular product to meet the standards of the customer.

SPECIFIC NIP PRESSURE: See AVERAGE SPECIFIC NIP PRESSURE.

SPECIFIC WOOD CONSUMPTION: Measure of wood consumption for a unit of paper production, usually in terms of ton per ton on a bone dry basis. As utilization of high-yield pulps and secondary fiber generally increases for a variety of paper products, the average specific wood consumption decreases.

SPEED-UP: Increase in paper machine speed.

SPIRAL LAID DANDY ROLL: Dandy roll in which a surface wire wraps around the circumference of the roll in spiral fashion, producing lines in the paper parallel with the grain of the paper.

SPLICE: Union of two webs of paper to make a continuous sheet, as during the winding of rolls. See also BUTT SPLICE, LAP SPLICE.

SPLICING: Act of producing a splice.

SPLIT-TOP FELT: Utilization of two top felts on a conventional cylinder board machine to replace the traditional long top felt, and thus improve the pressing efficiency of the drum, primary and main presses.

SPOILER BARS: See DRYER BARS.

SPOOL: See REEL SPOOL.

SPOOL STARTER: Device on a drum reel which brings the empty spool up to speed before the spool comes in contact with the web on the rotating drum. Most commonly, the starter consists of a rubber tire which is driven by the drum and brought to bear against the spool by a pneumatic cylinder.

SPOUTING: Throwing up of columns of liquid on the fourdrinier due to pressure pulses caused by table rolls or foils. See also STOCK JUMP.

SPRAY DYEING: Process of spraying dye stuff solution onto the paper web as it passes over the suction box area of the fourdrinier.

SPREADER BAR: Adjustable curved bar on a winder that is wrapped by the sheet following slitting and serves to spread the web and prevent interweaving of web edges as rolls are wound. Syn. Camber Bar.

SPREADER ROLL: See BOWED ROLL.

SPREADING: Process of smoothing a non-slit web or separating webs following slitting so that rolls can be wound without interweaving. See also FAN-TYPE SPREADER, BOWED ROLL, SPREADER BAR, WORM ROLL.

SPRING ROLL: Guide roll with spring bearings.

SQUEEZE ROLLS: Type of two-roll press in which little if any additional loading is added to the top roll, i.e., a press with very little nip loading.

SQUIRTS: High-pressure water jets located over the wire near each edge just prior to the couch roll, used to trim the edges of the wet sheet.

STACK: See CALENDER STACK.

STACKED DRYERS: Arrangement of dryer cylinders on the paper machine in which the cylinders are mounted in tiers to a height of ten or more. This arrangement is more typical of multiply board machines than of fourdrinier machines.

STACKING: Getting the sheet threaded through the calender stack.

STAPLING: Fibers being removed from suspension and accumulating across the lands (solid area between holes) of a perforated roll within a headbox, causing fiber flocs in the downstream flow. Stapling is usually associated with insufficient rotational speed of the perforated roll. See also SCOOPING.

STARTUP: Beginning operation of a paper machine. Syn. Restart.

STATIONARY SYPHON: See SYPHON.

STEAM CALENDERING: Machine calendering in which the web is made to pass through a steam shower before it enters one or more calendering nips.

STEAM CYLINDER: See DRYER CYLINDER.

STEAM ECONOMY: Measure of steam usage during paper drying, usually calculated as mass of steam per unit mass of water evaporated.

STEAM JOINT: Special rotary fitting through which steam is admitted and condensate is removed at the end of a dryer cylinder. Syn. Steamfit.

STEAM RECOMPRESSION: Mechanical compression of low-pressure steam up to a higher pressure. Sectional pressure control of paper machine dryer sections based on steam recompression is a viable alternative to the cascade and thermocompressor systems now in common use.

STEAM SEPARATOR: Pressure-coded vessel into which condensate and blow-through steam are discharged from a dryer group. It is internally baffled to facilitate separation of liquid and vapor. From the separator, the condensate is returned to the boiler house and the steam is re-used in the dryers.

STEAM SHOWER: Array of steam jets across the paper machine, commonly used to heat the wet sheet during pressing operations or to heat and surface dampen the sheet prior to calendering. Syn. Thermal Shower.

STEP FLOW CHANNEL: Series of flow chambers of decreasing diameter interconnected by steps, utilized as a headbox turbulence generator.

STOCK JAMS: Filled areas in the forming fabric that do not drain water.

STOCK JUMP: Disturbance on the fourdrinier caused by an upward impulse, either due to a pressure pulse or from the abrupt breaking of a vacuum that causes an upward bounce of the forming fabric. See also SPOUTING.

STOCK METERING: Controlling the mass flow rate of papermaking constituents, which depends on control of both consistency and volumetric flow rate.

STOCK PROPORTIONING: Metering of different stock flows in the correct proportions to make up a specified blend for delivery to the paper machine.

STOCK WAVE: See WAKE EFFECT.

STRAIGHT-THROUGH PRESS: Simple press arrangement consisting of a horizontal sheet run through a series of vertical press nips.

STRATIFIED JET: Slice jet in which two or more individual stock flows are merged together in the converging channel. Although some intermingling of fibers occurs between strata, the emerging jet is layered.

STRATIFIED WEB: Paper or board web that has been intentionally produced with a nonuniform cross-sectional structure. Syn. Structured Web, Multistrata Paper.

STRATIFIED WEB FORMING: Any of three different methods: by forming separate mats and combining them into a single web; by forming successive layers on top of a base mat; and by forming the web from a stratified jet delivered by one headbox supplied with separate furnishes.

STREAMLINE FLOW: Liquid flow in which particles within the liquid follow well-defined continuous paths.

STRETCH ROLL: Roll incorporated into every forming wire run, press felt run or dryer fabric run which moves up and down (or backward and forward) as a unit and controls tension in the run. See also HITCH ROLL.

STRINGS: String-like accumulations of fibers which can form at protuberances or irregularities within the papermaking system. If strings break free and are not re-dispersed, they will form "worms" on the wire.

STRIPPING: See PEELING.

STRUCTURE: See SHEET STRUCTURE, ROLL STRUCTURE.

STUB ROLL: Narrow-width paper roll formed on the winder for the purpose of completing the machine fill, usually returned to the beater.

STUFF: Low-consistency, beaten fiber suspension containing additives, ready to be delivered to the paper machine as the papermaking furnish. Syn. Machine Furnish, Machine Stock.

STUFF BOX: Small, elevated tank which receives stock from the machine chest, then supplies this stock from a constant head compartment to the paper machine approach system, and returns a small overflow to the machine chest.

STUFF GATE: See BASIS WEIGHT VALVE.

SUCTION BOX: (1) Device connected to a vacuum source for removing water from a wet felt, most commonly consisting of a rectangular box with a slotted cover over which the felt runs. (2) Stationary suction chamber inside a rotating perforated couch roll or suction press roll.

SUCTION BOX DECKLE: Movable flap inside a suction box which allows for lateral adjustment of the suction area.

SUCTION COUCH: Large, perforated roll around which the fourdrinier forming fabric passes at the end where the sheet is transferred. It is often the main drive roll for the fourdrinier section and contains one or two stationary suction boxes for sheet dewatering.

SUCTION FORMER: Type of multiply former that utilizes a rotating cylinder mold without a vat. Initial formation usually takes place under a hydraulic head; internal suction boxes are used to obtain further fiber deposition and dewatering.

SUCTION PICKUP: System for transferring the wet sheet from the fourdrinier to the press section in which the sheet is picked off the wire by a felt wrapping a suction roll at the point of contact.

SUCTION PRESS: Two-roll wet press in which one roll consists of a rotating perforated shell with internal stationary suction box.

SUCTION ROLL: Roll consisting of a hollow perforated shell rotating about a stationary suction box, used for such paper machine applications as suction pick-up, felt turning roll, suction couch and as part of a suction press.

SUCTION ROLL FORMER: Roll former that uses a vacuum-augmented suction or couch roll arrangement to aid in sheet drainage. See also ROLL FORMER.

SUCTION ROLL NOISE: Noise generated by the rapid filling of suction holes with air as the holes come off the trailing packing strip of the suction box. The noise is most severe when a straight line of holes are opened at the same time.

SUCTION ROLL STRIP: Packing strip that provides a seal between the stationary suction compartment and the rotating shell of a suction roll.

SUCTION STEAM: Blow-through steam which is drawn into the thermocompressor and boosted in pressure.

SUNDAY DRIVE: Slow-speed drive used to keep certain paper mill equipment running at reduced speed during shutdowns.

SUPERCALENDERING: Off-machine calendering operation utilizing a stack consisting of alternating chilled iron and fiber rolls. The fiber rolls (called bowls or filled rolls) are commonly constructed of highly compressed cotton or other cellulosic material.

SUPERING: Mill jargon for supercalendering.

SUPPLY AIR: See AIR SUPPLY.

SUPPORTED SLEEVE: Cylindrical wire-covered sleeve that may be fitted over the body of a dandy roll in certain cases.

SURFACE APPLICATION: Operation involving application of a suitable material to the surface of paper or paperboard to change certain of its characteristics.

SURFACE COLORING: Application of a coloring agent (dye) to the surface of paper either on the paper machine or as an off-machine operation. Syn. Surface Staining.

SURFACE DRIVE: Power transmission from one moving surface to another due to pressure and friction between the surfaces, e.g., as occurs at the windup station of a drum reel or two-drum winder.

SURFACE HARDENING: Slight hornification of the paper surface due to excessively hot temperatures employed in the early stages of drying.

SURFACE SIZING: Sizing of the paper web by means of surface application of a suitable agent, usually a starch solution. Syn. External Sizing.

SWEAT DRYER: Cylinder at the end of the dryer section over which the paper sheet runs and through which cooling water is circulated. Water is condensed onto the surface of the roll (either from the humid dryer ventilation air or from steam showers) and this moisture film is transferred to the surface of the paper to assist the subsequent calendering operation. Syn. Chilled Roll, Sweat Roll. See also DAMPING ROLL.

SWEATING: Condensation of moisture on surfaces colder than the dew point of the ambient atmosphere.

SWEETENER STOCK: Long-fibered stock added to white water as a filter aid prior to its clarification through a disk-type vacuum saveall.

SWIMMING ROLL: Type of variable crown roll consisting of a stationary shaft supporting a rotating shell. Inside the roll is a chamber sealed by two longitudinally running axial seals into which oil is introduced under pressure to oppose the nip load. Syn. Antideflection Roll.

SWING ROLL: Mechanically driven wrapped roll which conducts the sheet from one paper machine section to another. It provides sheet storage and acts as a "shock absorber" while waiting for the drive to respond to a tension change.

SYPHON: Device to remove condensate from a dryer cylinder. "Stationary syphons" attached to an outside journal are typically employed if the condensate collects in a puddle. "Rotating syphons" attached to the interior surface are used for rimming conditions.

SYPHON SHOE: Part of the syphon assembly which is closest to the internal surface of the dryer cylinder.

SYSTEM RETENTION: See RETENTION.

T

TABLE CONFIGURATION: Selection and placement of drainage elements on the fourdrinier. Syn. Table Arrangement, Table Layout.

TABLE HARMONICS: Spacing of drainage elements on the fourdrinier to control sheet pulse frequency, and thereby optimize microturbulence down the table.

TABLE ROLL: Solid or grooved roll underneath the fourdrinier wire that supports the wire and assists drainage by virtue of hydrodynamic suction forces created as the wire passes over the roll.

TABLE ROLL BAFFLE: See DEFLECTOR.

TAIL: Small continuous strip taken from the full-width web at the front side of the paper machine. A wet-end tail taken after the presses is carried through the dryer sections on ropes during threading; once the tail is running through smoothly, the strip is widened rapidly to the full sheet width. A dry-end tail is used to carry the web from the dryers to the calender stack and from the calender stack to the reel. Syn. Leader, Tail End.

TAIL CUTTER: Device to cut a tail. A high-velocity squirt is used after forming; a knife device is used at the dry end.

TAKE-UP ROLL: Positioning roll in a fabric or filter cloth run whose main function is to take up slack and thus maintain tension in the run.

TAPERED INLET FLOWSPREADER: Principal design of flowspreader utilized in the paper industry. It consists of a tapered manifold (referred to as the "cross header") having a 5 to 10% recirculation flow at the end, with a large number of small-diameter laterals through which the stock flows to the headbox. Syn. Tapered Manifold.

T-BAR SUPPORT: Method of foil blade support where a T-shaped slot on the underside length of the foil blade fits into a T-shaped projection on the supporting structure.

TEMPERATURE-GRADIENT CALENDERING: Calendering technique wherein the paper web is passed through a single nip formed by two very hot iron rolls. The surface fibers are selectively heated, plasticized, and compressed while the middle of the web remains cool, resilient and relatively bulky.

TENDING SIDE: Operating or working side of the paper machine. Syn. Front Side.

TENSIOMETER: Device for measuring dry-end web tension. It senses the force exerted by the moving web on a turning roll by means of load cells (force transducers) mounted in the roll supports and calculates the true tension from the geometry of the configuration. See also LOADCELL ROLL.

TENSION: See SHEET TENSION.

TENSION CONTROL: Control of web tension at transfer points on the paper machine by adjusting the relative speed between sections. Automatic tension control is possible in those cases where web tension can be measured.

TENSION CYCLE: Variation in forming fabric tension as a function of position on the fourdrinier. Typically, tension varies from a minimum value just after the last driven roll on the return run to a maximum value ahead of the couch roll.

TENSION RELAXATION: Time-dependent reduction in tension following imposition of a step strain (with corresponding step change in tension), a phenomenon characteristic of viscoelastic materials such as wet paper. Tension relaxation in the wet paper is most pronounced in the dryer section subsequent to the draw imposed leaving the press section. Syn. Stress Relaxation.

THEORETICAL PRODUCTION (for a paper machine): Calculated tonnage for a specified speed, trim and grammage over a 24-hour period.

THERMAL BONDING: Process of achieving bonding within a dry-lay nonwoven by utilizing thermoplastic material in the structure which melts or becomes thermoplastic at a temperature lower than that affecting the carrier fiber.

THERMAL WATERMARKING: Imprinting of a heated die onto paper formed from thermoplastic synthetic fibers.

THERMOCOMPRESSOR: Type of jet ejector in which relatively high-pressure motive steam imparts some of its momentum to low-pressure steam. The thermocompressor is made up of three basic components: (1) the nozzle in which the motive steam is allowed to accelerate to high velocity, (2) the mixing section in which the motive steam entrains the load gas, and (3) the diffuser in which the jet momentum is converted into an increase in pressure. Syn. Jet Compressor, Steam Jet Booster.

THERMOCOMPRESSOR STEAM SYSTEM: Method of reusing blow-through steam and flash steam from a dryer section by increasing its pressure through a thermocompressor, and then injecting it back into the same dryer section or another dryer section.

THERMOPLANISHING: See GLOSS CALENDERING.

THICKENING: Designation for a fiber dewatering and forming process in which the fibers are linked to each other in a network and a progressive thickening of the whole fiber network takes place. The fiber mat resulting from thickening has a felted structure. See also FILTRATION.

THICKNESS CALENDER: Type of calender consisting of two cast iron rolls with an adjustable gap intended to give paper or board a predetermined caliper.

THIN STOCK: See APPROACH FLOW.

THREADING: Starting a new sheet through the paper machine by passing a small strip from one section to another. Threading is still a manual operation between some wet-end sections, but rope carriers are virtually always used to thread the dryers. See also AIR FOIL THREADING, VACUUM BELT THREADING, AIR THREADER PIPE.

THROUGH DRYING: Process in which hot, unsaturated gas is forced through a wet, porous material (e.g., a paper web) by imposing a pressure differential across the material. As the hot gas passes through, heat is transferred to evaporate the water; the gas leaves at a reduced temperature and with increased water vapor content. The intimate contact between the hot gas and the web, coupled with the large internal surface area of the porous material, produces exceptionally high drying rates.

TIGHT DRAW: Sheet transfer with high web tension. See also DRAW.

TINCTORIAL VALUE: Relative intensity of color produced in the paper product by dyeing.

TISSUE MACHINE: Paper machine of special design for the production of tissue grades.

TOE-IN: Included angle between top and bottom cutting components in a shear slitter system.

TOP FELT: Felt which contacts the top side of the web.

TOP LINER: (1) Lighter, cleaner, better-quality layer of stock (often applied by a secondary headbox) on top of a relatively coarse base sheet. A duplex structure is typical of most linerboard grades where the basic requirements are high levels of stiffness and burst resistance, with good appearance and printability on one surface. (2) Outside liner of multiply paperboard, the better quality side.

TOP LIP: See SLICE.

TOPPING: Method of adding dyes in sequence to the paper stock in order to produce a color lake of increased fastness and fullness.

TOP-WIRE FORMER: Device that sits atop a conventional fourdrinier and provides upwards drainage capability. With some designs, the top wire former is equipped with an integral headbox capable of adding a ply of stock on top of the previous sheet. See also TWIN-WIRE FORMER, HYBRID FORMER, DANDY ROLL FORMER.

TORN-OFF PAPER: Paper that is torn off the surface of the reel for various reasons. See also SLAB-OFF LOSSES.

TOUR BOSS: Shift foreman for paper mill operations.

TRACKING: Process of following the back-and-forth movement of paper machine clothing as it runs on the machine. The objective is always "centered tracking".

TRACTION: See WEB TRACTION.

TRAILING EDGE: That edge of a foil, suction box, etc. that is last to be in contact with a section of moving web on the paper machine, i.e., the edge nearest the reel.

TRANSFER BELT: Novel press fabric which is designed to replace the traditional granite roll surface in the 3rd press position for lightweight sheets; it does not absorb moisture, but is flexible and compressible, and allows closed transfer of the sheet to the single dryer fabric.

TRANSFER FELT: See PICKUP FELT.

TRANSFER PRESS: Press nip in which the wet sheet is transferred from the pickup felt to the press felt.

TRANSVERSAL FLOW PRESS: Any press design with dominant vertical flow (i.e., flow perpendicular to the felt).

TRAVEL: Amount of lateral oscillation of a forming fabric, felt or dryer screen while running on the paper machine.

TRAVERSING GAUGE: See SCANNING GAUGE.

TRAY: See SAVEALL TRAY.

TRAY WATER: Water passing through the forming fabric of a paper machine which contains various concentrations of fines and fillers depending on location.

TRIM: Width of finished paper produced on a paper machine.

TRIM CHUTE: Conduit for pneumatic conveying of trimmings to the broke pit or other receptacle.

TRIM EFFICIENCY: Trim divided by fill, usually expressed as a percentage.

TRIMMINGS: Narrow strips or pieces of paper and board removed during processing that are repulped as broke. See also EDGE TRIMMINGS.

TUB SIZING: On-machine or off-machine application of sizing solution for high-quality papers. The sheet is run through a shallow bath containing starch and other additives and the excess is removed by passing through a light nip. Air-impingement drying of the size is often employed to avoid disturbing the surface film.

TUNNEL DRYER: Large, insulated enclosure through which paper or paperboard is passed during air-impingement drying.

TURBULENCE: Irregular motion of fluids, in which local velocities and pressures fluctuate in a random manner. Turbulence can be characterized by two parameters: "scale", the size of the predominant eddies, and "intensity", the average magnitude of random velocity fluctuations. See also MICROTURBULENCE.

TURBULENCE GENERATOR: Term sometimes applied to the section of a hydraulic headbox after the mixing chamber which influences and maintains stock turbulence.

TURBULENCE SPECTRA: Method of characterizing the turbulence in a slice jet by fast-response impact probes. The information is presented as a curve relating the wavelength ("turbulence scale") to the energy per unit wave length ("turbulence intensity"). The objective in headbox design is to maximize the intensity at the small-scale end of the spectrum and eliminate the large-scale features.

TURBULENT FLOW: See TURBULENCE.

TURNING ROLL: Roll in a press felt run which is wrapped by the web-supporting pickup felt and markedly changes the direction of travel. The turning roll is often equipped with a suction box to prevent drop-off of the sheet.

TURNTABLE: Rotating platform, commonly used within a paper roll handling system to discharge rolls in different directions.

TURN-UP: Wrapping of the spool with the paper web to begin a new reel.

TWIN-WIRE FORMER: Paper or paperboard forming device in which the headbox slice jet impinges into the converging gap between two wires. Depending on the particular former design, the initial drainage can take place in one direction or in both directions. The dewatering action is due to the pressure set up by the tension in the two wires and by drainage elements outside of the wires. See also TOP-WIRE FORMER, ROLL FORMER, HYBRID FORMER.

TWO-COMPONENT WET-END SYSTEM: See MULTICOMPONENT WET-END SYSTEM.

TWO-DRUM WINDER: Common design of winder in which the windup station consists of back and front metal drums to support and drive the paper rolls. The wound-in tension or density of the rolls is principally controlled by the torque difference between the two drums. Syn. Bedroll Type Winder.

U

UNACCOUNTED LOSSES: That percent of production loss on the paper machine which represents the difference between theoretical production and the sum of scaled on-grade production and all classified losses.

UNDERLINER: Ply of multiply paperboard that is next to the top liner ply. The furnish for the underliner may be of intermediate quality between the top liner and the filler plies.

UNIFLOW VAT: Cylinder former in which the incoming dilute stock flows in the same direction as the cylinder rotation. Syn. Direct Flow Vat.

UNWINDING: Process which encompasses supporting the unwinding roll, braking (i.e., controlling the tension of the web), and acceleration/deceleration (i.e., increasing or decreasing web speed).

UNWIND STAND: Component of the winder that supports the reel and from which the sheet is fed into the slitter-winder. The unwind stand also provides braking to control acceleration and deceleration. Syn. Back Stand, Unwinder.

UPTAKE: Absorption of water by a fibrous structure.

V

VACUUM-ASSISTED FOIL UNIT: Foil unit in which a low level of suction can be applied. See also WET BOX.

VACUUM BELT THREADING: Method of threading the tail at the dry end of the paper machine utilizing a series of transfer belts. The tail is held to the transfer belts by vacuum and is trajected by its weight and velocity between belt units and directly to the in-running nip.

VACUUM BLOWER: Type of vacuum pump having twin impellors which rotate in opposite directions and are driven by timing gears. Each impellor alternately traps and then expels a definite measured amount of air, resulting in the evacuation of four equal volumes with each revolution of the main shaft. Syn. Rotary Lobe Blower, Cycloidal Vacuum Pump.

VACUUM BOX: See SUCTION BOX.

VACUUM CAPACITY: Air flow at a specified vacuum level.

VACUUM EXHAUSTER: Type of vacuum pump having a series of impellors mounted on a shaft which pulls in air and sets it in motion. A diffuser surrounds each impellor and serves to convert the velocity into higher pressure. Since one large unit can usually provide enough capacity for an entire paper machine, it is often referred to as a "central vacuum system". Syn. Centrifugal Exhauster, Centrifugal Blower.

VACUUM PUMP: Compressor for exhausting air or noncondensible gases from a space that must be maintained at subatmospheric pressure. See also LIQUID-RING VACUUM PUMP, VACUUM EXHAUSTER, VACUUM BLOWER.

VACUUM SUCTION FORCES: Suction forces causing drainage on the fourdrinier produced by suction foils and suction boxes under the wire.

VACUUM SYSTEM: Vacuum pumps and associated piping which are an integral component of an overall paper machine system. Adequate vacuum pumping capability must be provided for all vacuum-assisted drainage elements, suction boxes, and felt-conditioning boxes in both the forming and pressing sections.

VAPOR ABSORPTION: Transfer of water vapor, given off during the paper drying process, into the ventilation air.

VAPOR PRESSURE: Partial pressure of water vapor in the atmosphere. At normal levels, the vapor pressure is almost directly proportional to the absolute humidity.

VAPOR SIZING: Proposed treatment of paper with chemical vapors (e.g., certain silanes or fatty acids) that are absorbed by or chemically reacted with the surface fibers to develop sizing.

VARIABLE CROWN ROLL: Press or calender roll equipped so that the linear load can be distributed along the nip face as desired, most commonly by means of a hydraulic arrangement in the upper section of the roll shell that displaces the deflection to an internal stationary beam. Syn. Controlled Crown Roll. See also CONTROLLED DEFORMATION ROLL.

VAT: Tank in which a cylinder former is mounted and which contains the stock suspension from which the sheet is made.

VAT FORMER: See CYLINDER FORMER.

VATMAN: One of the operators in the manufacture of handmade paper, the individual who forms the sheets on the mould.

VAT SECTION: Section of a multi-cylinder board machine where the web is formed on one or more cylinder formers.

VELIN DANDY ROLL: See WOVE DANDY ROLL.

VELOCITY FORMING: Forming on a fourdrinier characterized by the gentle landing of the slice jet onto the wire with a minimum of stock bounce or jump.

VENTILATION: Process of supplying or removing air, to or from a space, by either natural or mechanical means in order to maintain an acceptable level of air quality. See also HOOD VENTILATION, MACHINE ROOM VENTILATION.

VERTICAL PRESS: Arrangement of press rolls, one on top of the other.

VIRGIN FIBER: Pulp used for papermaking that has not previously been used in any paper or board product. Syn. Primary Fiber.

VORTEX: Spinning motion of water. A "free vortex" is the normal pattern obtained when water flows from a basin into a drain.

VORTEX BREAKER: Baffle positioned in a tank above a pump suction line to prevent funnel formation and air entry into the suction pipe.

W _____

WAD BURNING: Damage caused by a wad of paper becoming lodged at the ingoing press nip which creates high frictional forces that melt and fuse the synthetic fibers on the wet felt surface, thereby forming "burned streaks".

WAKE EFFECT: Instability of fiber distribution in the forming zone of the fourdrinier due to non-coalesced jets from the slice rectifier roll of the headbox. Ridges and valleys are visible in the slice jet before impingement.

WAKE RATIO: Calculated distance the slice rectifier roll should be set back from the slice for no effect on the jet, divided by the actual distance of the roll from the slice.

WAREHOUSING: Storage and retrieval of paper rolls.

WARM-UP PERIOD: Running time prior to operational startup to bring system up to operating temperature; especially applicable to the headbox where slice distortion due to stress caused by temperature variation can be a problem on paper machine startups.

WASH ROLL: First outside roll on the return run of the forming fabric, which is showered from inside of the fabric and doctored to remove stock particles retained by the fabric. On some fourdriniers, the edge trims (or full-width sheet during startups and breaks) are removed from the forming fabric at this point.

WASH UP: Cleaning of the wet end of the paper machine during shutdown.

WATER BOX: Sturdy trough or pan contacting a paper machine roll by means of a reinforced rubber lip, commonly used for application of water or sizing solution at the calender stack. Liquid flows from the pan to the roll, which transfers it to the web.

WATER CREPING: See SECONDARY CREPING.

WATER JET SLITTER: Slitter which utilizes a high-velocity water jet to sever the web. This type of slitter is used selectively in the converting of tissue and board.

WATER-LOGGED: See FLOODED.

WATERMARK: Design formed among the fibers of the sheet as a result of the wet paper web coming into contact with the pattern of a dandy roll or marking roll. The paper becomes thinner and more translucent where the fibers are displaced by the raised design.

WATER VAPOR: Water in the gaseous state, especially when it is below the boiling point and diffused in air or other gases.

WEB: Term applied to the full width of the paper sheet in the process of being formed, pressed, dried, finished or converted. Syn. Sheet.

WEB HANDLING: Process of tracking the web, maintaining its tension at the proper level and keeping it wrinkle-free. Syn. Web Control.

WEB INSTABILITY: Any irregular behavior of an unsupported travelling web, including bouncing, floating and oscillation.

WEBSTER-TYPE FORMER: Former in which the sheet is formed between the external surface of a rotating cylinder and a forming fabric wrapping that cylinder. The cylinder may be solid or porous, and may be covered with fabric or felt. (Named for Canadian inventor.)

WEB SEPARATION: See SLITTING.

WEB TENSION: See SHEET TENSION.

WEB TRACTION: Pulling friction of the paper web as it moves over a roll or other surface.

WEB TRANSFER: See SHEET TRANSFER.

WEB WRINKLES: Out-of-plane deformations of the web that are transferred over rollers from one web span to the next.

WET BOX: Any vacuum-assisted drainage element for the fourdrinier that utilizes an interior seal leg. These low-vacuum elements produce up to 20 inches of water vacuum. Syn. Wet Suction Box, Forming Box.

WET BROKE: See BROKE.

WET BULB TEMPERATURE: Indicated temperature of a moving air stream as measured with a thermometer whose sensing element is covered with a wet wick. The wet bulb temperature along with the ambient temperature (dry bulb temperature) is used to determine the humidity and other psychrometric properties of air by reference to standard tables.

WET CREPING: Creping of a wet or partially dried paper web.

WET DRAW: Draw between sections at the wet end of the paper machine. See also DRAW.

WET END: That portion of the paper machine which includes the headbox, wire part, and press section.

WET-END ADDITIVES: Chemicals added to the papermaking furnish including internal additives and agents which serve as processing aids on the wet end. See also PAPERMAKING ADDITIVES.

WET-END BALANCE: Accounting of the distribution of stock and water inputs and outputs around the fourdrinier or other forming sections.

WET-END BARRING: Machine-direction grammage variation which takes place at relatively high frequencies above 10 Hz, due to wet-end hydraulics and mechanics including the phenomenon known as "wave amplification on the wire".

WET FELT: Designation correctly applied to any press felt, but more often applied to the felt used in the first press nip. See also FELT, PRESS FELT.

WET PACK: Process whereby paper is tub sized and then held in roll form for a certain length of time before it is dried.

WET ROLLING: Any pressing or smoothing operation carried out on the wet web.

WET-STRENGTH BROKE: Broke from wet-strength papermaking operations. Because of its high wet strength, the broke is difficult to repulp, and special techniques are usually employed depending on the particular type of wet strength treatment.

WETTING: Increasing the moisture content of paper; the opposite of drying. See also MOISTURE PICKUP, REHUMIDIFYING.

WETTING SHOWER: Arrangement of water sprays in the dry-end broke repulper which wet the sheet immediately to prevent flotation and allow the sheet to be quickly drawn into the vortex.

WET-UP: Adding water uniformly to a felt after installation or just prior to a startup.

WET WEB ADHESION: Adhesion between the wet web and any supporting surface, such as a forming fabric or press roll. The amount of adhesion depends on the characteristics of both the wet web and the surface. See also RELEASE PROPERTIES, PEELING ANGLE.

WET WEB SATURATION: Method of adding polymer solutions or dispersions (usually latex) to wet webs in the high grammage range from 250 to 1500 g/m^2. The pressed sheet is run through a tub of polymer (i.e., the saturation process) and then through a pair of squeeze rolls for redistribution and removal of excess polymer.

WHALES: Large air bubbles at the surface of a pulper which prevent submergence of a broke sheet.

WHIPPER: Roll equipped with extended bars, commonly used on multiply board machines to condition the felt by beating (in conjunction with showering of the felt).

WHITE WATER: General term for any stock filtrate or process water that contains fiber fines. On the papermachine, white water is produced during the forming and dewatering of the web. "Rich white water" contains a high concentration of fiber fines, while "lean white water" contains a low concentration. Syn. Back Water. Also see WIRE PIT WATER.

WHITE WATER CONSISTENCY PROFILE: Graph showing white consistency after each drainage element along the fourdrinier.

WHITE WATER LOOP: Paper machine process circuit in which white water is taken from a storage tank and utilized as stock dilution, and then subsequently separated from the stock and returned to the storage tank.

WHITE WATER SYSTEM: System of tanks, pumps and piping for handling all recirculated process water streams. A white water system is said to be "open" if a large proportion of the total white water flow leaves the system, and "closed" if only a small proportion leaves the system.

WIDENING: Usually refers to the treatment by which a felt or fabric is mechanically worked out to greater than normal operating width.

WIDE-NIP PRESS: Press in which the sheet runs through a wide nip formed by a rotating roll and a fixed concave support shoe. The shoe is continuously lubricated and acts as a slipbearing for a rubber blanket which runs between the shoe and the felt.

WIDTH (of a paper roll): Dimension of the web in the cross direction.

WINDAGE: Air carried along by a paper dryer fabric.

WINDER: Equipment that receives paper machine reels and breaks them down (by slitting and winding) into suitable size rolls that may be either sent directly to the customer or processed through additional coating, calendering or sheeting operations. See also TWO-DRUM WINDER.

WINDER SPECIFICATIONS: Misnomer referring to the specifications for the diameter and width of rolls produced from the winder. The specifications may also include a range of roll hardness.

WINDER TENSION CONTROL: Control of web tension between the unwind stand and the winding drums. See also BRAKING.

WINDING: Process which changes a material manufactured continuously from web form into roll form for further processing.

WINDING DRUMS: Pair of independently driven drums on which the paper rolls are wound on a winder. The difference in speed between the two rolls is used to control the roll structure. Syn. Bed Rolls.

WINDUP STATION: That part of the winder which provides a means of winding up rolls of paper side-by-side on small-diameter cores. Syn. Windup Stand.

WIRE: Endless belt of woven wire cloth for the drainage of stock and forming of a fiber web. In current practice, few metallic wires are used, but the term is often applied to synthetic forming fabrics.

WIRE CHANGE: Removal of a worn-out or defective forming fabric (or forming wire) and replacement with a new one.

WIRE LIFE: Service life of a forming fabric or forming wire.

WIRE LIFE EXTENDER: Corrosion inhibitor which is added to the paper machine white water system to extend the service life of a metal forming wire.

WIRE LOADING: Process of applying and incorporating a mineral or synthetic filler into the wet web as it is being formed on the fourdrinier.

WIRE PART: Paper machine forming unit, along with all ancillary equipment.

WIRE PIT: Rich white water silo equipped with long, open supply channels, usually located underneath the fourdrinier wire. Free-draining water from the forming section of the wire falls onto collecting trays, which funnel the water into the channels. A relatively long period of channel flow is then desirable to release entrained air and dissipate turbulence, before the wire pit water is recombined with the stock flow.

WIRE PIT WATER: Rich white water from the saveall trays underneath the fourdrinier forming zone. It is used as dilution for the machine chest stock in the approach system. Syn. Tray Water.

WIRE RETENTION: See SINGLE-PASS RETENTION.

WIRE RETURN ROLLS: Rolls located on the underside of the fourdrinier to guide and control the forming fabric on its return run.

WIRE SPEED: Speed at which the forming fabric runs and the speed of the initially formed wet web. The wire speed is less than the machine speed (i.e., reel-up speed) because of the draws between sections.

WIRE TURNING ROLL: Solid roll which is generously wrapped by the forming fabric, located immediately after the couch roll on the fourdrinier. It forms a short inclined section with the couch roll which provides the takeoff point for the suction pickup. The wire turning roll is driven and usually provides a large portion of power transmission for the entire fourdrinier. Syn. Forward Drive Roll.

WORKING FACE (of a press roll): Length of press roll surface over which the load is distributed.

WORM ROLL: Spreading and conditioning roll for a felt having a raised spiral on the roll surface running outward in both directions from the middle of the roll.

WOUND-IN TENSION: Tension in the paper web as it is wound into rolls, caused by the nip pressure between the roll and the winding drums, and the torque differential between winding drums. Syn. Residual Tension.

WOVE DANDY ROLL: Dandy roll that is surfaced with a fine wire mesh that leaves no pattern in the paper sheet. Syn. Velin Dandy Roll.

WRAP: Angle of circumference of a roll or cylinder with which the paper web is in contact. Syn. Angle Of Wrap.

WRAP AROUND: Paper wrapping around any roll of the paper machine following a break. Syn. Wrap-Up.

WRAP-UP: See WRAP AROUND.

WRINGER PRESS: Press nip used on the first press felt run to dewater and condition the press felt.

Y

YANKEE CYLINDER: Dryer cylinder of large circumference with a highly polished surface, commonly used for such applications as drying of tissue, cast coating, and glazing of board. Syn. Yankee Dryer.

YANKEE HOOD: Hood enclosing the Yankee dryer which provides recirculating high-velocity hot air impingement to the web. For a modern tissue machine, the air impinges at a temperature approaching 500°C and velocity of 8500 meters per minute.

YANKEE MACHINE: Paper machine that uses a Yankee cylinder as the principal method of paper drying.

YARDAGE: Length of paper expressed in lineal yards.

Z

ZONE-CONTROL ROLL: See CONTROLLED DEFORMATION ROLL.

Chapter 14
Paper Product Properties
(Includes Characteristics, Testing, Defects, etc.)

ABRASION RESISTANCE: Ability of a paper or board surface to resist scratching or wearing away through contact with another sheet surface or with some other object. Syn. Scuff Resistance, Wear Resistance.

ABRASION TEST: Means of studying the erasability of paper where weight loss due to abrasion is plotted against the number of wear cycles. A break in the curve corresponds to the point where the abrasive wheel breaks through the surface film of size into the interior of the paper sheet.

ABRASIVENESS: Property of a substance which enables it to abrade surfaces, almost the exact opposite of softness. The abrasiveness of paper products is affected by their furnish and finishing.

ABSORBENCY: (1) Property of a paper that causes it to take up or imbibe liquid with which it is in contact. (2) Rate at which paper will absorb a specified quantity of water.

ABSORBENT: [adj] Term applied to unsized, bulky papers which are used to absorb water solutions or other liquids. Examples of absorbent papers are blotting and toweling products and base papers. Syn. Bibulous.

ABSORPTION COEFFICIENT: Capacity of a unit thickness of paper to absorb spectral light energy. The absorption coefficient can be derived from basic optical measurements using the Kubelka-Munk equation corrected for basis weight.

ACCELERATED AGING: Artificial, rapid method of simulating the changes that occur in paper during natural aging, usually by storing paper samples for a specified period at a relatively high temperature. Syn. Heat Aging. See also RELATIVE STABILITY, HUMIDIFIED HEAT TREATMENT.

ACCELERATED AGING TEST: Test method carried out on a sample of paper (or other product) before and after accelerated aging as the basis for evaluating its permanence or useful service life.

ACCELERATED TEST: Test in which conditions are intensified to reduce the time required to obtain necessary data. The objective is to simulate within a few hours the results expected during long-time service.

ACCURACY: See TEST ACCURACY.

ACID FASTNESS: Resistance of dyed paper to color change when exposed to acid conditions.

ACID FREE PAPER: Paper which contains no acidity. Acid-free paper typically has good aging characteristics and has no detrimental effect on materials that are in contact with it. Syn. Anti-Acid Paper.

ACIDITY (of paper): Residual chemical acidity in paper as determined by taking a water extract and then either measuring the pH of the extract or titrating the extract with alkali.

ACID PAPER: Paper manufactured with sheet acidity; most often associated with rosin-alum internal sizing. Syn Acidic Paper.

ACID-RESISTANT: [adj] Term applied to paper which has been specifically treated to resist the action of acids.

ACOUSTICAL TESTING: Determination of paper properties by means of measuring ultrasonic wave propagation speed in various directions within the sheet. See also ULTRASONIC SHEET TESTER.

AGING: Change in properties over a time span which is dependent on storage conditions. Aging with respect to paper and board usually implies a deterioration. See also PERMANENCE.

AGING TEST: See ACCELERATED AGING TEST.

AIR CONDITIONING: Controlling an atmosphere to suit particular requirements, which may include cleaning, humidifying or dehumidifying, cooling or heating, and circulation.

AIR-DRIED PAPER: Paper dried by exposure to air.

AIR FRACTION: Ratio of the volume occupied by air spaces to the gross volume of a sheet of paper, a measure of sheet porosity. Air spaces consist of pores, voids and recesses. See also SOLID FRACTION.

AIR LEAK TESTER: Class of instrument used to measure the surface roughness of paper. It consists of a constant-pressure air source and a gauge head that clamps down on the paper sample. Roughness is indicated by the volume flow rate of air that leaks between the paper and the gauge head or by the time it takes for a predetermined volume to leak through.

AIR PERMEABILITY: Index of sheet porosity, obtained by measuring the flow rate of air through a sample sheet (of specified dimensions) under specified conditions of pressure difference, temperature and humidity.

AIR RESISTANCE: Resistance of a paper sheet to the passage of air under specified conditions. Air resistance has an inverse relationship to air permeability.

AIR RESISTANCE TESTER: See DENSOMETER.

AIR SHEAR BURST: Irregular machine-direction separation of the sheet inside a paper roll during winding due to air entrapment (e.g., because of improper drum grooving) causing shear deformation.

AIR VOLUME (of paper): See AIR FRACTION.

ALKALI FASTNESS: Resistance of dyed paper to color change when in contact with alkali or alkaline adhesive.

ALKALINE-FILLED PAPER: Paper containing calcium and/or magnesium carbonate and having a pH in the range from 7.5 to 9.5. This paper has a reserve buffering capacity that can neutralize acidity absorbed from the atmosphere.

ALKALINE PAPER: Paper manufactured with sheet alkalinity, most commonly associated with the presence of calcium carbonate filler.

ALKALINITY (of paper): Residual chemical alkalinity in paper as determined by taking a water extract and then either measuring the pH of the extract or titrating the extract with acid.

ALKALI PROOF: [adj] Term applied to papers that resist changes in color caused by contact with alkaline materials.

ALL-DIRECTION STRETCH: See CROSS CREPING.

ALUM SPOTS: Defects in paper caused by undissolved particles of alum being retained in the sheet during forming and subsequently crushed into powder during calendering.

ANGLE OF INCIDENCE: Angle from the perpendicular at which a beam of light strikes a surface.

ANISOTROPIC PAPER: Paper with a grain, having different properties in different directions. Machine-made paper is anisotropic.

ANISOTROPIC RATIO: Ratio of machine-direction to cross-direction measurements of a paper property, which is generally indicative of the degree of fiber orientation; however the anisotropic ratio will typically be different for different properties.

ANNULAR RINGS: Pattern of rings on the end of a paper roll due to slight differences in sheet width as the paper is being wound. The cause is a deviation of the slitter edge from its vertical plane due to run-out or wobbliness.

ANTI-ACID PAPER: See ACID FREE PAPER.

ANTIQUARIAN PAPER: Large-size, hand-made paper (53 X 30 inches) which was manufactured in England up to 1936.

ANTIQUE FINISH: Rough paper finish obtained by operating with reduced pressure during wet pressing and calendering.

APPARENT DENSITY: Weight per unit volume of sheet, commonly calculated by dividing the grammage by the caliper. Syn. Apparent Specific Gravity.

APPEARANCE: Subjective judgement of a paper or board sheet surface based on visual assessment of formation, color, finish, and cleanliness.

ASH CONTENT: Amount of residue after complete combustion, usually expressed as a percentage of the original moisture-free weight. The ash content of a paper sample is indicative of its filler content and/or coating application. See also IGNITION FACTOR.

ASHING: Placing a sample (e.g., paper) in a crucible and heating in a muffle furnace at a temperature (usually 900°C) sufficient to produce a carbon-free ash in 10–15 minutes.

ASHLESS PAPER: Paper that leaves negligible residue after complete combustion. Syn. Ash-Free Paper.

AS-MADE GRAMMAGE: Grammage of paper as it is produced on the paper machine, as opposed to grammage after exposure of the paper to the ambient environment or after conditioning in a standardized environment.

B _____

BAGGY PAPER: Slack area in the middle section of a finished paper roll, usually caused by a moisture streak which makes the paper thinner in this area. Syn. Baggy Roll.

BALLISTIC WET WEB TESTER: Simple, rapid wet web tester utilizing the measurement of the energy lost by a steel ball dropped through a wet handsheet that is clamped perpendicular to the vertical axis.

BARK SPECKS: Common type of dirt in paper caused by the presence of bark fragments, usually associated with groundwood papers.

BARRING: Appearance of periodic, cross-direction "bars" of lower caliper and higher finish on the surface of the paper as it leaves the calendering operation, usually associated with vibrations in the calender stack, but sometimes due to other causes. Syn. Chattermarking.

BARRING PATTERN: Frequency and amplitude of caliper nonuniformities as displayed by a machine-direction caliper gauge.

BARRING SEVERITY: Range of caliper variation due to barring.

BASE PAPER: Paper that is chemically converted into products such as vegetable parchment and vulcanized fiber.

BASIS WEIGHT: Weight of paper product per ream or per specified area. The existence of different ream sizes is a source of confusion when comparing basis weights for different products. The preferred term is now "grammage".

BELL: See FOAM MARK.

BENDING: Mechanical distortion of paper or paperboard as occurs when wrapping a small-diameter core or spool. Syn. Flexing.

BENDING NUMBER: Narrowest score that can be used on a paperboard which will not cause cracking when the paperboard is folded, a measure of bending quality.

BENDING QUALITY: Relative ability of a scored paperboard to be folded without cracking.

BENDING RESISTANCE: Necessary property of some paper and board grades; determined by measuring the bending force required to deflect a rectangular test piece according to standard procedures. Syn. Stiffness.

BETAMETER: Instrument for measuring paper grammage continuously on the machine, based on the amount of beta ray absorption from a radioactive source.

BETA RADIATION: Electrons which have been emitted from an atomic nucleus.

BIAXIAL STRENGTH: Maximum resistance to fracture when paper is subjected to tension loading in both the machine and cross-machine directions, and where the biaxial stress ratio can be varied. (Note that the burst test is fundamentally a biaxial strength test, except that the biaxial stress ratio cannot be varied.)

BIAXIAL STRESS RATIO: Ratio of the tension applied to a paper sample in the machine direction to that in the cross-machine direction. See also BIAXIAL STRENGTH.

BIBULOUS: See ABSORBENT.

BLACKENING: See CALENDER BLACKENING.

BLISTER: Paper defect consisting of small soft areas protruding from the sheet surface, usually because of too rapid evaporation during the early stages of drying.

BLISTER CUT: Cut in the paper web occurring when the paper around a blister accumulates at the entrance of a calender nip and is then carried through in a creased condition.

BLOOD PROOF: [adj] Term applied to certain butcher papers that are resistant to penetration by blood.

BLOTCH: Lump of stock or other foreign material imbedded in the sheet, most commonly a broke chip.

BODY DAMAGE: Paper roll defect in the form of dents and gouges to the body of the roll caused by poor roll handling practice. Body damage may not be apparent until the roll wrap is removed.

BOGUS: [adj] Term applied to papers and paperboards made principally from secondary fiber to differentiate them from the same grades made from virgin fiber.

BONDED AREA: External fiber surface area which is involved in interfiber bonding in a sheet of paper.

BONDING INDEX: Measure of the bonding strength of fibers within a paper sheet based on short-span tensile curves. It is calculated in percentage as the difference between the dry and wet tensile divided by the dry tensile, all values taken at the short span distance corresponding to the "fiber length index".

BOOK BULK: Overall thickness of a given number of sheets measured under specified conditions.

BOTTOM SIDED SHEET: Sheet that is dyed significantly deeper on the wire side, due either to preferential dyeing of the long fiber or negligible affinity of the filler for dye.

BREAKING LENGTH: Length of a strip of paper which would break of its own weight when suspended vertically, as calculated from the tensile strength and grammage of the paper; it is essentially a tensile strength measurement which is independent of grammage.

BRIGHTNESS: Reflectivity of a paper sample using light of specified wave length (457 nm), commonly used as an index of whiteness. See also REFLECTANCE, REFLECTIVITY, DIRECTIONAL BRIGHTNESS, DIFFUSE BRIGHTNESS.

BRIGHTNESS METER: See REFLECTANCE METER, SPECTROPHOTOMETER.

BRIGHTNESS REVERSION: Loss of brightness due to natural or accelerated aging. Syn. Yellowing, Color Reversion.

BRILLIANCY: Term referring to the relative brightness of a color which corresponds to the lightness-darkness value of the Munsell System.

BRISTOW TESTER: Benchtop instrument for the measurement of liquid absorption into a paper or board sample under dynamic conditions. It consists of an open distributor (headbox) containing a liquid which is brought into gentle contact with a sample strip mounted on a one-meter rotation wheel.

BRITTLENESS: Property of paper which causes it to fail or break when deformed by bending. It is a subjective property, not measurable by present testing methods.

BROKEN EDGE: Small nicks or tears at the edge of paper sheets or rolls due to faulty processing or handling, most commonly because of dull slitter knives.

BUBBLE: Area of delamination in multiply paperboards.

BUCKLE: See RIDGE.

BUCKLING: Type of yielding failure of paper or paperboard under compression in the form of bends, kinks or other deformations.

BUILT-IN STRESS OR STRAIN: See DRIED-IN STRAIN, WOUND-IN TENSION.

BULK: Volume per unit weight of paper product. Bulk is the reciprocal of apparent density. Syn. Apparent Specific Volume.

BULKING: [adj] Term describing papers and boards that are light in weight in relation to their thickness. These products are generally given little calendering and contain no fillers.

BULKING CALIPER: Thickness of a pack of sheets divided by the number of sheets. The bulking caliper tends toward an average caliper reading. Syn. Bulking Thickness.

BULKING INDEX: Number obtained by dividing the caliper of a single sheet by its grammage.

BULKING NUMBER: Number of sheets constituting one inch of thickness under specified applied pressure.

BULKING PRESSURE: Specified pressure to which a pack of sheets are subjected during a bulking caliper measurement.

BULK MODULUS: Ratio of the pressure applied to a paper sample to the fractional change in its volume under specified conditions. See also COMPRESSIBILITY.

BULK SOFTNESS: Softness of paper related to crumpling, as distinct from surface softness. See also SOFTNESS.

BULKY: [adj] Term applied to papers that have a large volume in relation to their grammage. A bulky paper is generally more absorbent, more opaque, but less strong than a more dense paper of the same grammage. See also DENSE.

BUNCH PLATING: Plating carried out in such a way as to give a special finish to each side of the sheet.

BURNISHED FINISH: Usually synonymous with a glazed finish. However, it more specifically applies to flint or friction glazing.

BURNT PAPER: See OVER-DRIED PAPER.

BURST INDEX: Measure of bursting strength that is independent of sheet grammage, basically determined by dividing bursting strength by the grammage of the sample.

BURSTING STRENGTH: Resistance of a paper sheet to deformation by an expanding rubber diaphragm, as measured by the hydraulic pressure at the point of rupture.

BURST: Rupture of the sheet inside a paper roll during winding due to a number of causes. See also AIR SHEAR BURST, CALIPER SHEAR BURST, CROSS-MACHINE BURST, CORE BURST.

BUTYL CARBITOL TEST: Time required for complete absorption of one drop of butyl carbitol (diethyleneglycol monobutyl ether), used for measuring the resistance of paperboard to ink.

C

CALENDER BLACKENING: Undesirable paper condition caused by a combination of high paper moisture content and high calendering pressure. Under transmitted light the calender-blackened areas appear glassy, while under reflected light they appear as darkened areas.

CALENDER-CRUSH FINISH: Surface finish obtained by wetting the paper during the calendering operation.

CALENDER CUT: Defect in the paper caused by a wrinkle in the paper as it passes through the calender, appearing as a slit, or as a glazed or discolored line leaning toward one edge of the sheet.

CALENDERED PAPER: Paper that has been subjected to some type of calendering treatment.

CALENDER FINISH: Any paper finish obtained by means of calendering, including machine calendering, supercalendering and friction calendering.

CALENDER-MARKED: [adj] Applied to paper on which marks from the calender rolls have been impressed.

CALENDER SPOTS: Imperfections in paper in the form of glazed or indented spots, often transparent; caused by small flakes of paper which either adhere to the calender roll surface or to the paper passing through the calender stack.

CALENDER STREAKS: Continuous streaks of darkened paper occurring in the machine direction, caused by uneven drying and pressing preliminary to calendering. For coated paper, calender streaking refers to relatively high gloss bands occurring in the machine direction, where non-uniform coating weight may also be a contributing factor.

CALENDER WRINKLE: Crease in paper produced when the sheet folds over on itself during calendering.

CALIBRANT: Any reference material, specimen or device used for calibration. See also CALIBRATION STANDARD.

CALIBRATION: Determination of the output value for specified scale readings of a measuring device with respect to that of reference standards.

CALIBRATION STANDARD: Reference material, specimen or device used to calibrate test instruments at some predetermined level. Sometimes, calibration standards are built into the instrument.

CALIPER: Thickness of a paper sheet, measured under specified conditions. See also BULKING CALIPER, SINGLE-SHEET CALIPER.

CALIPER GAUGE: Micrometer with specified foot area and squeeze pressure, for determining paper sheet caliper.

CALIPER SHEAR BURST: Irregular machine-direction separation of the sheet within a paper roll occurring during winding between areas of relatively low and high caliper, caused by differential layer-to-layer slippage as the paper is processed through the nip formed between the roll of paper and the drum.

CAPILLARITY (of paper): Time required for a liquid to rise by a specified amount in a test strip that is held vertically with one end immersed in the liquid. See also CAPILLARY RISE.

CAPILLARY RISE: Distance a liquid will rise in a strip of paper or board that is held vertically for a specified time with one end immersed in the liquid. See also CAPILLARITY.

CHAIN LINES: See LAID LINES.

CHALKY APPEARANCE: Term descriptive of a coated surface that has no gloss.

CHATTERMARKING: See BARRING.

CHEMICALLY RESISTANT: [adj] Descriptive term for papers that are resistant to the action of various chemicals.

CHEMICAL PROPERTIES (of paper): Grouping of properties that includes certain characteristics of the fiber such as alpha-cellulose content, pentosan content, cuene·viscosity, and copper number, as well as properties related to the nonfibrous constituents such as pH, acidity, rosin content, ash content, starch content, and moisture content.

CHEMICAL TESTS: Tests carried out on paper and board to quantify and monitor their chemical properties.

CHEVIOT PAPERS: Lightly colored papers containing a small percentage of highly colored fibers which provide a granite effect. See also GRANITING, SILURIAN EFFECT.

CHROMA: In the Munsell color system, that attribute of color which corresponds to the degree of vividness of a hue. Syn. Saturation.

CLEANLINESS (of paper): Freedom from dirt and debris.

CLOSE FORMATION: See FORMATION.

CLOTH FINISH: Surface finish produced by pressing the weave of cloth such as linen or burlap against the paper during manufacture. See also LINEN FINISH.

CLOUD FINISH: Decorative effect obtained by adding white pulp fibers to the surface of colored paper during the sheet forming stage.

CLOUDY FORMATION: See FORMATION.

COBB TEST: Test for paper absorbency or degree of sizing in which a tared paper sample is clamped underneath a ring and liquid is poured onto the sample and allowed to remain for a specified time. The sample is then removed, blotted off and re-weighed, the gain in weight being used as the test measurement. (After R.M. Karapetoff Cobb)

COCKLE: Puckered area where excess moisture caused that portion of the sheet to dry more slowly than the surrounding area.

COCKLE CUT: Sheet defect cause by a cockled area (i.e., slack area) folding over on itself in the machine direction as it goes through the calender stack.

COCKLE FINISH: Hard, rough surface which is characteristic of paper that has been air-dried without applied tension. The extent of cockle depends on the paper furnish, the amount of moisture lost during air drying, and the temperature of the drying air.

COCKLING: Undesirable condition of unevenness and rippling in the surface of paper due to improper drying.

COEFFICIENT OF FRICTION: Resistance of a surface to slippage, an important property for certain paper products.

COHERENT VARIATIONS: Usually refers to low-frequency, machine-direction variations that are in phase across the the width of the paper machine.

COLD COLORS: Bluish tone paper colors which evoke a cool psychological reaction, as opposed to reddish-hue colors which produce a warm response.

COLD PRESSED FINISH: Rough finish given to loft-dried heavyweight ledger paper by pressing in a hydraulic press.

COLD STORAGE: Recommended conditions for laboratory storage of pulping raw materials and pulp/paper samples at 4°C and 85% relative humidity.

COLOR: Attribute of visual perception that can be described by color names, such as red, yellow, blue, etc. or combinations of these; it depends primarily on the spectral reflectivity of the specimen and the spectral character of the illuminant.

COLOR ATTRIBUTES: See COLOR PERCEPTION, MUNSELL COLOR SYSTEM.

COLORED FIBERS: Designation for a paper defect caused by contamination from dyed fibers that have remained in a papermaking system from a run of stock other than white.

COLOR FASTNESS: Property of a dyed paper to retain its color in normal storage or to resist changes in color when exposed to deleterious influences, such as heat and light.

COLOR PERCEPTION: Ability to discern color difference or variation based on 3 attributes: (1) Hue—visual sensation that distinguishes one color from another. (2) Brightness—relative position on a light-to-dark tone scale. Also called luminosity or tone value. (3) Saturation—relative presence or absence of gray. Also called purity, intensity, or chroma.

COLOR SPECIFICATIONS: Quantitative description of paper colors, most commonly by applying the Munsell system or the CIE system (i.e., utilizing tristimulus values).

COLOR VARIATION: Changes in paper color during a production run due to changes in system pH, filler retention, refining, etc.

COLUMN STRENGTH: Maximum resistance to deformation under edgewise compression of straight strips of paperboard or multiply board. Syn. Column Crush.

COMPACTNESS: Component of sheet formation which refers specifically to the frequency of fine irregularites in the sheet structure. When fibers and fillers are firmly and closely matted, the sheet is described as "compact".

COMPARABILITY: Limit within which agreement may be expected 95% of the time between two test results obtained under essentially the same conditions from samples of different materials having the same level of the measured property, but perhaps being markedly different in other properties.

COMPOSITE: Structural transition between an open paper network and a condensed plastic film. See also CRITICAL ADHESIVE VOLUME CONCENTRATION.

COMPOSITE PROFILE: Profile obtained when several cross direction plies are run together through a profilograph. The composite profile provides essentially an average profile.

COMPRESSIBILITY: Percentage decrease in sheet caliper produced by a specified loading under standard conditions. In printing, compressibility specifically refers to the property of paper by which its surface contour changes under printing pressure to effect complete contact with the printing surface.

COMPRESSION STRENGTH: Maximum resistance to deformation under edgewise compression loading. A number of testing modes for compression strength are used including straight strip (column strength), fluted strip (concora test), and ring (ring crush). Syn. Crushing Resistance, Compression Resistance.

CONCORA TEST: Force required for edgewise compression of a straight strip of linerboard or a fluted sample of corrugating medium.

CONDITIONED PAPER: Paper that has reached equilibrium with a standardized environment. Syn. Seasoned Paper.

CONDITIONING DOWN: Conditioning of a paper sample when the equilibrium moisture content is approached from a higher moisture level.

CONDITIONING UP: Conditioning of a paper sample when the equilibrium moisture content is approached from a lower moisture level.

CONFORMANCE: Verification by testing that a sample or lot is in agreement with specification requirements.

CONTACT ANGLE: Angle at which the surface of a liquid meets the surface of a solid, such as paper. A large angle (above 90°) indicates that the liquid has little tendency to penetrate, while a small angle (less than 70°) indicates extensive wetting and spreading.

CONTRAST GLOSS: Ratio of specularly reflected light to diffusely reflected light at specified equal angles of incidence and reflection.

CONTRAST RATIO: Ratio of the diffuse reflectance of a paper sheet when backed by a black body to that of the sheet when backed by a "white" body. The contrast ratio is taken as a measure of sheet opacity.

COPPER NUMBER: Index of chemical stability for paper, expressed as the number of grams of copper reduced from the cupric to the cuprous state by 100 grams of paper fiber.

CORE BURST: Irregular separation of the sheet near the core of a paper roll due to layer-to-layer slippage of the paper when the initial wraps of paper are not sufficiently tight.

CORRUGATING MEDIUM TEST (CMT): See FLAT CRUSH RESISTANCE.

CORRUGATIONS: (1) Undesirable twisting effects on the paper caused by unequal tension; the sheet is subjected to localized stretching and forms rope-like patterns in the machine direction. Syn. Ropes. (2) Paper roll defect consisting of a soft spot bracketed by hard spots on either side.

COTTON CONTENT: [adj] Applied to papers containing at least 25% cotton fiber content, up to 100%. Syn. Rag Content.

CRACKING: Fissuring in the crease when a sheet of paper is sharply folded.

CRACKLE: See RATTLE.

CRASH FINISH: Paper finish resembling coarse linen, obtained by embossing.

CREASABILITY: Property of a paper sheet to resist cracking when sharply bent, and to permit a smooth crease without wrinkles.

CREASE RETENTION: Ability of paper to remain in position after folding.

CREASING STRENGTH: Ability of a paper sheet to retain tensile strength after folding and creasing under a specified load.

CREPE RATIO: Measure of the amount of crepe in a paper sample, usually expressed as percentage elongation of the stretched sheet.

CREPE WRINKLE: Bunching up of paper accordion-fashion in the machine direction in a manner similar to creped tissue. Crepe wrinkles often occur near the core of a roll because of insufficient initial tension during winding.

CRIMP MARK: Deformation at the edge of the paper roll caused by extreme pressure applied to the crimp. This problem may be caused by excessive pressure when applying the heads or by the weight of rolls when stacked too high.

CRITICAL ADHESIVE VOLUME CONCENTRATION: Polymer/fiber ratio in a paper sheet at which physical properties change rapidly from those expected for a paper sheet to those more typical of a plastic film, i.e., where the binder continuum dominates and cancels autoadhesive entanglement forces between fibers.

CROSS-DIRECTION PROFILE: Graphical representation of a paper property as a function of sampling position across the machine. A profile can show single-point values, composite values, or mean values based on a number of measurements.

CROSS-DIRECTION VARIATION: Variation of sheet properties in the cross-machine direction, generally assumed to be stable with time and capable of being measured directly.

CROSS-MACHINE BURST: Irregular cross-direction separation of the sheet inside a paper roll during winding which does not extend to the edge of the sheet, caused by excessive wound-in tension. Syn. Tension Burst.

CROSS SECTIONING: Cutting a microtome cross section of paper or board in either the machine direction or cross direction for microscopical examination of sheet structure.

CRUSHED FINISH: Mottled effect due to lumpy formation, produced by applying high pressure with the dandy roll.

CRUSHED ROLL: Badly flattened or misshapen paper roll resulting from mishandling. Syn. Flat Roll.

CRUSHING RESISTANCE: See COMPRESSION STRENGTH.

CULL: Defective paper.

CURL: Out-of-plane deformation so that the paper sheet is curved rather than flat. The axis of curl is usually in the machine direction. See also EDGE CURL, STRUCTURAL CURL, WRAP CURL.

CURLING TENDENCY: Tendency of the sheet to curl due to internal stresses, uneven moisture distribution and non-uniform fiber orientation.

CUSHION: Compressibility or resiliency of paper.

CUT: Any rupture of the sheet which does not result in a sheet break. See also BLISTER CUT, CALENDER CUT, DRY CUT, FIBER CUT, HAIR CUT, SLITTER CUTS, etc.

D _____

DANDY BARRING: Barring on the sheet caused either by the dandy puddling in excess water on the sheet surface or from the dandy rotating too slowly (i.e., dandy dragging).

DANDY LICKS: Glazed translucent spots on the surface of paper caused by filled areas in the dandy roll. They repeat at distances equivalent to the dandy roll diameter.

DANDY MARK: Localized dulling on the sheet surface caused by uneven pressure from the dandy roll.

DANDY PICK: Paper defect caused by the dandy roll picking up fibers from the sheet or otherwise disturbing sheet formation to leave thin spots or other imperfections.

DEACIDIFICATION: Process to impart an alkaline chemistry to acidic paper (in order to slow down embrittlement).

DEAD SPOTS: Localized areas of low finish in an otherwise highly finished paper sheet.

DEFECTIVE SLITTER EDGE: See BROKEN EDGE.

DEFECTIVE SPLICE: Imperfect splice which can cause web breaks. Typically, the tape is applied in such a way that it sticks to the ply underneath or on top. Where the splice protrudes, it is usually caused by too little tension applied when winding is resumed.

DEGREE OF FIBER ORIENTATION: See FIBER ORIENTATION, ANISOTROPIC RATIO.

DEGREE OF SIZING: Resistance of a paper surface to liquid penetration.

DELAMINATION: Separation of plies of multiply board.

DELAMINATION RESISTANCE: See PLYBOND.

DELAMINATION STRENGTH: Force at right angles to the plane of the sheet required to maintain the delamination of paper into two layers once it has started.

DENSE: [adj] Term applied to papers that have a high weight in relation to their volume. High density often indicates high strength, except in the case of a highly filled sheet. See also BULKY.

DENSIMETER: Device to measure the specific gravity of a wide range of solid materials. Typically, the mechanism of buoyancy in a liquid is utilized; the mass of the solid is measured in air and again while suspended in a liquid.

DENSITY MONITOR: Device that plots the density changes in a roll of paper during winding or unwinding processes.

DENSOMETER: Instrument that measures the air resistance of paper in terms of the time required for a given volume of air to pass through a given area of paper under controlled conditions. Syn. Air Resistance Tester.

DENTED ROLL: See BODY DAMAGE, END DAMAGE.

DESTRUCTIVE TEST: Test carried out on paper or paperboard that results in destruction of the sample. Virtually all standard laboratory strength tests are of the destructive type.

DETERMINATION: Process of carrying out the series of operations specified in a test method whereby a single value is obtained.

DIELECTRIC RESISTANCE: Degree to which paper resists penetration by an electrical charge, an important property for electrical insulating papers.

DIFFUSE BRIGHTNESS: Brightness measurement obtained where the reflective surfaces are in many planes and at different angles so the reflected light is scattered in as many directions. Syn. Elrepho Brightness.

DIFFUSE TRANSMISSION: Light emerging from the opposite side of an object that has been scattered during transmission through the object. (Such an object is said to be "translucent".) Light transmission by paper is mostly diffuse transmission.

DIMENSIONAL PROPERTIES (of paper): Grouping of paper properties that includes grammage, caliper, bulk, and dimensional stability.

DIMENSIONAL STABILITY: Ability of paper to retain its dimensions in all directions under stress of handling and adverse changes of humidity.

DIRECTIONAL BRIGHTNESS: Brightness measurement utilizing essentially parallel beams of light to illuminate the paper surface at an angle of 45°. Syn. Institute Brightness, G.E. Brightness.

DIRECTIONALITY: Dominant orientation of fibers within a sheet of paper. See also GRAIN, FIBER ORIENTATION, ANISOTROPIC RATIO.

DIRT: Foreign matter embedded in a sheet of paper that has contrasting color to the rest of the sheet when viewed by reflected or transmitted light, e.g., bark, cinder, scale, shive, rust, grease, etc. Syn. Dirt Specks, Specks.

DIRT ANALYSIS: Identification of dirt specks in pulp or paper to determine the source of dirt. Syn. Speck Analsis.

DIRT COUNT: Quantitative assessment of the dirt content of a representative area of paper product based on manual counts or optical scanning devices.

DISCOLORATION: Unintended alteration in the color of paper, for example by the action of light and air.

DISHED: [adj] Describes a stack of paper sheets that lies in a decidedly concave condition rather than flat.

DISHED ROLL: See TELESCOPED ROLL.

DOUBLE CALENDERED: [adj] Term applied to coated paper that is processed through the supercalenders twice in order to achieve the desired finish.

DOUBLE THICK (DT): [adj] Term applied to paper products made by bonding two thicknesses of paper together.

DRAG SPOTS: Thin streaks in the paper sheet occurring in the machine direction, caused by agglomerations of stock adhering to the slice lip.

DRAPABILITY: Ease of buckling or three-dimensional deformation. Good drapability corresponds to low elastic stiffness.

DRIED-IN STRAIN (of paper): Difference between the percentage shrinkage that would occur without restraint and the percentage shrinkage in the same direction that actually does occur on the paper machine.

DRIP MARK: Characteristic mark on paper surface caused by water falling or dropping onto the paper web while draining on the fourdrinier.

DROP TEST: Time required for measured droplets of water to be absorbed by a paper surface, a measure of degree of sizing.

DRY CUT: Split in the web in the machine direction or at a slight angle, up to a meter in length. There is usually no evidence of wrinkling.

DRY FINISH: Unglazed, fairly rough surface obtained when paper is passed through the calenders without dampening.

DRY-FORMED PAPERS: Papers formed by a dry process utilizing cellulosic fibers, where the end products resemble conventional papers. See also DRY-LAY NONWOVENS.

DRY GRAMMAGE: See OVEN-DRY GRAMMAGE.

DRY INDICATOR METHOD (for degree of sizing): Test for water resistance in which one side of a test specimen of paper is made to contact water. The time required for complete penetration is indicated by the development of color on the opposite side (from application of a water-sensitive dry indicator powder).

DRY RUB RESISTANCE: Ability of a dry paper to withstand rubbing or scuffing without disruption of surface fibers.

DULL FINISH: Paper finish with good smoothness, but lacking in luster (e.g., English finish).

DUMBBELLS: Type of wet-lay nonwoven sheet defect consisting of paired clumps of fibers connected by one or more fibers. This problem can usually be traced to snags in the approach piping which capture fibers that are at least 2 to 3 times the nominal fiber length; the free ends whip in the flow and accumulate nominal fibers at both ends; the resultant dumbbell eventually becomes so large that fluid drag plucks it from the snag and delivers it to the sheet.

DUPLEX FINISHED: [adj] Describes paper having a different finish on each side.

DUPLEX PAPERS: Papers having a different color on each side. Syn. Split-Color Papers.

DUPLEX SUPER: [adj] Describes paper that has been supercalendered in a single-finishing stack.

DURABILITY: Ability of a paper to retain its original qualities under continuous usage. See also PERMANANCE.

DUSTING: Condition where fine particles of fiber, filler, or coating material leave the sheet during finishing, converting or printing.

DYE STREAK: Paper defect in the form of a colored streak, caused by undissolved dye particles in the papermaking system.

DYNAMIC LABORATORY FORMER: Laboratory sheet machine that produces paper having the non-uniformities and anisotropies found in commercial machine-made papers.

DYNAMIC PUNCTURE TESTER: Apparatus which determines the amount of energy required to drive a hemispherically shaped striking head through a firmly held sheet of paper at high velocity. The energy values obtained for sack and bag papers are said to correlate well with drop tests.

DYNAMIC STRENGTH: Resistance of paper to very rapid rates of straining.

E _____

EDGE CRACK: Ragged perforation at the edge of a sheet caused by a misaligned or damaged slitter.

EDGE CURL: Curl at the edges of a sheet.

EDGE TEAR RESISTANCE: Force required to initiate and propagate a tear in a test specimen, where the force is applied in the plane of the sheet at a tearing angle of 12°.

EDGEWISE COMPRESSION STRENGTH: See COMPRESSION STRENGTH.

EFFECTIVE CALIPER: Calculated value of paper caliper (e.g., from the simultaneous solution of expressions for bending stiffness and tensile stiffness). Effective caliper can be visualized as the distance between two imaginary planes that pass midway between the peaks and valleys of the topside and wire-side surface roughness profiles. (From V.C. Setterholm)

EGGSHELL FINISH: Relatively rough finish typical of book grades. A special felt is used to imprint the surface before the paper is dried.

ELASTICITY: Property of a material which enables it to undergo deformation and return to its original dimensions when the deforming force is removed. This property should not be confused with the properties of extensibility or stretch which for paper are primarily concerned with permanent deformation.

ELASTIC LIMIT: Smallest value of a stress that will produce a permanent deformation. This applies strictly only to truly elastic materials. For a viscoelastic material such as paper, the elastic limit depends on the rate of stress, having a high value for an instantaneous shock loading, but a much lower value for a more sustained stress.

ELASTIC MODULUS: See ELASTIC STIFFNESS.

ELASTIC PARAMETERS: Refers to the nine elastic stiffness measurements that can be made on machine-made paper. These measurements are related to various strength and physical properties of the paper.

ELASTIC STIFFNESS: Maximum slope of the stress-strain curve. A total of nine elastic stiffness measurements are required to fully characterize machine-made paper. Syn. Elastic Modulus, Young's Modulus.

ELASTIC STRETCH: Elongation due to tension, which is not retained when tension is relaxed.

ELECTRICAL PROPERTIES (of paper): Grouping of paper properties that includes conductance and dielectric properties.

ELECTRON MICROSCOPE: Device which produces a magnified image of an object by virtue of selective transmission, reflectance or emission of electrons by the object.

ELMENDORF TEAR RESISTANCE: Force required to propagate a tear in a test specimen where the force is applied perpendicular to the plane of the sheet at an angle of 90°. Syn. Internal Tearing Resistance.

ELONGATION: See STRETCH.

ELREPHO BRIGHTNESS: See DIFFUSE BRIGHTNESS.

EMBEDDING: Technique for immobilizing a paper sample within a surrounding transparent mass so that microtome sections of the sheet can be taken without distortion or disruption of the paper structure. The embedding material is usually a synthetic resin.

EMBOSSED FINISH: Patterned finish imparted to paper through an embosser, with subsequent calendering.

EMBOSSING TENDENCY: Tendency of paper to take a permanent set (i.e., become embossed) from contact with a letterpress printing form.

EMBRITTLEMENT: Irreversible condition of aged paper defined by the paper's inability to withstand more than one fold along the same line without breaking.

EMPIRICAL TESTS: Tests that are dependent on arbitrary instrument design and carefully defined procedure as to size of sample and other variables.

END DAMAGE: Paper roll defect in the form of gouges or indentations at the ends of the roll, caused by poor roll handling practices.

END-USE TESTS: Tests which relate to the end uses of the particular paper product, such as erasability, creasability, grease resistance, flame resistance, etc.

ENGLISH FINISH: Smooth surface with low gloss, generally considered to be the best finish obtainable on the paper machine.

EQUAL-SIDEDNESS: Similarity in surface properties between the two sides of paper. See also TWO-SIDEDNESS.

EQUILIBRIUM AIR: Air having a temperature and humidity such that it will not affect the moisture content of the paper.

EQUILIBRIUM MOISTURE CONTENT: Moisture content of paper that is in equilibrium with the prevailing atmospheric conditions.

ERASABILITY: Property of a sheet of paper that resists surface disruption by erasure.

EXPANSIMETER: Test equipment to measure the expansions and contractions of test specimens of paper or board by means of micrometers.

EXPANSION (of paper): Change in dimension, usually in the cross direction, of a sheet of paper due to absorption of moisture. See also HYGROEXPANSIVITY.

EXPANSIVITY: Index of a paper's ability to change dimensions with variation in moisture content. Syn. Expansiveness.

EXTENSIBILITY: Ability to stretch and absorb energy without rupture, an important property of sack papers.

EXTENSIBLE PAPER: Sack paper having a high level of extensibility, usually as a result of compaction on the paper machine.

EXTENSOMETER: Device designed to measure deformation of paper samples subjected to tensile stress.

F _____

FADEOMETER: Instrument used to measure the lightfastness of paper, inks, and other materials under controlled and reproducible conditions.

FAST COLOR: Paper color which is resistant to change from aging or from exposure to light, heat, or other adverse conditions.

FASTNESS: Resistance to change, e.g., light fastness, color fastness.

FATIGUE FAILURE: Rupture after repeated stress applications. (The folding endurance test is a measure of fatigue failure.)

FATIGUE STRENGTH: (1) Maximum cyclic load that a material can withstand for a specified number of cycles before rupture occurs. (2) Residual strength after being subjected to a specified cyclic loading.

FEATHER EDGE: Deckle edge where the caliper and grammage taper off from the body of the sheet toward the edge. Syn. Scarfed Edge.

FEATHERING: Ink spread from the edges of a pen stroke, due to insufficient sizing of paper.

FEATHERWEIGHT: [adj] Denotes paper that is lightweight in relation to its bulk.

FEEL: Subjective judgement of paper surface, stiffness or suppleness, based on touching and handling a sheet of paper.

FELT FINISH: Surface impression applied to paper at the wet press with felts having a special weave.

FELT MARK: Felt pattern impressed into the sheet during pressing reflecting the coarse or grainy character of a worn or filled felt.

FELT SIDE: Side of the paper web that has not been in contact with the forming fabric; the top side on fourdrinier machines.

FIBER-BASED SYNTHETIC PAPERS: Paper-like products constructed from synthetic fibrous materials, which can be produced by the extrusion of polymers (spunbonded products), from synthetic fibers (using special forming techniques), or from synthetic pulps (using the conventional papermaking process).

FIBER CONTENT: Content of cellulosic material, usually expressed as a percentage of the moisture-free paper. The fiber content is usually determined by weighing a moisture-free sample before and after ignition, assuming all volatile matter as fiber. See also ASH CONTENT, IGNITION FACTOR.

FIBER CUT: Sheet defect occurring during calendering due to the presence of a very coarse fiber (shive) near the surface. The fiber sustains an excessive share of the nip load, thus causing a cutting effect in the sheet.

FIBER LENGTH INDEX: Measure of the length of fibers in a paper sheet based on short-span tensile curves. It is defined as the total span (measured from extrapolated zero) at the position on the wet curve where the tensile value is one-half of the fiber strength index.

FIBER ORIENTATION: Alignment of fibers in the machine direction. The directionality of paper must be taken into account in measuring such paper strength properties as tear, tensile and folding endurance. The ratio of machine-direction and cross-direction strength values is indicative of the degree of orientation.

FIBER ORIENTATION DIAGRAM: Graphical depiction of the fiber orientation in a sheet of paper in polar coordinates, i.e., the distance from the center of the diagram to the edge of the curve at any angle represents the number (or percentage) of fibers lying in that direction. Typically, the upper half of the diagram shows fiber orientation in the top part of the sheet and the lower half shows the wire side of the sheet. See also MEAN ORIENTATION ANGLE.

FIBER ORIENTATION INDICES: See ORIENTATION INDEX, MEAN ORIENTATION ANGLE.

FIBER STRENGTH INDEX: Measure of the tensile strength of fibers within a paper sheet based on short-span tensile curves. It is defined as the intercept value on the tensile scale when the wet and dry short-span tensile curves are extrapolated to an intersecting point beyond the nominal zero point.

FILLED BOARD: Paperboard made on a multiply machine with different stock used for the inner plies (filler plies) from that of the liners. See also SOLID BOARD.

FILLED SHEET: Paper sheet containing a significant percentage of mineral or synthetic filler. Syn. Loaded Sheet.

FILLER CONTENT: Mineral filler content of paper, usually expressed as a percentage of the moisture-free substance. The filler content of uncoated paper is determined by weighing a moisture-free sample before and after ignition, assuming all residual ash as filler. See also ASH CONTENT, IGNITION FACTOR.

FILLER DISTRIBUTION: Filler content of the paper web (usually measured as percent ash) as a function of transversal strata position from the top side to the wire side.

FILLER SPLIT: Inadequate bonding between filler plies of multiply board.

FILM PAPER: Paper-like product made by forming a plastic film, stretching the film, and paperizing the film (i.e., treating the film to give it paper-like properties).

FINES DISTRIBUTION: Fines content (i.e., minus 200 mesh fraction) or filtration resistance of a paper web as a function of transversal strata position from the top side to the wire side.

FINISH: (1) Paper surface characteristics, mainly imparted by mechanical means. A "high finish" means high gloss; a "low finish" means without luster. (2) General surface quality as determined by color, brightness, texture, and appearance.

FISH EYES: Paper defect in the form of translucent spots, caused by the presence of slime, undissolved rosin, or other foreign materials in the sheet which become glazed by calendering.

FLAMEPROOF: [adj] Term applied to papers that have been treated with inorganic salts to retard oxidation to the extent that the paper will not support combustion. The paper will char and can be destroyed by heat, but will not act as a flame propagator. Syn. Flame-Resistant, Non-Combustible, Non-Flammable.

FLAT CRUSH RESISTANCE (of corrugated board)**:** Compressive force required to collapse a flute when applied perpendicular to the plane of the board, usually expressed as a pressure.

FLAT FINISH: Smooth, low-gloss finish.

FLATNESS: (1) Condition of paper or paperboard when it has no curl, cockle or waviness. (2) Lack of gloss.

FLAT ROLL: See CRUSHED ROLL.

FLAW: Defect in a paper sheet.

FLAW-CARRYING CAPACITY: General strength of a paper web that enables it to run with minimum breaks on a paper machine (or on a printing press) in spite of the presence of multiple flaws in the paper. See also FRACTURE RESISTANCE.

FLEXING: See BENDING.

FLEXING STRENGTH: See FOLDING ENDURANCE.

FLIMSY: [adj] Term describing very thin, lightweight papers such as tissues or manifolds.

FLUORESCENCE: Ability to emit radiant energy at wavelengths different than those which were absorbed, a property of papers which have been treated with an optical brightener.

FOAM MARK: Defect in paper caused by a bubble of froth in the stock emerging from the headbox which breaks up before the suction boxes. Syn. Bell.

FOLDABILITY: Ability of a heavy paper or paperboard to be folded without cracking. See also Creasability.

FOLDING ENDURANCE: Paper strength test measured as the number of double folds that a test strip under specified tension can withstand before failure.

FOLDING QUALITY: Assessment of the appearance of a fold. In one test method, a solid ink film is printed along the folding area and several folded sheets are placed together to form a small book. Backbone samples that exhibit a considerable amount of broken ink film are considered to be of poor folding quality.

FOLDING STRENGTH: See FOLDING ENDURANCE, CREASING STRENGTH.

FOLD NUMBER: See FOLDING ENDURANCE.

FORCED DRAPE TESTING: Method for evaluating the drapability or hand of tissue papers in which a sample is draped around the top of a rod and forced through the annulus created between the rod and a circular opening. Drapability is related to the work required to force the specimen through the annulus.

FORMATION: Degree of uniformity of the fiber distribution in a sheet of paper. A uniform fiber distribution is described as "close formation"; an irregular distribution is said to have "wild formation" or "cloudy formation", or may be described as a "snowstorm". Syn. Mass Distribution. See also LOOK-THROUGH, COMPACTNESS, FORMATION INDICES.

FORMATION INDICES: Quantitative measurements of formation by various methods, for example by the STFI, QNSM, and MK formation testers.

FORMATION NUMBER: Standard deviation of sheet mass variation (on a micro scale) about a mean value, expressed as a percentage (i.e., as percent variation).

FORMATION TESTER: Device for quantitatively measuring the uniformity of fiber distribution or mass distribution of paper. Most such devices operate by light transmission and are therefore limited to the testing of lightweight sheets.

FOXING: Staining of paper by mold or mildew because of unfavorable storage conditions.

FRACTURE RESISTANCE: Force required to propagate a tear, where the force is applied in the plane of the sheet and the tearing angle is 0°. In essence, fracture resistance is a tensile test with a cut put at one edge of the test strip.

FRACTURE TOUGHNESS: Generic term referring to the resistance of a material containing flaws or defects (collectively called "cracks") to stable or unstable crack growth. See also FLAW-CARRYING CAPACITY.

FREE SHEET: Paper made from freely draining stock. (This term should not be confused with "woodfree paper".)

FROZEN STRESSES: Tensional stresses imposed on paper during drying that remain after the paper is dried.

FUGITIVE COLOR: Color that is unstable with exposure to light or to the action of acids, alkalis and oxidizing agents.

FUGITIVE SIZING: Sizing which is lost after aging of the paper. See also SIZING REGRESSION.

FUNCTIONAL TESTS: See USE TESTS.

FUNDAMENTAL PROPERTIES (of paper): Those properties of paper which are independent of dimensions, procedures, or instrument design, and should be capable of correlation with the paper-making process.

FUZZ: Hairiness or fibrous projections on the surface of the sheet. Lint is similar in appearance, but is not attached to the surface.

FUZZINESS: Tendency of a paper to develop fibrous projections on its surface.

G _____

GALVANIZED SURFACE: Variation in the apparent gloss of the sheet surface, where scattered areas are of higher or lower gloss.

GALVANIZED WIRE SIDE: Surface streakiness resembling galvanized iron on the wire side, traceable to differences between jet and wire speed or water following the wire around the breast roll.

GAP TEST: Test made on a roll of paper to assess the amount of wound-in tension. The outer layer of a roll sitting on the floor is cut and the gap between the two broken edges is measured as an indication of the tension which would be required to stretch the paper to fill the gap.

G.E. BRIGHTNESS: See DIRECTIONAL BRIGHTNESS.

GEOMETRIC MEAN VALUE (of paper strength properties): Square root of the product of machine-direction value times cross-direction value. The geometric mean value for machine-made paper is usually a good approximation of the value obtained on an isotropic sheet made from the same furnish.

GLAZED FINISH: High gloss or polish applied to a paper surface either during manufacture (e.g., with a Yankee dryer) or as an off-machine finishing operation (e.g., using a friction calender). See also BURNISHED FINISH.

GLOSS: Angular selectivity of surface-reflected light; the light-reflecting property of a surface which causes a shiny appearance. Syn. Sheen, Luster. See also SPECULAR GLOSS, CONTRAST GLOSS.

GLOSS FINISH: Extra smooth finish applied to paper, generally to achieve superior printability. Syn. Mirror Finish.

GLOSSIMETER: Instrument for measuring the ratio of light reflected from a surface in a definite direction to the total light reflected in all directions. Syn. Glossmeter, Glarimeter.

GLOSS PAPER: Paper having a shiny or lustrous appearance.

GLOSS RETENTION: Percent of original gloss retained by a specimen after aging under specified conditions.

GLOSSY-COATED PAPERS: All papers that have a gloss reading between 50 and 80.

GLUEABILITY: Strength of glued joint under standard conditions, an important property for some board grades, which depends on surface wettability, surface absorbency and shear plane strength.

GLUE ON ROLL END: Minor paper roll defect in which glue used in roll wrapping is inadvertently transferred to the end of the roll. Such glue is usually colored so that it can be easily spotted by the unwind operator and removed by sandpapering. If not removed, the condition will cause plies to stick together and precipitate a break. Syn. Stuck End, Blocked End, Glued End.

GRAIN: Alignment of fibers. See also DIRECTIONALITY, FIBER ORIENTATION.

GRAIN DIRECTION: Direction of predominant fiber alignment, i.e., the machine direction.

GRAINY: [adj] Term used to describe the rough surface of a paper sheet, usually applied to paper which has undergone considerable cross shrinkage during drying.

GRAINY EDGES: Outer edges of the paper web on the paper machine which are subject to lateral shrinkage. Grainy edges are more obvious on rougher and heavier paper grades.

GRAMMAGE: Mass per unit area of paper, expressed as grams per square meter. Grammage is the preferred term by the ISO. The terms "basis weight" and "substance" are also commonly used.

GRAMMAGE TOLERANCE: Allowable variation in grammage established by trade custom. Syn. Weight Tolerance.

GREASE PENETRATION TEST: See TURPENTINE TEST.

GREASE-RESISTANT: [adj] Term applied to papers that are resistant to absorption of greases and oils.

GREASY SPOTS: Spots on the surface of paper that cause a pen to skip, resulting from too much grease in the animal glue used for surface sizing of the sheet.

GREEN PAPER: Newly-manufactured paper that has not been conditioned.

H

HAIR CUT: Sharp, smooth-curved cut in the paper, having no definite length or direction which is caused by an animal hair or synthetic fiber getting into the web and cutting the sheet during calendering.

HAND: Feel, drape, or "handle" of tissue papers.

HANDLE: Vague term indicating a papermaker's subjective impression when a single sheet of paper is held or moved by hand, encompassing such properties as "stiffness", "feel", "rattle", etc. See also HAND.

HANDLING DAMAGE: Any physical damage which occurs to rolls or packages of paper during storage and movement.

HANDLING STIFFNESS: Ability of a paper to resist bending during handling.

HANDMADE FINISH: Rough finish resembling handmade paper.

HANDMADE PAPER: Paper formed on individual wire moulds by hand manipulation.

HARD-CALENDERED: [adj] Term applied to papers and boards that have been heavily calendered.

HARDNESS: Property of a paper or paperboard sheet which resists indentation by objects pressed against its surface.

HARD PAPER: Hard sized paper with a firm, smooth writing surface and relatively poor ink receptivity.

HARD SIZED: [adj] Describes paper that is heavily sized to icrease its resistance to liquid penetration. Opposite to slack sized. Syn. Well Sized.

HARD SPOTS: Localized hard areas on a paper roll or reel which correspond to the high spots on the cross machine caliper profile.

HARD WRINKLE: Foldover that has been calendered into a hard crease. In roll stock, a hard wrinkle is one present in the roll of paper as shipped from the mill.

HEAT AGING: See ACCELERATED AGING.

HEAT CURL TEST: Degree of curl when a sample of paper is exposed to heat on one side under specified conditions. Nearly all papers will show some curl with this test because of the contraction of the exposed fibers; it is a high degree of curl that relates to problems.

HEAVY WEIGHTS: Papers in the higher grammage categories for a particular grade.

HIGH-FILLER PAPER: Paper containing over 30% filler by weight.

HOLDOUT: Extent to which a paper or board surface resists penetration by liquids.

HOLE: Sheet flaw consisting of a small open area with ragged edges. A relatively clean hole is usually due to a hole or deposit on the forming fabric. See also SLUG HOLE, SLIME HOLE, PINHOLE, WIRE HOLE.

HUE: See COLOR PERCEPTION, MUNSELL COLOR SYSTEM.

HUMIDIFIED HEAT TREATMENT: "Accelerated aging" of paper or board in a humidified atmosphere. Comparison of accelerated aging methods with natural aging indicates that some moisture should be present in an accelerated aging atmosphere for the most representative results.

HYGROEXPANSIVITY: Property of paper which causes it to expand and contract in concert with changes in its moisture content, as when the relative humidity of the surrounding atmosphere is variable. See also DIMENSIONAL STABILITY.

HYGRO-INSTABILITY: Tendency to change dimension as a result of moisture change.

HYGROMETER: Instrument to measure the relative humidity of air at a specific location or within a controlled environment.

HYGRO-STABILITY: Ability of paper or paperboard to retain its dimensions while its moisture content changes.

I

IGNITION FACTOR: Ratio of original filler weight to ash weight after ignition in a muffle furnace at 900°C, a characteristic property of mineral fillers. The ignition factor must be taken into account when the ash residue from paper is taken as a measure of the original filler content.

IMITATION HANDMADE PAPER: Machine-made paper that is manufactured to have the appearance of handmade paper.

IMPACT STRENGTH: Ability of paperboard to resist failure when an object is dropped onto a supported specimen from successively increasing heights.

IMPERFECTIONS (in paper): Local irregularities or nonuniformities in sheets or rolls of paper.

IMPERVIOUS: [adj] Describes paper that resists penetration by moisture, grease, oil and chemicals.

IMPULSE TESTER: Apparatus which subjects a paper strip to a straining rate of 10 m/s and measures the impulse or momentum transferred through the strip before the strip breaks. Test values on bag or sack papers are said to correlate well with drop test results.

IMPULSE TO RUPTURE: Strength test for paper, measured under prescribed conditions as the integrated product of the tensile force applied to cause rupture and the time interval over which the force acts on the test specimen.

INDENTED PAPER: Paper or board that has raised areas formed into the wet sheet on the paper machine by impression rolls. The soft and bulky sheets are used mainly in protective packaging applications.

INDIA TINT: Light buff color often selected for printing papers.

INDIRECT MEASUREMENT: Measurement of a related property which is used to predict the value of the needed property. For example, electrical resistance can be used to indicate the moisture content of paper.

INHERENT CURL: Curl due to dried-in strains which result from shrinkage. Paper with inherent curl once released will immediately curl because one side will tend to expand under compressive stress while the other side will tend to contract, having been dried under tensile stress.

INITIAL TEAR RESISTANCE: See EDGE TEAR RESISTANCE.

INK ABSORPTION: See INK PENETRATION TEST, INK WIPE TEST.

INK ABSORPTIVITY: Property of paper that characterizes the rate and amount of ink vehicle penetration into the paper substrate after deposition from the press plate or blanket.

INK FLOTATION SIZING TEST: Method of evaluating the degree of internal sizing by floating a test sample of paper on a colored writing ink and measuring the time for ink penetration through the paper.

INK HOLDOUT: Tendency of paper to resist the inward migration of freshly printed ink.

INK PENETRATION TEST: Amount of ink that has penetrated a specified area of paper in a specified time, a measure of sizing.

INK RECEPTIVITY: Ability of a paper surface to uniformly and adequately transfer ink from the printing plate or blanket. Uniform ink coverage over a wide range of film thickness is characteristic of a paper sheet having good ink receptivity.

INK RESISTANCE: Resistance of a paper surface to ink penetration.

INK WIPE TEST: Test for ink absorption in which a special ink is spread evenly over a sample of coated paper and left for a specified time; the excess ink is then removed by rubbing with cotton wool. A reflectance reading is taken and compared with the reflectance of the unstained paper. The darker the stain, the higher is the ink absorption.

IN-PLANE TEAR RESISTANCE: Force required to propagate a tear in a test specimen where the force is applied in the plane of the sheet at a tearing angle of 12°.

INTERFIBER BOND STRENGTH: Energy required to delaminate a sample strip of paper or paperboard when the force is applied at 90° in a peeling mode.

INTERNAL BOND STRENGTH: Maximum tensile force per unit area which a test specimen of paper or paperboard can withstand when the force is applied over the entire test area perpendicular to the plane of the sheet. Syn. Z-Strength.

INTERNAL TEAR RESISTANCE: See ELMENDORF TEAR.

ISOTROPIC PAPER: Paper having random orientation of fibers and identical properties in all directions within the plane of the sheet. Examples of isotropic papers are laboratory handsheets and handmade paper.

IVORY: Cream-white color commonly used for boards and bristols.

IVORY FINISH: Finish obtained by calendering the sheet through a stack of rolls onto which beeswax has been applied.

J

JUST-PERCEPTIBLE DIFFERENCE: Difference in color that is just large enough to be perceived in almost every trial.

K

KEROSINE NUMBER: Quantitative measurement of the amount of kerosine absorbed by a test specimen under specified conditions, used to indicate the bituminous saturating capacity of felt papers.

KID FINISH: Soft vellum-like finish resembling in appearance and feel undressed kid leather. It is similar to a smooth eggshell finish, but with a finer surface texture.

KIT TEST: Procedure for determining the degree of repellancy and/or the antiwicking characteristics of papers and boards which are treated with fluorochemical-type sizing agents. Solutions are made up with different penetrating abilities. The measurement is reported in terms of the highest numbered solution (i.e., most penetrating) that will stand on the surface for 15 seconds without causing pronounced darkening.

KUBELKA-MUNK EQUATION: Empirical relationship between optical reflectance measurements and the light scattering and light absorbing properties of a material. (Named for the authors of the theory of scattering and absorption of radiation.)

L

LAID LINES: Continuous watermark in the form of closely spaced parallel lines either with or perpendicular to the grain. Syn. Chain Lines, Chain Marks.

LAID PAPER: Paper having laid lines.

LATERAL POROSITY: Permeability of paper in a direction parallel with the plane of the sheet. Syn. Transverse Porosity.

LENGTH (of a paper roll): Distance between ends measured in the machine direction.

LEVELNESS: Point-to-point variations in paper thickness which occur on a macro scale (as distinct from roughness which measures variations in paper thickness on a micro scale).

LIGHT ABSORPTION: Process by which light energy is transferred to the incident surface.

LIGHT-ABSORPTION COEFFICIENT: Measure of the ability of a material to absorb light. With respect to paper, the absorption coefficient is used as a measure of the presence of colored components in the sheet.

LIGHT BOX: Shallow box equipped with internal light source and glass window to which sheets of lightweight paper are attached for viewing formation and other see-through features.

LIGHTFASTNESS: Ability of paper to resist change in color, fading and yellowing upon exposure to light.

LIGHT SCATTERING: Process by which incident light energy is absorbed and then re-emitted without appreciable change in wave length. Syn. Optical Scattering.

LIGHT-SCATTERING COEFFICIENT: Measure of the ability of a material to scatter incident light. With respect to paper, the scattering coefficient is used as a measure of how much free unbonded area exists in the sheet.

LIKE-SIDEDNESS: Similarity in surface character between wire and felt sides of the paper, especially with respect to smoothness, brightness, color and surface strength.

LINEN FINISH: Finish resembling linen fabric obtained off-machine by compressing sheets of paper between alternate sheets of linen cloth or by embossing a continuous web with an engraved steel roll.

LINT: Small fiber particles that separate or "dust off" from the paper during manufacturing, printing and converting operations. Syn. Dust, Fluff.

LIQUID PENETRATION TESTER: Instrument which indicates the penetration of liquid into a paper sample (and hence the sizing effectiveness) by measuring the light reflectance or transmittance of the sample.

LIVELINESS: Speed of bending recovery, a component of "handle"

LOAD: Tensile or compressive force applied to a paper sample. See also STRESS.

LOADED SHEET: See FILLED SHEET.

LOADING RATE: Rate at which stress is imposed onto a sample, e.g., during a tensile test. (Note that some instruments are capable of being operated either with a constant rate of loading or a constant rate of straining.) In the SI system, the units are kN/m·s.

LOCALIZED WATERMARK: Watermark appearing at specific intervals on the web, so that each cut sheet will have one mark.

LOGS: Type of wet-lay nonwoven fabric defect consisting of bundles of fibers with aligned cut ends that were never dispersed, either due to a fiber supply problem or gross under-agitation during initial dispersion.

LOOK-THROUGH: Structural appearance of a sheet of paper when viewed under diffuse, transmitted light. See also FORMATION.

LOOSE CORE: Core of a roll that can be moved easily by hitting the end or twisting the core with a torque wrench, due to insufficient wound-in-tension at the core.

LOOSE WINDING: Loose condition of a paper web in a roll caused by inadequate web tension during winding.

LOT: Quantity of paper (of a single type, grade, grammage, etc.) about which it is desired to make a judgement (usually regarding conformance to specifications) by examining or testing a small fraction, called a sample. Each lot is generally identified by "lot number".

LOW FINISH: Low gloss finish such as antique or machine finish.

LUMINANCE: Reflectivity of a paper sample measured in green light (wave length 557 nm). Since the eye is most sensitive to green light, this measurement corresponds approximately to how bright a given paper sample appears to the average observer. (As opposed to brightness which is a measure of bleaching effect.).

LUMINOSITY: See COLOR PERCEPTION.

LUSTER: See GLOSS.

M _____

MACHINE-DIRECTION PROFILE: Variation in property of a paper or paperboard web along a straight line in the machine direction. The term is sometimes applied to the machine-direction variation of the mean value of a property over the entire cross direction of the web, which more specifically is the "machine-direction mean profile".

MACHINE-DIRECTION VARIATION: Variation of web properties in the machine direction (or with time). This type of variation can be measured directly.

MACHINE FINISH: Finish obtained from on-machine calendering.

MACHINE-GLAZED (MG): [adj] Term applied to paper or board having one side (usually the wire side) smooth and glossy as a result of having been dried in contact with a highly-polished Yankee cylinder.

MACHINE-IMPRINTED: [adj] Term applied to paper that has had a design or mark impressed into the wet web by means of metal to rubber rolls. See also INDENTED PAPER.

MACHINE MARK STRIPES: Machine direction stripes caused by a localized disturbance during formation, spaced across the web so that each finished roll will have at least one stripe. These stripes are used in the enforcement of tariff regulations in certain countries. Syn. Water Lines, Tariff Regulation Stripes.

MACROSCOPIC: [adj] Large enough to be observed with the naked eye.

MANILA: [adj] Term indicating a color tone formerly obtained in paper manufactured from manila hemp stock. Under present usage, it only describes a particular straw-yellow color.

MARBLE SURFACE: Decorative surface effect obtained on paper by dripping dyestuff solution onto the stock as it is being formed on the fourdrinier, usually at some short distance before the first suction box.

MASS DISTRIBUTION: See FORMATION.

MATTE COATED PAPERS: Coated papers with gloss readings between 7 and 20.

MATTE FINISH: Finish with good smoothness, but devoid of gloss.

MATURING: Aging of paper and board which leads to an improvement in product quality or uniformity.

MEALY FORMATION: See MOTTLED FORMATION.

MEAN ORIENTATION ANGLE: Index of fiber orientation within a paper sheet, calculated from the weighted average of individual fiber orientation angles within a quadrant.

MECHANICAL CURL: Curl caused by mechanical stress on paper other than that of swelling or shrinkage due to changing moisture content.

MECHANICAL DECKLE EDGE: Imitation deckle edge imparted to dry paper by abrasion or other mechanical processing of the edge.

MECHANICAL PROPERTIES: Measured behavior of paper under various types of stress.

MEDIUM FINISH: Finish for uncoated paper resembling a smooth, vellum finish. Any intermediate finish between high and low.

MELLOW: [adj] Term applied to paper with a soft, resilient feel.

METAMERISM: Difference in color between two paper samples under a certain light source after a good color match has been achieved under another light source (e.g., fluorescent lighting vs. daylight). This phenomenom often occurs when different colorants are used to produce the respective colors.

MICROGRAPH: See PHOTOMICROGRAPH.

MICROMETER: Thickness gauge. The foot area and squeeze pressure of a micrometer for measuring paper thickness (caliper) are standardized.

MICROSCOPE: Optical instrument for producing a magnified image of a small object.

MICROSCOPICAL TEST (of paper): Grouping of tests which includes determination of the type of fibers used in the paper, qualitative analysis of the filler present, and identification of dirt specks and spots.

MICROSCOPY (of paper): Science and interpretive use of the microscope for paper examination, fiber differentiation, fiber length analysis, identification of foreign matter, etc.

MICROSECTIONING: See SECTIONING.

MICROSMOOTHNESS: Degree of irregularities with respect to microscopic areas of the paper surface.

MICROSTRUCTURAL ANALYSIS: Prediction of the elastic and inelastic response of paper in terms of the mechanical behavior of the fibers and the fiber network structure of the paper.

MICROSTRUCTURE: Structure of a suitably prepared specimen (of paper, fibers, fillers, etc.) as revealed by a microscope.

MICROTOME: Instrument for cutting an ultra-thin section of paper or board for microscopical examination.

MIL: See POINT.

MOISTURE CONTENT (DRY BASIS): Moisture in a material (e.g., pulp, paper), expressed as the ratio of moisture weight to weight of moisture-free material. Syn. Moisture Ratio.

MOISTURE CONTENT (WET BASIS): Moisture in a material (e.g., pulp, paper) as a percentage of the weight of the wet material. (Although commonly used, the wet basis is less satisfactory than the dry basis where the change is constant for any given increment of moisture gain or loss.)

MOISTURE DETERMINATION: Test to measure the moisture content of a sample (of paper, pulp, chips, etc.), usually carried out by weighing the sample before and again after drying in an oven at 105°C. The moisture content (wet basis) is calculated as the difference in sample weight divided by the original wet sample weight.

MOISTURE METER: Device which is held against a paper roll to indicate its moisture content. Most devices of this type measure either electrical resistance or capacitance and should be calibrated against similar papers of known moisture content.

MOISTUREPROOF: [adj] Term applied to papers that are very resistant to the passage of liquid water or water vapor, i.e., papers that exhibit low water/vapor permeability.

MOISTURE REGAIN: Moisture content (dry basis) at equilibrium.

MOISTURE-VAPOR TRANSMISSION RATE (MVTR): Measure of water vapor permeability for paper. This property is usually measured by sealing a test specimen over a cup containing anhydrous calcium chloride (a powerful deliquescent), placing the assembly for two hours in a cabinet at 38°C and 90% relative humidity, and determining the moisture pickup.

MOISTURE WELTS: Machine-direction ridges in rolls of paper caused by surface expansion due to uneven moisture absorption from the atmosphere. Syn. Weather Wrinkles.

MOLD RESISTANT: [adj] Term applied to papers that have been treated to resist attack by fungi and bacteria.

MOTTLED FINISH: Finish with glossy and dull spots.

MOTTLED FORMATION: Sheet formation with look-through appearance of curdled milk, most commonly due to a crushing effect during pressing. Syn. Mealy Formation.

MOTTLED SHADE: Decorative effect produced on the surface of paper by adding a small proportion of heavily-dyed fibers to the furnish. See also VEINED PAPER.

MULLEN TESTER: Instrument for measuring the bursting strength of paper samples. The sample is clamped between two concentric rings, and hydraulic pressure is applied to one side through a rubber diaphragm.

MUNSELL COLOR SYSTEM: System for color specification utilizing uniform perceptual spacing of the three defining attributes: hue, chroma (saturation), and value (lightness-darkness).

N

NATURAL COLORED: [adj] Term applied to papers made from unbleached pulp stock to which no coloring has been added. In the case of natural kraft papers, the color varies from tan to brown.

NIP-INDUCED DEFECTS: Roll defects caused by nonuniform nip pressure during winding operations, including bursts, bags, offsets, wrinkles, and corrugations.

NOMINAL GRAMMAGE: Labelled grammage of a paper product. Due to unavoidable variation on the paper machine, the actual grammage will vary up to plus or minus 5%. Syn. Nominal Weight. See also GRAMMAGE TOLERANCE.

NON-CELLULOSE PAPERS: See SYNTHETIC PAPERS.

NONDESTRUCTIVE TEST: Any test method for paper or paperboard (e.g., visual, microscopic, ultrasonic, gauging, etc.) that does not affect the mechanical properties of the sample.

O

OFF COLOR: [adj] Describes paper that does not match the color of a reference sample. Syn. Off Shade.

OFFSET: Paper roll defect which can be seen as an abrupt change in the sheet edge position at the end of the roll, usually caused by a sudden change in sheet tension during winding.

OFFSET CORE: Paper roll defect in which the core is protruding or recessed into the roll. Syn. Core Slippage, Telescoped Core.

OIL PENETRATION TEST: Time required for complete penetration of a specified oil into a sample of paper, under standardized conditions, used as a measure of oil-based ink receptivity.

OIL REPELLANCY: Ability of a paper surface to resist penetration by oil.

OIL REPELLANCY TEST: Control test for surface repellancy in which three drops of a specified oil solution are placed on a test sheet and allowed to stand for 15 minutes. Darkening of the fibers under any of the spots indicates failure. By using a number of oil solutions of decreasing concentration until failure occurs, it is possible to rate the sheet for repellancy.

OIL WICKING: Conveying oil by capillary attraction.

OIL WICKING TEST: Test for resistance to oil wicking in which a test specimen of paper is suspended so that one end is barely below the liquid surface in a container of dyed oil. The wicking height is measured after 24 hours and compared to a standard.

ON-LINE MEASUREMENTS: Measurements of paper properties that are made continuously by sensors on the paper machine. Most on-line measurements are indirect measurements.

OPACIMETER: Instrument for measuring the opacity of paper.

OPACITY: Property of a sheet of paper which obstructs the passage of light, as opposed to transparency, usually determined as a contrast ratio on a reflectance meter. See also OPACITY (PAPER BACKING), OPACITY (WHITE BACKING).

OPACITY (PAPER BACKING): Ratio (expressed as a percentage) of the amount of light reflected from a single sheet of paper with a black backing to the amount of light reflected from the same sheet of paper backed by an opaque pile of the same paper, measurements being made under standardized conditions. Formerly called "Printing Opacity".

OPACITY (WHITE BACKING): Ratio (expressed as a percentage) of the amount of light reflected from a single sheet of paper with a black backing to the amount of light reflected from the same sheet of paper backed by a standard white body (usually having an absolute reflectance of 89%), measurements being made under standardized conditions. Formerly called "TAPPI Opacity".

OPAQUE PILE: Pile of paper sheets of sufficient thickness that the addition of more sheets does not affect the reflectance reading.

OPTICAL CONTACT: Close contact between two objects (e.g., two fibers in a paper sheet) such that a beam of light passing from one to the other does not pass through a layer of air between them.

OPTICAL PROPERTIES: Grouping of paper properties that includes brightness, opacity, color, gloss, and light scattering coefficient.

OPTICAL SCATTERING: See LIGHT SCATTERING.

OPTICAL SMOOTHNESS: Ability of a paper sheet surface to reflect incident light.

OPTICAL TESTS: Tests carried out on paper and board products to quantify and monitor their optical properties.

ORANGE PEEL: Pebbly-grained paper surface.

ORIENTATION INDEX: Relative index of fiber orientation in a paper sheet, defined as the ratio of the fiber strength index in the machine direction to that in the cross direction. See also FIBER STRENGTH INDEX.

ORIENTATION OF FIBERS: See FIBER ORIENTATION.

ORTHOTROPIC: [adj] Term applied to materials that have different properties in three mutually perpendicular directions. While paper can certainly be viewed as an orthotropic material, it is more often considered as a two-dimensional, anisotropic material.

OUTLYING TEST DETERMINATION: Test value that appears to deviate markedly from other values determined on the same sample or near-identical samples. For mill testing, it is common practice to disregard an "outlier". For research work, statistical or nonstatistical rules can be applied to assess whether the value can be disregarded or not.

OUT-OF-ROUND ROLL: Slight flattening of a roll due to mishandling or storage on the bilge. A severely out-of-round roll is referred to as a "crushed roll".

OUTTURN SAMPLE: Sample of paper made on a particular run, which can either be sent to the customer as representative of a subsequent paper shipment or kept by the mill for reference purposes.

OVEN-DRY GRAMMAGE: Calculated value of moisture-free grammage for paper and paperboard based on grammage and moisture content measurements. Syn. Dry Grammage.

OVER-DRIED PAPER: Paper that has been excessively dried to the extent that it has become brittle and lost some of its inherent strength. Syn. Burnt Paper.

P _____

PAPER DIRECTIONALITY: See GRAIN DIRECTION.

PAPER HYGROSCOPE: See SWORD HYGROMETER.

PAPERIZATION: Treatment of a plastic film to produce paper-like properties. The aim is to ensure good opacity and provide a surface with good printability. Paperization can be achieved either on the surface or throughout the whole sheet. Surface paperization may involve surface treatment with solvent, chemical or flame; mechanical or electrical methods; or coating with clays and other materials. Bulk paperization can be achieved by forming the plastic or by compounding it with fillers or mixtures of plastics.

PAPER MECHANICS: Study of paper under the action of forces, in order to formulate general rules of behavior for paper under the influence of any type of stress.

PAPER PHYSICS: Study of paper physical properties, in order to gain a fundamental understanding in terms of basic principles and laws.

PAPER QUALITY: Degree of excellence with respect to those properties and characteristics which are important to the user of the paper product.

PAPER QUALITY INDEX: Weighting and summation of all measured properties relevant to the end use of the paper product.

PAPER STRENGTH: Vague term, unless a particular strength property has been specified. The term is often ambiguously applied to papers that must withstand considerable stress.

PAPER TEST: See TEST.

PARCHMENT FINISH: Dull, smooth, undulating surface finish resembling true parchment, produced by bunch plating a hard sheet.

PASTED BOARD: Paperboard made up of two or more thicknesses (of the same or different stocks) which have been bonded together with an adhesive in an off-machine operation.

PATCH MARK: Watermark made by a patch sewed onto the forming fabric or onto the dandy roll of the fourdrinier.

PATENT COATED: [adj] Describes multiply paperboard that has been vat lined on one or both sides with white fibers. (Note that patent coated board is not pigment coated.)

PATTERN: Surface characteristic of paper which comes about through some type of variation in either smoothness, gloss, or color, or any combination of the three.

PEN AND INK TEST: Simple test of the writing qualities of a sheet of paper carried out by drawing several lines of ink on the paper surface. Lack of good writing quality is indicated by feathering or spreading of the ink beyond the point of contact of the pen.

PENESCOPE TEST: Measurement of liquid penetration into paper under specified liquid head (pressure). Since pressure increases the rate of penetration, this test is useful for determining the degree of sizing for paperboards.

PERFECT: [adj] Term applied to paper that is free of defects.

PERFORMANCE TESTS: See USE TESTS.

PERMANENCE: Ability of paper to retain its desirable properties during normal aging or after prolonged exposure to light, humidity and high temperature. Permanence can be evaluated by carrying out accelerated aging tests. Syn. Aging Resistance. See also DURABILITY.

PERMEABILITY: Ability to allow fluid movement through paper under a pressure gradient when the fluid permeates the paper and is present on both sides of the sheet. The permeability is inversely related to the resistance offered by the paper to fluid movement. Syn. Permeance.

pH (of paper): See ACIDITY (of paper), ALKALINITY (of paper).

PHOTOMICROGRAPH: Photographic reproduction of an object or sample (e.g., paper cross section, individual fibers, etc.) as seen through a microscope or equivalent optical instrument. Syn. Micrograph.

PHOZY: [adj] Term applied to tissue papers that are too fluffy or loosely bonded.

PHYSICAL PROPERTIES: Overall grouping of paper properties that includes dimensional, mechanical, optical, surface, permeable, electrical, and thermal properties, but generally excludes chemical properties.

PICK RESISTANCE: Resistance of the surface of paper to lifting or pulling away of the fibers or coating when being printed. It is a measure of the surface strength or fiber bonding strength of the paper. Syn. Surface Strength, Surface Bonding Strength, Surface Cohesion.

PICK TESTER: See SURFACE STRENGTH TESTER.

PIN HOLE: Any of those defects in paper most commonly caused by fine particles of sand, clay, or hardened size, which when the paper is calendered, are crushed and fall out leaving holes. Very hard grit may adhere to the steel rolls and produce pin holes at every revolution.

PIPING: Hard edges on the paper web due to insufficient roll crown during calendering.

PITCH SPOTS: Dirt specks in paper which have their origin in the resins contained in the wood for pulp manufacture.

PLATE FINISH: Smooth or glossy finish obtained by placing a stack of steam-seasoned paper sheets between two metal plates and passing the pile (called a "book") through a high-pressure nip. The finish varies depending on the characteristics of the plates, the pressure applied, and the number of times the book is passed through the nip.

PLATING: Technique to achieve special surface effects wherein the paper sheets are placed between two layers of a material, such as linen cloth or burlap. Metal plates are added for rigidity and the "book" is then run between heavy rolls so that the paper takes on the impression of the plating material.

PLIABILITY: Subjective property of tissue papers which is a function of softness, smoothness and drapability.

PLYBOND: Generally, the bonding strength between adjoining plies of multiply paperboard. More specifically, plybond is the resistance to ply separation when a tensile force is applied perpendicular to the plane of the multiple plies. Syn. Ply Adhesion, Delamination Resistance.

POINT: Term denoting 0.001 inches of paper thickness, e.g., nine-point corrugating medium has a caliper of 0.009 inches. Syn. Mil.

POISSON'S RATIO: Ratio of lateral contraction to elongation of a paper sheet when it is subjected to tensile stress.

POLISH: High gloss.

POOR START: Paper roll defect characterized by an obvious difference in appearance between paper near the core and the remainder of the role; most often caused by low web tension during the start of roll winding.

POP TEST: Colloquialism for the bursting strength test.

PORES (of paper): Openings that extend entirely through the sheet. (An opening that extends only from one side of the sheet is sometimes called a "dead-end pore", but is more often referred to as a "recess".) The pore volume of most papers is a small fraction of the total air volume; the large portion consists of voids and recesses.

POROSITY: Percentage of air space within a sheet of paper. This property is evaluated by determining the air permeability.

POWDERING: Condition where fine particles of pigment (either filler pigment or coating pigment) leave the sheet during finishing, converting or printing. See also DUSTING.

PRECISION: See TEST PRECISION.

PRECISION STATEMENT: Statement that qualifies a test method with respect to repeatability within a laboratory, comparability between materials and reproducibility between laboratories.

PRECONDITIONING: Conditioning of paper samples at 39°C and 20% relative humidity prior to standard conditioning. Preconditioning "on the dry side" ensures that the samples are "conditioned up" to the final equilibrium condition, which will avoid most of the hysteresis effect.

PRESSURE BULKER: Test equipment that measures the bulk of a number of sheets of paper under a specified pressure.

PRIMARY STANDARD: Certified reference material used for standardization or calibration purposes.

PRINTABILITY: Ability to accept and preserve a printed image with minimum rub-off, set-off and show-through. Although tests are available to measure specific aspects, relative measurement of printability is a subjective judgement based on the legibility and show-through of printed sheets. Printability is dependent on such sheet properties as smoothness, absorbency, moisture content, formation, opacity and brightness. See also PRINT DENSITY, SHOW-THROUGH.

PRINT DENSITY: Optical contrast between printed and unprinted surfaces of a sheet of paper, an important aspect of printability. This contrast is usually measured from a solid print and is dependent on the brightness of the paper. Heavier inking on the printing plate will improve print density, but also has the adverse effect of increasing show-through.

PRINT EVENNESS: Variance in tone of solid and dark-grey print areas as judged subjectively or measured by optical scanning or image analysis, an important aspect of print quality in newspaper printing.

PRINTING OPACITY: See OPACITY (PAPER BACKING).

PRINTING RATING: Relative printing quality of paper based on comparisons made with a proof press.

PRINTING SIDE: Designation for the felt side or top side of an uncoated, fourdrinier-made paper, which normally has slightly better printability than the wire side.

PROFILE: See CROSS-DIRECTION PROFILE, MACHINE-DIRECTION PROFILE.

PROFILER: See PROFILOGRAPH.

PROFILOGRAPH: On-machine or off-machine measuring and recording equipment for obtaining cross-direction and machine-direction profiles of various paper properties, such as grammage, moisture content, and caliper. Syn. Profiler.

PROFILOMETER: See SURFACE ANALYZER.

PROOF PRESS: Press used to take sample impressions from a printing plate. A proof press can be used for printability comparisons between different papers.

PROOF TESTING: Printing paper by means of a proof press and evaluating the results with respect to print density and showthrough, or by means of ranking different printed paper samples.

PUCKER: Bumpy, cockle-like defect in paper due to uneven contraction during drying.

PULP CONTENT: Fiber content of a paper or paperboard sheet by weight percentage, exclusive of filler, coating and other material.

PUNCTURE RESISTANCE: Ability of a paper sheet to resist puncture, as measured by standard procedures.

R

RAG CONTENT: See COTTON CONTENT.

RAG PAPER: Paper that contains at least 25% cotton fiber in the furnish.

RAILROADS: Sheet defect that is visible as a narrow machine-direction band, either in the form of a wrinkle on paper machines or as a blow on multiply machines. Syn. Railroad Tracks.

RANDOM ERROR: Chance variation in all test work despite the closest control of variables.

RANDOM ORIENTATION: Total lack of fiber alignment within a paper sheet, i.e., a sheet without grain or directionality. See also ISOTROPIC PAPER.

RANDOM VARIATION: Variation in machine-made paper properties that are neither pure machine-direction (MD) nor cross-direction (CD) in origin and cannot be measured directly. The random variation is estimated by subtracting the MD and CD components from the overall variation. Because the random variation also includes measurement and analysis errors, it is sometimes referred to as "residual variation".

RANKING: Arrangement of a series of samples in order of intensity or degree with respect to some designated attribute.

RATTLE: Crackling sound produced by shaking or crumpling a sample of paper, indicative of sheet hardness or stiffness; considered a desirable attribute for certain papers such as bonds, but objectionable in some other grades.

READABILITY: Smallest incremental difference that can be read from a test instrument. Readability can sometimes be improved by the use of a magnifying lens or vernier scale; but it is useless to have a readability that is better than the test sensitivity.

READING: Numerical value indicated on the scale, dial or digital display of a measuring instrument.

RECESSES: Minute openings in paper which are connected to one surface only. See also PORES, VOIDS.

REDUCIBLE SULFUR: Those forms of sulfur in paper or paperboard which under certain conditions can be reduced to sufide and cause tarnishing of polished metals. "Reducible" forms under test conditions include sulfide, elemental sulfur, thiosulfate and polysulfide.

REEL SAMPLE: Sample of paper taken from the reel just after manufacture. Typically, one full-width, cross-direction strip made up of several plies is taken from each finished reel for testing or reference purposes. Syn. Outturn Sample.

REFLECTANCE: Ratio of the intensity of the light reflected by a paper test specimen to the intensity of light reflected by a perfectly reflecting, perfectly diffusing surface.

REFLECTANCE METER: Generic term applied to all instruments capable of measuring the reflectance of light. Typically, it refers to an instrument for measuring the reflectance of pulp and paper sheets at two specific wave lengths, sufficient for determining brightness and opacity values. There are two major categories of refectance measuring instruments, namely diffuse and directional, referring to the illuminating and viewing geometries of the instruments. Syn. Reflectometer. See also SPECTROPHOTOMETER.

REFLECTIVITY: Reflectance of material that is sufficiently thick that an increase in thickness does not alter reflectance.

REFRACTIVITY: Ability of a material to bend light rays from a straight course, measured by its refractive index. The higher the refractivity of fillers or coating pigments used in a sheet of paper, the higher will be the scattering coefficient of the sheet.

RELATIVE HUMIDITY (of paper): Relative humidity of air that is in immediate contact with paper and closed off from any other contact (usually measured with a sword hygrometer). The equilibrium of this air is a measure of the equilibrium of the paper.

RELATIVE STABILITY (of paper): Effect of a specified heat treatment on the folding endurance of paper. This accelerated aging test infers information regarding the aging qualities of the paper.

RELAXATION: See STRESS RELAXATION.

REPEATABILITY: Difference within which two tests are expected to agree 95% of the time when testing is done by one tester on the same sample using the same apparatus under controlled conditions. See also REPRODUCIBILITY.

REPLICATES: Two or more measurements made at different times on the same sample or near-identical samples.

REPLICATION: Act of repeating a measurement or series of steps to obtain a measurement.

REPRESENTATIVE SAMPLE: Sample collected in such a manner that it has characteristics of the whole material. The designation "representative" implies that the population has been properly sampled.

REPRODUCIBILITY: Difference within which two tests are expected to agree 95% of the time when testing the same sample at different locations. The reproducibility figure includes the expected variance between testers and test instruments. See also REPEATABILITY.

RESIDUAL VARIATION: See RANDOM VARIATION.

RESILIENCY: Ability of a material such as paper to regain its original form after deformation by bending, compression, tension, etc. Syn. Elasticity.

RESISTANCE TO LIQUID PENETRATION: Property of a paper to resist passage of liquid into or through the sheet, usually measured by the time required for complete penetration. See also COBB TEST, INK PENETRATION, OIL PENETRATION.

RESOLUTION: Capability of making distinguishable the individual features of an object, as with an optical microscope. Syn. Resolving Power.

RESONANCE STIFFNESS TESTER: Device that vibrates one end of a variable-length paper sample strip at constant frequency and measures the amplitude of the free end. The length of the sample strip at the point of maximum amplitude is proportional to the paper's stiffness.

RETENTIVENESS: Ability of filter papers to retain fine precipitates during analytical work.

RETREE: Sheets of paper with slight imperfections that are sold as seconds. The term is usually applied only to handmade paper.

RIDGE: Paper roll defect consisting of a ring around the circumferance of the roll, caused by a band of higher caliper and grammage which originates from nonuniform headbox slice delivery. Syn. Rope Mark, Bar, Buckle.

RIGIDITY: See STIFFNESS.

RING CRUSH: Resistance to compression, parallel to the axis, of a short cylinder (i.e., a test strip bent into a ring) of paper or board.

ROLL DAMAGE: See BODY DAMAGE, END DAMAGE.

ROLLED EDGE: Refers to paper with curl at the edge of the web or sheet.

ROLLING SHEAR STRENGTH: Resistance of a paperboard to delamination when passed through a series of loaded nips of opposing steel and rubber-covered rolls. The number of passes under standard conditions before failure is called the "rolling shear strength index".

ROLL QUALITY: General term used to describe the overall mechanical condition of a roll of paper, its conformance to diameter and width specifications, and freedom from defects. Assessments of roll quality are primarily made by a visual inspection, sometimes supplemented by "sounding" of the roll or by roll hardness measurements.

ROPE MARKS: See RIDGES.

ROPES: (1) See CORRUGATIONS. (2) Type of nonwoven fabric defect consisting of assemblages of fibers with nonaligned ends, which are clearly more agglomerated than the general dispersion; caused by equipment vortices that are approximately as long as the fiber.

ROSIN SPECKS: Translucent, amber-colored specks in paper caused by incomplete emulsification of rosin size or by precipitation of the size before it is uniformly dispersed in the stock.

ROUGH FINISHED PAPER: Paper with little or no calendering.

ROUGHNESS: Index of paper surface irregularities, usually determined by measuring under standardized conditions the rate of pressurized air flow between the paper surface and a solid ring pressed against the surface. Roughness and smoothness indices are inversely related.

ROUGHNESS PROFILE: See SURFACE ANALYZER.

ROUGHNESS RATIO: Means of characterizing a surface (e.g., a paper surface), defined as the ratio of the real surface area to the geometric surface area.

ROUGHNESS TESTER: See ROUGHNESS, AIR LEAK TESTER.

ROUND ROBIN TESTING: Method of monitoring bias between testing stations, in which nearly identical paper samples are sent periodically to each station within an organization for testing, and the reported results are compended by a centralized laboratory. Values far from the mean value are usually indicative of poorly calibrated equipment or faulty procedures.

RUNNABILITY: (1) Ability to run paper successfully through user operations. For printing papers, it is the ability to run the paper through the presses without breaks and without reductions in press speed. (2) For corrugating medium, the ability of the sheet to withstand the stresses and strains of the corrugating operation without fracture of the flutes.

RUNNABILITY TEST: Corrugating medium test in which a sample strip is run through a test corrugator at constant speed and increasing tension. The number of flutes which pass through the tester without fracture is taken as the "index of runnability performance".

S

SAD COLORS: Colors which are muted or dulled by the action of chemicals or by mixing with other colors.

SAMPLE: Portion of material taken from a larger quantity for the purpose of estimating properties or composition of the larger quantity. See also REPRESENTATIVE SAMPLE.

SAMPLE ROOM: Area where paper (and/or pulp) samples representative of filled orders are stored systematically for reference purposes in case of repeat orders or complaints.

SAMPLING: Gathering or collecting a small portion of material that is representative of a large mass of the same material.

SATIN FINISH: Smooth paper surface suggestive of satin.

SATURATING CAPACITY: See KEROSINE NUMBER.

SATURATING PROPERTIES: Properties of an impregnating paper that determine the rate at which an impregnating material will be picked up and the maximum amount of material that can be picked up. The saturating properties are related to penetration rates.

SATURATION: See CHROMA.

SCAB MARK: Glazed impression resulting from stray paper being carried through the calender with the main sheet.

SCALE: (1) That part of a measuring instrument which contains a series of marks and numbers to facilitate reading the value of the quantity which is being measured. (2) Device for measuring weight or mass.

SCRAP IN ROLL: Edge trimmings or random pieces of paper which fall onto the web during winding. Scrap in roll can cause a web break or damage to an offset press blanket under certain circumstances.

SCUFFING RESISTANCE: Ability of a paperboard surface to resist abrasion forces.

SCUFF MARK: Mark caused by differential movement between the paper web and dryer fabric, usually manifested as fuzz on the sheet surface.

SEALABILITY: Ability of a paper or board to be sealed by adhesive, heat, pressure or other means.

SEASONED PAPER: See CONDITIONED PAPER.

SECOND: Paper product which does not meet target specifications, but which is marketable as a lower quality item at a lower price.

SECTIONING: Process of cutting an ultra-thin section (usually a cross section) of paper or board for microscopic examination. Also called Microsectioning.

SELF-SIZING (of paper): Decrease in wettability of paper and board with time or heating.

SENSITIZED: [adj] Term applied to paper that has been treated with a chemical agent to make it sensitive to light or to the action of a particular chemical.

SENSORY PROPERTIES: Properties of paper that are apparent to the human senses of sight and feel, such as color, brightness, gloss, opacity, smoothness, texture, etc.

SHEAR: Applied forces which tend to cause two contiguous parts of a body to slide relative to each other in a direction parallel to their plane of contact.

SHEAR PLANE STRENGTH: Resistance of paperboard to in-plane shear forces. Syn. Internal Shear Strength. See also ROLLING SHEAR STRENGTH.

SHEEN: See GLOSS.

SHEET: General term for paper or board in any form or quantity, which with appropriate modifying words can describe more or less precisely product characteristics, applications and properties.

SHEET SPLITTER: Laboratory device for transverse sectioning of paper or board samples into two or more discrete layers, making possible many types of analyses of sheet structure.

SHINERS: Translucent spots in paper due to agglomerations of filler particles or fiber bundles which become visible as defects upon calendering.

SHORT COLUMN TEST: Determination of edgewise compressive strength, parallel to the flutes, of corrugated board. See also COMPRESSION STRENGTH.

SHORT-SPAN TENSILE ANALYSIS: Technique for evaluating basic structural properties of paper including the strength of fibers making up the sheet, their average length, the extent of their orientation in the sheet, and the strength of inter-fiber bonding. The data for this analysis are obtained by measuring the tensile strength of wet and dry paper strips over a range of short spans from essentially zero to 1 mm. See also SHORT-SPAN TENSILE CURVES, FIBER STRENGTH INDEX, FIBER LENGTH INDEX, BONDING INDEX.

SHORT-SPAN TENSILE CURVES: Graphical depiction of tensile strength as a function of short spans from essentially zero to 1 mm for wet and dry paper strips.

SHOW-THROUGH: Undesirable effect of a printed image being visible through the reverse side of a paper sheet, an important aspect of printability. This factor depends on the opacity and porous structure of the paper, as well as the level of ink application. Syn. Print-Through.

SIMULATED WATERMARK: Pattern in paper that resembles a watermark, but which has been produced mechanically or with a substance that increases the transparency of the paper.

SINGLE-LINED: [adj] Descriptive term for multiply boards that have been vat lined on one side only.

SINGLE-SHEET CALIPER: Caliper test carried out under standard conditions on a single sheet thickness.

SIZE SPECKS: Transparent or glazed spots in the paper, normally of different color from the rest of the sheet; caused by undispersed particles or agglomerations of sizing materials carrying through the sheet.

SIZING REGRESSION: Gradual loss of sizing with natural ageing. See also FUGITIVE SIZING.

SIZING TEST: Any of several liquid penetration tests. See also COBB TEST, CONTACT ANGLE, DROP TEST, PENESCOPE TEST, DRY INDICATOR METHOD, INK FLOTATION TEST, WATER IMMERSION TEST, LIQUID PENETRATION TESTER.

SKIM: [adj] Term applied to liner plies on paperboard denoting a light vat lining, e.g., skim ivory top.

SKIN: Glossy, hard finish on paper or board.

SKIPPED SUCTION: Marked variation in moisture content and sheet finish caused by skipping vacuum in the suction boxes or suction couch.

SLACK EDGES: Paper roll defect in which one or both edges of the roll are soft or slack due to lower sheet caliper.

SLACK SIZED: [adj] Term applied to lightly sized paper or to paper that has not undergone sufficient sizing. Syn. Soft Sized.

SLACK START: Roll defect in which paper near the core has marked indentations, caused by insufficient tension at the start of winding.

SLENDERNESS RATIO: Means of characterizing a material with respect to its edgewise compressive strength, defined as the effective unsupported length divided by the least radius of gyration of the cross-sectional area. For a strip of paper or paperboard, the slenderness ratio is equal to the square root of twelve times the ratio of length to thickness.

SLICE MARK: Defect in paper formation caused by an irregularity or deposit on the slice lips.

SLICK: [adj] Vague term applied to coated papers with characteristics of smoothness, gloss, slipperiness, and to some degree, of color and brightness.

SLICK FINISH: Jargon for a smooth finish.

SLIME HOLE: See SLIME SPOT.

SLIME SPOT: Dark, semi-transparent, unsightly spot in paper caused by inclusion of a slime growth in the sheet. Often, part of a slime spot is picked out leaving a hole in the sheet.

SLIP: Property of paper related to texture, involving the minimizing of surface friction. See also COEFFICIENT OF FRICTION.

SLIPPERY: [adj] Term applied to paper with a low coefficient of friction. Some alkaline papers are notably slippery due to alkaline sizes.

SLIP TEST: Measure of paper surface slipperiness by appropriate procedure. One simple test utilizes an adjustable inclined plane onto which a strip of paper is attached. Another strip of paper is wrapped around a block of wood which is placed on the inclined plane. The angle of incline at which the block begins to slide is taken as the measure of slipperiness.

SLUG HOLE: Hole in the sheet resulting from a group of fibers becoming superimposed on the sheet and being picked out in the presses or dryers.

SMASHED BULK: Thickness of a specified number of sheets after sufficient pressure has been applied to remove essentially all air between sheets. Smashed bulk is an important property of book papers.

SMITH NEEDLE: Instrument which measures the layer-to-layer pressure in a paper roll by measuring the force required to insert a needle into the edge of the roll. A tightness profile can be obtained by taking measurements at different diameters.

SMOOTHNESS: See ROUGHNESS.

SNAILING: Streaks or marks in the paper sheet caused by bubbles that form in front of the dandy roll; also by excess water in the web at the dandy roll.

SNAP: Vague property of paperboard that is a combination of stiffness and resiliency. Snap is judged by flexing a corner of a sheet and letting the bent corner snap back into position, and thereby forming an idea of the tone and speed of recovery. See also SPRINGBACK, SNAP TEST.

SNAPOMETER: See SNAP TEST.

SNAP TEST: Quantitative measurement of "snap" using a piece of test apparatus called a "snapometer", in which a specimen of paperboard is bent back and held by means of a trigger catch; it is then released driving a ball up an inclined tube, the distance of ball travel being used as the measure of snap.

SNOWSTORM: Appearance of paper (under transmitted light) having a wild, non-uniform formation. Syn. Wild Formation.

SOFT END: Localized sponginess in a paper roll caused by lower sheet caliper and/or light grammage near the edge of the sheet.

SOFTNESS (of paper): Subjective property of such paper products as tissues and toweling which relates to a soothing feel (velvet-like) and the yielding sensation when paper crumples easily (high compressibility and absence of stiffness). See also SURFACE SOFTNESS.

SOFT ROLL: Badly wound roll, without proper wound-in tension.

SOFT SIZED: See SLACK SIZED.

SOFT SPOT: Localized sponginess in a paper roll caused by corresponding lower caliper of the sheet.

SOLID BOARD: Paperboard made on the paper machine with the same material throughout. Syn. Plain Board. See also MULTIPLY BOARD, PASTED BOARD, FILLED BOARD.

SOLID FRACTION: Ratio of the volume occupied by solid material (fiber, filler, size, etc.) to the gross volume of a sheet of paper. See also VOID FRACTION.

SONIC SHEET TESTER: See ULTRASONIC SHEET TESTER.

SOUNDING (of a reel): Striking the reel at various points across its width with the hand or billy club. The sound heard during the process relates to the density of the roll. A distinctly different sound is perceived when a "soft" spot is struck.

SPECIFIC TENSILE STRENGTH: See TENSILE INDEX.

SPECIMEN: Test unit or portion of a test unit upon which a single or multiple determination is carried out. Syn. Test Piece.

SPECKS: See DIRT.

SPECTROPHOTOMETER: Instrument that measures light reflectance across the visible spectrum. It can be used to produce a spectrophotometric curve for a color sample, or it can describe the color in terms of the tristimulus.

SPECTROPHOTOMETRIC CURVE: Graph of reflectance as a function of wavelength, which can serve as a precise "fingerprint" of any color sample, but is not very helpful in color matching work.

SPECULAR GLOSS: Reflectance at specified equal angles of incidence and reflection, the most common measurement or characterization of gloss.

SPECULAR REFLECTANCE: Light reflected at an angle equal to the angle of incident light. It is specular reflectance that characterizes a mirror-like surface.

SPONGY SHEET: Sheet that is bulky and compressible, usually with little or no sizing.

SPOT: Any small area of the paper having a different appearance from the overall sheet.

SPRINGBACK: Extent to which a sheet can return to its original flat condition after being folded for a certain time interval under specified conditions.

SQUARE SHEET: Paper or paperboard with relatively equal tensile and tear strength values in the machine direction and cross direction. See also ISOTROPIC PAPER.

STAGGERED WINDING: Roll defect characterized by an irregular pattern at the end of the roll, caused by sidewise movement of the web during winding.

STANDARD GRAMMAGE: Sheet grammage that has been standardized for a certain paper product. Syn. Standard Weight.

STANDARDIZED: Accepted as standard by general agreement.

STANDARD TEST PROCEDURE: Detailed procedure established by industrial or governmental authority or by custom or agreement to serve as a model in the measurement of a specific property or quantity.

STARRED ROLL: Paper roll defect seen as arms of "wavy paper" radiating from the core when viewed from the end of the roll (i.e., tightly wound paper surrounding loosely wound paper); caused by uneven tension during winding.

STATIC ELECTRICITY: Electrical charge that builds up on paper and other electrical insulating materials through contact with other substances, especially at low relative humidities when ability to dissipate the charge to ground is reduced. Electrostatic charging of paper is troublesome because it causes sheets to stick together and electrical shock to operators can be hazardous.

STEAM FINISHED: [adj] Describes paper that has been sprayed with steam prior to machine calendering or supercalendering in order to increase the density, smoothness and gloss of the sheet.

STEAM SEASONING: Hanging paper sheets in a steam room, a procedure commonly undertaken prior to plate finishing.

STIFFNESS: Bending resistance, a desirable property of certain paper and board grades; determined by measuring the bending moment of a test strip under standard conditions. Syn. Rigidity, Flexural Stiffness.

STRAIN: See STRETCH.

STRAINED FORMATION: Defect in paper caused by excessive stress or draw of the wet sheet, seen as small light spots in the sheet with displaced fibers forming a lump on the upstream edge of the light spot. (Mainly associated with open draw machines.)

STRAINING RATE: Rate at which a sample strip is strained, e.g., during a tensile test, usually measured as a percentage stretch per unit time. (Note that some instruments are capable of being operated either with a constant rate of straining or a constant rate of loading.)

STREAKS: Continuous narrow bands running in the machine direction of the paper web having properties different from the rest of the web; e.g., high-moisture streaks, high-grammage streaks.

STRENGTH PROPERTIES: Mechanical properties of a material which permit it to resist parting or distortion under the application of force. Paper strength properties include tear strength, tensile strength, folding endurance, burst strength, shear plane strength, toughness, etc.

STRESS: Specifically, the uniaxial load applied to a paper sample, divided by the cross-sectional area of the specimen. In practice, the terms "stress" and "load" are often used interchangably when applied to paper. See also LOAD.

STRESS CONCENTRATION: Condition in which an applied stress to a web or section of a sheet becomes highly localized, usually induced by a discontinuity of the web in the vicinity of a crack, cut or hole.

STRESS RELAXATION: Progressive reduction in stress required to maintain a constant elongation of paper, typical behavior for a viscoelastic material.

STRESS-STRAIN CURVE: For any material, the graphical depiction of the stress (tension, load) response to various levels of imposed strain (stretch, elongation). For paper at various moisture contents, the shape of the curve is greatly influenced by the loading rate (or straining rate). Syn. Load-Elongation Curve. Stress-Strain Diagram.

STRESS-STRAIN PROPERTIES: Properties defined by the stress vs. strain relationship for a paper or board sample, such as tensile strength, stretch at break, tensile energy absorption, and elastic modulus.

STRETCH: Increase in length, usually expressed as a percentage of the original length. Syn. Elongation, Strain, Deformation, Extension.

STRETCH AT BREAK: Increase in length of a test specimen at the moment of rupture in the standardized tensile test, expressed as a percentage of the original length. Syn. Maximum Stretch.

STRUCTURAL CURL: Curl resulting from structural differences between the two sides of the paper or otherwise related to paper structure.

STUCK WEB: Roll defect where one or more web layers stick together, most commonly caused by water on the web after machine processing has been completed.

SUBJECTIVE GLOSS: One method of measuring gloss, essentially the ratio of the reflectance measured at the angle of incident light to the reflectance measured at right angles to the surface of the specimen.

SUBJECTIVE TESTS (of paper)**:** Grouping of judgemental observations of paper carried out by the papermaker to assess the product, but which cannot be given numerical values. They include such properties as feel, rattle, snap, look-through, and softness.

SUBSTANCE: See GRAMMAGE.

SUPER GLAZED FINISH: Very glossy paper finish.

SUPERIMPOSED PROFILES: Succesive machine-direction or cross-direction profiles of a paper property that are recorded on the same chart with the same scale of coordinates, so that the chart shows a number of overlapping profiles.

SURFACE ANALYZER: Device which traces a profile of paper surface irregularities and contours and calculates a root-mean-square value as an indication of surface roughness. Syn. Profilometer.

SURFACE pH: pH value of the surface layer of paper.

SURFACE PROPERTIES: Grouping of paper properties that includes roughness, surface strength, erasability, and abrasion resistance.

SURFACE SOFTNESS: Feeling of softness when stroking the surface of paper.

SURFACE STRENGTH: See PICK RESISTANCE.

SURFACE STRENGTH TESTER: Device that measures the pick resistance of paper by printing either with increasing speed or increasing tackiness of ink until fibers are picked from the surface. Syn. Pick Tester. See also WAX PICK.

SWORD HYGROMETER: Blade inserted into a paper stack to measure the relative humidity of the paper. The traditional instrument contains a taut fiber that expands or contracts to indicate a scale reading; this is being displaced by an instrument with electrical sensors. Syn. Paper Hygroscope.

SYNTHETIC PAPERS: Papers made without natural cellulosic fibers. See FILM-BASED SYNTHETIC PAPERS, FIBER-BASED SYNTHETIC PAPERS.

SYSTEMATIC ERROR: Error in testing which may arise from personal bias, instrumental bias, or distortion in the principle or theory of the test method.

T

TACTILE PROPERTIES: Grouping of paper properties that includes surface softness, bulk softness, and handle.

TAPPI OPACITY: See OPACITY (WHITE BACKING).

TARE WEIGHT: Weight of an empty container, which can be subtracted from the gross weight of the loaded container to calculate the net weight of the contents.

TARIFF REGULATION STRIPES: See MACHINE MARK STRIPES.

TEAR INDEX: Measure of tear strength that is independent of sheet grammage, basically determined by dividing Elmendorf tear resistance by the grammage of the sample.

TEARING STRENGTH: Force required to tear a paper specimen under specified conditions. A number of test methods are used to evaluate this property. See also ELMENDORF TEAR RESISTANCE, EDGE TEAR RESISTANCE, FRACTURE RESISTANCE, IN-PLANE TEAR RESISTANCE.

TEAR OUTS: Samples torn from the paper web for testing or inspection.

TELESCOPED CORE: See OFFSET CORE.

TELESCOPED ROLL: Roll in which the ends instead of being flat and relatively smooth, are convex or concave; due to insufficient tension control during winding. Syn. Dished Roll, Offset Roll, Slipped Roll.

TENDER: [adj] Term used to describe low-strength paper, especially a paper whose strength has deteriorated.

TENSILE AT FOLD: Residual tensile strength of a paper sample after it has been heat treated and given a sharp fold. This test is used to assess the durability of magazine cover papers which are often printed heatset and folded while still hot and dry.

TENSILE ENERGY ABSORPTION: (TEA) Integrated area under the tensile-stretch curve; a measure of the total energy that can be absorbed before failure, an important property of sack papers. The TEA is taken as an index of toughness.

TENSILE ENERGY ABSORPTION INDEX: Measure of TEA which is independent of sample grammage, obtained by dividing the TEA by the grammage.

TENSILE INDEX: Tensile strength measurement in units of kNm/kg. The tensile index divided by the acceleration due to gravity (9.807 m/s^2) equals the breaking length in meters. Syn. Specific Tensile Strength. See also BREAKING LENGTH.

TENSILE STIFFNESS: Elastic stiffness of paper or paperboard subjected to tension. Syn. Extensional Stiffness.

TENSILE STRENGTH: Force required to break a narrow strip of paper when both the length of strip and rate of loading are closely specified.

TENSION BURST: See CROSS-MACHINE BURST.

TEST: Procedure carried out to measure any of a wide range of paper or paperboard properties (or properties of other materials) under various conditions.

TEST ACCURACY: Difference between the test value and the true value. (In practice, assessment of test accuracy is often difficult because the "true value" may not be easily determined.)

TEST DETERMINATION: Process of carrying out a series of operations specified in a test method whereby the value for a single test specimen is obtained.

TESTING: Determining whether a product or material meets certain requirements by subjecting a representative sample to physical, chemical, and optical tests under specified conditions.

TEST MEASUREMENT: Single quantitative value obtained from a test determination. More than one test measurement is commonly required in a test method.

TEST METHOD: Detailed, step-by-step procedure for carrying out a test procedure and determining test results. See also STANDARD TEST PROCEDURE.

TEST PRECISION: Measure of the variation that can be expected when repeated tests (i.e., replicates) are made on the same specimen or on a near-duplicate specimen.

TEST PRINT: Printed sheet from a proof press. A comparative series of test prints can provide the basis for evaluating relative printability.

TEST RESULT: Value obtained for one test unit of a sample material. This value may be a single determination or an average.

TEST SENSITIVITY: Smallest change in the property being measured that can be detected, usually expressed as the smallest incremental difference.

TEST SHEET: Sheet of paper (or strip of paper) specifically selected for testing because it is representative of a production run or representative of one position on the paper machine.

TEST SPECIMEN: See SPECIMEN.

TEST UNIT: Area of paper sufficient to obtain a single adequate set of test results for all the properties to be measured. See also SPECIMEN.

TEXTURE (of paper): Surface finish and smoothness.

THERMAL PROPERTIES: Grouping of paper properties that includes thermal conduction, specific heat, thermal expansion, and flammability.

THICKNESS: See CALIPER.

THIN SPOTS: Low-grammage areas of the paper sheet.

TINNY PAPER: Paper that exhibits a high degree of rattle.

TINTED: [adj] Term descriptive of lightly dyed paper. See also TINTED WHITE.

TINTED WHITE: [adj] Term descriptive of essentially white paper that has been lightly tinted (usually with blue or blue-violet dyes) to override the yellowish cast typical of many pulp furnishes.

TOLERANCE: Permissable degree of variation from a specified standard.

TONED PAPER: Paper colored very slightly from the white or natural color.

TONE VALUE: See COLOR PERCEPTION.

TOOTH: Patterned roughness in the form of minute depressions between fibers or groups of fibers on the surface, a characteristic of some low-finish papers which facilitates pencil or crayon marking. Tooth can be produced on the paper machine during forming or pressing. Syn. Bite.

TOP SIDE: Side of the paper web that is not in contact with the forming fabric on fourdrinier paper machines.

TOP SIDED SHEET: Sheet that is dyed significantly deeper on the top side due to preferential dyeing of the short fiber or clay filler.

TOP SIZING: Surface sizing of a paper that has already been internally sized.

TORSION: Twisting deformation of a solid body. The force causing torsion is known as "torque".

TORSION SHEAR STRENGTH: Resistance of a paper sample to in-plane shear rupture under torsion.

TORSION TEAR TESTER: Essentially a heavy-duty Elmendorf-type tear tester, used for testing high-grammage boards.

TOUGHNESS: See TENSILE ENERGY ABSORPTION.

TRANSIT DAMAGE: Damage occurring to paper rolls during shipment.

TRANSLUCENT: [adj] Ability of paper to transmit light without being transparent.

TRANSMITTANCE: Fraction of incident light that passes through a specimen under specified conditions.

TRANSPARENCY: Property of a material which transmits light rays so that objects can be seen more or less distinctly through a sample specimen.

TRANSPARENCY RATIO: Ratio of near regular transmittance to near hemispherical transmittance, an important measurement to characterize the transmittance properties of glassine papers. (Hemispherical transmittance is measured by placing a light collecting sphere behind the sample.)

TRISTIMULUS: Definition of a paper color in terms of the relative amount of each of the three primary colors (i.e., their dominant wave lengths) reflected from its surface.

TRISTIMULUS COLORIMETER: Reflectance meter for measuring optical properties (tristimulus) which can be correlated with a psychophysical description of color.

TURNOVER: Cracked edge or slight tear at the edge of the web that has been folded over during slitting, winding or printing.

TURPENTINE TEST: Time required under specified conditions for colored turpentine to soak through a test specimen of paper, as indicated by the first definite staining on the underside. The test is taken as a measurement of resistance to grease penetration.

TWIN-WIRE PAPER: Paper manufactured on a twin-wire machine.

TWO-SIDEDNESS: Difference in surface properties between the felt and wire sides of fourdrinier-made paper, due to a marked gradient in fiber composition and wire marking of the bottom surface. Papers formed on twin-wire machines exhibit far less two-sidedness. See also EQUAL-SIDEDNESS.

U _____

ULTIMATE STRETCH: Stretch at rupture.

ULTRASONIC SHEET TESTER: Device which measures nondestructively the longitudinal ultrasonic pulse wave propagation speed in sheet materials, and from the results then calculates various physical properties. Syn. Sonic Sheet Tester.

ULTRASONIC STIFFNESS: Elastic stiffness of paper as measured nondestructively by the longitudinal ultrasonic pulse wave propagation speed within the sheet.

UNCALENDERED: [adj] Descriptive term for paper that is reeled directly from the dryers without any calendering.

UNCOATED PAPER: Paper that has not been pigment coated. (Paper only surface sized is considered uncoated.)

UNGLAZED FINISH: Low-gloss machine finish.

UNIFORMITY: Assessment of paper variablity in all aspects; most commonly applied to sheet formation, color and finish.

UNIVERSAL TESTING MACHINE: Testing machine which is capable of performing a variety of tensile and compression tests for a wide range of materials. These machines are used in the testing of combined board and corrugated board.

UNSIZED PAPER: Paper produced without internal size or surface size, which is generally very absorbent. Syn. Waterleaf Paper.

USE TESTS (of paper): Tests made on paper based on the element of utility, i.e., those tests which simulate conditions that the paper may be subjected to in use. This grouping includes proof press testing of printing paper, laminating performance of paper on small laminating machines, and measurement of water-vapor resistance on boxboard after fabrication into a finished package. Syn. Functional Tests, Performance Tests.

V _____

VALUE: See COLOR PERCEPTION, MUNSELL SYSTEM.

VANCEOMETER: Test for ink receptivity in which an oil vehicle is applied to a paper surface followed by measurement of 70° specular gloss at specified time intervals to indicate penetration.

VAPOR PERMEABILITY: Ability of paper to allow passage of vapor through the sheet.

VARIATION OF PAPER PROPERTIES: Machine-made paper has three components of variability. See MACHINE-DIRECTION VARIATION, CROSS-DIRECTION VARIATION, RANDOM VARIATION.

VAT LINED: [adj] Term applied to any multiply paperboard in which one or both of the liner plies is of a different color or furnish than the other plies.

VEINED PAPER: Paper containing a small quantity of multi-colored fibers, which provide a marble-like surface appearance. Certain grades are known as silurian or granite papers. See also MOTTLED SHADE.

VELLUM FINISH: Dull, toothy finish typically applied to text papers.

VELVET FINISH PAPERS: Blade-coated papers that are processed through a conventional supercalender to develop smoothness and achieve caliper reduction, but with a minimum of gloss development.

VISCOELASTIC MATERIAL: Material that exhibits both viscous and elastic behavior, of which paper (especially wet paper) is a good example; it has the ability to store energy of deformation. The application of stress to paper gives rise to strain that approaches its equilibrium value slowly (i.e., the paper "creeps"); the application of a set strain gives rise to stress that decays in a time-dependent fashion (i.e., the tension "relaxes").

VISUAL EFFICIENCY: Overall reflectivity of paper, a function of reflectance over the visual spectrum, defined as the ratio of the luminosity of light reflected from the specimen to the luminosity of light reflected from a perfect, diffuse reflecting body. (As contrasted to papermaker's brightness, which is based on measurement at a single wavelength in the blue region of the spectrum.)

VOID FRACTION: See AIR FRACTION.

VOIDS: Minute air spaces in paper which are not connected to either surface. (Sometimes, all air spaces in paper are collectively referred to as voids.) See also PORES, RECESSES.

W _____

WARM COLORS: Reddish tone paper colors which evoke a warm psychological reaction, as opposed to bluish-hue colors which produce a cool response.

WARP: Loss of flatness for paperboard sheets or corrugated board.

WATER BLEED FASTNESS: Resistance of dyed paper to color change when it becomes wet, an important property for paper towels.

WATER-DAMAGED ROLL: Any paper roll exposed to wetting, ranging in severity from light staining to saturation of the paper. If the damage is superficial, the roll can often be salvaged after the wetted areas have dried.

WATER FINISH: Relatively high-gloss, on-machine finish produced by applying water to the calender rolls.

WATER LINES: See MACHINE MARK STRIPES.

WATER IMMERSION SIZING TEST: Weight of water absorbed by a sample of paper after it has been immersed for a given time under specified conditions, a measure of sizing effectiveness.

WATERLEAF PAPER: See UNSIZED PAPER.

WATER REPELLENCY: Ability of a treated paper sheet surface (e.g., waxed or varnished) to resist penetration by water.

WATER RESISTANT PAPER: Paper made water resistant by high-energy refining of the fiber furnish and surface sizing. Syn. Waterproof Paper.

WATER SENSITIVITY: Tendency for paper to weaken from contact with press moisture in lithography, causing it to pick, to release small coating or size particles, or to curl.

WATER SPOT: Paper defect caused by a drop of water falling on the sheet. Syn. Drop Mark.

WAVINESS: Distortion of a paper sheet surface at the cross-direction edges.

WAX PICK: Test that duplicates the pulling stress applied to the surface of paper as it travels through a printing press. Waxes of varying adhesive strength are melted and applied to the surface of a test specimen. The rating given to a particular paper corresponds to the highest numbered wax that does not disturb the surface when pulled off. Syn. Pluck.

WAX PICKING POINT: Approximate temperature at which waxed surfaces in contact with each other (e.g., waxed paper) will begin to stick together.

WAX SPOTS: Transparent spots in a paper sheet caused by poor dispersion of wax.

WEAR RESISTANCE: See ABRASION RESISTANCE.

WEATHER WRINKLES: See MOISTURE WELTS.

WEAVING: Paper roll defect in which the moving web, in unwinding, oscillates from side to side instead of tracking consistently over the guide rolls of the printing or converting unit.

WEB CONTENT CHART (for paper rolls): Graph relating sheet caliper and roll diameter with web length. Most commonly, web length (on the Y-axis) is shown as a function of sheet caliper (on the X-axis) for different roll diameters.

WEIGHT TOLERANCE: See GRAMMAGE TOLERANCE.

WELTS: See MOISTURE WELTS, WINDER WELTS.

WET ASHING: Thermal and chemical treatment of a sample (e.g., paper) within an aqueous medium until the water solution becomes clear, thus ensuring complete decomposition of all organic matter. This technique is used in place of conventional ashing for certain analytical methods.

WET CURL: Curling of paper from the application of liquid water as in lithographic printing.

WET EDGES: Edges of paper rolls that have been wetted at some time during handling or storage. Such rolls will not unwind properly because the wraps of paper will be cemented together in the wetted area.

WET-END FINISH: Any finish applied to the wet paper web by machine rolls and presses at the wet end of the paper machine (e.g., antique, eggshell, vellum).

WET PICK RESISTANCE: Resistance of paper to picking after it has absorbed moisture.

WET RUB RESISTANCE: Ability of a paper sheet with a moistened surface to withstand rubbing or scuffing without surface disruption.

WET SOAK PAPER: Distinctive surface-sized paper produced by tub sizing the web, wet winding the sheet at about 35% moisture, and storing the wet paper for several hours to obtain optimum and uniform penetration of size. Finally, the paper is passed through a special air dryer to remove the moisture. Syn. Wet Pack Paper.

WET STREAKS: Continuous ribbons of markedly higher moisture content paper within the machine-direction web. Two common causes are plugged areas in suction boxes, and filled areas in wet felts.

WET STRENGTH: See WET TENSILE STRENGTH.

WET STRENGTH PAPER: Paper that retains a high proportion of strength properties when wet. At least 15% of the dry tensile strength must be retained to qualify as a wet strength paper.

WET STRENGTH RETENTION: Ratio of the tensile strength of a paper sample in the wet state to the tensile strength of the same paper in the dry, conditioned state.

WET TENSILE STRENGTH: Tensile strength of a wetted strip of paper under specified conditions, usually reported as a percentage of the dry tensile strength; commonly applied for measuring the quality of wet strength treatment.

WETTABILITY: Ability of a paper surface to be wetted by a liquid (typically water).

WHITENESS: Extent to which a sheet of paper approaches theoretically perfect white due to high brightness, high light scattering and minimum perceivable hue. In practice, the terms brightness and whiteness are used interchangeably.

WICKING: Ability of paper to absorb water by capillary attraction.

WILD FORMATION: See FORMATION.

WINDER WELTS: Grain-direction ridges that form in paper during winding due to uneven expansion of the paper caused by high tension and/or non-uniform moisture content of the paper. In severe cases, winder welts develop into winder wrinkles.

WINDER WRINKLES: Machine-direction creases formed on the sheet during winding, due to uneven moisture, improper tension, and/or imperfect alignment of the roll shaft.

WIRE HOLE: Hole in the paper sheet associated with a defect in the forming fabric, usually by a hole in the fabric or a pitch deposit that plugs the fabric.

WIRE MARK: Impression left in a sheet of paper by the mesh of the forming fabric.

WIRE SIDE: Side of a sheet of paper that was in contact with the forming fabric during manufacture.

WOOD-CONTAINING PAPER: Paper made from a furnish containing mechanical pulp to a greater or lesser extent.

WOOD-FREE PAPER: Paper containing a minimum of 90% chemical pulp furnish (i.e., essentially free of mechanical pulp). The term "freesheet" is used in Europe.

WORMINESS: Formation defect on cylinder-formed sheets appearing as twisted lines in the machine direction.

WORMS: Formation defect in paper appearing as irregular lines of higher grammage, often caused by "strings" in the papermaking stock.

WOVE PAPER: Paper which does not show any marks of laid lines.

WRINKLE: Defect in paper caused by creases during manufacture.

XYZ

YELLOWING: Reduction of paper brightness as a result of aging or exposure to light.

YELLOWNESS: Difference between luminance and brightness values expressed as a percentage of reflectivity, a measure of how yellow (off white) a paper is.

YOUNG'S MODULUS: See ELASTIC STIFFNESS.

ZERO-SPAN TENSILE STRENGTH: Tensile force required to rupture a specimen of paper when the distance between the clamps is essentially zero; used as an index of individual fiber strength within the sheet.

Z-STRENGTH: See INTERNAL BOND STRENGTH.

Chapter 15
Papermachine Clothing

BASE CLOTH: Loosely woven fabric into which a batt of fibers is needled in the process of manufacturing a felt.

BATT: Web of fibers produced by carding. Syn. Batting.

BATT-ON-BASE FELT: Variety of needled felt in which the batt is needled into a base cloth.

BATT-ON-MESH FELT: Variety of needled felt in which the batt is needled into the spun yarn top layer of a duplex base cloth, the bottom layer of which consists of a coarse open structure woven from relatively stiff synthetic yarns. The open structure retains its void volume in the press nip and provides a space for the water expressed from the pressed paper web.

BOARDY: [adj] Term used to describe press felts which have the body and stiffness to resist any tendency to distort or rope up.

BOWING: Felt or fabric distortion on the paper machine characterized by a seam which runs ahead at the center.

BULGE: Slack place in a felt or fabric.

BULKING: Crimping, curling, or looping yarn so that it becomes bulked, i.e., occupies a greater volume for the same mass of fiber.

BURR: Rough edge along the wearing surface of the bottom warp knuckle of a forming fabric. The more frequently seen burrs occur on the trailing edge and are called "drag burrs". Burrs on the leading edge are called "creep burrs".

C

CARDING: Process by which textile fibers are separated and laid essentially parallel in a web form (called a "batt") or they are condensed into a continuous untwisted strand of fibers (called a "sliver").

CLEANABILITY: Ability of a dryer fabric to be kept free of deposits and maintain a specified level of permeability. Generally, the more open designs are easier to maintain. Inclusion of spun yarns in the weave reduces cleanability.

CLIPPER SEAM: Seam for dryer fabrics that uses the principle of the belt fastener, with metal hooks clenched into cloth and a hinge wire (called a "pintle") joining the two sides of the seam.

COIL FABRIC: See SPIRAL FABRIC.

COMBINATION FELT: Variety of needled felt in which the batt is needled to a two-layer, rigid base fabric of large void volume. This clothing essentially makes any press nip into a fabric press without the need for separate felt and fabric runs.

CONVENTIONAL FELT: Traditional woven construction using spun yarns in both the machine and cross directions which has been "fulled" to build bulk and stability. The fiber content is predominantly wool with small percentages of synthetic.

COUNT: Number of shute filaments per inch in a fabric. See also MESH.

CREASE: Sharp, long projection of a forming fabric running lengthwise or crosswise.

CREEP: Sliding action of the forming fabric on a drive roll surface caused by contraction of the fabric as the tension is reduced.

CRIMP: (1) Corrugation in either a warp or shute strand which holds the strands in position, one against the other. See also KNUCKLE. (2) Natural or induced waviness in fibers or strands. All textile staple fibers have crimp to permit them to be processed into yarns.

CROSS STABILITY: Dimensional stability in the cross direction, an important requirement for papermachine clothing.

D

DENT: Indentation in a forming fabric, which can generally be identified as either a pimple or a jam.

DEWATERABILITY: Ability of a press felt to release water to a suction box, usually assessed by running a saturated felt over a slotted vacuum pipe under specified conditions to measure the water released.

DOUBLE-LAYER FABRIC: Fabric construction with two discrete layers; the sheet side is designed to produce the desired forming surface and the underside is designed to optimize drainage and running life. It is woven with one shute yarn and two warp yarns that are stacked one above the other; this produces a fabric with about 50% more thickness than a single-layer weave.

DOUBLE TWILL: Fabric weave in which each strand goes over two strands and under two strands in a repeating pattern.

DRAG WEAR: Fabric wear caused by sliding movement between the fabric and a bearing surface.

DRAINAGE (of a forming fabric): Amount of water that will drain through a specified area of forming fabric at constant pressure and temperature. (Drainage is related to open area, but only in a general way.)

DRAINAGE COEFFICIENT (of a forming fabric): Quantity of water passing through a specified area of forming fabric in relation to the quantity of water passing through the same area without interposition of the fabric, usually expressed as a percentage.

DRAPE: Qualitative property of a fabric associated with its folding, bending and handling characteristics.

DUPLEX FABRIC: Forming fabric having shute strands lying in two or more distinct planes.

DUPLEX WEAVE: Basic weave pattern for dryer fabrics consisting of two layers of shute yarns woven together with warp yarns that are common to both faces of the cloth. A common method of producing different permeabilities is to keep the number of warp yarns constant and change the number, size or type of shute yarns.

E _____

EDGE CRACKING: Breakage of strands at the edge of a forming wire or fabric due to rapid flexing.

EDGE RAVELING: Loose machine-direction yarns at the edge of a dryer fabric, the most common form of dryer fabric damage.

ENDLESS WOVEN FABRIC: Fabric that is woven in the shape of a tube, using a circular loom in which the shute takes a circular path. Syn. Tubular Fabric.

EXTRA-WEFTED FABRIC: See SHUTE-SUPPORT FABRIC.

F _____

FABRIC: Any material made on a loom or on a knitting or needling machine, usually a planar structure.

FABRIC EDGE WEAR: Damage and fraying at the edge of a forming fabric, a major cause of fabric removal.

FABRIC STABILITY: Resistance to stretching or wrinkling under running tension.

FABRIC WEAR: Gradual removal of material from contacting surfaces during the service life of a forming fabric.

FABRIC WRINKLING: Sharp up or down creases typically running on the diagonal of a forming fabric, usually the result of machine misalignment or cocking of the fabric during installation.

FELT FINISH: Relative ranking of the smoothness of the sheet-side surface of the felt. Terms used are coarse, medium, fine, and superfine.

FELT ROUGHNESS: Relative coarseness or fineness (i.e., denier) of the filaments making up the batt of a press felt at the paper contacting surface. Syn. Felt Fineness.

FIBER SUPPORT INDEX: Calculated measurement of the number of support points at a forming fabric surface per unit fiber length. (The formula proposed by R.L. Beran utilizes the MD and CD mesh counts and indices "a" and "b" describing surface geometry.)

FILAMENT: (1) Long, continuous fiber that can be measured in meters, or in the case of man-made fibers, in kilometers. (2) Single strand of the several that constitute a multifilament yarn.

FILLING: See SHUTE.

FILLINGLESS FELT: Felt construction in which the batt is needled into a set of carefully aligned warps. During manufacture, special shute threads may be used to stabilize the warps, which are chemically dissolved after the felt is finished. Syn. Knuckle Free Felt. See also MINIMUM SHUTE FELT.

FINENESS: Relative characterization of a forming fabric with respect to strand count; the greater the number of MD and CD strands per inch, the finer is the fabric.

FLAT WARP: Warp strand flattened on both the paper side and the inside of a forming fabric, so that the cross section is approximately oval shaped.

FRACTIONAL PERMEABILITY (of a dryer fabric): Permeability of a dryer fabric in relation to the permeability of an unrestricted, infinitely short, frictionless orifice, usually expressed as a percentage.

FRAME (of a forming fabric): Opening in the forming fabric defined by the axis of the crossing strands at the top surface of the mesh. See also WINDOW.

FULLING: Process to develop the felting properties of a woolen fabric, in which friction and pressure are applied to the fabric while it is running in a hot soapy solution. Syn. Felting.

H _____

HARNESS: See SHED.

HEATSETTING: Heating and stretching treatment given to a forming fabric after weaving to improve its dimensional stability. Syn. Heat Stabilization.

J _____

JAMS: Indentations in the forming fabric caused by stock coming between the fabric and a roll. "Downward jams" are indentations toward the inside of the fabric. "Upward jams" are indentations toward the outside of the fabric.

K _____

KNUCKLE: Crimped portion in a monofilament strand. The "warp knuckle" is the crimped portion of a warp strand as it passes either over or under a shute strand. The "shute knuckle" is the similar portion of a shute strand. See also CRIMP.

KNUCKLE FREE FELT: See FILLINGLESS FELT.

L _____

LONGITUDINAL STABILITY: Dimensional stability in the machine direction, an important requirement for paper machine clothing.

LOOM: Machine for weaving cloth.

LOOP SEAM: Any seam for a dryer fabric which is sewn to the back of the fabric and consists of a row of loops woven into a webbing. The ends of the fabric are joined by threading a monofilament through the loops.

M _____

MESH: Number of filament strands per square inch of fabric, designated by two numbers: the first indicates the number of warp filaments and the second the number of shute filaments per lineal inch

(e.g., 80/60). If only one number is given, it refers to the number of warp filaments. Syn. Strand Number, Mesh Number. See also COUNT, MESH COUNT.

MESH COUNT: Number of meshes or openings per square inch either warpwise or shutewise, measured by multiplying the number of warp filaments by the number of shute filaments. For example, an 80/60 mesh has 4800 openings per square inch.

MESH FABRIC: General term for a fabric having large open areas between yarns.

MINIMUM SHUTE FELT: Felt construction in which the shute of the base cloth is reduced to the minimum amount of fine threads that will stabilize the fabric during the needling and finishing operations. This felt construction has high permeability to water.

MODULUS: Load required to stretch a fabric to twice its original length, calculated from a stress-strain diagram. The shipped length of a fabric is, in part, determined by modulus and slack side operating tension required to keep the fabric from slipping on the machine.

MONOFILAMENT: Long continuous single strand of natural or synthetic fiber.

MULTIFILAMENT: Yarn made up of two or more monofilaments of natural of synthetic fiber.

N _____

NAP: Downy or fuzzy finish given to a fabric by brushing or scratching the surface to raise part of the fiber from the body of the yarn. The nap is usually brushed level and cropped.

NARROWING: Reduction in width of a felt or fabric, often associated with bowing.

NEEDLING: Process in which a loose batt is punched and fixed into the surface of a fabric to give a firm, but porous structure. Needling machines are equipped with a large number of notched and barbed needles that force the batt downwards into the fabric and fix it in this position.

NEEDLING TRACKS: Marks left in a felt after the needling process.

NONWOVEN FELT: Essentially an all-needled fiber batt of 100% synthetic construction. This construction offers the least flow resistance of any felt.

NYLON: Polyamide synthetic fiber used in the construction of forming fabrics and other types of paper machine clothing.

O

ON-MACHINE-SEAMED PRESS FELT (OMS PRESS FELT): Open-ended felt that is installed on the paper machine by pulling one end through the press section by means of ropes, putting in a pin-seam pin, and giving the surface batt a quick "touch-up".

OPEN AREA: Major characteristic of a forming fabric determined by the number of holes per square inch (mesh count) and the size of the holes. Most forming fabrics have between 20 and 30% open area.

OPEN-ENDED CLOTHING: Paper machine clothing manufactured and installed with the two ends unattached. Dryer fabrics are normally supplied in this configuration.

P

PATCHING: Repair of small holes and slits on forming fabrics, involving a number of techniques.

PERMEABILITY: Measure of the flow rate of air through a dryer fabric or dry press felt under specified conditions. The units and conditions normally used are cubic feet of air which will flow in one minute through one square foot of fabric when the pressure drop across the fabric is equivalent to 0.5-inch water column.

PICK LINE: Cross machine yarns of a felt or fabric.

PICK STACKING: Alignment of yarns relative to each other in the weave structure of a felt. The "pick stacking ability" of a felt refers to its ability to maintain this alignment during the service life.

PIMPLES: Indentations in the forming fabric caused by small hard objects coming between the fabric and a roll. "Downward pimples" are indentations toward the inside of the fabric. "Upward pimples" are indentations toward the outside of the fabric.

PIN SEAM: See WARP LOOP SEAM.

PINTLE: Connecting cable for a fabric seam.

PLAIN WEAVE: Basic weave in which each shute strand passes alternately under and over each successive warp strand, and each warp strand over and under each successive shute strand.

PLANAR WEAVE: Refers to a press felt base weave in which the yarn layers are woven perpendicular to each other without shute knuckles on the sheet-side surface of the weave. This arrangement allows for more warp yarns which can improve pressure uniformity in the nip.

POLE: Wooden or metal rod, slightly longer than the width of the forming fabric, on which the fabric is wound for shipping or strung for installation.

POLYESTER: Synthetic plastic material. Polyester monofilament is the principal material used for the manufacture of forming fabrics. Various forms of polyester are also used extensively in the construction of other types of paper machine clothing.

POWER FABRIC: Coarse fabric running underneath a forming fabric which transmits power and provides a wearing surface over the suction boxes. Modern double and triple layer fabrics, in effect, have a power fabric built into the forming fabric.

R

RIDGE: Long, narrow projection on the surface of a forming fabric, running lengthwise or crosswise.

ROUND WARP: Warp strand having a circular cross section.

RUNNING ATTITUDE: Orientation of a forming fabric with respect to sheet support and wear surfaces; most fabrics provide different characteristics on each surface.

S

SATEEN: Forming fabric weave with either a 4/1 or 1/4 construction. The name is also applied to certain 3/1 or 1/3 constructions that are not twills. See also WEAVE CONSTRUCTION, TWILL.

SATURATED MOISTURE: Amount of water absorbed by a press felt under static conditions, taken as a measure of the ability of a felt to receive water from the paper sheet in the nip.

SEAM: Joint where the ends of a forming fabric or dryer screen are fastened together to make an endless belt.

SHAFT: See SHED.

SHED: In weaving, the term refers to the opening formed for the passage of the loom shuttle by raising some warp threads and depressing others. The term is more often used (in the paper mill) to characterize the resulting fabric weave; it is the number of warp yarns (or the number of sets of yarns in double-layer weaves) before the weave pattern repeats. For example, a 5-shed fabric is one in which a return crossover of the shute yarn occurs for every 5 warp yarns. Syn. Harness, Shaft.

SHUTE: Strand (monofilament, multifilament, yarn) that runs the width of the fabric; i.e., in the cross direction. Syn. Weft, Woof, Filling, Pick.

SHUTE-FACED FABRIC: Fabric having a preponderance of shute showing on the outside surface.

SHUTE-RUNNER: Forming fabric in which the shute strands are running principally on the inside of the fabric and are in contact with the abrasive surface.

SHUTE-SUPPORT FABRIC: Double-layer fabric with an additional small shute yarn woven into the top layer to reduce the distance that a paper-making fiber needs to bridge for support. Syn. Extra-Wefted Fabric.

SHUTTLE: Device used in weaving operations to carry the shute strand back and forth between the warp strands.

SLACK AREA: Large section of the forming fabric having markedly less tension than the rest. Syn. Baggy Area.

SLACK TENSION: Tension in the slack area.

SLEAZY: [adj] Term applied to dryer fabrics with low diagonal stiffness which tend to narrow up on the paper machine.

SLIPPAGE: Relative movement between the forming fabric and any rotating surface it contacts.

SNAKING: Oscillation of a dryer fabric on the paper machine, typically a rather jerky back-and-forth motion. This problem can be related either to installation technique or guide configuration.

SPIRAL FABRIC: Dryer fabric design in which rectangular, monofilament warp strands are formed into helical loops and connected by shute cables threaded through the loops. Syn. Coil Fabric.

SPIRAL SEAM: Seam for dryer fabrics in which a row of spirals on both ends of the fabric are held in place by the machine direction yarns, and are connected by threading a monofilament through the spirals.

SPUN YARN: Yarn made by carding, twisting together and drawing out staple fibers into a continuous strand.

STABILITY: Ability of a felt or fabric to maintain its original dimensions during its service life.

STAPLE FIBER: Short lengths of fiber, rather than one continuous strand or filament.

STRAND: Specified length of monofilament, multifilament, yarn, etc. which forms an element of woven material. (A multilayer forming fabric may contain as many as 84,000 machine direction strands and 325,000 cross direction strands.)

STRAND NUMBER: See MESH.

STRATIFIED BATT: Two-layered batt structure utilizing a finer batt fiber on the sheet-side surface of a felt while a coarser batt beneath it is more resistant to compaction.

STRINGING: Installing a forming fabric or wire on the paper machine.

STUFFER YARN: Bulky spun yarn that is inserted between the layers of a monofilament or multifilament dryer fabric in order to retard air flow and control permeability.

SURFACING: Treatment given to a forming fabric to reduce wire marking, in which the sheet-side knuckles are lightly sanded to smooth the surface.

T

TIGHT AREA: Large section of the forming fabric having markedly greater tension than the rest.

TRIPLE-LAYER FABRIC: Forming fabric consisting of a fine, plain-weave structure atop an underlying coarse structure; the two layers are held together with a shute "binder yarn".

TRIPLEX WEAVE: Basic weave pattern for dryer fabrics consisting of three layers of shute yarns woven together with two sets of warp yarns. Each set of warp yarns weaves between two of the three layers of shute yarns (as in the duplex weave) and the center layer of shute yarn is common to both sets of warp yarns.

TWILL: Fabric weave that creates a pattern of diagonals on the surface. All fabrics with a 2/1, 1/2 or 2/2 construction are twills; certain 1/3 and 3/1 constructions are also twills.

TWINNING: Tendency for two adjacent strands to move closer together in certain four-shed fabric weaves. Syn. Pairing.

V

VOID VOLUME (of a felt): Percent of volume occupied by air spaces within the bulk of the felt while in compression (i.e., at mid-nip of the press).

W _____

WARP: Strand that runs the length of the fabric; i.e., in the machine direction.

WARP-FACED FABRIC: Fabric having a preponderance of warp showing on the outside surface.

WARP LOOM SEAM: Seam for dryer fabric in which loops are formed from the machine-direction yarns on both sides and joined by threading monofilaments through the loops. Syn. Pin Seam.

WARP-RUNNER: Forming fabric in which the warp strands are principally running on the inside of the fabric and are in contact with the abrasive surface.

WATER RETENTION CAPACITY: Quantity of water which the forming fabric carries along on its return run, dependent on the wettability and capillarity of the fabric structure.

WEAVE: Type or style of weaving. Examples are plain weave, twill and sateen.

WEAVE CONSTRUCTION: Numerical designation for a single-layer fabric weave; it is the number of strands over and under during each repeating pattern of machine direction strand travel. For example, the designation 3/1 refers to a 4-shed fabric in which each shute strand goes over 3 warp strands and under one in a repeating pattern. See also SHED.

WEAVING: Producing a cloth or fabric on a loom.

WEB: Layer or lap or batt.

WEFT: See SHUTE.

WINDOW (of a forming fabric): Actual open area defined by a frame. (Sometimes "window" is used as a synonym for "frame".)

WOOF: See SHUTE.

WRINKLE: Sharp, long projection running diagonally across the forming fabric or in a lengthwise direction.

Y _____

YARN: Continuous strand of twisted fibers for use in weaving and knitting.

Chapter 16
Paper and Paperboard Grades

A

ABRASIVE BACKING PAPERS: Well-sized kraft papers used as the backing for sand, aluminum oxide, silicon carbide, garnet and other abrasives. Animal glue is the usual adhesive.

ABSORBENT GRADES: Grouping of paper and board products, all requiring absorbency as a principal property, including saturating papers, towelling, tissue and hygienic disposables.

ACOUSTICAL BOARD: Thick, bulky board, usually formed on a wet machine from a coarse fibrous furnish of wood, straw, bagasse, cornstalks and similar materials and dried in a tunnel dryer. Two or more layers of the board are subsequently glued together to form the required thickness, and then the combined board is cut into tiles of relatively small size.

ADDING-MACHINE PAPER: Writing paper or book paper in tightly-wound, narrow rolls (coils) for use on adding or tabulating machines.

AIR-MAIL PAPER: Lightweight writing paper. See also ONIONSKIN.

ALBUM PAPERS: Soft-surface, medium-weight paper with antique finish, principally used for making photograph albums. A basic requirement is the ability to take paste without cockling.

ARCHIVAL PAPER: See PERMANENT PAPER.

ARTICULATING PAPER: Paper impregnated with vegetable wax and nontoxic coloring, used by dentists to check the "bite" of teeth by marking those areas of interference or heavy contact between teeth and dentures.

ARTIST PAPERS: General category of papers including art parchment, drawing paper and boards, mat board, tracing paper and poster board.

ART PAPER: Designation of high-quality coated paper used for fine-screen, four-color printing.

ART PARCHMENT: Hard-sized, heavy sheet of cotton fiber or vegetable parchment, clear or mottled, used for diplomas, award certificates, announcements, programs, menus and other work requiring extra fine printing.

ASBESTOS BOARD: Paperboard, usually manufactured on a multiply machine, containing varying amounts of asbestos fiber depending on end use; mostly used as a fire retardant barrier in construction.

ASPHALT PAPERS: General classification for papers that are coated or saturated with asphalt or other bituminous material. The substrate is usually kraft paper.

B

BAG PAPER: High-strength, well-formed paper used for conversion into bags or sacks of all types. The furnish and grammage depend on the size of the bag and the nature of the contents to be packaged. Typically, bag paper is made from well-refined unbleached kraft pulp and given special handling on the paper machine to retain or enhance sheet extensibility. See also SACK PAPER.

BAKERS WRAP: Lightweight wrapping paper made from bleached chemical pulp, used for packaging bakery goods. The product requires reasonable strength, high finish and good white color.

BANKNOTE PAPER: See CURRENCY PAPER.

BIBLE PAPER: Dense, lightweight, opaque printing paper used in such products as bibles, dictionaries and encyclopedias where low bulk is important. It is made from a good-quality, bleached long-fibered furnish, often containing linen, cotton or flax fiber and heavily loaded with titanium dioxide or other fillers for maximum opacity. Requirements are good printability and strength and reasonable permanence. Syn. India Paper.

BINDERS BOARD: Solid board used for book covers, made on a wet machine from mixed paper furnish. Requirements are rigidity, uniformity, strength, high density and smoothness.

BLANKING PAPER: Plain, uncoated, wet-strength poster paper used to fill edges on billboards or placed between printed sheets of multi-sheeted posters. Printability is not a requirement for blanking paper. See also Poster Paper.

BLANKS: Term applied to a wide range of paperboards, coated and uncoated, solid or filled, mostly used for display work. Blanks may be manufactured directly on a wet machine or multiply machine, or they may be produced from pasting together two or more layers of fourdrinier paper. The principal requirement is for stiffness, but other properties such as smoothness and printability are important for some applications.

BLOTTING PAPER: Unsized, porous, bulky paper of little strength, originally used to absorb excess ink quickly from freshly written letters or manuscripts. Now, blotting paper is more often used for advertising display work.

BOND PAPER: High-quality, wood-free, hard-sized writing or printing paper, sometimes containing cotton fibers and often watermarked. In order to withstand handling and filing, the principal requirements are strength and durability.

BOOK PAPERS: Class of printing papers (exclusive of newsprint and groundwood specialties), usually made from blended chemical and mechanical pulps, and sized or coated for good printability. The properties of specific grades are tailored to meet the demands of the printing process and the product end-use. See also OFFSET PAPERS, LIGHTWEIGHT PRINTING PAPERS, ROTOGRAVURE PAPERS, PUBLICATION PAPERS.

BOXBOARD: Paperboard used to fabricate boxes. The general requirements are stiffness and durability. Syn. Rigid Paperboard, Setup Paperboard, Nonbending Paperboard. See also FOLDING BOXBOARD.

BRAILLE PAPER: High-quality paper made from chemical pulp, used for printing or writing by the Braille process, in which raised dots are embossed onto the surface. Requirements are smoothness and high tensile strength.

BRISTOLS: General term for paperboards made either on a fourdrinier or multiply machine that are 0.006 inches or greater in thickness. Many coated and uncoated grades are available for indexing, printing, folders, post cards, covers, etc.

BUILDING BOARD: Any of a general grouping of paperboards used in the building trade, including wallboard, gypsum board, plasterboard, panel board, insulating board and acoustical board.

BUILDING PAPERS: General grouping of papers used in the building trade, mostly consisting of converted products such as sheathing, roofing and moisture-barrier papers.

BUREAUCRACY PAPERS: Papers produced to meet government specifications and sold principally to government department buyers.

BUSINESS PAPERS: Grouping of papers for financial and administrative applications. Included under this heading are ledger papers, currency papers, safety papers, bonds, onionskins, copying papers, stationery, etc.

BUTCHERS WRAPS: Wide range of well-sized or waxed papers used to wrap meat, having the characteristics of chemical purity, resistance to grease and meat juices, and relatively high strength.

C _____

CABLE PAPER: Insulating material for electrical wires, consisting of a strong, acid-free kraft paper with non-conducting properties, which is sometimes creped.

CARBONIZING TISSUE: Raw stock for carbon paper, consisting of a strong, closely-formed, non-porous lightweight paper product made from chemical pulps. The prime requirement is to take carbon inks without penetration.

CARBONLESS PAPER: Paper that has been specially treated or coated to provide copies without the use of interleaved carbon papers or carbon coating.

CARBON PAPERS: Papers coated with a specially prepared ink compounded from waxes, colors and oils. Specific grades are suitable for use as typewriter carbons, pencil carbons, one-time carbons, duplicator carbons, and heat-transfer carbons.

CARDBOARD: Vague term referring to paperboards over 0.006 inches caliper, where stiffness is the prime requisite.

CARLINER: Heavy kraft paper used to line freight cars to protect contents against dirt and the sides of the car. Often it is a laminated sheet with asphalt as the binder.

CATALOG PAPERS: Basically lightweight newsprint used for catalogs, directories, and other forms of commercial printing, but usually containing fillers and a higher percentage of long-fibered pulp to retain opacity and strength. Some grades of catalog paper are given higher finishes, and a few are coated. Syn. Groundwood Printing Papers.

CELLULOSE WADDING: Absorbent material formed from layers of highly creped tissue, used in hospital and sanitary applications.

CHART PAPER: See MAP PAPER.

CHEMICAL REACTION PAPERS: Papers that produce a visible image by the reaction of relatively colorless materials which come into contact under pressure.

CHIPBOARD: Multiply board made from 100% low-grade secondary fiber, used for applications where stiffness is the main requisite, and appearance and strength are less important.

CIGARETTE PAPER: Well-formed tissue paper free of pinholes, having relatively high strength, stretchability, opacity and porosity, used solely as a wrapper in the manufacture of cigarettes. It is formed from well-beaten flax stock containing varying amounts of calcium carbonate filler.

COARSE PAPERS: See INDUSTRIAL PAPERS.

COATED FREE SHEET: Publication grade in which the coating raw stock contains no more than 10% mechanical pulp.

COATED GROUNDWOOD PAPERS: Publication grades in which the coating raw stock contains more than 10% mechanical pulp.

COATED NATURAL KRAFT (CNK): Coated simplex sheet which constitutes the fastest growing boxboard grade.

COIL PAPER: Unbleached kraft paper used as layer insulation between wires and as wrap around insulation. Requirements are strength and flexibility, high dielectric strength, and freedom from metallic and other conducting particles. Syn. Layer Insulation Paper.

COMMERCIAL PRINTING PAPERS: Classification of printing papers for such end uses as annual reports, advertising materials, booklets, calenders, and leaflets.

COMMODITY PAPERS: Mass produced grades, especially the lower-quality printing grades.

COMMUNICATION PAPERS: Vague classification encompassing various grades of writing and book papers.

CONDENSER TISSUE (or CONDENSER PAPER): Lightweight, dense, well-formed paper made from highly-refined kraft, used as a capacitor dielectric. Essentially the same product is used as raw stock for carbonizing and (with wet strength treatment) for tea bags. Syn. Capacitor Paper.

CONSTRUCTION PAPER: (1) General classification for papers, felts and boards used by the construction industry for insulation, roofing and underlay, etc. These grades often contain mineral fiber. General requirements are low thermal conductivity, fire resistance, permanency, and resistance to insects and vermin. (2) Newsprint-type sheet of high grammage and bulk, typically used for kindergarten cutouts and artwork.

CONTAINERBOARD: General term referring to either corrugated board or fiberboard used in the manufacture of shipping containers.

COPYING PAPERS: General classification encompassing plain (passive) and treated (sensitized) copying papers. The two major categories of plain copy machines use either "liquid toners" or "dry toners", referring to the material creating the image. Wet copying requires paper with a smooth, non-porous surface; whereas dry copying papers have more texture and must be manufactured with a certain tolerance to the heat which is applied to fix the dry toner. The major treated copying papers are thermal paper, diazotype paper, and blueprint paper. Syn. Reproduction Papers, Reprographic Papers.

CORRESPONDENCE PAPERS: Writing papers with attractive finishes. Distinctive finish and good writing quality are the principal attributes.

CORRUGATING MEDIUM: Lightweight board used for the fluted inner plies of corrugated box board, having requirements only of stiffness and runnability through the fluter. Corrugating medium is usually manufactured on a fourdrinier machine from high-yield semi-chemical pulp at nine-point thickness. Syn. Fluting Medium.

COVER PAPERS: Heavier-weight, fine-quality, coated and uncoated printing papers made from high-grade wood or cotton fibers, available in a variety of grammages. Cover papers are used for the covers of brochures and catalogs and also for such products as folders, cards, posters and menus.

CREPE PAPERS: Industrial and decorative papers that have been creped during manufacture or conversion, and are distinctive primarily as a result of the creping process. Industrial crepe papers consist mainly of wrapping, cushioning and filtering grades. The brightly-colored, decorative crepe papers, with very high creping ratios, are used for artistic arrangements and commercial displays.

CULTURAL PAPERS: Vague classification of paper according to its use for cultural purposes such as writing and printing, as opposed to industrial (i.e., non-printing) applications.

CURRENCY PAPER: Durable, high-quality paper used for printing currency, bonds and other government securities. U.S. currency paper is produced on a fourdrinier machine from well-beaten cotton and flax pulp; it is tub-sized with animal glue, loft-dried and plate finished. Currency papers usually incorporate distinctive safety and security features to protect against counterfeiting. Syn. Banknote Paper.

CUTTING PAPERS: Papers used in the garment industry in the cutting of fabrics. Included in this category are "separating tissue" (used on the cutting table to separate different bolts of cloth), "underlay paper" (kraft paper placed on the cutting table before material is laid out), and "anti-fusion paper" (waxed paper placed between layers of synthetic fabrics to reduce friction and heat during cutting).

D

DAMASK PAPER: Writing paper with a finish resembling linen.

DECORATIVE PAPERS: Papers manufactured with embossed or printed designs, used for gift-wrapping and other decorative purposes.

DECOR PAPERS: Papers made in a variety of solid shades and printed patterns, used as the surface sheet in laminates for application in the construction and furniture industries.

DIAZOTYPE BASE PAPER: Smooth, sized paper manufactured from bleached chemical pulp having high tear and folding strength. Suitable papers for diazotype coating also must be chemically inert and free from metallic ions that could adversely affect the photochemical process.

DIRECTORY PAPER: See CATALOG PAPERS.

DIRECT PROCESS PAPER: Fine paper designed to be treated with a light-sensitive or heat-sensitive coating for various reprographic processes.

DISPOSABLES: Term generally applied to nonwoven products up to about 1970, then abandoned because of its negative connotations for environmentalists.

DOCUMENT PAPER: High-quality, hard-finished, permanent paper, usually made from rag furnish.

DRAWING PAPERS: Medium to high-grade papers with furnishes varying from combination mechanical/chemical pulp to 100% cotton fiber.

Some are made with a smooth finish, while others have sufficient "tooth" to take a light touch of a pencil or crayon. Specific properties are tailored to the end use, but all grades generally require good texture, close formation, good erasability and freedom from specks.

DRY FELT: See FELT PAPER.

DRY-LAY NONWOVENS: Nonwovens that are produced by dry forming methods, usually from 100% long-fibered, synthetic staple. See also NONWOVENS.

DUPLICATOR PAPERS: Classification of papers used in making copies from a prepared master. Included in this group are papers for office-scale letterpress and offset printing, spirit duplicating paper and mimeographing paper.

E

ELECTRICAL INSULATION PAPER: General classification encompassing the wide range of papers, tissues, boards, and vulcanized products used by the electrical industry for various insulating purposes.

ELECTROSTATIC COPY PAPERS: See XEROGRAPHIC BONDS.

ENVELOPE PAPERS: Papers used in the making of envelopes, of which there are many types having a wide variation in grammage, appearance and finish depending on the particular requirements. All envelope papers must lie flat without curling and have good folding properties, good writing and printing surfaces, sufficient opacity for privacy, and adequate strength to resist mail and system handling.

EXCELSIOR: Newspaper or other lightweight paper that has been thinly shredded in such a way as to be fluffy and free from dust. It is used in the packing of fragile articles. Syn. Shredded Paper.

F

FACIAL TISSUE: Extremely soft tissue paper especially made for facial application, from a furnish of bleached sulfite or kraft.

FACSIMILE PAPER: High-quality, treated paper used to produce high-resolution copies from reception of electrical impulses sent over telephone lines. Syn. Fax Paper.

FELT PAPER: Absorbent felted sheet, usually formed on a wet machine from a mixed furnish of secondary fiber, mineral fiber and/or animal fiber; used as base stock for tarred paper, felt and sheathing, and for various saturating papers and boards. Syn. Dry Felt.

FIBERBOARD: (1) Solid board made on a wet machine from a variety of furnishes, used in the construction of shipping containers. (2) Sheets made by laminating paperboard to a thickness which provides the desired degree of stiffness.

FILTER PAPER: Porous, unsized paper of high chemical purity, usually made from cotton linters or chemical wood pulp or blends of the two stocks. While certain types of filter papers are adaptable to a wide range of industrial uses, others are tailor-made for specific applications.

FINE PAPER: General classification referring to white, uncoated printing and writing grades which contain no more than 25% mechanical pulp in the furnish. Most furnishes are wood-free. Specific grades are offset, tablet, envelope, bond, ledger, mimeo, duplicating, and various book stocks.

FLOCKING TISSUE: Highly-finished tissue used extensively in textile manufacturing plants to protect and support fabrics through printing processes.

FLONG PAPER: See MATRIX BOARD.

FOIL PAPER: Decorative barrier wrapping material consisting of metal foil laminated to a paper substrate.

FOLDER STOCK: Board or bristol, used for manufacturing file folders, which has been surface sized for durability. Requirements are stiffness, folding endurance, tearing strength, noncurling properties and uniform high finish.

FOLDING BOXBOARD: Paperboard suitable for conversion into folding cartons. In addition to general requirements of stiffness and durability, it must possess strength properties that permit scoring and folding. Syn. Carton Board.

FOODBOARD: Solid or multiply board used for food packaging, usually made from 100% bleached virgin pulp furnish.

FOOD WRAPPER: Any totally-clean paper suitable for wrapping food, including baker's wrap, butchers wrap, glassine, greaseproof, vegetable parchment, and a wide variety of waxed, coated, lacquered, and laminated grades.

FRENCH FOLIO: Opaque, hard-sized, smooth-finished, manifold-type paper, not as strong as onionskin.

FROZEN FOODBOARD: Foodboard that has been made water-resistant and diffusion-resistant by coating or impregnating with wax, or by coating or lining with other barrier materials.

FRUIT WRAPS: Tissues or lightweight papers used to wrap fruit for packing, made from a variety of furnishes and sometimes treated with oil or chemicals depending on specific requirements.

FUNCTIONAL PAPERS: Papers designed to be converted into such products as bags, boxes, wrappings, and tapes, and whose primary purpose is to fulfill the specified function rather than being printed, although often they will carry a printed message as well.

G

GLASSINE: Glossy, transparent paper used for protective wrappings or converted into waxed paper. It is produced from greaseproof paper by dampening and heavy pressure during subsequent supercalendering.

GRADES (of paper): See PAPER GRADES.

GRAPHIC PAPERS: See PRINTING PAPERS.

GREASEPROOF PAPER: Dense, non-porous paper made from highly refined sulfite pulp.

GREETING CARD STOCK: Specialty papers tailored to the specifications of greeting card manufacturers.

GROUNDWOOD CONVERTING PAPERS: Grades of paper containing varying amounts of mechanical pulp which are primarily converted into products such as salesbooks, notebooks, tablets, office forms, computer print-out forms and way-bills.

GROUNDWOOD PAPERS: General classification of printing, converting and specialty papers containing varying amounts of mechanical pulp.

GROUNDWOOD PRINTING PAPERS: See CATALOG PAPERS.

GROUNDWOOD SPECIALTIES: Specially developed grades of paper (usually uncoated printing grades) that contain varying amounts of mechanical pulp. See also MECHANICAL PRINTING PAPERS.

GUMMING KRAFT: Substrate for gummed sealing tape. It is similar to kraft wrapping paper except that it is hard sized to prevent the subsequent adhesive layer from penetrating too deeply into the paper.

GYPSUM BOARD: Multiply board made from 100% low-grade secondary fiber, used for the outer surfaces of plaster board.

H

HANGING RAW STOCK: Bulky, hard-sized, toothy-surfaced groundwood paper, which is manufactured in a wide range of grammages for conversion into wallpaper. It is usually coated by the converter and then printed and/or embossed. Syn. Hanging Paper, Wallpaper Base.

HARD PAPER: Paper which is impregnated with phenolic resins and used to form such products as plates, pipe and molded pieces. The formed products are dried and cured at high temperature and pressure. Syn. Bakelite Paper.

HEAT SEAL PAPERS: Papers coated with thermoplastic adhesives that utilize heat to reactivate the adhesive. Heat seal paper grades are widely used in packaging applications.

I

IMPREGNATING PAPERS: See SATURATING PAPERS.

INDEX BRISTOL: Rigid board made from chemical pulp, used principally for index record cards and business cards.

INDIA PAPER: See BIBLE PAPER.

INDUSTRIAL PAPERS: Vague classification of papers used in industrial applications, as opposed to papers used for cultural purposes. Prime examples are linerboard, corrugating medium and bag paper. Syn. Coarse Papers.

INDUSTRIAL TISSUES: General designation of tissue papers that includes condenser, carbonizing, and wrapping grades. Syn. Specialty Tissues.

INTERLEAVING TISSUE: Classification of paper according to use, rather than to any particular type of paper. Included under this heading are onionskin paper, flocking tissue, separating tissue, and a wide range of other plain, treated and/or embossed papers for interleaving of printed work, carbon papers, aluminum sheets and siding, other metal sheeting, and various glass, rubber and plastic products.

INTERMEDIATE GRADE: Any paper grade between the upper and lower extremes of a paper quality scale or converting scale. In printing paper, for example, newsprint and lightweight coated paper represent the lowest and highest quality, and such grades as supercalendered and pigmented are classed as intermediate grades.

IVORY BOARD: High-quality coated bristol typically used for menus and display work involving half-tone printing.

K

KRAFT PAPER: (1) Paper made almost wholly from kraft pulp. (2) Paper with high mechanical strength made almost wholly from unbleached softwood kraft pulp. It usually refers to wrapping paper.

L

LABEL PAPERS: Uncoated or coated-one-side sheets used for the manufacture of labels and other end uses. The base stock may be wood free or contain some mechanical pulp. Requirements are good opacity, ability to accept adhesive without curling, stiffness for proper feeding through the printing process, and generally good strength and stability.

LAYER INSULATION PAPER: See COIL PAPER.

LEATHERBOARD: Specialized grade of board used in shoe soles, made from at least 50% leather pulp (pulp manufactured from leather waste) with the remainder consisting of mixed waste paper.

LEDGER PAPERS: Semi-stiff, durable writing papers made from various combinations of rag and chemical pulps, used for bookkeeping, records, policies, legal documents, and long-life forms. The uses tend to overlap with those of bonds.

LENS TISSUE: High-grade tissue made from various long-fibered stock furnishes that are totally free of unbleached and mechanical pulps. The requirements are a high degree of softness and freedom from abrasive contaminants. It is used for cleaning, wiping and polishing optical lenses and other delicate instruments.

LIGHTWEIGHT COATED (LWC) **PAPERS:** Coated papers of relatively low grammage, generally under 72 g/m². See also ULTRA LIGHTWEIGHT COATED PAPERS.

LIGHTWEIGHT PAPERS: Uncoated papers of low grammage, generally under 40 g/m².

LIGHTWEIGHT PRINTING PAPERS: All grades of dense, thin, strong and opaque paper suitable for printing. Most lightweight printing papers are made from long-fibered stock and loaded with titanium dioxide to meet opacity requirements. The important advantage of lightweight printing paper is the savings in postage for mailed catalogs and other pieces.

LINERBOARD: Lightweight board used as the liners or facings for corrugated box stock and for wrapping applications. It is generally of two-ply construction, typically manufactured from high-yield unbleached kraft on a fourdrinier machine equipped with a secondary headbox; the thin top layer being of relatively better quality for appearance and printability. The main requirements are stiffness and strength. Syn. Facing.

M

MAGAZINE COVER: Machine-finished or supercalendered, coated or uncoated cover paper with both surfaces suitable for letterpress or offset printing. Strength must be sufficient for rough handling with emphasis on good folding endurance.

MAGAZINE PAPERS: Wide range of coated and uncoated printing papers used for periodicals, covering the gamut from catalog papers to publication grades.

MANIFOLD PAPER: Lightweight bond paper used primarily for 2nd and 3rd copies by interleaving with carbon paper on the typewriter. See also FRENCH FOLIO, ONIONSKIN.

MAP PAPER: Hard sized, wood-free printing paper with good dimensional stability and high strength properties, especially with respect to tearing resistance, folding endurance and abrasion resistance. It also may have some wet strength. Syn. Chart Paper.

MAT BOARD: Solid, light-colored board, lined or faced with plain or fancy papers, and manufactured in various grammages and finishes; used for mounting pictures.

MATRIX BOARD: Thick, laminated sheet made on a wet machine usually from secondary furnish, used for making molds from which stereo-type printing plates are made. Syn. Stereotype Dry Mat, Flong Paper.

MECHANICAL PRINTING PAPERS: Printing papers made from a principal furnish of mechanical pulp. These grades are distinguished from newsprint by their higher brightness, improved surface smoothness, and different grammages and end-uses.

MEDIUM-WEIGHT COATED (MWC) **PAPERS:** All publication grade papers above 72 g/m².

METALLIC PAPERS: Papers that are dusted with metallic powders (most often aluminum or bronze) immediately after being coated with lacquer or other adhesive. Sometimes the metallic powders are mixed with the adhesive prior to application.

METALLIZED PAPER: Paper that has been coated with a molecular layer of aluminum by condensing aluminum vapor against a lacquer coated surface within a vacuum chamber. This product is highly regarded by the packaging industry because it combines the appearance of metal foil with the handling properties of paper.

MILLBOARD: Generic term for heavy paperboard made from mixed waste paper on an intermittent board machine.

MIMEOGRAPH PAPER: Paper for duplication by the mimeograph process; it can be made from a wide variety of furnishes depending on the characteristics desired in the sheet. The necessary properties are rapid ink absorption, a minimum of fuzz or lint, and sufficient stiffness for automatic feeding. Some qualities are slack sized, but others are suitable for pen and ink signatures.

MOLDED PULP PRODUCTS: Contoured products such as egg cartons, fruit baskets, plates, etc, which are made by depositing a pulp slurry onto a suitably shaped mold while dewatering the stock by suction or pressure, and then drying the wet preform either in an unrestrained state or between heated dies.

N

NAPKIN STOCK: Tissue or lightweight paper that is converted into napkins. A semi-creped paper with properties of body, bulk, stretch, softness and opacity is generally used for production of single-ply napkins. A dry creped tissue that has been lightly calendered produces the optimum in feel and softness required for the finest-quality multiply napkins.

NEWS: Term applied to both newsprint and reclaimed newspaper stock.

NEWSBOARD: Low-grade multiply board made from waste news, used mainly as a backing material. See also CHIPBOARD.

NEWSPRINT: Machine-finished, unsized paper composed mainly of mechanical pulp, commonly used for printing newspapers.

NOISELESS PAPER: Bulky, unsized paper made from rag and chemical pulp blends, used for theater programs, studio manuscripts and other applications where the rustle and rattle of paper is objectionable. Syn. Silent Paper.

NONWOVENS: Fabric-like materials formed by felting together (by various wet and dry forming methods) a conglomeration of staple fibers, some of which are significantly longer than those typically used in papermaking. Among the many fibers used by the nonwoven manufacturing industry are acrylic, rayon, polyester, polypropylene, wood pulp, cotton, nylon, glass, vinyon, metallic, saran, and cellulose acetate. Syn. Nonwoven Fabrics, Formed Fabrics, Bonded Fiber Fabrics. See also DRY-LAY NONWOVENS, WET-LAY NONWOVENS, DISPOSABLES.

O

OFFSET PAPERS: Any type of printing paper that is specifically manufactured for the web offset printing process. The general requirements are a reasonably smooth surface, adequate surface strength (i.e., resistance to pick), cleanliness of surface, and resistance to the softening effect of water.

ONIONSKIN: Durable, hard-sized, manifold-type paper that is thin and usually quite transparent, made from well-beaten cotton fiber or chemical wood pulp. It is often used for air-mail correspondence.

OPAQUE CIRCULAR: High-opacity printing papers available in a wide range of grammages and finishes; these are basically offset papers that have been made highly opaque through the addition of certain fillers.

ORGANIC FELT: Roofing felt which is formed principally from wood fibers, as distinct from glass fiber roofing felt.

P

PACKAGING PAPERS: Broad classification of papers which includes wrapping papers, sack papers and bag papers.

PAPERBOARD SPECIALTIES: Paperboards that are made expressly for a particular end use. Examples are binder's board (for book covers), bottle-cap board, automobile board (for panels, etc.), various shoe boards, and various trunk boards (for luggage construction).

PAPER GRADES: Classifications of paper and board products according to quality, use, appearance, performance, or other relevant characteristic, or on the basis of a combination of factors. Certain grades are standardized within the industry.

PAPER TEXTILES: Fabrics woven or knitted from paper yarns, principally used for open-mesh vegetable bags and fruit packing baskets. The yarns used are generally made from tightly twisted kraft paper, either treated or untreated, which has high tensile strength.

PAPETERIE PAPER: Bright, white, bulky, soft textured paper with good folding qualities, allowing for a smooth, soft fold without cracking, used for a wide range of social correspondence.

PAPIER MACHÉ: Molding material prepared from repulped waste papers to which adhesives have been added, typically used to make relief maps.

PARCHMENT: Writing sheet made from the skins of sheep, goats and other animals. A number of grades of paper are manufactured to simulate the mottled appearance of true parchment. Syn. Skin Parchment.

PARCHMENTIZING PAPER: Waterleaf sheet prepared expressly for conversion into vegetable parchment.

PARCHMENT PAPER: See VEGETABLE PARCHMENT.

PARCHMENT WRITING: See ART PARCHMENT.

PERMANENT PAPER: Any high-quality, wood-free paper that is manufactured in such a way that it more effectively resists the effects of aging. Generally, the paper is acid-free and has been buffered with three to five percent calcium carbonate. Syn. Archival Paper.

PERSONAL PAPERS: General grouping of paper grades that includes napkins, tissues and towelling.

PHOTOGRAPHIC BASE PAPER: High-quality wet-strength paper having good dimensional stability. It must be chemically inert and free from impurities which could adversely affect the photosensitive coating or the photographic image.

PIGMENTED PAPER: Paper which has been given a thin pigmented coating, usually at the size press. The coat weight normally does not exceed 5 g/m^2 on either side. Pigmented papers bridge the quality gap between groundwood papers and publication grades. In the trade, they are referred to as machine finished, pigmented (MFP) grades. Syn. Semicoated Printing Paper, Slightly Coated Paper.

PLASTIC PAPERS: Varied grouping which includes solid plastic sheets and papers made from mixtures of plastic and cellulose fibers. Most products in this grouping are functional grades, but generally they also have good printing properties.

POSTER PAPER: Well-sized printing paper suitable for a limited period of outdoor use.

PRESSBOARD: Hard-calendered board, usually made on an intermittent board machine from 100% chemical pulp, having characteristics of high chemical purity, high density, even thickness, surface smoothness, high strength, and good electrical insulation properties; used for pressing fabrics and as layer insulation in electrical transformers. Syn. Transformer Board, Textile Board.

PRESSURE SENSITIVE PAPERS: Papers coated with an adhesive which is activated by contact or pressure. During converting, printing and handling, the adhesive side must be protected by specially treated release papers or coatings.

PRINTING PAPERS: Papers that are suitable for printing, such as book paper, bristols, newsprint, bond, etc. The designation does not denote a class of paper. Syn. Graphic Papers.

PROCESSED PAPERS: General grouping of papers that have undergone converting operations to prepare them for specific end uses. Examples are embossed papers, impregnated papers, laminated papers, and functionally coated papers.

PUBLICATION GRADES: Coated printing papers encompassing a wide range of grammages and qualities. General grade categories are numbered from 1 to 5, where No. 1 is the highest quality and No. 5 the lowest quality. Nos. 1 through 3 are wood-free. Within each quality level, the sheets are manufactured for a specific printing process.

R _____

REINFORCED PAPER: Designation for any paper that has been reinforced by bonding or laminating another material to it. Most commonly, it refers to a multiply laminated paper in which the layers are bonded together by means of asphalt or adhesive to which a reinforcing material such as glass fibers has been added.

RELEASE PAPERS: Grades of vegetable parchment, glassine and other papers that are used for protective backings and which have been chemically treated to release readily from tacky and pressure-sensitive adhesive surfaces. Wax impregnated release papers are widely used by the food, baking and candy industries for handling sticky products. Syn. Separating Papers.

REPRODUCTION PAPERS: See COPYING PAPERS.

REPROGRAPHIC PAPERS: See COPYING PAPERS.

ROLL SPECIALTIES: General grouping of paper products that are sold in the form of small rolls, including accounting and adding machine rolls, addressograph rolls, teleprinter rolls, thermal paper rolls, and teletype and ticker tapes.

ROOFING FELT: Saturating paper usually made on a single-cylinder machine from a waste paper stock often made freer draining by the addition of defibrated wood particles. It is specifically designed for conversion into asphalt saturated papers. See also ORGANIC FELT.

ROTOGRAVURE PAPER: Any type of printing paper that is specifically manufactured for rotogravure printing. The principal requirement is exceptional smoothness on both sides.

ROTONEWS: Upgraded newsprint, suitable for printing by the rotogravure process. The required surface smoothness is achieved by utilizing lower-freeness mechanical pulp in the furnish and high-intensity machine calendering.

RUST-INHIBITOR PAPERS: Wrapping papers used for steel articles that have been impregnated or coated with synthetic rust-inhibitor chemicals.

S _____

SACK PAPER: Similar to bag paper, but usually heavier and stronger. See also BAG PAPER.

SAFETY PAPER: Paper which incorporates antifalsification characteristics, i.e., paper that is designed to reveal alterations or attempts at alteration. Syn. Antifalsification Paper.

SANITARY TISSUE: General designation for such products as facial and bathroom tissues.

SATURATING PAPERS: Soft, porous papers that are manufactured specifically to be saturated with solutions or compounds of various types for conversion into decorative laminates and industrial specialties. Syn. Impregnating Papers.

SECURITY PAPER: Any paper product in which security features are incorporated into the sheet to deter counterfeiting, such as watermarks of various types, flourescent fibers, color reactive stains, and marks which are only detectable by ultra violet light or by water.

SEMICOATED PRINTING PAPER: See PIGMENTED PAPER.

SENSITIZED PAPERS: Papers that have been treated with a chemical solution to make them surface reactive to light, chemicals or gases. Included in this group are various copy and photographic papers.

SEPARATING PAPERS: See RELEASE PAPERS.

SEPARATING TISSUES: See CUTTING PAPERS.

SHREDDED PAPER: See EXCELSIOR.

SPECIALTY PAPERS: Grades of paper made with specific characteristics to adapt them to definite and comparatively restricted end uses. Included under this category are technical papers, saturating grades, and certain decorative and laminating papers. Syn. Specialties.

SPINNING PAPER: Paper with a high degree of fiber orientation having particularly high tensile strength in the machine direction, suitable for spinning into twine or cord.

STATIONERY: Relatively soft and bulky paper with good appearance, used for personal correspondence; usually made from chemical pulp furnish, but highest quality includes cotton fiber.

STEREOTYPE DRY MAT: See MATRIX BOARD.

STRAWBOARD: Board made from straw pulp, generally used as corrugating medium because of its high rigidity.

SUPERNEWS: Term sometimes applied to uncoated groundwood specialties.

T _____

TAG STOCK: Paperboard used for making tags of various types, as well as other products. It is made from a variety of furnishes depending on requirements. Certain grades may be hard sized, coated or made with wet strength additives. Typically, desired properties include good strength, especially with respect to tear, tensile and folding endurance, durability, moisture resistance and a good printing surface. Syn. Tagboard.

TAPE PAPER: See GUMMING KRAFT.

TECHNICAL PAPERS: Grouping of specialty paper grades that includes filter papers, carbonless papers, heat sensitive papers, facsimile papers and some duplicating papers. Technical papers often contain such non-cellulose fibrous materials as glass, mica, carbon, metal and ceramic.

TEST LINER: Linerboard which conforms to a test specification. Syn. Test Board.

TEXT PAPERS: Fine quality uncoated printing papers made from high-grade wood or cotton fibers, available in a variety of common grammages. They are used primarily for the inside pages of books, brochures and catalogs.

THERMAL PAPER: Lightweight paper with a one-sided application of heat sensitive coating, used for facsimilies, computer printouts and medical imaging applications.

THIN PAPERS: Grouping of dense, lightweight sheets that includes bible paper, onionskin, manifold paper, carbonizing tissue, condenser paper and cigarette paper.

TICKET STOCK: Wide range of papers and boards used to make tickets, some of which incorporate security features.

TISSUE: General designation covering a wide range of low-weight sheets. See also SANITARY TISSUE, INDUSTRIAL TISSUE.

TOILET TISSUE: Bathroom tissue made from 100% chemical wood pulp or mixtures of chemical and mechanical pulps in a variety of finishes and constructions. General requirements are adequate strength, softness, clean appearance, freedom from coarse particles and easy disintegration under the flushing action of water.

TOUGH CHECK: Very strong multiply paperboard usually made from unbleached kraft pulp and often coated on one or both sides, used for shipping tags and other applications where toughness is required.

TOWELING: Creped, lightweight, absorbent paper usually made from lightly-refined kraft with addition of some mechanical pulp. Fast absorbency and water holding capacity are prime requisites. Some grades are treated with wet-strength resins to prevent wet disintegration.

TRACING PAPER: High quality, lightweight, highly transparent drafting paper made from all-rag pulp or a mixture of rag and chemical pulps. The transparency can be achieved by long beating of the pulp (making essentially a greaseproof-type paper) or by treating the sheet with oils or synthetic resins. Syn. Vellum.

TYPEWRITER PAPER: Adequately sized paper having good erasure properties and able to withstand the impact of the type of a typewriter.

U _____

ULTRA LIGHTWEIGHT COATED (ULWC) **PAPERS:** Coated papers of very low grammage, generally under 58 g/m².

V _____

VALUE-ADDED GRADES: Designation usually applied to mechanical printing papers that have been upgraded to meet customer specifications by such means as supplemental brightening, addition of fillers, web sizing, supercalendering, etc. and by offering a wide range of grammage.

VEGETABLE PARCHMENT: High quality product obtained by parchmentizing a waterleaf sheet formed from purified cellulose fibers. The sheet is then dried, surface-sized and calendered to

VEGETABLE PARCHMENT: (cont):
the extent required for the finished product. Vegetable parchment is either greaseproof or grease resistant, has high wet strength and resistance to disintegration by chemical agents. It is widely used in food packaging, as a printing parchment, and as release paper.

VELLUM: (1) High-quality parchment made from calf skin. (2) High-grade paper sheet which resembles parchment.

VULCANIZING PAPER: Waterleaf paper made of rag and/or chemical pulp, with high chemical purity and controlled cupriethylenediamine viscosity.

W

WADDING: Soft bulky material commonly made up of several layers of creped paper, used in a variety of forms for protection of items during shipment.

WALLPAPER BASE STOCK: See HANGING RAW STOCK.

WATER-COLOR PAPER: High-quality, tub sized sheet for water color work, generally made from 100% rag stock, with a toothy surface to simulate an oil painting canvas.

WAXED PAPERS: Large group of papers which have been treated in a conversion process with wax or waxy materials to varying degrees. Base stocks are usually bleached kraft and sulfite papers, including vegetable parchment, greaseproof and glassine. Petroleum waxes are used, augmented as necessary by resin and polymer additives to improve the properties. Because of their barrier properties and low cost, waxed papers are extremely important in the protection and preservation of a wide range of food items, and also such non-food items as cosmetics, soap and tobacco.

WAXING PAPER or **WAXING TISSUE:** Any paper used as base stock for saturating or coating with wax.

WET-LAY NONWOVENS: Nonwovens that are produced on some variation of conventional papermaking machinery, most often on a fourdrinier or cylinder former. Wet-lay nonwovens generally contain some natural pulp, whereas dry-lay nonwovens are frequently made from 100% long-fibered synthetics. See also NONWOVENS.

WRAPPING PAPER: General classification of papers having sufficient strength and appropriate properties for enveloping and protecting almost any shape and size of contents. Some wrapping papers have a decorative function.

WRAPPING TISSUE: Designation covering a wide variety of tissue products used for wrapping and packaging merchandise. The general requirements are for strength, good formation and cleanliness. Sheet weight is generally in the 16 to 28 g/m² range.

WRITING PAPER: Broad classification of paper that is suitable for pen and pencil writing as well as for certain printing purposes. Writing papers are made in a wide range of qualities.

XYZ

XEROGRAPHIC BONDS: Bond papers that have been developed to meet the requirements of high-speed electrostatic office copiers.

Chapter 17

Paper Coating

(Includes Pigmented and Functional Coating)

A _____

ACRYLIC BINDERS: Family of synthetic resins based on esters of acrylic and methacrylic acid, used as coating color binders. Coatings made from acrylics generally have good printability and excellent resistance to heat, light, and chemical degradation. Syn. Acrylic Emulsions.

ADHESIVE: See BINDER.

ADHESIVE DEMAND: Amount of binder required by a particular pigment to stick the particles together. In most coating layers, there is sufficient binder present to fill the spaces between the pigment particles completely. Syn. Binder Demand.

ADHESIVE RATIO: Parts of binder used for each 100 parts by weight of pigment, a basic parameter for coating color formulation.

AFTER-DRYERS: Dryer section positioned on a paper machine after the size press or coating operation.

AIR FLOTATION DRYER: Drying equipment for two-sided coated paper which utilizes two opposing air streams to suspend the substrate as it passes through the heating chamber. Syn. Floater Dryer, Air Suspension Dryer.

AIR IMPACTOR: Thin jet of air applied to a freshly coated sheet to smooth and spread the coating color.

AIR KNIFE: Thin horizontal jet of air angled from a pressurized slot. Syn. Air Blade, Air Doctor.

AIR KNIFE COATING: Method of coating in which an excess of aqueous pigmented dispersion is applied to the sheet by an applicator roll (or other method), and the excess is then immediately removed by means of a thin flat jet of air which doctors the surface and also serves to smooth out irregularities. Syn. Air Blade Coating, Air Brush Coating, Air Jet Coating, Air Doctor Coating.

ALGINATE: Derivative of seaweed used as a thickener in coating formulations.

ALKALI-REACTIVE BINDERS: Synthetic acrylic/vinyl acetate binders for coating color which swell under alkaline conditions, yielding desirable thixotropic and pseudoplastic flow properties. These binders are used as replacements for casein and soy protein, which are more in demand as protein food sources.

ALKYD RESINS: Synthetic heat-set resins formed by condensation reaction from complex alcohols and acids, used in functional coatings.

ALPHA PROTEIN: See SOY PROTEIN.

ALUMINUM STEARATE: Insoluble soap used as a coating lubricant.

AMMONIUM STEARATE: Soluble soap used as a coating lubricant.

ANGLE OF ATTACK: Angular relationship between the air knife jet and the tangent line at the point of impingement on the backing roll. Syn. Lip Angle, Alpha Angle.

ANTIBLOCKING AGENT: Material used in a coating formulation or as overcoating to prevent blocking.

ANTISTATIC AGENT: Additive in coating formulations, used to decrease or eliminate static build-up on surfaces. Many antistatic agents impart conductive properties. See also CONDUCTIVE AGENTS.

APPLICATOR: Device for applying coating color to the raw stock, which may be a roll, brush, dip tank, or spray.

APPLICATOR ROLL: Rotating roll which picks up a layer of coating color (e.g., from a pan or by contact with an intermediary pickup roll) and then contacts the sheet, and thereby transfers color to the sheet. Syn. Coating Roll.

APPLICATOR ROLL STREAKS: Streaks of non-uniform coating due to interrupted coating flow from the supply system to the applicator roll.

AQUEOUS: [adj] Made with or containing water, as e.g., an aqueous dispersion.

ASPECT RATIO (of particles): Ratio of the diameter of a particle to its thickness, a useful concept to characterize pigments. For example, the aspect ratio of clays falls between 5 and 15.

ATTACK DISTANCE: Distance that the air jet travels from the nozzle to the coating in an air knife coater. Syn. Lip Distance.

B

BACK COATING: Reverse side contamination of a single coated sheet, caused by accidental application of coating color to the backing roll.

BACKING ROLL: Roll that supports and guides the web during processing operations carried out by a blade, air knife, brush, another roll, etc. Syn. Backup Roll, Impression Roll. See also BREAST ROLL.

BACKING ROLL MARK: Defect in blade coated paper corresponding to a gouge mark in the backing roll. The sheet retains an excess of coating in the affected area. Syn. Butterfly.

BACKING ROLL SPOT: Defect in blade coated paper caused by a particle stuck to the coater roll of a coating press. The center areas of the mark appear lighter, while the edges appear heavier.

BACKUP ROLL: See BACKING ROLL.

BARRIER COAT: Coating application on the side of the paper opposite to the printing surface to provide increased sheet opacity.

BARRIER COATING: See FUNCTIONAL COATING.

BARRIER MATERIAL: Paper coating or laminate that functions primarily to impede the transmission of air, water, water vapor, light, etc.

BASE BOARD: Board that will ultimately be covered or coated.

BASE COAT: First applied coat of multiple applications.

BASE STOCK: See COATING RAW STOCK.

BASE STOCK STABILITY: Ability of a base stock to retain surface properties following wetting by an aqueous coating. (Generally, a paper intended for coating must be well formed and wet-rolled, as any imperfections of the original wet sheet, even if removed or hidden during dry rolling, will reappear on coating.)

BEAD COATER: See MENISCUS COATER.

BENT-BLADE COATER: Coater that employs a bent or extended blade for metering and leveling the coating. Unlike the more conventional stiff blade (which is positioned at a large angle relative to the backing roll), the bent blade is positioned at a smaller angle so that the side of the blade produces a troweling action over a relatively large area. The action of the bent blade is suitable for medium to high coat weights.

BINDER: Component of coating dispersion that serves to bind the pigment particles together in the coating, bind the coating to the rawstock, reinforce the rawstock and fill the pores in the pigment structure. Syn. Adhesive.

BINDER MIGRATION: Movement of water soluble components into the sheet following application of coating color, leaving on the surface a coating lower in binder content than the original formulation.

BINDER SPECKS: Defect in coated paper caused by non-uniform coating binder distribution, which gives a grainy or textured appearance to the coated surface and causes variations in ink receptivity.

BITUMEN: Any mineral pitch such as asphaltum or coal tar.

BITUMINOUS COATING: Mixture containing asphalt and solvent, used as a functional coating material.

BLADE COATER: Any coating equipment in which the thickness of application is controlled by means of an angled blade which doctors off excess color and smooths the surface. See also HIGH-ANGLE BLADE COATER, LOW-ANGLE BLADE COATER.

BLADE CONTACT ANGLE: Angle between the blade and the plane of the sheet that is being coated.

BLADE CREASE: Blade coating defect caused by a machine direction wrinkle in the raw stock. The crease itself is devoid of coating because of greater localized blade pressure.

BLADE CUT: Blade scratch that is deep enough to sever the paper.

BLADE LOADING: Pressure exerted by the blade tip on the surface being coated.

BLADE MARK: See BLADE STREAK.

BLADE PUDDLE COATER: Trailing blade coater consisting essentially of a one-sided trough, the bottom of which holds a flexible blade. In operation, the trough containing coating color is forced against the backing roll around which the coating raw stock is drawn in a downward direction. A pond 10 to 15 cm deep is maintained on the paper and the amount of pickup is controlled by the pressure on the blade.

BLADE SCRATCHES: Blade coating defect in the form of fine hair-like indentations in the coated paper surface which may have a length up to several hundred meters in the machine direction, most commonly caused by grit caught under the blade as a result of poorly dispersed coating color.

BLADE STREAK: Blade coating defect in the form of a broad indentation in the coated paper surface which may have a length up to several hundred meters in the machine direction, usually caused by a buildup behind the coating blade. Syn. Blade Mark.

BLISTERING: Separation of coating from raw stock in the form of eruptions, usually caused by too rapid drying of the coating.

BLISTER RESISTANCE: Property of a coated paper which withstands the vapor pressure generated internally during rapid heating in the ovens of web-fed heatset printing presses and allows the pressure to leak away through the combined coating and ink layers.

BLOCKING: Tendency of two sheets (e.g., coated paper) in intimate contact to adhere to each other, thus causing tearing or picking when the sheets are separated.

BLOCKING RESISTANCE: Ability of a given material (e.g., coated paper) to resist the blocking effects of temperature, pressure and humidity.

BLUSHING: Change in a solvent coating from a clear or colored appearance to a white, greyish or iridescent appearance during drying.

BODY: See CONSISTENCY.

BODY STOCK: See COATING RAW STOCK.

BREAST ROLL: Backing roll that provides support for the substrate but does not create counter-pressure (as in a press nip).

BRISTLE MARK: Indentation in the surface of coated paper impressed by a bristle that came off the coating brushes and adhered to one of the calender rolls.

BRUSH COATING: Early method of coating in which the coating color is first applied to the sheet by an applicator roll and then spread and worked into the sheet by means of fixed, oscillating or rotary brushes. This method is now little used.

BRUSH FINISH COATING: Pigmented coating formulated with a high wax content where the coated paper is run dry or partially dried through a brush calender.

BRUSH MARK: Defect in coated paper caused by a mark left in the coating by any of the brushes used for spreading the coating color.

BUBBLE COATING: Coating containing minute bubbles which have been intentionally introduced into the coating color. The dried coating is a uniformly porous structure providing air/adhesive interfaces that have excellent light-scattering properties.

BULKING VALUE: Ability of a pigment constituent to add volume to a coating dispersion.

BUMP: Each successive coating layer of a multi-station same-side coating operation.

BURN OUT TEST: Qualitative test of coating uniformity. A double-folded sample of coated paper is subjected to a heated reagent, which shows any defects such as marks or streaks, and heavy or light coat weight. Iodine is used for starch-containing coatings and acid for coatings without starch.

C _____

CASEIN: Protein material obtained from coagulated cow's milk, used as a binder in coating formulations. Up until 1950, casein was the most widely used coating binder, but relatively high cost now limits its use to more specialized coatings.

CAST COATING: Method of producing a high gloss finish of mirror-like quality (on one side of the sheet), in which a freshly coated paper is pressed onto the surface of a highly polished Yankee drying cylinder and carried on the cylinder until the coating is dried.

CHARM-FLEX WRINKLE: Defect on cast coated paper occuring when the web is misaligned prior to the applicator roll causing a wrinkle in the draw.

CHILL DRUM: Large-diameter, double-shell drum used to cool and provide surface finish to extruded thermoplastic coatings or laminates. The outer wall provides for maximum heat transfer from the melt to the water circulating between the two walls; and the solidified coating is directly influenced by the drum's surface. The inner wall is designed to be the structural support for the entire assembly.

CHILL ROLL: Water-cooled, hollow rotating cylinder which reduces the temperature of a moving web by surface contact.

CLAY COATING: Aqueous pigmented coating utilizing clay as the main constituent.

COATED ONE SIDE (C1S): [adj] Term applied to paper that has been coated on one side only.

COATED PAPERS: Papers in which one or two surfaces have been treated with a pigment/binder dispersion to improve printability and/or appearance. Some manufacturers apply this designation only to papers in which more than 10% of the total sheet structure is made up of coating material and where pigment amounts to more than 50% of the coated material; thus excluding film-coated papers and functional coated papers.

COATED TWO SIDES (C2S): [adj] Term applied to paper that has been coated on both sides.

COATING: (1) Cover substance on the surface of paper or board. (2) Applying coating color or functional material to the surface of a paper.

COATING ADDITIVES: Supplemental ingredients in coating formulations which modify the handling properties of the dispersion or improve the coating itself. Additives can be considered under the general classifications of insolubilizers, lubricants, thickeners, dispersants, preservatives, defoamers, and dyes. Syn. Modifiers.

COATING BANDS: Bands of heavy coating extending in the machine direction due to localized excess application and/or insufficient doctoring.

COATING BLISTER: See BLISTERING.

COATING CLAY: Tiny platelets of mineral clay, usually kaolin and china clay, which typically make up 80% of the dried coating.

COATING COLOR: Term applied to all aqueous pigmented coating dispersions before their application to paper. Sometimes referred to simply as "color". Syn. Coating Slip.

COATING COLOR STRAINER: Screening or filtering device through which the coating color is pumped to remove undispersed pigments or oversize particles before the color is applied to the web.

COATING COMPOSITION: Formulation or recipe for the coating color.

COATING DEFECTS: Imperfections in the coated paper surface which detract from the sheet's appearance or printability.

COATING FORMULA: List of ingredients and the actual amounts to be used in making up a batch of coating color. Syn. Coating Furnish, Coating Recipe.

COATING FORMULATION: Precise way in which a coating color or functional coating mixture is prepared for practical use, including the exact proportions of the various constituents. Sometimes used interchangably with "coating formula".

COATING HOLDOUT: Extent to which the coating rawstock resists inward migration by the freshly-applied coating color.

COATING KITCHEN: Centralized paper mill facility for storage, dispersal and mixing of coating formulations. The typical sequence of operations is to meter each component from storage into a high-viscosity mixer, blend thoroughly and extract into holding tanks. In a modern facility, the operational sequence is computer controlled. Both batch and continuous systems are used. Syn. Color Room.

COATING LAYER: Single application of coating.

COATING LUMP: Discolored, shiny, hard and brittle spot on the coated paper caused by excess color applied to the localized area.

COATING MACHINE: Independent equipment for applying pigmented or functional coatings to webs. Syn. Off-Machine Coater.

COATING MAKEDOWN: Metering and blending together the various components of a coating formulation, either as a continuous process or batch process.

COATING MIXER: Device for rapidly producing pigment-vehicle dispersions. Syn. Disperser, Dispersion Mill. See also IMPACT MILL, COLLOID MILL, KNEADER.

COATING MOTTLE: Small-scale variation in the gloss of a supercalendered coated sheet, giving a galvanized look. Often, coating mottle is caused by inadequate smoothness of the coating raw stock.

COATING OPERATION: Continuous application of a substance to the surface of paper or board.

COATING PAN: Container from which coating is picked up (e.g., by a fountain roll, metering roll, or gravure cylinder) for application to the paper surface.

COATING PIGMENTS: Very finely divided mineral materials which constitute 60 to 90% of the coating layer. Fine grades of clay are most commonly used. Other pigments used are titanium dioxide, calcium carbonate, talc, zinc oxide, and satin white.

COATING PLANT: Section of the paper mill where off-machine coating operations are carried out.

COATING PUDDLE: Generally, the volume of coating liquid stored between two surfaces. Most often, the term refers to the volume between two gate rolls, where the puddle is contained by "edge dams".

COATING RAW STOCK: Base sheet on which coating is applied. The specifications for the coating raw stock are usually quite stringent, requiring good formation and freedom from defects. Syn. Body Stock, Body Paper, Body Board, Base Stock.

COATING SLIP: See COATING COLOR.

COATING SPLASH: Localized irregular areas of high basis weight on the coated sheet due to coating color inadvertently spattering onto the sheet during the coating operation.

COATING STATION: That part of the paper machine or coating machine where pigment coatings are applied.

COATING STREAK: Defect in blade coated paper caused by a localized decreased clearance between roll and blade and the resulting thinner coating at this point. The root cause is usually an object stuck between the roll and the blade.

COATING STRUCTURE (of a pigmented coating): Manner in which pigment particles are packed and the distribution of binder and air spaces around them.

COAT WEIGHT: Amount of coating added to the rawstock in g/m² or other units of weight per unit area.

CO-EXTRUSION COATING: Functional coating process in which two extruded heated resin films are combined into a single multilayer coating material (without intermixing of the two melted resins) before being applied to the substrate.

COLLOID MILL: Type of high-shear mixer used for coating color dispersion.

COLOR: See COATING COLOR.

COLOR IMMOBILIZATION: "Setting" of the coating color on the base sheet, i.e., when dewatering into the sheet and binder migration are minimal.

COLOR IMMOBILIZATION POINT: Point within the coating drying process where the coating layer is totally immobilized. Research indicates the immobilization point for most colors is 75 to 78% solids. Syn. Gel Point.

CONDUCTIVE AGENT: Additive to coating color that imparts conductive properties to the substrate.

CONDUCTIVE COATING: Pigmented coating containing additives that impart conductivity to the substrate. Conductive coatings are used in the production of facsimile papers and certain copying papers.

CONGEALING POINT (of waxes): Temperature at which molten wax, when allowed to cool under prescribed conditions, ceases to flow. This property relates to the handling and utilization characteristics of the wax.

CONSISTENCY: Property of a coating color that resists deformation or flow. Consistency is not a fundamental property, but a combination of viscosity, plasticity, and other phenomena. (For a Newtonian fluid, consistency is the same as viscosity.)

CONTACT COATER: Any coater in which the metering device (blade, roll, bar) is in physical contact with the coating raw stock.

CONVERSION COATING: Off-machine coating.

COUPLING AGENT: Specialty chemical used in coating formulations which serves as a "molecular bridge" to improve the bonding between a filler, fiber, or pigment and the surrounding matrix. Examples are silanes, titanates, and zircoaluminates.

COVERAGE: (1) Degree to which the surface fibers are covered up and concealed by a coating. (2) Degree of continuity and thickness of an applied coating.

CRACKING: Defect in coated paper in the form of fissures in the surface of the coating, caused by stresses imposed during printing or converting operations.

CRATERS: Small blemishes in coated paper, caused by the breaking of air bubbles after the coating has been applied. Syn. Foam Spots.

CRAZING: Disruption of the coating in the form of fine wrinkles and minute surface cracks.

CROW'S FEET: (1) Surface distortion of wet waxed paper caused by the wax film being too soft as the freshly dipped sheet enters the water bath. (2) Defect on cast coated paper related to light coating weight due to increased drum speed with no change in coating viscosity.

CURING: Chemical reaction occurring by heating that stabilizes or changes the composition of a coating (or saturant). The effect may be similar to that achieved by drying, but the action is not by vehicle removal.

CURTAIN COATING: Method of applying functional coatings in which the hot melt coating is pumped through a slot die in the form of a falling film or curtain. The horizontal sheet passes through the curtain at high speed and the coating is deposited directly on the paper surface where it solidifies by cooling.

D _____

DECORATIVE COATING: Coating applied for aesthetic purposes.

DIFFERENTIAL ROLL COATING: Method of coating application using multi-roll units on which the speed of the rollers relative to each other and to the moving web can be altered. The various rollers always rotate in the direction of web movement. Syn. Transfer Roll Coating.

DILATANCY: See SHEAR THICKENING.

DILATANT FLUID: Non-Newtonian fluid exhibiting a non-linear relationship between shear stress and shear rate. Specifically, the shear rate increases less rapidly with successive incremental changes in shear stress, i.e., the apparent fluid viscosity increases. An example of a dilatant fluid is a raw starch slurry at 55–60% solids.

DILUENT: Fluid that dissolves another substance or dilutes a solution. Syn. Solvent, Thinner.

DIP: Bath through which the web passes in dip coating.

DIP COATING: Method of coating in which the web passes beneath a roll submerged in a bath containing the coating color. The roll may be either partially submerged (single-sided coating) or totally submerged (two-sided coating). Syn. Immersion Coating, Submersion Coating.

DIP ROLL: Partially or fully submerged roll that guides the sheet in a dip coater.

DISPERSIBILITY: Relative ease or difficulty in obtaining complete dispersion of a particular pigment within a coating color formulation.

DISPERSING AGENT: See DISPERSANT.

DISPERSION: (1) Process of maintaining individual particles in suspension, usually by a combination of mechanical and chemical action. (2) Resultant suspension from such a process.

DISTRIBUTOR ROLL: Roll on some designs of coater (principally roll coaters) that serves to reduce the coating film thickness and to distribute the film more evenly onto the surface of the applicator roll. Some coaters employ a series of distributor rolls that may be of varied diameter, and/or turning with different peripheral speed, with or without oscillating motion.

DOCTOR ROLL: See METERING ROLL.

DOG HAIRS: Defect in coated paper consisting of protruding fibers which are longer than those commonly known as fuzz.

DOUBLE BUMP COATER: Two-station, same-side coater.

DOUBLE-COATED PAPERS: Papers which have an extra heavy coating, which may or may not have been applied in two operations. They may be double coated on one or both sides.

DRAW ROLLS: Web-wrapped, driven rolls in the interior of an off-machine coater that are designed to split the machine into tension zones and to aid in the threading operation.

DRUM PICK: Surface void on cast coated paper where the coating sticks to the drum at the takeoff point, caused by excessive drum temperature or poor adhesive bond to the base coat.

DRUM SCAB: Surface void on cast coated paper where coating splash or a lump has adhered to the casting surface.

DRYER DWELL TIME: Amount of time, specified in seconds, that a functional coating must remain under heated conditions for solidification and curing.

DRYING CRACKS: Fine cracks on the surface of coated paper caused by too rapid evaporation of the moisture in the coating.

DRY WAXING: Application of wax up to 20% pickup in such a way that it is combined almost entirely within the sheet. Dry waxing is actually a saturating process. The wax is typically applied by a kiss coater to one side of the sheet.

DULL COATED: [adj] Term applied to papers that have been coated with calcium carbonate or blanc fixe and not supercalendered. From a gloss standpoint, dull coated paper lies between uncoated and regular coated sheets.

DUPLEX COATER: Coating machine which coats both sides of the paper simultaneously. Syn. Two-Sided Coater, Double Coater.

DWELL TIME: Time between application of excess coating color and removal of the excess by a blade, air knife, or rotating rod. Long dwell times are undesirable because the layer of coating color nearest the web becomes greatly dewatered prior to removal of excess color and undergoes significant rheological change.

E _____

ELECTROSTATIC COATING: Noncontact coating method in which a controlled deposit of solid or liquid coating particles is applied on a dielectric substrate by an opposing electrical charge. This method is used principally in the manufacture of carbon papers, sandpapers and flock finishes.

EMULSION COATING: Any coating process in which the substrate is coated with plastics and resins applied in the form of an emulsion.

ENAMEL: Term used for a glossy, shiny-surfaced paper.

ENAMELED PAPER: Loosely, any coated paper.

EVENER ROLL: Component of a coating machine which evens out the layer of coating color applied to the paper web.

EXCESS COATING SYSTEM: Coating system that applies an unmetered or partially metered volume of coating color onto the substrate which is greater than the desired or finished amount. A post-coating metering device (e.g., blade, air knife, rod) removes the excess color and conditions or finishes the remaining coating.

EXTRUDATE: Web of hot coating as it emerges from the slot of an extruder.

EXTRUSION COATING: Method of coating used primarily for the application of polyethylene plastic onto a paper substrate. Heated resin is extruded through a slot as a hot film, and is combined immediately with the paper between a pair of rolls, creating a permanent bond between the plastic film and the paper.

F

FILM: Thin application of coating.

FILM COATING: Coating consisting of a pigmented sizing solution, usually applied at the size press. Typically casein is used for the sizing rather than starch because of its greater moisture resistance, which is important if the paper is subsequently printed by the offset process (where dissolution of the binder would result in pigment piling up on the offset blanket during printing). Syn. Skin Coating, Wash Coating, Pigment Sizing.

FILM SPLITTING: Separation of a fluid body into two parts resulting from its adherence to separating solid surfaces. For example, when a wet sheet is peeling off a roll and leaves moisture behind on the roll, the film of moisture at the interface is "splitting" between the sheet and roll surface. Film splitting during roll coating is characterized by a surface with "pile pattern" or "orange peel", especially if the coating color viscosity is too high or if nip pressure (in a size press coater) is excessive.

FISH EYES: (1) Round, transparent spots in the coated surface of pigment coated paper, usually caused by excess defoamer of an oil-base type. (2) Undissolved particles in a solvent coating application.

FLAKING: Defect in coated paper or board where the coating material separates from the sheet in the form of flakes.

FLINT GLAZING: Oldest method of achieving a highly polished coated surface in which the coated paper web travels slowly over a smooth, flat wood or stone surface and a smooth stone or stone burnisher is drawn back and forth over the paper. The method is extremely slow and little used in current practice.

FLITTING: Flapping of the web on the outgoing side of the nip, a condition encountered for some types of roll coaters.

FLOATER DRYER: See AIR FLOTATION DRYER.

FLOCK FINISH: Decorative finish obtained by deposition of short colored fibers on a tacky coating. Several kinds of fibers can be used, and the particular effect depends somewhat on the characteristics of the fibers.

FLOODED NIP APPLICATION: Any roll application of coating color in which the nip between the applicator roll and the backing roll is flooded with coating to develop a hydraulic pressure.

FLOW COATING: Method of applying surface finishes by pouring the coating over the surface and allowing the excess to drain away.

FLOW-ON COATING: Coating applied to the wet web as it is being formed on the paper machine.

FLOW-OUT: Tendency of the coating color applied by a gravure coater to spread into the non-coated areas to form a more favorable coating profile.

FLUIDITY: Ability of a fluid to flow; the reciprocal of viscosity. Syn. Mobility.

FLUIDIZER: Additive used in coating formulations to reduce the viscosity and thixotropy of the coating color.

FOAM COATING: Process whereby a water-based solution of starch or pigmented coating is foamed and applied to the paper web at a roll-to-roll nip or a blade-roll nip.

FOAM SPOTS: See CRATERS.

FOGGING: See MISTING.

FORMULATION: See COATING FORMULATION.

FOUNTAIN BLADE COATER: Blade coater in which the coating color is pumped or extruded through a machine slot directly onto the web prior to the metering blade. Color that is doctored off by the blade is returned to the central reservoir and is refiltered before it is re-applied to the web.

FOUNTAIN COATER: Hot melt coater, in which the coating flows under pressure through a slot, forming a thin sheet which is deposited onto the underside of the web. Syn. Slot Orifice Coater.

FOUNTAIN ROLL: Roll which picks up coating color from a pan and deposits all or part of this amount onto another roll. Syn. Pan Roll, Pickup Roll.

FRICTION CONTROL AGENT: Chemical applied directly to the surface of paper (or as a component in a coating) to either decrease or increase friction. Emulsified mineral oils are common agents for decreasing friction, whereas colloidal silica is used for imparting antiskid properties.

FUNCTIONAL COATING: Coating applied to paper, usually for the purpose of providing a barrier to water, water vapor, air, or grease. Functional coating materials include waxes, asphalt, lacquer, varnish, resins, glues and various plastics. Syn. Barrier Coating.

G

GATE ROLL COATER: Size press-type two-sided coater that utilizes gate rolls to meter a film of coating onto each applicator roll. In this arrangement, the sheet does not pass through a pond of coating color.

GATE ROLLS: Pairs of rolls which perform three functions on a coater: they act as fountain and metering rolls, and they form the bottom of the coating puddle.

GATE ROLL SIZE PRESS: Size press that utilizes gate rolls to meter a film of starch onto each applicator roll. In this arrangement, the sheet does not pass through a pond of sizing solution.

GEL POINT: See COLOR IMMOBILIZATION POINT.

GLOSSING AGENT: Additive to coating color which enhances gloss on the coated surface.

GRAVURE COATING: Roll coating method in which the applicator roll is supplied with coating color from a metal roll engraved with small closely spaced cells or depressions (called the "gravure cylinder").

GUMMING: Coating the surface of paper with a substance that when wetted becomes an adhesive.

H

HAIR MARK: Defect on coated paper due to a bristle (usually from a brush coater) which adheres to the soft calender roll (bowl) and marks or indents the paper on every revolution.

HELICOID CYLINDER: Gravure coating cylinder which utilizes recessed helical grooves (instead of cells) to achieve relatively heavy laydowns.

HIDING POWER: Ability of a pigmented coating to obscure the substrate background.

HIGH-ANGLE BLADE COATER: Blade coater in which the blade rides on both the color and the surface fibers, and the coat weight control is based on the surface void volume of the paper. This volume is controlled by regulating the compression force on the coater blade.

HIGH FINISH: [adj] Term applied to papers with a smooth, hard coating.

HIGH-SOLIDS COATING COLOR: Aqueous pigmented coating dispersion in the 50 to 65% solids range.

HOLD DOWN ROLLS: Adjustable-position web-entry and web-exit rolls which form the wrap angle with the applicator roll and provide the necessary counterpressure when a coating is applied in the kiss coating method. Syn. Entry and Exit Rolls, Lead-In and Lead-Out Rolls, Fly Rolls.

HOT MELT: Any functional coating material that can be applied to the web in a molten state.

HOT MELT COATING: Coating of the web with melted wax, resin, plastic or similar substance followed by cooling. The hot melts are applied at temperatures ranging from 80° to 230°C.

HOT WAXING: Paperboard wax coating in which considerable wax penetration below the surface is encouraged. See also DRY WAXING.

HYDROPHILIC ROLL COATER: Type of transfer roll coater used for on-machine single-sided applications of starch and light pigment coatings. It utilizes a chrome-plated transfer roll that has been treated with a proprietary etching process enabling it to carry wet films 3 to 15 microns thick. The coating is transferred to the sheet against a rubber-covered backing roll.

I

IMMERSION COATING: See DIP COATING.

IMPACT MILL: Type of coating mixer utilizing a double-acting rotor which operates on the principle of impact and attrition rather than shear.

IMPRESSION ROLL: See BACKING ROLL.

INSOLUBILIZER: Additive used in coating formulations to make the dried coated film less sensitive to water.

INTERMEDIATE ROLLS: See TRANSFER ROLLS.

INVERTED BLADE COATER: Coater in which the coating color is applied with a transfer roll and simultaneously leveled and metered by means of a flexible blade.

K _____

KISS ROLL: Generally, any roll contacting the sheet or forming a nip with very light pressure. Syn. Kiss Applicator.

KISS ROLL COATING: Coating operation in which the web passes over the applicator roll without any backup support. Idler rolls are positioned to allow the web a small angle of wrap, 5° to 15°, and the only force keeping the web in contact with the roll surface is the vertical component of the web tension.

KNEADER: Batch mixer for thick coating color consisting of two arms rotating in opposite directions in a vessel with a divided trough. Some designs of kneaders utilize sigma blades (heavy helical shaped blades).

KNIFE COATING: Coating method in which the coating material is maintained in a puddle atop the substrate (usually with backing roll or moving blanket support) and behind an angled knife. The coating material flows out through the adjustable nip between the knife and the substrate. If no backing roll is used for the web, the process is called "floating knife coating".

L _____

LACQUER: Cellulosic derivative substance used as a functional coating for paper, principally applied in a solvent coating operation.

LAYDOWN: Application of coating color.

LEAFING: Orientation of clay platelets in pigmented coatings during drying so that the major dimensions of the particles are parallel to the sheet surface.

LEVELING AGENT: See LUBRICANT.

LOADCELL ROLL: Idling roll fitted with one or two load sensing transducers which measure the pull of the material against the roll due to web tension. Syn. Tension Sensing Roll.

LOW-ANGLE BLADE COATER: Blade coater in which the blade is supported by the color film between the blade and the paper. Coat weight control is based on regulation of the color film thickness and compression of the paper.

LUBRICANT: Component of coating color which serves to lubricate the wet coating and/or the dried coating. For example, soluble stearate soaps (e.g., sodium and ammonium stearate) lubricate the wet coating so that it can be picked up evenly by the applicator roll, and in turn, deposited evenly onto the web. Wax emulsions and insoluble stearate soaps (e.g., calcium and aluminum stearate) principally lubricate the dry coating during supercalendering to give reduced dusting and improved gloss. A lubricant for a wet coating is sometimes called a "leveling agent", while a lubricant for a dry film is better described as a "plasticizer".

M _____

MACHINE COATED: [adj] Term applied to papers that are coated by equipment that is integral to the paper machine.

MAYER ROD: Small-diameter rotating cylinder which has a helical winding of a continuous strand of wire, sometimes used with a turning rod coating system.

MENISCUS COATER: Coater which functions by lowering the web-carrying roll into the coating liquid and then raising it just above the liquid surface to form and maintain a meniscus. The amount of liquid deposited depends on the surface tension and viscosity of the coating material and the web speed. Syn. Bead Coater.

METALLIC COATING: Pigmented coating for paper in which the pigment consists of metallic flakes (e.g., aluminum or bronze powder) and the vehicle is lacquer or a casein solution.

METERING ROLL: Reverse rotating roll that shears excess coating from another roll in order to create a pre-determined thickness of coating on the surface of the roll being wiped. (Note that this roll is never used to remove excess coating from the substrate.) Syn. Doctor Roll, Wiping Roll. See also REVERSE ROLL COATING.

MIGRATION: Physical movement of a coating solvent (along with soluble components) from one position within the sheet to another layer. Typically during pigment coating, capillary forces within the sheet structure cause migration of water souble components into the smaller pores of the sheet, leaving behind at the surface a formation richer in pigment particles. See also BINDER MIGRATION.

MISTING: Entrainment of small droplets of coating color in the deflecting air jet of an air knife coater, usually occurring at higher machine speeds. Syn. Fogging.

MODIFIERS: Ingredients added to coating color to change its properties. See also COATING ADDITIVES.

N

NECK-IN: For extrusion and coextrusion curtain coating, the narrowing of the curtain of resin between the time the melt leaves the die and when it is deposited on the substrate.

NEWTONIAN FLOW: Fluid flow that conforms with Newton's Law which states that the shear stress (i.e., force applied) and shear rate (i.e., flow rate) are always proportional. Since the proportionality constant between shear stress and shear rate is the fluid viscosity, it is apparent that fluid viscosity is constant with increasing shear stress. Newtonian flow is typical for simple fluids, which are referred to as Newtonian fluids.

NEWTONIAN FLUID: See NEWTONIAN FLOW.

NON-CONTACT COATER: Any coater in which the metering device does not contact the coating raw stock. The prime example is the air knife coater.

NON-NEWTONIAN FLUID: Fluid that does not conform with Newton's Law. There are three types of non-Newtonian fluids: see PLASTIC FLUID, PSEUDOPLASTIC FLUID, DILATANT FLUID. In addition, non-Newtonian fluids may exhibit time-dependent behavior: see THIXOTROPIC FLUID.

O

OFFSET GRAVURE COATER: Gravure coating system that employs one or more transfer rolls between the gravure cylinder and the substrate. The purpose of these "offset cylinders" is to improve the wet coating flow-out characteristics, reduce or remove gravure patterning, and enable the unit to apply a more uniform and thinner coating film.

OPAQUE WAXING: Type of wet waxing in which the wax contains a high opacifying filler, usually titanium dioxide. The objective is to achieve water-vapor resistance without transparency.

ORANGE PEEL: See FILM SPLITTING.

ORGANOSOL: See VINYL DISPERSIONS.

OVERCOAT: Coating applied beyond the edge of the sheet which is retained on the backing roll or other backing surface.

P

PAN: See COATING PAN.

PAN ROLL: See FOUNTAIN ROLL.

PARIS WHITE: Very pure form of calcium carbonate, used as a coating pigment.

PARTICLE BINDER: Binder in which the adhesive ingredients (most commonly latex) are present as an emulsion, rather than in solution.

PASTE DISPERSION COATING: Protective coating of vinyl resin particles in a dispersed state surrounded by organic liquid. The organic liquid can be a plasticizer, a plasticizer plus a suitable diluent, or a plasticizer plus a solvent. The protective film forms when the temperature is raised, but the mechanism depends on the composition of the organic liquid.

PATTERN COATING: Special case of hot-melt coating in which folding-grade paperboard is coated in a way that leaves areas of the board uncoated so that those areas are free to accept adhesive in the subsequent carton-sealing operation. The hot melt is premetered on a gravure roll equipped with doctor blade and transferred to a patterned silicone rubber pad from which it is applied to the paperboard.

PICKUP ROLL: Roll that runs partially submerged in a pan of coating color, thus picking up a layer of color on its surface, which it then transfers through a light nip to another roll, usually the applicator roll. If the pickup roll applies coating directly to the web, it is referred to as the applicator roll.

PIGMENT COATING: Coating consisting of fine mineral particles (usually clay) along with binders and other components.

PIGMENT SIZING: See FILM COATING.

PIGMENT VOLUME: Volume occupied by a specified mass of pigment particles, usually determined by liquid displacement.

PIGMENT VOLUME CONCENTRATION: Ratio of pigment volume to total solids volume in a color dispersion, expressed as a percentage. The "critical pigment volume concentration" is that value of the PVC where the binders and other additives just fill the voids between pigment particles.

PILE PATTERN: See FILM SPLITTING.

PITS: Tiny wells or indentations in the surface of coated paper from various causes. Pits appear as white specks in printed areas.

PLASTIC FLUID: Non-Newtonian fluid exhibiting a linear relationship between shear stress and shear rate; but a finite shear stress (known as the "yield stress") is required to initiate flow. An example of a plastic fluid is flocculated (non-dispersed) coating color.

PLASTICIZING: Softening a material by incorporation of a plasticizer or by heating.

PLASTICIZER: Additive used in coating formulations to increase the elasticity and flexibility of the dried coating. Syn. Softener, Calendering Agent. See also LUBRICANT.

PLASTISOL: See VINYL DISPERSIONS.

PLATING: Coating application that contours the surface of the base sheet, (i.e., applies almost equal amounts to hills and valleys) and thus achieves a uniform coating thickness, but not necessarily a smooth level surface. Plating is characteristic of air knife coating.

POLISHED DRUM COATING: Similar to cast coating, except that a polished drying cylinder other than a Yankee cylinder is used to smooth and dry the coating. See also CAST COATING.

POLYVINYL ACETATE LATEX (PVAc): Synthetic binder for coating color. Coatings made with PVAc have excellent gluability, high brightness and good printability; and contribute to substrate stiffness.

POSITIVE ANGLE DOCTOR BLADE: Doctor blade wiper that is pointed toward the direction of roll rotation. Syn. Trailing Angle Doctor Blade.

POST-COATING FINISHING DEVICE: Device (e.g., brush, blade, air knife) that treats or conditions the surface of a wet coating to create a change in its physical appearance.

POST-COATING METERING: Removal of the superfluous part of a wet coating layer from a substrate, leaving a residue which conforms to the desired wet laydown value.

PRECAST COATING: Method of coating in which coating color is applied directly to a highly polished Yankee dryer surface and allowed to dry. The web is treated with adhesive and pressed against the dried coating so that the coating is stripped off and adheres to the paper.

PRECOAT: Film coating applied to the sheet on the machine, so that a lighter coating can subsequently be applied off-machine to make up the total coating weight.

PRE-METERED COATING SYSTEM: Coating system (e.g., gravure coating, reverse roll coating, size press coating) that applies a pre-determined volume of coating color onto the substrate which equals the desired laydown level; post-coating metering is not required.

PREPOLYMERS: Mixtures of organic compounds, usually in the form of viscous liquids, which when activated by heat or ultraviolet radiation polymerize into solids. Prepolymers are utilized as solventless functional coatings.

PRESERVATIVES: Additives used in coating or sizing formulations to retard spoilage of the adhesives (by putrefaction) in the formulation and/or in the finished sheet.

PRESSURE COATING: Coating applied at a size press, or by any other method involving a two-roll nip.

PRIME COAT: First coat in a double or multiple coating sequence.

PRINT-ON COATING: Printing-like method of coating by means of applicator rolls which transfer an accurately measured, evenly distributed film of high-solids coating mixture directly onto the paper.

PROTECTIVE COATING: Transparent coating, typically a lacquer or varnish, applied to an outer surface to protect against moisture, chemical attack or abrasion.

PSEUDOPLASTIC FLUID: Non-Newtonian fluid exhibiting a non-linear relationship between shear stress and shear rate, in which the shear rate increases more rapidly with successive incremental changes in shear stress, i.e., the apparent fluid viscosity decreases with increasing shear stress. An example of a pseudoplastic fluid is starch paste.

PSEUDO-PLASTICITY: See SHEAR THINNING.

PUDDLE-BLADE COATER: See BLADE PUDDLE COATER.

PYROXYLIN COATING: Lacquer coating (cellulose tetranitrate dissolved in a solvent) used as a protective coating over printed stock such as book covers, box coverings, labels, and food wrappers.

R _____

RAILROAD TRACKING: Coating surface defect consisting of long machine-direction striations as viewed under low-angle light, due to excessive localized drying rates which cause variable binder migration.

RAW WEIGHT: Grammage of raw stock before coating.

RECEPTIVITY INDEX: Measure of the surface receptivity of blade coating raw stock. It is the slope of the line obtained when the quantity of test fluid applied is plotted against the square root of the contact time for test conditions similar to those under which commercial trailing blade coaters normally operate. The intercept is a measure of surface roughness and is referred to as the "surface roughness factor".

RECIRCULATING COATING SYSTEM: Coating system that supplies more liquid to the coating puddle, pan, or tank than is being supplied to the material, thus creating an overflow which is returned to the reservoir.

REINFORCING AGENT: Additive used in coating formulations to increase the strength of the dried film.

RELATIVE SEDIMENT VOLUME (RSV): Ratio of the sediment volume to the solid pigment volume. Adhesive demand of a pigment depends on void volume which is equal to (1–1/RSV). Lower RSV corresponds to lower pigment demand. See also SEDIMENT VOLUME.

RELEASE COATING: Coating substance having a low surface tension or low surface energy. The major release coating materials are silicone resins in solutions, emulsions and 100% solids forms. Other materials used to a lesser extent are wax or rosin-wax emulsions, chrome complexes of fatty acids, and fluorocarbons.

REPLENISHMENT COATING SYSTEM: Coating system which maintains the amount of coating color contained in a puddle, pan or tank, but without overflow or recirculation.

REVERSE ANGLE DOCTOR BLADE: Doctor blade wiper that is directed opposite to the direction of roll rotation.

REVERSE ROLL COATING: Method of single-side coating where the applicator roll turns against the surface being coated (backed by a rubber-covered "pressure roll"). The pickup by the applicator roll is controlled by an adjustable doctor and the peripheral speed of the applicator roll is two to three times that of the pressure roll, thus tending to wipe off and smooth the coating surface.

REWETTING AGENT: Additive in coating formulations that permits controlled wetting of the coated surface. Wetting is necessary when the coated paper is subjected to gluing, saturating or multicoat operations.

RHEOLOGY CONTROL AGENT: See VISCOSITY MODIFIER.

RHEOPEXY: Behavior of certain non-Newtonian fluids characterized by a time-dependent buildup of resistance to shear at constant shear rate.

ROD COATING: See TURNING ROD COATING.

ROLL COATING: Method of coating both sides of the web by direct transfer in a nip from rubber applicator rolls. The coating color is metered and spread onto the applicator rolls by means of metering and distributing rolls.

ROTATIONAL VISCOMETER: Instrument that measures liquid viscosity by turning a spindle immersed in the liquid; the resistance to turning is measured by deflection of a spring within the instrument.

RUNNING-IN: Operating a newly installed coating blade against the substrate at slow speed prior to actual production operation in order to ensure a smooth, uniform and non-streaking profile.

S

SEDIMENT VOLUME (SV): Fractional volume occupied by the wet pigment after settling or centrifugation of a pigment dispersion.

SETBACK: Increased viscosity with aging, a problem in handling some starch dispersions and coating colors. Syn. Retrogradation.

SHAFT COATING: Method of coating both sides of the web in which the coating color is metered and applied in a two-roll nip and is then spread and leveled by a series of rollers (i.e., rotating shafts) that contact both sides of the web.

SHAFT STREAKS: Craters formed during shaft coating because of action by the shaft. The craters typically collect in lines on the paper.

SHEAR BLOCKING: Behavior of certain non-Newtonian fluids characterized by a maximum shear rate that cannot be exceeded irrespective of the magnitude of the shearing force.

SHEAR THICKENING: Viscosity increase of non-Newtonian fluid under shear stress. This phenomenon occurs with some organic dispersions. Syn. Dilatancy.

SHEAR THINNING: Viscosity reduction of non-Newtonian fluid under shear stress. Clay slurries, in particular, exhibit pronounced shear thinning behavior. Syn. Pseudo Plasticity.

SHELF LIFE: Length of time between delivery (or manufacture) and end use during which a material will perform according to specifications.

SHORT DWELL: [adj] Term applied to certain blade coaters where the coating color is in contact with the sheet for a relatively short period of time before the excess is metered off by the blade.

SHORT DWELL COATER: Blade coater consisting of a captive pond just before the blade. The pond is slightly pressurized to promote adhesion of the coating to the paper web. Excess color is channeled over a deflector at the incoming side and collected in a return pan before being returned to the color tank.

SINGLE COATED: [adj] Term describing paper that has been coated once on one or both sides. The term should not be confused with "coated one side".

SIZE PRESS COATER: Coater that works on the same principle as a size press, with either vertical, horizontal or inclined arrangement of rolls. Syn. Two-Roll Coater, Roll Pressure Coater.

SKIPS: Randomly patterned surface areas of coated paper that are devoid of coating, indicative of several possible operating problems.

SLIP: Viscous dispersion of a pigment, such as clay in water.

SLOT ORIFICE COATER: See FOUNTAIN COATER.

SLURRY FILTER: Strainer-type device designed to remove oversize particles and agglomerates from coating color. High-frequency, low-amplitude vibrations are often employed during filtration to offset the dewatering tendency of the high-solids pigment dispersion and thus maintain fluidity.

SLURRY PIGMENTS: Paper-coating pigments in slurry form. Approximately 25% of coating pigments are supplied to the mill in the form of a high-solids (about 70%) slurry.

SMOOTHING ROLL COATING: Coating method in which the applied coating color is smoothed out with small rolls that contact the web, some of which rotate in the web direction and some opposite to the web direction.

SOLIDIFICATION SECTION: Section of a coating line where the liquid layer is solidified. There are three basic solidification techniques depending on the type of coating formulation: evaporation of diluents, polymerization of the liquid, and cooling of thermoplastic materials.

SOLIDS CONTENT: Percentage by weight of nonvolatile matter in a coating, adhesive or other aqueous dispersion.

SOLID STATE COATING: Functional coating consisting entirely of coating solids, binders, modifiers and other solid agents, which may be made from a solid thermoplastic material or from a liquid mixture that polymerizes into a solids. Syn. Non-Diluted Coating.

SOLVENT: Liquid used to dissolve a substance and place it in solution. The term usually refers to an organic solvent.

SOLVENT COATING: Coating operation with resin, plastic, etc. dissolved in a volatile solvent. The solvent is subsequently evaporated and recovered leaving behind a functional coating.

SOUR-COATED PAPER: Coated paper which has an offensive odor due to the use of decomposed casein in the coating mixture.

SOY PROTEIN: Extract from soy beans, used as a binder in pigment coating applications. Several types of soy protein are available commercially including unmodified, hydrolyzed, chemically modified, and enzyme treated. Syn. Alpha Protein.

SPANISHED EMBOSSING: Application of coating color to an embossed paper surface which is then wiped with a doctor blade. The color concentrates in the depressions left by the embossing.

SPANISHING: Type of knife coating in which a thin coating layer is deposited on a smooth substrate by means of a flexible scraper.

SPITS: Random spots of excess coating on the surface of coated paper, most commonly due to splashing of the coating color. Syn. Coating Splash.

SPLIT COATING: Coating of one side of a sheet with two applications simultaneously.

SPOT COATING: Coating applied only to a specified area of the sheet.

SPRAY COATING: Method of applying low-viscosity coatings by means of an atomizing process which breaks up the liquid into minute droplets which flow together on the substrate to form a continuous coating film. This method is rarely used for paper substrates.

SPREAD COATING: Coating method in which the coating material (e.g., resins, plastics, adhesives) is maintained in a puddle atop the substrate (which is usually backed with a horizontal support) and behind a vertical plate. The coating material is drawn through the adjustable gap by the forward movement of the web.

SQUEEZE ROLL COATER: See SIZE PRESS COATER.

STALACTITES: Projections of coating buildup extruding from under the coating blade at the outgoing nip. This problem leads to sheet defects such as scratches and streaks. Syn. Feathering, Whiskers.

STEARATES: Fatty acid soaps (mainly of stearic acid) used as coating color lubricant additives and sometimes as internal sizing agents. See also AMMONIUM STEARATE, ALUMINUM STEARATE, LUBRICANT.

STRIATIONS: Pattern of lines or streaks on a coated surface due to uneven application of coating.

STRIKE THROUGH: Penetration of coating through a porous substrate and subsequent offsetting onto a backing roll or surface.

STRUCTURED PIGMENT: Clay that has been structurally modified by thermal or hydrothermal chemical reactions. The most common structured pigment is calcined clay.

STYRENE-BUTADIENE LATEX: Synthetic binder used as the sole adhesive for high-quality pigmented coatings or in combination with various natural or synthetic binders. This versatile binder can be used for all grades of pigmented paper; the color can be applied by any coating unit; and the resultant coating can be printed by any method.

SUBMERSION COATING: See DIP COATING.

SUBSTRATE: Web that is being coated. Typical substrates are coating raw stocks, plastic films, foils, and laminates.

SURFACE ROUGHNESS FACTOR (for blade coating raw stock)**:** See RECEPTIVITY INDEX.

SURFACE VOID VOLUME: Void volume of the surface of paper in relation to a reference plane pressed against the surface. This characterization of surface roughness relates to the amount of coating color retained by the sheet when it is leveled with a high-angle blade. Syn. Surface Roughness Volume.

SUSPENSION: Dispersion of fine solid particles in a liquid.

SYNTHETIC BINDERS: Binder materials of synthetic origin including styrene-butadiene latex, polyvinyl alcohol, and acrylic and polyvinyl acetate emulsions.

T _____

TENSION SENSING ROLL: See LOADCELL ROLL.

THERMAL COATING: Heat sensitive coating applied in the manufacture of thermal papers.

THERMOPLASTIC COATING: Material such as wax, asphalt or plastic applied to a substrate to make it heat sealable. See also HOT MELT COATING.

THICKENING AGENT: Additive used in coating formulations to control the viscosity of the coating color and its water retention properties. Syn. Thickener.

THIN: [adj] Term applied to coatings lacking in viscosity or concentration.

THIXOTROPY: Characteristic behavior of some non-Newtonian fluids, in which a reversible decrease in shear stress occurs over time at a constant rate of shear. A fluid exhibiting thixotropy may be termed a thixotropic fluid, but thixotropy is not a basic type of flow.

TRAILING BLADE: Blade that is pointing in the direction of rotation of the metering roll.

TRAILING BLADE COATING: Any coating method in which excess coating color is removed and the coating is smoothed by a flexible blade bearing against a metal or rubber-covered backup roll for the web. Various trailing blade coating methods differ with respect to how the coating is applied to the web and how long it contacts the web; and with regard to the particulars of the blade itself, its thickness, sharpness, extension from its holder, flexibility, angle of approach to the backup roll, and blade tip loading.

TRANSFER ROLL: Roll that meters and conditions the coating after receiving it from a fountain roll or other transfer roll, and then carries it onto another roll. The transfer roll usually rotates in the same direction as the receiving roll since film splitting is the prime intermediate metering method. Syn. Intermediate Roll.

TRANSFER ROLL COATER: See DIFFERENTIAL ROLL COATING, HYDROPHILIC ROLL COATER.

TROWELING: Spreading and leveling a coating application by means of a blade, bar, rollers, brushes, etc.

TURNING ROD COATING: Any coating method in which a small-diameter turning rod is positioned against the sheet to doctor off excess coating. The turning rod rotates slowly against the direction of sheet travel, so is self-cleaning and eliminates scratches. Syn. Metering Bar Coating.

TWO-BLADE COATER: Coater in which both sides of the web are coated simultaneously by two flexible blade units. The web runs vertically, first through the "applicator nip" consisting of two opposed fountain applicators. Two opposed flexible blades are located immediately above the applicators to smooth out the applied color and doctor off the excess, which is directed into pans located on either side of the web. Syn. Twin-Blade Coater.

TWO-ROLL COATER: See SIZE PRESS COATER.

TWO-SIDED COATER: Coater which coats both sides of the sheet at the same time.

U _____

UNCOATED WEIGHT: See RAW WEIGHT.

V _____

VACUUM COATING: Method of applying very thin layers of certain metals and metal compounds to a material which is enclosed in an extremely low-pressure environment. The common term for a product that has received a vacuum deposited laydown is "metallized".

VARNISH: Generic term for any liquid preparation that, when spread upon a surface, dries to form a hard, lustrous coating. It usually consists of natural or synthetic resins dissolved in a volatile solvent.

VEHICLE: Liquid portion of a coating including the binder.

VINYL DISPERSIONS: Film-forming coatings which are suspensions of vinyl resins in organic liquids that do not dissolve the resin at ordinary temperatures. If the liquid phase consists only of plasticizer, the dispersion is termed a "plastisol". If the dispersing liquid contains volatile components, the dispersion is termed an "organisol".

VISCOMETER: Instrument for measuring the viscosity of a liquid or semi-liquid substance. See also ROTATIONAL VISCOMETER, CAPILLARY VISCOMETER.

VISCOSITY: Resistance to flow.

VISCOSITY MODIFIER: Agent added to coating color to either reduce or increase fluid viscosity. Syn. Rheology Control Agent. See also FLUIDIZER, THICKENING AGENT.

VOIDS: Pinholes or defects that destroy the continuity of a functional coating.

VOID VOLUME: Volume of air in a coating structure, caused by displacement of evaporated water. The void volume and distribution of void spaces has a major impact on the properties of a coating.

W _____

WASH COATING: See FILM COATING.

WATER-BASE COATING: Coating for printing or specialty papers consisting of a solid phase dissolved or dispersed in water. The solid film or layer that remains and adheres to the paper substrate after the water is evaporated may be composed of a combination of adhesives, inorganic minerals or organic compounds. Examples of water-base coatings are aqueous pigmented coatings and sizing solutions.

WATERFALL WETTING: Pressurized application of coating color to the surface of a high-speed gravure cylinder to overcome the adhering air barrier, generally used in combination with a coating pan.

WATER RETENTION AGENT: Agent added to coating color to better retain water within the coating after application, and therefore decrease migration to the surface or into the base sheet.

WAX COATING: Applying a coating of wax to a paper web.

WEB TURNBARS: Air lubricated angle bars which invert the moving web on a coater so that the opposite side of the substrate can be coated.

WET ANGLE: Degrees of rotation during which a coating remains on a wetted cylinder before being transferred or deposited.

WET COVERAGE: Coating or adhesive thickness in the wet state as applied to a surface. Though not measurable, it can be calculated by dividing the volume applied by the area covered. Syn. Wet Mil.

WET STREAKS: Blade coating defect in the form of heavy lines of coating that appear more opaque than the surrounding sheet, most commonly caused by a scratch on the backing roll that gives localized low blade pressure.

WET WAXING: Application of wax as a surface film to one or both sides of the paper where the total amount of wax applied varies between 8 and 16 g/m².

WHISKERS: See STALACTITES.

WIPE RATIO: (1) Relative surface speed of the substrate in relation to the applicator roll in a reverse roll coater. (2) Relative speed of any two reverse direction rolls.

WIPING ANGLE: Angle of the doctor blade with the tangent of the gravure cylinder on a gravure coater.

XYZ _____

YIELD VALUE: Stress necessary to deform a plastic material.

Chapter 18
Paper Finishing and Converting
(Includes Handling and Shipping)

ACETATE LAMINATING: Adhering a thin, clear layer of acetate over printed matter to provide a glossy, protective film.

ADHEREND: Body (or surface) that is being held to another body (or surface) by an adhesive.

ADHESION PROMOTER: Substance applied lightly to a laminating substrate in order to enhance the bonding effect from a subsequently applied adhesive. Syn. Primer.

ADHESION STRENGTH: Force required to cause a separation at the interface of two bonded surfaces or laminates. Syn. Bonding Strength.

ADHESIVE FAILURE: Separation occurring within a multilayer structure due to lack of adherence between materials.

ADHESIVENESS: Measure of how well a gummed paper adheres to another specified surface under prescribed conditions, but not necessarily indicative of how well it adheres to other surfaces nor for how long it will maintain its adhesiveness.

AGAINST THE GRAIN: Folding or feeding paper at right angles to the grain of the paper.

AIR BAGS: Inflatable, disposable bags used to brace loads of paper rolls in rail cars.

AIR FLOAT: Principle of partially supporting piles of paper sheets using low-pressure air to reduce sliding friction. Syn. Flying Carpet.

AIR SWORD: Hollow blade with small holes through which low-pressure air is blown; used to separate stacks of sheeted paper.

ANCHOR COAT: Coating applied to a substrate prior to the application of a pressure-sensitive adhesive to improve anchorage. See also BOND COAT.

ANGLE CUT PAPER: Paper that has been cut at an angle to the machine direction, such as envelope blanks.

ANIMAL GLUE: Proteinaceous material of animal origin (hides, bones, etc.) which is processed for use in adhesives.

ANTI-PENETRANT: Chemical agent added to an adhesive to decrease penetration into the substrate.

ANTISTATIC AGENT: Material used on or in paper to reduce the accumulation of static electricity, and thus minimize the attraction forces between sheets, with other surfaces, or of air-borne dust.

ASEPTIC CARTONS: Laminated paperboard cartons which can keep unrefrigerated juice, milk and other specialty food products fresh for up to six months.

BACK GUARD: Vertical protective framework mounted on the lifting carriage of a high-lift truck to prevent the load or any part of the load from falling back toward the truck operator.

BACKING: Ply of paper, cloth, or other sheeting used as a lining for a sheet material.

BAG: Flexible container made of paper, film or similar material. There is a size distinction between bags and sacks; bags are small containers and sacks are larger containers.

BANDING: Process of applying a metal or fiberglass-reinforced band to secure a package, bale, or palletized load. Syn. Strapping.

BASIC SIZE: Standard dimensional sheet, a ream weight of which has traditionally been used as the basis weight for the paper. For example, 30 lb newsprint refers to the weight of a ream (500 sheets) of basic-size 2 ft by 3 ft sheets.

BEADING: Forming the edge of paper into a tight roll for reinforcement as on the lip of a paper cup.

BENDER: Term for boxboard that has the ability to be scored and folded 180° without rupture of the top liner. Syn. Bending Board.

BITE: Ability of the adhesive to penetrate through the surfaces of the adherends.

BLANK: (1) Piece of board from which a container will be made by further operations. (2) Folding carton after cutting and scoring, but before folding and gluing.

BOND COAT: Initial coating layer, designed to improve the adherence of succeeding coats.

BONDING STRENGTH: Measure of the strength of a bond between two adherends. Syn. Adhesion Strength.

BOND TIME: Time required for a laminate to develop tearing bond after initial preparation.

BOTTOM PAPER: Paper attached to the under surface of a setup box.

BOWED EDGES: Convex or concave edges on trimmed sheets, usually due to wavy or tight edges on the roll being cut, and thus uneven "draw" of the knife.

BOX: Rigid container having closed faces. See also CARTON, CORRUGATED BOARD BOX, SOLID-BOARD BOX.

BOX BLANK: Any pre-cut section of boxboard, in the flat, to be formed into a set-up box or portion of a box.

BOX CAR: General-service freight car, fully enclosed and having doors on both sides.

BRACKET TRIMMER: Machine to trim cut-size papers that is equipped with automatic spacers.

BREAKER ROLL: See DECURLER.

BREATHER: Plastic strip placed across the corner of a stack of sheets to relieve pressure during automatic counting.

BROKEN REAM: Less than a full ream, i.e., less than 500 sheets of paper.

BRUSH DETECTOR: Hole detector which works on the contact principle. The paper web is passed over a grounded metal roller and is contacted by a series of individual metallic brush elements held in place by a large brush housing. When a hole occurs, one or more of the bristles contact the metal roller producing a ground in the circuit.

BUNDLE: (1) Measuring unit for paper or paperboard equal to 50 lbs. The number of sheets in a bundle will depend on the size and grammage of the sheets. (2) Two or more articles bound together without compression to form a package.

BUTT DROP: Drop test of a filled sack onto its bottom, in which stresses occur predominantly in the cross direction of the paper.

BUTT SPLICE: Type of splice formed by placing the trimmed ends of two paper webs together and pasting a strip over and under the juncture; used for thick webs where a lap splice would cause problems in subsequent processing. Syn. Butted Splice, Butted Joint.

C _____

CANT: Full-width web for such converted products as toilet tissue and towelling prior to being sawed into individual packages.

CARLOAD LOT: Quantity of paper in rolls or skids to make up a full freight carload, usually 36,000 to 100,000 lbs.

CARRIER DRUM: Driven roll (or rolls) on certain winding machines that supports and often drives the wound roll (or rolls).

CARTON: (1) General term for a folding paperboard box. See also FOLDING CARTON. (2) Packaging unit of paper sheets, containing a number of reams. For small-sized sheets, the term applied is "junior carton".

CASE: Large packaging unit of paper sheets, containing a number of cartons of small-sized sheets or a number of reams of large-sized sheets.

CASE LOT: Quantity of paper sheets required for a case.

CHOP ANGLE: Angle at the point of contact between the rotating knife of a single rotary cutter and the plane of the sheet on the leading side.

CLAMP TRUCK: Moving equipment for roll paper that employs two opposed clamps which grab and hold the roll during transport. Syn. Grab Truck.

CLAMP TRUCK DAMAGE: Gouging and perforation of paper rolls due to improper use of clamp trucks, mostly as a result of rough, unpadded clamp edges.

COHESIVE FAILURE: Separation of a multi-layer structure occurring either within one of the layered materials or in the adhesive.

COIL: Small, narrow roll of paper, such as for an adding machine or cash register.

COLD CORRUGATING PROCESS: Manufacture of corrugating medium at room temperature with little or no heating of the paperboard components.

COLD PRESSING: Bonding of two or more sheets together in a press using a suitable adhesive without the application of heat.

COLD WATER WAXING: Process of coating paperboard in which the board or blanks are contacted with hot paraffin and then immediately immersed in cold water to prevent penetration. This process produces a high gloss finish.

COMBINED BOARD: Laminated product consisting of two or more layers of paper, paperboard or corrugated board.

COMBINER: Machine for making paperboard by pasting or laminating two or more sheets of paper together. Syn. Combining Unit.

COMBINING ADHESIVE: Adhesive used with either a corrugator or combiner.

COMBINING UNIT: See COMBINER, ROLLER PRESS, LAMINATING MACHINE.

COMBINING WINDER: Winder which is capable of bringing together two or more webs into a common roll. It differs from a conventional winder mainly at the unwind station where multiple unwinds and associated control equipment are utilized.

COMBINING WINDING: Process of combining two or more webs into one roll, the most common example being the assembling of 2-ply or 3-ply tissue.

COMPOSITE CANS: Containers produced by the spiral or convoluted winding of two or more binder-coated paperboard strips around a mandrel. Depending on the intended service, the board is first laminated with plastics or foil, or coated with hot melts or other specialty coatings. The formed tube is cut on the mandrel to desired sizes. Either metal or plastic caps are used to seal the ends. See also CONVOLUTE WINDING, SPIRAL WINDING.

COMPRESSION TEST ESTIMATION: Estimation of how much compression strength a box will have before it is made, based on corrugated board strength, box design criteria and other relevant inputs.

CONDITIONING: Treatment given to high-grade printing papers in which moisture is added to the roll web so that any expansion takes place before the paper is cut into sheets. Typically, the paper is subjected to high-velocity impingement of humidified air as the web passes over successive drums; the driest areas of the sheet preferentially absorb moisture from the air, and the resultant web has a higher and more uniform moisture content without built-in stresses and has virtually no static electrical charge.

CONTAINERIZATION: Unitizing, grouping or consolidating of multiple units into a larger container for efficient movement.

CONVERTER: Plant that carries out converting operations and produces end products such as bags, envelopes, corrugated boxes, etc. An "independent converter" is not affiliated with a primary producer of paper and board. Syn. Converting Plant.

CONVERTER WASTE: Waste paper in the form of cuttings and discards that are created as a byproduct of converting operations. Converter waste is usually a homogeneous grade, available in predictable volume, and free of most contaminants.

CONVERTIBILITY: Ability to convert paper into different products or different roll forms without problems.

CONVERTIBILITY EFFICIENCY: Ratio of the actual flat crush value of combined board to that predicted by the Concora test of the corrugating medium.

CONVERTING: Seconday processing or manufacturing of end products utilizing basic grades of paper and board as the major raw materials. (Printing of newspapers, magazines, books, etc. is generally considered apart from converting; however many converting plants utilize printing as one stage of a converting process.)

CONVERTING OPERATION: In the broadest sense, any operation which takes place after the paper is made that changes the dimensions of the product, the shape of the product, the surface characteristics of the product, or the properties of the product. Converting operations are usually grouped according to whether the paper is handled in roll form (called "wet converting") or made into actual products (called "dry converting").

CONVERTING PAPERS: Paper mill products that may undergo subsequent converting operations and be transformed into other products with properties and characteristics quite distinct from the original papers.

CONVERTING PLANT: See CONVERTER.

CONVERTING WINDER: Winder that converts a parent roll into smaller rolls of different sizes.

CONVOLUTE WINDING: Style of winding in which a tube of fixed length is formed by having each ply placed directly over the previous ply, i.e., the length of tube is equal to the width of paper from which it is wound.

CORE WASTE: Paper left on a roll after all the usable paper has been run out.

CORRUGATED BOARD: Structure formed from one or more paperboard facings (sometimes erroneously called liners) and one or more adjoining corrugated members (fluted portion), used for making corrugated board boxes and other products.

CORRUGATED BOARD (cont):
The various structures are:
  SINGLE FACE: Formed by one corrugated member glued to one flat facing.
  SINGLE WALL (or **DOUBLE FACE**): Formed by one corrugated member glued between two flat facings.
  DOUBLE WALL: Formed by three flat facings and two intermediate corrugated members.
  TRIPLE WALL: Formed by four flat facings and three intermediate corrugated members.
Syn. Corrugated Combined Board, Containerboard, Corrugated Fiberboard.

CORRUGATED BOARD BOX: Rigid shipping container, made of corrugated board, having closed faces and completely enclosing the contents. The designation of box, as opposed to carton, infers that it meets the requirements as an outer shipping container.

CORRUGATED WRAPPING: Usually single face corrugated board; sometimes just the fluted corrugated medium.

CORRUGATING: Imparting of a wavelike shape to paper or board by passing the heated and steam-softened web between two intermeshing metal rolls cut with alternate ridges and grooves. Syn. Fluting

CORRUGATIONS: See FLUTES.

CORRUGATOR: Combination of several machine units running in line with each other which take linerboard and corrugating medium in roll form and convert them into corrugated board sheet blanks.

COTTONING: Formation of web-like filaments of adhesive between various machine parts or between machine parts and the receiving surface during transfer of liquid adhesive onto the receiving surface.

COUNT: Number of sheets required to make up a standard unit of a particular kind of paper.

COUNTING: Determination of the number of sheets in a stack by manual or mechanical counting of the individual sheets.

CREASING: Impressing a groove into heavy paper or paperboard to facilitate folding.

CROSS CUTTING: Action of the knife section of a sheeter. Syn. Chop Cutting.

CROSS LAMINATE: See LAMINATE.

CURING: Changing the physical properties of an adhesive or other substance by chemical reaction (condensation, polymerization or vulcanization), usually initiated by the action of heat and/or catalyst (with or without pressure).

CUSTOM SHEETING: Service provided by certain paper mills or converters, who receive rolls of paper from a customer, cut and trim it to the customer's specifications, and ship the sheeted paper back to the customer.

CUT-OFF: On a corrugator, the length of the sheet being made.

CUTOFF KNIFE: Device on a sheeter for cutting across the web, of which three types are common in the industry: single rotary (also called fixed bed knife), electromechanical double rotary, and electric double rotary.

CUTSCORING: Partially cutting through heavy paper or board to facilitate folding.

CUT SIZE SHEETS: Generally refers to business and writing papers that have been rotary trimmed or guillotine cut to dimensions of 8½ x 11 or 8½ x 14 inches and wrapped in packages of 500 sheets. The term may also be applied to other papers up to a maximum of 16 x 21 inches.

CUT STOCK: Material which has been cut to proper dimension, such as paper, paperboard or corrugated board.

CUTTER: See SHEETER.

CUTTER BROKE: Waste and trimmed edges from the cutter operations. This broke is combined with other broke streams and is repulped and re-used as furnish to the paper machine.

CUTTER DUST: Small particles of fiber and paper dust that result from the cutting operation. These particles adhere to the edges of the paper and, due to relative sheet movement, are carried into the sheet pile and onto the paper surfaces to cause later problems during printing.

CUTTER SET: Matched rolls put on the sheet cutter, so that an equal number of sheets is cut from each roll simultaneously.

CUTTER WRINKLES: Random creases or folds in the sheet running at slight angles to the machine direction, caused by the baggy condition of paper being cut or uneven feed into the cutter pull rollers.

CUTTING TOLERANCE: Permitted variation in sheet length after sheeting.

CUT TO REGISTER: Paper cut in a manner that allows the watermark to appear in a specified position on the finshed sheet.

D

DEAD KNIFE: Fixed blade of a cutter against which the rotating knife cuts.

DECURLER: Equipment for mechanically removing curl from roll paper by passing the web under tension over a bar or small-diameter roll (called a "breaker roll") that stretches the sheet in the direction opposing the curl.

DEFECT DETECTOR: See FLAW DETECTOR.

DEHYDRATION: Loss of moisture from paper subsequent to manufacture due to exposure in a high-temperature and/or low-humidity environment.

DELAMINATION: Separation of layers in a laminate.

DELIVERY TABLE: Surface upon which paper sheets from a sheeter are automatically stacked following cutting.

DEXTRIN: Carbohydrate, produced by hydrolysis from starch, used as an adhesive for gummed papers.

DIE CUTTING: Stamping out paper or board in a specified shape or size by means of a steel die.

DIPPING: Essentially the same as tub sizing, but always carried out off-machine by converters on narrow purchased rolls.

DIP SHEAR CUTTING: Manufacturer's term to describe knife movement during guillotine cutting.

DISHING: Forming a pile (of paper sheets) in which the sides are higher than the center.

DOG EAR: Corner of sheet which becomes folded during sheeting operations and remains this way during trimming. When the foldover is unfolded, it extends beyond the corner of the sheets.

DOLLY: Low platform or structure mounted on small wheels or casters, used for moving loads short distances.

DOUBLE FACE: See CORRUGATED BOARD.

DOUBLE FACER: Principal component of a single-wall corrugator which brings the fluted medium together with the faces and applies adhesive.

DOUBLE POPS: Refers to a burst test on corrugated board when one liner bursts first and the second one later. (Note that the burst test on corrugated board is solely a function of the quality of the facings and is insensitive to the quality of the fluted medium.) Syn. Double Burst.

DOUBLE ROTARY CUTTER: Sheet cutter having two rotating knives.

DRAW: Displacement of the cut sheet by the thickness of the knife during paper trimming, a source of inaccurate cut size.

DRAW ROLLS: Wrapped, driven rolls which pull the paper web from the unwind stand into the cutting section of a sheeter. If a nip is used, the term "squeeze rolls" may be applied. Where one roll in the nip is wrapped, it may be called a draw roll and the other called a squeeze roll.

DRILLING: Piercing stacks of paper precisely with a high-speed, hollow drill. Looseleaf notebook paper is an example of drilled paper.

DROP TESTS: Procedures for evaluating various shipping sack or bag constructions by the repetitive dropping of filled sacks or bags at different heights and orientations, and assessing any failures. See also BUTT DROP, FACE DROP.

DRY CONVERTING: Converting operations in which such end products as bags, envelopes, and boxes are produced. See also WET CONVERTING.

DRYING TIME: Time between application of an adhesive and reaching equilibrium with the moisture in the substrate or in the air.

DRY LAMINATING: Joining together two substrates to form a multiply structure using a dry bonding agent.

DUNNAGE: Bracing or supports for holding a load in position during transport for the purpose of preventing damage to the load.

DUPLEX SHEETER: Sheeter which simultaneously produces two different-length sheets.

E

EDGE PROTECTORS: Heavy board covering used to protect the ends of rolls against damage during handling and transit. See also END BANDS.

EMBOSSER: Machine that operates in a similar manner to a single-nip supercalender, except that the chrome-plated upper steel roll has a pattern engraved on it and is designed to be steam-heated. The lower roll, whose diameter is typically double that of the upper roll, consists of soft fibrous material, and serves as a backing roll for the paper web as it receives the pattern from the upper roll. Syn. Embossing Calender.

EMBOSSING: Passing a web between a steel roll with a raised surface pattern and a soft roll (e.g., paper, cotton, rubber, plastic, etc.), sometimes with a matching indented surface. See also FRICTION EMBOSSING, HOT EMBOSSING, PRINT EMBOSSING, SPANISHED EMBOSSING.

END BANDS: Wraps of heavy paper at the ends of rolls to provide protection against damage. See also EDGE PROTECTORS.

ENVELOPE: Flexible container, usually made of paper, having two faces and joined at three edges to form an enclosure. The non-joined edge provides an opening for filling which may later be closed by a gummed flap, tie string or other method.

EXTENDER: Low-cost material added to a coating or adhesive to reduce the concentration of the active ingredients.

EXTRAS: Sheets in excess of 500 within a ream of paper.

EXTRUSION LAMINATING: Joining together two interfacing webs utilizing a continuous extruded film of molten plastic as the bonding agent. The plastic material gives the entire structure additional strength and protective properties.

F _____

FACE: Any of the plane surfaces of a container.

FACE DROP: Drop test of a filled sack on its flat side, in which the paper is exposed to biaxial stress, i.e., forces are applied in both the machine direction and cross direction.

FACING: (1) One of the two outer layers of a laminate. (2) Linerboard used as any flat member of corrugating board (sometimes erroneously termed liner).

FANNING: (1) Inspecting stacks of paper manually for defects. (2) Riffling of sheets in a trimmed pile to relieve any "welding" together of edges from trimming.

FAULT DETECTOR: See FLAW DETECTOR.

FEATHERING: See STRINGINESS.

FESTOON SPLICE: Splice formed between two stationary webs while the machine remains at full or limited production. A festoon or accumulator roller system stores material during normal operation, and this reserve material feeds the machine when the rollstands are inoperative during roll changes.

FIBER DRUM: Cylindrical shipping container designed for use as an unsupported outer package. The body is formed by winding adhesive-coated paper around a mandrel or cylindrical form until the required thickness is built up.

FIBER TEAR: Separation within the fibrous sheet structure when a glued assembly is pulled apart, as opposed to a failure at the paper/adhesive interface or within the adhesive layer.

FILM: Thin, unsupported, non-fibrous plastic membrane.

FINGERLESS SINGLE FACER: Single facer without the fingers which on traditional designs hold the fluted medium in place until it bonds to the single facing. The fingerless design utilizes a positive hold to the lower corrugating roll, either by application of vacuum or positive pressure.

FINISHED PRODUCTION: Tonnage produced from the paper mill in finished form. Finished production is equal to the on-grade paper machine production less trim and broke losses during winding and less finishing broke losses.

FINISHING: Vague term within the paper industry referring to any of the following: (1) imparting surface finish. (2) occurring in the finishing room. (3) applying the final operations in a production process. (4) preparing for shipment.

FINISHING BROKE: Discarded paper resulting from any finishing operation.

FINISHING DEFECTS: Various product defects that can arise during sheet finishing operations, such as out-of-square sheets, folded corners, poorly trimmed sheets, short-count reams, etc.

FINISHING OPERATIONS: Wide range of operations to prepare paper products for shipment, including winding, slitting, cutting, sorting, counting, cartoning, palletizing, and wrapping. Some specific finishing operations could also be described either as converting operations or packaging operations.

FINISHING ROOM: Area of the paper mill in which paper from the paper machine is further processed into packages for shipment. Syn. Finishing Department.

FINISHING ROOM EFFICIENCY: Shipped tons divided by the tons off the winder, expressed as a percentage.

FIRM GLUING: Term applied to corrugated board box construction, indicating when mutilation of the surface fibers accompanies separation of joined areas.

FLAP: Closing member of a box, carton or envelope.

FLAT BUNDLING: Method of packaging paper sheets in which the desired quantity is placed between two sheets of heavy paperboard, then wrapped with heavy water-proof paper and securely tied or strapped.

FLAW DETECTOR: Sensing device for continuously surveying the moving web and detecting flaws in the sheet. Under this general heading are included hole detectors, wrinkle detectors, lump detectors, and spot detectors.

FLOATING LOAD: Arrangement of paper packages in a freight car that allows some shifting without damage if the car is bumped in transit.

FLOW POINT: Temperature during heating at which a gelled material (e.g., adhesive paste) begins to exhibit liquid properties. Syn. Pour Point.

FLUFF OUT: Partial disengagement of the corrugated medium from the corrugating roll following fluting, just prior to contact with the glue applicator roll.

FLUTE CONTOUR: Flute configuration which is characterized by the thickness dimension, the number of flutes per lineal unit length, and the take-up ratio. The four standard contours are referred to as A-flute, B-flute, C-flute, and E-flute.

FLUTES: Undulations formed into the corrugating medium during the manufacture of corrugating container board. Syn. Corrugations.

FLUTING: See CORRUGATING.

FLYING SPLICE: Mechanism on the unwind stand of a coating or converting machine which allows the lead end of a new roll of paper to be connected (spliced) to the tail end (or near the tail end) of an expiring roll without stopping or slowing down the machine.

FLY KNIFE: Rotating knife of a cutter.

FOIL: Thin metal membrane.

FOLDER: Machine or machine component which carries out a folding operation on such items as cartons, envelopes, and bags.

FOLDER-GLUER: Machine for folding a box blank (which has previously been slotted and scored) and gluing it to form a three-dimensional structure.

FOLDING CARTON: Paperboard container, manufactured by means of cutting and scoring operations, which is shipped in collapsed form and not set up until used. Syn. Folding Paper Box.

FOLDING-TYPE SPREADER: Spreading system wherein a slitted web wraps one bowed roll to separate the adjacent webs, and then wraps a second spreader roll or bar to regain parallel running, thus setting the web spacing and equalizing the stresses on the edges of the webs.

FOLIO-SIZE SHEETS: Paper sheets that are 17 x 22 inches.

FORK-LIFT TRUCK: Self-loading truck designed to lift a load on large forks, carry it and deposit it at relatively high levels.

FORMAT: Essentially, the specified form in which paper and paperboard products are sold. For sheets, the format includes sheet dimensions and grain orientation. For rolls, the format includes roll width, diameter or mileage, and core specifications.

FORMER: That part of a machine for manufacturing paper bags around which the web of paper is formed and seam pasted or heat sealed into a tube.

FRACTURES: Disruptions in the structure of corrugated medium during the fluting operation due to tensile and bending stresses.

FREIGHT RULES: Carrier regulations which constitute the ground rules governing the manufacture, marketing, sales, production, and end uses of corrugated board shipping containers. In the USA the principal regulations are embodied in Rule 41 of the "Uniform Freight Classification" for rail transport and Item 22 of the "National Motor Freight Classification" for truck transport.

FRICTION: Resisting force to movement that arises when one surface slides or tends to slide over another surface. See also STATIC FRICTION, KINETIC FRICTION.

FRICTION EMBOSSING: Passing a web between a heated steel roll with a raised pattern and a smooth paper roll run without gearing. Syn. Slip Embossing.

G _____

GLUE JOINT: Specific portion of a fabricated product which comprises the adhering parts.

GLUING: See FIRM GLUING.

GRAIN LONG: [adj] Describes a paper sheet which has its longest dimension parallel to the paper grain. Syn. Long Grain.

GRAIN SHORT: [adj] Opposite of grain long. Describes a paper sheet which has its shortest dimension parallel to the paper grain. Syn. Short Grain.

GUILLOTINE: Machine equipped with a heavy removable knife for trimming or dividing stacks of paper with a downwards slicing action. Syn. Trimmer, Trimmer Press.

GUMBALLING: Formation of large sticky agglomerates, as sometimes occurs during dispersion of certain adhesives.

H _____

HARDENER: Substance added to an adhesive to promote the curing reaction. Syn. Hardening Agent.

HARD FOLD: Method of preparing large paper sheets for shipment in which a small number of sheets at a time are folded over by hand and compressed with a round stick. The sheets retain a crease.

HIGH-LOWS: Defect in corrugated board due to the formation of flutes of inconsistent height, most commonly caused by the inability of the corrugating machine to provide sufficient heat and moisture to properly condition the medium at the prevailing speed.

HOLE DETECTOR: Equipment that views a running web to detect clear voids, but does not detect other sheet flaws. Both contacting and non-contacting types are used.

HOT EMBOSSING: Embossing with heated rolls or plates.

HOUSEHOLD ROLL: Small roll of packaging material for household use.

HUMECTANT: Substance that promotes retention of moisture.

I _____

IMPREGNATING: Process of running a web of paper or paperboard through a liquid bath in which the sheet becomes saturated. The liquid may be molten asphalt or wax, a solution, or an oil. Syn. Saturating.

IMPREGNATION TIME: Time required for a liquid of definite composition and viscosity to penetrate completely from one face of a sheet of paper to the other under specified conditions.

INCLINE IMPACT TEST: Performance test for corrugated board shipping containers which simulates the forces applied to a packaged product when it is subjected to sudden starts and stops in a carrier vehicle.

INSPECTION: Surveillance for faulty product, which may be carried out manually or automatically during papermaking, coating, or conversion operations.

INTERFACE: Area of contact between two surfaces.

INTERFACING: Bringing two surfaces into contact.

J _____

JACKET: Hollow metal covering for process equipment containing circulating steam or water, used for heating or cooling the process stream.

JOB LOT: Order of paper made up from overs and seconds, sold at a reduced price. Syn. Odd Lot.

JOGGING: Producing a smooth-sided pile of paper sheets by jarring the sides of the pile against a smooth flat vertical surface.

JOINT: (1) That part of a box where the ends of the sheet are joined together by taping, stitching or gluing. (2) Any laminated area.

K _____

KINETIC FRICTION: Resisting force to continuance of one surface sliding over another surface, after movement has begun.

KNIFE EDGE: That edge of a paper sheet that has been cut with a rotary knife.

L _____

LABELER: Mechanical device or machine, available in many styles and types, for applying labels to packages.

LABYRINTH: Forming nip between two corrugating rolls wherein fluting of corrugating medium takes place.

LAMINANT: Bonding agent used to combine two or more interfacing web materials into a laminate. The laminant is often selected for its barrier qualities.

LAMINATE: Laminated product. Where two or more layers of paper or paperboard are combined to achieve greater thickness and rigidity, the product is called "combined board". Often, other substances like thin sheets of metal or plastic are fused with paper. If some of the layers are oriented at right angles to the remaining layers with respect to the grain direction or direction of greatest strength, the product is called a "cross laminate". If all the layers have the same orientation, the product is called a "parallel laminate". See also LAMINATED PAPER.

LAMINATED PAPER: Laminated product in which at least one layer is paper.

LAMINATING: Fusing together two or more similar or dissimilar interfacing webs into a product of the desired thickness and quality. See also WET LAMINATING, DRY LAMINATING, EXTRUSION LAMINATING, PRESSURE LAMINATING, THERMOPLASTIC LAMINATING.

LAMINATING MACHINE: Machine for bonding together two or more continuous webs of layers of material.

LAMINATION: (1) Process of laminating. (2) Any layer in a laminate.

LAP SPLICE: Type of splice that utilizes an overlap between the ends of the web that are spliced. This general method is used in the majority of splices.

LAYERING: Conversion operation in the manufacture of certain tissue products in which several low grammage sheets are formed into a multiply sheet. The added bulk and void spaces between plies provide additional softness. The layers may be laminated in a quilted fashion through embossing.

LAY FLAT: Non-warping and non-wrinkling characteristics of laminates.

LEANING FLUTES: Nonsymmetrical flutes, a fabrication defect during manufacture of corrugated board.

LIFT: Maximum number of sheets of paper placed at one time under the knife of a cutting machine.

LINER: Paperboard sheet with a soft finish inserted in a container, usually covering all side walls, to cushion and protect the contents.

LOG: Full-width, small-diameter tissue roll from the winder prior to being sawn into individual tissue rolls.

LONG GRAIN: See GRAIN LONG

LOWERATOR: Platform elevator which can only move loads from a higher elevation to a lower elevation, typically utilized in paper mills to move rolls or pallets from the finishing room area to a lower warehouse area.

LUMP DETECTOR: Equipment that views a running web to detect raised caliper imperfections. Both contacting and noncontacting types are used.

M _____

MARKS: Numbers, symbols and other information placed on the outer surface of a paper roll or package to facilitate identification, handling and shipment.

MATRIX EMBOSSING: Embossing both sides of the web.

MERCHANT BRAND: Paper marketed and sold under the brand name of the merchant (distributor), converter or customer. Syn. Private Brand. See also MILL BRAND.

MILL BRAND: Paper marketed and sold under the brand name of the manufacturer. See also MERCHANT BRAND.

MILL EDGE: (1) Sheet edge produced by slitters or cutters, as contrasted with that produced by a guillotine which provides a smoother and more accurate cut. (2) Slightly rough edge of untrimmed sheets.

MILL LINING: Off-machine operation of pasting a paper lining onto a finished paperboard web. (The corresponding on-machine operation is called "vat lining".)

N _____

NIPPING ROLLER: Soft-covered roller which can be pneumatically or hydraulically loaded against a driven metal roller. Syn. Nip Roll, Pressure Roll.

O _____

OFFCUT: Part of a sheet removed during processing, the size of which is large enough to be salvaged for purposes other than repulping.

OFF SQUARE: [adj] Term applied to paper sheets which have been cut or trimmed so that two or more corners deviate from an exact 90° angle.

OPEN ASSEMBLY TIME (for laminating operations): Maximum time interval between application of adhesive to one or both substrates and the bringing together of the substrates within which a satisfactory bond can be achieved. Syn. Open Time.

OPPOSITE DIMENSION: Dimension of a paper sheet at right angles to the grain direction.

OUTER SHIPPING CONTAINER: Any container which meets the handling requirements of Rule 41 of the Uniform Freight Classification. See also FREIGHT RULES.

OUT-OF-JOG: [adj] Term applied to a stack of paper sheets with protruding sheets.

OUTSIDES: Defective paper sheets which are placed at the top and bottom of a pile of paper sheets during packaging.

OUTSIDE WASTE: Wastepaper from the outside of a paper roll consisting of the wrapper plus unusable paper from the outer plies of the roll.

OVERCUTTING: Producing oversize sheets at the bottom of a cut pile, usually caused by incorrect settings on a guillotine trimmer.

OVERSIZE PAPER: Paper intentionally cut to a larger size for subsequent trimming to a specified size.

P _____

PACKAGE: Individually wrapped unit of paper product.

PALLET: Tray or platform for lifting and moving materials, used in conjunction with a fork lift truck. There is a clear distinction between a pallet and skid. The cheaply-made and expendable pallet consists of support boards nailed on top and bottom to either 2 x 4's or to 4-inch square blocks. See also SKID.

PALLETIZING: Operation of stacking uniform packages or bales on a pallet.

PAPER WASTE: Portions of the paper roll that are unusable for various reasons, but are salvaged for return (as broke) to the paper or board mill. See also CORE WASTE, TRIM WASTE, OUTSIDE WASTE.

PARAFFINING: Application of paraffin to paper or paperboard.

PARALLEL LAMINATE: See LAMINATE.

PARENT REAM: Large-size ream, from which smaller-size reams are cut by a guillotine.

PASTE: Adhesive having a characteristic plastic-type consistency. The term is also applied to any preparation of similar consistency.

PEELING BOND: Adhesive bond between two paper surfaces that can be pulled apart without tearing of the interfacial fibers, as distinct from a "tearing bond" where fibers are pulled out during separation.

PEEL WASTE: Damaged outer wraps of containerboard rolls.

PHENOLIC RESIN: Synthetic resin produced by condensation of phenol with formaldehyde, used for thermosetting laminates and as a component in adhesives, lacquers and varnishes.

PILE CURL: Aggregate tendency of a pile of similarly oriented sheets to curl, when the top of the pile is unrestricted.

PIN ADHESION: Compression test which measures selectively the force required to separate either the inside or outside facing of corrugated board. "Support pins" and "pressure pins" are inserted in a sample which is then placed on the plates of a compression machine and the force required for separation is determined.

POLYMERIC IMPREGNATED BOARD: Usually refers to corrugated board in which the fluted medium has been impregnated with a polymeric material during the fluting and assembly process.

POT LIFE: Period of time during which a mixed batch of adhesive remains usable. At the end of its pot life, an adhesive is said to be "over the hill" or "kicked".

POUR POINT: See FLOW POINT.

PRECISION SHEETER: Sheeter that accurately cuts and piles the sheets without the need for trimming.

PRESS TRIMMING: Precision trimming of paper piles using a guillotine or similar type of trimmer.

PRESSURE LAMINATING: Combination of dry and thermoplastic laminating processes in which two webs, one or both of which have been previously treated with a pressure bonding agent, are combined under pressure. Three types of pressure bonding agents are used: pressure sensitive, thermally activated, and pressure activated.

Q _____

QUIRE: 24 or 25 sheets (depending on grade) or 1/20th of a ream.

R _____

REAM: Unit package of paper containing either 480 or 500 sheets depending on the grade.

REAM MARKER: Small rectangular slip of paper inserted in a stack of paper to mark off a ream.

REAM WEIGHT: Weight of a given ream of paper. The ream weight is the traditional measurement of basis weight.

REAM WRAPPED: [adj] Describes paper that is packaged in reams.

RECTANGULARITY: See SQUARENESS.

RECTIFYING: Adding sheets to a partial ream to bring it up to the standard number of sheets.

REJECT GATE: Fast-acting mechanism on a precision sheeter which allows single or multiple sheets to be rejected either by manual control or by a signal from any flaw detector.

REPROCESS WINDING: Winding operation that makes necessary changes to rolls which for one reason or another were not wound in finshed form on the paper machine winder.

REREELER: Type of winder for handling reels directly from the paper machine. It is on the rereeler that breaks in the web are spliced to allow continuous operation on a subsequent coater or other converting operation. Some of these machines take two reels and wind them into one large continuous reel.

REWINDER: Equipment which slits and rewinds paper into smaller rolls, or simply rewinds a defective roll for salvage. Syn. Tertiary Winder. See also SALVAGE WINDER.

RIGHT SIDE (of paper): Side of a sheet of paper from which a watermark can be read; this is the top or felt side for machine-made paper, but the wire side for handmade paper.

RIGID BOXES: See SETUP BOXES.

RIPPLE FINISH: Dimpling effect on the sheet surface achieved by passing the web through an embossing nip composed of male and female steel rolls.

ROLL CURL: See WRAP CURL.

ROLLER PRESS: Equipment to effect bonding of a laminate by passing the web assembly between pressure-loaded rollers, as distinct from a platen press where the assembly is placed between two loaded flat surfaces. Syn. Roll Press, Combining Unit, Combining Nip.

ROLLSTOCK: Designation for paper or paperboard in roll form, especially rolls that are utilized in finishing and converting operations.

ROTARY PAPER: Designation for paper in roll form. See also ROLLSTOCK.

S _____

SACK: Flexible container made of paper, film or similar material. There is a size distinction between bags and sacks; bags are small containers and sacks are larger containers.

SALVAGE WINDER: Equipment for rewinding rolls that have previously been wound in an unsatisfactory way. Syn. Reclaim Winder.

SAMPLE BOOK: See SWATCH BOOK.

SCORING: Impressing a crease into paperboard between two metal surfaces to facilitate a subsequent folding operation. The scoring allows the paperboard to be readily folded with minimum cracking.

SCOTCH: Wooden wedge or "stopblock" placed under a paper roll to prevent slipping or rolling.

SEALED: [adj] Describes paper that is contained in sealed packages.

SEALING STRENGTH (of petroleum wax): Force necessary to separate strips of paper sealed together with wax when the force is applied at an angle of 180° under specified conditions. The sealing strength of wax is related to its performance in the manufacture of heat-sealable waxed papers.

SENIOR-SIZE SHEETS: Any sheets larger than folio size.

SET TIME: Time required after application of an adhesive to achieve a specified bonding strength. Syn. Rate Of Set.

SETTING: Converting an adhesive into a fixed or hard state. Depending on the particular adhesive, the mechanism of setting may be by chemical action (e.g. condensation, polymerization, oxidation, vulcanization, gelation, hydration) or by physical action (e.g. evaporation of volatile constituents).

SETUP BOXES: Boxes that are manufactured and shipped in finished form, as contrasted with folding cartons that are shipped flat. Syn. Rigid Boxes.

SHAFTLESS MOUNTING: Method of roll mounting utilizing two independent core chucks to support the roll at each end.

SHEET: Single piece of pulp, paper or board, generally rectangular in shape.

SHEET CALENDERING: Process of passing individual sheets of paper or board through a calender stack using sheet feed equipment, for the purpose of applying a finish or glaze to the sheets.

SHEETER: Equipment assembly consisting of an unwind stand, cutter/slitter, delivery section, and piler, which is used to cut paper from parent rolls into sheets of specific length and width, but sometimes requiring further trimming to finished size. Syn. Conventional Sheeter, Cutter, Slitter-Cutter, Cross Cutter, Rotary Sheeter. See also PRECISION SHEETER, SIMPLEX SHEETER, DUPLEX SHEETER.

SHEETING: Cutting a continuous web across the grain into sheets. Sheeting traditionally has been a separate operation following slitting; but in current practice, sheeting and slitting are often carried out on the same machine. Syn. Rotary Sheeting.

SHEET ROLL: Roll of paper destined to be finished into sheets on finishing room equipment.

SHORT GRAIN: See GRAIN SHORT.

SILICATING: Treatment of paperboard with sodium silicate to impart a smooth hard finish. The same treatment is given to paper sheets used as interleaving for sticky materials.

SIMPLEX SHEETER: Sheeter which cuts to a single sheet length during a production run.

SINGLE FACE: See CORRUGATED BOARD.

SINGLE FACER: Corrugator or portion of a corrugator which produces single-face corrugating board.

SKATING: Riding on a layer of air; as for example when a high-speed web wraps a drum where the air carried on the underside of the web becomes entrapped and serves as a slip bearing. Syn. Air Flotation.

SKID: Platform used for handling and moving material, consisting of a solid wooden floor nailed securely to two runners. See also PALLET.

SKIVER WINDER: Winder in which two or more small-width rolls are joined by means of gluing adjoining overlapping skived edges in order to form one or more rolls of salable width. This salvage operation is most commonly carried out on corrugating medium trim rolls where differences in appearance between rolls is not important.

SKIVING: Cutting off a thin layer; for example, removing a portion of paperboard thickness. When two edges of a web are joined by lapping, the overlapping edges are skived to obtain a continuous sheet of uniform thickness.

SLABBING: Cutting slabs or lifts of paper out of a roll which is later cut to size on a guillotine.

SLIPPAGE: Relative movement between two adherends during the bonding process.

SLIP SORTING: Ultimate method of manual inspection of paper sheets in which each individual sheet is transferred from one stack to another so that the entire surface can be inspected. Syn. Overhauling.

SLITTER-CUTTER: See SHEETER.

SLITTER EDGE: Sheet edge produced by a slitter.

SLITTING TOLERANCE: Permitted variation in web width after slitting.

SLOT: Cut made through a sheet with little or no stock removed, as applied for example in the making of folding cartons.

SLOTTER: Machine for making slots in paperboard forms, which may utilize either a die press, slitter or saw depending on design.

SOFT FOLD: Paper finishing operation in which a large number of sheets are folded over together within a stack in such a manner that no permanent crease marks are retained.

SOLID FIBER BOX: Rigid shipping container made of solid board, having closed faces and completely enclosing the contents. Designation as a box, as opposed to carton, infers that it meets requirements as an outer shipping container.

SORTING: Operation of inspecting sheets of paper, either manually or automatically (by electrical, mechanical or optical methods), to identify and remove imperfect sheets.

SPIRAL WINDING: Style of continuous winding in which the paper web advances at an angle to the mandrel, with each ply partially overlapping the previous plies. The endless formed tube slides along the mandrel and is cut into required lengths.

SPOT DETECTOR: Photoelectrical device that views a running web to detect any local appearance change.

SQUARED PAPER: Sheets of paper that have been guillotine-trimmed square on all four sides or on two adjoining sides.

SQUARENESS: Degree to which successive sheets will align one on top of the other regardless of original orientation. Syn. Rectangularity.

STACKER: Equipment that automatically forms an even-sided, well jogged pile of paper sheets which can subsequently be fed into finishing equipment without further handling or jogging.

STACKING: Producing a pile of sheets by placing one upon another.

STAIR-STEP CUT: Difference in cut sheet lengths which occurs during sheeter operations when several webs are fed through a driven roll nip to the cutter section. Syn. Multi-Ply Effect.

STARVED JOINT: Joint which has received an insufficient amount of adhesive to produce a satisfactory bond.

STATIC FRICTION: Force that resists initial movement of one surface sliding over another surface.

STIFFENING AGENT: Special compound used for ply bonding of two-ply fluted corrugating medium which imparts high strength and performance characteristics to the flute.

STIPPLING: Embossing treatment to reduce the high gloss of paper by running the sheet between rollers with countergrained surfaces.

STOCK: Paper in inventory or storage.

STOCK SIZE: Any of the common paper and board sheet sizes that are likely to be stocked by suppliers.

STOCK WEIGHTS: Common paper and board grammages that are likely to be stocked by suppliers.

STRAPPING: See BANDING.

STRIKE-THROUGH (in adhesion): Defect in color or appearance when adhesive applied to one surface of a paper sheet migrates to the other side before setting. This problem occurs with porous sheets and thin adhesives.

STRINGINESS: Property of an adhesive that causes it to draw filaments or threads when adhesive-transfer surfaces are separated. The resultant condition on the adherends from the application of a stringy adhesive is called "webbing". The resultant condition of cobweb-like filaments between machine parts that transfer the adhesive is called "feathering".

SUBSTRATE: Underply or inner ply of a laminate; the surface to which adhesive is applied.

SWATCH: Colored paper used as a sample or specimen.

SWATCH BOOK: Grouping of paper samples, usually in bound form, which displays the grammages, colors, finishes, and other particulars of the collection; used as an aid in the selection of grades. Syn. Sample Book.

T _____

TACK: Stickiness of an adhesive or pulling resistance between two adherends when the adhesive still exhibits viscous or plastic flow; as opposed to "bond" when the adhesive is dried.

TACKIFIER: Resin which can be added to pressure sensitive adhesive emulsions to increase bonding or improve other properties.

TAKE-UP RATIO: Ratio of the linear footage of corrugated medium to the linear footage of linerboard required for the manufacture of corrugated board. Depending on the flute contour used, the ratio will generally fall in the 1.3 to 1.6 range. Syn. Take-Up Factor, Draw Ratio.

TEARING BOND: Adhesive bond between two paper sheet surfaces in which interfacial fibers are pulled out from one or both sheets during separation without failure of the adhesive, as distinct from a "peeling bond" where separation occurs strictly within the adhesive layer.

TENSION ZONE: Section of a web-fed machine which has the capability of processing material at the same or different tension level as the other sections of the machine. A tension zone requires a driven roll, often in combination with a nipping roll, to "isolate" the tension.

THERMOPLASTIC LAMINATING: Form of wet laminating in which the bonding agent is a thermoplastic material, usually some type of wax.

TIE LAYER: Functional layer within a laminate that also serves as the bonding material between adjacent layers, usually formed from an extrudable adhesive resin.

TIER: One layer of cartons or packages on a pallet.

TOP PAPER: Paper attached to the top of a set-up paper box lid.

TRANSFER UNWIND: Unwind station in which support for the expiring roll is transferred from one arm to another so that a new roll may be brought into position for a splice.

TRANSPARENTIZING: Method of making a paper web more transparent by replacing the air-fiber interface with one that has a refractive index close to that of cellulose.

TRIMMER: See GUILLOTINE.

TRIM WASTE: Waste paper resulting from trimming a stack of paper sheets or trimming off an edge from a continuous web.

TUB COLORING: Method of dyeing paper by passing the web through a bath or flooded nip, removing the excess dye solution in a nip, then drying the web by suitable means. See also DIPPING.

TURRET UNWIND: Unwind station that handles small rolls at modest speeds, having two independently driven unwind positions, one at either end of opposing rotating arms.

U

UNDERCUTTING: Condition of undersized sheets at the bottom of a pile, which may occur during guillotine trimming due to incorrect settings.

UNDER-RUN: Amount of paper under that required to fill an order.

UNITIZING: Grouping or arranging a number of items in a specified manner so that they are capable of being handled as a unit. An example of unitizing is the stacking of paper packages on a pallet or skid and then wrapping and banding them securely together.

UNIT LOAD: Items packaged in such a way that they can be handled as a unit. Syn. Unitized Load.

UNTRIMMED: [adj] Describes paper produced on the sheeter without subsequent trimming.

V

V-BOARD: Water resistant and water vapor resistant classes of corrugated board, manufactured with wet-strength linerboard and corrugated medium and utilizing a laminated sheet with a water barrier as the outer face.

VIBRATION TEST: Performance test for corrugated board shipping containers intended to simulate the motions and shocks to which packaged products are subjected when shipped in railroad cars or motor trucks.

W

WASHBOARDING: Form of thickness loss on corrugated board caused by contraction of adhesive during drying which pulls a lightweight liner downwards toward the profile of the flute.

WEBBING: See STRINGINESS.

WEB CORE LOSS: Amount of material omitted from a roll due to the presence of a core.

WET CONVERTING: Converting operations carried out on the roll web, such as coating, laminating, corrugating, impregnating and embossing.

WET LAMINATING: Joining together two webs while the bonding agent is still in liquid form.

WIND DIRECTION: Rotation of a roll in the direction it was wound.

WITH THE GRAIN: Folding or feeding paper parallel with the grain of the paper.

WRAP CURL: Curl in the grain direction caused by the paper setting in this conformation while wound in a roll. Syn. Roll Set, Roll Curl.

WRAPPING STATION: Area in a paper mill finishing department where stacks of paper or rolls are wrapped in preparation for shipping.

Chapter 19
Printing

ADDITIVE PRIMARY COLORS: Red, green and blue. Various combinations of these respective areas of the electromagnetic spectrum allow perception of color over the entire visible range. See also SUBTRACTIVE PRIMARY COLORS.

ANGLE BAR: Bar or roll placed within the sheet run of a printing press at an angle of 45° to the direction of sheet travel. The sheet is passed over the angle bar to change its direction of travel by 90°. Two angle bars are placed in series to effectively move the web in a lateral direction by whatever amount is desired.

ANTI-OFFSET SPRAY: Fine-particle spray applied to printed sheets approaching the delivery table to create a barrier or partition between sheets and prevent transfer of wet ink from the printed face to the neighboring unprinted back.

ANTIOXIDANT: Ink additive used to reduce drying on the press and also to reduce skinning.

ANTI-SKINNING AGENT: Material added to ink to retard skin formation.

ARTWORK: Illustrative material for reproduction.

AUTOPASTER: See FLYING PASTER.

AUXILLIARY ROLL STAND: Second roll stand on a web press, permitting one stand to be reloaded while another continues to unwind.

B

BACKING UP: Printing the reverse side of a sheet already printed on one side.

BACKLASH: Unsatisfactory condition for an indirect printing unit when larger-than-normal spacing occurs between successive gear teeth on a common drive unit; this allows the position of one driven cylinder to change in reference to another driven cylinder (e.g., the blanket cylinder relative to the plate cylinder).

BACK PRINTING: Reverse-side printing on a sheet. A designation of back printing infers printing of secondary importance or printing which is read after the "front printing". Syn. Backer, Reverse Side Printing, Backed-Up Printing.

BALANCE: Visual relationship between the various elements on a printed page, including type, artwork, and space.

BIMETAL PLATE: Printing plate composed of two metals in layers. One metal serves as the base for the image area; the second metal the non-image area.

BINDER: Material in an ink film which holds the pigment to the printed page.

BITE: (1) Affinity of a particular paper surface to accept ink. (2) Specific action of acid on metal (i.e., depth of removal) during a stage of etching.

BLANKET: Multiply fabric laminated and coated with rubber, utilized in offset-lithography. It is clamped around the cylinder which receives the image from the plate and transfers (or offsets) it to paper.

BLANKET CONTAMINATION: General term that simply indicates the presence of foreign or undesirable materials on the offset blanket. See also DUSTING, LINTING, WHITENING, MILKING.

BLANKET CREEP: Movement of the blanket in the impression nip.

BLANKET CYLINDER: Cylinder on which the blanket is mounted on an offset press. Syn. Offset Cylinder.

BLANKET GAIN: Slight enlargement of lines and dots on the offset blanket due to the tendency toward spreading when the image is transferred from the plate to the blanket.

BLANKET GLAZE: Hardened surface layer which forms on the offset blanket from the oxidation of drying oils or buildup of other materials from paper or ink. Glazed blankets are less ink receptive and contribute toward reduced print quality.

BLANKET-TO-BLANKET PRESS: Offset lithographic perfecting press in which the paper web runs between two blanket cylinders, each acting as an impression cylinder for the other. Syn. Unit Perfecting Press.

BLANKET WRAP: Angle subtended by the paper and blanket cylinder as the paper is peeled off following the printing nip. For a specified sheet tension, a large amount of blanket wrap is indicative of high ink tack. Since the effect is more prominent in the solid print areas, high blanket wrap will cause localized stretch and contribute to problems with running and side-to-side register as well as cutoff register.

BLANKET WRAPAROUND: Wrap of the blanket cylinder with several layers of paper, caused by a web break downstream from the press nip which eliminates the take-off tension, while the incoming sheet follows its normal path into the press nip until the press can be stopped. A severe wraparound causes damage to the blanket.

BLEEDING: (1) Extension of the printed image beyond the trim edge of the sheet or page. (2) Diffusion of color from printed areas into surrounding areas.

BLIND: Image area on a plate that will not accept ink.

BLISTERING: Eruptions in the surface of coated printing papers during heatset printing.

BLISTER PICK: Partial delamination during printing of parts of the paper strata below the printed surfaces resulting in a round or oval shaped area resembling a blister.

BODY: Term referring to the viscosity, consistency or covering power of an ink or vehicle.

BODY GUM: Essentially a very stiff oil which when added to an ink formulation increases tack.

BUCKLES: Wave-like distortions of book pages that originate near the spine (backbone) of a book, caused by changes in the moisture content of the paper after binding.

C _____

CAKING: Accumulation of ink particles on rollers and plates, caused primarily by the inability of the vehicle to hold the pigment in suspension. Syn. Filling Up.

CAMERA-READY COPY: Final paste-up ready to be photographed without further alteration. Syn. Master Copy, Reproduction Copy.

CARBON BLACK: Ink pigment consisting of minute carbon particles derived from partial combustion of natural gas.

CATCHING UP: See SCUMMING.

CELLS: Individual depressions, chemically etched into the surface of a gravure printing cylinder, which retain and transfer ink in the gravure printing process.

CHALKING: Lithographic printing defect associated with coated papers, characterized by poor adhesion of print to the paper as evidenced by a tendency toward rub-off following the first stages of drying. Typically, ink adhesion improves during the final drying stages. Syn. Powdering.

COATING PICK: Disturbance of the surface of coated paper during printing which results in the lifting or complete removal of coating particles or fragments.

COLD TYPE: Non-metallic composition or typesetting methods other than hot metal type.

COLLATING: Assembling sheets or signatures in proper sequence for binding.

COLLECTING: Problem in lithographic printing characterized by filling in of halftones and incomplete printing of solids, due to excessive tack of ink, dust in the environment, and/or linty paper.

COLOR CONTROL: Measures taken at each step of a color printing process to match color tones with standards.

COLOR PROCESS WORK: Individual negatives and plates made by means of photographic separations for 2, 3, and 4 color printing.

COLOR PROOFS: Set of proofs consisting of an impression of each color plate singly and in successive combination with other proofs as the job is to be printed.

COLOR SEPARATION: Negative exposed through one of the tri-color filters and usually reproducing one of the primary (red, yellow and blue) colors.

COMBINATION PLATE: (1) Printing plate imaged with both halftone and line work. (2) Printing plate imaged with two or more unrelated forms for simultaneous printing.

COMBINATION RUN: Two or more print jobs handled together to effect savings.

COMPOSING: Transfering text to a medium which will produce type directly or indirectly.

COMPOSITION: Any composed typographic matter ready for printing.

CONCEALED LOSS: Damage to a paper roll or other paper product that is not evident upon delivery to the customer, but is discovered upon opening the wrappers or packages.

CONTACT PRINTING: See IMPACT PRINTING.

CONTINUOUS TONE: Any image consisting of blacks and intermediate shades of gray that is not made up of halftone dots.

CONTRAST: Differences in tone, as for example between highlights and shadows.

CONVERTIBLE PRESS: Type of multi-unit sheet-fed press in which reversing equipment is provided between two adjacent units so that the sheet may be turned over, thus allowing either two-color printing on one side or perfecting.

COOLING ROLLER: Roller through which cold water is circulated, typically used to cool the printed web as it leaves the drying oven. Syn. Chill Roll.

COPY: Any finished written material to be used in the production of printing such as manuscript, captions, tabular matter, etc.

CRAWLING: Tendency of some inks to form a discontinuous film by drawing up into droplets or irregular patterns before drying.

CROCKING: Smudging or rubbing off of ink.

CROPPING: Eliminating portions of copy, usually on a photograph.

CROSS HAIRS: Register marks used in accurate positioning or overlaying of images.

CROWS FEET: Failure of a solid print to bridge spaces created by cracks or crevices in the coating surface.

CRYSTALLIZED: [adj] Term applied (incorrectly) to a dried ink film that does not trap an overlap inking. (The meaning in chemistry is completely different.)

CURVED PLATE: In letterpress printing, an electrotype or stereotype which is backed up and precurved to fit the cylinder of a rotary press.

CUSHION FORM ROLLER: Special form roller used to inhibit excessive bounce at plate gaps, consisting of a soft-covered roller to which a harder veneer elastomer coating is applied. Cushion form rollers are expensive to manufacture and cannot be reground due to the thinness of the elastomer coating. See also FORM ROLLER.

CUT: In letterpress printing, a photoengraving.

CUT OFF: Length of a print in web printing, usually corresponding to the circumference of the plate cylinder.

CYLINDER: Heavy, accurate rotating member of a press to which a plate and/or blanket is attached and around which the paper travels to receive the printed impression. Three cylinders are utilized on an offset press: plate cylinder, blanket cylinder and impression cylinder.

D _____

DAMPENERS: Rollers that distribute dampening solution.

DAMPENING SOLUTION: Mixture of water, gum and etching chemicals, used for wetting the non-image areas of the lithographic plate so that they will not accept ink. Syn. Fountain Solution.

DEEP ETCHING: Making printing plates in offset-lithography where the image areas are slightly recessed below the surface.

DELIVERY: Portion of a printing press where the freshly-printed sheets are piled as they leave the impression section of the press. Syn. Delivery Platform, Delivery Table.

DENSITOMETER: Instrument designed to accurately measure the optical density of photographic images or colors in color printing. (The densitometer measures the absorbance properties of individual colorants, but it cannot measure color in the more general sense as measured by a colorimeter or viewed by the human eye.)

DENSITOMETRY: Application of densitometer readings to the control of halftone printing and evaluation of printing inks.

DESENSITIZATION: Chemical treatment of non-image areas of a lithographic plate to make them ink-repellent.

DEVELOPING: Making an image visible after exposure.

DIE-STAMPING: Intaglio process for the production of letterheads, business cards, etc.

DIRECT LITHOGRAPHY: Printing by direct transfer from the lithographic plate to the paper.

DIRECT PRINTING: Any printing process where ink is transferred directly from the printing plate to the paper.

DISTRIBUTION ROLLER SYSTEM: Series of contacting rollers which transfer the ink from the fountain section and deliver it to the form rollers of an offset press as a uniform film. Some of the rollers are driven by the press gears and others are friction driven; some also oscillate from side to side as the press rotates.

DOPING: Changing ink characteristics by adding driers, extenders, thinners, antioxidants, etc.

DOT: Individual element of a halftone.

DOT GAIN: Increase in dot size due to wet ink expansion, a characteristic of lithographic printing.

DOT SKIP: Missing of dots in halftone printing. Syn. Speckle Skip.

DOT SLURRING: Smearing or elongation at the trailing edges of halftone dots.

DOUBLING: Appearance of superfluous halftone dots on a print during multicolor offset printing, caused by the ink image on the sheet transferring to the blanket of a following unit in which misregister occurs.

DRAWDOWN: Application of a thin film of ink to a piece of paper by means of a spatula, used to assess the color value. Syn. Pull Down.

DRIER: In inkmaking, any substance added to hasten ink hardening. A typical drier consists mainly of lead and manganese salts which exert a catalytic effect on the oxidation and polymerization of the vehicles employed.

DROPOUT HALFTONE: Halftone in which dots have been intentionally deleted from the extreme highlights to increase contrast.

DRYBACK: Decrease in the gloss of ink that occurs during the drying of offset inks.

DRYING: That property of the ink vehicle by which hardening results.

DRYING OIL: Constituent of inks which has the property of hardening to a tough film by oxidation and polymerization.

DRYING OVEN: Oven through which the printed web passes after contacting the last printing unit, used for heat-set inks.

DRY OFFSET: Printing process similar to conventional offset, except that it employs a relief plate and does not require a water-dampening system. Syn. Letterset.

DRY PICKING: Occurrence of picking in the absence of water introduced by the printing process.

DRY PRINTING PROCESS: Multi-color printing of a web in which each ink layer is solidified prior to application of the next colored ink. Multicolor rotogravure is an example of a dry printing process.

DRY TRAPPING: Action of a paper surface in accepting sufficient ink during an overlap printing of a previous dried printing to yield an overprint of satisfactory optical density and uniform coverage. See also TRAPPING, WET TRAPPING.

DUCTOR ROLLER: Common device to deliver the ink from the fountain to the distribution system of an offset press. The ductor roller alternately contacts the fountain roller and the first roller of the distribution section.

DUMMY: Page by page layout for a pamphlet, magazine, book, etc.; essentially a "preview" of a piece of printed work. Syn. Mock-Up.

DUPLICATOR: Term commonly applied to a small offset press or to other office-scale printing presses.

E _____

ELECTROSTATIC INK TRANSFER: Technique applied to rotogravure printing in which an applied voltage to the web produces a distorted meniscus in the ink cells which bulge the ink into better contact with the paper web.

ELECTROSTATIC PRINTING: Printing by the xerographic method. The image is controlled by means of electric charge on the surface to be printed, while the atomized or powdered ink is given the opposite charge.

EMULSIFICATION: Inadvertent mixing of fountain solution into the ink system (causing "gray image") or ink into the dampening system (causing "plate scum") during lithographic printing.

ENGRAVER'S SPREAD: Layout on which all finished artwork that is to appear on a printed plate has been mounted in the exact position for the plate.

ENGRAVING: (1) General term applied to any printing plate prepared by an etching process. (2) Process of making such a plate.

ETCHING: Chemical dissolution of metal in the image or non-image areas of a plate or printing cylinder. In lithography, the non-image areas are etched (desensitized) to make them water-receptive and ink-repellent. In gravure, the image areas are etched (photoengraved) into copper plates or cylinders.

EXHAUST OVERPULL: Difference between the volume rate of air entering the dryer and the amount removed by the exhaust system. The exhaust overpull enters the dryer from the pressroom.

EXPOSING: Allowing light to selectively imprint an image onto a coated plate or film.

EXTENDER: Inorganic pigment used to impart transparency, opacity or working qualities to an ink.

F _____

FANNING-IN OF IMAGE: Narrowing of a printed image at the trailing edge of a printed sheet, caused by the sheet stretching in the cross direction during printing and then snapping back.

FANNING-IN OF WEB: Decrease in web width after printing one color, so that succeeding colors print "longer".

FANNING-OUT OF IMAGE: Widening of a printed image at the trailing edge of a printed sheet, caused by the sheet narrowing during printing and then snapping back.

FANNING-OUT OF WEB: Increase in web width after printing one color, so that succeeding colors will print "short".

FAR SIDE: Non-operating side of the press.

FIBER PICK: Disturbance of the sheet surface during printing with waterbased inks resulting either in the lifting of fibers or the complete removal of fibers. Syn. Fiber Lift, Fiber Rise, Fiber Roughening.

FIBER PUFFING: Roughening of the paper surface during heatset drying; mainly a problem with coated groundwood papers. Syn. Heatset Roughening, Fiber Lifting.

FILL-IN: Distortion seen in tonal prints due to filling in of the voids (reverse dots) in the tone area; caused by paper, ink and/or either excessive ink application and printing pressure. Syn. Flooding.

FILLING UP: See CAKING.

FLATBED CYLINDER PRESS: Press having a flat printing plate with an impression cylinder.

FLEXOGRAPHY: Method of relief printing employing hard rubber plates and volatile inks, as well as special procedures. This method is used primarily by the packaging industry.

FLOW: Property of an ink which allows it to level out as would a true liquid. Inks of poor flow are described as short or buttery in body; while inks of good flow are said to be long.

FLYING: See MISTING.

FLYING PASTER: Mechanism on the unwind stand of a printing press which allows the lead end of a new roll of paper to be connected (pasted) to the tail end (or near the tail end) of an expiring roll without stopping or slowing down the press. Syn. Flying Splice, Autopaster.

FOLDER: Device at the delivery end of the press or collator which folds signatures or forms.

FOLIO: Sheet of paper folded once.

FORMAT: Arrangement of printed matter and artwork, including size and style of type, page margins, column width, etc.

FORMER-FOLDER: Equipment typically used on newspaper presses to form a section of the newspaper. At the entrance, the printed webs are laid one upon another and slit into ribbons, each ribbon being two pages wide. Each ribbon then passes over a former into a pair of nipping rollers that make the first fold in the machine direction of the paper. The paper is then cut to the correct length and given a second fold (in the cross direction) as it passes through a second set of nipping rollers.

FORM ROLLER: Ink or dampening roller that contacts the printing plate.

FOUNTAIN: That part of the printing press that feeds ink into the distribution system. In lithography, it is also the part which feeds the dampening solution to the dampening rollers.

FOUNTAIN SOLUTION: See DAMPENING SOLUTION.

FOUR COLOR PROCESS: Method of printing color illustrations through the use of four separate plates: black, blue, red and yellow.

FRONT (of press): Delivery end of the press.

FUGITIVE INK: Ink which changes in color when exposed to light.

G _____

GALLEY PROOF: Proof taken of typed matter before it has been made into pages.

GATHERING: Operation of collating folded signatures in consecutive order.

GHOSTING: Variations in ink gloss, density or color associated with a ghost image from another area of the copy. Particular types of ghosting may be traceable to either mechanical or chemical causes. See also GLOSS GHOSTING.

GLOSS GHOSTING: Gloss variations on back printing due to non-uniform drying and setting of ink, caused by interference from volatile drying accelerators used for the first side printing.

GLOSS INK HOLDOUT: Measurement of gloss on a sample of coated paper that has been printed and dried, which is used to assess the required ink application to achieve the desired gloss level. For economic reasons, printers prefer to use the minimum amount of ink.

GRAINY HIGHLIGHTS: Printing defect in which dots in a light tone area either are missing or are of defective shape, due to a deficiency in printing smoothness. This defect mainly applies to gravure printing. Syn. Salt and Pepper, Speckling.

GRAPHIC ARTS: Products, techniques and crafts associated with printmaking and the production of printed matter.

GRAVURE: Method of printing utilizing a plate or cylinder with minute engraved or etched depressions on the surface to hold ink and then transfer the ink to a paper surface. The depth and area of the depressions vary, thus yielding more or less ink onto the paper. See also INTAGLIO.

GREASING: See SCUMMING.

GRIPPER EDGE: Leading edge of the paper which is picked up by the grippers.

GRIPPERS: Metal fingers which grip the paper and carry it through a sheet-fed printing press to the delivery end.

H _____

HALFTONE: Print or printing plate in which details and tone value of an image are recorded by means of tiny dots of varying size, shape and proximity.

HEATSET DRYER FLUTING: Closely-spaced machine-direction ridges occurring on printed sheets from a heatset dryer. This problem occurs with lightweight coated paper in areas of heavy ink coverage. Syn. Corrugations, Streaks, Striations.

HEATSET INKS: Inks for high-speed printing which set rapidly when they are heated and quickly cooled.

HEATSET OFFSET: Offset printing using drying ovens for rapid drying of a two-sided print after each color application.

HEATSET PRESS: Printing press utilizing a heated chamber (often called a "drying oven") to dry the inks. In multi-color printing, wet ink is printed on wet ink and a separate drying cycle is employed for each side of the sheet.

HEATSET ROUGHENING: Roughened or raised surface area of a printed sheet comparable to a fiber or fiber bundle in size, occurring in the dryers of heatset presses, particularly in areas of heavy ink coverage. Syn. Fiber Puffing.

HELIOTEST: Method of grading comparative halftone prints produced under specified conditions. The "missing dots" are counted in the variable halftone printed areas, and the results are expressed as the distance (mm) to obtain 20 missing dots.

HICKEY: Blemish in the image area of offset prints appearing as a white area around a dark center, caused by specks of dirt, hardened ink or other extraneous matter adhering to the printing plate.

HICKEY PICKER: Specialized roller which contacts the inked printing plate to remove dust, lint, paper particles and bits of dried ink before they can be transferred to the printing substrate along with the ink.

HIGHLIGHTS: Lightest or whitest parts in a printed picture, represented in an engraved plate or halftone by the finest dots or absence of dots.

HUMPING: Appearance and effect of an out-of-round roll as it unwinds on the press roll stand causing web vibration and varying web tension.

I _____

IMAGE: Visual display or graphic representation on a printing plate or other carrier.

IMAGE CARRIER: Surface that carries the image to be inked and printed.

IMPACTLESS PRINTING: See NONIMPACT PRINTING.

IMPACT PRINTING: Any form of printing involving solid physical contact between the paper (or other printing substrate) and an image-carrying device (e.g., printing plate or blanket) which is inked. Syn. Contact Printing, Impression Printing.

IMPRESSION: (1) Pressure applied in the printing nip, usually given in pounds per lineal inch or mils of "squeeze". (2) Inked image printed on paper as it runs through the press.

IMPRESSION CYLINDER: Cylinder which backs the paper at the point of impression. Syn. Back Cylinder.

IMPRESSION TOLERANCE: Ability in letterpress printing to produce acceptable print quality over a wide range of impression pressure.

INDIRECT PRINTING: Any printing method where the ink is transferred from the image carrier to an intermediate surface and then to the stock being printed. All commercial indirect presses are offset presses, most commonly rotary offset presses.

INFEED ROLLER: Any of three rollers (two driven, one free) mounted in series on the roll stand, used to smooth the web and control its tension and speed as it feeds from the roll into the first printing unit. Syn. Metering Unit.

INK: Dye solution or pigment dispersion in the form of liquid, paste or powder which is applied and dried on a substrate. See also PRINTING INK.

INK DRYING: Final hardening or stabilizing of an ink film by actions (depending on the type of ink) of oxidation, penetration, evaporation, polymerization, gelation, and precipitation.

INK DRYING CURL: Curl toward the printed side parallel to the grain, caused by drying of heavy ink printing or varnish.

INK FIXING: Printing on "safety papers" treated with chemicals that will react with the ink to produce very insoluble compounds that are difficult or impossible to erase.

INK FOUNTAIN: Container which supplies ink to the ink rollers.

INK GLOSS: Gloss measured on the printed ink film. The surest way to obtain a glossy ink film is to print the proper ink on a smooth glossy paper surface.

INKING: Application of ink to the image carrier by rollers, by immersion, or by a squeegee. In letterpress and lithography, inking is commonly by rollers. Gravure cylinders are commonly immersed in a fountain of ink.

INK JET PRINTING: Non-impact printing process in which images are produced by a high-velocity stream of microscopic ink droplets from a pressurized ink system.

INK MILEAGE: Area of printed solid of specified optical density that can be printed on a designated paper with one unit weight of a given ink under conditions that produce a satisfactory level of print quality. Basically, a measure of how much ink is required for a given print job.

INKOMETER: Instrument for measuring ink tack in terms of the force required to split an ink film between rollers under specified conditions.

INK REQUIREMENT: Amount of a specified ink required to produce a print of acceptable optical density in the tone and solid areas.

INK RUB RESISTANCE TEST: Test to measure the relative rub-off from a test paper after printing with a standard ink under specified conditions.

INK SET: Condition of printed sheets when, although the ink is not fully dry, they can be handled without smudging.

INK TRAIN: Series of rollers that take ink from the ink fountain of an offset press, spread it to an even film of required width, and apply it to the plate during press operation.

INK TRANSFER: Amount or percentage of ink transferred from the printing plate (or other image carrier) to the paper (or other receiving surface) as a result of a printing impression.

IN-LINE CONVERTING: Carrying out converting operations on the printed web (such as coating, laminating, embossing, sheeting, folding, hole punching and die cutting) before the web is removed from the printing press.

INTAGLIO: Any method of printing in which the printing elements are below the plate surface. The main method of intaglio printing is gravure.

K _____

KISS IMPRESSION: Printing performed with only slight pressure, the normal procedure for quality printing.

L _____

LAYOUT: Arrangement of the various elements of the printed page. Syn. Makeup.

LETTERPRESS: Printing method in which raised image areas are inked and pressed on paper. Syn. Relief Printing.

LETTERSET: See DRY OFFSET.

LINEN TESTER: Fixed-focus magnifier, typically used to examine halftone print details.

LINTING: Release of surface lint or removal of partially or poorly bonded fibers from uncoated paper surfaces during printing, causing the accumulation of fibers on offset blankets, printing surfaces or rollers. See also DUSTING.

LINTING TENDENCY: Relative measure of the linting propensity of an uncoated paper used for web offset printing.

LITHOGRAPHY: Printing process in which the printing and non-printing parts are in the same plane (planographic). The process utilizes a metal plate or other flat surface which is chemically treated so that ink will adhere to the image to be printed and will be repelled by the non-image areas. Often the image is photographically transferred to the printing plate. Syn. Litho Printing. See also OFFSET LITHOGRAPHY.

LIVERING: Irreversible increase in the body of inks resulting from physical or chemical changes during storage.

LONG INK: Ink that has good flow in the fountain.

LOW SPOT: Nonprinting area on an offset press due to unevenness in the blanket, plate, cylinder or packing.

M _____

MAKEREADY: Preparation of the press to obtain proper printing impression.

MAKEUP: See LAYOUT.

MASS TONE: Color of ink in bulk. Opaque inks print nearly the mass tone, while transparent inks are much darker in bulk than the printed color.

MENISCUS: Curvature of a liquid surface within a cell or capillary caused by surface tension and wetting.

METERING UNIT: See IN-FEED ROLLERS.

MIDDLETONES: Tonal range between highlights and shadows of a halftone reproduction.

MILKING: Coating buildup on the non-image areas of a blanket, usually due to insufficient water resistance of the coating on the paper being run.

MISREGISTER: Degree of inexactness of register. See also REGISTER.

MISTING: Flying off of tiny ink droplets from the rollers. Syn. Flying.

MOTTLE: Gross, random non-uniformity in the visual density and/or color and/or gloss of a printed area. This type of printing defect is due primarily to non-uniform ink receptivity or absorptivity, although deficient printing smoothness may also be involved.

N _____

NEAR SIDE: Operating side of a press.

NEGATIVE IMAGE: Image in reverse of the original copy. All direct printing methods use a negative image plate. In offset printing, the printing plate retains a positive image.

NONIMPACT PRINTING: All forms of printing where the paper (or other printing substrate) is not contacted. Examples are xerography, ink jet printing, and thermal printing. Syn. Noncontact Printing, Impactless Printing.

O _____

OFFSET: Short for offset lithography. (Other offset printing methods are used, but these have specific designations.)

OFFSET LITHOGRAPHY: Lithographic printing system in which the planograghic printing plate transfers the image to a rubber-covered blanket which, in turn, transfers the image to the paper.

OFFSET PRESS: Indirect rotary press having a plate cylinder, a blanket cylinder and an impression cylinder. Either planographic or relief plates are used.

OFFSET PRINTING: Any printing method in which the image is transferred to a rubber-covered blanket which, in turn, transfers the image to the paper. The foremost offset printing method is offset lithography; another example is letterset or dry offset.

OFFSETTING (of ink): Condition where part of the ink from a printed surface sets off on the back of the next sheet in a pile. See also SET-OFF.

OIL-BASE INK: Type of ink commonly used for letterpress and lithographic printing. The ink in newspapers is set by oil absorption into the sheet body. For higher quality printing, special oil vehicles are used which dry (set) by polymerization/oxidation reactions.

OPTICAL DENSITY: Degree of opacity of an ink film.

ORIGINAL: That which is to be reproduced by printing or reprographic methods.

OVERPRINTING: Printing on an area that already has been printed.

P _____

PACKING: Material used to build up the surface of a plate, blanket or impression cylinder.

PASTER: Splice connecting two webs together. See also FLYING PASTER.

PASTE-UP: Assemblage of the various elements (text, artwork, etc.) on a page in preparation for photographing a printing job. Syn. Mechanical.

PEENED EDGES: Minute edge curl condition in a pile of paper caused by a dull trimmer knife not cutting cleanly. This condition can cause erratic feeding of sheets to a printing press due to mechanical clinging of these edges. Syn. Welded Edges.

PERFECTING PRESS: Press which prints both sides of the web in the same pass through the unit. In offset printing, two printing units oppose each other so that both sides are printed at the same time. Non-offset presses utilize two printing couples in series for perfecting work. See also BLANKET-TO-BLANKET PRESS.

PHOTOENGRAVING: Type of relief printing plate made by photographing the material on sensitized metal.

PICKING: Pulling off of particles of paper as the web leaves the printing nip, due to high ink tack or low surface strength of the paper. Syn. Plucking.

PIGMENT: Minute solid particles, which when dispersed in the vehicle, give ink its color, body and opacity.

PILING: Condition in offset lithography where ink collects and cakes on the plate, rollers, or blanket instead of transferring readily, usually as a result of incorrect ink formulation.

PLANOGRAPHIC PRINTING: See LITHOGRAPHY.

PLATE: In printing, the image carrier or image transfer medium.

PLATE BLINDING: Short plate life due to image loss, usually attributed to excessive pressures or the abrasiveness of the ink and/or paper.

PLATE CYLINDER: Cylinder on a rotary press to which the printing plates are mounted.

PLATEN PRESS: Letterpress printing press utilizing two flat surfaces.

POSITIVE IMAGE: Image which corresponds to the original subject in all respects.

POWDERING: See CHALKING.

PRESENSITIZED PLATE: Plate ready for exposure when received by the offset printer.

PRESS: Abbreviation for printing press.

PRESS PROOF: Final proof taken on the press after proper make-ready.

PRESSROOM: Area in which printing operations are carried out.

PRINTED GLOSS: Gloss of printed areas; this property is generally dependent on the gloss of the paper, the ink holdout, and the ink formulation.

PRINT EMBOSSING: Embossing process in which ink is applied to the raised pattern on the steel engraving roll.

PRINTING: Making a copy of lettering and/or images on a surface such as paper.

PRINTING COUPLE: Plate cylinder and opposing impression cylinder.

PRINTING INK: Colored or pigmented liquid or paste composition (most commonly carbon black suspended in an oil vehicle) that dries to a solid film after application as a thin layer by printing equipment. See also OIL-BASE INK, WATER BASE-INK, SOLVENT-BASE INK.

PRINTING PRESS: Equipment in which an image is transferred to paper or other planar material.

PRINTING PRESSURE: See IMPRESSION.

PRINTING SMOOTHNESS: (1) Degree of contact between the paper surface and the printing surface. (2) Relative ease by which good printing contact may be obtained. (Printing smoothness is a function of paper roughness, levelness and compressibility.)

PRINTING SUBSTRATE: Any printing surface, including paper, paperboard, plastic, metal, etc.

PRINTING TRAIN: Series of rollers and cylinders that carry ink through the printing unit and onto the paper.

PRINTING UNIT: One complete printing cylinder assembly, including (e.g., for an offset press) water and ink trains, plate cylinder, blanket cylinder and impression cylinder.

PRINT QUALITY: Degree to which the appearance and other properties of a print approach those of the desired result.

PROCESS COLOR: Loose term for full color printing.

PROCESS COLORS: Yellow, magenta (process red), and cyan (process blue) are the three basic process colors. These colors, usually in combination with black, provide the means to reproduce four-color process photography.

PROCESS PRINTING: Printing and overprinting from two or more halftone plates with different colors to produce intermediate colors and shades. Typically, four plates are used, printing yellow, magenta, cyan and black.

PULL DOWN: See DRAW DOWN.

R _____

REDUCERS: Varnishes, solvents, waxy or greasy compounds that are added to ink to control tack or consistency on the press.

REGISTER: Correct positioning of printed matter on a paper surface to meet the needs of its end use. Such positioning may be with reference to the edges of the sheet or with reference to previously printed matter, as for example during a sequence of multicolor printing.

RELIEF PRINTING: See LETTERPRESS.

REPROGRAPHY: Copying and reproduction of graphic materials.

ROLLER STRIPPING: Condition in lithography when the inking rollers are wetted by the fountain solution and become ink repellent.

ROLL STAND: Equipment that supports the roll of paper as it unwinds to feed the web into the press.

ROLL-TO-ROLL PRESS: Printing press in which the unprinted web is fed from a roll and the printed web is reformed into a roll. Syn. Reel-To-Reel Press.

ROTARY PRESS: High-speed press using curved printing plates and a curved impression cylinder. Rotary presses may be sheet-fed or web-fed.

ROTOGRAVURE: High-production gravure printing process using a rotary gravure press. Often abbreviated to "roto".

RUB-OFF: Loss of ink from dry prints due to rubbing against other objects. Rub-off against readers' hands, household linen, etc. (as, for example, from newspapers) is a common aggravation.

RUN: Total number of copies printed at one time.

RUPTURE PICK: Disturbance of the paper surface during printing which results in the removal of a continuous strip of material.

S _____

SCREEN: Number of lines or dots to the inch in halftone engravings.

SCREEN ANGLE: Angle at which the screen is turned to avoid a noticeable dot pattern. In color work, the angle must be changed for each color to avoid total dot overlap.

SCREENING: Process of separating continuous tones into halftones by means of line grids, with a fineness up to 300 lines per inch. The choice of screen depends on the printing method used (for example, letterpress is limited to relatively coarse screens), the fineness of detail desired in the printed reproduction, and the surface character of the paper used.

SCUMMING: In lithography, the printing of unwanted ink in non-image areas, due either to mechanical wear of plates or to chemical degradation of the desensitizing film on plates. Syn. Catching Up, Image Spread, Thickening, Filling, Greasing.

SELECTIVE WETTABILITY: Behavior of a lithographic plate during printing press operation whereby the image areas are wetted by ink and the non-image areas are wetted by fountain solution.

SEPARATION NEGATIVE: One of a set of color separation negatives. See also COLOR SEPARATION.

SET-OFF: Transference of ink from freshly printed matter to any other contacted surface. "First-impression set-off" is due to the ink smudged by first-side prints onto the second impression cylinder. "Companion page set-off" is the smudging of ink between opposite printed pages. See also OFF-SETTING.

SHADOWS: Darkest parts of a picture.

SHARPNESS: Clarity of the printed image.

SHEET-FED PRESS: Any printing press requiring paper in sheet form, as opposed to printing from rolls.

SHORT INK: Ink that does not flow freely.

SICCATIVE: Reagent that catalyzes or promotes oxidation of oils; a drier.

SIGNATURE: Section of a book, brochure, or magazine, etc. obtained by folding a single printed sheet to form 8, 12, 16 or more pages.

SILK SCREEN PRINTING: High-quality printing method utilizing fine-mesh silk onto which special photographic negatives are adhered. A squeegee drawn across the screen forces ink through the open image areas. Syn. Screen Process Printing.

SKINNING: Formation of a dried layer of ink on the surface of a quantity of ink after a period of standing.

SKIPS: Missing dots in gravure printing due to lack of ink transfer from individual cells of the gravure cylinder to the paper during impression. See also SPECKLE.

SLURRING: Smearing or elongation of halftone dots or type and line images at their trailing edges.

SMASHED BLANKET: Blanket with a localized area of low caliper.

SMEARING: Unwanted transfer of "non-dry" ink from a printed area to some other (usually adjoining) area of the paper; as distinct from smudging which is the transfer of "dry" ink.

SMUDGING: Unwanted transfer of "dry" ink from a printed area to some other area of the paper; as distinct from smearing which is the transfer of "non-dry" ink.

SNAP: Visual contrast between the printed image and paper surface.

SNOWFLAKING: In lithography, the appearance of fine white specks in a printed area, caused by water droplets remaining in the printing nip during impression.

SOAKINESS: Extreme absorbency of ink, where some ink penetrates through to the opposite side of the sheet; equivalent to strike-through.

SOLID PRINT: Image produced from a section of printing plate that is completely covered with ink; equivalent to a 100% tone of a single color.

SOLVENT-BASE INK: Ink commonly used for gravure and flexographic printing in which highly volatile solvents set the dyes and pigments on the paper surface rapidly by evaporation. However, some applications are restricted by environmental controls on solvent discharges.

SPECKLE: Presence of small white specks in a printed area due to cell skipping (in gravure printing) or to nonprinted depressions in the paper.

SPECKLING: See GRAINY HIGHLIGHTS.

SPLITTING: Large areas of the paper sheet tearing loose from the paper web and sticking to the offset blanket. Splitting usually occurs in the solid print areas.

SPOILAGE: Paper spoiled during the printing run. The printer usually allows for at least 5% spoilage when ordering paper for a particular run.

SPOT COLOR: Color printing in which one or more colors are located in certain areas. There is no blending of colors from different plates as in process printing.

SQUEEZE: Amount of vertical deflection of roll surfaces in a printing nip, used as a relative indication of printing pressure.

SQUEEZE-OUT: Lateral migration of ink beyond the edges of image areas in relief printing, caused by excess ink and/or excess impression.

STEREOTYPE: Letterpress plate made of rubber, plastic or metal which is made from a molded matrix. Often abbreviated to "stereo".

STICKING OF SHEETS: Problem in lithographic printing where successive sheets stick together, caused either by using excessive ink or poorly formulated ink.

STOCK: Paper or other material to be printed.

STRIKE-IN: Penetration of the ink vehicle into the paper, an important factor in the drying of most printing inks.

STRIKE-THROUGH: Undesirable penetration of the ink vehicle from the printed surface through to the reverse surface, due to a highly porous paper sheet structure and/or an excessive level of ink application.

STRIPPING: See ROLLER STRIPPING.

SUBLIMATION: Property of an ink pigment to change directly from a solid to a vapor when heated and return to the solid state when cooled. Sublimation in stacks of drying paper can cause ghosting and tinting.

SUBTRACTIVE PRIMARY COLORS: Colors obtained (yellow, magenta, cyan) when light is transmitted through three separate filters, each corresponding to one of the additive primary colors.

T _____

TACK: Adhesion of ink to other surfaces, specifically the printing plate and paper. Tack is primarily a property of the ink itself.

TACK REDUCERS: See REDUCERS.

TAIL-END HOOK: Curl that develops at the back edges of printed sheets as a result of printing heavy solids close to the back edge.

TANDEM ROLL STAND: Dual or single roll stands, one behind the other, for feeding multiple webs through the press at the same time.

TEMPERATURE CONDITIONING: Bringing paper to pressroom temperature before it is unwrapped and printed.

TINTING: In lithography, the appearance of small ink dots in the background (non-printed areas), most commonly caused by an imbalance between ink and fountain solution which results in emulsification of ink particles in the fountain solution. Another possible cause is sensitization of the plate surface by paper coating ingredients (e.g., proteins).

TONE: (1) Uniform printed area formed by minute dots. With black ink, a gradation of tones can be achieved from pure white through all shades of grey to solid black. (2) Percentage of the uniform printed area which is inked. A 50% tone usually consists of a checkerboard pattern of printed and unprinted squares. Above this value, the un-inked areas are usually in the form of circular dots of decreasing diameter. And conversely, below 50% the inked areas are usually in the form of circular dots of decreasing diameter. Syn. Dot Area. See also HALFTONE.

TONE DISTORTION: Discrepancy between a tone area on the printing plate and its corresponding tone area in the printed image. For various reasons, the printed area may either have heavier coverage than the plate or lighter coverage.

TRANSPARENT INK: Ink which lacks hiding power and permits previous printing to show through. Where two such colors are superimposed, they can blend to form a third, e.g., transparent yellow over blue to form green.

TRAPPING: Action of an image-receptive surface in accepting sufficient ink during printing to yield a print of satisfactory optical density and uniform coverage. See also DRY TRAPPING, WET TRAPPING.

TWO-COLOR PRINTING: Printing in two colors, usually black for definition and another color for effect.

TYMPAN: Sheets of paper placed between the impression surface of a platen or cylinder press and the paper to be printed.

TYPOGRAPHY: Art of printing, with reference to style, format and aesthetics of the printed page. See also GRAPHIC ARTS.

V _____

VARNISH: Substance used as a vehicle or base in the making of inks, often consisting of boiled linseed oil or resins.

VEHICLE: Liquid component of a printing ink, often an oil or varnish. It carries the pigment, provides flow properties, and supplies binder for the finished film.

W _____

WAFFLING: Bands with an embossed-like appearance on the printed sheet where repetitious heavy offset printing has caused stretching and deformation due to tack forces as the paper separates from the blanket.

WALKING OFF: Weakening or disappearance of printed image parts during a press run, due to failure of the corresponding image areas of the plate to accept ink.

WASHING: Appearance of a tinted scum on the unprinted section of the sheet during lithographic printing, usually due to using an ink that is too short.

WATER-BASE INK: Desirable type of ink from a pollution control point of view in which the water vehicle is absorbed into the sheet to set the pigments. Unfortunately, since pulp fibers swell in the presence of water, it is difficult to obtain consistent high-quality prints.

WATER-INK BALANCE: Relative amounts of dampening solution and ink applied to the paper in lithographic printing applications.

WATERLOGGED INK: Lithographic ink that has picked up enough emulsified water to adversely affect its flow and workability.

WEATHERABILITY: Ability of printing to withstand sunlight and temperature/moisture changes, mainly a property of the ink.

WEB COMPENSATOR: Movable roller on a web run that changes the web distance between two successive printing units, typically used to control register.

WEB LEAD: Amount of paper in the press when threaded.

WEB OFFSET PRESS: Offset lithographic press in which paper is fed from a roll, as opposed to sheet-fed.

WEB PRESS: General term applied to any high-speed press that prints from a continuous roll of paper. Syn. Web-Fed Press.

WEIGHT: In typography, the degree of blackness.

WELDED EDGES: See PEENED EDGES.

WET PICKING: Picking in the presence of water introduced by the printing process. Wet picking results from the loss of surface strength due to dampening of the sheet surface prior to the moment of impression.

WET PRINTING PROCESS: Multicolor printing of a web in which successive colors are printed before the preceding colors are dry.

WET TRAPPING: Action of a paper surface which carries one or more printed and undried images in accepting sufficient ink during subsequent overlap printing to yield an overprint of satisfactory optical density and uniform coverage. Wet trapping necessitates that each freshly deposited ink film be immobilized on the image surface before the next ink layer is deposited, and that succeeding inks have somewhat less tack. See also TRAPPING, DRY TRAPPING.

WHISKERING: Problem in gravure printing when "filaments" of low-viscosity ink extend from printed characters into the non-image areas. Whiskering is believed to be an electrical phenomenon, or at least to be aggravated by electrostatic forces.

WHITENING: Accumulation of pigment materials from the paper in the non-image area of the offset blanket. This term is general in nature and does not infer the mechanism by which the accumulation developed.

WHITE PAPER: Paper that is devoid of printing.

Chapter 20
Water & Effluent Treatment

A

ABATEMENT: Measures taken to reduce or eliminate pollution.

ACCLIMATION: Adaptation by an organism to changes in its environment.

ACRE-FOOT: Unit of volume commonly applied to holding ponds, equal to the quantity of water required to cover one acre to a depth of one foot ($43,560 \text{ ft}^3$).

ACTIVATED CARBON: Carbon which has been treated with high-temperature steam to produce a porous structure; it is an excellent adsorbent. Syn. Activated Charcoal.

ACTIVATED SLUDGE: Biological floc formed in aerated organic wastewaters by the growth of zoogleal bacteria and other microorganisms and accumulated in high concentration by returning the floc previously formed.

ACTIVATED SLUDGE LOADING: Weight or mass of biochemical oxygen demand in the feed wastewater per unit of treatment volume.

ACTIVATED SLUDGE PROCESS: High-rate biological effluent treatment process that converts dissolved and colloidal organic matter into biological floc by saturating it with air and activated sludge.

ACUTE TOXICITY: Poisonous effect produced by an effluent within a short period of time (usually up to 96 hours), possibly causing severe biological damage to the receiving water. See also LETHAL THRESHOLD.

ADSORBABLE ORGANIC HALIDE (AOX): Measure of the amount of organically combined halides (i.e., fluoride, chloride, bromide and iodide) in a wastewater sample. This test (involving the adsorption of chlorinated organics onto activated carbon) is tending to displace the TOCl test as a regulatory guideline.

ADSORBATE: Gaseous or dissolved solid substance which is condensed in the form of a film of molecules on the surface of an adsorbent such as charcoal or silica.

ADSORBENT: Porous molecular structure (e.g., activated carbon or silica gel) or a synthetic resin having the ability to attract and hold molecules or charged particles (cations or anions) on its surfaces.

ADSORPTION: Attachment of molecules or charged particles to the chemically active groups on the surfaces and in the pores of such materials as activated carbon and synthetic resins.

ADVANCED WASTEWATER TREATMENT: Any remedial process applied to the wastewater following biological treatment to further reduce the pollution load or remove specific contaminants that may be deleterious to the receiving water. Syn. Tertiary Treatment, Polishing.

AERATION: Bringing about intimate contact between air and water to promote oxygen uptake by the water.

AERATION EFFICIENCY: Usually defined in terms of the amount of oxygen transferred from the air to the liquid per unit amount of energy expended, at standard conditions of zero dissolved oxygen and 20°C.

AERATION LAGOON: Impounding basin for aerobic biological oxidation which utilizes a number of aerators to continuously solubilize oxygen into the wastewater flowing through the basin. Because a significant concentration of oxygen is maintained in the wastewater, biological activity is relatively high and a retention time on the order of 3 to 5 days is sufficient. Syn. Aerated Stabilization Basin.

AERATOR: Equipment for aeration. See also AIR DIFFUSER, CASCADE AERATOR, SURFACE AERATOR, MECHANICAL AERATOR.

AEROBES: Microorganisms requiring oxygen for respiration.

AEROBIC: [adj] Requiring (or tolerant to) the presence of free molecular oxygen.

AEROBIC BIOLOGICAL OXIDATION: Any waste treatment or process utilizing aerobic organisms, in the presence of air or oxygen, to reduce the pollution load or the oxygen demand of organic substances in wastewater or sludge.

AEROBIC DIGESTION: Process in which microorganisms, in the presence of air or oxygen, obtain energy by oxidation of their cellular protoplasm into carbon dioxide and water. Aerobic digestion corresponds to the endogenous phase of biological treatment. Syn. Contact Stabilization.

AIR DIFFUSER: Submerged perforated pipe distributor for injecting small bubbles of air into wastewater. See also AIR SPARGER.

AIR SPARGER: Device for injecting large bubbles of air into wastewater, commonly used in combination with mechanical aerators. See also AIR DIFFUSER.

AIR STRIPPING: Method of deodorizing condensates by direct contact with a stream of air, taking advantage of the greater volatility of the contaminants relative to water. Air stripping is less effective than steam stripping.

AIR-TO-SOLIDS RATIO: Important operating parameter for flotation clarifiers. Obviously, the amount of air must be adequate for efficient solids separation, but the ratio varies with the characteristics of the suspension.

ALGAE: Simple plants containing chlorophyll, many of which are microscopic. Under conditions that favor their growth, algae can form large nuisance colonies in water bodies.

ANAEROBES: Microorganisms which do not require or cannot tolerate oxygen in their life process.

ANAEROBIC: [adj] Requiring (or tolerant to) the absence of free molecular oxygen.

ANAEROBIC BIOLOGICAL TREATMENT: Any waste treatment or process utilizing anaerobic microorganisms in the absence of air to reduce the pollution load or the oxygen demand of organic substances in wastewater or sludge.

ANAEROBIC CONTACT PROCESS: Anaerobic biological waste treatment process in which active microorganisms are removed from the treated effluent and returned to the process to enhance the rate of treatment.

ANAEROBIC DIGESTION: Process in which microorganisms in the absence of oxygen stabilize the biodegradable materials, principally by conversion to methane and carbon dioxide.

ANION INTERCHANGE: Displacement of one negatively charged particle by another on an anion exchange material.

ANOXIC: [adj] Lacking in oxygen; sometimes used as a synonym for "anaerobic".

ANTIFOULANT: Any of a broad class of water treatment chemicals used to control fouling or scaling.

AQUEDUCT: Large conduit or flow channel for carrying water.

AQUIFER: Rock or sediment stratum (geological formation) which is saturated and sufficiently permeable to transmit economic quantities of water to springs or wells. There are two major types of aquifers: unconfined and confined (usually called "artesian"). The water table forms the upper surface of an unconfined aquifer, while an artesian aquifer is confined by a layer of relatively impermeable material. Syn. Water-Producing Zone.

ARTIFICIAL WATERCOURSE: Surface watercourse constructed by human agencies.

ASSIMILATION: (1) Conversion or incorporation of absorbed organic material into protoplasm. (2) Ability of a body of water to purify itself of organic pollution.

ATTRITION: Rubbing of one resin particle against another in a resin bed, causing diminution of resin particle size.

AUTOMATIC SAMPLING: Collecting prescribed samples either continuously or at preset time intervals by a mechanical apparatus operating without direct manual control.

B _____

BACKFLOW: (1) Water flow in a channel or conduit in a direction opposite to normal flow. (2) Any reverse flow, such as occurs in backwashing.

BACKWASH: Part of the operating cycle of an ion-exchange process or a mixed media filter wherein reverse upward flow of water expands the bed, washing out the lighter insoluble contaminants and separating a mixed bed into its components. In the case of the ion-exchange process, the backwash step prepares the bed for regeneration.

BASE EXCHANGE: Exchange of cations on an ion-exchange resin or other prepared medium, e.g., replacement of an undesirable ion, such as calcium or magnesium, with a more desirable one, such as sodium or hydrogen. The reaction is reversible if the concentrations are changed.

BASIN: Shallow depression through which liquids pass or in which they are detained for treatment or storage.

BED: Volume of mixed media in a water filter or ion-exchange resin in a water softener.

BED DEPTH: Depth of mixed media or resin through which water is transported during treatment.

BELT SCREEN: Continuous belt or band of wire mesh, bars, plates, or other screening medium supported between upper and lower rollers, which runs through a water channel and screens out gross debris. The material caught is deflected continuously into a receptacle by gravity, sprays, brushes or other means. Syn. Band Screen.

BENTHIC: [adj] Situated on or associated with the bottom of a water body. Syn. Benthonic.

BENTHIC ORGANISMS: Bottom-dwelling aquatic organisms.

BICARBONATE: Any salt containing the bicarbonate radical (HCO_3). It often refers to calcium bicarbonate in water systems.

BICARBONATE ALKALINITY: Hydroxyl ions (OH^-) in water solution resulting from the hydrolysis of carbonates or bicarbonates.

BIOACCUMULATION: Buildup of contaminants in living organisms above a natural background level.

BIOACCUMULATIVE: [adj] Term applied to chemically stable substances which tend to become concentrated in the food chain.

BIOASSAY: Employment of living organisms to determine the biological effect of a wastewater, chemical agent, or condition. Typically, a number of individuals of a sensitive species are placed in water containing varying concentrations of a contaminant for a specified period of time.

BIOCHEMICAL: [adj] Pertaining to chemical change resulting from the metabolism of living organisms (i.e., biological activity or action).

BIOCHEMICAL OXYGEN DEMAND (BOD): Amount of oxygen consumed in natural aerobic biological processes. See also BOD_5.

BIOCHEMICAL PROCESS: Process by which microorganisms, through their metabolic activity, break down complex organic materials into simple, more stable substances. Syn. Biological Process.

BIOCONVERSION: Conversion of soluble organic waste into biomass, the type of conversion occurring in high-rate biological oxidation processes.

BIODEGRADABLE: [adj] Describes organic material that can be decomposed by the action of microorganisms.

BIOFILM: See ZOOGLEAL FILM.

BIOGAS: Gaseous product resulting from the digestion (usually anaerobic) of organic materials. It has a methane content of 55 to 70% and carbon dioxide content of 30 to 45%, and often contains hydrogen sulfide. Syn. Marsh Gas, Swamp Gas.

BIOLOGICAL CONTACTOR: Partially-submerged, rotating discs with high specific surface area upon which a zoogleal film can develop, designed so that the surface alternately contacts wastewater and air to promote biological oxidation and oxygen transfer.

BIOLOGICAL FILTER: Inert medium with air-exposed surfaces covered by zoogleal films that absorb and adsorb fine suspended, colloidal, and dissolved solids from wastewater as it flows or trickles through. The effectiveness is due to biological action, not from filtering action in the conventional sense.

BIOLOGICAL FLOC: Flocculent colony of microorganisms rich in a polysaccharide slime matrix, typical of the prevailing biomass during the log growth phase or declining growth phase of biochemical oxidation. This biological floc has poor settling characteristics. Syn. Biologically Active Floc, Microbial Floc.

BIOLOGICAL OXIDATION: See AEROBIC BIOLOGICAL OXIDATION.

BIOLOGICAL PROCESS: See BIOCHEMICAL PROCESS.

BIOLOGICAL PURIFICATION: Biological treatment, a duplication of nature's own purification process, by which microorganisms convert organic matter in wastewater into more stable and more benign forms.

BIOLOGICAL SLIME: See ZOOGLEAL FILM.

BIOLOGICAL SLUDGE: Sludge with a low ash content. Syn. Biosludge. See also ACTIVATED SLUDGE, BIOLOGICAL FLOC, BIOMASS.

BIOLOGICAL WASTEWATER TREATMENT: Any form of wastewater treatment in which microorganisms are cultivated to oxidize or stabilize the organic matter present. Examples are aerobic and anaerobic lagoons, aeration lagoons, activated sludge process, biological filters, and biological contactors. Syn. Biotreatment.

BIOMASS: Insoluble organic material resulting from bioconversion; the mass of biological material in the system. Syn. Biosolids.

BIOTA: All living organisms (flora and fauna) within an ecosystem.

BLOOM: Large masses of microscopic and macroscopic plant life, such as green algae, occurring in bodies of water.

BOD$_5$: Shorthand for 5-day biochemical oxygen demand, a laboratory test that determines the amount of oxygen consumed by biological action from a sample of wastewater during a 5-day standardized incubation period, usually expressed in units of milligrams oxygen per liter of wastewater (or ppm). It is generally assumed that 60–70% of the ultimate oxygen demand is reflected in the 5-day test result.

BOD LOAD: Amount of BOD passing into a treatment system or receiving water, expressed in weight or mass per unit time (e.g., lbs/day, kg/day).

BOOSTER PUMP: Pump installed in a pipeline to increase the pressure of the liquid on the discharge side of the pump, commonly used in water distribution systems.

BRACKISH WATER: Mixture of fresh and salt water.

BREAK POINT: Point at which impurities first appear in the effluent of a granular carbon adsorption bed.

BREAKTHROUGH: First appearance of certain ions in the outflow water from an ion exchange bed, which indicates that the ion exchange capacity of the resin is near exhaustion and regeneration is necessary.

BRINE: (1) Very salty water having a dissolved salt content above 30g/l. (2) Solution of sodium chloride (NaCl), often used as an ion exchange regenerant.

BULKING: Phenomenon occurring in activated sludge plants whereby the sludge occupies excessive volumes and will not concentrate readily, usually due to the presence of filamentous organisms.

C _____

CAKE: High-solids residue from a filter, centrifuge or other dewatering device.

CAPACITY: Adsorption ability possessed by an ion exchange resin, reported as weight of ions adsorbed per unit volume of adsorbent.

CARBONATE: Any salt of carbonic acid. It often refers to calcium carbonate in water systems.

CARBONATE ALKALINITY: Alkalinity caused by the presence of carbonate ions, expressed in milligrams of equivalent calcium carbonate per liter.

CARBONATE HARDNESS: Hardness caused by the presence of carbonates and bicarbonates of calcium and magnesium in water. See also HARDNESS.

CARBONATION: Diffusion of carbon dioxide gas through a liquid to render the liquid stable with respect to precipitation or dissolution of alkaline constituents.

CARBONIC ACID: (H_2CO_3) Weak acid formed by the dissolution of carbon dioxide (CO_2) in water.

CARCINOGEN: Material that induces cancerous growth in an organism.

CASCADE AERATOR: Steps of an inclined plane with staggered projections over which water flows in contact with air.

CENTRATE: Liquid remaining after removal of solids as a cake in a centrifuge.

CENTRIFUGATION: Dewatering of sludge using a continuous horizontal centrifuge. Typically, cake consistencies in the 20% to 30% range are attainable depending on the gravitational force applied, detention time in the unit, and the nature of the sludge.

CHANNEL: Natural or artificial waterway having a definite bed and banks to contain the water.

CHEMICAL OXYGEN DEMAND (COD): Rapid chemical test to determine the oxygen demand of all organic matter present in a sample of wastewater. The limitation of the test is its inability to differentiate between biologically oxidizable and biologically inert organic matter.

CHEMICAL SLUDGE: Sludge obtained by treatment of raw water or wastewater with inorganic coagulants.

CHEMICAL TREATMENT (of water): Any water or wastewater treatment process involving the addition of chemicals to achieve a desired result, for example coagulation, flocculation, sludge conditioning, or disinfection.

CHLORINATED PHENOLS: By-product compounds of lignin chlorination that are toxic to aquatic organisms. These chemical substances are also lipophilic (fat soluble) and can therefore accumulate in living organisms.

CHLORINATION: Application of gaseous chlorine to water, sewage or organic waste, usually for purposes of disinfection.

CHLORINATOR: Metering device for adding gaseous chlorine or chlorine water to water or wastewater.

CHRONIC TOXICITY: Long-term toxicity.

CLARIFICATION: Process of removing turbidity and suspended solids by settling. Chemicals can be added to improve and speed up the settling process through coagulation and flocculation. Syn. Sedimentation.

CLARIFIED WASTEWATER: Wastewater from which most of the settleable solids have been removed by sedimentation.

CLARIFIER: See SEDIMENTATION CLARIFIER.

CLEAR WELL: Reservoir containing filtered or clarified water.

COAGULATION: Agglomeration of particles by salts (e.g., lime, alum) that produces small, closely-packed sediments. (N.B. In many cases, the terms "coagulation" and "flocculation" are used interchangeably.)

COLIFORM: Bacteria that are most abundant in sanitary sewage and in streams containing feces and other bodily waste discharges.

COLIFORM ORGANISMS: Group of bacteria recognized as indicators of fecal pollution.

COLOR (of water): Designated as either "true color" or "apparent color". True color is associated only with substances in solution. Apparent color is caused by suspended matter as well as dissolved substances.

COLOR BODIES: Complex molecules that impart color to a solution.

COMBINED SEWER: Sewer intended to receive both wastewater and storm or surface water.

COMPLIANCE: Affirmative indication or judgement that a mill or plant has operated within the discharge limits imposed by government standards.

COMPRESSION FLOTATION: Thickening action which occurs at the surface of a flotation separator. The distinction between "free flotation" and "compression flotation" becomes more pronounced as the particulate concentration in a suspension increases.

CONDENSATE TREATMENT: See AIR STRIPPING, STEAM STRIPPING.

CONDITIONED SLUDGE: Sludge which has been biologically, chemically, or physically modified to facilitate subsequent handling, processing or disposal operations.

CONTAMINANTS: Generally, all foreign components present in another substance. All mineral and organic substances in water are usually considered as contaminants.

CONTINGENCY PLANNING: Flexibility to cope with unforeseen problems, including the provision of backup and alternative processes.

CONTROLLED DISCHARGE: Regulation of effluent flow rates to ensure maintenance of receiving water quality.

COOLING TOWER: Equipment for efficiently contacting hot process water or wastewater with atmospheric air in order to transfer heat into the air (in the form of water vapor) and thus cool the water.

D _____

DECOLORIZATION: Treatment of wastewater to remove color.

DECOMPOSITION: Breakdown of complex chemical structures into basic compounds by chemical or biological action. Syn. Chemical Breakdown.

DEEP WELL DISPOSAL: Pumping of wastewater into confined underground strata to a depth ranging from a few hundred feet to several thousand feet below the ground surface.

DEGREE OF TREATMENT: Measure of the removal effected by a specific treatment, whether directed towards suspended solids, BOD, toxicity, color or any other specified parameter.

DEIONIZATION: Process of selectively removing charged constituents or ionized salts (both inorganic and organic) from solution by ion exchange. Separate steps are required for anions and cations. See also ION EXCHANGE, DEMINERALIZATION.

DEMINERALIZATION: Process of complete or near-complete removal of all ions; the term is usually restricted to ion exchange processes. See also DEIONIZATION.

DENITRIFICATION: Biological process in which nitrites and nitrates are decomposed into nitrogen gas.

DESIGN LOADING: Flow rate and constituent concentration on which the design of a process or piece of equipment is based. Loadings above the design level usually infer lower operating efficiency.

DESORPTION: Removal of a sorbed substance; the reverse of absorption or adsorption.

DETENTION TIME: Period of time that water or wastewater is retained within a basin, tank, or reservoir for storage, settling, or completion of a chemical or biological reaction.

DETOXIFICATION: Treatment of waste to modify or remove toxicity.

DEWATERED SLUDGE: Sludge which has been concentrated to the point where the handling properties are those of a solid rather than a liquid. See also THICKENED SLUDGE.

DIATOMACEOUS-EARTH FILTRATION: Treatment process for raw water to remove colloidal suspended solids in which a built-up layer of diatomaceous earth (mostly skeletons of diatoms) serves as the filter medium.

DIFFUSED AERATION: Injection of air under pressure into a liquid through a diffuser to form small air bubbles.

DIFFUSER: Porous tube or plate through which gas is forced and divided into minute bubbles for diffusion into liquids. When the gas is air, the device may be called a "diffusion aerator".

DIFFUSER OUTFALL: Distributed discharge of wastewater effluent through a long submerged perforated pipe.

DIGESTED SLUDGE: Organic sludge digested under anaerobic conditions until the volatile content has been reduced substantially, usually by more than 50%.

DIGESTION: Biological decomposition of organic matter.

DILUTION FACTOR: Ratio of the quantity of discharge effluent to the average quantity of dilution water available in the receiving water, usually expressed as a percentage. Syn. Available Dilution.

DIOXIN: Name given to a family of chlorinated cyclic compounds of which more than 70 members have been identified as likely carcinogens. Their cancerous character is determined apparently by the location of chlorine atoms in the cluster. Attention is often focussed on 2,3,7,8 tetrachlorodibenzo-p-dioxin (2378 TCDD) because it is extremely toxic and bioaccumulative.

DISCHARGE: Flow from a tank, stack, or treatment process.

DISCHARGE PERMIT: Formal authorization, issued by a regulatory agency, stipulating limiting conditions for effluent discharge into the environment.

DISINFECTION: Destruction of harmful or objectionable microorganisms, usually by chemical or thermal methods.

DISSOLVED OXYGEN (DO): Molecular oxygen in solution, a vital constituent of natural waters, measured in milligrams per liter, parts per million or percent saturation. The level of dissolved oxygen in a particular body of water reflects the dynamic equilibrium between such factors as absorption, respiration, photosynthesis and decomposition. See also OXYGEN SATURATION.

DISSOLVED SOLIDS: Total amount of dissolved material, organic and inorganic, contained in raw water or wastewater. In the laboratory, the dissolved solids content of any water can be determined by evaporating a filtered sample to dryness and weighing the residue.

DISTILLATE: Condensed vapors which form the product from a distillation operation.

DIVERSITY: Number of species present in an ecosystem and their numerical composition.

DIVERSITY INDEX: Ratio of the total number of individuals of all species present to the number of species present at a site, used in biological studies as a measure of the health of an aquatic community.

DOSAGE: Specified amount of a substance to be added to a unit volume of liquid. In practice, the terms "dosage" and "dose" are used interchangeably.

DOUBLE BELT FILTER: Device for dewatering sludge that utilizes two endless or seamed porous belts (upper and lower), usually of polyester wire mesh merging at one point and enclosing the cake between the belts. This "sandwich arrangement" then passes through a series of squeeze rolls before the belts separate to discharge the dewatered cake.

DRAIN: Channel or pipe which carries away run-off water, spills, or wastewater.

DRAWDOWN: (1) Amount that the water surface in a well is depressed when water is being pumped, a function of the pumping rate and the porosity of the stratum. (2) Lowering of the water table caused by pumping of groundwater from wells.

DREDGING: Removal of sediment.

DUMP: Land site where solid waste is disposed of in a haphazard manner, not protective of the environment.

E _____

ECOLOGICAL IMPACT: Total effect of an environmental change on the ecology of an area.

ECOLOGY: Interrelationships of living things to one another and to their environment (or the study thereof).

ECOSYSTEM: Composite balance of all living organisms and their ambient environment within a well-defined compass.

EFFLUENT: Out-flowing stream from a process or confined space. The term is most often applied to liquid discharges into receiving waters. Syn. Effluent Stream.

EFFLUENT QUALITY: Physical, chemical and biological characteristics of an outflow stream.

EFFLUENT SEEPAGE: Diffuse discharge of wastewater into substrata or surface water bodies.

EFFLUENT STANDARD: Maximum allowable concentration or mass of a specified constituent that may be discharged.

EMBAYED: [adj] Term applied to an outfall when there is inadequate flushing action to prevent buildup of the effluent in the adjacent receiving water.

EMBAYMENT: Deep indentation in a shoreline forming a bay.

EMISSION: Any discharge of liquid, solid or gaseous material.

EMISSION STANDARD: Maximum amount of pollutant legally permitted to be discharged into the environment from a specified source.

END-OF-PIPE: [adj] Term applied to treatments of wastewater which are external to the mill, as contrasted to treatment processes within the mill.

ENDOGENOUS PHASE: Terminal phase of an aerobic treatment process when a small portion of the organic material remains unstabilized and endogenous respiration is dominant.

ENDOGENOUS RESPIRATION: Process in which microorganisms consume their own cell material for energy.

ENVIRONMENT: Sum of all external conditions and influences affecting the life and development of an organism.

ENVIRONMENTAL CHEMISTRY: Study of the sources, reactions, transport, effects and fates of chemical species in the water, soil and air environments.

ENVIRONMENTAL IMPACT: Untoward effect of industrial activity (e.g., emission of pollutants) on the quality of the environment and on the stability of the ecological processes that maintain it.

ENVIRONMENTAL IMPACT STATEMENT (EIS): Report which identifies and assesses the direct beneficial and detrimental impact of a proposed action on the environment. The filing of such a report is required by the EPA and other regulatory agencies.

EQUALIZATION: (1) Controlling the flow of effluent discharge at a rate proportional to the receiving stream. (2) Controlling the flow of wastewater into a treatment process at a rate determined by the capacity of the process.

EQUALIZING BASIN: Holding and blending basin for waste streams in which variations of flow and/or composition can be averaged out before the wastewater enters the treatment unit.

ESTUARY: Water passage where the tide meets a river current.

EUTROPHIC: [adj] Term applied to water that has an optimal or nearly optimal concentration of nutrients for plant or animal growth.

EUTROPHICATION: Undesirable enrichment of a receiving water, causing excessive growth of aquatic plants and eventual choking and deoxygenation of the water body.

EVAPORATION POND: Shallow, artificial pond where concentrated waste is pumped, permitted to dry, and either removed or buried by additional sludge.

EXCESS SLUDGE: Sludge produced in the activated sludge process which is not needed for recirculation, and is removed from the process. Syn. Waste Sludge.

EXHAUSTION: State of an ion exchange resin when it can no longer remove specified ions to the required degree.

EXTENDED AERATION PROCESS: Modification of the activated sludge process which utilizes longer aeration periods to promote reduction in biomass by endogenous respiration.

EXTERNAL WASTEWATER TREATMENT: Treatment of wastewater outside of the normal mill processing sequence, as distinct from internal treatment.

EXTERNAL WATER TREATMENT: Water treatment applied to most of the raw water before it enters the mill.

F

FACULTATIVE BACTERIA: Bacteria having the ability to grow and metabolize either when oxygen is present or when it is absent.

FACULTATIVE LAGOON: Biological treatment lagoon for wastewater with an aerobic upper section and an anaerobic bottom section, in which the principles of both aerobic and anaerobic processes apply.

FAUNA: Animal life taken as a whole that is characteristic of a specific environment.

FILAMENTOUS ORGANISMS: Bacterial, fungal, and algal species that grow in thread-like colonies. These growths if prevalent in activated sludge or biological filters will reduce the settleability and dewaterability of the resultant biomass.

FILL AREA: That portion of a landfill site which has been or will be filled with solid waste.

FILTER BED: Filter media consisting of layers of particles which gradually increase in size from the top downward. See also RAPID SAND FILTER, MIXED-MEDIA FILTER.

FILTER PLANT: Section of the mill where the processes, devices and structures for water treatment are situated.

FIXED SOLIDS: Solids in any category (i.e., dissolved, settleable, nonsettleable) that are left as residue after ignition at 600°C. The portion of fixed solids in a sample is an indication of the inorganic content. Syn. Non-Volatile Solids.

FLASH DISTILLATION: Technique for removing volatiles from contaminated condensate which utilizes a heat exchanger to pressurize the condensate. The pressure is then released through a throttling valve causing the volatiles to flash off along with a predetermined quantity of water vapor.

FLOATABLE SOLIDS: Low-density solids that float on the surface.

FLOCCULANT: Chemical additive for promoting flocculation. Syn. Flocculating Agent.

FLOCCULATION: Formation of suspended solids into large, loose, open masses that are primarily tied together by bridging via polyelectrolytes. (N.B. In many cases, the terms "coagulation" and "flocculation" are used interchangeably.)

FLOCCULENT SETTLING: Sedimentation in which the separation process is accompanied by changes in particle size due to flocculation.

FLORA: Plant life taken as a whole that is characteristic of a specific environment.

FLOTATION: Method of separating suspended solids from wastewater by the introduction of minute air bubbles which become attached to the particles and float them to the surface where they form a scum and are removed by a skimming device.

FLOTSAM: Debris from natural causes or human activity that floats on oceans, lakes and rivers.

FLOWAGE: Movement of liquid through a series of structures or basins such as occurs in a treatment plant.

FLOW-THROUGH TIME: Average time required for an incremental volume of liquid to pass through a basin or treatment process from inlet to outlet.

FLUME: Channel section of known geometry which is used as a measuring device for open-channel flow (based on the relationship between flow rate and upstream water depth). Syn. Control Flume. See also PARSHALL FLUME.

FOAM FRACTIONATION: Method of removing toxic substances from pulp mill waste by introducing small air bubbles into the wastewater to generate a foam (in which the toxic substances are concentrated) and subsequently skimming off the foam for special treatment.

FOOD CHAIN: Sequence of species in order of increasing complexity and decreasing numbers, with the more-complex species feeding on the less-complex species.

FOOD-TO-MICROORGANISM RATIO (F/M RATIO): Measure of organic loading for the activated sludge process, usually defined as the daily mass of 5-day BOD in the secondary effluent to the mass of volatile suspended solids in the aeration tanks.

FREEBOARD: Space provided above the resin bed in a deionization unit to allow for expansion of the bed during backwashing without loss of resin particles.

FREE SETTLING: Separation of independent particles from a suspension by gravity settling, i.e., sedimentation without coagulation or flocculation.

FRESH WATER: Water of low mineral or salt content.

FRESH WATER BODIES: Lakes, rivers, streams and estuaries with a fresh-water surface layer harboring fresh-water fauna.

FURAN: Name given to a family of toxic chemicals that are related to dioxin and are often found with dioxins.

G _____

GRAPPLE DREDGE: Floating derrick with a grapple-type bucket for removing material below water.

GRIT: Heavy mineral matter, such as sand, gravel or cinders, in wastewater.

GRIT CHAMBER: Enlargement of a sewer channel to reduce the velocity of flow and allow gravity settling of inorganic solids.

GROUNDWATER: Subsurface freshwater in an aquifer; all fresh water below the water table.

H _____

HARDNESS: Measure of a water's ability to precipitate soap; the combined concentration of calcium and magnesium ions, expressed as calcium carbonate.

HAZARDOUS WASTE: Any waste that is potentially damaging to the environment because of its toxicity, corrosivity, chemical reactivity, radioactivity or other detrimental properties.

HEAVY SLUDGE: Sludge in liquid form, but with a high solids content.

HIGH-RATE BIOLOGICAL PROCESS: Treatment process for wastewater that combines efficient removal of BOD with a low flow-through time. The principal mechanism of BOD removal is bioconversion of soluble waste into biomass.

HIGH-VOLUME, LOW-CONCENTRATION (HVLC): [adj] Term applied to large wastewater flows containing a relatively small amount of contaminants.

HUMIC ACID: Any of numerous complex organic acids derived from decaying organic matter, a common constituent of surface waters.

HYDRAULIC DREDGE: Scow equipped with a centrifugal pump. The suction line from the pump reaches the bottom to be excavated, and the pump discharge connects to a pipeline that conveys the dredged material to a place of deposit. Syn. Suction Dredge.

HYDRAULIC JUMP: Abrupt rise in water level occurring in an open channel when water flowing at high velocity is retarded.

HYDRAULIC JUMP STICK: Simple device to obtain approximate flow measurements in an open channel of uniform dimensions, such as a mill sewer. It has a sharp edge for depth measurement and a blunt edge to create the "hydraulic jump" (difference in readings between blunt and sharp edges) necessary to measure flow velocity.

HYDRAULIC LOADING: Rate at which wastewater is fed into a treatment process, either in terms of a volumetric flow rate or volumetric flow rate per unit surface area.

HYDRO-GEL: Highly hydrated sludge (i.e., having properties approaching those of a viscous jelly-like product) which does not dewater well by mechanical processes. Hydro-gels are formed from such substances as wood flour, fiber debris, ray cells, alumina hydrate, starches, dextrins, and proteins. Syn. Hydrous Gel, Hydrous Sludge.

HYDROLOGY: Applied science dealing with the occurence, distribution, circulation and characteristics of natural waters and their relationship with the environment.

HYDROUS SLUDGE: See HYDRO-GEL.

I _____

IMHOFF CONE: Graduated, cone-shaped glass container used to measure the volume of sediment accumulated during a specified settling time in a sample of wastewater or other liquid.

IMMEDIATE OXYGEN DEMAND: Amount of oxygen consumed by a wastewater effluent immediately upon being introduced into a receiving water containing dissolved oxygen. The reactive agent may be a product of prior biochemical action or a chemical substance that is extremely reactive with oxygen (i.e., a strong reducing agent).

INCLINED PLATE SEPARATOR: See LAMELLA SEPARATOR.

INCLINED TUBE SETTLER: Sedimentation clarifier utilizing a series of inclined tubes to improve the efficiency of solids removal.

INCUBATION: Supporting a viable culture of microorganisms at suitable conditions for growth and reproduction.

INDUSTRIAL WASTE: Liquid waste from an industrial process, as distinct from municipal, domestic or sanitary wastes.

INFILTRATION: Flow of water downward from the land surface into and through the upper soil layers.

INFILTRATION CAPACITY: Maximum rate at which infiltration can occur under specific conditions of soil moisture.

INFILTRATION RATE: Maximum rate at which soil layers (under specified conditions) can absorb water, defined as the volume of water passing into the soil per unit area and unit time.

INFLUENT: Any stream entering a unit operation; the term is typically applied to wastewater as it flows into a basin or treatment process.

INHIBITION INDEX: Measure of inhibitory toxicity. A value near unity indicates no inhibitory effect; a value of 0.5 is sometimes taken as the transition between moderate and severe inhibition.

INHIBITORY TOXICITY: Reduction in the rate of general metabolism of microorganisms due to constituents in the wastewater.

INITIAL DILUTION ZONE: Specified area of a receiving water adjacent to the point of waste discharge, which is usually excluded from receiving water guidelines. Syn. Mixing Zone.

INTAKE: Opening, with or without a screen or grating, through which raw water enters a conduit for gravity conveyance to a sump.

INTERNAL WASTEWATER TREATMENT: Reduction of pollution by means of steps taken within the normal mill process, as distinct from external treatment.

INTERNAL WATER TREATMENT: Specialized water treatment for a limited amount of the mill water supply, e.g., boiler water treatment.

ION EXCHANGE: Replacement of an ion in a mineral or resin lattice with another ion that is present in an aqueous solution.

ION EXCHANGE PROCESS: See DEIONIZATION, DEMINERALIZATION.

ION EXCHANGE RESINS: Insoluble, synthetic polymers with appended functional groups that are capable of ion exchange, used in water treatment for deionization and demineralization.

ISOPLETHS: Contours of constant concentration; for example, showing water pollutant concentrations on a survey chart in an area of receiving water adjacent to an industrial plant.

J _____

JAR TEST: Laboratory procedure for evaluating coagulation, flocculation and sedimentation characteristics of wastewaters.

JOINT TREATMENT: Combined treatment of municipal and industrial wastewaters.

L _____

LAGOON: Any holding or detention pond used to contain wastewater for storage, sedimentation or biological treatment.

LAMELLA SEPARATOR: Sedimentation clarifier utilizing a series of inclined thin plates to improve the efficiency of solids removal. Syn. Inclined Plate Separator.

LAND APPLICATION: Disposal of wastewater onto land under controlled conditions, such as by irrigation or infiltration.

LAND FARMING: Systematic use of the upper soil zone to manage certain biodegradable industrial wastes.

LANDFILL: Disposal of solid waste by depositing onto a suitable land site, followed by compacting and covering with an appropriate layer of soil.

LEACHATE: Liquid that has percolated through solid waste or other media and has extracted dissolved or suspended material from it.

LEACHING: Process by which soluble materials in the soil are dissolved and carried away by percolating water.

LETHAL THRESHOLD: Maximum amount of a toxic substance tolerated by a test fish without causing death. See also MEDIAN TOLERANCE LIMIT.

LIME PRECIPITATION: Any of several processes for decolorization of pulp mill effluent based on the low solubility of the calcium salts of the colored weak acids present. Typically, the colored substances in caustic extraction effluent and other specific colored effluents are precipitated with minimal amounts of lime slurry followed by dewatering in admixture with lime mud and burning of the colored organics in the lime kiln.

LOADING: See POLLUTION LOAD.

LOG GROWTH PHASE: Initial phase of aerobic treatment processes during which the bacterial population increases logarithmically with time; i.e., that phase in which the growth rate is a function only of cell division time, not of food supply.

LOSS ON IGNITION: Percentage difference between the weight before and after burning, an indication of percent organics in a sample.

LOW-VOLUME, HIGH-CONCENTRATION (LVHC): [adj] Term applied to small wastewater flows containing large amounts of contaminants, especially volatile organics.

M _____

MAIN SEWER: Sewer to which one or more branch sewers are tributary.

MANIFOLD: Pipe with numerous branches to convey fluids between a large pipe and several smaller pipes, or to permit selection of flow diversion from one of several sources or to one of several discharge points.

MARINE WATER: Generic term for all receiving waters having a certain measurable level of sea salt, including coastal and estuarine waters.

MARSH GAS: See BIOGAS.

MAXIMUM SUSTAINED YIELD: Maximum rate at which groundwater can be withdrawn perennially from a particular source.

MECHANICAL AERATOR: Device that mixes atmospheric oxygen into a liquid by the mechanical action of a paddle, turbine, spray, etc. See also SURFACE AERATOR.

MEDIAN TOLERANCE LIMIT: In bioassays, the concentration of pollutants or wastewater at which 50 percent of the test animals can survive for a specified period of exposure, usually 96 hours. Syn. Median Lethal Concentration, Median Effective Concentration.

MESOPHILIC BACTERIA: Bacteria which grow best within the temperature range of 20 to 40°C.

METABOLISM: Sum of all the interrelated chemical processes occurring in living organisms.

METABOLIZING: In biological processes, converting food, such as soluble organic waste, into cellular matter and gaseous by-products.

METHANE: (CH_4) Colorless, flammable, non-toxic gaseous hydrocarbon produced during anaerobic decomposition of organic waste.

MICROBE: See MICROORGANISM.

MICROBIAL FILM: See ZOOGLEAL FILM.

MICROBIAL FLOC: See BIOLOGICAL FLOC.

MICROORGANISM: Organism observable only through a microscope. Large, visible types may be distinguished as "macroorganisms". Syn. Microbe.

MIXED LIQUOR: Mixture of wastewater and recirculated sludge in the aeration tank undergoing activated sludge treatment.

MIXED LIQUOR SUSPENDED SOLIDS (MLSS): Suspended solids in a mixture of activated sludge and organic matter undergoing activated sludge treatment in an aeration tank.

MIXED-MEDIA FILTER: Modified rapid sand filter utilizing two or more dissimilar granular materials (e.g., anthracite and sand) blended by size and density to produce a deep, composite filter medium hydraulically graded after backwash from fine to coarse in the direction of normal flow. Syn. Multi-Media Filter.

MONITORING: Routine observation, sampling and testing as appropriate to determine efficiency of treatment, compliance with standards and requirements, and environmental impact. Syn. Surveillance.

MULTIROLL PRESS: Mechanical equipment for dewatering sedimentation sludge consisting of four small rolls ("press rolls") bearing against a center roll ("mother roll"). The entering mixture is fed from a vertical chute into the space between the inlet press roll and mother roll and is carried around the mother roll through three press nips.

MUNICIPAL WASTE: Office, shop and street waste, but excluding domestic waste.

MUTAGEN: Material that induces genetic change.

N _____

NATURAL PURIFICATION: Naturally-occurring processes in a receiving water which result in reduced population of microorganisms, stabilization of organic constituents, restoration of dissolved oxygen level and return of resident biota to normal diversity. Syn. Self-Purification.

NEUTRALIZATION: Restoration of a balanced condition between hydrogen and hydroxyl ions in solution by controlled addition of acid or alkali.

NONSETTLEABLE SOLIDS: Solid material that remains in suspension for an extended period of time. In the laboratory, the portion of solids remaining in suspension after one hour of settling are usually designated as nonsettleable solids.

NUTRIENT: Substance assimilated by a microorganism which promotes growth, especially either nitrogen or phosphorus in wastewater.

O

OCEAN DISPOSAL: Barging of waste out to sea and dumping in deep water.

OPEN CHANNEL: Natural or artificial waterway in which water flows with a free surface.

ORGANIC LOADING: Measure of the amount of organic material in the wastewater influent to a biological treatment process, expressed as mass per unit time per unit surface area or per unit mass of microorganisms. See also FOOD-TO-MICROORGANISM RATIO.

ORGANIC SCREEN: Special anion resin with a high porosity which is placed within a water treatment sequence prior to demineralization in order to remove organic molecules which would foul the demineralizer anion resin.

OUTFALL: Mouth of a sewer, drain or conduit where effluent is discharged into the receiving water.

OVERHEADS: Vapor leaving the stripping column.

OXIDATION POND: Shallow, artificial basin in which wastewater is oxidized by the action of aerobic microorganisms, with oxygen transfer primarily by natural absorption from the air. If significant amounts of air are mixed into the wastewater by artificial means, the designation "aeration pond" or "aeration lagoon" is more appropriate. Syn. Oxidation Lagoon, Stabilization Pond.

OXYGENATION CAPACITY: Amount of oxygen that an aerator is capable of supplying to a liquid under specified conditions. See also AERATOR EFFICIENCY.

OXYGEN SAG CURVE: Profile of dissolved oxygen along the course of a stream which shows the depression resulting from the addition of a BOD effluent and the subsequent recovery from reoxygenation through absorption of atmospheric oxygen and through biological photosynthesis.

OXYGEN SATURATION: Maximum concentration of dissolved oxygen that a water or wastewater can contain in equilibrium with the atmosphere. Fresh water at 20°C has a saturation concentration of 8.9 ppm.

OZONATION: Treatment of water or wastewater with ozone for purposes of disinfection and odor control.

P

PARSHALL FLUME: Flow-measuring device for open channels consisting of a contracting length on the upstream side, a throat and an expanding length on the downstream side. Typically, the liquid level in the contracting length is sufficient to indicate the liquid flow rate.

PATHOGEN: Material that produces disease in an organism.

PCB: Generic term covering a family of partially or wholly chlorinated biphenol compounds. Before their toxic properties were identified, PCB's were widely used as insulating materials in power transformers and other products.

PENSTOCK: Pipeline which carries water from a higher elevation source under pressure to the turbine in a hydroelectric power generating station.

PERCOLATION: Flowing or trickling of a liquid downward through a contact or filtering medium. The liquid may or may not fill the pores of the medium.

PHENOLS: Family of cyclic organic compounds, by-products of lignin degradation, which have toxic properties.

PHOTOSYNTHESIS: Mechanism by which chlorophyll-bearing plants utilize light energy to produce carbohydrates and oxygen from carbon dioxide and water (the reverse of respiration).

PIG: Ram-like cylindrical object (often with brushes on the surface) that is forced through a pipeline by fluid pressure to remove buildups of sludge or other deposits. The technique of utilizing a pig is known as "pigging". See also PROGRESSIVE PIGGING.

PLANKTON: Small, floating or weakly-swimming animals (zooplankton) and plants (phytoplankton) in a body of water.

PLASTIC MEDIA: Honeycomb-like formed products with high surface area, used in trickling filters in place of crushed stone as a forming surface for zoogleal film.

POLLUTANT: Any causative factor which renders water unfit for a given use.

POLLUTION ABATEMENT: See ABATEMENT.

POLLUTION LOAD: Effluent volume and strength, especially in terms of its solids or oxygen-demand characteristics. The term may also refer to some objectionable physical or chemical characteristics of the wastewater that are particularly harmful to the receiving water.

POTABLE WATER: Water suitable for domestic purposes, especially human consumption.

PRETREATMENT: Operations such as screening, grit removal, equalization, skimming, or neutralization that prepare the wastewater for major treatment. Syn. Preliminary Treatment.

PRIMARY EFFLUENT: Treated wastewater leaving primary treatment.

PRIMARY SLUDGE: Sludge from primary treatment.

PRIMARY TREATMENT: Removal of settleable and floatable solids from the wastewater, usually either by means of sedimentation or flotation operations.

PRIMARY TREATMENT EFFICIENCY: Percentage reduction in suspended solids in the primary effluent as compared to the incoming wastewater.

PROCESS WATER: Water which is utilized within a pulp/paper mill or other industrial plant for sealing, cooling, dilution, cleaning, washing or other related purposes.

PROGRESSIVE PIGGING: Strategy of pipeline cleaning in which a series of successively fatter and denser pigs are run through the line to gradually reduce the buildup and prevent hangup of the pig. See also PIG.

R

RACE: Channel transporting water, most often applied to a supply channel for hydraulic equipment. On the outflow side, it is called a "tailrace". A channel designed specifically for industrial water is called a "millrace".

RADIAL-FLOW TANK: Any circular tank (e.g., a sedimentation clarifier) in which the direction of flow is from the center to the periphery, or vice versa.

RADIAL INWARD FLOW: Flow from the periphery of a circular tank to the center.

RADIAL OUTWARD FLOW: Flow from the center of a circular tank to the periphery, as for example the flow in clarifier tank.

RAPID INFILTRATION: Method of removing color from wastewater, where topography and soil structure are suitable, in which wastewater percolates from a supply basin down through porous subsoil strata before it enters the receiving water. The color is removed by adsorption and precipitation onto soil particles. Because the soil strata become rather rapidly saturated, it is necessary to operate a number of basins intermittently, allowing time for the regeneration of adsorbing surfaces by natural means.

RAPID SAND FILTER: Type of filter used mainly in raw water treatment plants, in which water that has been previously treated by coagulation and sedimentation is passed downward through a filtering medium consisting of sand and/or anthracite coal particles resting on a bed of gravel. The filter is cleaned periodically by reversing the flow of water upward. See also MIXED-MEDIA FILTER.

RAW EFFLUENT: Wastewater discharged into a receiving water without treatment.

RAW SLUDGE: Sludge freshly withdrawn from a sedimentation process, prior to further treatment. Syn. Undigested Sludge.

RAW WASTEWATER: Wastewater before it receives any treatment. Syn. Raw Sewage.

RAW WATER: Untreated water, especially water that is entering the initial stage of a treatment process.

RECEIVING WATER: Any stream or body of water that receives treated or untreated wastewater.

RECLAIMED WASTEWATER: Treated wastewater used for some beneficial purpose such as irrigation or recreation.

RECOVERY: Rise in water level in a pumping well and nearby observation wells after groundwater pumpage has stopped.

REFUSE: See SOLID WASTE.

REGENERANT SOLUTION: Chemical solution of high concentration used to restore the activity of an ion exchanger. See also REGENERATION.

REGENERATION: (1) Restoration of the activity of an ion exchanger by displacing the ions adsorbed from the treated water (usually divalent or trivalent ions) by less-firmly-adsorbed ions (monovalent ions) from the regenerant. (2) Restoration of a molecular adsorbent, such as activated carbon, most commonly by steaming or thermal treatment; also referred to as "reactivation" or "revivification".

REOXYGENATION: Replenishment of oxygen in a receiving water by such natural means as photosynthesis by aquatic plants and atmospheric aeration.

RESIDUALS MANAGEMENT: Imprecise term meaning pollution control or waste treatment. Syn. Waste Management.

RESPIRATION: Biological oxidation within a life form, the typical energy source for animals (the reverse of photosynthesis).

RETURN SLUDGE: Settled activated sludge that is returned to mix with the wastewater entering the treatment process.

RINSE: Operation which follows regeneration, the flushing out of excess regenerant solution.

ROTATING BIOLOGICAL CONTACTER: Type of biological filter consisting of a series of closely spaced corrugated plastic discs anchored to a rotating horizontal shaft and supported above a trough through which wastewater is channeled. The discs alternately move through wastewater and air, thus feeding and aerating the zoogleal film that builds on the surfaces.

S _____

SALINITY: Concentration of dissolved salts in a water sample, often expressed as mg/liter of chlorine.

SALVAGE: Extraction of usable materials from a mixture of waste.

SANITARY SEWER: Independent system handling only domestic wastewater.

SCUM: Extraneous matter that has risen to the surface or formed on the surface of a liquid, often having a foul, filmy appearance. The term "skimmings" refers to scum that has been removed.

SECCHI DISC: Circular disc (20 cm in diameter) divided by painting into four quadrants of alternating white and black, used to measure turbidity in a water body. The disc is slowly lowered into the water, and the depth at which the disc is no longer visible is noted as the Secchi disc reading of turbidity.

SECONDARY EFFLUENT: Treated wastewater leaving secondary treatment.

SECONDARY SLUDGE: Sludge from secondary treatment.

SECONDARY TREATMENT: Biological treatment of wastewater for removal of BOD, the second step in most waste treatment systems.

SECONDARY TREATMENT EFFICIENCY: Percentage reduction of BOD_5 in the secondary effluent as compared to the wastewater entering secondary treatment.

SEDIMENT: Solid material settled from a liquid suspension. An example is the sludge from a clarifier.

SEDIMENTATION: Gravity settling, a process for removing settleable material. Sedimentation may be carried out without chemical additives (called "plain sedimentation" or "free settling"), or following coagulation and flocculation. Syn. Settling, Subsidence.

SEDIMENTATION BASIN: Basin in which wastewater is retained for a sufficient time to allow suspended solids to settle out. Syn. Settling Basin.

SEDIMENTATION CLARIFIER: Tank which continually receives a dilute suspension and produces a relatively clear overflow. Many configurations are available, the most common being circular tanks with diameters up to 500 feet and having slowly rotating rakes. The supernatant overflows at the periphery while the denser layer of slurry is withdrawn at the bottom. See also SEDIMENTATION THICKENER.

SEDIMENTATION THICKENER: Tank which is similar to a sedimentation clarifier except that provision is made for concentrating the sludge layer, usually by providing greater tank depth. The construction is more robust and torque requirement of the rake is greater.

SEDIMENT CONCENTRATION: Weight percent of sediment in a water/sediment mixture. Low concentrations are generally expressed in parts per million.

SEEDING: Inoculating wastewater with biological sludge for the purpose of introducing favorable organisms, and thereby accelerating the initial stages of digestion.

SELECTIVE CONDENSATION: Two-pass condensing of volatile-rich evaporator vapors in such a manner that the quantity of volatile contaminants in the uncondensed steam fraction is continuously enriched by volatile compounds distilled from the condensate. As a result, the condensate in the first condensing section is effectively steam-stripped and requires no further treatment.

SEPTIC: [adj] Anaerobic; often referring to the foul-smelling or putrid ambience of anaerobic conditions.

SETTLEABLE SOLIDS: Material in wastewater that settles out of suspension after an extended time period. In the laboratory, settleable solids are usually designated as the portion that settles out after one hour.

SETTLING: See SEDIMENTATION.

SEWAGE: Flow in a sewer. Syn. Wastewater.

SEWER: System of drain channels and pipes that collects and delivers wastewater to a treatment plant or receiving water.

SHOCK LOADING: Sudden change in the composition of wastewater entering a treatment facility which may be beyond the ability of the system to assimilate.

SKIMMING: Removing floating solids and scum from the surface of a liquid, either by means of a shallow overflow or a mechanical device.

SKIMMING TANK: Tank designed so that floating matter will rise and remain on the surface until removed, while wastewater discharges continuously under a vertical baffle (scum board).

SLEEK: [adj] Iridescent appearance of the surface of water to which wastewater has been discharged, due to a thin oily film.

SLOUGHING: See UNLOADING.

SLUDGE: Slurry separated from water or wastewater during processing.

SLUDGE CAKE: Air-dried or dewatered sludge at sufficiently high dryness to be handled as a solid.

SLUDGE DIGESTION: Biological process by which organic sludge is decomposed or converted into more stable organic matter.

SLUDGE PIT: Receiving cavity at the bottom of a sedimentation clarifier from which the sludge is pumped. Syn. Sludge Sump.

SLUDGE VOLUME INDEX: Indicator of the settling properties of flocculated microorganisms, measured as the volume of mixed liquor suspended solids after a one-liter sample has been allowed to settle for 30 minutes.

SLUICING: Causing water to flow at high velocity for whatever purpose, for example, to wash up a stock spill.

SOFTENING: Removing calcium and magnesium ions by ion exchange or precipitation/settling.

SOLIDS: In water and wastewater treatment, any dissolved or suspended material. See also SUSPENDED SOLIDS, DISSOLVED SOLIDS, VOLATILE SOLIDS, FIXED SOLIDS.

SOLIDS LOADING: Rate at which suspended solids are fed into a treatment process, usually in terms of mass flow rate per unit area.

SOLIDS RETENTION TIME (SRT): Average residence time in days of suspended solids (ss) in a biological treatment process, calculated by dividing the total weight of ss in the system by the total weight of ss leaving the system per day.

SOLID WASTE: Useless, unwanted or discarded material with insufficient liquid to be free flowing. Syn. Refuse.

SOLID WASTE DISPOSAL: Ultimate disposition of refuse that cannot be salvaged or recycled, usually by landfill or incineration.

SORPTION: Attachment of molecules or particles to a solid material by either absorption or adsorption.

SPARGER: See AIR SPARGER.

SPECIFIC FILTER LOADING: Amount of suspended solids that can be removed by a filter before backwashing is required, typically expressed as mass (or weight) per unit area per cycle.

SPILL: Accidental discharge of untreated wastewater or hazardous material that has the potential to harm the environment.

SPILL COLLECTION SYSTEM: System designed to collect spills of fiber and spent liquor while minimizing inclusion of dilution water.

SPILL POND: Holding or equalizing basin to handle emergency conditions; e.g., spills of concentrated waste. Syn. Holding Pond, Diversion Pond.

STABILIZATION: Process of converting organic matter in wastewater or solid waste into inert, harmless material.

STEAM DISTILLATION: See STEAM STRIPPING.

STEAM STRIPPING: Essentially a multistage distillation separation using direct steam as the heat source. Steam stripping is commonly applied to such concentrated wastewater streams as digester and evaporator condensates in order to remove methanol, reduced sulfur gases and other volatile components. Syn. Steam Distillation.

STERILIZATION: Complete destruction of all bacteria and other organisms in water (or in products, containers, etc.).

STREAM STANDARDS: Set of criteria defining the desired chemical, physical, and biological conditions of a stream; usually established by government regulation.

STRIPPING: Any distillation process for removing the more volatile constituents from a liquid mixture. See also Air Stripping, Steam Stripping.

STRIPPING COLUMN: Multi-tray distillation column in which contaminated condensate is contacted with steam to remove volatile compounds.

SUBLETHAL TOXICITY: Nonbeneficial change which occurs in an organism as a result of exposure to a toxicant which need not result in the death of the organism.

SUCTION DREDGE: See HYDRAULIC DREDGE.

SUMP: Depression or tank that serves as a receptacle for liquids at the lowest point of a recirculation, salvage or disposal system.

SUPERNATANT LIQUID: Layer of liquid essentially free of suspended solids above the sludge surface in a clarifier thickener or in a digester unit.

SURFACE AERATOR: Equipment located near the liquid surface which provides pumpage and agitation in order to expose the liquid to air. Oxygen is transferred through rapid surface turnover and turbulent lifting of liquid.

SURFACE LOADING: Measure of wastewater feed rate to a sedimentation clarifier in terms of volumetric flow rate per unit area. See also Hydraulic Loading.

SURFACE WATER: Generic term for fresh water sources that include lakes, rivers and reservoirs.

SUSPENDED SOLIDS: Insoluble solids that either float on the surface or are in suspension in water, wastewater or other liquids. Suspended solids may be further classified into floatable solids, settleable solids and nonsettleable solids.

SUSPENSOIDS: Colloidal particles remaining in suspension under all conditions.

T _____

TAILRACE: Channel for carrying water away from a turbine or industrial usage.

TAINTING: Taste and odor impairment of fish flesh and fat. (Numerous agents in industrial effluents can cause tainting, including compounds contained in digester and evaporator condensates.)

TERATOGEN: Specific substance identified as causing birth defects.

TERMINAL SETTLING VELOCITY: Rate at which a suspended particle will settle when it is not hindered in any way.

TERTIARY TREATMENT: See ADVANCED WASTEWATER TREATMENT.

THERMAL POLLUTION: Degradation of receiving water quality by introduction of heated effluent. Thermal pollution can generally be controlled by cooling towers.

THICKENED SLUDGE: Sludge which has been concentrated to a higher solids level but maintains the general properties of a fluid or hydro-gel.

THICKENER: See SEDIMENTATION THICKENER.

THROUGHPUT VOLUME: Amount of water passed through an ion exchange bed before exhaustion of the resin is reached.

TOLERANCE: Capability of an organism to withstand adverse conditions in its environment.

TOTAL ORGANIC CARBON (TOC): Measure of the amount of combined organic carbon in a wastewater sample, usually measured instrumentally.

TOTAL ORGANIC CHLORINE (TOCl): Measure of the amount of organically combined chlorine in a wastewater sample. See also ADSORBABLE ORGANIC HALIDE.

TOTAL OXYGEN DEMAND (TOD): Quantitative measure of all oxidizable material in a sample of wastewater as determined instrumentally by measuring the depletion of oxygen after high-temperature combustion.

TOTAL SOLIDS: Total of dissolved and suspended solids in a wastewater sample.

TOXICANT: Specific substance identified as being poisonous or harmful to plant or animal life.

TOXICITY: Quality or degree of being poisonous or harmful to plant or animal life.

TOXICITY EQUIVALENTS (TEQ): Concentration of total dioxins and furans corrected for the toxicity of each species relative to 2378 TCDD. See also DIOXIN.

TOXICITY LEVEL: Classification of degree of toxicity for a wastewater based on the concentration resulting in a lethal threshold. For example, "slightly toxic" is 1 to 10 g of wastewater per liter; "very toxic" is less than 1 mg/liter.

TOXIC WASTE: Waste which has an adverse effect on the receiving water biota because of its toxic properties.

TRACER SOLUTIONS: Chemical solutions typically used for effluent flow calibration or for measuring retention times in vessels or holding ponds. The tracer material is injected into a stream at a precisely measured rate; and samples are subsequently taken at appropriate points downstream where tracer dispersion is complete. Accurate analysis indicates the degree of dilution which has occurred, and this fact is used to determine flow rates or other desired information.

TRACE SUBSTANCE: Element or chemical compound occurring at a concentration level of a few parts per million or less.

TRASH: Debris that can be removed from water or wastewater streams by coarse screens.

TRASH RACK: Very coarse screening element to remove leaves, sticks, weeds and fish from a water intake. The screening element may consist of a line of rugged parallel bars (called a "bar screen"), rods, wires, grating, wire mesh, or a perforated plate, and the openings may be any shape.

TRAVELLING SCREEN: Revolving screen installed or constructed in a wastewater channel to catch and remove suspended trash.

TREATED SLUDGE: Sludge whose characteristics have altered by such chemical or biological means as digestion or wet oxidation. See also DIGESTED SLUDGE.

TRICKLING FILTER: Type of biological filter consisting of a bed of rocks, plastic media or other substrate exposed to atmospheric air and through which wastewater is percolated. A zoogleal film builds up on the media through bioconversion of the wastewater, and periodically, biomass is sloughed off to be collected in a subsequent sedimentation step.

TUBE SETTLER: See INCLINED TUBE SETTLER.

TURBIDITY: Cloudiness in water due to suspended and colloidal organic and inorganic material.

U ────────────────────────

ULTIMATE BIOCHEMICAL OXYGEN DEMAND: Total quantity of oxygen required for complete biochemical decomposition of organic waste.

ULTRAFILTRATION: Separation process sometimes applied to remove specific contaminants from wastewater in which large dissolved molecules or colloidal suspended solids are separated from water on the basis of their inability to pass through a membrane along with the bulk of the water.

UNDERFLOW: Thickened sludge removed from the discharge well of a clarifier.

UNLOADING: Periodic or continuous disattachment of the accumulated zoogleal film from the medium on which it grows in a biological filter. Syn. Sloughing.

V ────────────────────────

VACUUM BREAKER: Device for relieving a vacuum formed in a pipeline and preventing back-siphonage, often in the form of a vent line.

VOLATILE SOLIDS: Solids in any category (i.e., dissolved, settleable, nonsettleable) that are volatized at 600°C. The portion of volatized solids in a sample is indicative of the organic content.

V-PRESS: Sludge dewatering press in which material enters through an intake hopper at the widest point between two side-by-side but non-parallel large revolving discs which are covered with perforated screen plating. The faces become progressively closer together as the discs rotate toward a point of minimum separation, thus squeezing out liquid. The pressed material is discharged continuously as the gap between the discs expands.

W ────────────────────────

WASTE: See SOLID WASTE, WASTEWATER.

WASTEWATER: Spent or used water carrying wastes in the form of suspended and dissolved solids.

WASTEWATER IRRIGATION: Disposal of wastewater by distribution over the surface of the ground.

WASTEWATER TREATMENT: Series of chemical, physical or biological processes that render wastewater suitable for discharge into a receiving water.

WASTEWATER TREATMENT FACILITIES: Structures, equipment and processes used to collect, convey and treat industrial wastewater and dispose of the effluent and sludge.

WATER ANALYSIS: Determination of the physical, chemical and biological characteristics of water.

WATERCOURSE: Natural or artificial channel through which water flows before discharging into a stream or body of water.

WATER INTAKE: Physical structure capable of withdrawing water from a source such as a lake.

WATER POLLUTION: Change in the condition of water which is detrimental to some beneficial use.

WATER QUALITY CRITERIA: Those specific values of water quality associated with an identified beneficial use of the water under consideration. Syn. Water Standards.

WATERSHED: Area drained by a given stream. Syn. Drainage Area, Catchment Area.

WATER SOFTENING: See SOFTENING.

WATER TABLE: Upper level of groundwater.

WATER TREATMENT: Series of chemical and physical processes to render water acceptable for an intended use.

WATER TREATMENT PLANT: Central mill facility for external treatment of incoming raw water.

WEIR: Containment device placed across a stream to determine the flow rate, generally calculated from the upstream height above the crest in relation to the geometry of the weir opening. Several different designs of weirs are used depending on the particular application.

WORKING FACE: That area of a landfill operation at which placing, confining or compacting of solid waste is actually being undertaken.

XYZ

ZEOLITE: Porous aluminum-sodium silicate granules, used as a cation exchange resin.

ZERO DISCHARGE: (1) Total recycle of all water used in the process. (2) Discharge of treated effluent with constituents and properties essentially the same as the receiving water.

ZONE SETTLING: Sedimentation occurring when the particles form a loose aggregation held together by weak attractive forces. The whole mass settles, thus producing a distinct interface between the clarified liquid and the sedimentation particles.

ZOOGLEAL FILM: Colony or mass of bacteria embedded in a jellylike substance formed by the swelling of cell membranes through absorption of water. Syn. Biofilm, Biological Slime, Microbial Film.

Chapter 21
Air Pollution Abatement

A
_____

ABATEMENT DEVICE: Equipment used to reduce the emission from a source polluting the air.

ACID RAIN: Precipitation having a pH lower than 5.6, which can occur as a result of atmospheric pollution. The principal anions causing acid rain are sulfate, nitrate, and chloride. Syn. Acid Deposition.

AEROSOL: Fine dispersion of solid or liquid particles suspended in a gaseous phase, for example smoke, fog, or haze.

AIR: Mixture of gases that surrounds the earth. Dry air is composed of approximately 79% nitrogen and 21% oxygen by volume (or 77% nitrogen and 23% oxygen by weight) along with a small amount of carbon dioxide and traces of other constituents.

AIR CONTAMINANTS: Solid, liquid or gaseous materials or combinations thereof, which by their presence in the ambient air may produce undesirable effects on humans, animals, vegetation, surfaces or materials.

AIR MASS: Wide-spread body of air having approximate horizontal homogeneity; i.e., where the physical properties, level for level, are about the same over a wide area.

AIR POLLUTION: Presence in the atmosphere of one or more contaminants in combinations, in such quantities, or of such duration as to be potentially injurious to human, plant, or animal life, or to property, or which unreasonably interferes with the comfortable enjoyment of life or property, or the conduct of business.

AIR POLLUTION CONTROL: Measures taken to maintain the purity of the ambient air within accepted standards.

AIR POLLUTION CONTROL EQUIP-MENT: Any equipment which prevents or controls the emission of any contaminant. Syn. Emission Control Equipment.

AIR QUALITY INDEX: Characterization of air quality by a single number on a scale from 0 to 500. The index incorporates five factors: total suspended particulates, sulfur dioxide, nitrogen dioxide, carbon monoxide and ozone. An index value of 100 or less represents acceptable air quality from a health standpoint.

AIR SHED: Geographical region whose meteorology is interrelated and whose ambient air quality is related to the same pollutional sources and meteorological influences.

AIR-TO-CLOTH RATIO: Ratio of volume flow to the effective filter surface area, a design factor for baghouses. Units are CFM/ft^2 or m^3/h·m^2.

AMBIENT AIR: Surrounding environmental air.

AMBIENT AIR MONITORING: Network of air sampling stations to determine the nature and extent of air pollution and the trends in the level of atmospheric contamination within a specified area.

AMBIENT AIR QUALITY: General, qualitative term used to describe the state of the outside air.

AMBIENT CONDITIONS: Prevailing conditions of temperature, moisture, pollution, etc. in the surrounding atmosphere.

ATMOSPHERE: Envelope of air that surrounds the earth; one of the traditional subdivisions of the earth's physical environment. Different layers of the atmosphere have been designated by meteorologists as homosphere, heterosphere, stratosphere, mesosphere, thermosphere, troposphere, and ionosphere.

ATMOSPHERIC ASSIMILATION: Photochemical reactions whereby chemical substances in the atmosphere are mixed, diffused, and chemically reacted, thus tending to maintain concentrations at reasonably constant levels within defined atmospheric regions.

ATMOSPHERIC CONVECTION: Process by which circulation is created and maintained within a layer of the atmosphere, due either to surface heating of the bottom of the layer or to cooling of its top.

ATMOSPHERIC DIFFUSION: Process by which a fluid or gas permeates or moves through its environment; process by which puffs of gaseous/particulate contaminant (i.e., pockets of high concentration) expand in size and thus are reduced in concentration.

ATMOSPHERIC EDDIES: More or less circular motions in the atmosphere. Of primary interest with respect to air pollution dispersion are mechanical eddies (caused by obstructions in the path of the wind) and thermal eddies (caused by unequal heating of the air by the earth's surface).

ATMOSPHERIC PRESSURE: Ambient pressure exerted by the earth's atmosphere at a specific point. At sea level, the pressure is approximately 101.3 kPa (or 760 mm Hg or 14.7 psi), but it varies within a small range depending on meteorological conditions. Syn. Barometric Pressure.

ATMOSPHERIC STABILITY (or INSTABILITY): Vertical distribution of temperature.

ATMOSPHERIC TURBULENCE: Any flow of air in the atmosphere that is not horizontal; i.e., any flow that tends to have a mixing action and encourage the spread of pollutants in the atmosphere. Factors associated with atmospheric turbulence are convection, instability, diffusion, and eddies.

B _____

BACKGROUND CONCENTRATION: Concentration of constituents in normal ambient air.

BAFFLE CHAMBER: Chamber within a duct or flue that is designed to promote the settling of coarse particulates by changing the direction of gas flow and/or by reducing the gas velocity. Syn. Settling Chamber, Dropout Box.

BAG FILTER: Fabric filter for high-efficiency separation of dry particulates from a gas stream, used to recover valuable material as well as to control atmospheric pollution. Typically, the filter medium is slipped over a tubular wire frame, and the particle-laden air is introduced inside the tube to allow larger particles to settle or be projected into the dust hopper before the carrier gas enters the tubes. Syn. Fabric Filter, Fabric Collector.

BAGHOUSE: Multiple banks of bag filters within a housing through which gas passes continuously for removal of particulates. A small number of individual filters are taken out of service on a rotating basis for backflushing and/or mechanical shaking of solid material into a collection hopper. Three basic designs are used: reverse air, pulse jet, and shaker-deflate.

BAG LIFE: Time between replacement of filter media in a baghouse.

BAROMETER: Instrument for measuring atmospheric pressure.

BAROMETRIC PRESSURE: See ATMOSPHERIC PRESSURE.

BOLOMETER: Energy detecting device which can be mounted opposite to an energy source in a stack and be used as a particulate monitor where the degree of energy attenuation is a function of the particulate concentration.

BOUNDARY LAYER EMISSION MONITORING: Measurement of atmospheric emissions from large heterogeneous area sources.

BUBBLER: Absorption apparatus used in gas sampling, usually consisting of a series of absorbing columns filled with specific amounts of reagent through which the gas is dispersed in the form of fine bubbles.

C _____

CARBONYL SULFIDE: (COS) Odorless gas present in small concentrations (up to 30 ppm) in the flue gases of some kraft recovery furnaces. It is detected by some analyzers incorrectly as part of the total reduced sulfur component.

CASCADE IMPACTOR: Particulate sampling device in which contaminated air is drawn through a series of jets against a series of microscope slides. Particulates adhere to the slides which are coated with an adsorbing medium. The jet openings are sized to obtain a size distribution of particulates.

CATCHALL: See ENTRAINMENT SEPARATOR.

CERAMIC THIMBLE: Particulate filtration element of a stack sampling system, especially suitable for high-temperature (500–600°C) use.

CHAMBER: (1) Compartment or space enclosed by walls, often prefixed by a descriptive word indicating its function, such as grit chamber or baffle chamber. (2) Independent compartment in an electrostatic precipitator.

CHARGED DROPLET SCRUBBER: Particulate removal device which combines features of the electrostatic precipitator and wet scrubber.

CLIMATE: Aggregate of weather including all meterological activity occurring over a relatively long period of time.

COLLECTION DEVICE: Device used to collect a particulate or gaseous sample.

COLLECTION EFFICIENCY: Percentage of material by weight removed from the emitted gas stream by an abatement device.

COLLECTOR: Device for removing and retaining contaminants from air or other gases. The term is typically applied to cleaning devices in exhaust systems.

COLLECTOR ELECTRODE: Grounded collection surface in an electrostatic precipitator.

CONTINUOUS SAMPLING: Sampling without interruption over the span of operations or for a predetermined period.

CONTINUOUS SOURCE MONITORING: Measuring the concentration of a specific airborne contaminant on a continuous basis within an exhaust gas stream by means of a probe or sensing element mounted within the exhaust duct. Effective devices are available for a number of gaseous contaminants, but reliable instruments for continuous particulate monitoring have not yet been perfected.

CONTROLLED OPEN BURNING: Open burning of approved materials undertaken with adaquate supervision in a specified time under climatic conditions favorable for complete combustion.

CORONA: Discharge of electricity due to ionization of particulates (and of the surrounding air) in an electrostatic precipitator when the voltage gradient exceeds a certain critical value. Syn. Corona Discharge.

CORONA CURRENT: Electrical current equivalent to the rate of charge transferred to the particulates (and to the surrounding air) in an electrostatic precipitator as measured by the current flow from the transformer to its electrical section, in milliamperes of direct current.

CUMULATIVE SAMPLE: Sample obtained by increments over a period of time which accumulates into a single whole.

CURRENT DENSITY: Measure of particle charging in an electrostatic precipitator, defined as the current per unit area in the charging region, commonly in units of milliamperes (ma) per square foot of plate area.

CYCLONE SEPARATOR: Device for removing particulates from a gas stream utilizing centrifugal force. It consists of a cylindrical or conical structure without moving parts in which the velocity of an inlet gas stream is transformed into a confined vortex from which centrifugal forces tend to drive the suspended particles to the wall of the cyclone body. Syn. Cyclonic Collector.

D _____

DEPOSIT GAUGE: Instrument used to measure the amount of settleable particulate matter deposited on a given area during a given time. Deposition rates are most commonly expressed in units of tons per month per square mile.

DESULFURIZATION: Control of sulfur dioxide (SO_2) emissions.

DILUTION AIR: Cooling air or other external air introduced to a pollution abatement system purposely or otherwise. The amount of dilution air usually must be accounted for in the calculation of the outlet concentration of contaminant.

DISCHARGE ELECTRODE: Electrode having regions of intense electrical field for ion generation in an electrostatic precipitator.

DISPERSION: Action of mixing plumes or other atmospheric emissions into the ambient air, thereby reducing the pollution concentration.

DROPLET: Small liquid particle that will remain suspended in a gas under turbulent conditions.

DROPOUT BOX: See BAFFLE CHAMBER.

DRY CATCH: (1) Particulate collected by an abatement device without the use of water and which is uncontaminated by condensed moisture. (2) Solid particulate caught in the probe and on the filter during stack testing.

DRY COLLECTOR: Any type of collecting device that recovers particulate matter in a dry condition.

DRY SCRUBBER: Dust collection device in which the filter medium is a slowly-moving, vertical column of gravel. Syn. Gravel Bed Filter, Dry Granular Filter.

DUCT SYSTEM: All parts of an air pollution control system, other than the abatement device, including connection to the source, dampers, duct, expansion joints, structural duct supports, fan and stack.

DUST: Organic or inorganic particles formed from operations other than combustion processes.

DUST COLLECTOR: Any device used to remove particulate matter from exhaust gas streams.

DUST COMPOSITION ANALYSIS: Determination of the chemical nature of dust collected or to be collected, typically reported in weight percent of anions and cations, or elements and compounds.

DUST DEPOSITION: Particulate matter that settles out of the atmosphere. Syn. Deposited Matter, Dust Deposit, Dust Fall, Fallout.

DUST LOADING: Particulate concentration in the gas stream; weight of particulates per unit volume of gas, in grains per cubic feet or g per kg of gas.

E

EFFECTIVE MIGRATION VELOCITY:
Experimentally-determined design factor for electrostatic precipitators related to the average migration velocity of particulates.

ELECTRIC MOBILITY: Ratio of the constant velocity of a particle to the electrical force that produces the velocity. Electric mobility depends on the net charge carried by the particle.

ELECTRIFIED FILTER BED: Dry scrubber in which the incoming gas-borne particulates become electrically charged as they pass through a set of high-voltage ionizing discs and are subsequently captured by an electrically polarized gravel bed filter.

ELECTRODES: Charged surfaces, e.g., the discharge and collector devices in an electrostatic precipitator.

ELECTROSTATIC PRECIPITATOR: High-efficiency dust collection device which uses an electric field to charge particles and then force them to a collecting surface. Often referred to simply as a precipitator, or abbreviated still further to "precip".

EMISSION CONTROL EQUIPMENT: See AIR POLLUTION CONTROL EQUIPMENT.

EMISSION MONITORING: See SOURCE SAMPLING.

EMISSION SOURCE: See SOURCE.

ENTRAINMENT: Entrapment and carrying along of finely divided liquid droplets with the gas stream during separation of a gas (or vapor) from a liquid.

ENTRAINMENT SEPARATOR: Apparatus used to remove entrained liquid droplets from a gas stream. The most common design consists of porous wire mesh or glass fiber pads through which the gas flows. Syn. Catchall.

EVAPORATIVE COOLING: Reducing the temperature of a gas stream by utilizing its sensible heat to evaporate water. Typically, the water is sprayed into the gas stream from atomizing nozzles.

EXPOSURE: Subjecting a receptor to an environment containing a harmful concentration of one or more air pollutants.

F

FABRIC FILTER: See BAG FILTER.

FALLOUT: See DUST DEPOSITION.

FALLOUT JAR: See DEPOSIT GAUGE.

FIELD: Basic collection unit of an electrostatic precipitator, generally having an independent electrical portion connected to a transformer/rectifier.

FILTRATION (of air): Method of measuring the amount of suspended particulates in ambient air. A "high-volume sampler" is used to draw known, large volumes of air through a filter medium over a specified period (commonly 24 hours). The tared filters are weighed after the sampling period to determine the amount of accumulated material.

FLANGE-TO-FLANGE: [adj] Descriptive term for an abatement device from inlet to outlet, excluding all the rest of the pollution control system. The term may be applied to dimensions, pressure drop, collection efficiency, etc.

FLOATING-HEAD GAS HOLDER: See GAS HOLDER.

FLUID BED SCRUBBER: Scrubber in which the dust-laden gases flow upward through a mobile packing consisting of small-diameter plastic spheres (resembling ping pong balls). Under the influence of countercurrent gas and liquid flow, the spheres move in violent random motion, thus providing a self-cleaning action. Syn. Turbulent Contactor.

FOG: Visible liquid aerosol.

FUGITIVE EMISSION: Emission resulting from a leak in equipment or piping.

FUMES: Vapors from burning or vaporizing substances.

FUMIGATION: Meteorological event by which an emission released at an elevated height is brought to ground level with little dispersion.

G

GAS ANALYSIS: Determination of the gaseous components of an emission, such as water vapor (H_2O), oxygen (O_2), carbon dioxide (CO_2), carbon monoxide (CO), nitrogen oxides (NO_x), sulfur oxides (SO_x), etc.

GAS HOLDER: Surge vessel for noncondensible gases to equalize flow to an incineration process in a kraft mill using batch digesters. Two basic types are used: The "vaporsphere" consists of a spherical tank compartmentalized by a plastic diaphragm that rises and falls to maintain a constant pressure in the surge compartment. The "floating head" design utilizes an open-ended cylinder that floats in a tank of water with the open end down to seal a gas compartment; the cylinder rises and falls as gases enter or leave the compartment.

GAS SCRUBBER: See SCRUBBER.

GRAIN LOADING: Dust loading in units of grains per standard cubic foot of dry gas.

GRAINS: Measure of particulate weight. There are 7,000 grains in a pound.

GRAVEL BED FILTER: See DRY SCRUBBER.

GRAVIMETRIC METHOD: Method of analysis that involves determination of weight; e.g., any method that involves weighing a sample collected over a specified time frame.

GROUND LEVEL CONCENTRATION: Amount of solid, liquid or gaseous material per unit volume of air, measured from 0 to 2 meters above the ground.

H _____

HAZE: Aerosol in sufficient concentration in the atmosphere to cause loss of visibility.

HIGH-VOLUME SAMPLER: Vacuum unit with a filter element on the intake side, designed to sample large volumes of air, usually over a 24-hour period. Typically, samplers are set initially to draw 55 to 65 cfm. As particulates accumulate on the filter media, the resistance to air passage increases and the flow rate diminishes.

HOPPER: Chamber underneath a dry-catch abatement device for gathering the dust collected by the device. They are typically pyramidal in shape.

HYDROGEN SULFIDE: (H_2S) Common gaseous pollutant from kraft mills having a characteristic, disagreeable odor of rotten eggs. It is a major odor pollutant, being detectable by smell in concentrations as low as one part per billion.

I _____

IMPACTION: See IMPINGEMENT.

IMPINGEMENT: Method for collecting particulate matter in which the gas being sampled is directed forcibly against a surface. With "dry impingement", the particulate is retained upon the surface against which the stream is directed; this collecting surface may be treated with a film of adhesive. "Wet impingement" occurs within a liquid body and the liquid retains the particulate matter. Syn. Impaction.

IMPINGERS: Portion of a sampling train in which the condensing vapors and fine particulates that pass through the filter are captured. See also IMPINGEMENT.

INCINERATION OF NONCONDENSIBLES: Destruction of kraft mill noncondensible vapors by burning in the lime kiln or power boiler.

INCINERATOR: Device to treat combustibles by burning. In the case of gases or vapors, the objective is often to destroy pollutants. For liquids and solids, reduction of bulk is often the objective since the ash residue is easier to dispose of as landfill.

INERTIAL SEPARATOR: Class of dry collector in which the gas flow is made to follow a path that particles, because of their inertia, cannot easily follow. Syn. Mechanical Collector.

IN SITU MEASUREMENT: Measurement in place under actual conditions as opposed to laboratory simulation.

INTERELECTRODE SPACE: Space between the discharge and collector electrodes of an electrostatic precipitator.

INTERMITTENT SAMPLING: Successive sampling when the duration of sampling and the intervals between sampling are not specified and are not necessarily regular.

INVERSION: Atypical atmospheric condition in which a warm air mass moves over a cool one, thus preventing the rising and dispersion of pollutants throughout a well mixed atmosphere. An inversion can create a trapped and highly polluted layer of air.

ISOKINETIC SAMPLING: Drawing a small gas sample from a larger gas stream at the same velocity at which the larger gas stream is moving. Isokinetic sampling is necessary for accurate measurement of dust loading.

M _____

MAXIMUM ALLOWABLE CONCENTRATION: Highest pollutant concentration considered harmless to healthy adults during working hours, assuming that they breath uncontaminated air during nonworking time.

MERCAPTANS: Family of compounds that have structures similar to alcohols except that the oxygen is replaced by sulfur. The simplest structure, methyl mercaptan (CH_3SH), having the characteristic disagreeable odor of rotten cabbage, is a common odor pollutant in kraft mills; it is detectable by smell in concentrations as low as one part per billion. Syn. Thioalcohols.

METEOROLOGY: Science concerned with the atmosphere and its phenomena.

MIGRATION VELOCITY: Velocity of a charged particle perpendicular to a collection surface in an electrostatic precipitator. Syn. Drift Velocity. See also EFFECTIVE MIGRATION VELOCITY.

MIST: Suspension of finely divided liquid droplets in a gas stream.

MULTICLONE: Large number of small-diameter cyclone separator tubes within a large housing.

N _____

NITROGEN OXIDES: (NO_x) Air pollutants created by chemical combination of nitrogen and oxygen during combustion processes. Syn. Oxides Of Nitrogen.

NUISANCE THRESHOLD: Concentration of an air pollutant that is considered objectionable. In the case of an odor, it is the concentration that can be detected by a human being.

O _____

ODOR: Sensation of smell perceived as a result of olfactory stimulation by an odorous material.

ODOR ABATEMENT: Measures taken to reduce or eliminate the emission of objectionable odors. Syn. Odor Control.

ODOR INTENSITY: Amplitude of the signal generated at the olfactory cells (of a human receptor). For a broad range of odorous materials, the odor intensity is proportional to the log of the concentration. This means, for example, that to achieve a 90% reduction in odor intensity, it is necessary to reduce concentration by 99.8%.

ODOR POLLUTION: Presence of odor in the ambient air to a degree deemed unpleasant and undesirable by receptors.

ODOR THRESHOLD: Minimum concentration of an odorous substance in air that can be detected by a human being.

OPEN BURNING: Uncontrolled combustion of refuse where the products of combustion and other contaminants are discharged directly to the open air. See also CONTROLLED OPEN BURNING.

P _____

PACKED COLUMN: Vertical column filled in random fashion with packing material of high surface area, used for gas absorption.

PARTICLE: Single, continuous unit of solid or liquid material with dimensions larger than molecular dimensions. A particle may also consist of several single units adhering together (i.e., an agglomerate).

PARTICLE SIZE ANALYSIS: Determination of a weight distribution of particulate matter according to ranges of mean particle diameter.

PARTICULATES: All airborne solid or liquid materials emitted by a pollution source other than uncombined water. Particulates are composed of settlable matter (i.e., material that will deposit onto the earth's surface within a reasonable period of time) and suspended matter (i.e., material that will remain in the atmosphere until washed out by precipitation). Terms denoting specific particulates include dust, flyash, smoke, soot, aerosols, droplets, mist, fog and fumes. Syn. Particulate Matter.

PEAK CONCENTRATION: Highest concentration of a particular air pollutant during a period of monitoring.

PENETRATION: Percent by weight of emission which passes through an abatement device, equal to one hundred minus the collection efficiency.

PLATE COLUMN: Multistage wet scrubber used for absorbing gases The absorbing liquid travels down a vertical column over a series of plates each of which represents a discrete contact stage. The gas travels up through contacting devices on each plate. Syn. Tray Column.

PLUME: Visible emission from a stack. The shape and concentration distribution of plumes are dependent on meteorological conditions. Looping, coning, fanning, fumigating, and lofting are among the designations for various shaped plumes.

POINT SOURCE: Any identified, confined source of emissions, such as a vent line or stack.

POST TREATMENT: Secondary cleaning of a gas stream after it passes through the primary collection device.

POTENTIAL EMISSION: Emission that is anticipated if an emission control device is bypassed or nonfunctional.

PRECIPITATOR: See ELECTROSTATIC PRECIPITATOR.

PRECLEANING: Removing pollutants with a less efficient device ahead of a primary collection device to reduce the load on the primary device.

PRESSURE DROP: Commonly used term for the loss of static pressure within a piping or duct system, or across an abatement device.

PREVAILING WIND: Conventionally, the direction from which the wind blows during the greatest proportion of the time. See also RESULTANT WIND.

PRIMARY POLLUTANTS: Pollutants emitted directly into the air from identifiable sources, as opposed to pollutants formed later in the atmosphere by photochemical means.

PROBE: Tube used for sampling inside stacks or ducts.

PULSE-JET BAGHOUSE: Baghouse design in which particulate matter collects on the outside of the bags, and is cleaned periodically by blasts of high-pressure air.

R _____

RAPPERS: Devices on electrostatic precipitators to move or vibrate the electrodes adequately for the collected dust to fall off. Specific types of rappers used by various manufacturers include mechanical hammers, electrical solenoids, and pneumatic cylinders.

RECEPTOR: Any person, animal, plant, piece of property, etc. upon which an air pollutant creates a harmful effect.

RE-ENTRAINMENT: Return of dust particles from an electrostatic precipitator collector surface to the gas stream during rapping, resulting in carry-through of some collected dust.

RESISTIVITY: Impedance offered to electric charge transfer across a dust layer in an electrostatic precipitator, a property of the dust itself that affects collection efficiency.

RESPIRABLE-SIZE PARTICULATES: Particulates in the size range that permits them to penetrate the lungs upon inhalation.

RESULTANT WIND: Vectorial average of all wind directions and speeds at a given place for a specified period.

REVERSE AIR BAGHOUSE: Baghouse design in which the dirty gas stream flows into the bags, with particulates collected on the interior. The bags are cleaned periodically by blowing clean air back through the bags, so that particulate matter drops into a hopper below.

RINGELMANN NUMBER: Crude guide to the condition of a plume from a combustion process. The plume is compared and numbered according to a series of cards that present varying shades of grey from white (Ringelmann Number 0) to black (Ringelmann Number 5).

ROTARY VALVE: Rotary device containing radial pockets, used to remove the dry catch from the hopper of an abatement device while preventing inflow of air or outflow of gases. Syn. Star Valve. See also AIR LOCK.

RUN: Subdivision of a monitoring test which corresponds to one observation at a single point in a sample location.

S _____

SAMPLING TRAIN: See TEST TRAIN.

SCRUBBER: (1) Dust collector that utilizes particle wetting. (2) Equipment for absorption of gaseous pollutants. (Generally, the design criteria for removal of gases and particulates are quite different; it is unlikely that one piece of equipment could be utilized for simultaneous removal of both types of pollutants.)

SECONDARY POLLUTANTS: Various chemical products of polluted air reactants, principally those which form in atmospheric photochemical reactions.

SECONDARY SHAVEOFF: Technique for increasing the efficiency of a cyclone separator by taking advantage of the high-velocity secondary spiral in the outlet tube. Essentially, the dust-rich layer at the outer boundry (at least 10% of the flow) is "shaved off" for further treatment, while the main gas stream is carried out the stack.

SETTLING CHAMBER: See BAFFLE CHAMBER.

SHAKE-DEFLATE BAGHOUSE: Baghouse design in which bags are cleaned by mechanically shaking them.

SIGNIFICANT EMISSION LEVEL: Baseline emission rate for a specified pollutant, above which the pollution effect is considered significant for regulatory purposes.

SMOG: Heavy smoke cloud generated by air pollutants. A photochemical smog is the result of sunlight promoting reactions involving hydrocarbons, ozone and nitrogen oxides.

SNOW: Mill jargon for recovery furnace fume or other light-colored particulates appearing at ground level.

SOURCE: Any point or place from which air pollutants are being emitted.

SOURCE SAMPLING: Sampling of individual stack effluent streams to measure specific emission rates and determine if regulatory limitations are being met. Syn. Emission Monitoring.

SPECIFIC COLLECTION AREA: Basic design factor for an electrostatic precipitator; the total collection plate area divided by the volume flow rate.

STACK DILUTION RATIO: Measure of dispersion at some specified point, defined as the ratio of the pollutant concentration in the stack effluent to that in the ambient air downwind from the source. The ambient air concentration is a function of the distance from the stack and atmospheric conditions.

STACK EFFLUENT: Gas stream discharged to the atmosphere through stacks of some form.

STACK GAS: Total aggregate of gaseous, liquid and solid materials being emitted from a source.

STACK TEST: Emissions measurement according to standardized procedures. Generally, a gas sample is drawn from the source isokinetically through a probe to a filter for the dry catch (particulate) and through liquid-filled impingers for the wet catch (condensibles). Syn. Stack Sampling.

STANDARD CONDITIONS: Reference conditions for compressible fluids. For flue gases, it often refers to dry gas conditions at a temperature of 60°F (15.6°C) and pressure of 1 atmosphere. For ventilation air, it refers to 50% relative humidity, 70°F (21°C) and 1 atmosphere. In some cases, standard conditions are defined as 0°C and 1 atmosphere.

STATIC PRESSURE: Pressure in a fluid unrelated to the movement of the fluid, usually measured in relation to the ambient atmospheric pressure. Some loss of static pressure occurs during fluid flow in a duct due to fluid friction.

T _____

TEST TRAIN: Complete stack sampling equipment including probe, filter, impingers, and sampling rate control apparatus. Syn. Sampling Train.

TOTAL REDUCED SULFUR (TRS): Total of all reduced sulfur compounds including hydrogen sulfide (H_2S), methyl mercaptan (CH_3SH), dimethyl sulfide (CH_3SCH_3) and dimethyl disulfide (CH_3SSCH_3).

TRANSFORMER/RECTIFIER SET: Combination electrical device used in electrostatic precipitators to transform low voltage to high and to rectify alternating current to direct.

TRANSMISSOMETER: Device mounted within a flue that measures variable light transmission as an indication of flue gas dust loading. These instruments are subject to error because of the variability of particle size and shape and their effects on light transmission. See also BOLOMETER.

TRANSPORT VELOCITY: Velocity required within a duct or pipe to prevent settling of particles or particulates.

TRAY COLUMN: See PLATE COLUMN.

V _____

VAPOR: Gaseous form of substances that are normally solid or liquid at ambient temperatures.

VAPORSPHERE: See GAS HOLDER.

VENTURI SCRUBBER: High-efficiency scrubbing device which requires a high pressure drop for removal of fine particulates.

VOLATILE ORGANIC COMPOUNDS: Category of air pollutant from kraft pulp mills, derived from digester relief gases and noncondensibles from spent liquor evaporation. Typical constituents are alcohols, terpenes and phenols. Some of these organic vapors undergo photochemical reactions in the atmosphere.

W _____

WET-BOTTOM PRECIPITATOR: Electrostatic precipitator in which the collected dust is discharged into a pool of circulating liquid (e.g., strong black liquor in kraft mills).

WET CATCH: In stack testing, the portion of the emission caught in the wet impingers. This emission can include very fine particulates which pass through the filter, but it is mostly condensible matter which is in vapor form at the filter temperature.

WET ELECTROSTATIC PRECIPITATOR: Precipitator in which cleaning of the collector electrodes is by washdown rather than rapping. Washdown may be continuous or intermittent.

WIND ROSE: Diagram that shows the distribution of wind direction experienced at a given location over a considerable period. The most common form shows a circle from which 8 or 16 lines emanate, one for each compass point. The length of each line is proportional to the frequency of wind from that direction; the frequency of calm conditions is entered in the center.

Chapter 22

Energy Conversion and Electrical Systems

A

ALTERNATING CURRENT: Electric current the direction of which reverses at regular recurring intervals. Unless otherwise specified, it is a periodically varying current with successive half waves of the same shape and area.

ALTERNATOR: Obsolete term for an alternating-current generator.

ANODE: Positive terminal of an electrolytic cell; a collector of electrons.

AVAILABILITY FACTOR: Measure of the maximum theoretical efficiency of a thermal system, defined as the difference in temperature between the heat supplied and heat exhausted divided by the absolute temperature of the heat supplied.

AXIAL-FLOW TURBINE: Turbine in which the direction of steam flow is parallel to the rotary shaft, with the blades fitted perpendicular to the shaft.

B

BACK-PRESSURE TURBINE: Steam turbine in which the exhaust steam is not immediately condensed but is conducted away for general heating applications or for industrial process use.

BASE LOAD: Minimum amount of electric power that is supplied continuously over a given period of time.

BASE-LOAD POWER PLANT: Generating station operating at essentially constant output to supply all or part of the base load of a system.

BOTTOMING CYCLE: Cycle or process added to a conventional energy cycle in which relatively low level heat is utilized to generate additional electricity. An example would be the utilization of low-pressure exhaust steam to provide incremental power.

BREAKER: Electric current interrupter.

BY-PRODUCT POWER: Noncondensing power generated when process steam is expanded through a turbine generator on its way from the boiler to the process.

C

CAPABILITY: Maximum level of electric power which a generating plant can produce under specified conditions for a given period of time, without exceeding approved limits of temperature and stress.

CAPACITOR: Device for storing electrical charge within an alternating current circuit. It serves to oppose a change in voltage.

CAPACITY: Design level of electric power production (i.e., the rated load) for a generating plant as stated by the manufacturer's name plate ratings. Sometimes used interchangably with the term "capability". Syn. Capacity Rating. See also NAME PLATE RATING.

CAPACITY FACTOR: Ratio of the average generating plant load for a given period of time to the capacity.

CATHODE: Negative terminal of an electrolytic cell; a source of electrons.

CIRCUIT: See ELECTRIC CIRCUIT.

CIRCUIT BREAKER: Device for automatically breaking the normal current in a circuit under fault conditions such as a short circuit.

COEFFICIENT OF PERFORMANCE (COP): Index of performance for a heat pump or similar device equal to the energy output divided by the amount of "virgin energy" required to drive the system.

COGENERATION: Sequential prodution of two forms of energy, usually steam and electricity. Syn. Combined Heat and Power.

COMBINED CYCLE: Electric power generation system that utilizes a gas turbine to drive a generator; and the hot exhaust from the gas turbine is used to produce steam in a boiler, which in turn, is used to drive a steam turbine connected to a generator. Thus, electricity is produced by both a gas turbine and a steam turbine.

CONDENSER: Obsolete term for a capacitor.

CONDENSING TURBINE: Steam turbine in which the steam passing through the turbine expands to very low pressure and discharges to a condenser where the exhaust steam is cooled and condensed into water.

CONNECTED LOAD: Sum of the ratings of electric power consuming equipment connected to a supply system, or any part of the system under consideration.

CURRENT: Movement of charges through a conductor in response to a difference in electrical potential; the rate of transfer of electricity.

CYCLE: (1) Periodic change in alternating current, e.g., from positive to negative and back to positive. (2) Thermodynamic process following the progress of the working medium (e.g., water/steam) from its starting point through the entire process. In a closed cycle, the working medium is returned to the starting point and re-used; in an open cycle, it is discharged.

D _____

DEMAND: Rate at which electric energy is consumed by a system or piece of equipment, usually in units of kilowatts. It may be an instantaneous rate; but more commonly, it is an average rate for a designated period of time (e.g., 30 minutes).

DEMAND FACTOR: Ratio of the peak demand to the connected load for a system or part of a system under consideration.

DIRECT CURRENT: Unidirectional current; the term usually infers an essentially non-pulsating current.

DISCHARGE: Complete or partial removal of an electric charge from a system or body.

DISTRIBUTION: Act or process of delivering electric power to the sources of demand.

E _____

ELECTRIC CHARGE: Positive or negative potential of a body or system for transferring electrical energy, equivalent to its net excess or deficiency of electrons.

ELECTRIC CIRCUIT: Any closed conductive path containing voltage and current sources, resistors and/or other components.

ELECTRIC DISTRIBUTION SYSTEM: Network of transformers, wiring and auxiliaries for delivering electric power to the various points of use.

ELECTRIC POWER: Rate at which electrical energy is generated, transferred, or converted into other forms of energy, equal to the product of the current and the voltage drop, usually expressed in kilowatts.

ELECTRODE: Electrical conductor by which electrons enter or leave a medium (liquid, solid, gas or vacuum). See also ANODE, CATHODE.

ELECTROMOTIVE FORCE: See VOLTAGE.

ENERGY: Capacity or ability to do work. Different types of energy are known as potential energy, kinetic energy, internal energy and flow energy (pressure volume energy). Sources of energy are solar, gravity, mechanical, chemical, nuclear, geothermal, electrical, biological, etc. The first law of thermodynamics states that energy can neither be created nor destroyed, but can be converted to different forms.

ENERGY AUDIT: Systematic assessment of existing energy consumption levels within an industrial plant or process in relation to optimum levels, thereby identifying opportunities for energy conservation.

ENERGY BALANCE: Accounting of the distribution of energy input and output.

ENERGY CONSERVATION: Any action or program undertaken to limit or reduce energy consumption. Examples of industrial energy conservation are utilization of alternative fuel sources, system closure, utilization of waste heat, and proper sizing of pumps and other equipment for maximum energy efficiency. See also ENERGY MANAGEMENT.

ENERGY CONSUMPTION: Term meaning energy utilized. More correctly, energy is not consumed, but is converted to a different form, ultimately ending up as low level heat. Energy is neither created nor destroyed.

ENERGY CONVERSION: Changing of energy from one form to another. One example is fuel combustion in which chemical energy is converted into heat energy. Another example is the conversion of the thermal energy of hot combustion gases or boiler steam into mechanical energy or electrical energy in a turbine or turbine-generator. In all conversions, some energy is lost in the form of unusable heat.

ENERGY EFFICIENCY: Ratio of useful work output to energy input, usually expressed as a percentage.

ENERGY INTENSITY: Amount of energy required to produce a product, usually expressed as the energy utilized per unit of production.

ENERGY INTENSIVE: [adj] Term descriptive of a process that uses large amounts of energy, for example any mechanical pulping process.

ENERGY MANAGEMENT: Monitoring and control of energy generation and utilization, toward the objective of more economical generation and more efficient utilization. In practice, the terms "energy management" and "energy conservation" are used interchangably.

ENERGY SELF-SUFFICIENCY: Ability of a mill to meet its total energy requirements (i.e., all electric power and process heat) with steam generated from its own organic solids and hog fuel. (A kraft mill using fossil fuel only for firing the lime kiln is nominally energy self-sufficient. But strictly speaking, for total self-sufficiency, the kiln should be fired with mill woodwaste.)

EXTRACTION STEAM TURBINE: Steam turbine from which steam is extracted at different pressures from intermediate stages of the turbine for use in industrial processes. The turbine may be either a back-pressure or condensing type.

F _____

FREQUENCY (of alternating current): Number of cycles through which the current passes per second; the reciprocal of the period.

G _____

GAS TURBINE: Turbine in which the working medium is a pressurized, hot gas.

GENERATING PLANT: Plant equipped with prime movers, generators, and auxiliary equipment (e.g., pumps, stokers, fans, pulverizers, etc.) for converting mechanical, chemical or nuclear energy into electrical energy. Syn. Generating Station. Power Plant.

GENERATING UNIT: Generator together with its prime mover.

GENERATOR: Machine which transforms mechanical power into electrical power. Syn. Electric Generator.

GRID: Utility's power generation, transmission and distribution system, including transmission lines, transformer stations, etc.

GROUNDED PARTS: Those parts of an electric apparatus connected to ground or that may be considered to have the same potential as earth.

GROUNDING (of electrical systems): Connection of one terminal of each electrical system to earth. See also STATIC GROUNDING.

H _____

HEAT ENERGY: See INTERNAL ENERGY.

HEAT PUMP: Device which raises heat to a higher temperature level. Heat pumps that transfer heat from a cooler reservoir to a hotter one using freon or other refrigerants are called "closed-cycle heat pumps". Compressors used to upgrade process steam or other process fluids are called "open-cycle heat pumps".

HYDRAULIC TURBINE: Device used to transform the energy of flowing water into rotating mechanical power.

HYDROELECTRIC POWER: Electric power generated by falling or flowing water. Often abbreviated to "Hydro Power". Syn Hydraulic Power.

I _____

IMPEDANCE: Ratio of the impressed voltage to the current that flows in an alternating current circuit, taking into consideration the magnitudes of the signals and the phase relationships between them.

INDUCTOR: Device which causes an induced counter electromotive force within an alternating current circuit. It serves to oppose a change in current flow.

INTERLOCK SYSTEM: System of electrical inputs and outputs that are related and interconnected to perform a defined function, such as the startup or shutdown of a series of interdependent operations. An interlock system will cause a predictable set of operations when process limits are exceeded, power is lost, mechanical equipment fails, or components fail either individually or in combination.

INTERNAL ENERGY: Energy possessed by a body by virtue of its internal state which is a function of its temperature. It is sometimes referred to loosely (and erroneously) as "heat energy".

INTERRUPTIBLE POWER: Power made available under agreements that permit curtailment or cessation of delivery by the supplier. A certain amount of advance notice, usually at least one hour, must be given.

K _____

KINETIC ENERGY: Energy possessed by a body by virtue of its motion, equal to $\frac{1}{2} mv^2$ where m is the mass of the body and v its velocity.

L

LANDFILL GAS: Gas generated from a landfill site, typically a mixture of methane, hydrogen and carbon dioxide having a unit heating value about half that of natural gas.

LIMIT SWITCH: Switch fitted to moving machinery which will cut off the power supply if the equipment moves outside its prescribed area of operation. The term also applies to a protective action within a control circuit.

LOAD: Amount of electric power delivered or required by power consuming equipment at any specified point or points in a system.

LOAD CURVE: Time plot of power supplied or consumed, illustrating the variations in demand during the period covered.

LOAD FACTOR: Ratio of average power to peak power, usually expressed as a percentage.

LOAD LEVELING: Adjusting electric power requirements to reduce fluctuations and ensure that a relatively uniform load is supplied by the generating plant or utility. See also PEAK-DEMAND MANAGEMENT.

LOAD SHEDDING: Reduction in load by shutting down certain non-essential pieces of equipment denoted as "load shedding equipment". Load shedding is sometimes required as part of "peak-demand management".

LOSSES: General term applied to power and energy losses in an electrical distribution system, occurring as waste heat in transformers, conductors and apparatus.

LOW-GRADE HEAT: Thermal energy at a temperature below 100°C, which has a low availability factor. Syn. Low-Level Heat. See also AVAILABILITY FACTOR.

N

NAMEPLATE RATING: Full-load continuous power demand of a piece of electrical equipment under specified conditions as designated by the manufacturer on a name plate attached to the equipment.

NATURAL GAS: Mixture of low-molecular-weight gases, principally methane and ethane, which is generated from fossil deposits below the surface of the earth.

O

OUTAGE: Failure in an electric power system.

OVERLOAD PROTECTION DEVICE: Device which operates on excessive current to cause and maintain an interruption of current flow in a particular circuit.

P

PARALLEL GENERATION: Industrial power generation in which the alternating current frequencies are exactly equal to and are synchronized with the utility service grid.

PEAK DEMAND: Greatest demand that occurred during a specified period of time.

PEAK-DEMAND EFFICIENCY: Measure of energy management control, defined as the number of occurrences of peak demand during a specified period divided by the total number of possible occurrences.

PEAK-DEMAND MANAGEMENT: Attempt to reduce the system peak demand by maintaining a relatively level load. Syn. Peak-Demand Control.

PERIOD (of alternating current): Time required for the current to pass through one cycle. The reciprocal of frequency.

PLANT FACTOR: Ratio of average electric load to rated capacity for a generating plant.

POTENTIAL DIFFERENCE: See VOLTAGE.

POTENTIAL ENERGY: Energy stored in such a way that it can be recovered in a more useful form at a later time. The foremost example is the gravitational potential of water stored in a high-elevation reservoir.

POWER: See ELECTRIC POWER.

POWER DISTRIBUTION SYSTEM: Arrangement of unit substations in the mill which take moderately high voltage from the main incoming transformer bank and reduce it to the working voltage of nearby equipment.

POWER FACTOR: Measure of the degree to which the alternating current and voltage are out of phase. If in phase the power factor is 100%, but typical mill operation is between 92 and 95%.

POWER PLANT: See GENERATING PLANT.

PRIME MOVER: Engine, turbine, water wheel or similar machine which transforms pressure or thermal energy into useful mechanical energy, and is commonly utilized to drive an electric generator.

PURCHASED ENERGY: All forms of energy (e.g., fossil fuel, hog fuel, electrical power, etc.) that are purchased to supplement the energy supplied from mill sources.

PURCHASE POWER: Dependable power available for purchase from the utility.

R _____

RESISTANCE: Property of a given material that limits the amount of current flowing through the material in response to a fixed potential difference.

RESISTOR: Electrical component that shows a specific resistance to current flow.

RHEOSTAT: Resistor which is provided with a means to readily vary its resistance.

S _____

SHAFT POWER: Mechanical power in the form of a rotating shaft. Syn. Brake Power.

SINGLE-PHASE CIRCUIT: Circuit energized by a single alternating voltage and usually supplied through two wires.

STARTER: Electrical equipment that controls the acceleration of a motor.

STATIC GROUNDING: Forming an electrical path to earth for components in hazardous areas to avoid buildup of dangerous voltages from static-generating elements.

STEAM POWER: Energy or power derived from steam pressure. The term is commonly applied to electrical or mechanical power generated through the use of steam turbines. See also THERMAL POWER.

SUBSTATION: Assembly of equipment through which electrical energy is passed for transmission, transformation, distribution or switching.

SWITCH: Device for making, breaking, or changing connections in an electric circuit.

T _____

THERMAL POWER: Power generated by expanding combustion gases or from steam produced from a boiler fueled by fossil fuels, wood waste, peat, or other combustible materials.

THERMODYNAMICS: Study of the general laws governing the properties of matter and the processes involving energy change.

THREE-PHASE CIRCUIT: Three-wire circuit energized by alternating-current voltages that differ in phase by one third of a cycle or 120°.

THYRISTOR: Semiconductor device used to control the supply of power between a source and a load.

TIE LINE: Circuit connecting the mill electrical system into the utility grid.

TOPPING CYCLE: Cycle or process installed ahead of a conventional energy cycle to extract additional mechanical energy using high-level heat, usually for conversion to electrical power. With reference to a conventional boiler-steam turbine combination, a topping cycle might utilize a gas turbine ahead of the boiler.

TRANSFORMER: Device that transforms electrical energy from one voltage and current level to another (through the principle of mutual inductance).

TRANSMISSION: Act or process of transporting electrical energy from the supply source to the point of consumption.

TRIP: Automatic opening of an electric circuit due to changes in current or voltage or other electrical conditions.

TURBINE: Device for converting the thermal or hydraulic energy of a flowing fluid into the mechanical power of a rotary shaft. See also AXIAL-FLOW TURBINE, BACK-PRESSURE TURBINE, GAS TURBINE, HYDRAULIC TURBINE, CONDENSING TURBINE, EXTRACTION-STEAM TURBINE.

TURBINE-GENERATOR: Rotary type unit consisting of a turbine and an electric generator. Usually abbreviated to "turbogenerator".

TURBOALTERNATOR: Alternating-current generator which is driven by a steam turbine.

V _____

VOLTAGE: Driving force that causes current to flow through a conductor. Syn. Potential Difference, Electromotive Force.

W _____

WASTE ENERGY: Energy in the form of steam, hot exhaust gases, hot-water streams and refuse that is lost from a process without being fully utilized.

WASTE HEAT: Thermal energy in the form of relatively low-temperature exhaust gases and process effluents that are released to the environment from an electric generation plant or industrial process.

WINDING: System of insulated conductors forming the current-carrying element of a machine or transformer and designed to produce a magnetic field or be influenced by one. An electric machine operates by magnetomotive forces arising from currents flowing in groups of windings suitably mounted on the stator and rotor.

Chapter 23
General Industry Terminology

ANALYSIS: (1) Determination of the nature of a thing by separating it into constituent parts. (2) Methodical examination of a problem, breaking it down into elements and interrelationships. (3) Derivation of new information by bringing together and processing basic data.

ANNEALING: Process of holding a material at a temperature near, but below, its melting point, the objective being to permit stress relaxation without distortion of shape.

APPLIED RESEARCH: Investigation focussed on obtaining specific scientific knowledge having direct commercial application to products or processes.

A PRIORI: [adj] Based on theory or supposition, rather than facts.

AUXILIARY EQUIPMENT: Equipment that works in conjunction with a key piece of equipment.

AVAILABILITY: Portion of total operating time during which the equipment or process has been available for full production; a measure of reliability, a key index of production performance. See also UTILIZATION.

B

BASIC RESEARCH: Investigation directed to the discovery of scientific knowledge without any obvious commercial objectives (even though the investigation may be in a field where future commercial exploitation is possible). Syn. Fundamental Research, Pure Research.

BATCH PROCESS: Process in which materials remain virtually stationary in equipment or vessels while being treated or reacted; as opposed to a continuous process.

BENCH SCALE PROCESS: Manufacturing process carried out in a laboratory on a research bench utilizing typical laboratory equipment with glassware and plasticware. Products are usually made in quantities of grams.

BIONICS: Study relating the functions, characteristics, and phenomena of living systems to the development of electronic or physical systems.

BIOTECHNOLOGY: Technical exploitation of biological processes. The pulp and paper industry employs biological processes for waste water treatment, and to a limited extent, for production of by-product chemicals.

BLOCK DIAGRAM: Representation of a system by annotated boxes and interconnecting lines. See also FLOW SHEET.

BOTTLENECK: See PRODUCTION BOTTLENECK.

BRAINSTORMING: Team or group discussion to promote creativity and generate useful concepts. Syn. Ideation.

BUZZ WORD: Colloquialism for a current "hot topic".

C

CAPACITY: Production capability of a single piece of process equipment, unit operation, process line, or entire mill.

CASCADING: Arranging process units so that the outflow from one unit provides the inflow to another unit.

CATWALK: Narrow raised walkway for reaching otherwise inaccessable areas, such as above the fourdrinier.

CERTIFICATION: Program to substantiate the qualifications or competence of personnel in a specified vocational area by documentation of experience and/or learning.

CHEMICAL ENGINEERING: Branch of engineering dealing with the design and operation of plants and equipment that chemically convert basic raw materials into a variety of products.

CHEMICAL PROCESS INDUSTRIES (CPI): Large group of companies that exploit chemical and engineering principles to separate or change materials into salable products.

CIRCUIT: Directed route taken by a flow from one point to another.

CLOSED CIRCUIT: Circuit through which a flow makes a complete journey and returns to its origin.

COLOR CODE: Any system of colors used to identify the different materials carried within pipes.

COMMISSIONING (of new plant or equipment): Startup of new plant equipment, monitoring of all components, verification of equipment performance, and shakedown operation; usually carried out cooperatively by plant and contract engineering personnel.

COMPARABLE DATA: Two or more data sets using the same bases, standards, and/or definitions for purposes of comparison.

COMPLIANCE: Affirmative indication or judgement that a supplier of a product or service has met the requisite specifications.

CONTINUOUS PROCESS: Process in which the flow of materials being treated or reacted is continuous (with relatively little fluctuation) through equipment or vessels; as opposed to a batch process.

CONTROLLABILITY: Qualitative term indicating the relative ease or difficulty of operating a process within certain defined limits.

COUNTER: Device that registers a single occurrence and from which a total number of occurrences can be determined for any specified time period.

D _____

DATA: Raw facts and figures which are capable of being processed into information.

DATABASE: Repository of information, such as contained in files, library or computer discs. Syn. Data Bank.

DATA PROCESSING SYSTEM: Equipment, methods and procedures (and sometimes including personnel) organized to accomplish a specified set of data processing functions.

DECIBEL: Measurement of relative sound intensity. It is a dimensionless unit which expresses the ratio of two numerical values on a logarithmic scale with reference to a base level. The reference base for the decibel was chosen as the threshold of audibility for a person with good hearing.

DECISION: Determination of future action.

DEDICATED PILOT PLANT: Single-purpose pilot plant in which equipment is assembled and piped together to do a specific job; it is a true small-scale model of the expected large plant.

DEMONSTRATION PLANT: Large-scale pilot plant that is designed to utilize commercial equipment, operate continuously, demonstrate the full technology of a process, and substantiate the final commercial plant design. The demonstration plant is usually scaled to produce from 10 to 25% of the commercial plant capacity.

DETENTION TANK: See SURGE VESSEL.

DEVELOPMENT: Industrial activities associated with the application of knowledge for beneficial purposes of a commercial nature. More specifically, the coordinated activities of design, improvement, testing and engineering in the course of bringing a technical innovation into fruition.

DOWNSTREAM: [adj] Descriptive term for any portion of a product stream which has advanced past a reference point in the process; or descriptive of an event that occurs later to a particular portion of the process under consideration.

E _____

EMERGENCY SHUTDOWN: Immediate shutdown of an operating system or piece of equipment that has exceeded a safe limit with respect to speed, temperature, pressure, vibration or other condition.

ENGINEERING: Economic application of science to social purposes.

ENVIRONMENTAL AUDIT: Thorough examination (usually by independent investigators) of a plant's environmental practices to objectively assess compliance with environmental regulatory requirements.

ERGONOMICS: Science that deals with the relationship of a person to the workplace, both in the plant and in the office, and is concerned, in particular, with the safety, health and productivity of people on the job. Syn. Human Engineering, Biomechanics.

EXCESS CAPACITY: Productive capacity not in use because potential volume cannot be marketed economically.

EXEMPTION: Relief from specific regulatory requirements, usually granted by the agency having jurisdiction.

EXPANSION: Increase in the capacity of a plant or process unit, usually as a direct result of installing additional equipment. The term is used in a generic sense for all projects ranging from the removal of a production bottleneck to the entire replacement of an existing plant with a larger one.

EXTRACTIVE INDUSTRY: Enterprise that takes products directly from nature, e.g., lumber, liquified oxygen, clay, etc.

F

FEEDSTOCK: General term for any process stream entering a unit operation; sometimes applied to a stock stream at an appropriate point within a pulp or paper mill process.

FILTER AID: Material such as diatomaceous earth which is added to a solution being filtered in order to maintain a porous structure in the filter cake.

FILTER CAKE: High solids residue which builds up on the filter medium during liquid filtration.

FILTRATION: Separation of particles from a fluid, such as air or a liquid, by passing the fluid carrier through a medium that will not allow passage of the particles.

FLAGSHIP MILL: Most impressive or most up-to-date pulp and/or paper mill within a multi-mill company. It is the mill which sets a standard for other mills in the organization.

FLOW REGIME: Physical configuration exhibited by a two-phase mixture (e.g., gas and liquid) flowing in a conduit. For example, the liquid might occupy the bottom of the conduit with the gas phase flowing above; or a liquid phase could dominate with bubbles of gas distributed throughout.

FLOWSHEET: Diagram that illustrates process design. It shows schematically the equipment used and the steps by which the raw material is changed into a finished product. Syn. Flow Diagram, Flow Chart. See also BLOCK DIAGRAM.

FOREST PRODUCTS: Any products derived from trees, e.g., lumber, plywood, pulp, paper, etc.

FUNCTIONAL DESIGN: Design of a process or system in terms of broad components describing operations and interrelationships, as opposed to engineering design which specifies equipment and ancillary devices.

G

GREENFIELD MILL: Pulp and/or paper mill constructed on a previously undeveloped site. Syn. Grassroots Mill.

H

HAZARDOUS MATERIAL: Any material or substance that is potentially damaging to the health and well-being of man. Classifications include toxins, corrosives, radioactives, flammables, explosives, and oxidizers.

HEATER: Any contrivance which is designed specifically to add heat to a liquid, gas, moving web, etc.

HOUSEKEEPING: General plant upkeep with emphasis on maintaining working areas in clean and orderly condition.

HYDRAULICS: Branch of science and technology dealing with the mechanics of fluids, especially low-viscosity liquids.

HYDRAULIC STRUCTURE: Generic term for any engineered structure designed to hold or control water, such as a clarifier or headbox.

I

INDUSTRIAL HYGIENE: Science and art devoted to the recognition, evaluation and control of those environmental factors and contaminants in the workplace which may cause occupational sickness, impaired health or well-being, or significant discomfort and inefficiency among workers or members of the community.

INDUSTRIAL MARKETING: Process of delivering products and services from their origin to industrial uses. It includes such functions as defining the product mix, establishing prices and credit terms, advertising and promotion, selling, distribution and technical service.

INDUSTRIAL MINERAL: Any rock, mineral or naturally occurring substance of economic value, exclusive of metallic ores, mineral fuels and gemstones. Examples of interest to the pulp and paper industry are clays, limestone, saltcake, soda ash and titanium dioxide.

INERT GAS: Non-reactive gas for industrial purposes. For simple movement of material, the main requirement is for an oxygen content of less than 5%. Sometimes, boiler flue gas is utilized.

INFEED: (1) Material supplied to the initial stage of a process. (2) Material metered into a machine.

INFORMATION SYSTEM: See MANAGEMENT INFORMATION SYSTEM, OPERATIONS INFORMATION SYSTEM.

INTEGRATION: Consolidation of manufacturing operations to achieve cost savings in such departments as material handling and administration, as for example the integration of pulping and papermaking operations. Additional "backward integration" of pulp production with mechanical wood processing and "forward integration" of papermaking with finishing and converting operations are other examples. A fully integrated forest products mill might incorporate all operations from log handling to the packaging of consumer paper products.

INVENTORY: On-hand stock of raw materials and finished products.

INVENTORY CONTROL: Steps taken to maintain proper levels of raw materials and finished goods.

L _____

LOGGING: Entering of process data onto tabular reports for future reference and analysis.

LOSS CONTROL: Prevention and/or reduction of losses arising from industrial accidents. Good loss control includes identifying the hazards present and taking actions to eliminate or reduce them.

LOST-TIME ACCIDENT: On-the-job mishap that causes the worker to be away from the job for a day or more. Records of plant safety are usually based on the number of lost-time accidents.

M _____

MANAGEMENT: Executive authority that operates a business.

MANAGEMENT INFORMATION SYSTEM: System for providing all levels of management with timely and reliable information required for planning, control and evaluation of performance. Syn. Millwide Information System. See also OPERATIONS INFORMATION SYSTEM, TOTAL INFORMATION SYSTEM.

MARKET RESEARCH: Study of one or more industrial markets including their size, growth rates, technological requirements, competition, impact of external forces, etc.

MATERIAL BALANCE: Accounting for mass flows into and out of a system and for changes in inventory of mass in the system. Material balances in the pulp and paper industry are commonly carried out with respect to water and chemicals.

MATERIAL FLOW: Progressive movement of material through a process system.

MECHANICS: Branch of physics which studies the behavior of systems or materials under the action of forces.

METRICATION: Conversion from customary units of measurement (typically English or imperial units) into metric units (usually SI units).

METRIC SYSTEM: Rational system of measurement developed in France about 200 years ago. Several variations of the metric system have been used over the years. In 1960, a modernized version called SI (from Systeme International d'Unites) was established as the international standard.

METRIC TON or **TONNE:** Mass or weight equal to 1000 kg, or approximately 2200 lbs.

MILL: Group of buildings housing machinery where raw materials are converted or refined into finished products. Syn. Plant, Factory. See also PULP MILL, PAPER MILL.

MILL SERVICES: Generally refers to such operational requirements as steam supply, electrical power, compressed air, externally treated water, etc.

MODERNITY: Quality of being modern or up-to-date, used interchangeably with "relative obsolescence" as a qualitative indication of a mill's competitiveness. The principal factors affecting modernity are the chronological age of mill equipment and the cost-effectiveness of operations.

MODULAR CONSTRUCTION: Offsite prefabrication and preassembly of plant facilities and equipment. Every construction project includes some modular techniques whether consisting simply of structural materials or (at the other end of the scale) a totally self-contained plant or unit transported to the job site.

MODULAR SYSTEM: Operating machinery system made up of a number of independent units, each with its own drive.

MOTHBALLING: Preparation and placement of industrial equipment into long-term storage.

MULTIPURPOSE PILOT PLANT: Location or building filled with small process equipment (e.g., tanks, reactors, columns, heat exchangers, centrifuges, dryers, pumps, conveyers, etc.), all available for hooking up in a desired configuration to do specific jobs.

N _____

NOISE CONTROL: Maintenance of sound within a range that is comfortable for humans in plants and offices.

NOMOGRAPH: Graph from which can be read the value of a dependent variable (using a straight-edge) when the values of two or more independent variables are given.

NOZZLE: Tapering tube or slot opening for accelerating and directing a fluid.

O _____

OFF-LINE: [adj] Term applied to equipment that is out of service or shut down.

OLFACTORY FATIGUE: Loss of ability to detect an odor (e.g., of a toxic gas) because of continued exposure.

OPERABILITY: Ability to maintain continuity and control of manufacturing operations.

OPERATIONS INFORMATION SYSTEM: Mill-wide system for collecting, processing and communicating data which are useful for technical, financial and management control. See also MANAGEMENT INFORMATION SYSTEM, TOTAL INFORMATION SYSTEM.

OPERATIONS RESEARCH (OR): Application of scientific methods, techniques and tools toward solving problems within operating systems. A number of mathematical techniques are utilized that provide a scientific approach to the analysis of complex situations.

OPERATOR: Pulp or paper mill employee who is responsible for the operation of equipment or a unit process.

ORGANIZATION CHART: Pictorial representation of the formal relationships amongst designated individuals within an enterprise, showing lines of communication, division of responsibility, and delegation of authority.

OSHA: Acronym for the Federal Occupational Safety and Health Act (USA) which has forced industry to critically re-examine its equipment, processes and work environment from the standpoint of operator safety and well-being.

P _____

PARAMETER: Variable to be considered, measured or controlled in a given situation.

PARAMETER OF OPERATION: Setting, adjustment, or condition that varies with the circumstances of its application.

PHASE: Portion of a physical system having definable boundaries which can be physically separated from the rest of the system. The basic phases are solid, liquid and gas, but two-phase liquid systems are also common.

PHYSICAL DISTRIBUTION MANAGEMENT: Concept of business logistics which integrates the functions of packaging, handling, storage, shipping, inventory control and finance.

PILOT PLANT: Scaled-down version of an expected final plant design, at least of the critical portions. (It is not a scaled-up version of laboratory apparatus.) Syn. Semi-Works. See also DEDICATED PILOT PLANT, MULTIPURPOSE PILOT PLANT, BENCH SCALE PROCESS, DEMONSTRATION PLANT.

PROCESS: Sequence of operations leading toward a particular result.

PROCESS DESIGN: See PROCESS ENGINEERING.

PROCESS ENGINEERING: Process design and optimization. Process design includes the basic design concept, preliminary economics, process calculations, process flow sheet and equipment design parameters. Process optimization includes troubleshooting, removal of production bottlenecks, quality improvement, and cost reduction.

PROCESS LAG: Time interval between two related actions. Syn. Dead Time.

PROCESS OPTIMIZATION: Running a production limited process closely to a specified restraint.

PRODUCT DIFFERENTIATION: Creating real differences in a product to gain market advantage. For example, product differentiation for newsprint might include specification of higher brightness and greater tear strength.

PRODUCTION: (1) Plant output. (2) Amount or rate of plant output. See also PAPER MACHINE PRODUCTION.

PRODUCTION BOTTLENECK: Any hindrance to higher production rates.

PRODUCTION CONTROL: Procedures for processing the available fibrous raw material through the various conversion steps into a uniform, high-quality product, in the most expeditious manner with regard both to the volume input of raw material and the yield of product.

PRODUCTION LINE: Series of machines and equipment within a plant carrying out sequential operations for conversion of materials or for their packaging into products.

PRODUCTIVITY: Ratio relating output (goods and/or services) to one or more of the inputs (e.g., labor, capital, energy, etc.) associated with the output. Productivity is often expressed by an index derived from a ratio that compares standard input or output to actual input or output.

PROJECT ENGINEERING: Engineering design and coordination aspects of building a plant facility including capital cost estimates, application for capital expenditure, scheduling, design supervision, equipment selection, contractor relationships, purchasing and field supervision, and equipment inspection.

PROTOTYPE: Model of a process (or product, or system, etc.) suitable for evaluation of design, cost, performance, etc.

R

RAW MATERIAL: Incoming material to a manufacturing plant, where it is processed into a salable product. Wood chips are a raw material for the manufacture of pulp. Pulp, in turn, is a raw material for the manufacture of paper or rayon fiber.

REBUILD: Machine which has been extensively modified and updated by disassembling specific sections and reassembling them utilizing modern components and technology; a machine that has been restored to a modern standard of productivity.

RECYCLING: Process of utilizing one or more of the components from discarded or waste material. The term sometimes includes the recovery of chemical energy.

RELATIVE DENSITY: See SPECIFIC GRAVITY.

RELATIVE OBSOLESCENCE: See MODERNITY.

RELIABILITY: Ability of a component device, equipment, or plant to give a specified performance for a given time.

RETROFIT: Modification of older equipment to incorporate recent design improvements. (A contraction of retroactive refit.)

RISK ASSESSMENT: Systematic analysis of plant designs and proposals in order to identify hazards, evaluate the possible consequences of these hazards, compute the probabilities that these hazards will occur, and evaluate the overall risk.

S

SAFETY AUDIT: Survey of plant operations with the specific objectives to identify unsafe acts and conditions, and take corrective actions.

SHAKEDOWN OPERATION: Operation of process equipment for the major purpose of diagnosing and correcting problems, as during the start-up of a new mill.

SIMULATION: Representation of a physical system using a computer so that the outcome of a proposed action on the system may be predicted. Information provided to the computer represents process data, the processing done by the computer represents the process itself, and the information produced by the computer represents the results of the process.

SINGLE-LINE MILL: Pulp mill with one production line.

SI UNITS: International system of units (Système International d'Unites) derived from seven base units for length (meter), mass (kilogram), time (second), electric current (ampere), temperature (kelvin), amount of substance (mole) and luminous intensity (candela). The system also includes two other classes of units: supplementary units and derived units.

SOUND: Vibrational energy that causes sensation in the organs of hearing. It travels through air (or other materials) in waves, by the compression and rarefaction of molecules. Sound waves are, therefore, a series of pressure variations that radiate from a source. Sound has three predominant characteristics: pitch, quality and intensity.

SPECIFIC GRAVITY: Dimensionless number which characterizes the density of a material in relation to water, defined as the ratio of the density of the material to the density of pure water. Syn. Relative Density.

STANDARDIZATION: (1) Process of bringing items into conformity with quantitative or qualitative criteria commonly used and accepted as authoritative. (2) Activity to control unnecessary proliferation in procedures or materials in such a manner as to minimize operating costs to a company.

STARVED: [adj] Term applied to a piece of process equipment that is not receiving its allotted share of the process stream or the requisite quantity of feed material.

STATUS QUO: Existing state of affairs.

STEADY STATE: Characteristic of a system in which conditions at each point do not change significantly with time. Steady state is attained after initial transients and fluctuations have disappeared.

STRATEGIC PLANNING: Long-term planning concerning products, processes and the general direction of the organization.

SURGE: Any abrupt periodic increase in flow rate or pressure within a system.

SURGE TANK: Vessel within a system which has sufficient capacity to dampen out surges in flow rate or pressure from the upstream side to provide a leveling effect on the downstream side operation. Syn. Detention Tank, Equalization Tank.

SYSTEM: Stand-alone assemblage of components or sub-systems being considered (as distinct from surrounding components).

SYSTEM ENGINEERING: Engineering approach which takes into consideration all of the elements of the control system and the process itself.

SYSTEMS APPROACH: Approach (in design, optimization, problem solving, etc.) which takes into account the over-all situation, rather than focusing on the narrow implications of the task at hand.

T

TECHNICAL AUDIT: Investigation into all aspects of a process or operation with the objective of showing where the operation can be improved and determining what must be done to improve it.

TECHNICAL INNOVATION: Creation and implementation of new technology.

TECHNICAL INTEGRATION: Integration of manufacturing processes. Examples in the forest products industries are integration of wood processing with pulp production and integration of pulping and papermaking operations.

TECHNICAL SERVICE: Usually refers to technical assistance provided by a vendor firm to a customer to overcome specific problems related to utilization of a product.

TECHNICAL STANDARDS PROGRAM: Program within a multi-plant company to develop, establish and promote technical standardization. As such, it provides common terms of reference (e.g., test methodology, round-robin testing, file headings, reporting forms and methods, product specification guidelines, etc.) required for effective technical communication.

TECHNOLOGICAL FORECASTING: Clear statement based on valid judgements made about the technology that will be in practice five to ten years into the future; used as the basis for technical development programs.

TECHNOLOGY: Scientific knowledge applied to industrial processes.

TECHNOLOGY ASSESSMENT: Organized approach toward establishing an early-warning system to control, direct and, if necessary, restrain technological development so as to maximize the public good while minimizing the public risks. This concept includes allocating scientific resources, setting technological priorites and seeking more benign alternatives to the technology at hand.

TONNE: See METRIC TON.

TOTAL INFORMATION SYSTEM: System capable of supplying all the information, in a useful form, which is available to an organization. See also MANAGEMENT INFORMATION SYSTEM, OPERATIONS INFORMATION SYSTEM.

TRADE NAME: Company name or term which identifies a particular product or service, and which is protected by registration and copyright.

TRADE TERMINOLOGY: Words or phrases used by a particular industry which have a specific meaning within that industrial context, and which may be at variance with the common dictionary definition.

TRANSIENT STATE: Temporary abnormal condition of a process, such as during startup or grade changes, when parameters of operation are being rapidly changed from one level to another.

TRANSPORT PROCESS: In chemical engineering, any fundamental process involving mass transfer, momentum transfer or heat transfer.

TURNDOWN: Reduction in throughput.

TURNDOWN CAPABILITY: Ability of equipment or process systems to function effectively at relatively low levels of throughput (as compared to design).

TURNDOWN RATIO: Level of operational throughput, usually expressed as a percentage of design capacity.

TURNKEY DELIVERY: Complete package service by an equipment vendor which usually includes engineering, manufacture, erection, project management, and commissioning.

U

UNIT OPERATION: One of the processing steps that materials undergo in a chemical process plant. Pulp washing and liquor evaporation are examples of unit operations.

UPSTREAM: [adj] Descriptive term for that portion of the product stream which has not yet reached a reference point in the process; or descriptive of an event that occurred previously to a particular portion of the product stream under consideration.

UP TIME: Time during which equipment is operational.

UTILIZATION: Portion of time during which a department is utilized for full production (within the limit of its availability), a key index of production performance.

V

VALUE-ADDED PRODUCT: Basic product that has been further refined, upgraded, or embellished to increase its market value. In the paper industry, the term refers to a basic paper grade that has been converted into a higher priced product by such secondary processes as coating, laminating, saturating, or finishing.

VALUE ENGINEERING: Organized analysis of operations, systems, methods, constructions, equipment and supplies to achieve required functions at the lowest cost without compromising performance, reliability, quality and maintainability. It is the study of alternatives within an overall design strategy. Syn. Value Analysis.

Chapter 24

Maintenance, Mechanical & Corrosion

A _____

ABRASION: Wear damage caused by one surface rubbing against another surface or by the cutting action of hard particles that are trapped between two rubbing surfaces. This latter type of abrasion is characterized by the presence of grooves on the abraded surface.

ABSORBENT: Material which when in contact with a liquid or gas can extract from it certain substances with which it has a chemical or physical affinity.

ADHESIVE WEAR: Damage resulting when two metallic surfaces rub together and material from the weaker surface (not necessarily the softer surface) is transferred onto the stronger surface, or remains between the two surfaces as loose particles.

ADJUSTABLE SPEED EQUIPMENT: Equipment whose speed can be adjusted infinitesimally over a wide range either by electrical or mechanical means, and when adjusted is unaffected by load changes.

AGITATION: Production of fluid motion for blending, mixing, heat transfer, or other purpose.

AGITATOR: Mechanism for keeping liquids and slurries in motion by mixing and stirring, most commonly a propellor-like device. See also TURBINE AGITATOR.

AIR BINDING: Accumulation of air in a conduit or pump which interferes with free passage of liquid or stock.

ALLOY: Mixture of two or more metals, perhaps including one or two non-metallic components (e.g., carbon, silicon), which has been formulated to provide durability, anticorrosiveness, or other desirable properties for a specific type of application.

ALTERNATING CURRENT DRIVE: Variable speed drive consisting of an induction motor powered from a frequency inverter, allowing the current frequency to be controlled and hence the shaft speed.

ANCHORING: Attachment of process equipment or machinery to the floor or mounting base, most commonly by means of anchoring bolts (bolts set into a cement base).

ANODIC PROTECTION: Method of electrolytic corrosion control in which the potential of a metal is maintained within a passive range.

ANODIZING: Application of a protective oxide film on light metal surfaces by passing a high-voltage electric current through a chemical bath in which the metal is suspended and serves as the anode.

ANTIFRICTION: [adj] Term generally applied to bearing surfaces employing a rolling contact rather than a sliding contact.

ANTIFRICTION BEARING: Any bearing having the capability of reducing friction effectively, usually by employing a rolling contact instead of a sliding contact.

APPRENTICE: Any learner or beginner; usually refers to a novice mill tradesman who is learning his trade under the guidance of a journeyman.

ARMATURE: That part of an electric rotating machine that includes the current-carrying winding. In an alternating-current generator, electromotive force is induced by magnetic flux rotation. In a motor, magnetic lines of force are cut which converts electrical energy into shaft energy.

ASPERITIES: Minute raised imperfections on a finished surface. Interlocking asperities are a major cause of friction between two sliding surfaces.

AUTOMATIC VALVE: Valve with a remote-controlled actuator, used to regulate the flow of a process fluid in accordance with the requirements of the process. The actuator is normally an air-operated diaphragm or piston; springs oppose the force of air pressure to hold the plug or vane in position against the forces of fluid flow, and act to return the valve to a closed postion when the air pressure is reduced.

AXIAL-FLOW IMPELLOR: Impellor design which draws material in and discharges material in an axial direction. For a top-entry turbine agitator configuration (e.g., in a stock chest), the axial flow impellor draws from the top and discharges toward the bottom.

B _____

BACK PRESSURE: Ambiguous term that usually refers to the pressure on the downstream side of a piping system or piece of equipment. (However, sometimes it refers to the upstream pressure.)

BALANCING (of rolls): Improving the mass distribution of a rotating roll in such a way that the free centrifugal forces do not exceed permissable tolerances (to avoid troublesome vibrations).

BALL VALVE: Quick-opening valve used for on-off service which provides a very tight shut-off. The name derives from its spherical gate.

BASE SPEED: Lowest speed setting for a variable speed drive.

BEARING: Machine part which supports the load of a turning shaft. Bearings range in sophistication from a simple sleeve to ball and roller bearing assemblies which operate at very high speeds. See also ANTIFRICTION BEARING, THRUST BEARING.

BEDPLATE: Plate or framing used as the foundation of a machine, upon which the machine is attached or mounted.

BIOLOGICAL CORROSION: Chemical attack occurring directly from the metabolic activity of bacteria where they are present and active. Examples include sulfate reducers and filamentous iron and sulfur bacteria. Syn. Bacterial Corrosion.

BLEEDING: Continuous or intermittent slow draining of a fluid in order to remove it or prevent accumulation.

BLIND FLANGE: Flange for closing off the end of an open pipe.

BOROSCOPE: Straight-tube telescope with built-in high-intensity light source used to visually inspect cylindrical cavities such as heat exchanger tubes for corrosion, scaling and/or fabrication defects.

BREAKDOWN MAINTENANCE: Repair of equipment after it has failed.

BRUSH (on an electrical machine): Piece of carbon that maintains sliding electrical contact and conveys electric current between the stationary part of the machine and the rotor.

BUSHING: Soft metal support lining for a shaft, a type of bearing.

BUTTERFLY VALVE: Throttling valve deriving its name from the winglike action of the disc which operates at right angles to the flow.

BY-PASS: Auxiliary loop in a pipeline or process flow sequence for diverting flow around a valve or piece of equipment.

C _____

CARBONIZATION: Formation of a carbonaceous residue in lubricating oils and other hydrocarbon fluids by chemical reduction.

CASING: (1) Protective outer covering for machinery or equipment. (2) For a pump, the housing for the impellor or rotor.

CATHODIC POLARIZATION: Method to protect bleach plant washers and other process equipment from corrosion in which electrons are used as an antichlor. Electrons are fed from a rectifier to the washer in the form of an electric current. At the washer surface, the electrons react with chlorine to form relatively harmless chloride ions. Syn. Electrochemical Protection, Electrochemical Potential Control.

CATHODIC PROTECTION: Method of electrolytic corrosion control in which the structure to be protected is flooded with electrons so that the entire structure becomes a cathode, thus eliminating the myriad of minute galvanic cells all over the metal surfaces caused by grain orientation, different metallic compounds, inclusions, varying stress levels, temperature differences, differing electrolyte composition, etc.

CAVITATION: Condition in which vapor or gas bubbles occur locally in liquids, normally in an area where pressure decreases abruptly. Cavitation in centrifugal pumps results in poor pumping efficiency and accelerated erosion and corrosion of the impeller and pump housing.

CAVITATION EROSION: Pitting caused by the rapid formation and collapse of vapor bubbles near to a metal suface. The finer scale of cavitation pitting distinguishes it from corrosion pitting.

CENTRALIZED OIL SYSTEM: Type of lubrication system for machines having many bearings and hard-to-reach or hazardous points. A typical system consists of a central reservoir, a pump, and the related piping that delivers the lubricant to the machine elements. Like once-through oiling, it is an all-loss system. See also CIRCULATING-OIL SYSTEM.

CENTRIFUGAL PUMP: Pump is which a revolving wheel or impeller forces liquid to revolve in a casing and therefore exerts a centrifugal force on the casing which is equal to the discharge pressure or head.

CHAIN DRIVE: Chain and sprocket assembly used to transmit power (usually from one rotary shaft to another), move materials or operate equipment. The sprocket wheel may have a single row or multiple rows of teeth (sprockets). The chain is made up of individual links with rollers (spindles), bushings and interconnecting links.

CHECK VALVE: Valve which permits fluid flow in one direction only. It automatically stops back flow when the fluid in the line reverses.

CHIME RINGS: Removable end rings on a fabric or mesh-covered cylinder, used to hold and secure the edges of the cover.

CIRCULATING-OIL SYSTEM: Common type of lubrication system for paper machines in which oil from a central reservoir is pumped and metered continuously to each bearing to remove heat, moisture and other possible contaminants; and is then drained by gravity back to the reservoir. The retention time in the storage tank is sufficient to allow for heat dissipation and separation of contaminants; an in-line filter is also provided for removal of contaminants.

CLADDING: Process of covering one material with another under high temperature and pressure. Metal cladding is commonly used in pulp mills for digester linings.

CLEARANCE: Distance between adjacent moving and stationary surfaces of process machinery.

CLEARANCE SEAL: Seal which limits leakage between a rotating or reciprocating shaft and a stationary housing by means of a controlled annular clearance between the two.

CLINGAGE: Material left inside equipment after draining.

CLUTCH: Component of a drive unit for the engagement and disengagement of the shaft, especially when running. Many different designs are used depending on the application.

CODE VESSEL: Pressure vessel which was manufactured in conformance to specified ASME codes for the required pressure and temperature conditions.

COMMUTATOR (on an electrical machine): Cylindrical ring or disc assembly of individually insulated conducting members (commutator segments) with exposed surfaces for contact with the current-collecting brushes.

COMPOSITE VALVE: Valve which utilizes a composite fiber-resin lining for handling abrasive and corrosive fluids.

COMPRESSED AIR: See UTILITY AIR.

COMPRESSOR: Machine used to increase the pressure of a gas or vapor.

CONDITION MONITORING: See PREDICTIVE MAINTENANCE.

CONDUIT: Pipe or channel for conveying fluids or for carrying electrical cable.

CONTRACT MAINTENANCE: Maintenance labor supplied to a manufacturing plant by a contractor. Depending on requirements, the contractor may also supply supervisory personnel. The contract work force may be hired for specific short term jobs, or they may work along with a plant's regular maintenance employees on a longer term basis.

CORRECTIVE MAINTENANCE: All maintenance carried out to correct or repair faults in equipment. It may be carried out as part of a planned program in response to observations (during condition monitoring) or as an unplanned event in response to acute requirements.

CORROSION: Gradual destruction of metals, alloys, and nonmetals by chemical action. Uniform or general corrosion is the most common type and is characterized by the same rate of deterioration over the entire wetted or exposed surface. See also BIOLOGICAL CORROSION, CREVICE CORROSION, CORROSION-EROSION, GALVANIC CORROSION, INTERGRANULAR CORROSION, PITTING CORROSION, STRESS CRACKING, WELD-ASSOCIATED CORROSION.

CORROSION CONTROL: Any steps taken to reduce or minimize corrosion. In general, corrosion control may be accomplished by (1) using improved alloys or nonmetals, (2) modifying the process chemistry to reduce the corrosivity of the environment, (3) isolating the metal or nonmetal from its environment by the use of protective coatings, and (4) applying electrolytic corrosion control methods.

CORROSION COUPONS: Small metal plates which are exposed to a corrosive environment for a specified time. After exposure, the plates are weighed to indicate the degree of corrosion. Metal loss is usually reported in units of mg/cm² per month.

CORROSION-EROSION: Accelerated attack of a metal surface due to a combination of corrosive action and high fluid velocity where the erosion prevents the formation of a passive surface on alloys that require passivation to prevent corrosion.

CORROSION INHIBITOR: Chemical substance that when added to the water solution in contact with a metal will effectively stifle, decrease or even prevent the reaction of the metal with its environment. Inorganic inhibitors (such as phosphates, nitrates, silicates and chromates) are used extensively in cooling, petrochemical and related fields, but their application in pulp and paper mills has been minimal. Some organic inhibitors (such as mercaptobenzothiazole) have received FDA approval for paper applications and have been used successfully for extending the life of fourdrinier metal wires.

CORROSION RATE: Rate of metal loss due to corrosion. A variety of units are used, usually based on loss of metal thickness, e.g., mils per year or mm per year.

CORROSIVITY: Ability of a solution, agent or environment to cause corrosion.

COUNTERSHAFT: Secondary shaft which is driven by the main shaft and supplies power to the machine part.

COUPLING: Device for connecting shafts together for power transmission. A large number of designs are used including rigid couplings, flexible couplings, and couplings incorporating overload protection.

CREVICE CORROSION: Localized chemical attack on the portion of a metal surface which is partially shielded, such as around gaskets, lap joints, bolts, rivets, etc. This type of corrosion may be accelerated by dirt deposits, scratches, changes in acidity, and lack of oxygen. Syn. Concentration Cell.

CRITICAL JOB: Any job on the "critical path". The latest time that one critical job can be completed is the earliest time that the next critical job can be started. There is no free time or overlap between successive critical jobs.

CRITICAL PATH: Schedule identifying the starting and finishing times of all the "critical jobs" that must be completed in succession in order for a project to be completed at the earliest date. Any other path through the project is known as a "slack path".

CRITICAL PATH METHOD: Graphical method used in planning and scheduling a complex series of related operations to determine the sequence of jobs that has the most critical bearing on the completion time for the overall project.

D _____

DEAD SHAFT ROLLER: Any roller which rotates on internal bearings around two stationary stub shafts.

DEAD-TIGHT: [adj] Non-leaking.

DELIVERY: Volumetric flow rate of fluid discharged by a pump, most commonly in units of gallons per minute (gpm).

DESIGN ALLOWANCE: Increment in equipment capability included in specifications to meet unusual or unpredictable operating conditions.

DESIGN CRITERIA: (1) Objectives, results and/or limits which must be met by equipment or facilities in performance of their intended function. (2) Engineering guidelines specifying procedures, allowances, margins, materials, etc. Syn. Design Standards.

DESIGN MARGIN: Increment in equipment capability to compensate for imprecise design and to compensate for normal deterioration.

DIAPHRAGM PUMP: Pump consisting of a flexible membrane which is pushed and/or pulled to contract or enlarge an enclosed cavity. Flow is directed through this cavity by check valves.

DIAPHRAGM VALVE: Throttling type valve that utilizes a flexible elastomer diaphragm forced down into a seat as the open-close mechanism.

DIRECT CURRENT DRIVE: Variable speed drive powered by direct current from a thyristor rectifier taking current from an AC supply. Speed control is achieved by using thyristors to alter the armature voltage or the field voltage.

DIRECT DRIVEN: [adj] Refers to equipment which is coupled directly to a motor or other prime mover without gears or auxiliary apparatus.

DISCHARGE HEAD: Essentially the pressure developed by a pump.

DOG: Any of various simple devices for holding and grappling.

DRIVE: Means by which a machine is given motion or power, or by which power is transferred from one part of a machine to another.

DROPPING POINT: Temperature at which grease passes from a semi-solid to a liquid state. Dropping point helps to determine the maximum temperature at which a grease will lubricate and remain in a bearing without running out.

DRY-RUNNING SEAL: Seal that operates without the presence of liquid at the sealing surface.

DUMP VALVE: On-off type valve usually located at the bottom of a tank, used to dump the contents or for wash-outs.

DYNAMIC BALANCE CONDITION: Condition of a roller which can rotate at high speed without whip or vibration.

E

EDDY CURRENT TESTING: Method of non-destructive testing in which a metallic material is subjected to an electromagnetic field which induces eddy currents in the metal. Structural discontinuities, as well as composition and permeability variations, alter the path of the current and cause a voltage imbalance. By electronic analysis of this imbalance, the magnitude and nature of the condition is determined.

EJECTOR: Device that uses a moving fluid to develop suction for moving a second fluid. Syn. Eductor.

ELBOW: Pipe fitting which incorporates a 45° or 90° bend into the line. A 90° elbow is also referred to as an "ell".

ELECTROCHEMICAL METALLIZING: High-current method of depositing metal on a conductive surface without heat build-up and without having to immerse the part in a plating bath.

ELECTROCHEMICAL PROTECTION: See CATHODIC POLARIZATION.

ELECTROLYTIC CORROSION: Generic term for all types of corrosion associated with electric current flow in an electrolyte. Syn. Electrochemical Corrosion.

ELECTROLYTIC CORROSION CONTROL: Generic term covering all potentiometric methods of corrosion control. See also CATHODIC PROTECTION, ANODIC PROTECTION, CATHODIC POLARIZATION.

ELECTROMAGNETIC VARIATOR DRIVE: Variable speed drive consisting of an inner and outer rotor and a magnetizing coil. The motor-driven inner rotor creates eddy current, which generates a magnetic field causing the outer rotor attached to the drive shaft to rotate. Speed is controlled by varying the magnetizing current.

ELECTROPOLISHING: Electrochemical metal removal process which consists of submerging the surface to be polished in an electrolyte solution, making it one electrical potential, and supplying an electrode of the opposite potential. Metal is removed from the high points at a greater rate than from the low points; thus the surface becomes smoother and has less area. This process (which is the opposite of electroplating) is commonly applied to headbox interiors.

EROSION: General term for several related types of wear caused by movement of a surface relative to a fluid containing particles, i,e., particles of solid or liquid carried in either liquid, gas or vapor.

EXPANSION JOINT: Pipe connector which compensates for thermal movements in the piping. Expansion joints of the bellows type or slip/packed type have tended to replace pipe loops in recently designed piping systems.

EXPLOSION-PROOF: [adj] Term applied to an electrical device (e.g., motor, control panel, etc.) that is housed in an extremely rigid enclosure which will not rupture, even if there is an internal explosion due to ignition of a combustible mixture.

F

FAULT-TRACING: See TROUBLE-SHOOTING.

FEMALE THREAD: Internal thread of a pipe fitting, valve, machine part, etc. for making a screwed connection.

FIBERGLASS-REINFORCED PLASTICS (FRP): Composite materials that are commonly used in the fabrication of process vessels and equipment, consisting of a thermosetting polymer reinforced with glass (and other) fibers. These materials have excellent resistance to corrosion and, when appropriate additives have been incorporated, good resistance to heat and fire. At least six types of FRP resins can be used depending on the specific requirements.

FITTING: (1) Any special attachment to a piece of equipment. (2) Any connecting piece for pipe, tubing or other conduits.

FLANGE: Projecting rim on a pipe or piece of mechanical equipment, often used for bolted connections.

FLOW CHANNEL: Conduit for conveying fluids.

FORGING: Metal part which has been worked into a specified shape by such operations as hammering, pressing, rolling, etc. usually from a heated slug or blank.

FRAMING: Supporting structure of a paper machine or building.

FRETTING: Removal of extremely fine particles by the action of adhesive forces between bearing surfaces, which occurs when bearings (or other contacting surfaces) are subjected to slight vibration or back-and-forth movement. Syn. Fretting Corrosion.

G

GALVANIC CORROSION: Chemical attack occurring when two dissimilar metals are in electrical contact, both exposed to a conductive solution. It can be recognized by increased attack close to the junction of the two metals.

GASKET: Deformable material that is used between two static surfaces to prevent leakage. See also STATIC SEAL.

GATE VALVE: On-off type valve utilizing a tapered disc-shaped closing element that moves perpendicular to the flow direction. Some gate valves use a wedge-shaped disc.

GAUGE (also GAGE): Measuring instrument.

GEARBOX: Housing for a gear drive or speed-changing gears.

GEAR DRIVE: Drive shaft which transmits motion or torque by direct contact between companion gears (e.g., bevel gears).

GEARS: Toothed machine elements that mesh with other gears or chains to transmit power or to change the speed and/or direction of a turning shaft.

GLAND: Cavity of a stuffing box.

GLAND FOLLOWER: Axially moving part of a stuffing box which is forced against the seals by means of a manual adjustment, resulting in an increase in radial sealing force.

GLAND WATER: Water piped into the gland which serves to lubricate, cool and seal the gland. Syn. Seal Water.

GLOBE VALVE: Throttling type valve utilizing a movable disc-type element and a stationary ring seat in a spherical compartment.

GREASE: Plastic solid to semi-fluid lubricant which is a dispersion of a thickening agent and other additives in a fluid lubricant. Greases are used instead of oils where a lubricant is required to maintain its original position in a mechanism, especially where opportunities for frequent relubrication may be limited. However, because of their essentially solid nature, greases do not perform the cooling and cleaning functions associated with the use of a fluid lubricant.

H _____

HANGER: Device for supporting a pipe line.

HARDNESS INDICES: Numbers which represent the relative hardness of a material as determined by any of several methods. The Pusey and Jones index is commonly used for measuring the hardness of rubber-covered rolls; the Brinell index for metal rolls.

HEAT BUILDUP: Accumulation of thermal energy (i.e., increase in temperature) generated within a material as a result of hysteresis. Heat buildup is a common problem with certain coverings used for high-speed paper machine rolls.

HYDRAULIC DRIVE: See HYDROSTATIC DRIVE.

HYDRAULIC FLUID: Fluid used within a hydraulic system for transmitting force and motion. Various types are used depending on the requirements of the system including rust-and-oxidation inhibited oils, water-in-oil emulsions and water/glycol solutions.

HYDROSTATIC: [adj] Relating to the pressure from overlying or confined liquids.

HYDROSTATIC DRIVE: Type of variable speed drive consisting of a hydraulic motor in which speed is controlled by variation in flow. Flow is controlled either by a variable volume pump or a control valve. Syn. Hydraulic Drive.

I _____

IMMERSION TEST: Test to characterize the chemical resistance of elastomeric or plastic roll cover materials in which the changes in certain physical properties are measured after specimens have been immersed in chemical solutions under specified conditions for various lengths of time.

IMPELLOR: Rotating set of vanes designed to impart motion to a fluid. In a centrifugal pump, the impellor rotates in the casing to impart centrifugal action to the liquid.

INFRARED INSPECTION: Utilization of thermal imaging equipment to observe differential patterns of infrared radiation for the purpose of providing specific information concerning a structure, piece of equipment or process. See also THERMOGRAPHY, THERMOGRAPHIC DOCUMENTATION.

INTERGRANULAR CORROSION: Chemical attack at the grain boundaries or adjacent areas of a metal which has lost elements necessary for corrosion resistance, usually as a result of improper heat treatment of the metal.

INTRINSICALLY-SAFE: [adj] Term applied to electrical components which operate with minimal amounts of power and are current-limited so that even with a short circuit the power will not be great enough to create a spark which can ignite a combustible mixture.

J _____

JACKSHAFT: Auxiliary shaft between two other shafts.

JET MIXER: Mixing system in which the driving force is hydraulic rather than mechanical, consisting of a centrifugal pump, piping and jet nozzles to circulate and mix the contents of a tank. Some applications employ air or other gas introduced through a pipe connected to the suction inlet, as for example with biological oxidation.

JOISTS: Parallel beams used to support floor and ceiling loads, which are in turn supported by vertical beams, girders, or bearing walls.

JURY RIG: Any temporary or expedient contrivance or repair job. Syn. Makeshift, Stopgap.

K

KEY: Small square steel bar which makes a tight fit with a keyway.

KEYWAY: Machined slot on a shaft or cylinder to hold a "key". Keyways with keys can be used to lock a gear, coupling or cylinder on a shaft and/or they can be used to align them and be the power transmission device.

L

LABYRINTH SEAL: Clearance-type seal in which the fluid being sealed must traverse a tortuous path in order to escape.

LANTERN RING: Ring or sleeve around a rotating shaft which provides a flow path for lubrication or flushing liquid. Lantern rings are commonly used in pump stuffing boxes with gland water.

LEAKAGE RATE: Quantity of fluid passing through a seal in a given length of time.

LEAK TESTING: Nondestructive evaluative technique carried out by filling a vessel, tank, pipe or other device with a fluid (usually water) and placing it under pressure. The pressurization simulates operational stresses, and any leakage may be interpreted as a precursor to failure.

LIVE SHAFT ROLLER: Any roller having its shafts permanently attached to the body of the roller, and both the shaft and roller revolve about external bearings. Syn. Integral Shaft Roller, Rotating Shaft Roller.

LOADCELL: Device which converts a force into a proportional voltage. The loadcell with a recording device constitutes a strain gauge. Syn. Force Transducer.

LOCK-OUT: Use of locks to positively stop and secure a machine, process or system in order to protect workers from unexpected startups, release of hazardous energy (e.g., electric, compressed air, steam, hydraulic, mechanical, etc.), or release of harmful substances.

LUBRICANTS: Substances used for lubrication, principally categorized as oils or greases. Generally, an oil tends to flow and a grease tends to stay put, but these terms are sometimes inadequate to describe a modern high-performance lubricant which adapts to changing requirements during actual service.

LUBRICATION: Reducing the friction where one surface contacts or rubs against another.

LUBRICITY: Ability of a material to lubricate.

LUG: Projecting metal part for holding or supporting something, or to serve as a handle.

M

MAGNETIC PARTICLE TESTING: Technique of nondestructive testing used for detection of flaws on or close to the surface of ferromagnetic (iron or carbon steel) materials. The method utilizes the principle that electric current flowing through or around a segment induces a magnetic field within the segment. Defects interrupt the continuity of the field, producing polarity which creates magnetic poles at each side of the discontinuity. When iron powder is applied, a visual indication of the size and shape of the defect is created.

MAINTAINABILITY: Relative ease or difficulty of carrying out maintenance work as quantified by the "mean time to repair". Maintainability is largely determined at the design stage by such factors as general accessibility, access openings, and lifting arrangements.

MAINTENANCE: Any activity intended to keep equipment in satisfactory working condition including repairs, replacements, adjustments, measurements and tests. See also BREAKDOWN MAINTENANCE, CORRECTIVE MAINTENANCE, PREDICTIVE MAINTENANCE, PREVENTIVE MAINTENANCE, SCHEDULED MAINTENANCE.

MAINTENANCE PLANNING: Staff function within a maintenance organization responsible for ordering and control of materials and inventories, scheduling of labor, preparation of workloads, and improvement of repair methods.

MALE THREAD: External thread of a pipe fitting, valve, machine part, etc. for making a screwed connection.

MECHANICAL SEAL: Device which prevents leakage of fluids along rotating shafts. The primary seal is formed by two contacting surfaces that create a very difficult leakage path. In all cases, one face is held stationary in a housing, while the other is fixed to the shaft and rotates with the shaft.

MECHANICAL VARIATOR DRIVE: Variable speed drive in which speed is controlled by varying the ratio between an electric motor and the drive shaft by means of mechanical linkages.

METALLURGY: Science and technology of metals and alloys. Also refers to the metallic composition of process equipment and vessels.

MONOLITHIC LININGS: Continuous corrosion-resistant tank linings, typically consisting of mixtures of liquid thermosetting resins and inert fillers reinforced with glass flakes and glass or synthetic fibers.

MOTOR: Fixed-speed electric drive, in which the rotational speed of the shaft depends on the frequency of the current supplied (usually either 50 or 60 Hz) and the number of poles in the motor's stator.

MUFFLER: Device to control gas flow noise by back pressure control of gas expansion. Syn. Silencer.

MULTITRADING: Overlapping of maintenance tradesmen's responsibilities without legalistic wrangling over who does what.

N

NET POSITIVE SUCTION HEAD (NPSH): Parameter which defines the suction lift capability of a centrifugal pump. It is defined as the total suction head determined at the suction nozzle less the vapor pressure of the liquid, in units of feet or meters. In other words, it is the absolute pressure (in terms of liquid head) available above the vapor pressure of the liquid at the pump suction.

NIPPLE: Short length of pipe or tube for joining piping elements.

NON-CODE VESSEL: Pressure vessel which was manufactured before the current pressure vessel codes were developed.

NONDESTRUCTIVE TESTING (NDT): Techniques for assessing the condition of equipment without shutdowns or dismantling, including vibration analysis, acoustical analysis, infrared thermography, dye penetrant, radiographic inspection, eddy current testing, leak testing, magnetic particle testing and optical holography.

NOZZLE: Pipe connection to a vessel serving as an inlet, outlet or vent.

O

OFFSET: Arrangement of fittings or bends changing an alignment of piping or ducting to another line parallel to the original line.

OILER: Member of the lubrication crew.

ON-OFF VALVE: Valve that is operated either fully open or shut. It is normally not used for throttling.

OPERATIONAL RELIABILITY: Measure of the performance of a piece of equipment in terms of its ability to operate without problems under specified external conditions. It is dependent partly on the characteristics of the equipment and partly on the effectiveness of maintenance.

OPTICAL HOLOGRAPHY: Nondestructive testing technique which uses coherent light (i.e., light of a single wave length) to measure surface displacements during loading of a structure, vessel or other component. If discontinuities are present, the surface displacement will not be uniform, and this can be seen in a holographic image which overlays the object as changes in the amount of deflection on the order of a wavelength or smaller.

O-RING SEAL: Sealing ring with an O-shaped cross section, used as a gasket material or as a secondary seal in mechanical seals.

P

PACKING: Any of a variety of deformable materials for fitting into a stuffing box to make sealing contact with the shaft by adjusting a gland which compresses the material against the base of the stuffing box.

PASSIVATION: Changing from an active to a passive state with respect to corrosion. Passivation is generally associated with oxidizing media and the formation of thin protective-oxide films.

PASSIVITY: Very low corrosion rate in an environment where a high corrosion rate is normally expected. Passivity is a result of a continuing reaction between a metal and its environment. Even though a metal is passive, it is still corroding at a very low rate.

PAWL: Small metal lug tapered to a small angle which serves as the driving link or holding link of a ratchet mechanism.

PENETRANT DYE: Liquid used to indicate the presence of cracks in process equipment or structural members.

PINION: Smallest of a pair of gear wheels or the smallest wheel of a gear chain.

PIPE LOOP: Piping configuration that promotes bending to compensate for thermal movement in the piping. See also EXPANSION JOINT.

PITTING: Surface voids, commonly caused by mechanical erosion, cavitation, or corrosion.

PITTING CORROSION: Localized chemical attack on an unshielded area of metal surface.

PLANNED MAINTENANCE: See SCHEDULED MAINTENANCE.

PLASMA SPRAYING: Type of thermal spraying commonly employed for resurfacing Yankee cylinders in which the metal coating material is melted and transferred to the workpiece by means of a nontransferred arc, i.e., an arc between the electrode and constricted nozzle, but excluding the workpiece.

PLUG VALVE: On-off type valve in which the fluid passage is a hole in a rotatable plug fitted in a valve body. Syn. Cock, Plug Cock.

POSITIVE DISPLACEMENT: [adj] Term applied to any pump which exhibits an essentially constant rate of delivered flow regardless of pressure, and the only limitation to pressure is the strength of the structural parts.

PREDICTIVE MAINTENANCE: Measures taken to determine the condition of equipment on an ongoing basis, i.e., to assess the need for maintenance. Predictive maintenance is one aspect of preventive maintenance. Syn. Condition Monitoring, Condition-Based Maintenance.

PRESSURE RELIEF VALVE: Self-operated, quick-acting valve which opens when the pressure in a vessel or system exceeds a safe level and closes when the pressure falls below the danger point. Syn. Pop Valve, Safety Valve.

PREVENTIVE MAINTENANCE (PM): Programmed maintenance carried out to prevent the occurrence of faults and unnecessary wear and tear, or to detect faults before they cause damage or interrupt production.

PRIMING (of pumps): Filling the casing of a centrifugal pump with liquid and removing all air to enable the pump to operate. Priming is generally not a problem for pumps operating with a positive suction head, only those operating with a suction lift.

PROGRESSING CAVITY PUMP: Positive displacement pump commonly utilized for viscous and non-Newtonian fluids, consisting of an external helix element rotating within a stationary double internal helix stator.

PUMP: Device that raises or moves liquids. See also CENTRIFUGAL PUMP, RECIPROCATING PUMP, ROTARY PUMP, etc.

PUMP CHARACTERISTIC CURVES: Series of curves showing such performance characteristics as dynamic head, brake power, and efficiency as a function of pumping rate.

Q _____

QUICK OPENING VALVE: Any valve which opens and closes quickly. The term is often applied to a gate valve with a sliding stem operated through a fulcrum and lever.

R _____

RACE: Concentric channel between a rotating member and its stationary support, provided by grooves or rings on the two opposing sides (called the "inner" and "outer" sides), as for accommodating the balls in a ball bearing.

RADIAL-FLOW IMPELLOR: Impellor design (e.g., as on a turbine agitator) which draws material from either axial direction and discharges material in a radial direction.

RADIOGRAPHIC TESTING: Method of detecting discontinuities in a solid material by the use of x-rays and/or nuclear radiation. The amount of transmitted radiation depends on the type of material and its thickness. Variations in radiation intensity are recorded by a film placed behind the material.

RATCHET: Notched or toothed wheel operating with a catch or pawl which permits motion of the wheel in one direction only.

RECIPROCATING PUMP: Positive displacement pump which creates lift and pressure by displacing liquid with a moving member or piston. The chamber or cylinder is alternately filled and emptied by forcing and drawing the liquid by mechanical motion.

REDUNDANCY: In plant operations, the ability to start up a similar spare piece of equipment if the operating one fails.

REMANUFACTURE: Overhaul, rebuild or upgrade of existing equipment by the fabricator.

RESERVOIR: Container for storage of oil or hydraulic fluid in a circulating system.

RETAINER: Device that holds a mechanical component in place.

ROTARY PUMP: Positive displacement pump consisting of two intermeshing cams or gears which rotate in a close fitting casing. Liquid fills the spaces between the cam teeth, and as the cams rotate, the liquid is literally squeezed out the discharge.

ROTOR: Rotating member of a machine including the shaft.

RUPTURE DISC: Thin diaphragm designed to burst at a designated pressure; it serves as a deliberately weak element to protect vessels and piping systems against excessive pressure.

S

SAFETY VALVE: See PRESSSURE RELIEF VALVE.

SCAFFOLDING: Temporary or removable supporting framework used for working at considerable heights above the ground.

SCHEDULED MAINTENANCE: Maintenance carried out in accordance with an established plan, often incorporating aspects of predictive and preventive maintenance.

SCRAPPING: Retiring from use, as for obsolete machinery, worn out parts, or threadbare machine clothing.

SEAL: Device to prevent the movement of fluid from one chamber to another or to exclude contaminants.

SEAL ASSEMBLY (for a rotating shaft): Group of parts or unitized assembly including sealing surfaces, provision for initial loading, and a secondary sealing mechanism which accommodates the radial and axial movement necessary for installation and operation.

SEAL BUSHING: Type of seal consisting of a close-fitting sleeve within which the shaft rotates. Leakage is controlled by the clearance between the shaft and the bushing.

SEAL WATER: See GLAND WATER.

SEIZING: Abrupt increase in friction when lubrication fails. Seizing increases metal temperatures and may cause stoppage of machinery due to gross destruction and welding of working metal surfaces.

SELECTIVE LEACHING: Type of corrosion in which one element is removed from an alloy, thus leaving it porous and with poor mechanical properties.

SENSOR: Element or device which responds to changes in a process variable that is being monitored or controlled.

SERVICEABILITY: Capability of a machine, assembly, component, product or construction to perform the function for which it is designed and used.

SERVICE LIFE: Length of time that a machine or device can be operated or utilized economically or before breakdown.

SHAFT: Cylindrical piece of metal, typically used to carry rotating machine parts. See also COUNTERSHAFT, JACK SHAFT.

SHEAVE: Grooved wheel or pulley.

SHOCK-PULSE MEASUREMENT: Method of measuring the magnitude of mechanical shocks generated in damaged rolling bearings, producing a direct measurement of bearing condition.

SIGHT GLASS: Visual indicator of liquid level in a vessel consisting of a vertical glass tube (often calibrated in volumetric units) connected by means of special fittings to nozzles at the top and bottom of the vessel.

SILENCER: See MUFFLER.

SOLENOID VALVE: Valve that is actuated (i.e., opened and closed) by the magnetic action of an electrically energized coil causing movement of a plunger.

SOLID LUBRICANTS: Materials such as graphite, molybdenum disulfide, Teflon and mica with low shear properties which enable them to reduce friction between solid surfaces. These solids can be used in their natural form as powders, or they can be dispersed in lubricating fluids or grease.

SPALLING: Type of gear damage where parts of teeth are missing, caused by excessive loading or inadequate lubrication.

SPIDER: Any of various rotating constructions consisting of a frame or skeleton with radiating arms or members.

SPRAYER: Device used to form liquids into small droplets or mists.

SPRAY NOZZLE: Device attached to a pressurized pipe that is used to form a liquid stream into small droplets or mists. Depending on the nozzle design, the spray pattern may be flat or fan-shaped, hollow-cone or solid-cone.

STAINLESS STEELS: Steels that contain at least 11% chromium. Like all steels, stainless grades also contain carbon. Additional alloying elements can be present, notably nickel and molybdenum. The properties of a particular alloy depend mainly on its composition. However, stainless steels are classified according to their structural properties rather than their composition. The three established classifications are martensitic, ferritic, and austenitic. The stainless steels in the austenitic group are particularly well known in the chemical process industries because of their excellent resistance to corrosion.

STANDPIPE: Vertical cylindrical tank or large-diameter pipe installed in a water distribution system to provide buffer capacity and relief from pressure surges in the pipeline.

STATIC SEAL: Seal between two surfaces which have no relative motion.

STATOR: (1) Stationary part of a machine opposing a rotor or in which a rotor turns. (2) That part of an electric rotating machine that contains the stationary parts of the magnetic circuit and their associated windings.

STEAM TRACING: Method of protecting fluid within a pipe from freezing, by installing tubing carrying steam in contact with the fluid pipe.

STETHOSCOPE: Instrument for detection and study of sounds that are transmitted to the listener through rubber tubing connected to a disk or funnel-shaped endpiece. A stethoscope is often used for condition monitoring of a machine or machine part, but assessment is subjective and dependent on the skill of the user.

STRAIN GAUGE: See LOADCELL.

STRESS CRACKING: Combination of localized corrosion and either internal or applied stress which results in eventual failure via a cracking mode. The cracks follow intergranular and/or transgranular pathways within the metallic structure. The corrosion often shows branched cracking. Syn. Stress Corrosion.

STRESS FATIGUE: Failure of a material by cracking resulting from repeated cyclic stress. Suction rolls often fail by this mechanism.

STROBOSCOPE: Instrument for producing very short flashes of light at an adjustable, exact interval. When used to illuminate a piece of rotating equipment, with the flash rate the same as the rotational speed, the machine will appear to be stationary allowing for visual inspection of such rotating components as couplings or pinions. Stroboscopes are also used for balancing, high-speed photography and other applications.

STUFFING BOX: Cylindrical cavity and the enclosing stationary parts surrounding a shaft, designed to accept packing for the purpose of preventing leakage along the shaft.

SUCTION HEAD (for a pump): Vertical distance upward between the pump centerline and the free level of the liquid source.

SUCTION LIFT (for a pump): Operating condition when the source of supply is below the centerline of the pump. It is the vertical distance downward between the pump centerline and the free level of the liquid source.

SUCTION LINE: Line connecting a pump with its source of supply. Syn. Suction Pipe.

SURFACE FATIGUE: Common type of wear for machine components which are subjected to repeated or cyclic stress. Surface fatigue is characterized by pitting and spalling of the surface. In contrast to pits caused by corrosion, surface fatigue pits tend to have sharp, well-defined edges and associated cracks. Syn. Contact Fatigue, Fatigue Wear.

SYNTHETIC LUBRICANTS: Base fluids manufactured by chemical synthesis supplemented by performance additives. The base fluids are tailored, through specific chemical reactions, to meet predetermined physical and chemical requirements. Synthetic lubricants are man made, as opposed to mineral oils which are refined from crude oils.

T _____

TACHOMETER: Device for measuring rotational or lineal speed of machine components.

TEE: Pipe fitting (in the shape of the letter T) which allows for a perpendicular take-off from an existing pipe line.

THEODOLITE: Optical instrument used for establishing vertical reference planes, for setting out right angles across the paper machine and for plumbing vertical ways. It is basically a telescope mounted on a frame in such a way that it can be rotated a full 360° in both vertical (transiting) and horizontal (traversing) planes.

THERMAL SPRAYING: Generic term for all types of spraying in which metallic and nonmetallic materials are deposited in a semimolten or plastic condition to form a coating. The coating material may originally be in the form of powder or wire. The three major processes of thermal spraying are flame spraying, electric-arc spraying and plasma spraying, which are distinguished by the heat source and the propelling agent used to deposit the material to the substrate.

THERMOGRAPHIC DOCUMENTATION: Any videotape or any photographic, computer-generated, or graphic record of information derived from an infrared inspection.

THERMOGRAPHY: Practice of gathering information about a structure, system, process or object by observing images of differential patterns of infrared radiation, and recording and/or presenting the information.

THIRD PARTY MAINTENANCE: Type of contract maintenance in which the contractor is an independent service company that is not engaged in equipment fabrication activities and has no ties to specific equipment manufacturers.

THROTTLING: Controlled reduction of flow through a pipeline, usually by means of a suitable valve.

THRUST BEARING: Bearing which sustains axial loads and prevents axial movement of a loaded shaft.

THRUST LOAD: Force or pressure in the axial direction of a shaft.

TORQUE: Turning or twisting force.

TOTAL HEAD (for a pump): Pressure differential between the inlet and outlet of any operating pump. It is equal to the discharge head plus suction lift or minus suction head.

TOTALLY ENCLOSED MACHINE: Machine in which there is no access whatever to the inside of the casing, so that cooling must be effected by conduction to and subsequent dissipation from the exterior surface.

TRIBOLOGY: Study of friction and sliding surfaces toward the goals of reducing friction, improving the design of bearings and other wearing surfaces, and developing superior lubricants.

TROUBLE-SHOOTING: Locating and diagnosing problems and faults. Syn. Fault-Tracing.

TRUNNIONS: Opposing journals supported by bearings to provide a means of turning or swiveling.

TURBINE AGITATOR: Mechanical device that produces motion in a fluid through the rotary action of one or more impellors.

U

ULTRASONIC TESTING: Method of nondestructive testing in which a beam of ultrasonic energy is transmitted into a material, and surface or sub-surface discontinuities reflect back a small portion of that energy. The reflected energy, converted to an electrical pulse, is then displayed visually on a cathode ray tube allowing analysis of defects.

UNION: Pipe fitting for coupling or joining together two pipe sections which is designed to facilitate frequent connections and disconnections.

UNIVERSAL JOINT: Coupling that can transmit power through an angle without transmitting torque and speed fluctuations.

UTILITY AIR: Piped air that is used in process plants for tools, painting, hoists, pneumatic power cylinders and other maintenance equipment. The utility air system normally operates at 100–125 psig. Syn. Compressed Air, Mill Air.

V

VALVE: Device which controls fluid flow direction, pressure or flow rate.

VARIABLE SPEED DRIVE: Drive with infinitely variable shaft speed.

VENT: Opening provided in a vessel for the discharge or equalization of pressure.

VESSEL: Structural container in which materials are stored or processed, e.g., pressure vessels, reaction vessels, and storage vessels.

VIBRATION: Continuous oscillation or periodic motion with respect to a fixed reference.

VIBRATION ANALYSIS: Method of condition monitoring of rotating equipment involving periodic, planned vibration measurements combined with trending and analysis of results.

VIBRATION ISOLATION: Technique, utilizing a vibration mount or isolator, to reduce the force transmitted from a piece of vibrating equipment to the base. The isolation efficiency is measured by the percentage of generated force which is blocked by the isolators.

VORTEX TUBE: Tube which takes in ordinary compressed air and discharges two streams of air, one hot and one cold. By adjusting the relative flow rates of the two discharge streams, a range of air temperatures from -40 to 90°C can be obtained.

W

WATER-COOLED: [adj] Descriptive term for equipment indicating that it is designed to have water circulating through it to prevent overheating.

WEAR (of bearing surfaces): Progressive loss of material from a surface due to relative motion between that surface and a contacting material. Various mechanisms of wear are recognized as: Adhesive Wear, Abrasion, Surface Fatigue, Erosion, Cavitation Erosion, and Fretting. In addition, corrosion can be a factor in wear problems.

WELD: Union between metal surfaces which have been heated to a plastic or liquid condition and which may involve the addition of more metal and the application of pressure.

WELD-ASSOCIATED CORROSION: Chemical attack at a weld or in the heat-affected zone of a weld, either in the form of pitting corrosion, crevice corrosion or intergranular attack.

WELD OVERLAY: Corrosion resistant metal applied over another metal by various welding techniques.

WET FLUORESCENT MAGNETIC PARTICLE TESTING (WFMT): Highly sensitive nondestructive testing method for determining cracking in process vessels. It is a technique that has been effectively applied to the monitoring of continuous digester welds. Proper preparation of the surface is essential. The area is then magnetized using direct current, and a suspension of fluorescent iron particles is sprayed onto the magnetized area and illuminated by ultraviolet light. Because surface cracking creates flux-leakage fields in the magnetized area, the suspended iron particles outline the leakage. The particles are clearly visible in ultraviolet light, revealing the extend of cracking.

WINTERIZATION: Various techniques utilized in the design, installation and operation of equipment and piping in order to ensure continuity of plant operations during the coldest winter months. Generally, the basic objective is to keep fluids warm and moving.

WOODSTAVE PIPE: Piping systems made from narrow mating strips of wood (staves) which are placed side by side and banded with wire; often used for transport of water and pulp suspensions.

Chapter 25
Quality Control & Statistics

ACCEPTANCE TEST: Test performed on a representative sample of pulp, paper or raw materials to confirm that the product meets minimum standards, and which provides the basis for accepting or rejecting a quantity of the product.

ANALYSIS OF VARIANCE: Statistical procedure for measuring the variation attributable to different sources.

ARRAY: Arrangement of single observations or times in ranked order.

ATTRIBUTE SPECIFICATIONS: Specifications of a non-numerical nature which divide the unit of product into either an acceptable or defective classification. Examples are either having or not having the correct dimensions, or either containing or not containing a flaw.

AUTOCORRELATION COEFFICIENT: Statistic describing dependence between values in a time series with previous conditions or states. See also SERIAL CORRELATION.

AUTOCORRELATION FUNCTION: Plot of autocorrelation coefficients computed from a number of prescribed lags as a function of lag.

AUTOREGRESSION: Regression in which one serial variable is regressed upon one or more variables which precede it in time.

AVERAGE: See MEAN.

BIAS: Systematic or persistent error as opposed to a random error.

BIMODAL DISTRIBUTION: Distribution of data having two modes.

CAPABILITY INDEX: Measurement of quality performance in terms of meeting specifications with minimal variation. The C_p index is the ratio of the specification range to the natural process capability. The k index is the ratio of the actual deviation of the process average from target to half of the specification range. C_pk index combines the C_p and k indices to obtain a measure of performance in meeting specifications.

CENTRAL TENDENCY: Average or central value in a data set. See also INDEX OF CENTRAL TENDENCY.

CHI-SQUARE DISTRIBUTION: Set of continuous data that is skewed (to the right).

COEFFICIENT OF DETERMINATION (r^2): Square of the correlation coefficient which in regression analysis gives the proportion of the total squares attributable to the independent variable.

COEFFICIENT OF NONDETERMINATION: Equal to one minus the coefficient of determination ($1-r^2$) which in regression analysis gives the proportion of the total squares which are unexplained (i.e., not attributable to the independent variable).

COEFFICIENT OF VARIATION: See VARIATION.

COHERENCE: Estimate of the correlation between two time series, expressed as a function of frequency.

CONFIDENCE INTERVAL: Interval of values for which there is a specified percent chance (usually 95 or 99%) that it will contain the true value of the population parameter. The 95% and 99% confidence intervals correspond, respectively, to all values within two and three standard deviations of the mean value.

CONFIDENCE LEVEL: Probability that a confidence interval will contain the expected value. Syn. Significance Level.

CONFIDENCE LIMITS: Two statistics that define a confidence interval.

CONSUMER'S RISK: Probability that a lot of defective product will be accepted on the basis of a certain sampling testing program.

CONTROL CHART: Serial plot of operational data on graph paper typically enhanced with control limits placed at plus and minus three standard deviations from the target level.

CORRELATION: Association of two variables without implying the presence or the direction of dependence.

CORRELATION COEFFICIENT (r): Statistic which expresses the amount of interdependence or association between two data sets. It ranges in value between +1, which indicates perfect and direct association, to -1, which indicates perfect and inverse association. A value of 0 indicates a complete lack of interdependence. Direct association is called "positive correlation" and inverse association is called "negative correlation".

COVARIANCE: Measure of how two variables change in relation to each other. If both variables increase together, the covariance will be positive. If one variable increases while the other decreases, the covariance will be negative.

CRITICAL VALUE: Value of a statistic that lies at the junction between the region of rejection and the region of nonrejection.

CUMULATIVE SUM CHART: Statistical control chart on which is plotted the cumulative sum of deviations over a period of time for a particular process variable. Syn. Cusum Chart.

D _____

DEGREES OF FREEDOM: Number of items that can vary independently within a sample when the descriptive statistic is known.

DEVIATION: (1) Difference between an individual value in a data set and the mean for the data set. (2) Any departure from a desired or expected value or pattern. Syn. Error.

DISPERSION: Spread of values in a data set or frequency distribution as distinct from a clustering of values about the mean.

DUMMY VARIABLE: Variable sometimes introduced into a regression analysis which has two or more distinct levels; as contrasted with a normal variable which can take values over some continuous range.

E _____

ERROR: See DEVIATION.

EVOLUTIONARY OPERATION (EVOP): Technique for optimizing a production process by systematically introducing small changes into the process and then observing and evaluating the effects of these changes. The runs in each cycle usually satisfy a factorial design.

EXPERIMENT: In statistics, a planned set of trials which lead to a corresponding set of observations which constitute the results of the experiment.

F _____

FACTORIAL EXPERIMENT DESIGN: Experimental design that incorporates two or more independent variables. A complete factorial experiment would measure all the effects and interactions of all the factors. A fractional factorial experiment would measure only certain effects and interactions.

FISHBONE DIAGRAM: Diagram that illustrates various potential causes of a problem grouped under six fundamental headings: methods, materials, machines, manpower, measurement and environment. This technique is usually employed as a component of statistical process control. Syn. Ishikawa Diagram.

FLINCHING: Tendency of testers to falsify test results on a product that is borderline between acceptable and rejectable quality.

FREQUENCY DISTRIBUTION: Representation (usually graphical) of the probability or frequency with which a variable assumes specific values over the total range of the population.

G _____

GOODNESS OF FIT: Closeness of statistical estimates to the actual predictand data.

H _____

HISTOGRAM: Pictorial representation of the proportions of data occurring in various areas of the data scale, typically depicted by rectangles whose heights represent frequency and whose widths represent data values; essentialy a bar diagram of a frequency distribution.

HYPOTHESIS: Inference to be tested.

I _____

INDEPENDENT VARIABLE: Manipulated variable in an experiment.

INDEX OF CENTRAL TENDENCY: Statistic that describes the clustering tendency of data. Examples are mean, median and mode. Syn. Measure Of Central Tendency.

INDEX OF DISPERSION: Statistic that describes the spreading tendency of data about a central value. Examples are range, standard deviation and percentile. Syn. Measure Of Dispersion.

INFERENCE: Conclusion derived by reasoning from given information, usually including a number of facts.

ISHIKAWA DIAGRAM: See FISHBONE DIAGRAM.

L _____

LEAST SQUARES METHOD: Numerical method of fitting a function, such as a straight line, to a set of data in such a way that the sum of squares of residuals is minimized.

LEVEL OF SIGNIFICANCE: Probability of rejecting a true hypothesis. See also SIGNIFICANCE TEST.

M _____

MEAN: Sum of all the data divided by the number of data. The mean can be visualized as the center of gravity of the data. Syn. Average, Arithmetic Mean.

MEDIAN: Number characterizing the center of a data set in which approximately half the data are smaller than it and half are larger than it. The median can be visualized as splitting an ordered array of data into two equal parts: the data in one part being larger than the median, and the data in the other smaller.

MODE: Value in a data set that occurs more frequently than surrounding data.

MOVING AVERAGES: Averages of overlapping segments of a time series usually calculated at regular intervals in the time sequence.

MULTIPLE REGRESSION: Regression involving more than one predictor variable. Multiple regression coefficients describe the relative effect of each predictor variable upon the predictand, adjusting for the intercorrelations between the predictor variables.

N _____

NEGATIVE CORRELATION: See CORRELATION COEFFICIENT.

NEGATIVELY SKEWED DISTRIBUTION: Distribution with a "tail" on the left side.

NOISE: Random, residual or background variation in a time series that cannot be attributed to a detectable quality, pattern, or variation; as opposed to signal, which represents meaningful information.

NORMAL DISTRIBUTION: Bell-shaped, symmetrical distribution of data with the mean value (as well as the median and mode values) corresponding to the point where the distribution function is a maximum, and with approximately two thirds of the data within a distance of one standard deviation on each side of the mean.

NORMALIZED DATA: Set of data that has been converted to a population with a mean of zero and a standard deviation of 1.0 obtained by subtracting the mean and dividing by the standard deviation of the original data.

O _____

OBSERVATIONS: Results of the individual trials constituting an experiment.

ORTHOGONALITY: Property of an experimental design which ensures that the different classes of effects shall be capable of direct and separate estimation without any entanglement.

P _____

PARAMETER: Numerical measure that describes the characteristic of a population.

PARETO CHART: Graphical depiction of the quantitative relationship between an identified problem and its causes, usually applied as a tool of statistical process control.

PERCENTILE: Number that specifies the percentage of data in a data set smaller than it.

POPULATION: Aggregate from which a sample is chosen, i.e., the entire collection of objects, events, numbers, or subjects that are of interest to an experimenter.

POSITIVE CORRELATION: See CORRELATION COEFFICIENT.

POSITIVELY SKEWED DISTRIBUTION: Distribution with the "tail" on the right side.

PREDICTAND: In statistics, an output variable of a system which is predicted.

PREDICTOR: In statistics, an input variable of a system, values of which are used to estimate the predictands.

PROBABILITY INTERVAL: Upper and lower limits defining the range of values comprising a given fraction of a population of values.

PRODUCER'S RISK: Probability that a lot of on-specification product will be rejected on the basis of a sample testing program.

Q _____

QUALITY: Conformance to the customer's requirements with respect to such characteristics as function, reliability, serviceability, useful life, maintainability, and appearance.

QUALITY ASSURANCE (QA): Program to assure that manufactured products meet customer quality requirements. Quality assurance sets the policies, standards, methods, and specifications for monitoring the quality of production. (Note: The terms "quality assurance" and "quality control" are often used interchangeably without regard to differences in meaning.)

QUALITY AUDIT: Program to objectively and systematically survey a mill's quality control system and assess the effectiveness of its quality assurance program to satisfy both company and customer requirements.

QUALITY CIRCLE: Group of 3–10 employees who meet weekly, usually on a volunteer basis, to identify and solve work-related problems. Circle members make suggestions and initiate actions which help reduce costs and improve the quality of work life.

QUALITY CONTROL (QC): Day-to-day (or hour-to-hour) monitoring of production for conformance to the standards and specifications set under a quality-assurance program. (Note: The terms "quality control" and "quality assurance" are often used interchangeably without regard to differences in meaning.)

QUALITY MANAGEMENT: Integration of all functions affecting quality into a cohesive entity, a concept that depends on the involvement of all mill departments directly or indirectly concerned in developing and maintaining a quality standard. In particular, the actions of the production, technical, engineering and training departments must be coordinated toward unified quality objectives.

R _____

RANDOM SAMPLING: Sampling from a population such that any possible sample has an equal probability of being chosen.

RANGE: Refers either to the pair of data that are the largest and smallest values in a data set or to the difference between the largest and smallest values.

REGRESSION: General statistical term often represented by an equation which describes relationships where the values of one or more variables are expressed as a function of other variables.

REGRESSION EQUATION: Equation of a straight line which best fits the data points in a scatter plot.

REGRESSION LINE: Straight line which best fits the data points in a scatter plot.

RESIDUAL: Difference between an observation of actual data and an estimate obtained by applying a given function to a data set. Residuals represent the noise of a system and any signal not accounted for by the functional relationship.

S _____

SAMPLING FRACTION: Proportion of a population included in a sample. Syn. Sampling Density.

SCATTER PLOT: Graphical representation of the relationship between two variables.

SERIAL CORRELATION: Correlation between successive values in a time series (autocorrelation) or lagged correlation between two time series.

SIGNAL: Detectable pattern or variation in a time series caused by functional relationships, as opposed to background variation or noise.

SIGNIFICANCE TEST: Procedure adopted to assess whether some quantity which is subject to random variation differs from a postulated figure by an amount greater than that attibutable to random variation alone. Examples of significance tests are the t-test, F-test and chi-squared test. See also LEVEL OF SIGNIFICANCE.

SKEWED DISTRIBUTION: Distribution where more than 50 percent of the data fall on one side of the mean.

SPECIFICATIONS: Embodiment of control limits, the established minimum and maximum values of the various chemical and physical properties as applied to both raw materials and manufactured products.

STANDARD DEVIATION: Square root of the variance. Dispersion of data about the mean is usually described in units of standard deviations.

STANDARD ERROR: Estimate of how much a particular statistic of a sampled population can vary about its mean. Often used interchangeably with "standard deviation".

STATISTIC: Any form of numerical information, but most often applied to a value used to describe a characteristic of a population.

STATISTICAL ANALYSIS: Techniques utilized in statistical inference, e.g., calculation of standard deviations and percent variation, and analysis of variance.

STATISTICAL INFERENCE: Drawing of conclusions about a population on the basis of data obtained from a sample selected from the population.

STATISTICAL PROCESS CONTROL (SPC): Application of accepted statistical methods to determine if a given process is within the operating control limits established by those statistical methods.

STATISTICAL QUALITY CONTROL (SQC): Application of accepted statistical methods to determine if a given process is within the operating control limits established by those statistical methods and is producing a product that may be shown statistically to be acceptable for the end-use requirements.

STATISTICS: Principles and procedures developed for the collection, classification, summarization, interpretation, and communication of numerical data, and for the use of such data.

SYSTEMATIC SAMPLING: Sampling from a population by a systematic method as opposed to randomly, as for example, at equally timed intervals or equally spaced increments.

T _____

TIME SERIES: Set of data representing a regular sequence of occurrences or events which are indexed as a function of time.

U _____

UNIT OF PRODUCT: Entity of product to be inspected. It may be a sheet of paper or a roll of paper.

V _____

VARIABILITY: Degree to which data are dispersed around the mean of a distribution. See also VARIATION.

VARIANCE: Mean value of the squares of the deviations of an infinite set of observations about their mean. In practice, the variance is estimated from a finite sample of observations.

VARIATION: Standard deviation of a series of values divided by their mean, usually expressed as a percent. Syn. Coefficient Of Variation, Percent Variation.

W _____

WEIGHTED MEAN: Value obtained by multiplying each of a series of values by its assigned weight and dividing the sum of those products by the sum of the weights.

XYZ _____

ZERO CORRELATION: See CORRELATION COEFFICIENT.

ZERO DEFECTS: Program for improving product quality to such a consistent level of perfection that no failures are due to product defects.

Chapter 26

Cost Accounting & Engineering Economics

ACCELERATED DEPRECIATION: Method of depreciating an asset which produces higher depreciation in earlier years than in later years.

ACCOUNT: Summary of operations or transactions in terms of money or some other unit of measurement.

ACCOUNTANT: Person skilled in accounting, often referred to as a certified or licensed professional carrying out accounting functions.

ACCOUNTING: Information system about a specific entity, usually in financial terms and restricted to information that can be made reasonably precise.

ACCUMULATED DEPRECIATION: Sum of depreciation charges on an asset since it was acquired.

ACTUAL DEPRECIATION: True loss of value of an asset during service, as contrasted with depreciation calculated by a specified rate.

AMORTIZATION: Gradual repayment of borrowed capital.

ASSETS: Resources owned by a company that are utilized in achieving organizational objectives.

AUDIT: Inspection of records, assets, activities, and transactions to verify their existence and validate their accuracy.

BASE CASE: Situation expected to occur if no investment is made to correct a capacity or efficiency problem.

BREAK-EVEN ANALYSIS: Analytical technique used to determine the quantity of production that results in a zero level of earnings.

BREAK-EVEN CHART: See PROFIT-VOLUME CHART.

BREAK-EVEN POINT: Percentage of capacity at which the value of production just covers all variable and fixed costs.

BUDGET ESTIMATE: Approximation of costs for a proposed installation or alteration based on a well-defined process, flow diagrams, detailed equipment lists, and current valid site information. Its usual range of accuracy is plus or minus 15 to 25%. Syn. Preliminary Estimate.

CAPITAL ASSETS: Physical plant and equipment with a productive life of more than 1 year which are not bought and sold in the normal course of business.

CAPITAL EXPENDITURE: Expenditure of funds to acquire long-term assets. Syn. Capital Outlay, Capital Cost.

CAPITAL INTENSIVE: [adj] Requiring a high capital investment per ton of production or per employee. The pulp and paper industry is often characterized as being capital intensive.

CASH FLOW: Net passage of dollars into or out of a project as a result of operations, a measure of the rate at which invested money is returned as profit. (As distinct from depreciation which is merely a book transaction.)

COMPTROLLER: See CONTROLLER.

CONSERVATISM: Approach followed in the preparation of return-on-investment calculations for capital expenditures that tends to underestimate earnings where uncertainty exists.

CONTINGENCIES: Allowance in cost estimates for unforeseen elements of cost, usually in an amount shown statistically likely to occur.

CONTROL CHART: Graph that plots performance as a function of time. It distinguishes between abnormal and normal performance and helps to detect trends.

CONTROLLABLE COST: Cost that can be directly influenced and regulated by supervisory or managerial authority during a given time span.

CONTROLLER: Chief accounting officer of a business enterprise. Syn. Comptroller.

CONVERSION COST: Cost incurred in transforming raw materials into finished goods or in transforming a material from one state to another.

COST: Price paid for goods or services. Compare with EXPENSE.

COST ACCOUNTING: Systematic method of recording, allocating and summarizing cost data to determine the cost of making a product or of operating a department, and to provide an effective management control tool for overseeing operations.

COST-BENEFIT ANALYSIS: Economic analysis of a proposed system, installation, alteration, etc. to confirm that expected benefits exceed anticipated costs.

COST-BENEFIT RATIO: Ratio of the cost of a proposed system, installation, alteration, etc. to the anticipated economic benefits.

COST CENTER: Smallest segment of plant operations for which costs are accumulated.

COST CONTROL: Procedures by which management monitors a manufacturing operation to ensure efficient operation with respect to cost standards.

COST EFFECTIVE: [adj] Describes an action whose expected benefits exceed expected costs.

COST-EFFECTIVENESS ANALYSIS: Procedure of analyzing alternative courses of action to ensure that, in making a particular decision, unnecessary costs are avoided and maximum benefit is obtained.

COST INDEX: Means of expressing the relative cost of an item or service in terms of the cost at a particular base time. Some indices are designed to cover broad areas of building, construction, and equipments costs; others are highly specialized. Most cost indices reflect national averages, and therefore ignore local factors.

COST-PRICE SQUEEZE: Decreased profit as the difference between selling price and total production cost is reduced.

COST REDUCTION: Process of achieving increased profitability through improved design, better work methods, more complete utilization, new layout, incentive schemes, etc. The term is usually applied when little or no capital expenditure is required to obtain the benefit.

COST STANDARD: See STANDARD COST.

CURRENT COST: Estimated cost to replace an asset or to acquire equivalent production capacity.

D _____

DEAD COST: Cost which is necessary for doing business, but adds nothing to the value of the product.

DEPRECIATION: (1) Exhaustion of the useful service potential of an asset through the combined effects of utilization, wear and tear, aging and obsolescence. (2) Process used by accountants (more precisely called "Accounting For Depreciation") to allocate the original cost of a capital asset to the time period over which the asset is used to produce benefit. A number of depreciation methods are used depending on type of asset and accounting practice.

DETAILED ESTIMATE: Most accurate estimate of costs for a proposed installation or alteration. It is usually prepared after the process design has been essentially completed, and when the detailed design is well underway. Syn. Firm Estimate.

DIRECT COSTS: Costs of material and labor directly incurred in producing a product. In manufacturing, this term is often used interchangeably with "variable costs".

DISCOUNTED CASH FLOW (DCF): Method of analysis with respect to return-on-investment calculations that takes into account the time value of money by applying the concepts of compounded interest.

DISTRIBUTION COSTS: Costs involved in moving the product from the producer to the customer.

E _____

ECONOMETRIC MODELLING: Application of statistical methods to process and cost data to develop economic models for estimating future product costs and profits. Among the factors to be considered are economic indicators, product cost factors, and the relationships among production cost components.

ECONOMIC LIFE: Time span over which the benefits of an asset are expected to be received. Economic life may be limited by obsolescence, the physical life of equipment, or changing economic conditions.

ECONOMY OF SCALE: Greater profitability per unit product as the production capacity of a plant increases.

ENGINEERING ECONOMICS: Rational approach to optimum non-hazardous plant design based on economic principles.

ESCALATION: Provision in estimates for an increase in costs over those specified due to continued inflation or other causes.

ESTIMATE: Approximation of costs for a proposed installation or alteration, etc. Different types of estimates are characterized by their relative accuracy as follows:

order-of-magnitude	-plus or minus 40–50%
study	-plus or minus 25–40%
budget	-plus or minus 15–25%
project control	-plus or minus 10–15%
detailed	-plus or minus 5–10%

EXPENDITURE: Payment of cash. Syn. Disbursement.

EXPENSE: All costs incurred intentionally to produce revenue for a particular period.

F _____

FEASIBILITY STUDY: Investigation into all aspects of a proposed project (economic, technical, environmental, market) to determine if the project should be carried into the next stage or dropped.

FIXED COSTS: Plant operating costs that do not vary with volume of activity.

FUNCTIONAL DEPRECIATION: Higher-than-normal loss in value of an industrial property through extraordinary obsolescence, e.g., due to new process developments, mistakes in design, or poor selection of equipment.

G _____

GUESSTIMATE: Jargon for a quick order-of-magnitude estimate of doubtful accuracy. Guesstimates are used for deciding whether the economics are generally favorable to pursue a new idea or proposal.

I _____

INCREMENTAL COST: Added cost of manufacturing one additional tonne or unit of product without additional investment of facilities, normally equal to the unit variable cost. Syn. Marginal Cost.

INCREMENTAL INVESTMENT: Capital cost of adding increased production capability to an existing mill.

INCREMENTAL PRODUCTION: All production above an established or historical baseline level.

INCREMENTAL PROFIT: All profit on incremental production. If fixed costs are already allocated to baseline production, the apparent profit on incremental production will normally be much higher than on baseline production.

INSTALLED COST (of equipment): Cost of delivered equipment plus all costs incurred in getting it uncrated, laid on foundations, supported, and electrically wired. Typically, the installed cost does not include piping, utility hookup, insulation, instrumentation, painting or buildings; however, practices vary with regard to what is included.

M _____

MANAGER'S REPORT: Monthly or biweekly report on the status of operations, typically used to explain variances between standard costs and actual results.

MARGINAL COST: See INCREMENTAL COST.

MILL NET PROFIT (per unit product): Net realizable value minus the fully allocated cost per unit of production.

MILL NET VALUE: See NET REALIZABLE VALUE.

MODEL: Statement, equation or diagram which represents a basic set of facts and their interrelationships. Models range from basic hypotheses to highly complex systems.

N _____

NET PRESENT VALUE (NPV): Method of calculating the total theoretical profit discounted to the present that may be realized over the life of an investment.

NET REALIZABLE VALUE: Selling price of a product less reasonable further costs for marketing, warehousing, transportation, etc. It is the value realized by the producing plant. Often referred to as "mill net value" or simply, "mill net".

O _____

OBSOLESCENCE: Decreasing value of plant and equipment due to technological advance, rather than from physical deterioration.

OPTIMISM: Approach followed in the preparation of return-on-investment calculations for capital expenditures that foresees a favorable outcome for earnings where uncertainty exists.

ORDER-OF-MAGNITUDE ESTIMATE:
Approximation of costs for a proposed installation or alteration derived through the application of scale-up ratios and escalation factors to the known cost of a similar facility. Syn. Ratio Estimate.

OVERHEAD: Manufacturing costs which are not directly attributable to any single product, and are therefore allocated on some arbitrary basis believed to be equitable.

P _____

PAYBACK PERIOD: Length of time taken for an investment to generate sufficient extra net income to repay the expenditure involved, usually based on after tax net income. Syn. Pay-Out Time.

PRODUCT COST: Total manufacturing costs associated with a product, thus including all fixed and variable costs.

PROFIT: Accounting approximation of the earnings of a manufacturing concern after all expenses and deductions.

PROFITABILITY: General term related to the return on investment.

PROFIT CENTER: Segment of a business that is responsible for both revenue and expense.

PROFIT-VOLUME CHART: Diagram showing the expected relationship between cost and revenue at various volumes with profit being the residual. Syn. Break-Even Chart.

PROJECT CONTROL ESTIMATE: Detailed estimate of costs for a proposed installation or alteration, usually based on bid-issue drawings. Its purpose is to provide an accurate document against which to control costs. Syn. Definitive Estimate.

R _____

RATE OF RETURN: Abbreviation for "rate of return on investment".

RATE OF RETURN ON INVESTMENT:
Ratio which relates net profit for a period to the capital invested in the enterprise as a whole, or in divisions or segments of the enterprise. See also RETURN ON INVESTMENT.

RETURN ON INVESTMENT (ROI): Abbreviation for "rate of return on investment", but usually with reference to a single project and expressed as the ratio: net income divided by average cost of assets devoted to the project. It measures the efficiency with which capital resources are used. See also PAYBACK PERIOD.

RISK: Chance of encountering economic adversity with respect to a specific project or investment decision. Risk can be estimated from available information, as distinct from "uncertainty" which is unpredictable.

S _____

SENSITIVITY ANALYSIS: Technique for identifying key variables in a system and determining how changes in these variables will affect the output from the system.

STANDARD COST: Predetermined cost that is calculated on the basis of a desired level of operating efficiency.

STANDARD COSTING: Technique whereby standard costs are developed and used as a comparison for actual costs so that variances can be identified. Syn. Standard Cost System.

STARTUP COSTS: Those costs incurred between the end of plant construction and the start of normal operations less estimated standard costs (i.e., costs that would have occurred during an equal period of normal operation).

STUDY ESTIMATE: Approximation of costs for a proposed installation or alteration based on order-of-magnitude factors and knowledge of such specifics as location, site development, availability of construction materials, and scheduling. Syn. Factored Estimate.

T _____

THEORETICAL DEPRECIATION: Amount of depreciation (for an asset) calculated by application of a set formula or by use of tables.

U _____

UNCERTAINTY ANALYSIS: Technique to determine what range of return on investment is realistically possible from a specific project or investment decision and what the chances are for success or failure. The objective is to give the decision-maker a more reliable estimate of the risks involved and provide a more realistic basis for decisions.

UNIT COST: Cost of a unit of product or service; for example the cost of a kilowatt hour of electrical energy.

V _____

VALUE ANALYSIS: Technique focusing on design aspects that compares the cost of an installation or project with the value obtained from it as a basis of determining whether the outlay is justified. See also VALUE ENGINEERING.

VARIABLE COSTS: Costs that change as the volume of activity changes. Strictly speaking, variable costs are zero when there is no production. In manufacturing, the term is used interchangeably with "direct costs".

VARIANCE: Difference between a planned event (e.g., standard cost) and the actual outcome of the event.

Chapter 27
Abbreviations & Acronyms

A

AA	active alkali
AD	air dry
AIChE	American Institute of Chemical Engineers
AKD	alkylketone dimer
ANK	all natural kraft
AOX	adsorbable organic halides
APA	American Pulpwood Association.
API	American Paper Institute.
APMP	alkaline peroxide mechanical pulp(ing)
APPITA	Australia-New Zealand Pulp & Paper Industry Technical Assoc.
AQ	anthraquinone
ASA	alkenyl succinic anhydride
ASME	American Society of Mechanical Engineers
ASTM	American Society for Testing and Materials

B

BCTMP	bleached chemi-thermomechanical pulp(ing)
BD	bone dry
BKP	bleached kraft pulp
BLO	black liquor oxidation
BLRBAC	Black Liquor Recovery Boiler Advisory Committee
BLS	black liquor solids
BOD	biochemical oxygen demand
BP	boiling point
BPR	boiling point rise

C

C1S	coated one side
C2S	coated two sides
CC1S	cast coated one side
CCP	carbonless copy paper
CD	cross direction
CFM	cubic feet per minute
CMC	carboxymethylcellulose
CMD	cross machine direction
CMT	corrugated medium test or concora medium test
CNK	coated natural kraft
COD	chemical oxygen demand
COP	coefficient of performance
CP	chemically pure
CPI	chemical process industries
CPM	critical path method
CPPA	Canadian Pulp and Paper Association
CRMP	chemi-refiner mechanical pulp(ing)
CSF	Canadian standard freeness
CSP	combined strength parameter
CST	crude sulfate turpentine
CTH	constant temperature/humidity
CTLF	chemically treated long fiber
CTMP	chemi-thermomechanical pulp(ing)
CTO	crude tall oil

D

DARS	Direct Alkali Recovery System
DCF	discounted cash flow
DF	dilution factor
DMSO	dimethylsulfoxide
DO	dissolved oxygen
DP	degree of polymerization or differential pressure
DR	displacement ratio
DS	degree of substitution
DT	double thick
DV	dextrinizing value

E

EA	effective alkali
EF	English finish
EIS	environmental impact statement
EPA	Environmental Protection Agency (USA)
ESP	emergency shutdown procedure
EVOP	evolutionary operation
EuCePa	European Liaison Committee for Pulp and Paper
EW	excess wash liquor

F

FAS	formamidine sulfinic acid
FDA	Food & Drug Administration (USA)
FPM	feet per minute
FRP	fiberglass-reinforced plastic
FSP	fiber saturation point

G

GATF	Graphic Arts Technical Foundation (USA)
GRSP	gate roll size press
GW	stone groundwood

H

HC	high consistency
HCR	high consistency refining
HHV	higher heating value
HP	high pressure
HVAC	heating, ventilation & air conditioning
HVLC	high-volume, low-concentration

I

ICC	industrial corrugated containers
ID	inside diameter or inside dimension
IPC	Institute of Paper Chemistry (USA) [until 1989; now IPST]
IPST	Institute of Paper Science and Technology (USA) [formerly IPC]
IR	infrared
ISA	Instrument Society of America
ISO	International Organization for Standardization

L

LC	low consistency
LHV	lower heating value
LWC	lightweight coated
LP	low pressure
LTV	long-tube, vertical
LVHC	low-volume, high-concentration

M

MC	medium consistency
MD	machine direction
MF	machine finished
MFC	machine finished coated
MFP	machine finished pigmented
MG	machine glazed

MIS	millwide information system or management information system		PIMA	Paper Industry Management Association (USA)
MLSS	mixed liquor suspended solids		PIRA	Research Association for the Paper & Board, Printing and Packaging Industries (UK)
MVR	mechanical vapor recompression			
MVT	moisture vapor transmission		PITA	Paper Industry Technical Association (UK)
MVTR	moisture vapor transmission rate			
MWC	medium-weight coated		PIV	positive infinitely variable

N _____

NCG	noncondensible gases
NDT	nondestructive testing
NHV	net heating value
NPSH	net positive suction head
NPTA	National Paper Trade Association (USA)
NPV	net present value
NSSC	neutral sulfite semi-chemical

O _____

OCC	old corrugated containers
OCR	optical character recognition
OCS	outside chip storage
OD	oven dry or outside diameter or outside dimension
OEM	original equipment manufacturer
OMS	on-machine-seamed [*re. press felts*]
OR	operations research
ORP	oxidation-reduction potential
OSHA	Occupational Safety & Health Act (USA, 1970)

P _____

P&B	paper and board
PC	process control
PCB	polychlorinated biphenol
PCC	precipitated calcium carbonate
PGW	pressurized stone groundwood

PLI	pounds per lineal inch
PM	paper machine or preventive maintenance
PPB	parts per billion
PPM	parts per million
PPRIC	Pulp & Paper Research Institute of Canada (or Paprican)
PPTMP	pressure/pressure thermomechanical pulp(ing)
PRMP	pressure refined mechanical pulp(ing)
PSI	pounds per square inch
PSIA	pounds per square inch absolute
PSIG	pounds per square inch gauge
PVA	polyvinyl alcohol
PVAc	polyvinyl acetate
PVC	polyvinyl chloride

Q _____

QA	quality assurance
QC	quality control

R _____

RAA	residual active alkali
R&D	research and development
REA	residual effective alkali
RH	relative humidity
RMP	refiner mechanical pulp(ing)
ROI	return on investment
RPM	rotations per minute
RSV	relative sediment volume

S _____

SBK	semi-bleached kraft
SBL	strong black liquor
SC	supercalendered
SCAN	Scandinavian Pulp, Paper & Board Testing Committee
SCMP	semi-chemical mechanical pulp(ing) or sulfonated chemimechanical pulp(ing)
SEM	scanning electron micrograph
SGW	stone groundwood
SOP	standard operating procedure
SPC	statistical process control
SPCI	Swedish Association of Pulp & Paper Engineers
SQC	statistical quality control
SRT	solids retention time
SS	suspended solids
S&SC	sized & supercalendered
SSL	spent sulfite liquor
STFI	Swedish Forest Products Research Laboratory
SV	sediment volume

T _____

T4S	trimmed four sides
TA	total alkali
TAPPI	Technical Association of the Pulp and Paper Industry (USA)
TEA	tensile energy absorption

TEQ	toxicity equivalents
TF	thickening factor
TGW	thermogroundwood
TMCP	thermomechanical chemi-pulp(ing)
TMP	thermomechanical pulp(ing)
TOC	total organic carbon
TOCl	total organic chlorine
TOD	total oxygen demand
TOFA	tall oil fatty acids
TOR	tall oil rosin
TOX	total organic halides
TRMP	thermorefiner mechanical pulp(ing)
TRS	total reduced sulfur
TTA	total titratable alkali

U _____

UHYS	ultra high-yield sulfite
ULWC	ultra lightweight coated

V _____

VOC	volatile organic compounds

W _____

WBL	weak black liquor
WF	water finish
WRV	water retention value
WWE	wet web elongation
WWS	wet web strength
WWT	wet web tensile

INDEX

A

	Refer To Chapter		Refer To Chapter		Refer To Chapter
abaca	3	acetate	4	acidproof brick	8
abatement	20	acetate laminating	18	acid pulping	8
odor	21	acetate pulp	4	acid rain	21
pollution	20	acetic acid	4	acid-refined tall oil	6
abatement device	21	acetic anhydride	4	acid-resistant	14
abietic acid	6	acetone	4	acid size	5
abrasion	24	acetylated starch	5	acid-stable size	5
abrasion barker	1	acetyl radical	4	acid sulfite process	8
abrasion resistance	14	acetylating agent	4	acid tower	8
abrasion test	14	acid(s)	4, 8	acid treatment	10
abrasive	7	abietic	6	acidulating	4
abrasive backing papers	16	acetic	4	acidulating agent	4
abrasiveness	14	accumulator	8	acidulation	6
abrasive segment	7	carbonic	20	acoustical board	16
abrasivity (of mineral fillers)	13	cooking	8	acoustical testing	14
absorbency	11, 14	digester	8	acoustic leak detector	9
relative	11	fatty	6	acre-foot	20
water	11	formamidine sulfinic	10	acrylamide resins	5
absorbent	14, 24	formic	4	acrylic binders	17
absorbent capacity	11	glucuronic	4	acrylic fiber	3
absorbent grades	16	humic	20	activatable chemical	9
absorption	5	hydroxy	4	activated carbon	20
capillary	13	hypochlorous	10	activated sludge	20
ink	14	lignosulfonic	8	activated sludge loading	20
light	14	linoleic	6	activated sludge process	20
mechanical	13	mineral	4	activation	4
tensile energy	14	oleic	6	surface	11
vapor	13	peracetic	10	activation energy	8
absorption coefficient	14	raw	8	Arrhenius	4
accelerated aging	14	resin	6	activator	5
accelerated aging test	14	storage	8	active alkali	8
accelerated depreciation	26	sulfamic	10	active alkali-to-wood ratio	8
accelerated test	14	sulfuric	10	active surface area	13
acceleration ratio	13	sulfurous	8	activity	8, 13
accelerator	5	uronic	4	surface	5
		waste	10		
acceptance test	25			actual depreciation	26
accepted chips	1	acid-alkali cooking process	8	acute toxicity	20
accepted stock	12	acid cleaning	8	ac variable frequency drive	13
accept nozzle	12	acid dew point	9	adansonia fiber	3
accepts	12	acid dye	5	adaptation	5
screen	12	acid fastness	14	adding-machine paper	16
accessibility	4	acid free paper	14	addition reaction	4
acclimation	20	acid groups	4	additive(s)	13
account	26	acid hydrolysis	4	beater	13
accountant	26	acidification	4	coating	17
accounting	26	acid-insoluble ash	11	external	13
cost	26	acid-insoluble lignin	8	fuel	9
accumulated depreciation	26	acidity	5	internal	13
accumulator	8	acidity (of paper)	14	non-fibrous	5
heat	8	acid making	8	papermaking	13
steam	9	acid number	6	protective	10
accumulator acid	8	acid paper	14	wet-end	13
accumulator felling head	1	acid plant	8	additive primary colors	19
accuracy	14	acid-precipitated lignin	6	additive system	13
test	14	acid pretreatment	10	adherend	18

adhesion,
    bark   1
    pin   18
    wet web   13
adhesion promoter   18

adhesion strength   18
adhesive   17
    combining   18
    dry strength   5
adhesive demand   17

adhesive failure   18
adhesiveness   18
adhesive ratio   17
adhesive wear   24
adjustable speed equipment   24

adjusting color   13
adjusting rods   13
admixture   13
adsorbable organic halides   20
adsorbate   20

adsorbent   20
adsorption   5, 20
advanced wastewater treatment   20
aeration   20
    diffused   20

aeration efficiency   20
aeration lagoon   20
aerator   20
    cascade   20
    mechanical   20
    surface   20

aerial survey   1
aerobes   20
aerobic   20
aerobic biological oxidation   20

aerobic digestion   20
aerosol   21
affinity   4
afforestation   1
a-frame   1

after dryers   17
against the grain   18
agalite   5
agar   5
agave   3

aged chips   1
agent(s),
    acetylating   4
    acidulating   4
    antiblocking   17

    anti-skinning   19
    antistatic   17, 18
    bleaching   10
    bonding   5
    buffering   8

    chelating   10
    complexing   10
    conductive   17
    coupling   17
    debonding   12

dehydrating   4
deposit control   9
dispersing   17
dewatering   5
fixing   5

fluorescent brightening   5
foaming   5
freeze conditioning   1
friction control   17
glossing   17

leveling   17
oxidizing   10
peptizing   5
precipitating   5
reducing   10

reinforcing   17
rewetting   17
rheology control   17
sequestering   10
softening   5

stiffening   18
surface active   5
swelling   4
thickening   17
water retention   17
wetting   5

agglomeration   9
aggregate   9
aggregate ray   2
aging   14

    accelerated   14
    heat   14
aging test   14
    accelerated   14
agitation   24

    zone   12
agitator   24
    cross shaft   13
    filter vat   12
    turbine   24

agitator efficiency   12
agricultural residues   3
agriforestry   1
aid(s),
    drainage   5

    filter   23
    formation   13
    release   13
    retention   5
    washing   12

air   21
    ambient   21
    combustion   9
    compressed   24
    diffusion   13

    dilution   21
    entrained   13
    equilibrium   14
    excess   9
    exhaust   13

    felt   13
    infiltration   13
    makeup   13
    overfire   9
    primary   9

    roof   13
    saturated   13
    supply   13
    theoretical   9
    utility   24

    underfire   9
air bags   18
air balance   13
air binding   24
airborne web drying   13

air box   9
air bubbles   13
air cannons   1
air change   13
air classification   1

air cleaner   13
air conditioning   14
air contaminants   21
air content (of stock)   13
air cooling   13

air curtain   13
air-cushioned headbox   13
air deckle   13
air deficiency   9
air density separator   1

air diffuser   20
air doctor   13
air-dried chips   1
air-dried paper   14
air dry content   11

air dryer   10
air drying   13
air dry pulp   11
air dry weight   11
air entrainment   13

air exhaust   13
air float   18
air-float drying   12
air flotation dryer   17
air flotation separator   1

air foil threading   13
air forming   13
air fraction   14
air-fuel ratio   9
air heater   9

    recuperative   9
    regenerative   9
air impactor   17
air-impingement drying   13
air infiltration   9

air knife   17
air knife coating   17
air-laid sheet   13
air leak tester   14
air lock   8

air-mail paper	16
air mass	21
air pad	10, 13
air permeability	14
air pollution	21
air pollution control	21
air pollution control equipment	21
air ports	9
air pumping	13
air quality index	21
air resistance	14
air resistance tester	14
air shear burst	14
air shed	21
air showers	13
air sparger	20
air stripping	20
air supply	13
air threader pipe	13
air-to-cloth ratio	21
air-to-solids ratio	20
air-through drying	13
airveying	1
air volume (of paper)	14
album papers	16
alcohol	4
ethyl	6
polyvinyl	5
terpene	6
aldehyde	4
aldehyde starch	5
algae	20
alginate	17
alignment	13
hot-kiln	9
mechanical	13
optical	13
paper machine	13
alignment roll	13
aliphatic	4
aliquot	4
alkafide process	8
alkali	4
active	8
effective	8
excess	10
residual	8
total	8
total titratable	8
alkali analyzer	8
alkali cellulose	4
alkali fastness	14
alkali lignin	6
alkaline extraction stage	10
alkaline-filled paper	14
alkaline filler	5
alkaline paper	14
alkaline papermaking	5
alkaline peroxide mech. pulping	7
alkaline pulping	8

alkaline size	5
alkaline sulfite process	8
alkalinity	5
bicarbonate	20
carbonate	20
alkalinity (of paper)	14
alkali proof	14
alkali purification	8
alkali-reactive binders	17
alkali solubility	11
alkalization	4
alkane	4
alkenyl succinic anhydride	5
alkyd resins	17
alkyl	4
alkylation	4
alkylketene dimers	5
all-direction stretch	14
allowable cut	1
allowable working pressure	9
alloy	24
alphabet pulps	7
alpha-cellulose	4
alpha protein	17
alpha pulps	11
alternate pitting	2
alternating current	22
alternating current drive	24
alternator	22
alum	5
alumina	5
aluminate recovery process	9
aluminates	5
alumina trihydrate	5
alumino-silicate	5
aluminum chloride	5
aluminum oxide	7
aluminum resinate	5
aluminum stearate	17
aluminum sulfate	5
alum spots	14
ambient air	21
ambient air monitoring	21
ambient air quality	21
ambient conditions	21
amines	9
filming	9
neutralizing	9
amino resins	5
ammonia	8
ammonium base liquor	8
ammonium stearate	17
amorphous cellulose	4
amorphous region	2
amorphous silicas/silicates	5
amortization	26
amphipathic molecule	5
ampholytic starch	5
amphoteric	5
amylaceous	5
amylase	5

amylopectin	5
amylose	5
anaerobes	20
anaerobic	20
anaerobic biological treatment	20
anaerobic contact process	20
anaerobic digestion	20
analysis	23
break-even	26
chemical	4
chip size	1
cost-benefit	26
cost-effectiveness	26
dirt	14
dust composition	21
fiber	11
gas	9, 21
image	11
lost time	13
microbiological	5
microstructural	14
Orsat	9
particle size	21
qualitative	4
quantitative	4
sensitivity	26
short-span tensile	14
statistical	25
uncertainty	26
value	26
vibration	24
water	20
analysis of variance	25
analytical method	4
analyzer,	
alkali	8
optical fiber length	11
surface	14
anatase	5
anchor coat	18
anchoring	24
anemometer	13
angiosperm	2
angle,	
bar	12
blade contact	17
chip	1
chipper	1
chop	18
contact	14
fibril	2
foil	13
impact	13
jet impingement	13
mean orientation	14
microfibrillar	2
peeling	13
rake	13
screen	19
slope	1
wet	17
wiping	17

angle bar	19	apron	13	ashless paper	14
angle cut paper	18	apron board	13	ash retention	13
angle of attack	17	aqueduct	20	ash sluice	9
		aqueous	17	as-made grammage	14
angle of incidence	14	aqueous SO$_2$	8	aspect ratio (of fibers)	11
angle of outflow	13				
angle of repose	1	aquifer	20	aspect ratio (of particles)	17
angle of wrap	13	arabinan	4	aspenwax	5
anhydrous	5	arabinose	4	asperities	24
		aramid fiber	3	asphalt	5
anhydro	4	Arbiso process	8	asphalt papers	16
aniline dye	5				
animal fiber	3	arch	1	aspirating burner	9
animal glue	18	furnace	9	aspirator hole	13
animal size	5	archival paper	16	assets	26
		area,		capital	26
anion	5	basal	1	assimilation	20
anionic starch	5			atmospheric	21
anionic trash	13	bonded	14		
anion interchange	20	cross field	2	assist drive	13
anisotropic	2	cutover	1	asthma feeder	8
		effect. capillary x-sect.	2	atmosphere	21
anisotropic paper	14	effective refining	12	oxidizing	9
anisotropic ratio	14			reducing	9
annealing	23	equivalent black	11		
annual crop fiber	3	fill	20	atmospheric assimilation	21
annual cut	1	open	15	atmospheric convection	21
		projected	11	atmospheric diffusion	21
annual growth ring	2	recovery	9	atmospheric eddies	21
annual increment	1				
annular rings	14	slack	13, 15	atmospheric pressure	21
annular vessel	2	specific collection	21	atmospheric stability	21
anode	22	stock preparation	12	atmospheric turbulence	21
		tight	15	atom	4
anodic protection	24	arms,		atomization	9
anodizing	24	primary	13	atomizer	9
anoxic	20	secondary	13	atomizing medium	9
anthraquinone	8	armature	24	attack distance	17
anti-acid paper	14	aromatic	4	attemperation	9
		array	25	attribute specifications	25
antiblocking agent	17				
antichlor	10	Arrhenius activation energy	4	attrition	20
antideflection roll	13	articulated	1	attrition mill	1
antifoam	5	articulating paper	16	attrition-type repulper	13
antifoulant	20	artificial watercourse	20	audit	26
		artist papers	16	energy	22
antifriction	24				
antifriction bearing	24	art paper	16	environmental	23
anti-offset spray	19	art parchment	16	quality	25
antioxidant	19	artwork	19	recovery boiler	9
anti-penetrant	18	arundo	3	safety	23
		asbestine	3	technical	23
antiquarian paper	14				
antique finish	14	asbestos	3	auto causticizing	9
anti-skinning agent	19	asbestos board	16	autocorrelation coefficient	25
antistatic agent	17, 18	aseptic cartons	18	autocorrelation function	25
apparent density	1, 14	ash	5, 9	autohydrolysis	8
		acid-insoluble	11	automatic sampling	20
appearance	14				
chalky	14	chemical	9	automatic titration	8
applicator	17	fly	9	automatic valve	24
applicator roll	17	soda	8	autopaster	19
applicator roll streaks	17	sticky	9	autoregression	25
		ash content	9, 14	auto slice	13
applied research	23				
apprentice	24	ash control	12	auxiliary equipment	13, 23
approach flow	13	ash fusion characteristics	9	auxiliary fuel	9
approach system	13	ash hopper	9	auxiliary roll stand	19
a priori	23	ashing	14	availability	23
		wet	14	availability factor	22

available chlorine	10
available lime index	9
average	25
average fiber length	11
average specific nip pressure	13
axial	2
axial element	2
axial fan	9
axial-flow impellor	24
axial-flow turbine	22

B _____

baby dryer	13
baby presses	13
back coating	17
backcut	1
backfall	12
backflow	20
backflow steam	7
background concentration	21
back guard	18
backing	18
backing roll	17
backing roll mark	17
backing roll spot	17
backing up	19
backing wire	13
backlash	13, 19
back pressure	24
back pressure turbine	22
back printing	19
back side	13
back stand	13
back tender	13
backup roll	17
backwash	20
back water	13
bacteria,	5
facultative	20
filamentous	5
fimbriated	5
hydrogen-forming	5
iron	5
mesophilic	20
sulfate-reducing	5
sulfur	5
thermophilic	5
bacteria count	5
bactericide	5
baffle,	12
compaction	12
furnace nose	9
hanging	12
table roll	13
baffle chamber	21
bag	13, 18
bagasse	2

bag filter	21
Baggallay box	13
bagginess	13
baggy paper	14
baghouse	21
pulse-jet	21
reverse air	21
shake-deflate	21
bag life	21
bag paper	16
bakers wrap	16
balance	19
air	13
chemical	8
energy	22
heat	9
material	23
Sankey	13
steam	9
water	12
water-ink	19
wet end	13
balanced loop former	13
balancing (of rolls)	24
bale	12
baling	12
baling operation	12
baling press	12
ballistic wet web tester	14
ball mill	11
balloon swelling	2
balls	9
ball valve	24
balsam	6
bamboo	2
banding	18
band saw	1
banknote paper	16
bar angle	12
barium sulfate	5
bark	2
inner	2
bark adhesion	1
bark boiler	9
bark content	1
bark drying	1
barked wood	1
barker	1
abrasion	1
cutterhead	1
flail	1
hydraulic	1
mechanical	1
ring shear	1
Rosserhead	1
rotary drum	1
stationary friction	1
barker losses	1
barking	1
chemical	1

compression	1
dry	1
parallel	1
tumble	1
wet	1
barking cleanliness	1
barking drum	1
barking efficiency	1
bark pocket	1
bark press	1
bark reclaim	1
bark shredder	1
bark specks	14
barometer	21
barometric condenser	9
barometric leg	12
barometric pressure	21
barrelling	13
barrier coat	17
barrier coating	17
barrier material	17
barrier screening	12
barring	14
calender	13
dandy	14
wet-end	13
barring pattern	14
barring severity	14
bars	12
dryer	13
finger	7
spoiler	13
bar screen	12
bar width	12
baryte	5
basal area	1
base	4, 8
soluble	8
base board	17
base case	26
base cloth	15
base coat	17
base exchange	20
base load	9, 22
base-load power plant	22
base paper	14
base speed	24
base stock	17
wallpaper	16
base stock stability	17
basic dye	5
basic research	23
basic size	18
basic wood increment	1
basin	20
equalizing	20
sedimentation	20
basis weight	14
basis weight valve	13
basket cooking	8

basket screen	12	bending resistance	14	biological floc	20		
bast fiber	2	beneficiation	5	biological oxidation	20		
batch bleaching process	10	bent-blade coater	17	aerobic	20		
batch coloring	13	benthic	20	biological process	20		
batch cooking	8	benthic organisms	20	high rate	20		
batch digester	8	bentonite	5	biological purification	20		
batch digester scheduling	8	benzene	4	biological slime	20		
batch process	23	beta-cellulose	4	biological sludge	20		
batt	15	betameter	14	biological wastewater treatment	20		
stratified	15	beta radiation	14	biomass	20		
batt-on-base felt	15	bevel	7	biomass fuel	9		
batt-on-mesh felt	15	beveling tool	7	bionics	23		
baume hydrometer scale	9	Bewoid size	5	biopulping	8		
Bauer-McNett classifier	11	bhutang	2	biostat	5		
bauxite	7	bias	25	biosynthesis	4		
bead coater	17	biaxial strength	14	biota	20		
beading	18	biaxial stress ratio	14	biotechnology	23		
bearing	24	bible paper	16	birefringence	5		
antifriction	24	bibulous	14	bisulfite process	8		
thrust	24	bicarbonate	20	bisulfite pulp	8		
beatability	11	bicarbonate alkalinity	20	bite	18, 19		
beater	12	big-stick loader	1	bitumen	17		
breaker	12	bilge	13	bituminous coating	17		
laboratory	11	billet	1	bituminous emulsions	5		
beater additives	13	billy stick	13	black cook	8		
beater evaluation	11	bimetal plate	19	blackening	14		
beater roll	12	bimodal distribution	25	calender	14		
beater room	12	bin	1	black liquor	8		
beating	12	chip	1	heavy	9		
easy	11	live bottom	1	intermediate	9		
fast	11	binder(s)	1, 17, 19	oxidized	9		
hard	11, 12	acrylic	17	strong	9		
slow	11	alkali-reactive	17	thick	9		
beating curve	11	particle	17	unoxidized	9		
beating schedule	12	synthetic	17	weak	9		
beating time	12	binder migration	17	black liquor burning	9		
bed	20	binders board	16	black liquor evaporation	9		
char	9	binder specks	17	black liquor firing system	9		
electrified filter	21	bin discharger	1	black liquor oxidation	9		
filter	20	bioaccumulation	20	black liquor properties	9		
fuel	9	bioaccumulative	20	blackout	9		
slider	1	bioassay	20	black stock screening	12		
smelt	9	biocatalyst	5	blade,			
bed depth	20	biochemical	20	doctor	13		
bed load	12	biochemical oxygen demand	20	slitter	13		
bedplate	12, 24	ultimate	20	trailing	17		
bed rolls	13	biochemical process	20	blade coater	17		
bedroll-type winder	13	biochemistry	4	bent	17		
bell	14	biocide	5	fountain	17		
belt conveyor	1	nonoxidizing	5	high-angle	17		
		oxidizing	5				
belt conveyor scale	1			inverted	17		
belt filter	9	bioconversion	20	low-angle	17		
belt screen	20	biodegradable	20	two-	17		
belt thickener	12	biofilm	20	blade contact angle	17		
bench scale process	23	biofuel	9	blade crease	17		
bender	18	biogas	20	blade cut	17		
bending	14	biogasification	9	blade gap former	13		
bending factor	2	biological contactor	20	blade loading	17		
bending number	14	biological corrosion	24	blade mark	17		
bending quality	14	biological filter	20	blade puddle coater	17		

380

blade scratches	17	
blade streak	17	
blanc fixe	5	
blank	4, 18	
box	18	
blanket	19	
smashed	19	
blanket contamination	19	
blanket creep	19	
blanket cylinder	19	
blanket gain	19	
blanket glaze	19	
blanket-to-blanket press	19	
blanket wrap	19	
blanket wraparound	19	
blanking paper	16	
blank news	12	
blanks	16	
blazing	1	
bleachability	10	
bleachable grade pulp	8	
bleach chemical	10	
bleach demand	10	
residual	10	
bleached pulp	10	
bleach effluent	10	
bleachery	10	
bleaching	10	
chlorine-free	10	
chlorite	10	
continuous	10	
displacement	10	
dynamic	10	
electrochemical	10	
gas-phase	10	
grinder	10	
high-yield	10	
lignin-preserving	10	
multistage	10	
nitrogen dioxide	10	
refiner	7	
short-sequence	10	
viscosity-reducing	10	
bleaching agent	10	
oxidative	10	
bleaching effect	10	
bleaching index	10	
bleaching power	10	
bleaching sequence	10	
bleaching stage	10	
chlorine dioxide	10	
extraction	10	
hypochlorite	10	
oxygen	10	
peroxide	10	
bleaching time	10	
bleaching tower	10	
bleaching yield	10	
bleach liquor	10	
bleach liquor strength	10	

bleach plant	10	
closed cycle	10	
bleach requirement	10	
bleach response curve	10	
bleach sludge	10	
bleach washer	10	
bleeding	5, 19, 24	
bleed-through	13	
blend	12	
blending	12	
complete	12	
stock	12	
blending chest	12	
blend time	12	
blind	19	
blind-drilled press	13	
blind flange	24	
blinding	12	
blister	14	
coating	17	
blister cut	14	
blistering	13, 17, 19	
blister pick	19	
blister resistance	17	
block	1	
block diagram	23	
blocking	17	
calender roll	13	
shear	17	
blocking resistance	17	
blood proof	14	
bloom	20	
blotch	14	
blotting paper	16	
blow	8, 13	
cold	8	
blow back	7, 8	
blow boxes	12	
blowdown	8, 9	
blowdown valve	13	
blower	1	
soot	9	
vacuum	13	
blow gas	8	
blow-heat evaporator	9	
blow-heat recovery	8	
blowing	1, 13	
blowing-discharge chipper	1	
blowing roll	13	
blowline	8	
blowline refining	12	
blow out	7	
blow pipe	13	
blow pit	8	
blow pressure	8	
blow roll	13	
blow sample	8, 13	
blow tank	8	
blow-through steam	7, 13	
blow time	8	

blow unit	8	
blow valve	8	
blue glass	7	
blunger	5	
blushing	17	
board(s)	1, 13	
acoustical	16	
apron	13	
asbestos	16	
base	17	
binders	16	
box-	16	
building	16	
card-	16	
chip-	16	
combination	13	
combined	18	
container-	16	
corrugated	18	
fiber-	16	
filled	14	
food-	16	
forming	13	
fourdrinier	13	
gypsum	16	
ivory	16	
leather-	16	
liner-	16	
machine-made	13	
mat	16	
matrix	16	
mill-	16	
multiply	13	
news-	16	
particle-	1	
pasted	14	
polymeric impregnated	18	
press-	16	
solid	14	
straw-	16	
V-	16	
wood composition	1	
board foot	1	
board machine	13	
intermittent	13	
board mill	13	
boardy	15	
BOD_5	20	
BOD load	20	
body	17, 19	
body damage	14	
body gum	19	
body stock	17	
body wrap	13	
bogus	14	
boiler	9	
bark	9	
coal fired	9	
firetube	9	
multifuel	9	

boiler *(cont)*
    once-through 9
    packaged 9
    radiant-design 9
    rag 12
    recovery 9

    single-drum 9
    water tube 9
    wood waste 9
boiler code 9
boiler efficiency 9

boiler feed pump 9
boiler feedwater 9
boiler feedwater treatment 9
boiler house 9
boiler tubes 9

boiler water 9
boiling 9
boiling point 9
boiling point rise 9
boilout 9, 13

bole 1
bolometer 21
bolt 1
bond(s) 4, 7
    glycosidic 4

    hydrogen 4
    peeling 18
    vitrified 7
    tearing 18
    xerographic 16

bond coat 18
bonded area 14
    relative 11
bonded fiber surface area 11
bonding,

    chemical 13
    fiber 13
    solvent 13
    thermal 13
bonding agent 5

bonding index 14
    fiber 11
bonding potential 11
bonding strength 11, 18
bond paper 16

bond time 18
bone dry 11
bone dry unit 1
bone fiber 4
bone hard 13

book bulk 14
book papers 16
boom 1
    bundle 1
    heel 1

    knuckle 1
    loading 1
    log 1
boom logs 1
booster pump 20

borate-based kraft process 8
borax 5
bordered pit 2
bordered pit pair 2
boreal forest 1

borer hole 1
boroscope 24
boring method 11
borohydride 10
bottleneck 23

bottom colors 5
bottom felt 13
bottoming cycle 22
bottom liner 13
bottom paper 18

bottom roll 13
bottom sided sheet 14
boundary layer 13
boundary layer emission monit. 21
bound water 2, 11

bound water layer 11
bowed edges 18
bowed roll 13
bowing 15
bowl 13

box(es) 18
    air 9
    Baggallay 13
    blow 12
    broke 13

    corrugated board 18
    dropout 21
    dry 13
    dry suction 13
    feed 12

    fire 9
    flat 13
    flow 13
    light 14
    regulating 12, 13

    rigid 18
    rotary suction 13
    seal 12
    setup 18
    solid fiber 18

    stuff 13
    stuffing 24
    suction 13
    vacuum 13
    water 13

    wet 13
    wind- 9
box blank 18
boxboard 16
    folding 16

box car 18
box clippings 12
bracket trimmer 18
brackish water 20
braille paper 16

brainstorming 23
braking 13
    friction 13
    regenerative 13
branch tubes 13

break 13
    stretch at 14
breakage 1
break detector 13
breakdown 1

breakdown deck 1
breakdown maintenance 24
break end 13
breaker 12, 22
    circuit 22

    foam 12
    vacuum 20
    vortex 13
breaker bar section 7
breaker beater 12

breaker roll 18
breaker stack 13
break-even analysis 26
break-even chart 26
break-even point 26

breaking back 13
breaking length 14
break point 20
breakthrough 20
breast height 1

breast roll 13, 17
breast roll discharge 13
breather 18
breeching 9
brick 7
    acid proof 8

bricking 7
bridge crane 1
bridge tree 7
bridging 1, 9

bridle 1, 13
brightener 10
    optical 5
brightening 10
    steep 10

brightening stage,
    hydrosulfite 10
    hypochlorite 10
    peroxide 10
brightness, 14

    diffuse 14
    directional 14
    Elrepho 14
    G.E. 14
brightness meter 14

brightness reversion 10, 14
brightness stability 10
brilliancy 14
brine 20
bristle mark 17

bristol(s) 16
    index 16
Bristow tester 14
British sheet machine 11
Britt jar 11

brittleness 14
broadleaf tree 2
broke 13
    colored 13
    cutter 18

    dry 13
    finishing 18
    wet 13
    wet-strength 13
broke box 13

broke chips 13
broken edge 14
broken ream 18
broke pit 13
broker 13

broke recovery system 13
broomage 1
brown fiber 8
brown rot 2
brown stock 8

brown stock washing 12
bruising 11
brush 1
brush (on electrical machine) 24
brush calendering 13

brush coating 17
brush detector 18
brush finish coating 17
brushing 7, 11
brushing out 12

brush mark 17
bubble 14
bubble coating 17
bubbler 21
bucket elevator 1

bucking 1
buckle 14
buckles 19
buckling 14
budget estimate 26

buffer 4
buffering action 4
buffering agent 8
buffering ratio 8
buffer storage 12

building board 16
building papers 16
buildup 13
built-in stress or strain 14
bulge 15

bulk 14
    book 14
    smashed 14
bulk delignification 8
bulk density 1
    dry 1

bulk handling 1
bulkhead 1
bulking 14, 15, 20
bulking caliper 14

bulking index 14
bulking number 14
bulking pressure 14
bulking value 17
bulk modulus 14

bulk sampler 1
bulk softness 14
bulk storage 1
bulk volume 1
bulky 14

bullbuck 1
bull chain 1
bull nose 9
bull of the woods 1
bull screen 7

bull screen rakes 7
bull's eye 13
bump 17
bumping 8
bunching 1

bunch-loading 1
bunch plating 14
bundle 18
    fiber 12
    vascular 3

bundle boom 1
bundle deck 1
bundled logs 1
bunk 1
bunker 1

bunker C oil 9
bureaucracy papers 16
burkeite 9
burl 1
burn 7

burnability 9
burner 9
    aspirating 9
    sulfur 8
burning 9

    black liquor 9
    controlled open 21
    freeboard 9
    open 21
    slash 1
    wad 13

burning out 13
burnished finish 14
burnishing 13
burn out test 17

burnt cook 8
burnt lime 9
burnt paper 14
burr 7, 15
burr holder 7

burr impression 7
burring 7
burring interval 7
burr lead 7
burst 14

    air shear 14
    caliper shear 14
    core 14
    cross-machine 14
    tension 14

burst index 14
bursting strength 14
bushing 24
    seal 24
business papers 16

butchers wraps 16
butt 1
butt drop 18
butterfly valve 24
butting off 1

butting rolls 1
butt log 1
butt rigging 1
butt rot 2
butt splice 18

butt swell 1
butyl carbitol test 14
buzz word 23
by-pass 24
by-product 6
by-product power 22

C ——————————

cable logging 1
cable paper 16
cake 20
    filter 23
    sludge 20

caking 9, 19
calcination 9
calcined clay 5
calcined kaolin 5
calciner 9

    flash 9
    fluid bed 9
calcite limestone 9
calcium carbonate 5
calcium hydroxide 9

calcium hypochlorite 10
calcium oxide 9
calcium sulfate 5
calender 13
    deckling 13
    thickness 13

calender barring 13
calender blackening 14
calender coloring 13
calender cooling 13

calender-crush finish	14	
calender crushing	13	
calender cut	14	
calendered,		
double	14	
hard	14	
calendered paper	14	
calender finish	14	
calendering	13	
brush	13	
friction	13	
gloss	13	
machine	13	
matte	13	
moisture-gradient	13	
sheet	18	
soft	13	
steam	13	
temperature-gradient	13	
calender-marked	14	
calender nip	13	
calender roll	13	
calender roll blocking	13	
calender roll offsetting	13	
calender sizing	13	
calender spots	14	
calender stack	13	
calender streaks	14	
calender wrinkle	14	
calibrant	14	
calibration	14	
calibration pulp	11	
calibration standard	14	
caliper	14	
bulking	14	
effective	14	
single-sheet	14	
caliper gauge	14	
caliper shear burst	14	
calorific value	9	
camber	13	
cambium	2	
cambium shear	1	
camera-ready copy	19	
Canadian standard freeness	11	
can	13	
canal	7	
intercellular	2	
pit	2	
cane	3	
sugar	3	
cannister assembly	12	
canopy hood	13	
cant	1, 18	
cantilevered fourdrinier	13	
cantilevering	13	
capability	22	
turndown	23	
capability index	25	
capacitor	22	

capacity	20, 22, 23	
absorbent	11	
excess	23	
flaw-carrying	14	
heat	9	
hydraulic	12	
infiltration	20	
lime kiln	9	
oxygenation	20	
paper machine	13	
rated	9, 13	
saturating	14	
storage	12	
vacuum	13	
water retention	15	
capacity factor	22	
capillarity	14	
capillary	2	
capillary absorption	13	
capillary rise	14	
capillary system	2	
capillary viscometer	4	
capital assets	26	
capital expenditure	26	
capital intensive	26	
capping	8	
capping valve	8	
capstan wrap	13	
captive pulp	8	
carbohydrate	4	
carbon	9	
activated	20	
total organic	20	
carbonaceous	9	
carbonate	20	
carbonate alkalinity	20	
carbonate hardness	20	
carbonation	9, 20	
carbon black	19	
carbon dioxide	9	
carbon disulfide	4	
carbon fibers	3	
carbonic acid	20	
carbonization	24	
carbonizing tissue	16	
carbonless paper	16	
carbon monoxide	9	
carbon papers	16	
carbonyl group	4	
carbonyl sulfide	21	
carboxymethylcellulose	4	
carcinogen	20	
card	1	
cardboard	16	
carding	15	
carliner	15	
carload lot	18	
caroa	3	
carriage	1	
log	1	
skyline	1	

carrier drum	18	
carrying felt	13	
carrying roll	13	
carryover	8, 9	
carton(s)	18	
aseptic	18	
folding	18	
cascade aerator	20	
cascade evaporator	9	
cascade impactor	21	
cascade sequence	12	
cascade steam system	13	
cascading	13, 23	
case	18	
case hardening	13	
casein	17	
case lot	18	
cash flow	26	
discounted	26	
casing	7, 24	
castable	9	
cast coating	17	
catalog papers	15	
catalyst	4	
catchall	21	
catching up	19	
catfaces	1	
cathode	22	
cathodic polarization	24	
cathodic protection	24	
cationic dye	5	
cationic direct dyes	5	
cationic starch	5	
catwalk	23	
caustic	9	
caustic embrittlement	9	
causticity	8	
causticizer	9	
causticizing	9	
causticizing efficiency	9	
causticizing plant	9	
causticizing power (of lime)	9	
caustic soda	8	
caustic solubility	11	
cavitation	24	
cavitation erosion	24	
cell	2	
diaphragm	10	
epidermal	2	
flotation	12	
membrane	10	
mercury	10	
procumbent ray	2	
stone	2	
upright ray	2	
cellobiose	4	
cellophane	4	
cells	19	
comma	3	

cellulase	4
cellulolytic	4
cellulose	4
alkali	4
alpha	4
amorphous	4
beta	4
chemical	4
crystalline	4
ethyl	4
gamma	4
hemi-	4
holo-	4
hydrate	4
hydro-	4
ligno-	4
mercerized	4
mesomorphous	4
methyl	4
microbial	4
native	4
nitro-	4
oxy-	4
regenerated	4
water	4
cellulose acetate	4
cellulose acetate butyrate	4
cellulose ester	4
cellulose ether	4
cellulose fiber	4
cellulose film	4
cellulose nitrate	4
cellulose propionate	4
cellulose triacetate	4
cellulose viscosity	4
cellulose wadding	16
cellulosic	4
cell wall	2
cell wall check	2
centerline	13
offset parallel	13
paper machine	13
center stock	13
center winder	13
centerwind reel	13
centralized oil system	24
central tendency	25
centrate	20
centrifugal cleaner	12
centrifugal fan	9
centrifugal pump	24
centrifugal screen	12
gravity	12
centrifugation	20
ceramic fiber	3
ceramic pulpstone	7
ceramics	7
ceramic thimble	21
cereal straw	3
certification	23

chaff	3
chaffed fiber	3
chain drive	24
chain grinder	7
chain lines	14
chain saw	1
chain section	9
chalk	5
chalking	19
chalky appearance	14
chamber	21
baffle	21
combustion	9
grit	20
intermediate	13
mixing	13
pit	2
reception	13
seal	12
settling	21
change of state	9
channel	20
flow	24
open	20
channeling	12
char	9
char bed	9
charge,	
chemical	8
chip	8
digester	8
electric	22
electrokinetic	5
liquor	8
surface	5
charged droplet scrubber	21
charging	8
charging floor	8
charm-flex wrinkle	17
chart,	
break-even	26
control	25, 26
cumulative sum	25
organization	23
Pareto	25
profit-volume	26
web content	14
chart paper	16
chasing	1
chattermarking	14
check	1
cell wall	2
tough	16
checking	13
check valve	24
cheeking piece	13
chelating agent	10
chelation value	10
chemical,	
activatable	9

bleach	10
excess	10
makeup	8
residual	10
chemical accessibility	4
chemical analysis	4
chemical application	10
chemical ash	9
chemical balance	8
chemical barking	1
chemical bonding	13
chemical cellulose	4
chemical charge	8
chemical consumption	8, 10
chemical conversion	5
chemical cotton	4
chemical cycle	9
chemical diffusion	8
chemical engineering	23
chemical equation	4
chemical equivalent	4
chemical formula	4
chemical loss	9
chemically modified mech pulp'g	7
chemically resistant	14
chemically treated long fiber	7
chemical oxygen demand	20
chemical peeling	1
chemical process industries	23
chemical properties (of paper)	14
chemical pulp	8
chemical pulp demand	13
chemical pulping	8
chemical reaction	4
chemical reaction papers	16
chemical recovery	9
chemical residual	10
chemical shorthand	4
chemical sludge	20
chemical structure	4
chemical synthesis	4
chemical tests	14
chemical-to-wood ratio	8
chemical treatment (of chips)	1
chemical treatment (of water)	20
chemigroundwood	7
chemi-mechanical pulping	7
sulfonated	7
chemi-refiner mechanical pulp'g	7
chemi-thermomechanical pulp'g	7
chemistry,	
environmental	20
organic	4
photo-	4
stereo-	4
topo-	4
wet-end	5
chest	12
blending	12
machine	13
refiner	12

385

cheviot papers	14
chill drum	17
chill hardening	13
chill roll	17
chime rings	24
chimney	9
china clay	5
chip angle	1
chip bin	1
chipboard	1, 16
chip charge	8
chip chute	8
chip classification	1
chip classifier	1
chip cleaning	1
chip cleanliness	1
chip column	8
chip crushing	1
chip damage	1
chip destructuring	1
chip digger	1
chip dozer	1
chip filling	8
chip fines	1
chip fissures	1
chip grain length	1
chip grinding	7
chip inventory	1
chip irradiation	1
chip length	1
chip meter	8
chipper	1
blowing-discharge	1
conical	1
disc	1
drop feed	1
drum	1
horizontal feed	1
reducer	1
V-drum	1
chipper angle	1
chipper-canter	1
chipper infeed	1
chipper knife	1
chipper spout	1
chip packing	8
chip packing effectiveness	8
chip pile	1
chip pile rotation	1
chipping	1
chipping headrig	1
chip quality	1
chip quality index	1
chip reclaim	1
chip rot index	8
chips	1
accepted	1
aged	1
air-dried	1

broke	13
commercial	1
fresh	1
fuel	1
oversize	1
over-thick	1
pin	1
residual	1
undersize	1
whole-tree	1
chip screen	1
chip shredding	1
chip silo	1
chip size analysis	1
chip slicer	1
chip spreader	8
chip tester	1
chip thickness	1
effective	1
chip washer	1
chip width	1
chi-square distribution	25
chitin	4
chlor-alkali process	10
chlorate	10
chlorate cell liquor	10
chloride	9
chloride enrichment	9
chloride enrichment factor	9
chloride removal	9
chlorinated phenols	20
chlorination	20
hot	10
sequential	10
chlorination ratio	10
chlorination stage	10
chlorination stage, modified	10
chlorinator	20
chlorine	10
available	10
total organic	20
chlorine dioxide	10
chlorine dioxide bleach stage	10
chlorine dioxide generation	10
chlorine dioxide generator	10
chlorine dioxide plant	10
chlorine dioxide plant effic.	10
chlorine dioxide solution	10
chlorine dosage	10
chlorine evaporator	10
chlorine-free bleaching	10
chlorine hydrate	10
chlorine mixer	10
chlorine monoxide	10
chlorine number	10
chlorine water	10
chlorite bleaching	10
chlorolignin	10
choker	1
choking	13

chop	7
chop angle	18
chopper-fan	13
chroma	14
chromatic sensor	10
chromophores	10
chronic toxicity	20
chuck	13
chute	1
chip	1
cigarette paper	16
cinders	9
circuit	22, 23
closed	23
electric	22
single-phase	22
three-phase	22
circuit breaker	22
circularity	2
circular saw	1
circulating-oil system	24
circulation	8, 9
forced	8, 9
liquor	8
long	13
natural	9
short	13
circulation ratio	9
circulation system	13
circumferential valve	12
cladding	24
claflin refiner	12
clambunk	1
clamp truck	18
clamp truck damage	18
clarification	20
clarified wastewater	20
clarified white liquor	9
clarifier	9, 20
sedimentation	20
clash	7
classification,	
air	1
chip	1
fiber	11
classifier	9
Bauer-McNett	11
chip	1
clay	5
calcined	5
china	5
coating	17
delaminated	5
clay coating	17
cleanability	9, 15
cleaner(s)	12
air	13
centrifugal	12
core bleed type	12
flowthrough	12

cleaner(s) *(cont)*		
primary	12	
reverse-flow	12	
secondary	12	
cleaner head assembly	12	
cleaning	12	
acid	8	
chip	1	
felt	13	
stock	12	
cleaning efficiency	12	
cleanliness,		
barking	1	
chip	1	
cleanliness (of paper)	14	
cleanliness ratio	12	
clearance	12, 24	
plate	12	
clearance seal	24	
clearcutting	1	
cleared land	1	
clearing	11	
clear well	20	
cleavage	5	
cleavage reaction	4	
climate	21	
clingage	24	
clinker	9	
clipper seam	15	
clogging	13	
closed circuit	23	
closed cycle bleach plant	10	
closed draw	13	
closed-frame supercalender	13	
closed hood	13	
closed screening	12	
closed transfer	13	
closed transfer press	13	
close formation	14	
closure	13	
degree of	13	
cloth,		
base	15	
filter	12	
wire	12	
cloth finish	14	
clothing	13	
machine	13	
open-ended	15	
paper machine	13	
clothing lost time	13	
cloud finish	14	
cloudy formation	14	
cloverleaf press	13	
clutch	24	
coagulation	20	
hetero-	13	
coal-fired boiler	9	
coarseness	11	
fiber	11	
coarse papers	16	

coarse screening	12	
coat,		
anchor	18	
barrier	17	
base	17	
bond	18	
prime	17	
coated,		
dull	17	
machine	17	
patent	14	
single	17	
coated free sheet	16	
coated groundwood papers	16	
coated natural kraft	16	
coated paper(s)	17	
double	17	
glossy	14	
lightweight	16	
matte	14	
medium-weight	16	
sour	17	
ultra-lightweight	16	
coated one side	17	
coated two sides	17	
coater,		
bead	17	
bent-blade	17	
blade	17	
blade puddle	17	
contact	17	
double bump	17	
duplex	17	
fountain	17	
fountain blade	17	
gate roll	17	
high-angle	17	
hydrophilic roll	17	
inverted blade	17	
low-angle	17	
meniscus	17	
non-contact	17	
offset gravure	17	
puddle-blade	17	
short dwell	17	
size press	17	
slot orifice	17	
squeeze roll	17	
transfer roll	17	
two blade	17	
two-roll	17	
two-sided	17	
coating	17	
air knife	17	
back	17	
barrier	17	
bituminous	17	
brush	17	
brush finish	17	
bubble	17	

cast	17	
clay	17	
co-extrusion	17	
conductive	17	
conversion	17	
curtain	17	
decorative	17	
differential roll	17	
dip	17	
electrostatic	17	
emulsion	17	
extrusion	17	
film	17	
flow	17	
flow-on	17	
foam	17	
functional	17	
gravure	17	
hot melt	17	
immersion	17	
kiss roll	17	
knife	17	
metallic	17	
paste dispersion	17	
pattern	17	
pigment	17	
polished drum	17	
precast	17	
pressure	17	
print-on	17	
protective	17	
pyroxylin	17	
release	17	
reverse roll	17	
rod	17	
roll	17	
shaft	17	
smoothing roll	17	
solid state	17	
solvent	17	
split	17	
spot	17	
spray	17	
spread	17	
submersion	17	
thermal	17	
thermoplastic	17	
trailing blade	17	
turning rod	17	
wash	17	
water-base	17	
wax	17	
coating additives	17	
coating bands	17	
coating blister	17	
coating clay	17	
coating color	17	
high-solids	17	
coating color strainer	17	
coating composition	17	

coating defects	17	
coating formula	17	
coating formulation	17	
coating holdout	17	
coating kitchen	17	
coating layer	17	
coating lump	17	
coating machine	17	
coating makedown	17	
coating mixer	17	
coating mottle	17	
coating operation	17	
coating pan	17	
coating pick	19	
coating pigments	17	
coating plant	17	
coating puddle	17	
coating raw stock	17	
coating slip	17	
coating splash	17	
coating station	17	
coating streak	17	
coating structure	17	
coating system,		
excess	17	
pre-metered	17	
recirculating	17	
replenishment	17	
coat weight	17	
Cobb test	14	
cock	24	
cockle	14	
cockle cut	14	
cockle finish	14	
cockling	14	
coconut fiber	3	
code,		
boiler	9	
color	23	
code vessel	24	
coefficient,		
absorption	14	
autocorrelation	25	
contraction	13	
correlation	25	
drainage	15	
heat transfer	9	
light-absorption	14	
light-scattering	14	
slice	13	
coefficient of determination	25	
coefficient of friction	14	
coefficient of nondetermination	25	
coefficient of performance	22	
coefficient of variation	25	
co-extrusion coating	17	
coflocculation	5	
cogeneration	22	
coherence	25	
coherent variations	14	
cohesion	11	
degree of	11	
cohesive failure	18	
cohesiveness	11	
coil	18	
coil fabric	15	
coil paper	16	
coir	3	
cold alkali purification	8	
cold blow	8	
cold colors	14	
cold corrugating process	18	
cold deck	1	
cold grinding	7	
cold pressed finish	14	
cold pressing	18	
cold pulping	12	
cold soda process	7	
cold soda pulping	8	
cold storage	14	
cold type	19	
cold water waxing	18	
coliform	20	
coliform organisms	20	
collapsed fiber	11	
collapsing speed	13	
collating	19	
collecting	19	
collecting plates	9	
collection device	21	
collection efficiency	21	
collector	21	
dry	21	
dust	21	
collector electrode	21	
colloid	5	
protective	5	
colloidal system	5	
colloid mill	17	
colophony	6	
color(s)	14, 17	
adjusting	13	
bottom	5	
coating	17	
cold	14	
fast	14	
fugitive	14	
off	14	
process	19	
sad	14	
spot	19	
top	5	
warm	14	
color (of water)	20	
colorant	5	
color attributes	14	
color bodies	20	
color code	23	
color control	19	
colored broke	13	
colored fibers	14	
colored pigments	5	
color equilibration	13	
color fastness	14	
colorimeter	5	
tristimulus	14	
color immobilization	17	
color immobilization point	17	
coloring,		
batch	13	
calender	13	
continuous	13	
internal	13	
surface	13	
tub	18	
coloring strength	13	
color lake	5	
color matching	13	
color perception	14	
color process work	19	
color proofs	19	
color reversion	10	
color separation	19	
color specifications	14	
color variation	14	
color yield	13	
column,		
chip	8	
packed	21	
plate	21	
stripping	20	
tray	21	
column strength	14	
combination board	13	
combination felt	15	
combination plate	19	
combination run	19	
combination stage	10	
combination vat	13	
combination Yankee machine	13	
combined board	18	
combined cycle	22	
combined machine	13	
combined sewer	20	
combined SO_2	8	
combined strength parameter	11	
combiner	18	
combining adhesive	18	
combining unit	18	
combining winder	18	
combining winding	18	
combustibility	9	
combustible	9	
unburned	9	
combustible loss	9	
combustion	9	
complete	9	
fluidized bed	9	
heat of	9	
perfect	9	

combustion *(cont)*
    products of   9
    spontaneous   1
    wet   9
combustion air   9
combustion chamber   9

combustion gases   9
combustion rate   9
comma cells   3
commercial chips   1
commercial dryness (of pulp)   11

commercial match   13
commercial printing papers   16
commercial species   1
comminution   1
commissioning   23

commodity papers   16
communication papers   16
commutator   24
compactability   11
    wet fiber   11

compaction   13
    felt   13
compaction baffle   12
compaction factor   8
compactness   14

compactor   13
comparability   14
comparable data   23
complete blending   12
complete combustion   9

complete-tree utilization   1
complexing agent   10
compliance   20, 23
compose   19
composite cans   18

composite   14
composite profile   14
composite sample   11
composite tubes   9
composite valve   24

composition   19
    coating   17
    fiber   11
compound   4
    cyclic   4

    ionic   5
    monocyclic   6
    nonionic   5
    saturated   4
    unsaturated   4

compressed air   24
compressibility   11, 14
compressibility curve   11
compressing   11
compression barking (of chips)   1

compression damage (to chips)   1
compression flotation   20
compression modulus   13
compression ratio   7
compression strength   14

    edgewise   14
compression test estimation   18
compression wood   2
compressor   24
    jet   13
comptroller   26

concealed loss   19
concentration   4
    background   21
    critical adhesive volume   14
    ground level   21

    maximum allowable   21
    peak   21
    pigment volume   17
    sediment   20
    stress   14

concentration quotient   12
concentration yard   1
concentrator   9
    contaminant   12
concentricity   13

concora test   14
condensate   9
    contaminated   8
    residual   13
condensate receiver   9

condensate removal system   13
condensate return system   9
condensate treatment   20
condensation   9, 13
    heat of   9
    selective   20

condensation reaction   4
condenser   9, 22
    barometric   9
    direct-contact   8

    indirect   8
    jet   9
    surface   9
condenser tissue   16
condensible vapors   8

condensing turbine   22
conditioned paper   14
conditioned sludge   20
conditioning   11, 18
    air   14

    felt   13
    temperature   19
conditioning down   14
conditioning (of chips)   8
conditioning shoe   13

conditioning up   14
condition monitoring   24
conductive agent   17
conductive coating   17
conductive heat transfer   13

conductivity (of solutions)   8
conduit   24
confidence interval   25
confidence level   25
confidence limits   25

confluent pitting   2
conformability   11
conformance   14
congealing point   17
conical chipper   1

conical disc refiner   12
conical refiner   12
conifer   2
coniferin   6
connected load   22

conservation   1
    energy   22
conservatism   26
consistency   11, 17
consolidation   13

constant-rate drying   13
constant temp./humidity room   11
construction paper   16
consumer's risk   25
contact angle   14

contact coater   17
contact drying   13
contact printing   19
contact ratio   11
containerboard   16

containerization   18
contaminant concentrator   12
contaminants   12, 20
    air   21
contaminated condensate   8

content,
    air   13
    air dry   11
    ash   9, 14
    bark   1

    cotton   14
    dry solids   11
    equilibrium moisture   14
    fiber   14
    filler   14

    moisture   11
    pulp   14
    rag   14
    shive   11
    solids   17
    sulfonate   7

contingencies   26
contingency planning   20
continuous bleaching   10
continuous cooking   8

continuous coloring	13	conversion cost	26	calender	13
continuous diffusion washer	12	converter	5, 18	evaporative	21
continuous digester	8	converter waste	18	spray	8
Kamyr	8	convertibility	18	cooling roller	19
continuous grinder	7	convertibility efficiency	18	cooling tower	20
continuous process	23	convertible press	19	copolymer	4
continuous sampling	21	converting	18	copper number	14
continuous source monitoring	21	dry	18	coppice	1
continuous stirred tank	10	in-line	19	copy	19
continuous tone	19	wet	18	camera-ready	19
contoured plate	12	converting operation	18	copying papers	16
contraction	13	converting papers	18	cord	1
contraction coefficient	13	groundwood	16	cordage fiber	3
contract maintenance	24	converting plant	18	cordwood	1
contraries	12	converting winder	18	core	13
contrast	19	conveying medium	1	offset	14
contrast gloss	14	conveying wire	13	loose	14
contrast ratio	14	conveyor	1	peeler	1
control	4	belt	1	telescoped	14
air pollution	21	distribution	1	veneer	1
ash	12	flight	1	core bleed type cleaner	12
color	19	screw	1	core burst	14
corrosion	24	conveying,		core plug	13
cost	26	hydraulic	1	core shaft	13
deposit	9	pneumatic	1	core shaft slide	13
drainage	13	convolute winding	18	core slippage	13
drum differential	13	cook	8	core wood	2
electrolytic corrosion	24	black	8	core waste	18
inventory	23	burnt	8	corn husks	3
loss	23	hard	8	corn stalks	3
noise	23	soft	8	corona	21
pitch	5	water	8	corona current	21
production	23	cooker	5	corrective maintenance	24
quality	25	cooking	8	correlation	25
roll structure	13	basket	8	negative	25
slime	5	batch	8	positive	25
statistical process	25	continuous	8	serial	25
statistical quality	25	countercurrent	8	zero	25
tension	13	degree of	8	correlation coefficient	25
winder tension	13	extended	8	correspondence papers	16
control chart	25, 26	hydrothermal injection	8	corrosion	24
controllability	23	injection	8	biological	24
controllable cost	26	jet	5	crevice	24
controlled crown roll	13	sorption	8	electrolytic	24
controlled deformation roll	13	two-temperature	8	galvanic	24
controlled discharge	20	cooking acid	8	intergranular	24
controlled open burning	21	cooking curve	8	pitting	24
controller	26	cooking cycle	8	weld-associated	24
H-factor	8	cooking degree	8	corrosion control	24
convective drying	13	cooking liquor	8	electrolytic	24
convective heat transfer	13	cooking pressure	8	corrosion coupons	24
conventional felt	15	cooking time	8	corrosion-erosion	24
converging wedge former	13	cooking zone	8	corrosion inhibitor	24
conversion	1	cooler,		corrosion rate	24
chemical	5	gas	8	corrosivity	24
energy	22	sheet	12	corrugated board	18
enzyme	5	tube	9	corrugated board box	18
starch	5	web	12	corrugated wrapping	18
thermal	5	cooling,		corrugating	18
conversion coating	17	air	13	corrugating medium	16

corrugating medium test 14
corrugations 14, 18
corrugator 18
cost(s) 26
    controllable 26

    conversion 26
    current 26
    dead 26
    direct 26
    distribution 26

    fixed 26
    incremental 26
    installed 26
    marginal 26
    product 26

    standard 26
    startup 26
    unit 26
    variable 26
cost accounting 26

cost-benefit analysis 26
cost-benefit ratio 26
cost center 26
cost control 26
cost effective 26

cost-effectiveness analysis 26
cost index 26
costing,
    standard 26
cost-price squeeze 23

cost reduction 26
cost standard 26
cotton 3
    chemical 4
cotton content 14

cottoning 18
cotton linters 3
couch blotter 11
couch draw roll 13
coucher 13

couching 11, 13
couch marking 13
couch pit 13
couch press 13
couch roll 12, 13

couch trim 13
count 15, 18
    bacteria 5
    dirt 14
    fiber 11

    mesh 15
    plate 5
    shive 11
counter 23
    pocket 7

countercurrent bleach washing 10
countercurrent cooking 8
countercurrent flow 12
countercurrent washing 12
counterflow vat 13

counterknife 1
countershaft 24
counting 18
coupling 24
coupling agent 17

covariance 25
cover 13
    roll 13
    magazine 16
coverage 17

    wet 17
covered roll 13
cover papers 16
cracking 14, 17
    edge 15

    stress 24
    wet 9
crackle 14
crane 1
    bridge 1

    gantry 1
    jib 1
    mobile 1
    overhead traveling 1
    portal-type gantry 1

crane-way 1
crash finish 14
craters 17
crawler 1
crawling 19

crawl speed 13
crazing 17
creasability 14
crease 15
    blade 17

crease retention 14
creasing 18
creasing strength 14
creep 13, 15
    blanket 19

crepe papers 16
crepe pullout 13
crepe ratio 14
crepe wrinkle 14
creping 13

    crinkle 13
    cross 13
    dry 13
    micro- 11, 13
    primary 13

    secondary 13
    semi 13
    water 13
    wet 13
crevice corrosion 24

crill 11
crimp 11, 15
crimping 13
crimp mark 14
crimp ratio 11

crinkle creping 13
critical adhesive volume conc. 14
critical dryness 13
critical job 24
critical pair of properties 11

critical path 24
critical path method 24
critical point drying 11
critical speed (of rolls) 13
critical value 25

critical velocity 13
crocking 19
crook 1
cropping 19
cross-axis crown compensation 13

cross creping 13
cross cutting 1, 18
cross direction 13
cross-direction profile 14
cross-direction variation 14

cross field 2
cross field area 2
cross flow 13
crossflow heat exchanger 9
cross hairs 19

cross head 7
cross header 13
cross laminate 18
cross linkage 4
cross-machine burst 13

cross-machine direction 13
cross recovery 9
cross section 2
cross sectioning 14
cross shaft agitator 13

cross stability 15
crowding rolls 1
crown 1, 13
    negative 13
crown, amount of 13

crown closure 1
crown compensation,
    cross-axis 13
    roll-bending 13
crown curve 13

crown face 13
crown forest 1
crowning 13
crown shape 13
crow's feet 17, 19

crude soap washing 6
crude sulfate turpentine 6
crude tall oil 6
cruising 1
crumb 13

crumb pulp 12
crushed finish 14
crushed roll 14
crushing 13
    calender 13
    chip 1

crushing (of fibers) 11
crushing resistance 14
crystalline cellulose 4
crystallite 2

crystallization 10
crystallized 19
cuene 4
cull 1, 14
culled paper 13

cull roll 13
culm 3
cultural papers 16
culture 5
cumulative sample 21

cumulative sum chart 25
cunit 1
cuprammonium hydroxide 4
cuprammonium rayon 4
cupressoid pit 2

cupriethylenediamine hydroxide 4
cupriethylenediamine viscosity 4
curing 17, 18
curl 14
    edge 14

    fiber 11
    inherent 14
    ink drying 19
    mechanical 14
    pile 18

    roll 18
    structural 14
    wet 14
    wrap 18
curlator 12

curl index 11
curling 11
curling tendency 14
curl setting 7
currency paper 16

current 22
    alternating 22
    corona 21
    direct 22
current cost 26

current density 21
curtain chains 9
curtain coating 17
curve(s),
    beater 11

    bleach response 10
    cooking 8
    crown 13
    compressibility 11
    drying 13

    filling state 7
    load 22
    oxygen sag 20
    production rate 13
    pump characteristic 24

short span tensile 14
sigmoid adsorption 11
specific volume 7
spectrophotometric 14
stress-strain 14

curved plate 19
curved roll 13
curved screen 12
curvilinear surface 12
cushion 14

cushion form roller 19
custom sheeting 18
cut(s) 11, 14, 19
    allowable 1
    annual 1

    blade 17
    blister 14
    calender 14
    cockle 14
    dry 14

    fiber 14
    hair 14
    middle 1
    rotary- 1
    slitter 13

    stair-step 18
cut-off 18, 19
cutoff knife 18
cutoff saw 1
cutover area 1

cutpoint 13
cutscoring 18
cut size 18
cut stock sheets 18
cutter(s) 18

    double rotary 18
    edge 13
    guillotine roll 13
    slitter- 18
    tail 13

cutter broke 18
cutter dust 18
cutterhead 1
cutterhead barker 1
cutter-layboy 12

cutter set 18
cutter wrinkles 18
cutting 1, 11
    clear 1
    cross 1, 18

    die 18
    dip shear 18
    prime 1
    salvage 1
    seed tree 1

    selective 1
    under- 18
cutting papers 16
cutting rights 1
cutting tolerance 18

cut to register 18
cycle 22
    bottoming 22
    chemical 9
    combined 22

    cooking 8
    lime recovery 9
    temperature 8
    tension 13
    thermal 9

    topping 22
cyclic compound 4
cycling,
    kiln 9
    thermal 9

cyclone evaporator 9
cyclone furnace 9
cyclone quench flow 7
cyclone separator 1, 21
cyclone steam separator 7

cylinder 7, 19
    blanket 19
    dryer 13
    helicoid 17
    impression 19

    plate 19
    steam 13
    Yankee 13
cylinder drying 13
cylinder former 13

cylinder machine 13
cylinder on-top former 13
cylinder pressure 7
cylinder wrap 13
cymene 6

D _____

dam 7
    kiln 9
damage,
    body 14
    chip 1

    clamp truck 18
    compression 1
    end 14
    handling 14
    roll 14
    transit 14

damask paper 16
dampener 13
dampeners 19
dampening 13

dampening factor 13
dampening solution 19
damper 9
    pulsation 13
damping 13

damping roll	13	
damping stretch	13	
dancer roll	12	
dandy barring	14	
dandy licks	14	
dandy mark	13, 14	
dandy pick	14	
dandy roll	13	
laid	13	
spiral laid	13	
velin	13	
wove	13	
dandy roll former	13	
data	23	
comparable	23	
normalized	25	
data base	23	
data processing system	23	
dc variable-voltage drive	13	
deacidification	14	
deadburned lime	9	
dead beaten	12	
dead cost	26	
deadhead	1	
deadload	9	
dead spots	14	
dead knife	18	
dead shaft roller	24	
dead-tight	24	
dead wood	1	
deaeration	9, 13	
dealkalization	9	
deashing	12	
debarker	1	
debarking	1	
debarkability	1	
debonding agent	12	
debris	11	
fiber	11	
decadent wood	1	
decanter	6	
decanting hearth	9	
decay	2	
decayed wood	1	
decibel	23	
deciduous tree	2	
decision	23	
deck	1	
breakdown	1	
bundle	1	
cold	1	
mill	1	
decker	12	
deckle	13	
air	13	
jet	13	
machine	13	
maximum	13	
mechanical	14	
suction box	13	

deckle edge	13	
deckle frame	13	
deckle position	13	
deckle stain	13	
deckle strap	13	
deckling	13	
deckling calender	13	
decolorization	20	
decomposition	20	
thermal	4	
decorative coating	17	
decorative papers	16	
decor papers	16	
decorticator	3	
decrepitation	9	
decurler	18	
decurrent growth	1	
dedicated pilot plant	23	
deep etching	19	
deep well disposal	20	
defect detector	18	
defective slitter edge	14	
defective splice	14	
defective stand	1	
defects,		
coating	17	
finishing	18	
nip-induced	14	
zero	25	
defibering	12	
defibration	7	
defillers	12	
deflaker	12	
deflection	13	
deflector	13	
defloculants	5	
defloculation	13	
defoamer	5	
deforesting	1	
degradation	4	
degradation inhibitor	10	
degree of closure	13	
degree of cohesion	11	
degree of cooking	8	
degree of crystallinity	4	
degree of disintegration	11	
degree of fiber orientation	14	
degree of packing	8	
degree of polymerization	4	
degree of refining	12	
degree of sizing	14	
degree of substitution	4	
degree of sulfonation	7	
degree of swelling	11	
degree of treatment	20	
degrees of freedom	25	
degumming	3	
dehumidifying	10	
dehydrating agent	4	
dehydration	9, 18	

dehydrogenase	5	
dehydroxylated kaolin	5	
de-icing of logs	1	
deinkability	12	
deinking	12	
flotation	12	
hybrid	12	
wash	12	
deionization	20	
deknotting	12	
delaminated clay	5	
delamination	5, 11, 14, 18	
delamination resistance	14	
delamination strength	14	
delignification	8	
bulk	8	
extended	8	
initial	8	
nitrogen dioxide	8	
oxygen	8	
peroxide	8	
reductive alkaline	8	
residual	8	
delignification index	8	
delimber	1	
delimbing	1	
delivery	19, 24	
turnkey	23	
delivery table	18	
deluge showers	13	
demand	22	
adhesive	17	
bleach	10	
chemical pulp	13	
peak	22	
steam	9	
demand factor	22	
demineralization	20	
demonstration plant	23	
dendrology	1	
denier	3	
denitrification	20	
dense	14	
densification	1, 13	
densimeter	14	
densitometer	19	
densitometry	19	
density	1, 11, 12	
apparent	1, 14	
bulk	1	
current	21	
dry bulk	1	
fiber linear	11	
liquor	9	
optical	19	
packing	8, 11	
print	14	
relative	23	
roll	13	
solid	1	

density *(cont)*
   stand   1
   wood   2
density monitor   14
densometer   14
dent   15

dentate   2
dented roll   14
depithing   3
depletion   1
deposit   13

deposit control   9
deposit control agent   9
deposit gauge   21
deposits,
   fireside   9

   pitch   5
   slime   5
depreciation   26
   accelerated   26
   accumulated   26

   actual   26
   functional   26
   theoretical   26
deresination   8
derivative   4

derrick   1
desensitization   19
deshive refining   12
desiccant   10
design,

   factorial experiment   25
   functional   23
   process   23
design allowance   24
design criteria   24

design load   9
design loading   20
design margin   24
design pressure   9
design steam temperature   9

desilication   3
deslagging   9
desorption   20
destructive distillation   6
destructively dist'd turpentine   6

destructive test   14
desulfurization   21
desuperheater   9
detailed estimate   26
detector,

   acoustic leak   9
   break   13
   brush   18
   defect   18
   fault   18

   flame   9
   flaw   18
   hole   18
   lump   18
   shive   12
   spot   18

detention tank   23
detention time   20
detergent   5
determination   14

   moisture   14
   outlying test   14
   test   14
detoxification   20
detrimental substances   13

developing   19
development   23
deviation   25
   standard   25
devil-tooth plates   12

dewaterability   15
dewatered sludge   20
dewatering   12
dewatering agent   5
dew point   13

   acid   9
dextrin   18
dextrinizing   5
dextrinizing value   5
diagnostics   13

diagram,
   block   23
   fiber orientation   14
   fishbone   25
   Ishikawa   25
   Ross   8

diaphragm cell   10
diaphragm pump   24
diaphragm valve   24
diatomaceous earth   5

diatomaceous-earth filtration   20
diazotype base paper   16
dicotyledon   3
die cutting   18
dielectric drying   13

dielectric resistance   14
die stamping   19
differential drive   13
differential nip   13
differential pressure   13

differential roll coating   17
differential torque   13
diffuse brightness   14
diffused aeration   20
diffuse-porous wood   2

diffuser   8, 20
   air   20
diffuser outfall   20
diffuser tubes   13
diffuse transmission   14

diffusion   4
   atmospheric   21
   chemical   8
diffusion air   13
diffusion stage   10

diffusion washer,
   continuous   12
   pressure   12
diffusion washing   12
digested sludge   20

digester(s)   8
   batch   8
   continuous   8
   horizontal tube   8
   hydraulic   8

   inclined tube   8
   Kamyr continuous   8
   M & D   8
   piggyback   8
   rotary   8

   sawdust   8
   spherical   8
   steam phase   8
   two-vessel   8
digester acid   8

digester bumping   8
digester burping   8
digester charge   8
digester head   8
digester house   8

digester liquor   8
digester neck   8
digester performance efficiency   8
digester relief   8
digester screened yield   8

digester vent gases   8
digester yield   8
digestion   8, 20
   aerobic   20
   anaerobic   20

   sludge   20
dilatancy   17
dilatant fluid   17
diluent   17
dilution   9
   double   12, 13

dilution air   21
dilution/extraction washing   12
dilution factor   12, 20
dilution ring   12

dilution water   12
dilution zone   10
   initial   20
dimensional properties (fibers)   11
dimensional properties (paper)   14

dimensional stability   14
dimension lumber   1
dimer   4
dimethyl sulfide   6
dimethyl sulfoxide   6

dioxin   20
dip   17
dip coating   17
dipentene   6
dipolar molecule   4

dipping	18
dip roll	17
dip shear cutting	18
dipslide test technique	5
direct alkali recovery system	9
direct-contact condenser	8
direct-contact evaporator	9
direct costs	26
direct current	22
direct current drive	24
direct driven	24
direct dye	5
direct-heated hood	13
direction,	
cross	13
cross-machine	13
grain	14
machine	13
transverse	2
wind	18
directional brightness	14
directionality	14
paper	14
direct lithography	19
directory paper	16
direct printing	19
direct process paper	16
direct sizing	5
direct steaming	8
dirt	11, 14
dirt analysis	14
dirt count	14
disc chipper	1
disc filter	12
discharge	20, 22
breast roll	13
controlled	20
free	12
zero	20
discharge electrode	21
discharge head	24
discharge opening	13
discharge permit	20
discharge ratio	13
disc knotter	12
disc moisture	11
discoloration	14
disc oscillation	7
discounted cash flow	26
disc press	12
disc refiner	12
double	12
multi-	12
conical	12
disc runout measurement	7
disc screen	1
diseased wood	1
dished	14
dished roll	14
dishing	18

disinfection	20
disintegration	11
degree of	11
resistance to	11
disintegrator	11
disintegrator pump	9
dislocation	11
dispersant	5
disperse dye	5
disperser	9
dispersibility	11, 17
dispersing agent	17
dispersion	17, 21, 25
hot	12
index of	25
dispersions,	
rosin	5
vinyl	17
displacement bleaching	10
displacement heating	8
displacement pressing	13
displacement ratio	12
displacement washing	12
disposables	16
disposal,	
deep well	20
ocean	20
solid waste	20
disproportionation	5
dissociation	9
heat of	9
dissolution	4
dissolved oxygen	20
dissolved solids	20
dissolving pulp	4
dissolving tank	9
distillate	20
distillation	6
destructive	6
flash	20
steam	20
distilled tall oil	6
distribution	22
bimodal	25
chi-square	25
dp	4
fiber length	11
filler	14
fines	14
frequency	25
mass	14
negatively skewed	25
normal	25
positively skewed	25
skewed	25
steam	9
distribution conveyor	1
distribution costs	26
distribution roller system	19
distributor	9, 13

distributor roll	13, 17
ditch	7
dithionite	10
diversity	20
diversity index	20
diverted rolls	13
DMSO pulping	8
doctor	13
air	13
doctor back	13
doctor blade	13
positive angle	17
reverse angle	17
doctor blade holder	13
doctoring (the shade)	13
doctor roll	17
document paper	16
dog	1, 24
dog ear	18
dog hairs	17
doghouse	9
dolly	18
dolomite limestone	9
dominant trees	1
dope	4
doping	19
dosage	20
dot	19
dot gain	19
dot skip	19
dot slurring	19
double belt filter	20
double bump coater	17
double calendered	14
double-coated papers	17
double-disc refiner	12
double dilution	12, 13
double face	18
double facer	18
double felting	13
double-finishing supercalender	13
double-layer fabric	15
double pops	18
double rotary cutter	18
double screening	12
double sizing	13
double thick	14
double-tier dryers	13
double twill	15
double-wire press	12
doubling	19
dovetail support	13
downcomer	9
downflow tower	10
down-milling	1
downstream	23
downtime	13

dozer		1
dp distribution		4
dp number		4
draft		9
	forced	9
	induced	9
	natural	9
draft loss		9
drag		1
dragged		13
drag load		13
drag reduction		13
drag spots		14
drag wear		15
drain		20
	rapid	9
drainability		11
	dynamic	11
drainage		13, 15
drainage aid		5
drainage coefficient		15
drainage control		13
drainage factor		11
drainage profile		13
drainage rate		13
drainage resistance		11
drainage symmetry ratio		13
drainage table		13
drainage time		11
drainer		12
	inclined screw	12
	in-line	8
	rotary	12
drapability		14
drape		15
draw		13, 18
	closed	13
	open	13
	slack	13
	tight	13
	wet	13
drawdown		19, 20
draw-down tanks		8
drawing papers		16
draw rolls		17, 18
dredge,		
	grapple	20
	hydraulic	20
	suction	20
dredging		20
dregs		9
dregs washer		9
dried-in strain		14
dried pulp		11
drier		19
driftwood		1
drilling		18
drilling pattern		13
drip mark		14

drive		24
	ac variable frequency	13
	alternating current	24
	assist	13
	chain	24
	dc variable-voltage	13
	differential	13
	direct current	24
	electromagnetic variator	24
	gear	24
	helper	13
	hydraulic	24
	hydrostatic	24
	lineshaft	13
	mechanical variator	24
	paper machine	13
	sectional	13
	Sunday	13
	surface	13
	variable speed	24
drive roll		13
driving		1
driving force		8
drop,		
	butt	18
	face	18
drop feed chipper		1
drop leg		12
droplet		21
drop off		13
dropout box		21
dropout halftone		19
dropping point		24
drop test		14
drop tests		18
drum		9, 12, 13
	barking	1
	carrier	18
	fiber	18
	mud	9
	operating	1
	reel	13
	steam	9
	water	9
	winding	13
drum chipper		1
drum differential control		13
drum displacer washer		12
drum filter		12
drum grooving		13
drum internals		9
drum pick		17
drum press		13
drum reel		13
drum scab		17
drum submergence		12
dryability		13
dryback		19
dry barking		1
dry box		13
dry broke		13

dry broke repulper		13
dry bulk density		1
dry catch		21
dry coating process		17
dry collector		21
dry converting		18
dry creping		13
dry cut		14
dry end		13
dryer(s)		13
	after	17
	air	10
	air flotation	17
	baby	13
	double-tier	13
	Feeney	13
	felt	13
	float	17
	floating	13
	handsheet	11
	intercalender	13
	lead	13
	Lukenwald	13
	Minton	12
	pilot	13
	platen	13
	rotary hog fuel	1
	single-tier	13
	stacked	13
	sweat	13
	tunnel	13
	vacuum	12
dryer bars		13
dryer cylinder		13
dryer dwell time		17
dryer fabric		13
dryer head		13
dryer hood		13
dryer part		13
dryer performance		13
dryer pocket		13
dryer screen		13
dryer section		13
dryer wrinkle		13
dry felt		16
dry finish		14
dry finishing		13
dry-formed papers		14
dry forming		13
dry grammage		14
dry indicator method		14
drying		19
	air	13
	airborne web	13
	air float	12
	air-impingement	13
	bark	1
	constant-rate	13
	contact	13
	convective	13

drying *(cont)*

critical point 11
cylinder 13
dielectric 13
electro-assist 13
falling-rate 13

fan 13
festoon 13
flash 12
freeze 11
high-intensity 13

hog fuel 1
impingement 13
impulse 13
infra-red 13
ink 19

loft 13
machine 13
microwave 13
over- 13
radiant 13

steam 12
through 13
drying cracks 17
drying curve 13
drying intensity 13

drying oil 19
drying oven 19
drying plate 11
drying rate 13
evaporation 13

drying restraint 13
drying rings 11
drying system survey 13
drying time 18
dry laminating 18

dry-lay nonwovens 16
dry line 13
dryness 13
commercial 11
critical 13
theoretical commercial 11

dry nip operation 13
dry offset 19
dry picking 19
dry printing process 19

dry pyrolysis process 9
dry refining 11
dry rolling 13
dry rot 2
dry rub resistance 14

dry-running seal 24
dry scrubber 21
dry shredding 12
dry solids content 11
dry steam 9

dry-strength adhesive 5
dry-strength resins 5
synthetic 5
dry suction box 13
dry trapping 19

dry vat 13
dry waxing 17
dual press 13
dub 13
duct 9

ductor roller 19
ductors 13
duct system 21
duff 1
dull coated 17

dull finish 14
dulling 7
dumbbells 14
dummy 19
dummy variable 25

dump 20
dumper 1
dumping 8
flush 8
dump tank 8

dump valve 24
dunnage 18
duplex coater 17
duplex fabric 15
duplex finished 14

duplex papers 14
duplex sheet 13
duplex sheeter 18
duplex super 14
duplex weave 15

duplex winder 13
duplicator 19
duplicator papers 16
durability 14
dust 21

cutter 18
slitter 13
dust collector 21
dust composition analysis 21
dust deposition 21

dusting 3, 9, 14, 19
dust loading 21
dwell time 17
dryer 17
dye(s) 5

acid 5
aniline 5
basic 5
cationic 5
cationic direct 5

direct 5
disperse 5
liquid 5
penetrant 24
reactive 5

dyeing 13
spray 13
dye streak 14
dynamic balance condition 24
dynamic bleaching 10

dynamic drainability 11
dynamic drainage jar 11
dynamic laboratory former 14
dynamic mixer 10
dynamic modulus 13

dynamic puncture tester 14
dynamic strength 14

E

earlywood 2
easy beating 11
easy bleaching pulp 10
ecological impact 20
ecology 20

ecosystem 20
econometric modelling 26
economic life 26
economics
engineering 26
forest 1

economizer 9, 13
economy,
fuel 9
heat 9
steam 9, 13

economy of scale 26
eddy 13
eddy current testing 24
edge(s) 13

bowed 18
broken 14
deckle 13
defective slitter 14
feather 14

grainy 14
gripper 19
knife 18
leading 13
mill 18

peened 19
roll 13
rolled 14
slack 14
slitter 18

trailing 13
welded 19
wet 14
edge crack 14
edge cracking 15

edge curl 14
edge cutters 13
edge protectors 18
edger 1
edge raveling 15

edge relief 13
edge tear resistance 14
edge trimming 1
edge trimmings 13
edgewise compression strength 14

effect 9
effective alkali 8
effective caliper 14
effective capillary X-sec. area 8
effective chip thickness 1

effective migration velocity 21
effective power 12
effective refining area 12
effectivity 8
efficiency,

    aeration 20
    agitator 12
    barking 1
    boiler 9
    causticizing 9

    chlorine dioxide plant 10
    cleaning 12
    collection 21
    convertibility 18
    digester performance 8

    energy 22
    finishing room 18
    machine 13
    mixing 12
    peak demand 22

    primary treatment 20
    production rate 13
    recovery cycle 9
    reduction 9
    refining 12

    screening 12
    secondary treatment 20
    steam generating 9
    thermal 9
    trim 13

    visual 14
    washing 12
effluent 20
    bleach 10
    primary 20

    raw 20
    secondary 20
    stack 21
effluent quality 20
effluent seepage 20

effluent standard 20
efflux 4
efflux ratio 13
eggshell finish 14
ejector 24

elasticity 14
elastic limit 14
elastic modulus 14
elastic parameters 14
elastic stiffness 14

elastic stretch 14
elastomer 13
elbow 24
electrical double layer 5
electrical insulation paper 16

electrical properties (of paper) 14
electric charge 22
electric circuit 22
electric distribution system 22
electric mobility 21

electric power 22
electrified filter bed 21
electro-assist drying 13
electrochemical bleaching 10
electrochemical metallizing 24

electrochemical protection 24
electrode 22
    collector 21
    discharge 21
    selective ion 4

electrodes 21
electrokinetic charge 5
electrolysis 10
electrolyte 4
electrolytic corrosion 24

electrolytic corrosion control 24
electromagnetic variator drive 24
electromotive force 22
electron microscope 14
electrophoresis 5

electrophoretic mobility 5
electropolishing 24
electrostatic coating 17
electrostatic copy papers 16
electrostatic ink transfer 19

electrostatic interactions 5
electrostatic precipitator 21
electrostatic printing 19
element 2, 4
    axial 2
    vessel 2

elementary fibril 2
elements,
    fibrovascular 3
    forming 13

elephant grass 3
Elmendorf tear resistance 14
elongation 14
Elrepho brightness 14
elutriator 12

embayed 20
embayment 20
embedding 14
embossed finish 14
embosser 18

embossing 18
    friction 18
    hot 18
    matrix 18
    print 19
    spanished 17

embossing tendency 14
embrittlement 9, 14
    caustic 9
emergency shutdown 9, 23

emission 20
    fugitive 21
    potential 21
emission control equipment 21
emission monitoring 21
    boundary layer 21

emission source 21
emission standard 20
emitter 13
empirical formula 4

empirical tests 14
emulsification 19
emulsifier 5
emulsion 5
emulsion coating 17

emulsions,
    bituminous 5
    resin 5
    rosin 5
enamel 17

enameled paper 17
encrustation 9
end bands 18
end damage 14
end groups 4

endless woven fabric 15
end-of-pipe 20
endogenous phase 20
endogenous respiration 20
endothermic reaction 9

end point 4
end use tests 14
end wall 2
energy 22
    activation 8

    Arrhenius activation 4
    heat 22
    internal 22
    kinetic 22
    net specific 12

    potential 22
    purchased 22
    radiant 9
    specific 7, 9
    waste 22

energy audit 22
energy balance 22
energy conservation 22
energy consumption 22
energy conversion 22

energy efficiency 22
energy intensity 22
energy intensive 22
energy management 22
energy self-sufficiency 22

energy split 7
energy wood 1
engine 12

engineering	23
chemical	23
process	23
project	23
system	23
value	23
engineering economics	26
engine sizing	13
English finish	14
engraver's spread	19
engraving	19
entrained air	13
entrainment	21
air	13
entrainment separator	21
envelope	18
envelope papers	16
environment	20
standard	11
environmental audit	23
environmental chemistry	10
environmental impact	20
environmental impact statem't	20
enzyme	5
enzyme conversion	5
epidermal cell	2
epithelium	2
equalization	20
equalizing basin	20
equalizing tube	9
equal-sidedness	14
equation,	
chemical	4
Kubelka-Munk	14
regression	25
equilibrium	4
equilibrium air	14
equilibrium moisture content	14
equivalent black area	11
erasability	14
ergonomics	23
erosion	9, 24
cavitation	24
corrosion	24
error	25
random	14
standard	25
systematic	14
escalation	26
esparto grass	3
essential oil	6
ester	4
esterification	4
estimate	26
budget	26
detailed	26
project control	26

order-of-magnitude	26
study	26
estuary	20
etching	19
deep	19
ether	4
etherification	4
ethyl alcohol	6
ethyl cellulose	4
eucalyptus	1
eutectic point	9
eutrophic	20
eutrophication	20
evaporation,	
black liquor	9
evaporation drying rate	13
evaporation pond	20
evaporative cooling	21
evaporator	9
blow-heat	9
cascade	9
chlorine	10
cyclone	9
direct-contact	9
falling-film	9
flash steam	9
mechanical vapor compress.	9
multiple-effect	9
rising film	9
evener roll	17
evolutionary operation	25
excelsior	16
excess air	9
excess alkali	10
excess capacity	23
excess chemical	10
excess coating system	17
excess lime	9
excess lime factor	9
excess sludge	20
excess wash liquor	12
excurrent growth	1
exemption	23
exhaust air	13
exhauster	1
vacuum	13
exhaust gases	9
exhaustion	20
exhaust overpull	10
exothermic reaction	9
expander roll	13
expansimeter	14
expansion (of paper)	14
expansion	23
expansion joint	24
expansivity	14
expenditure	26
expense	26
experiment	25

explosion,	
furnace	9
smelt/water	9
explosion-proof	24
explosion pulping	8
exposing	19
exposure	21
extended aeration process	20
extended cooking	8
extended delignification	8
extended economizer rec. boiler	9
extended heat transfer surfaces	9
extended pit-aperture	2
extender	5, 18, 19
extensibility	14
extensible paper	14
extensometer	14
external additives	13
external fibrillation	11
external wastewater treatment	20
external water treatment	20
extracted permanganate	
number	10
extraction	8, 11
extraction stage	8, 10, 11
alkaline	10
oxidative	10
oxygen-enriched	10
extraction steam turbine	22
extraction washing	12
extractive	2
extractive industry	23
extractor,	
screw	12
trash	12
extractor press	13
extraneous materials	2
extras	18
extra-wefted fabric	15
extraxylary fibers	2
extrudate	17
extruder	7
extrusion coating	17
extrusion laminating	18
eye (of a refiner)	7

F

fabric	15
coil	15
double-layer	15
dryer	13
duplex	15
endless woven	15
extra-wefted	15
forming	13
mesh	15
power	15
serpentine	13
shute-faced	15
shute-support	15
spiral	15
triple-layer	15
warp-faced	15

fabric edge wear	15	
fabric filter	21	
fabric press	13	
fabric stability	15	
fabric wear	15	
face	6, 7, 12, 18	
crown	13	
double	18	
single	18	
working	13, 20	
face drop	18	
face length	12, 13	
facer,		
double	18	
single	18	
face-side showering	13	
face wire	12	
facial tissue	16	
facing	18	
facsimile paper	16	
factor,		
availability	22	
bending	2	
capacity	22	
chloride enrichment	9	
compaction	8	
dampening	13	
dilution	12, 20	
drainage	11	
excess lime	9	
fouling	9	
G-	8	
H-	8	
ignition	14	
intensity	12	
kappa	10	
length	11	
load	22	
Norden efficiency	12	
penetration	8	
plant	22	
power	22	
pulp weight	11	
roundness	2	
shape	11	
stowage	1	
substance yield	12	
surface roughness	17	
thickening	12	
factorial experiment design	25	
factor of safety	9	
facultative bacteria	20	
facultative lagoon	20	
fadeometer	14	
fail-safe operation	13	
failure,		
adhesive	18	
cohesive	18	
fatigue	14	

fall down	13	
faller	1	
falling-film evaporator	9	
falling-rate drying	13	
fallout	21	
fallout jar	21	
false pressure	8	
fan	9	
axial	9	
chopper-	13	
centrifugal	9	
forced-draft	9	
induced-draft	9	
fan drying	13	
fanning	18	
fanning-in of image	19	
fanning-in of web	19	
fanning-out of image	19	
fanning-out of web	19	
fan nozzle	12	
fan pump	13	
fan-type spreader	13	
farmer wood	1	
far side	19	
fast beating	11	
fast color	14	
fastness	14	
acid	14	
alkali	14	
color	14	
light-	14	
water bleed	14	
fast pulp	11	
fatigue,		
olfactory	23	
stress	24	
surface	24	
fatigue failure	14	
fatigue limit	9	
fatigue strength	14	
fatty acid	6	
fatty acid soap	6	
fault detector	18	
fault-tracing	24	
fauna	20	
feasibility study	26	
feather edge	14	
feathering	14, 18	
featherweight	14	
feculose	5	
feed box	12	
feeder	1	
asthma	8	
high-pressure	8	
low-pressure	8	
plug screw	7	
pocket	7	
rotary	1	
rotary pocket	8	
screw	1	

feed ring	7	
feedstock	23	
feedwater	9	
feedwell	9	
feedworks	1	
feel	14	
Feeney dryer	13	
feller-buncher	1	
feller-forwarder	1	
feller-skidder	1	
felling	1	
felling head	1	
accumulator	1	
felt(s)	13	
batt-on-base	15	
batt-on-mesh	15	
bottom	13	
carrying	13	
combination	15	
conventional	15	
dry	16	
fillingless	15	
knuckle free	15	
marking	13	
minimum shute	15	
nonwoven	15	
organic	16	
pickup	13	
press	13	
roofing	16	
split-top	13	
top	13	
transfer	13	
wet	13	
felt air	13	
felt cleaning	13	
felt compaction	13	
felt conditioning	13	
felt dryer	13	
felted structure	13	
felt filling	13	
felt finish	14, 15	
felt hairs	13	
felting	13	
double	13	
felt mark	14	
felt monitoring	13	
felt paper	16	
felt picking	13	
felt roll	13	
felt roughness	15	
felt run	13	
felt seam	13	
felt side	14	
felt stretcher	13	
female thread	24	
fenestriform pit	2	
fermentation	6	
festoon drying	13	
festooning	13	

festoon splice	18
fiber(s)	2
acrylic	3
adansonia	3
animal	3
annual crop	3
aramid	3
bast	3
bone	4
brown	8
carbon	3
cellulose	4
ceramic	3
chaffed	3
coconut	3
collapsed	11
colored	14
cordage	3
extraxylary	2
fruit	3
gelatinized	4
gelatinous	2
glass	3
hard	3, 4
hermetic	4
hull	3
hydrated	11
leaf	3
leather	3
libriform	2
long	12
man-made	3
metallic	3
mineral	3
natural	3
nonwood	3
orientation of	14
polyamide	3
polyethylene	3
polyolefin	3
polypropylene	3
recycled	12
rope	3
secondary	12
seed	3
septate	2
short	12
soft	3
staple	15
stem	3
synthesized	3
synthetic papermaking	3
textile plant	3
urena	3
vegetable	3
virgin	13
viscose rayon	3
vulcanized	4
white	12
xylary	2

fiber analysis	11
fiber anatomy	2
fiber axis ratio	11
fiber-based synthetic papers	14
fiber bonding index	11
fiberboard	1, 16
fiber bonding	13
fiber bundle	12
fiber classification	11
fiber coarseness	11
fiber composition	11
fiber content	14
fiber count	11
fiber crop	3
fiber curl	11
fiber cut	14
fiber debris	11
fiber drum	18
fiber flexibility	11
wet	11
fiber flocculation	11
fiber fractionation	11
fiberglass-reinforced plastics	24
fiberization	7
fiberizer	12
fiber length	11
average	11
fiber length analyzer	11
fiber length distribution	11
fiber length grid	11
fiber length index	14
fiber liberation	8
fiber linear density	11
fiber network	13
fiber network strength	11
fiber node	2
fiber number	11
fiber orientation	14
degree of	14
fiber orientation diagram	14
fiber orientation indices	14
fiber pick	19
fiber puffing	19
fiber recovery	12
fiber saturation point (of pulp)	11
fiber saturation point (of wood)	2
fiber shearing	11
fiber shedding	13
fiber source	1
fiber stiffness	11
fiber strength	11
intrinsic	11
fiber strength index	14
fiber structure	2
fiber support index	15
fiber surface	11
fiber suspension	13
fiber tear	18
fiber tracheid	2
fiber twist	11

fiber weight length	11
fibrary	2
fibrids	3
fibril	2
elementary	2
macro-	2
micro-	2
nano-	2
proto-	2
fibril angle	2
fibrilizer	12
fibrillar	2
fibrillation	11
external	11
internal	11
fibrilplasma fines	11
fibrovascular elements	3
field	21
cross	2
filament	15
filamentous bacteria	5
filamentous organisms	20
filer	1
fill	13
machine	13
fill area	20
filled board	14
filled in	13
filled roll	13
filled roll burnout	13
filled sheet	14
filler	13
alkaline	5
mineral	13
pearl	5
synthetic	5
filler content	14
filler distribution	14
filler pieces	12
filler ply	13
filler split	14
fillet	12
fill-in	19
filling	12, 13, 15
chip	8
felt	13
liquor	8
filling state curve	7
fillingless felt	15
filling up	19
film	17, 18
film coating	17
filming amines	9
film paper	14
film splitting	17
filter	12
bag	21
belt	9
biological	20
disc	12

filter *(cont)*
   double belt 20
   drum 12
   fabric 21
   gravel bed 21
   lime mud 9

   mixed-media 20
   precoat 9
   pressure 9
   rapid sand 20
   rotary vacuum 12

   slurry 17
   trickling 20
   valveless 12
filter aid 23
filter bed 20
   electrified 21

filter cake 23
filter cloth 12
filter paper 16
filter plant 20

filter tank 12
filter vat 12
filter vat agitator 12
filtrate 10
   washer 12

filtration 13, 23
   diatomaceous earth 20
filtration (of air) 21
filtration medium 12
filtration resistance 11
   specific 11

fimbriated bacteria 5
fin 9
fineness 15
fine paper 16

fines 1, 11
   chip 1
   fibrilplasma 11
   flour 11
fine screening 12

fines distribution 14
finger bars 7
fingerless single facer 18
finish 14
   antique 14

   burnished 14
   calender 14
   calender-crush 14
   cloth 14
   cloud 14

   cockle 14
   cold pressed 14
   crash 14
   crushed 14
   dry 14

   dull 14
   eggshell 14
   embossed 14
   English 14
   felt 14, 15

flat 14
flock 17
glazed 14
gloss 14
handmade 14

high 17
kid 14
ivory 14
linen 14
low 14

machine 14
matte 14
medium 14
mottled 14
parchment 14

plate 14
ripple 18
satin 14
slick 14
super glazed 14

unglazed 14
vellum 14
water 14
wet-end 14
finished,
   duplex 14
   steam 14

finished production 18
finishing 13, 18
   dry 13
   roll 13

finishing broke 18
finishing defects 18
finishing operations 18
finishing room 18

finishing room efficiency 18
fin tube 9
fire box 9
fireside deposits 9
firetube boiler 9

firing,
   fixed 9
   stationary 9
   suspension 9
   tangential 9

firing hood 9
firing rate 9
firm gluing 18
first-pass retention 13
fishbone diagram 25

fish eyes 14, 17
fitting 24
fixed costs 26
fixed firing 9
fixed solids 20

fixing agent 5
flag 13
flagship mill 23
flail barker 1
flakeboard 1

flakes 1
flaking 17
flame 9
flame detector 9
flame out 9

flame pattern 9
flameproof 14
flange 24
   blind 24
flanges 7

flange-to-flange 21
flap 18
flareback 9
flash calciner 9
flash distillation 20

flash drying 12
flashing 9
flash point 9
flash steam 9
flash steam evaporator 9

flash tank 9
flat band washer 12
flatbed cylinder press 19
flat box 13
flat bundling 18

flat car 1
flat crush resistance 14
flat finish 14
flatness 14
flat roll 14

flat screen 12
flat warp 15
flat wire washer 12
flavonoids 6
flaw 14

flaw-carrying capacity 14
flaw detector 18
flax 3
   seed 3
flax straw 3
flax tow 3

flex fatigue resistance 13
flexforming 13
flexing 14
flexing strength 14
flexography 19

flight conveyor 1
flimsy 14
flinching 25
flingers 7
flint glazing 17

flitting 17
floatable solids 20
floater dryer 17
floating dryer 13
floating-head gas holder 21

floating load 18
floc 13
   biological 20
   microbial 20
flocculant 20

flocculation	13, 20	
fiber	11	
hetero-	13	
pre-	13	
flocculation index	13	

flocculent settling	20
flock finish	17
flocking tissue	16
flong paper	16
flooded condition	13

flooded nip application	17
flooded nip shower	13
flooding shower	13
flora	20
flotation	20

compression	20
froth	12
flotation cell	12
flotation deinking	12
flotation purge	12

flotsam	20
flour fines	11
flow	19
approach	13
cash	26

countercurrent	12
cross	13
cyclone quench	7
gravity	12
laminar	13

material	23
Newtonian	17
plug	10
plug wiper	7
radial inward	20

radial outward	20
reverse	12
streamline	13
superficial	12
turbulent	13

flowability	1
flowage	20
flow box	13
flow channel	24
saw-blade	13
step	13

flow coating	17
flow evener roll	13
flow eveners	13
flow evening	13

flowing full	12
flow-limited pressing	13
flow-on coating	17
flow out	17
flow point	18

flow rate	12
flow regime	23
flow resistance	12, 13
flow sheet	23
flowspreader	13

tapered inlet	13
flowthrough cleaner	12
flow-through time	20
flue	9
flue gas	9

fluffability	11
fluffer	12
fluffing	12
fluff pulp	8
fluff out	18

fluid,	
dilatant	17
hydraulic	24
Newtonian	17
non-Newtonian	17

plastic	17
pseudoplastic	17
fluid-bed calciner	9
fluid-bed scrubber	21
fluidity	17

fluidization	9
fluidization point	12
fluidized bed combustion	9
fluidized bed recovery	9
fluidizer	17

fluidizing	9
fluid mechanics	13
fluid mobility	12
flume	1, 20
log	1
Parshall	20

fluorescence	14
fluorescent brightening agent	5
fluorescent whitening	5
fluorocarbon size	5

fluorochemicals	5
flush dumping	8
flute contour	18
fluting	18
heatset dryer	19

flutes	18
leaning	18
fly ash	9
fly bars	12
flying	19

flying paster	19
flying splice	18
fly knife	18
foam	12
static	12

foam breaker	12
foam coating	17
foam forming	13
foam fractionation	20
foaming agent	5

foam inhibition	12
foam mark	14
foam spots	17
foam stability	12
foam tank	12

fodder pulp	8
fog	21
fogging	17
foil	13, 18
foil angle	13

foil paper	16
foil unit	13
vacuum-assisted	13
fold,	
hard	18

soft	18
tensile at	14
foldability	14
folder	18, 19
former-	19

folder-gluer	18
folder stock	16
folding boxboard	16
folding carton	18
folding endurance	14

folding quality	14
folding strength	14
folding-type spreader	18
fold number	14
folio	19

French	16
folio-size sheets	18
foodboard	16
frozen	16
food chain	20

food-to-microorganism ratio	20
food wrapper	16
footage	13
forced circulation	8, 9
forced draft	9

forced-draft fan	9
forced drape testing	14
forest	1
boreal	1
crown	1

national	1
plantation	1
rain	1
virgin	1
forestation	1

forest economics	1
forest genetics	1
forest inventory	1
forest land	1
forest productivity	1

forest products	23
forestry	1
industrial	1
forest residuals	1
forest tree improvement	1

forest type	1
forging	24
fork-lift truck	18
formability	11
formaldehyde	4

formamidine sulfinic acid	10	coating	17	frequency distribution	25
format	18, 19	empirical	4	fresh chips	1
formation	14	formulation	17	fresh water	13, 20
close	14	coating	17	fresh water bodies	20
cloudy	14	fortified rosin	5	fretting	24
mealy	14	fortifying tower	8	friction	18
mottled	14	forward drive roll	13	coefficient of	14
strained	14	forwarder	1	kinetic	18
wild	14	forwarding	1	rolling	13
formation aid	13	fossil fuel	9	static	18
formation indices	14	fouling	9	friction braking	13
formation number	14	furnace	9	friction calendering	13
formation shower	13	fouling factor	9	friction control agent	17
formation tester	14	fountain	19	friction embossing	18
former	13, 18	fountain blade coater	17	front (of press)	19
balanced loop	13	fountain coater	17	front-end loader	1
blade gap	13	fountain roll	17	front side	13
converging wedge	13	fountain solution	19	frotation	12
cylinder	13	four color process	19	froth flotation	12
cylinder-on-top	13	fourdrinier	13	frozen foodboard	16
dandy roll	13	cantilevered	13	frozen stresses	14
dynamic laboratory	14	mini	13	fruit fibers	3
gap	13	roll-out	13	fruit wraps	16
hybrid	13	fourdrinier board	13	fuel	9
hydraulic	13	fourdrinier machine	13	auxiliary	9
		multi	13		
multiply	13			bio-	9
on-top	13	foxing	14	biomass	9
pressure	13	fractional permeability	15	fossil	9
roll	13	fractionator	12	hog	1
short	13	fracture resistance	14	fuel additives	9
suction	13	fractures	18	fuel bed	9
suction roll	13	fracture toughness	14	fuel chips	1
top-wire	13	frame (of a forming fabric)	15	fuel economy	9
twin-wire	13	frame saw	1	fuel value	9
vat	13	framing	24	fuel wood	1
Webster-type	13	free	5	fugitive color	14
former-folder	19	freeboard	12, 20	fugitive emission	21
formic acid	4	freeboard burning	9	fugitive ink	19
forming	13	free discharge	12	fugitive sizing	14
air	13	free fiber surface area	11	fulling	15
dry	13	free liquor	8	full-tree logging	1
flex-	13	free moisture	5	fully bleached pulp	10
foam	13	freeness	11	fully cooked pulp	8
high-consistency	13	Canadian standard	11	fume	9
multiply	13	freeness tester	11	fumes	21
stratified web	13	free pulp	11	fumigation	21
velocity	13	free rosin	5	functional coating	17
forming board	13	free settling	20	functional depreciation	26
phase-changing	13	free sheet	14	functional design	23
forming elements	13	coated	16	functional groups	4
forming fabric	13	free shrinkage	11	functional papers	16
forming roll	13	free SO_2	8	functional tests	14
forming section	13	free space	8	fundamental properties	14
forming shoe	13	free surface	13	fungicide	5
forming station	13	free water	2, 11	furan	20
forming wire	13	freeze conditioning agent	1	furfural	6
form roller	19	freeze drying	11	furnace	9
cushion	19	freight rules	18	cyclone	9
formula,		French folio	16	recovery	9
chemical	4	frequency (of alt. current)	22	Tomlinson	9

furnace arch	9	gelation	5	grade (of logs)	1
furnace explosion	9	gel point	17	grades of pulp	12
furnace fouling	9	generating plant	22	grade(s) (of paper)	16
furnace nose baffle	9	generating tube	9	absorbent	16
furnace screen	9	generating unit	22	intermediate	16
furnish	12	generator	22	publication	16
furnishing	12	chlorine dioxide	10	value-added	16
furnish layer	13	genetic tree improvement	1	waste paper	12
fusiform ray	2	geometric mean value	14	grafting	4
fuzz	14	G-factor	8	graft pulps	4
fuzziness	14	ghosting	19	grain	14
		gloss	19	against the	18
G		gilling	13	long	18
		gin	2	short	18
gaff	1	girdling	1	with the	18
galactan	4	gland	24	grain direction	14
galactomannon	4	gland follower	24	grain loading	21
galactose	4	gland water	24	grain long	18
galley proof	19	glass fiber	3	grains	21
		glassine	16	grain short	18
galvanic corrosion	24	glass transition	7	grainy	14
galvanized surface	14	glazed finish	14	grainy edges	14
galvanized wire side	14	glazing	13	grainy highlights	19
gamma-cellulose	4	flint	17	grammage	14
gampi	3	globe valve	24	as-made	14
gang sawing	1	gloss	14	dry	14
gantry crane	1	contrast	14	nominal	14
portal-type	1	ink	19	oven-dry	14
gap former	13	printed	19	standard	14
gap test	14	specular	14	grammage tolerance	14
garland chains	9	subjective	14	granite roll	13
gas analysis	9, 21	gloss calendering	13	graniting	13
gas cooler	8	gloss finish	14	granule	5
gas holder	21	gloss ghosting	19	graphic arts	19
gasification	9	glossimeter	14	graphic papers	16
gasket	24	glossing	13	grapple	1
gas-off	8, 10	glossing agent	17	grapple dredge	20
gas-phase bleaching	10	gloss ink holdout	19	grass	
gas scrubber	21	gloss paper	14	elephant	3
gas tempering	9	gloss retention	14	esparto	3
gas turbine	22	glossy-coated papers	14	lemon	3
gate roll coater	17	glucan	4	sabai	3
gate rolls	17	glucomannan	4	grate	9
gate roll size press	17	glucose	4	gravel bed filter	21
gate valve	24	glucoside	4	gravimetric method	21
gathering	19	glucuronic acid	4	gravity centrifugal screen	12
gauge	24	glue	5	gravity flow	12
gearbox	24	animal	18	gravity thickener	12
gear drive	24	glueability	14	gravure	19
gearing	13	glue joint	18	roto-	19
gears	24	glue on roll end	14	gravure coating	17
G.E. brightness	14	gluing	18	grease	24
gel	5	firm	18	grease penetration test	14
hydro-	20	glycoside	4	greaseproof paper	16
silica	10	glycosidic bond	4	grease-resistant	14
gelatin	5	go-devil	12	greasing	19
gelatinization	5	goodness of fit	25	greasy	12
gelatinized fiber	4	gooseneck	13	greasy spots	14
gelatinous	5	governor	7	green	1
gelatinous fibers	2	grab sample	11	greenchain	1

greenfield mill	23
green liquor	9
raw	9
green liquor pulping	8
green paper	14
greeting card stock	16
Grewin nozzle	13
grey stock	12
grid	22
fiber length	11
grinder	7
chain	7
continuous	7
hydraulic pocket	7
intermittent	7
magazine	7
pocket	7
ring	7
grinder bleaching	10
grinder pit	7
grinder pocket	7
grinder room	7
grinding,	
chip	7
cold	7
hot	7
pitless	7
roll	13
grinding in	12
grinding of wood	7
grinding pressure	7
grinding surface	7
grindstone	7
gripper edge	19
grippers	19
grit	7, 9, 17, 20
grit chamber	20
grizzly	9
grooved-roll press	13
groove marking	13
grounded parts	22
grounding	22
static	22
ground-lead logging	1
ground level concentration	21
ground skidding	1
ground slash	1
groundwater	20
groundwood	7
pressurized stone	7
refiner	7
stone	7
groundwood converting papers	16
groundwood papers	16
groundwood plant	7
groundwood printing papers	16
groundwood specialties	16
group(s),	
acid	4
carbonyl	4

carboxyl	4
end	4
functional	4
hemiacetal	4
hydroxyl	4
methoxyl	4
primary hydroxyl	4
secondary hydroxyl	4
growing stock	1
growth,	
decurrent	1
excurrent	1
old	1
rate of tree	1
second	1
growth rate	1
growth ring	2
growth-to-removal ratio	1
guesstimate	26
guide roll	13
guiding	13
guillotine	18
guillotine roll cutter	13
gum	2, 5
body	19
gumballing	18
gumming	17
gumming kraft	16
gum rosin	6
gum turpentine	6
gunk	12
guyline	1
gymnosperm	2
gypo	1
gypsum	5
gypsum board	16
gyratory screen	1

H

hackling	3
hair cut	14
hair mark	17
halftone	19
dropout	19
halfstuff	12
hammer	9
hammermill	1
hand	14
handed	13
handle	14
handling,	
bulk	1
material	1
roll	13
web	13
handling damage	14
handling stiffness	14
handmade finish	14
handmade paper	14
imitation	14

hand mold	13
handsheet	11
handsheet dryer	11
handsheet machine	11
handsheet press	11
hanger	24
hanging baffle	12
hanging raw stock	16
hangup	8
hard beating	11, 12
hard bleaching pulp	10
hardboard	1
hardburned lime	9
hard-calendered	14
hard cook	8
hardener	18
hard fiber	3, 4
hard fold	18
hard hardwood	2
hardness	13, 14, 20
carbonate	20
roll	13
hardness index (of sheet pulp)	11
hardness indices	24
hardness tester	13
hard-nip press	13
hard paper	14, 16
hard pulp	8
hard rolls	13
hard sized	14
hard spots	14
hard stock	12
hardwood(s)	2
hard	2
soft	2
tropical	1
hardwood pulp	12
hard wrinkle	14
harness	15
Harper machine	13
harvester	1
harvesting	1
mechanical	1
hatch	1
haul	1
haulback line	1
haul-up	1
hayout	13
hazardous material	23
hazardous waste	20
haze	21
head	8, 13
headbox	13
air-cushioned	13

headbox *(cont)*
    hydraulic 13
    lathe 13
    multichannel 13
    multilayer 13
    open 13
    pressurized 13
    primary 13
    secondary 13
headbox proper 13
header 9
    cross 13

heading 13
head loss 13
headrig 1
    chipping 1

hearth 9
    decanting 9
heartwood 2
heat,
    latent 13
    low-grade 22
    low-level 9
    sensible 13
    waste 22
heat accumulator 8

heat aging 14
heat balance 9
heat buildup 24
heat capacity 9
heat curl test 14

heat economy (lime kiln) 9
heat energy 22
heater 23
    air 9
heat exchanger 9
    crossflow 9
    plate 9
    spiral 9
    tube-in-shell 9
heat flux 9

heating surface 9
heating value 9
    higher 9
    lower 9
    net 9

heating zone 8
heat of combustion 9
heat of condensation 9
heat of dissociation 9
heat of reaction 9

heat of vaporization 9
heat pump 22
heat recovery 9
    blow 8
heat recuperation 9

heat regeneration 9
heat seal papers 16
heatset dryer fluting 19
heatset inks 19
heatset offset 19

heatset press 19
heatset roughening 19
heat setting 15
heat transfer 9
    conductive 13
    convective 13
    radiant 13
heat transfer coefficient 9
heatup rate 8
heavies 6

heavy black liquor 9
heavy metal ions 10
heavy sludge 20
heavy weights 14
hectare 1

heel 9
heel boom 1
helical 12
helical pulper 12
helical thickening 2

helicoid cylinder 17
heliotest 19
helper drive 13
hemiacetal groups 4
hemicellulose 4

hemp 3
    manila 3
    Mauritius 3
    New Zealand 3
    sunn 3

henequen 3
hermetic fiber 4
Herzberg stain 11
heterocellular ray 2
heterocoagulation 13

heteroflocculation 13
heterogeneous 2
hexosan 4
hexose 4
H-factor 8

H-factor controller 8
hickey 19
hickey picker 19
hiding power 17
high-alpha pulp 8

high-angle blade coater 17
high-consistency forming 13
high-consistency refining 12
high-density stock 12
high-density storage 12

higher heating value 9
high-filler paper 14
high finish 17
high flotation tires 1
highgrading 1

high-heat washing 12
high-humidity hood 13
high-impulse press 13
high-intensity drying 13
high-intensity mixer 10

high-lead logging 1
highlights 19
high lows 18
high polymer 4
high-pressure feeder 8

high-rate biological process 20
high-solids coating color 17
high-sulfonation mech. pulping 7
high-velocity air hood 13
high-volume, low-concentration 20

high-volume sampler 21
high-yield 8
high-yield bleaching 10
high-yield pulping 8
histogram 25

hitch roll 13
hivacs 13
hog 1
hog fuel 1
hog fuel drying 1

hoist 1
holdback 12
hold down rolls 17
holding ground 1
holding tank 9

holdout 14
    coating 17
    gloss ink 19
    ink 14
hole 14
    aspirator 13
    borer 1
    Hornbostel 13
    pin 14
    slime 14
    slug 14
    wire 14
hole detector 18
holey roll 13
Hollander 12

hollow-sphere pigment 5
holocellulose 4
holopulping 8
holopulps 11
homocellular ray 2

homopolysaccharide 4
honeycomb roll 13
hood 13
    canopy 13
    closed 13
    direct heated 13
    dryer 13
    firing 9
    high-humidity 13
    high-velocity air 13
    kiln 9
    open 13
    Yankee 13
hood ventilation 13
hood zero-pressure level 13

hopper	1, 21	hydraulic mass	8	hypochlorite brightening stage	10
ash	9	hydraulic pocket grinder	7	hypochlorous acid	10
hop vine	3	hydraulic pressure	13	hypo number	10
horizontal belt washer	12	hydraulics	23	hypo reactor	10
horizontal feed chipper	1	hydraulic structure	23	hypothesis	25
horizontal press	13	hydraulic thrust	7	hysteresis	11, 13
horizontal-tube digester	8	hydraulic turbine	22	moisture	11
Hornbostel hole	13	hydrocarbon	4		
hornification	11	hydrocellulose	4	**I**	
hot alkali purification	8	hydrocyclone	12		
				idler rolls	13
hot chlorination	10	hydrodynamics	13	ignition	9
hot dispersion	12	hydrodynamic specific volume	11	loss on	20
hot embossing	18	hydrodynamic suction forces	13	ignition factor	14
hot grinding	7	hydroelectric power	22	ignition temperature	9
hot kiln alignment	9	hydrofoil	12		
				image	19
hot logging	1	hydro-gel	20	fanning-in of	19
hot melt	17	hydrogenation	4	fanning-out of	19
hot melt coating	17	hydrogenation pulping	8	negative	19
hot pond	1	hydrogen bond	4	positive	19
hot pressing	13	hydrogen-forming bacteria	5		
				image analysis	11
hot rolling	13	hydrogen sulfide	21	image carrier	19
hot-stock refining	12	hydrology	20	imbibed water	11
hot-stock screening	12	hydrolysate	8	imbibition	11
hot waxing	17	hydrolysis	4	Imhoff cone	20
hot well	13	acid	4		
		pre-	4	imitation handmade paper	14
household roll	18			immediate oxygen demand	20
housekeeping	23	hydrolyzates	4	immersion coating	17
hue	14	hydrolyzed	5	immersion test	24
hull fiber	3	hydrolyzing	4	impact angle	13
humectant	18	hydrometer	9		
				impaction	21
humic acid	20	hydrophilic	5	impactless printing	19
humidification	13	hydrophilic roll coater	17	impact mill	17
humidified heat treatment	14	hydrophobic	5	impact printing	19
humidity	13	hydropyrolysis	9	impact strength	14
humping	19	hydrostatic	24		
				impedance	22
hurds	3	hydrostatic drive	24	impellor	24
hybrid deinking	12	hydrostatic pressure	13	axial-flow	24
hybrid former	13	hydrostatic test	9	radial-flow	24
hydrate	4	hydrosulfide	8	imperfections (in paper)	14
chlorine	10	hydrosulfite	10		
				impervious	14
hydrate cellulose	4	hydrosulfite brightening stage	10	impingement	21
hydrated fiber	11	hydrothermal injection cooking	8	jet	13
hydrated lime	9	hydrotrope	8	impingement drying	13
hydrated stock	12	hydrotropic pulping	8	impingers	21
hydrating	11	hydrous	5		
				impregnating	18
hydration	5	hydrous sludge	20	impregnating papers	16
water of	5	hydroxy acid	4	impregnation	8
hydraulic barker	1	hydroxyl group	4	impregnation time	18
hydraulic capacity	12	primary	4	impregnation vessel	8
hydraulic conveying	1	secondary	4		
				impregnation zone	8
hydraulic digester	8	hygroexpansivity	14	impression	19
hydraulic dredge	20	hygro-instability	14	burr	7
hydraulic drive	24	hygrometer	14	kiss	19
hydraulic entanglement	13	sword	14	nip	13
hydraulic fluid	24	hygroscopic	5		
				impression cylinder	19
hydraulic former	13	hygroscopicity	11	impression roll	17
hydraulic headbox	13	hygroscopic moisture	5	impression tolerance	19
hydraulic jump	20	hygro-stability	14	impress watermarking	13
hydraulic jump stick	20	hypochlorite	10	impulse	13
hydraulic loading	20	hypochlorite bleaching stage	10	press	13

impulse drying 13
impulse tester 14
impulse to rupture 14
incineration of noncondensibles 21

incinerator 21
inclined plate separator 20
inclined press 13
inclined separator 8
inclined screw drainer 12

inclined tube digester 8
inclined tube settler 20
inclined wire machine 13
incline impact test 18
included pit-aperture 2

incombustible 9
increment,
   annual 1
   basic wood 1
incremental cost 26

incremental investment 26
incremental production 26
incremental profit 26
incrustation 5
incubation 20

indented paper 14
independent variable 25
index (or indices),
   air quality 21
   available lime 9

   bleaching 10
   bonding 14
   bulking 14
   burst 14
   capability 25

   chip rot 8
   cost 26
   curl 11
   delignification 8
   diversity 20

   fiber length 14
   fiber orientation 14
   fiber strength 14
   fiber support 15
   flocculation 13

   formation 14
   hardness 11, 24
   inhibition 20
   kink 11
   orientation 14

   pulp strength 11
   quality 11
   receptivity 17
   sludge volume 20
   tear 14

   tensile 14
   tensile energy absorption 14
index bristol 16
index of central tendency 25
index of dispersion 25

index of order 4
India paper 16
India tint 14
indirect condenser 8
indirect measurement 14

indirect printing 19
indirect steaming 8
induced draft 9
induced-draft fan 9
inductor 22

industrial forestry 1
industrial hygiene 23
industrial marketing 23
industrial mineral 23
industrial papers 16

industrial tissues 16
industrial waste 20
inert 5
inertial pressure 13
inertial separator 21

inert gas 23
infeed 23
   chipper 1
infeed roller 19
inference 25

infiltration 20
   air 9
   rapid 20
infiltration air 13
infiltration capacity 20

infiltration rate 20
influent 20
information system 23
   management 23
   operations 23
   total 23

infrared drying 13
infrared inspection 24
inherent curl 14
inhibition index 20

inhibitor 4
   corrosion 24
   degradation 10
inhibitory toxicity 20
initial delignification 8

initial dilution zone 20
initial retention 13
initial tear resistance 14
injection cooking 8
ink(s) 19

   fugitive 19
   heatset 19
   long 19
   oil-base 19
   printing 19

   short 19
   solvent-base 19
   transparent 19
   water-base 19
   water-logged 19

ink absorption 14
ink absorptivity 14
ink drying 19
ink drying curl 19
ink fixing 19

ink flotation sizing test 14
ink fountain 19
ink gloss 19
ink holdout 14
inking 19

ink jet printing 19
ink mileage 19
inkometer 19
ink penetration test 14
ink receptivity 14

ink requirement 19
ink resistance 14
ink rub resistance test 19
ink set 19
ink train 19

ink transfer 19
ink wipe test 14
in-line converting 19
in-line drainer 8
in-line injector 10

in-line mixer 10
inner bark 2
inner pit-aperture 2
inorganic 4
in-plane tear resistance 14

inside showering 13
in situ measurement 21
insolubilizer 17
inspection 18
   infrared 24

installed cost 26
insulation 9
intaglio 19
intake 20
   water 20

integrated for/prod operations 1
integrated paper mill 13
integration 23
   technical 23
intensity factor 12

intensity of turbulence 13
intercalender dryers 13
intercellular canal 2
intercellular layer 2
intercellular space 2

interelectrode space 21
interface 18
interface opening 1
interfacing 18
interfiber bond strength 14

intergranular corrosion 24
interleaving tissue 16
interlock system 22
intermediate 4, 9
intermediate black liquor 9

intermediate chamber	13	
intermediate grade	16	
intermediate rolls	13, 17	
intermediate wood	2	
intermittent board machine	13	
intermittent grinder	7	
intermittent sampling	21	
internal additives	13	
internal bond strength	14	
internal coloring	13	
internal energy	22	
internal fibrillation	11	
internal sizing	13	
internal specific surface	11	
internal tear resistance	14	
internal valve	12	
internal wastewater treatment	20	
internal water treatment	20	
internode	3	
interruptible power	22	
inter-stage screening	12	
intertracheid pit	2	
intervessel pit	2	
interweaving	13	
intrinsically-safe	24	
intrinsic fiber strength	11	
intrinsic viscosity	4	
inventory	23	
chip	1	
forest	1	
liquor	9	
soda	9	
inventory control	23	
inversion	13, 21	
inverted blade coater	17	
investment,		
incremental	26	
rate of return on	26	
return on	26	
ion	5	
ion exchange	20	
ion exchange process	20	
ion exchange resins	20	
ionic compound	5	
ionization	5	
iron bacteria	5	
irreversible reaction	4	
Ishikawa diagram	25	
isoelectric point	5	
isokinetic sampling	21	
isomer	4	
isomerization	4	
isopleths	20	
isotropic	2	
isotropic paper	14	
istle	3	
ivory	14	
ivory board	16	
ivory finish	14	

J

jacket	13, 18	
jacking	13	
jack ladder	1	
jackshaft	24	
jackstrawed	1	
jammer	1	
jams	15	
jar,		
Britt	11	
dynamic drainage	11	
fallout	21	
jar test	20	
jet	13	
stratified	13	
jet compressor	13	
jet condenser	9	
jet cooking	5	
jet deckle	13	
jet impingement	13	
jet impingement angle	13	
jet mixer	24	
jet-to-wire speed ratio	13	
jet velocity	13	
jib crane	1	
jigging	7	
jobber	1	
job lot	18	
jog	12	
jogging	13, 18	
joint	18	
expansion	24	
glue	18	
rotary pressure	13	
starved	18	
steam	13	
universal	24	
jointless	13	
joint treatment	20	
joists	24	
Jordan refiner	12	
journal	13	
jumbo roll	13	
junker	12	
jury rig	24	
just-perceptible difference	14	
jute	3	
juvenile wood	2	

K

Kamyr continuous digester	8	
kaolin	5	
calcined	5	
dehydroxylated	5	
kaolinite	5	
kapok	3	
kappa factor	10	
kappa number	8	
karaya gum	5	
kenaf	3	

kerf	1	
kerosine number	14	
ketone	4	
key	24	
keyway	24	
kicker	1	
kid finish	14	
kiln	9	
kiln cycling	9	
kiln dam	9	
kiln hood	9	
kinetic energy	22	
kinetic friction	18	
kinetics	4	
reaction	4	
king roll	13	
kink index	11	
kinking	11	
kiss impression	19	
kiss roll	17	
kiss roll coating	17	
kite	12	
kit test	14	
Klason lignin	8	
Klason procedure	8	
kneader	17	
kneader pulper	12	
knife	1	
air	17	
chipper	1	
counter-	1	
cutoff	18	
dead	18	
fly	18	
knife coating	17	
knife edge	18	
knocking back	7	
knock-off shower	13	
knot	1, 2	
knots	12	
knotter	12	
disc	12	
knotter rejects	12	
knuckle	15	
knuckle boom	1	
knuckle-free felt	15	
k number	8	
Kollergang	12	
kozo	3	
kraft cooking liquor	8	
kraft high-yield pulp	8	
kraft lignin	6	
kraft paper	16	
kraft process	8	
borate based	8	
modified	8	
kraft pulp	8	
kraft recovery process	9	
Kubelka-Munk equation	14	

L

labeler	18
label papers	16
laboratory beater	11
laboratory sheet mold	11
labyrinth	18
labyrinth seal	24
lacing	13
lacquer	17
lagging	9
lagoon	20
aeration	20
facultative	20
laid dandy roll	13
spiral	13
laid lines	14
laid paper	14
lake	5
lamella	2
microfibrillar	2
middle	2
lamella separator	20
laminant	18
laminar flow	13
laminate	18
laminated paper	18
laminating	18
acetate	18
dry	18
extrusion	18
pressure	18
thermoplastic	18
wet	18
laminating machine	18
lamination	18
lance	9
land application	20
land farming	20
landfill	20
landfill gas	22
landing	1
lantern ring	24
lap	1
lap pulp	12
lap splice	18
laser slitter	13
latency	7
latency removal	7
latent heat	13
latent mechanical pulp	7
lateral movement	13
lateral porosity	14
laterals	13
latewood	2
latex	5
polyvinyl acetate	17
styrene-butadiene	17
lathe	7
lathe headbox	13
latices	5
launder ring	10
lay	1
lay-boy	12
lay down	17
layer	13
boundary	13
bound water	11
coating	17
electrical double	5
furnish	13
intercellular	2
tie	18
warty	2
layered structure	13
layering	18
layer insulation paper	16
lay flat	18
layout	19
L/b ratio	13
leachate	20
leach caster	8
leaching	12, 20
selective	24
lead dryer	13
leader	13
leading edge	13
leaf fiber	3
leafing	17
leakage rate	24
leak testing	24
leaning flutes	18
lean white water	13
least squares method	25
leatherboard	16
leather fiber	3
ledger papers	16
left-handed paper machine	13
leg,	
barometric	12
drop	12
seal	12
lemon grass	3
length (of a paper roll)	14
length factor	11
length/thickness ratio	11
lens tissue	16
lethal threshold	20
letterpress	19
letterset	19
levan	5
leveling agent	17
levelness	14
level of significance	25
level tank	8
libriform fiber	2
lick-up	13
lift	18
lifters	9
light absorption	14
light-absorption coefficient	14
light box	14
lightfastness	14
light scattering	14
light-scattering coefficient	14
lightweight coated papers	16
lightweight papers	16
lightwight printing papers	16
lightwood	1
lignan	6
lignification	1
lignin	4
acid-insoluble	8
acid-precipitated	6
alkali	6
chloro-	10
Klason	8
kraft	6
native	4
proto-	4
residual	8, 10
thio	6
lignin-preserving bleaching	10
lignocellulose	4
lignosulfonate products	6
lignosulfonates	8
lignosulfonic acid	8
like-sidedness	14
lily pad	1
limbing	1
lime	9
burnt	9
deadburned	9
excess	9
hardburned	9
hydrated	9
milk of	9
overburnt	9
quick	9
reburnt	9
slaked	9
underburned	9
lime availability	9
lime kiln	9
lime kiln capacity	9
lime mud	9
lime mud filter	9
lime mud washer	9
lime precipitation	20
lime reactivity	9
lime recovery cycle	9
lime slaker	9
limestone	9
calcite	9
dolomite	9
liming up	8
limit switch	22

limonene	6	liquor inventory	9	surface	20
lineal pressure	13	liquor nozzle	9	thermal	9
linear pit	2	liquor penetration	8	wire	13
linear polymer	4	liquor solids	9	loading boom	1
linen	3	liquor solids loading	9	loading rate	14
linen finish	14	liquor-to-wood ratio	8	load leveling	22
linen tester	19	liquor trap	8	load shedding	22
liner	13, 18	lithography	19	localized watermark	14
bottom	13	direct	19	lock-out	24
car-	16	offset	19	loft drying	13
test	16	lithopone	5	log(s)	1, 14, 18
top	13	live bottom bin	1	boom	1
under-	13	liveliness	14	bundled	1
linerboard	16	livering	19	butt	1
lines,		live shaft roller	24	de-icing of	1
laid	14	live steam	9	peeler	1
water	14	load	14, 22	pulp	1
lineshaft drive	13	base	9, 22	saw	1
lining	9	bed	12	sinker	1
mill	18	BOD	20	top	1
linoleic acid	6	connected	22	log boom	1
lint	14	dead-	9	log carriage	1
linting	19	design	9	log flume	1
linting tendency	19	drag	13	logger	1
lip,		floating	18	logging	1, 23
regulating	13	nip	13	cable	1
slice	13	overhung	13	full-tree	1
top	13	pollution	20	ground-lead	1
lip projection	13	process steam	9	high-lead	1
liquid cyclone	12	regulator	7	hot	1
liquid dye	5	swinging	9	salvage	1
liquid penetration tester	14	thrust	24	shortwood	1
liquid ring vacuum pump	13	unit	18	skyline	1
liquidus temperature	9	loadcell	24	tree-length	1
liquifier	5	loadcell roll	17	whole-tree	1
liquor	8	load curve	22	logging operations	1
ammonium base	8	loaded sheet	14	logging residues	1
black	8	loader	1	log growth phase	20
bleach	10	big-stick	1	log merchandising	1
chlorate cell	10	front-end	1	log pile	1
		self-	1		
cooking	8			log raft	1
digester	8	load factor	22	log rule	1
free	8	loading	13, 20	log scale	1
green	8	activated sludge	20	log tally	1
kraft cooking	8	blade	17	log yard	1
magnesium base	8	bunch	1	long butting	1
mixed	20	design	20	long-chain molecule	4
red	8	dust	21	long circulation	13
residual pulping	8	grain	21	long fiber	12
sluicing	8	hydraulic	20	chemically treated	7
sodium base	8	liquor solids	9	long-fiber fraction	7
spent pulping	8	lumen	13	long grain	18
spent sulfite	8	machine	13	long ink	19
wash	12	organic	20	longitudinal	2
white	8	shock	20	longitudinal stability	15
liquor charge	8	side	13	long pulp	12
liquor circulation	8	solids	20	longwood	1
liquor density	9	specific	12	look-through	14
liquor filling	8	specific edge	12	loom	15
liquor gun	9	specific filter	20	loop seam	15

loose core	14	
loose volume	1	
loose winding	14	
loss(es)	22	
barker	1	
chemical	9	
combustible	9	
concealed	19	
draft	9	
head	13	
radiation	9	
slab-off	13	
unaccounted for	9, 13	
web core	18	
loss control	23	
loss on ignition	20	
lost time	13	
clothing	13	
maintenance	13	
operating	13	
services	13	
lost-time accident	23	
lost time analysis	13	
lot	14	
carload	18	
case	18	
job	18	
lovacs	13	
low-angle blade coater	17	
lowerator	18	
lower heating value	9	
low finish	14	
low-grade heat	22	
low-level heat	9	
low-lignin pulping	8	
low-odor recovery boiler	9	
low-pressure feeder	8	
low spot	19	
low-sulfonation mech. pulping	7	
low-volume, high-concentration	20	
lubricant	17	
lubricants	24	
solid	24	
synthetic	24	
lubricating shower	13	
lubrication	24	
lubricity	24	
luffing	1	
lug	24	
Lukenwald dryer	13	
lumber	1	
dimension	1	
rough	1	
lumber recovery	1	
lumen	2	
lumen loading	13	
luminance	14	
luminosity	14	
lump breaker roll	13	
lump crusher	9	

lump detector	18	
luster	14	

M ——————————

maceration	2	
machine,		
board	13	
British sheet	11	
coating	17	
combined	13	
cylinder	13	
fourdrinier	13	
handsheet	11	
Harper	13	
inclined wire	13	
laminating	18	
mold	13	
multicylinder	13	
multiply	13	
off	13	
on	13	
open-draw	13	
paper	13	
pulp	12	
roll grinding	13	
tissue	13	
totally enclosed	24	
tree harvesting	1	
universal testing	14	
wet	12	
wetlap	12	
Yankee	13	
machine calendering	13	
machine chest	13	
machine clothing	13	
machine coated	17	
machine deckle	13	
machine direction	13	
machine-direction profile	14	
machine-direction variation	14	
machine drying	13	
machine efficiency	13	
machine fill	13	
machine finish	14	
machine-glazed	14	
machine-imprinted	14	
machine loading	13	
machine-made board	13	
machine mark stripes	14	
machine room	13	
machine room ventilation	13	
machine speed	13	
machine tender	13	
machine width,		
maximum trimmed	13	
maximum untrimmed	13	
machine winding	13	
macrofibril	2	
macromolecule	4	

macroscopic	14	
magazine	7	
magazine cover	16	
magazine grinder	7	
magazine papers	16	
Magnefite Process	8	
magnesia	8	
magnesium base liquor	8	
magnesium oxide	8	
magnetic particle testing	24	
wet fluorescent	24	
main line	1	
main press	13	
main sewer	20	
maintainability	24	
maintenance	24	
breakdown	24	
contract	24	
corrective	24	
planned	24	
predictive	24	
preventative	24	
scheduled	24	
third party	24	
maintenance lost time	13	
maintenance planning	24	
makeready	19	
makeup	19	
makeup air	13	
makeup chemical	8	
makeup water	9, 13	
making order	13	
making roll	13	
male thread	24	
maltose	5	
management	23	
energy	22	
peak-demand	22	
physical distribution	23	
quality	25	
residuals	20	
management information sys	23	
manager's report	26	
mancooler	13	
mandrel	7, 13	
manhole	9	
manifold	13, 20	
manifold paper	16	
manila	14	
manila hemp	3	
man-made fiber	3	
mannan	4	
mannogalactan	4	
mannose	4	
map paper	16	
marble surface	14	
marginal cost	26	
margo	2	
marine borer	1	
marine water	20	

mark(s)	18	M & D digester	8	meristem	2
backing roll	17	mealy formation	14	mesh	15
blade	17	mean	25	mesh count	15
bristle	17	weighted	25	mesh fabric	15
brush	17	mean orientation angle	14	mesomorphous cellulose	4
crimp	14	measuring tanks	8	mesophilic bacteria	20
dandy	13, 14	mechanical absorption	13	metabolism	20
drip	14	mechanical aerator	20	metabolizing	20
felt	14	mechanical alignment	13	metallic coating	17
foam	14	mechanical barker	1	metallic fiber	3
hair	17	mechanical curl	14	metallic papers	16
patch	14	mechanical deckle edge	14	metallic resinate	6
press	13	mechanical drive system	13	metallized paper	16
rope	14	mechanical harvesting	1	metallurgy	24
scab	14	mechanical printing papers	16	metamerism	14
scuff	14	mechanical properties	14	meteorology	21
slice	14	mechanical pulp	7	metering roll	17
wire	14	latent	7	metering unit	19
market pulp	12	mechanical pulping	7	methane	20
market pulp mill	12	alkaline peroxide	7	methoxyl group	4
market research	23	chemi	7	methyl cellulose	4
marking,		chemically modified	7	metrication	23
chatter-	14	chemi-refiner	7	metric system	23
couch	13	high-sulfonation	7	metric ton	23
groove	13	low-sulfonation	7	micelles	4, 5
shadow	13	pressure refined	7	microbe	20
shell	13	refiner	7	microbial cellulose	4
marking felt	13	semichemical	7	microbial film	20
marking roll	13	sulfonated chemi	7	microbial floc	20
marsh gas	20	thermo-refiner	7	microbiological analysis	5
Masonite pulping process	8	mechanical seal	24	microbiological survey	5
mass distribution	14	mechanical treatment	12	microbiology	5
mass tone	19	mechanical vapor compress evap	9	microcompressions	11
mat	13	mechanical vapor recompression	9	microcreping	11, 13
mat board	16	mechanical variator drive	24	microcrystalline wax	5
material balance	23	mechanical ventilation	13	microencapsulation	13
material flow	23	mechanics	23	microfibril	2
material handling	1	fluid	13	microfibrillar angle	2
matrix	2	paper	14	microfibrillar lamella	2
matrix board	16	nip	13	microfibrillar lamina	2
matrix embossing	18	median	25	microfibrillar structure	2
matte calendering	13	median tolerance limit	20	micrograph	14
matte coated papers	14	medium-consistency screening	12	micrometer	14
matte finish	14	medium finish	14	microorganism	5, 20
matting	13	medium-weight coated papers	16	microscope	14
				electron	14
mature wood	2	melamine-formaldehyde resin	5	microscopical tests	14
maturing	14	mellow	14	microscopy	14
Mauritius hemp	3	membrane cell	10	microsectioning	14
max allowable concentration	21	membrane wall	9	microslice	13
maximum deckle	13	meniscus	19	
maximum sustained yield	20	meniscus coater	17	microslice adjustment	13
maximum trim	13	mensuration	1	microsmoothness	14
max trimmed machine width	13	mer	4	microstructural analysis	14
max untrimmed machine width	13	mercaptans	21	microstructure	14
Mayer rod	17	mercerization	3	microtome	14
		mercerized cellulose	4	micro-turbulence	13
		merchandizer	1	microwave drying	13
		merchantable	1	middle cut	1
		merchant brand	18	middle lamella	2
		mercury cell	10	middle ply	13

middletones	19	high-intensity	10	molecular weight	4
midfeather	12	in-line	10	molecule	4
migration	17	jet	24	amphipathic	5
binder	17	peg	10	dipolar	4
migration velocity	21	static	10	long-chain	4
mil	14	mixing chamber	13	macro-	4
mildew	5	mixing efficiency	12	monitoring	20
mileage	13	mixing pump	13	ambient air	21
ink	19	mobile crane	1	condition	24
milking	19	mobile tower yarder	1	continuous source	21
milk of lime	9	mobility	12	emission	21
mill	11, 23	electric	21	felt	13
attrition	1	electrophoretic	5	monocotyledon	3
ball	11	fluid	12	monocyclic compound	6
board	13	mobility ratio	12	monofilament	15
colloid	17	mode	25	monolithic linings	24
flagship	23	model	26	monomer	4
greenfield	23	modernity	23	monosaccharide	4
impact	17	modified kraft process	8	monosulfite process	8
paper	13	modified starch	5	monument	13
pebble	11	modifiers	17	Morden	12
pulp	12	modular construction	23	mordant	5
rod	12	modular system	23	morphological properties	11
satellite chip	1	modulus	15	morphology	2
single-line	23	bulk	14	molecular	4
small log	1	compression	13	mothballing	23
millboard	16	dynamic	13	motive steam	13
mill brand	18	elastic	14	motor	24
mill deck	1	Young's	14	mottle	19
mill edge	18	moiety	4	coating	17
mill lining	18	moisture,		mottled finish	14
mill net profit	26	disc	11	mottled formation	14
mill net value	26	free	5	mottled shade	14
mill roll	13	hygroscopic	5	moving averages	25
mill services	23	saturated	15	Moxy process	8
mimeograph paper	16	moisture content	11	mucilage	5, 12
mineral	5	equilibrium	14	mucoid	5
industrial	23	moisture content (dry basis)	14	mud drum	9
mineral acid	4	moisture content (wet basis)	14	mud washer	9
mineral fiber	3	moisture determination	14	muffler	24
mineral filler	13	moisture-gradient calendering	13	Muhlsteph ratio	11
mineralogy	5	moisture hysteresis	11	muka	6
minifourdrinier	13	moisture meter	14	Mullen tester	14
minimum shute felt	15	moisture pickup	13	multichannel headbox	13
Minton dryer	12	moistureproof	14	multiclone	21
miscibility	5	moisture regain	14	multicomponent wet-end sys	13
misregister	19	moisture ratio	14	multicylinder machine	13
mist	21	moisture-vapor transmiss'n rate	14	multidisc refiner	12
misting	17, 19	moisture welts	14	multifilament	15
Mitscherlich pulp	8	molarity	4	multifourdrinier machine	13
mitsumata	3	mold	5, 12	multifuel boiler	9
mixed liquor	20	hand	13	multilayer headbox	13
mixed liquor suspended solids	20	laboratory sheet	11	multiple-effect evaporator	9
mixed-media filter	20	wove	12	multiple regression	25
mixed papers	12	molded pulp products	16	multiply board	13
mixed stand	1	mold machine	13	multiply former	13
mixer,		mold resistant	14	multiply forming	13
chlorine	10	mole	4	multiply machine	13
coating	17	molecular chain	4	multipurpose pilot plant	23
dynamic	10	molecular morphology	4	multiroll press	20

multiseriate	2
multiseriate ray	2
multistage bleaching	10
multistage refining	7
multi-stage sulfite process	8
multitrading	24
multitube section	13
municipal waste	20
Mumin tube	8
Munsell color system	14
mutagen	20

N _____

nameplate rating	22
nanofibril	2
NaOH solubility test	8
nap	15
napkin stock	16
narrowing	15
national forest	1
native cellulose	4
native lignin	4
natural circulation	9
natural colored	14
natural draft	9
natural fiber	3
natural gas	22
natural purification	20
naval stores	6
near side	19
neat liquids	4
neck (of a digester)	8
neck-in	17
needle shower	13
needling	15
needling tracks	15
negative correlation	25
negative crown	13
negative image	19
negatively skewed distribution	25
neps	11
net heating value	9
net positive suction head	24
net power	12
net present value	26
net realizable value	26
net specific energy	12
neutralization	4, 20
neutralization stage	10
neutralizing amines	9
neutral size	5
neutral sulfite process	8
never-dried pulp	11
news	16
blank	12
overissue	12
roto-	16
super-	16

newsboard	16
newsprint	16
Newtonian flow	17
Newtonian fluid	17
New Zealand hemp	3
nip	13
differential	13
press	13
reversing	13
nip action	13
nip impression	13
nip-induced defects	14
nip load	13
nip mechanics	13
nip-out roll	13
nipping roller	18
nipple	24
nip pressure	13
average specific	13
nip relieving	13
nip rolls	12
nip-type reel	13
nip-type winder	13
nip width	13
nitric acid pulping	8
nitrogen dioxide bleaching	10
nitrogen dioxide delignification	8
nitrocellulose	4
nitrogen oxides	21
N-number	12
node	2, 3
fiber	2
no-draw press	13
nodule	12
noise	25
suction roll	13
noise control	23
noiseless paper	16
no-load power	12
nominal grammage	14
nomograph	23
non-cellulose papers	14
non-code vessel	24
noncondensible gas	13
noncondensibles	8, 9
incineration of	21
non-contact coater	17
nondestructive test	14
nondestructive testing	24
non-fibrous additive	5
nonimpact printing	19
non-integrated paper mill	13
nonionic compound	5
non-Newtonian fluid	17
nonoxidizing biocide	5
nonporous wood	2
nonsettleable solids	20
nonwood fibers	3
nonwood pulp	8
nonwoven felt	15

nonwovens	16
dry-lay	16
wet-lay	16
Norden efficiency factor	12
normal distribution	25
normality	4
normalized data	25
nose baffle	9
no-sulfur pulping	8
notch	1
nozzle	9, 13, 23, 24
accept	12
fan	12
Grewin	13
liquor	9
slice	13
spray	24
nozzle ports	9
nozzle pump	9
nozzle slice	13
NSSC process	8
nubbin	7
nuisance threshold	21
number,	
acid	6
bending	14
bulking	14
chlorine	10
copper	14
dp	4
fiber	11
fold	14
formation	14
hypo	10
k-	8
kappa	8
kerosine	14
N-	12
permanganate	8
Reynolds	23
Ringelmann	21
Roe	10
roll	13
saponification	6
strand	15
nutrient	20
nylon	15

O _____

observations	25
obsolescence	26
ocean disposal	20
odor	21
odor abatement	21
odor intensity	21
odor pollution	21
odor threshold	21
off color	14
offcut	1, 18

off-grade paper	13	opaque pile	14	coliform	20
off-line	23	opaque waxing	17	filamentous	20
off-machine	13	OPCO process	7	organization chart	23
offset	14, 19, 24	open area	15	organosol	17
dry	19	open assembly time	18	organosolv pulping	8
heatset	19			orientation index	14
		open burning	21	orientation of fibers	14
offset core	14	controlled	21	original	19
offset gravure coater	17	open channel	20	o-ring seal	24
offset lithography	19	open-discharge refining	7	Orsat analysis	9
offset papers	16	open draw	13		
		open-draw machine	13	orthogonality	25
offset parallel centerline	13	open-ended clothing	15	orthotropic	14
offset press	19	open-frame supercalender	13	oscillator	13
offset printing	19	open headbox	13	OSHA	23
offsetting (of ink)	19	open hood	13	outage	13, 22
off square	18				
		operability	23	outer pit-aperture	2
oil,		operating drum	1	outer ply	13
bunker C	9	operating life	13	outer shipping container	18
drying	19	operating lost time	13	outfall	20
essential	6	operation(s),		diffuser	20
pine needle	6	baling	12	outlet device	8
pine	6	coating	17	outlying test determination	14
pine tar	6	converting	18	out-of-jog	18
residual fuel	9	dry nip	13	out-of-round roll	14
rosin	6	evolutionary	25	outside chip storage	1
tall	6	fail-safe	13	outsides	18
		finishing	18	outside waste	18
oil-base ink	19	integrated forest products	1	outturn sample	14
oiler	24	logging	1	ovality	9
oil penetration test	14	parameter of	23	oven-dry	11
oil repellancy	14	shakedown	23	oven-dry grammage	14
oil repellancy test	14	unit	23	oven-dry weight	11
oil system,		operational reliability	24	overall retention	13
centralized	24	operations information system	23	overburnt lime	9
circulating	24	operations research	23	overcoat	17
oil wicking	14	operator	23	overcooked	8
oil wicking test	14	opposite dimension	18	overcutting	18
		opposite pitting	2	over-dried paper	14
okra	3	optical alignment	13	over-drying	13
old growth	1	optical brightener	5	overfire air	9
oleic acid	6	optical contact	14	overflow	6
oleophilic	5	optical density	19	overhead	26
oleoresin	6	optical holography	24	overheads	20
		optical properties	14	overhead traveling crane	1
olfactory fatigue	23	optical scattering	14	overhung load	13
oligomer	4	optical sensor	10	overissue news	12
oligosaccharide	4	optical smoothness	14	overload protection device	22
once-through boiler	9	optical tests	14	overprinting	19
onionskin	16	optical whitening	5	overrun	13
		optimism	26	overs	13
on-line	13				
on-line measurements	14	orange peel	14, 17	oversize chips	1
on-machine	13	order-or-magnitude estimate	26	oversize paper	18
on-machine seamed press felt	15	organic	4	over-thick chips	1
on-off valve	24	organic chemistry	4	oxidant	10
		organic felt	16	oxidation	10
on-stream	13				
on-top former	13	organic loading	20	aerobic biological	20
opacifier	13	organic screen	20	biological	20
opacimeter	14	organic-to-inorganic ratio	9	black liquor	9
opacity	14	organisms,		wet	9
printing	14	benthic	20	oxidation pond	20
TAPPI	14				
opacity (paper backing)	14				
opacity (white backing)	14				
opaque circular	16				

oxidation-reduction potential	10	**paper(s)** *(cont)*		**paper(s)** *(cont)*	
oxidative bleaching agent	10	alkaline-filled	14	duplex	14
oxidative extraction stage	10	angle-cut	18	duplicator	16
oxidized black liquor	9	anisotropic	14	electrical insulation	16
oxidized starch	5	anti-acid	14	electrostatic copy	16
		Antiquarian	14	enameled	17
oxidized white liquor	9	archival	16		
oxidizing agent	10			envelope	16
oxidizing atmosphere	9	art	16	extensible	14
oxidizing biocide	5	articulating	16	facsimilie	16
oxidizing power	10	artist	16	felt	16
		ashless	14	film	14
oxycellulose	4	asphalt	16		
oxygen	10			filter	16
dissolved	20	bag	16	fine	16
oxygenation capacity	20	baggy	14	flong	16
oxygen bleaching stage	10	banknote	16	foil	16
		base	14	functional	16
oxygen delignification	8	bible	16		
oxygen demand,				gloss	14
biochemical	20	blanking	16	graphic	16
chemical	20	blotting	16	greaseproof	16
immediate	20	bond	16	green	14
total	20	book	16	groundwood	16
		bottom	18		
oxygen-enriched extract stage	10			handmade	14
oxygen enrichment	9	braille	16	hard	14, 16
oxygen pulping	8	building	16	heat seal	16
oxygen sag curve	20	bureaucracy	16	high-filler	14
		burnt	14	impregnating	16
oxygen saturation	20	business	16		
ozonation	20			indented	14
ozonation stage	10	cable	16	India	16
ozonator	10	calendered	14	industrial	16
ozone	10	carbon	16	isotropic	14
		carbonless	16	kraft	16
		catalog	16		
				label	16
P		chart	16	laid	14
		chemical reaction	16	laminated	18
package	18	cheviot	14	layer insulation	16
packaged boiler	9	cigarette	16	ledger	16
packaging papers	16	coarse	16		
packed column	21			lightweight	16
packing	8, 19, 24	coated	17	magazine	16
		coated groundwood	16	manifold	16
chip	8	coil	16	map	16
degree of	8	commodity	16	metallic	16
tower	8	communication	16		
packing density	8, 11			metallized	16
pads	13	conditioned	14	mimeograph	16
		construction	16	mixed	12
pallet	18	converting	18	noiseless	16
palletizing	18	copying	16	non-cellulose	14
pan	17	correspondence	16		
coating	17			off-grade	13
panel product	1	cover	16	offset	16
		crepe	16	over-dried	14
pan roll	17	culled	13	oversize	18
paper(s)	13	cultural	16	packaging	16
abrasive backing	16	cutting	16		
acid	14			papeterie	16
acid free	14	currency	16	parchmentizing	16
		damask	16	parchment	16
adding-machine	16	decor	16	permanent	16
air-dried	14	decorative	16	personal	16
air-mail	16	diazotype base	16		
album	16			photographic base	16
alkaline	14	directory	16	pigmented	16
		direct process	16	plastic	16
		document	16	poster	16
		drawing	16	preconditioned	13
		dry-formed	14		

paper(s) *(cont)*

pressure sensitive	16
printing	16
processed	16
rag	14
reinforced	16
release	16
reproduction	16
reprographic	16
roll	13
rotary	18
rotogravure	16
rough finished	14
rust inhibitor	16
sack	16
safety	16
saturating	16
seasoned	14
security	16
sensitized	16
separating	16
shredded	16
sour-coated	17
specialty	16
spinning	16
squared	18
synthetic	14
tape	16
technical	16
text	16
thermal	16
thin	16
tinny	14
toned	14
top	18
torn-off	13
tracing	16
twin-wire	14
typewriter	16
uncoated	14
unsized	14
veined	14
velvet-finish	14
vulcanizing	16
waste	12
water-color	16
waterleaf	14
water resistant	14
waxed	16
waxing	16
wet soak	14
wet-strength	14
white	19
wood-containing	14
wood-free	14
wove	14
wrapping	16
writing	16
paperboard	13
paperboard specialties	16
paper directionality	14

paper grades	16
paper hygroscope	14
paperization	14
paper machine	13
left-handed	13
right-handed	13
paper machine alignment	13
paper machine capacity	13
paper machine centerline	13
paper machine clothing	13
paper machine drive	13
paper machine furnish	13
paper machine production	13
paper machine production rate	13
paper machine productivity	13
paper machine runnability	13
paper machine sections	13
paper machine speed	13
papermaker	13
papermaking	13
alkaline	5
papermaking additives	13
papermaking materials	13
papermaking pulp	8
paper mechanics	14
paper mill	13
integrated	13
non-integrated	13
paper mulberry	3
paper physics	14
paper quality	14
paper quality index	14
paper stock	12
paper strength	14
paper structure	13
paper test	14
paper textiles	16
paper waste	18
papeterie paper	16
papier mache	16
papyrus	3
paraffin	5
paraffining	18
parallel barking	1
parallel generation	22
parallel laminate	18
parameter	23, 25
combined strength	11
parameter of operation	23
parchment	16
art	16
vegetable	16
parchment finish	14
parchmentizing	4, 12
parchmentizing paper	16
parchment paper	16
parchment writing	16
parenchyma	2
parent ream	18
parent roll	13

Pareto chart	25
Paris white	17
Parshall flume	20
partial pressure	8
particle	21
particle binder	17
particleboard	1
particle segregation	1
particle size analysis	21
particulates	21
respirable-size	21
parts per million	4
passivation	24
passivity	24
paste	18
pasted board	14
paster	19
auto-	19
flying	19
paster dispersion coating	17
paste size	5
paste-up	19
patching	15
patch mark	14
patent coated	14
pathogen	20
pattern	14
flame	9
pattern coating	17
pawl	24
payback period	26
pcb	20
peak concentration	21
peak demand	22
peak-demand efficiency	22
peak-demand management	22
pearl filler	5
pearl starch	5
peavey	1
pebble mill	11
pectin	4
peeler core	1
peeler log	1
peeler roll	13
peeling	13
chemical	1
sap	1
peeling angle	13
peeling bond	18
peeling force	13
peeling reaction	4
peel waste	18
peened edges	19
peewee	1
peg mixer	10
pelletization	9, 12
pen and ink test	14
pendant-tube superheater	9
penescope test	14
penetrability	8

419

penetrant dye	24	photosynthesis	20	pimples	15
penetration	8, 13, 21	phozy	14	pin adhesion	18
liquor	8	physical distribut'n managem't	23	pinching	13
penetration factor	8	physical properties	14	pin chips	1
penstock	20	physico-chemical mechanism	5		
				pineapple	3
pent house	9	piceoid pit	2	pinene	6
pentosan	4	piciform pit	2	pine needle oil	6
pentose	4	pick,		pine oil	6
peptization	5	blister	19	pine pitch	6
peptizing agent	5	coating	19		
				pine tar	6
peracetic acid	10	dandy	14	pine tar oil	6
percentile	25	drum	17	pin hole	14
percolation	20	fiber	19	pinion	24
perfect	14	rupture	19	pinoid pit	2
perfect combustion	9	wax	14		
				pin seam	15
perfecting press	19	pickaroon	1	pintle	15
perforated plate	12	picking	13, 19	piping	14
perforated roll	13	dry	19	pipe loop	24
perforation	2	felt	13	pirssonite	9
simple	2	wet	19		
				pit	2, 7, 13
perforation plate	2	pick line	15	blow	8
performance tests	14	pick resistance	14	bordered	2
perhydroxyl ion	10	wet	14	broke	13
period	22	pick stacking	15	couch	13
periodic	13	pick tester	14		
				cupressoid	2
peripheral speed	7	pickup	13	fenestriform	2
permanence	14	moisture	13	grinder	7
permanent paper	16	poor man's	13	intertracheid	2
permanent set	13	suction	13	intervessel	2
permanganate number	8	pickup felt	13		
				linear	2
extracted	10	pickup roll	17	piceoid	2
permeability	14, 15	pig	20	piciform	2
air	14	piggyback digesters	8	pinoid	2
fractional	15	pigment(s)	5, 19	simple	2
vapor	14	coating	17		
				sludge	20
pernicious contraries	12	colored	5	taxoid	2
peroxide	10	hollow-sphere	5	vestured	2
peroxide bleaching stage	10	plastic	5	wire	13
peroxide brightening stage	10	slurry	17	pita floja	3
peroxide delignification	8	structured	17		
		white	5	pit-aperture	2
personal papers	16			extended	2
perturbation	13	pigment coating	17	included	2
petroleum waxes	5	pigmented paper	16	inner	2
pH	4	pigment sizing	17	outer	2
surface	14	pigment volume	17		
				pit canal	2
pH (of paper)	14	pigment volume concentration	17	pit cavity	2
pH (of pulp)	11	pigtail	13	pitch	5, 7, 13
phase	23	pike pole	1	pine	6
phase-changing forming board	13	pile,		tall oil	6
phase shift	13	chip	1	white	12
phenol(s)	6, 20	log	1	pit chamber	2
chlorinated	20	opaque	14	pitch control	5
phenolic resin	18	ring-shaped	1	pitch deposits	5
phenology	2	wood	1	pitch pocket	2
phloem	2	pile curl	18		
				pitch spots	14
photochemistry	4	pile pattern	17	pits	17
photoengraving	19	piling	19	pith	2, 3
photographic base paper	16	pilot dryer	13	pith flecks	2
photographic survey	13	pilot plant	23	pitless grinding	7
photomicrograph	14	dedicated	23		
		multipurpose	23		

pit membrane	2	
pit pair	2	
pitting	24	
alternate	2	
confluent	2	
opposite	2	
pitting corrosion	24	
plain press	13	
plain roll	13	
plain weave	15	
planar weave	15	
plankton	20	
planned maintenance	24	
planning,		
contingency	20	
maintenance	24	
production	13	
strategic	23	
planographic printing	19	
plant,		
acid	8	
bleach	10	
causticizing	9	
chlorine dioxide	10	
coating	17	
converting	18	
demonstration	23	
filter	20	
generating	22	
groundwood	7	
power	22	
water treatment	20	
plantation forest	1	
plant factor	22	
plasma spraying	24	
plastic	4	
plastic fluid	17	
plasticizer	17	
plasticizing	17	
plastic media	20	
plastic papers	16	
plastic pigments	5	
plastic plate	7	
plastisol	17	
plastometer	13	
plate(s)	12, 19	
bed-	12	
bimetal	19	
collecting	9	
combination	19	
contoured	12	
curved	19	
devil tooth	12	
drying	11	
perforated	12	
perforation	2	
plastic	7	
presensitized	19	
refiner	12	
screen	12	
slotted	12	
splash	9	
target	8	
wave	12	
waveline	12	
wear	1	
plate blinding	19	
plate clash	7	
plate clearance	12	
plate column	21	
plate count	5	
plate cylinder	19	
plate finish	14	
plate heat exchanger	9	
platen	9	
tube	9	
platen dryer	13	
platen press	19	
plating	14, 17	
bunch	14	
plenum	9	
pliability	14	
plow	7	
plug	12	
plug flow	10	
plug screw feeder	7	
plug valve	24	
plug wiper flow	7	
plume	21	
ply	13	
filler	13	
middle	13	
outer	13	
plybond	14	
plywood	1	
pneumatic handling/conveying	1	
pocket	7	
bark	1	
dryer	13	
grinder	7	
pitch	2	
pocket counter	7	
pocket feeder	7	
rotary	8	
pocket grinder	7	
pocket ventilation	13	
pocket ventilator	13	
point	14	
boiling	9	
break	20	
break-even	26	
color immobilization	17	
congealing	17	
dropping	24	
eutectic	9	
fiber saturation	2, 11	
flash	9	
flow	18	
fluidization	12	
gel	17	
isoelectric	5	
pour	18	
radical deformation	9	
wax picking	14	
zero steam velocity	7	
point source	21	
Poisson's ratio	14	
polargraphic chemical sensor	10	
pole	1, 15	
pike	1	
polish	14	
polished drum coating	17	
polished white liquor	9	
pollutant(s)	20	
primary	21	
secondary	21	
pollution,		
air	21	
odor	21	
thermal	20	
water	20	
pollution abatement	20	
pollution load	20	
polyacrylamides	5	
polyaluminum hydroxy chloride	5	
polyamide fiber	3	
polycondensation (of lignin)	8	
polydisperse system	5	
polydispersity	4	
polyelectrolyte	5	
polyester	15	
polyethylene fiber	3	
polymer(s)	4	
high	4	
linear	4	
polymeric	4	
polymeric impregnated board	18	
polymerization	4	
degree of	4	
polymolecularity	4	
polymorph	4	
polyolefin fiber	3	
polyphenol	6	
polypropylene fiber	3	
polysaccharide	4	
homo-	4	
polysaccharose	4	
polystyrene	5	
polysulfide	8	
polysulfide pulp	8	
polyurethane	13	
polyvinyl acetate latex	17	
polyvinyl alcohol	5	
pond	13	
evaporation	20	
hot	1	
oxidation	20	
spill	20	
poor man's pickup	13	
poor start	14	

pope reel	13
pop test	14
population	25
pore	2
pores (of paper)	14
porosity	14
lateral	14
pulpstone	7
porous wood	2
portal-type gantry crane	1
port effect	13
positive angle doctor blade	17
positive correlation	25
positive displacement	24
positive image	19
positively skewed distribution	25
post	13
poster paper	16
post-coating finishing device	17
post-coating metering	17
post color value	11
post-consumer waste paper	12
post refining	7
post treatment	7, 21
potable water	20
potassium	9
potential difference	22
potential emission	21
potential energy	22
potentiometric titration	4
pot life	18
pour point	18
powdering	14, 19
power	22
bleaching	10
by-product	22
causticizing	9
effective	12
electric	22
hiding	17
hydroelectric	22
interruptible	22
net	12
no-load	12
oxidizing	10
purchase	22
scattering	11
shaft	22
steam	22
thermal	22
power distribution system	22
power fabric	15
power factor	22
power plant	22
base-load	22
power transmission	13
prebleaching	10
pre-breaker	12
precast coating	17
precipitate	5
size	5

precipitating agent	5
precipitator	21
electrostatic	21
wet-bottom	21
wet electrostatic	21
precirculation	8
precision	14
test	14
precision sheeter	18
precision statement	14
precleaning	21
precoat	17
precoat filter	9
preconditioned paper	13
preconditioning	14
preconverted starch	5
precursor	4
predictand	25
predictive maintenance	24
predictor	25
predryers	13
preflocculation	13
pregelatinized starch	5
preheating	7
preheating zone	9
prehydrolysis	4, 8
prehydrolyzed kraft pulp	8
pre-logging	1
pre-metered coating system	17
prepolymers	17
pre-refining	12
preretention tube	10
presensitized plate	19
preservative(s)	17
viscosity	10
press(es)	13, 19
baby	13
baling	12
bark	1
blanket-to-blanket	19
blind-drilled	13
closed transfer	13
cloverleaf	13
convertible	19
couch	13
disc	12
double-wire	12
drum	13
dual	13
extractor	13
fabric	13
flatbed cylinder	19
grooved-roll	13
handsheet	11
hard-nip	13
heatset	19
high-impulse	13
horizontal	13
inclined	13

main	13
multiroll	20
no-draw	13
offset	19
perfecting	19
plain	13
platen	19
primary	13
printing	19
proof	14
reverse	13
roller	18
roll-to-roll	19
rotary	19
sheet-fed	19
shrink-sleeve	13
size	13
slab	12
smoothing	13
straight-through	13
suction	13
transfer	13
transversal flow	13
V-	20
vertical	13
wash	12
web	19
web offset	19
wide-nip	13
wringer	13
pressability	13
pressate	12
pressboard	16
press felt	13
on-machine seamed	15
press impulse	13
press impulse concept	13
pressing	13
cold	18
displacement	13
flow-limited	13
hot	13
pressure-limited	13
press mark	13
press nip	13
press part	13
press proof	19
pressroom	19
press roll	13
press roll bounce	13
press trimming	18
pressure,	
allowable working	9
atmospheric	21
back	24
barometric	21
blow	8
bulking	14
cooking	8
cylinder	7

pressure, *(cont)*
    design 9
    differential 13
    false 8
    grinding 7
    hydraulic 13
    hydrostatic 13
    inertial 13
    lineal 13
    nip 13
    partial 8
    printing 19
    specific nip 13
    static 21
    vapor 13
pressure bulker 14

pressure coating 17
pressure differential 13
pressure diffusion washer 12
pressure drop 21
pressure filter 9

pressure foot 7
pressure former 13
pressure forming 13
pressure laminating 18
pressure-limited pressing 13

pressure/pressure TMP 7
pressure profile 13
pressure refined MP 7
pressure relief valve 24
pressure roll 13

pressure screen 12
pressure sensitive papers 16
pressure washer 12
pressurized headbox 13
pressurized refining 7

pressurized stone groundwood 7
press vibrations 13
presteaming 7, 8
pretreatment 20
    acid 10

prevailing wind 21
preventative maintenance 24
primary air 9
primary air port black-out 9
primary arms 13

primary cleaners 12
primary colors,
    additive 19
    subtractive 19
primary creping 13

primary effluent 20
primary headbox 13
primary hydroxyl group 4
primary pollutant 21
primary presses 13

primary refining 7
primary screens 12
primary sludge 20
primary standard 14
primary treatment 20

primary treatment efficiency 20
primary wall 2
primary winder 13
prime coat 17
prime cutting 1

prime mover 22
priming (of pumps) 24
printability 14
print density 14
printed gloss 19

print embossing 19
print evenness 14
printing 19
    back 19
    contact 19
    direct 19
    electrostatic 19
    impact 19
    impactless 19
    indirect 19
    ink jet 19
    nonimpact 19
    offset 19
    over- 19
    planographic 19
    process 19
    relief 19
    silk screen 19
    two-color 19
printing couple 19

printing ink 19
printing opacity 14
printing paper 16
    commercial 16
    groundwood 16
    lightweight 16
    mechanical 16
    semicoated 16
printing press 19
printing pressure 19

printing process,
    dry 19
    wet 19
printing rating 14
printing side 14

printing smoothness 19
printing substrate 19
printing train 19
printing unit 19
print-on coating 17

print quality 19
probability interval 25
probability screening 12
probe 21
process 23
    acid-alkali cooking 8
    activated sludge 20
    alkafide 8
    anaerobic contact 20
    Arbiso 8

    batch 23
    bench-scale 23
    biochemical 20
    biological 20
    bisulfite 8
    chlor-alkali 10
    cold corrugating 18
    cold soda 7
    continuous 23
    dry coating 17
    dry pyrolysis 9
    extended aeration 20
    four color 19
    ion exchange 20
    kraft 8
    Magnefite 8
    Moxy 8
    NSSC 8
    OPCO 7
    pulping 8
    Radfoam 13
    reject sulfonation 7
    soft 13
    solvent extraction 12
    sulfate 8
    transport 23
process color 19
process colors 19
process design 23
processed papers 16

process engineering 23
process lag 23
process optimization 23
processor 1
process printing 19

process steam 9
process steam load 9
process water 20
procumbent ray cell 2
producer 1

producer's risk 25
product cost 26
product differentiation 23
production 23
    finished 18
    incremental 26
    paper machine 13
    theoretical 13
production bottleneck 23
production control 23

production line 23
production planning 13
production rate 13
    paper machine 13
production rate curve 13

production rate efficiency 13
productivity 13, 23
    forest 1
    paper machine 13
products of combustion 9

profile(s) 14
  composite 14
  cross-direction 14
  drainage 13
  machine-direction 14

  pressure 13
  roll structure 13
  roughness 14
  superimposed 14
  white water consistency 13

profile adjusting screw 13
profiler 14
profiling sprays 13
profilograph 14
profilometer 14

profit 26
  incremental 26
  mill net 26
profitability 26
profit center 26

profit-volume chart 26
progressing cavity pump 24
progressive pigging 20
project control estimate 26
projected area 11

project engineering 23
promoter 5
  adhesion 18
proof(s),
  color 19
  galley 19

press 19
proof press 14
proof testing 14
properties,

  black liquor 9
  chemical 14
  critical pair of 11
  dimensional 11, 14
  electrical 14

  fundamental 14
  mechanical 14
  morphological 11
  optical 14
  physical 14

  psychrometric 13
  release 13
  saturating 14
  sensory 14
  slagging 9

  strength 14
  stress-strain 14
  surface 14
  tactile 14
  thermal 14

proportioner 13
proportioning 13
protective additive 10
protective coating 17
protective colloid 5

proteinaceous 5
protofibril 2
protolignin 4
protoplasm 2
prototype 23

pseudoplastic fluid 17
pseudo-plasticity 17
psychrometer 13
  sling 13
psychrometric properties 13

publication grades 16
pucker 14
puddle-blade coater 17
puddling 13
puff 9, 10

pull down 19
pulp(s) 8
  acetate 4
  air dry 11
  alpha 11

  alphabet 7
  bisulfite 8
  bleachable grade 8
  bleached 10
  calibration 11

  captive 8
  chemical 8
  crumb 12
  dissolving 4
  dried 11

  easy bleaching 10
  fast 11
  fluff 8
  fodder 8
  free 11

  fully bleached 10
  fully cooked 8
  graft 4
  hard 8
  hard bleaching 10

  hardwood 12
  high-alpha 8
  holo- 11
  kraft 8
  kraft high-yield 8

  lap 12
  latent mechanical 7
  long 12
  market 12
  mechanical 7

  Mitscherlich 8
  never-dried 11
  nonwood 8
  papermaking 8
  polysulfide 8

  prehydrolyzed kraft 8
  rag 12
  rayon 4
  reference 11
  refiner 7

reinforcement 13
roll 12
semi-bleach 10
semichemical 8
shivey 11

softwood 12
standard 11
sulfate 8
sulfite 8
synthetic 3

unbeaten 12
unbleached 10
virgin 8
wetlap 12
wood 8

yellow 12
pulpability 8, 12
pulp content 14
pulper 12
  helical 12
  kneader 12

pulper stock 12
pulper sweetener 12
pulp evaluation 11
pulp grades 12

pulping 12
  acid 8
  alkaline 8
  chemical 8
  cold 12

  cold soda 8
  DMSO 8
  explosion 8
  green liquor 8
  high-yield 8

  holo- 8
  hydrogenation 8
  hydrotropic 8
  low lignin 8
  mechanical 7

  nitric acid 8
  no-sulfur 8
  organosolv 8
  oxygen 8
  sawdust 8

  semichemical 8
  soda 8
  soda ash 8
  soda-oxygen 8
  solvent 8

  thermomechanical 7
  thermomechanical chemi- 7
  vapor phase 8
  whole-tree 8
pulping process 8
  Masonite 8
pulping reaction 8
pulp log 1
pulp machine 12
pulp mill 12
  market 12

pulp processability 12
pulp quality index 11
pulp roll 12
pulpstone 7
    ceramic 7

pulpstone bevel 7
pulpstone grade 7
pulpstone immersion 7
pulpstone jointing material 7

pulpstone porosity 7
pulpstone segment 7
pulpstone sharpening 7
pulpstone structure 7
pulp storage 12

pulp strength index 11
pulp substitute 12
pulp transport 12
pulp weight factor 11
pulpwood 1

pulpwood dealer 1
pulsation damper 13
pulse attenuator 13
pulse-jet baghouse 21
pulverizing 9

pump 24
    boiler feed 9
    booster 20
    centrifugal 24
    diaphragm 24

    disintegrator 9
    fan 13
    heat 22
    liquid ring vacuum 13
    mixing 13

    nozzle 9
    progressing cavity 24
    reciprocating 24
    rotary 24
    stock 12

    thick stock 12
    vacuum 13
pump characteristic curves 24
puncture resistance 14
punky 2

purchased energy 22
purchase power 22
purgeable shower 13
purging 9, 12
purging steam 9

purification,
    alkali 8
    biological 20
    cold alkali 8
    hot alkali 8
    natural 20

pusher 1
putrefaction 5
pyranose 4
pyranose ring 4

pyrite 8
pyrolysis 9
pyrolysis recovery 9
pyrometer 9
pyrosonics 9
pyroxylin coating 17

Q

qualitative analysis 4
quality 25
    ambient air 21
    bending 14
    chip 1

    effluent 20
    folding 14
    paper 14
    print 19
    roll 14
    wood 1

quality assurance 25
quality audit 25
quality circle 25
quality control 25

quality index,
    air 21
    chip 1
    paper 14
    pulp 11

quality management 25
quantitative analysis 4
quarter point problem 13
quarter section 1
quaternary 12

queen roll 13
quenching 8
quick lime 9
quick opening valve 24
quire 18

R

race 20, 24
rachis 3
Radfoam process 13
radial 2
radial-flow impellor 24

radial-flow tank 20
radial inward flow 20
radial outward flow 20
radial section 2
radiant-design boiler 9

radiant drying 13
radiant energy 9
radiant heat transfer 13
radiation loss 9
radical 4

radical deformation point 9
radiographic testing 24
rag boiler 12
rag content 14
ragger 12

rag paper 14
rag pulp 12
rag rope 12
rags 3
railroads 14

railroad tracking 17
rain forest 1
rake angle 13
ramie 3
random error 14

random orientation 14
random sample 11
random sampling 25
random variation 14
range 25

ranking 14
rapid drain 9
rapid infiltration 20
rapid sand filter 20
rappers 21

ratchet 24
rate,
    combustion 9
    corrosion 24
    drainage 13

    drying 13
    evaporation drying 13
    firing 9
    flow 12
    growth 1

    heatup 8
    infiltration 20
    leakage 24
    loading 14
    moisture-vapor
      transmiss'n 14

    production 13
    reaction 4
    reject 12
    steaming 9
    straining 14

    unit loading 12
    waste paper recovery 12
    waste paper utilization 12
rate constant 4
rated capacity 9, 13

rate of return 26
rate of return on investment 26
rate of tree growth 1
rathole 1, 9
rating,

    nameplate 22
    printing 14
ratio,
    acceleration 13
    active alkali-to-wood 8

    adhesive 17
    air-fuel 9
    air-to-cloth 21
    air-to-solids 20
    anisotropic 14

ratio, *(cont)*
aspect 11, 17
biaxial stress 14
buffering 8
chemical-to-wood 8
chlorine 10

circulation 9
cleanliness 12
compression 7
contact 11
contrast 14

cost-benefit 26
crepe 14
crimp 11
discharge 13
displacement 12

drainage symmetry 13
efflux 13
fiber axis 11
food-to-microorganism 20
growth-to-removal 1

jet-to-wire speed 13
L/b 13
length/thickness 11
liquor-to-wood 8
mobility 12

moisture 11
Muhlsteph 11
organic-to-inorganic 9
Poisson's 14
roughness 14

Runkel 11
slenderness 14
stack dilution 21
takeup 18
thickening 12

transparency 14
turndown 23
wake 13
wipe 17
rattle 14

raw acid 8
raw effluent 20
raw green liquor 9
raw material 23
raw sludge 20

raw wastewater 20
raw stock,
coating 17
hanging 16
raw water 20

raw weight 17
raw white liquor 9
ray 2
aggregate 2
fusiform 2

heterocellular 2
homocellular 2
multiseriate 2
uniseriate 2
ray crossing 2

ray margin 2
rayon 4
cuprammonium 4
rayon pulp 4
rayon rejects 12

ray tracheid 2
reaction 4
addition 4
chemical 4
cleavage 4

condensation 4
endothermic 9
exothermic 9
heat of 9
irreversible 4

peeling 4
pulping 8
reversible 4
stopping 4
substitution 4
topochemical 4

reaction kinetics 4
reaction mechanism 4
reaction network 4
reaction order 4

reaction rate 4
relative 8
reaction rate expression 4
reaction thermodynamics 4
reaction vessel 10

reaction wood 2
reactivation (of desiccant) 10
reactive dye 5
reactive size 5
reactivity 4
lime 9

reactor 8
hypo 10
readability 14
reading 14

reagent 4
ream 18
broken 18
parent 18
ream marker 18

ream weight 18
ream wrapped 18
reboiler 9
rebuild 23
reburning 9

reburnt lime 9
receiving water 20
reception chamber 13
receptivity index 17
receptor 21

receptor roll 13
recesses 14
rechipper 1
reciprocating screen 1
reciprocating pump 24

recirculating coating system 17
reclaim,
bark 1
chip 1
reclaimed waste paper 12

reclaimed wastewater 20
reclaiming 1
recovery 1, 20
blow-heat 8
chemical 9

cross 9
fiber 12
fluidized bed 9
heat 9
lumber 1

recovery area 9
recovery boiler 9
extended economizer 9
low-odor 9
recovery boiler audit 9

recovery cycle efficiency 9
recovery furnace 9
recovery process,
aluminate 9
kraft 9
pyrolysis 9

recovery system,
broke 13
direct alkali 9
rectangularity 18

rectification 13
rectifier roll 13
rectifiers 13
rectifying 18
recuperative air heater 9

recycled fiber 12
recycling 23
red liquor 8
redox potential 10
reducer chipper 1

reducers 19
reducible sulfur 14
reducing agent 10
reducing atmosphere 9
reductant 10

reduction efficiency 9
reductive alk. delignification 8
redundancy 24
reeds 3
reef roll 13

reel 13
centerwind 13
drum 13
nip-type 13
pope 13

reel building 13
reel drum 13
reeling 13
reel rail 13
reel sample 14

426

reel spool	13	
reel-up	13	
re-entrainment	21	
reference pulp	11	
refined sulfate turpentine	6	

refiner	12
Claflin	12
conical	12
disc	12
Jordan	12
sequential velocity	7
tickler	12
refiner bleaching	7
refiner chest	12
refiner cycling	7
refiner groundwood	7
refiner mechanical pulping	7
refiner plates	12
refiner pulp	7
sawdust	7
refining	12
blowline	12
degree of	12
deshive	12
dry	11
high-consistency	12
hot-stock	12
multistage	7
open-discharge	7
post	7
pressurized	7
primary	7
reject	7
refining degree	12
refining efficiency	12
refining energy split	7
refining frequency	7
refining intensity	12
reflectance	14
specular	14
reflectance meter	14
reflectivity	14
reforestation	1
reforming	13
refractivity	14
refractometer	9
refractoriness	9
refractory	9
refuse	20
regenerant solution	20
regenerated cellulose	4
regeneration	1, 20
heat	9
regenerative air heater	9
regenerative braking	13
register	9, 19
regression	25
multiple	25
sizing	14
regression equation	25

regression line	25
regrinding	7
regulating box	12, 13
regulating lip	13
regulator load	7
reheater	9
rehumidifying	13
reinforced paper	16
reinforcement pulp	13
reinforcing agent	17
reinjection	9
reject gate	18
reject rate	12
reject refining	7
rejects,	
knotter	12
rayon	12
screen	12
reject sulfonation process	7
relative absorbency	11
relative bonded area	11
relative density	23
relative humidity (of paper)	14
relative obsolescence	23
relative reaction rate	8
relative sediment volume	17
relative stability (of paper)	14
relaxation	14
stress	14
tension	13
release	1
release aid	13
release coating	17
release papers	16
release properties	13
reliability	23
operational	24
relief	8
digester	8
edge	13
side	8
relief printing	19
reload yard	1
remanufacture	24
reoxygenation	20
repeatability	14
repellancy,	
oil	14
water	14
replicates	14
replication	14
replenishment coating system	17
representative sample	14
reprocess winding	18
reproducibility	14
reproduction papers	16
reprographic papers	16
reprography	19
repulpability	12

repulper,	
attrition-type	13
dry broke	13
repulping	12
rereeler	18
research,	
applied	23
basic	23
market	23
operations	23
resenes	6
reservoir	24
residual	25
residual alkali	8
residual bleach demand	10
residual chemical	10
residual chips	1
residual condensate	13
residual delignification	8
residual fuel oil	9
residual lignin	8, 10
residual pulping liquor	8
residuals management	20
residual stand	1
residual variation	14
residue(s)	4
agricultural	3
forest	1
logging	1
wood	1, 8
resiliency	13, 14
resin(s)	2, 5
acrylamide	5
alkyd	17
amino	5
dry-strength	5
ion exchange	20
melamine-formaldehyde	5
phenolic	18
urea-formaldehyde	5
wet-strength	5
resin acid	6
resin acid soap	6
resin ducts	2
resin emulsions	5
resinous wood	2
resin tapping	6
resistance	22
abrasion	14
air	14
bending	14
blister	17
blocking	17
crushing	14
delamination	14
dielectric	14
drainage	11
dry rub	14
filtration	11
flat crush	14
flex fatigue	13

resistance *(cont)*
  flow 12, 13
  fracture 14
  ink 14
  pick 14
  puncture 14

  scuffing 14
  wear 14
  wet pick 14
  wet rub 14
resistance to disintegration 11

resistance to liquid penetrat'n 14
resistivity 21
resistor 22
resolution 14
resonance stiffness tester 14

respirable-size particulates 21
respiration 20
  endogenous 20
restraint 13
resultant wind 21

retainer 24
retention 13
  ash 13
  crease 14
  first-pass 13

  gloss 14
  initial 13
  overall 13
  single-pass 13
  system 13

  wet-strength 14
  wire 13
retention aid 5
retention time 10
  solids 20

retentiveness 14
reticulate 2
retree 14
retrofit 23
retrogradation 5

retting 3
return on investment 26
return sludge 20
reverse air baghouse 21
reverse angle doctor blade 17

reverse flow 12
reverse-flow cleaner 12
reverse press 13
reverse roll coating 17
reverse sizing 5

reversible reaction 4
reversing nip 13
reversion 10
  brightness 10, 14
  color 10

rewetting 13
rewetting agent 17
rewinder 18
Reynolds number 23
rheology 13

rheology control agent 17
rheopexy 17
rheostat 22
rhytidome 2
riceing 13

rich white water 13
rick 1
ricked 1
rider roll 13
ridge 14, 15

riding ring 9
riffler 12
rigging 1
  butt 1
right-handed paper machine 13

right side (of paper) 18
rigid boxes 18
rigidity 14
rimming 13
rimming speed 13

rimming thickness 13
ring crush 14
Ringelmann number 21
ring grinder 7
ring-porous wood 2

rings 9
  drying 11
  scalping 1
ring-shaped pile 1
ring shear barker 1

rinse 20
ripping 1
ripple finish 18
riser 9
rising film evaporator 9

risk 26
  consumer's 26
  producer's 26
risk assessment 23
rod coating 17

rodding 9
rod mill 12
Roe number 10
roll(s) 13
  alignment 13

  antideflection 13
  applicator 17
  backing 17
  backup 17
  beater 12

  bed 13
  blow 13
  blowing 13
  bottom 13
  bowed 13

  breaker 18
  breast 13, 17
  butting 1
  calender 13
  carrying 13

roll(s) *(cont)*
  chill 17
  controlled crown 13
  controlled deformation 13
  couch 12, 13
  couch draw 13

  covered 13
  crowding 1
  crushed 14
  cull 13
  curved 13

  damping 13
  dancer 12
  dandy 13
  dented 14
  dip 17

  dished 14
  distributor 13, 17
  diverted 13
  doctor 17
  draw 17, 18

  drive 13
  evener 17
  expander 13
  felt 13
  filled 13

  flat 14
  flow evener 13
  forming 13
  forward drive 13
  fountain 17

  gate 17
  granite 13
  guide 13
  hard 13
  hitch 13

  hold down 17
  holey 13
  honeycomb 13
  household 18
  idler 13

  impression 17
  intermediate 13, 17
  jumbo 13
  king 13
  kiss 17

  loadcell 17
  lump breaker 13
  making 13
  marking 13
  metering 17

  mill 13
  nip 12
  nip-out 13
  out-of-round 14
  pan 17

  parent 13
  peeler 13
  perforated 13
  pickup 17
  plain 13

roll(s) *(cont)*

press		13
pressure		13
pulp		12
queen		13
receptor		13
rectifier		13
reef		13
rider		13
scissored		13
self-skinning		13
set of		13
sheet		18
Sheraton		13
soft		14
solid		13
spreader		13
spring		13
squeeze		13
starred		14
stretch		13
stub		13
suction		13
swimming		13
swing		13
table		13
takeoff		12
take-up		13
telescoped		14
tension sensing		17
transfer		17
turning		13
variable crown		13
wash		13
water-damaged		14
wire return		13
wire turning		13
worm		13
zone control		13

roll back   7
roll balancing   13

roll-bend'g crown compensat'n   13
roll coater,

gate		17
hydrophilic		17
squeeze		17
transfer		17
two-		17

roll coating   17

differential		17
kiss		17
reverse		17
smoothing		17

roll cover   13
roll curl   18
roll damage   14

roll density   13
rolled edge   14
roll edges   13
roll ejector   13

roller   13

cooling		19
cushion form		19
dead shaft		24
ductor		19
form		19
infeed		19
live shaft		24
nipping		18

roller press   18
roller stripping   19

roll finishing   13
roll former   13
roll grinding   13
roll grinding machine   13
roll handling   13

roll hardness   13
roll hardness measurements   13
rolling,

dry		13
hot		13
wet		13

rolling friction   13
rolling shear strength   14
roll kicker   13
roll number   13

roll-out fourdrinier   13
roll paper   13
roll position   13
roll pulp   12
roll quality   14

roll specialties   16
roll specifications   13
roll splitter   13
roll stand   19

auxiliary		19
tandem		19

rollstock   18
roll structure   13
roll structure control   13
roll structure profile   13

roll-to-roll press   19
roll-type thickener   12
roll wrapping   13
roof air   13
roofing felt   16

rooster tails   13
rope carrier   13
rope fiber   3
rope marks   14
ropes   14

ropiness   13
roping (of a felt)   13
rosin   6

fortified		5
free		5
gum		6
tall oil		6
wood		6

rosin dispersions   5
rosin emulsions   5

rosin oil   6
rosin size   5
rosin specks   14
rosin spirits   6
Ross diagram   8

Rosserhead barker   1
rot   2

brown		2
butt		2
dry		2
soft		2
wet		2
white		2
wood		2

rotary-cut   1

rotary digesters   8
rotary drainer   12
rotary drum barker   1
rotary feeder   1
rotary hog fuel dryer   1

rotary paper   18
rotary pocket feeder   8
rotary press   19
rotary pressure joint   13
rotary pressure washer   12

rotary pump   24
rotary screen   1, 12
rotary slitter   13
rotary suction box   13
rotary vacuum filter   12

rotary vacuum washer   12
rotary valve   21
rotating biological contactor   20
rotating syphon   13
rotation   1

chip pile		1

rotational speed   7
rotational viscometer   17
rotogravure   19
rotogravure paper   16

rotonews   16
rotor   24
rough finished paper   14
rough lumber   1
roughness   14

felt		15

roughness profile   14
roughness ratio   14
roughness tester   14
roughwood   1

roundness   13
roundness factor   2
round reducer   1
round robin testing   14
round warp   15

roundwood   1
rub-off   19
run   13, 19, 21

combination		19
felt		13
side		13

Runkel ratio 11
runnability 14
    paper machine 13
runnability test 14

running attitude 15
running in 17
rupture disc 24
rupture pick 19
rushed 13

rust-inhibitor papers 16
rutile 5

S _____

sabai grass 3
saccharide 4
    mono- 4
    oligo- 4
    poly- 4

saccharification 4
saccharinic acids 4
sack 18
sack paper 16
sad colors 14

saddle 13
safety audit 23
safety paper 16
safety valve 24
saleable mass (of pulp) 12

salinity 20
salt 4
saltcake 9
saltcake-free 9
salt removal 9

salvage 20
salvage cutting 1
salvage logging 1
salvage winder 18
sample 14

    blow 8, 13
    composite 11
    cumulative 21
    grab 11
    outturn 14

    random 11
    reel 14
    representative 14
sample book 18
sampler 1

    bulk 1
    high-volume 21
sample plot 1
sample room 14
sample thief 1

sampling 14
    automatic 20
    continuous 21
    intermittent 21
    isokinetic 21

random 25
source 21
systematic 25
wedge 11
sampling fraction 25

sampling train 21
sand separator 8
sanitary sewer 20
sanitary tissue 16
Sankey balance 13

sap 2
sapling 1
saponification 6
saponification number 6
saponins 4

sap peeling 1
sapwood 2
sateen 15
satellite chip mill 1
satin finish 14

satin white 5
saturated air 13
saturated compound 4
saturated moisture 15
saturated solution 4

saturated steam 9
saturating capacity 14
saturating papers 16
saturating properties 14
saturation 14

    oxygen 20
    wet web 13
saveall 12
saveall tray 13
saw 1

    band 1
    chain 1
    circular 1
    cutoff 1
    frame 1
    web 1

saw-blade flow channel 13
sawdust 1
sawdust digester 8
sawdust pulping 8

sawdust refiner pulp 7
sawing 1
    gang 1
sawlog 1
sawmill residuals 1

sawyer 1
scab 13
    drum 17
scab mark 14
scaffolding 24

scalariform 2
scale 9, 14
    baume hydrometer 9
    belt conveyor 1
    log 1

soluble 9
    totalizing belt 1
scaler 1
scale of turbulence 13
scaling 8, 9, 13

scaling tendency 9
scalping rings 1
scalping screen 1, 12
scanning gauge 13
scarf 1

scarification 1
scattering power 11
scatter plot 25
scheduled maintenance 24
Schiel plot 13

Schopper-Riegler slowness 11
scissored rolls 13
sclereid 2
scooping 13
scoring 13, 18

scotch 18
scraper screen 12
scrap in roll 14
scrapping 24
screen(s) 12, 19

    bar 12
    basket 12
    belt 20
    bull 7
    centrifugal 12

    chip 1
    curved 12
    disc 1
    dryer 13
    flat 12

    furnace 9
    gravity centrifugal 12
    gyratory 1
    organic 20
    pressure 12

    primary 12
    reciprocating 1
    rotary 1, 12
    scalping 1, 12
    scraper 12

    secondary 12
    sidehill 12
    slag 9
    Somerville 11
    traveling 20
    vibratory 12

screen accepts 12
screen angle 19
screen basket 12
screening 12, 19

    barrier 12
    black stock 12
    closed 12
    coarse 12
    double 12

screening *(cont)*		second	14	semi-closed screening	12
fine	12	secondary arms	13	semicoated printing paper	16
hot-stock	12	secondary cleaners	12	semi-creping	13
inter-stage	12	secondary creping	13	senior-size sheets	18
medium-consistency	12	secondary effluent	20	sensible heat	13
probability	12				
semi-closed	12	secondary fiber	12	sensitivity analysis	26
		secondary headbox	13	sensitized	14
screening efficiency	12	secondary hydroxyl group	4	sensitized papers	16
screening quotient	12	secondary pollutants	21	sensor	24
screenings	12	secondary screens	12	chromatic	10
screen plate	12				
		secondary shaveoff	21	optical	10
screen rejects	12	secondary sludge	20	polargraphic chemical	10
screen room	12	secondary treatment	20	sensory properties	14
screen tailings	12	secondary treatment efficiency	20	separating papers	16
screw conveyor	1	secondary wall	2	separating tissues	16
screw extractor	12				
		secondary winder	13	separation negative	19
screw feeder	1	second growth	1	separator	13
scrub	1	section	1	air density	1
scrubber	21	breaker bar	7	air flotation	1
charged droplet	21	chain	9	cyclone	1, 21
dry	21				
		cross	2	cyclone steam	7
fluid bed	21	dryer	13	entrainment	21
gas	21	forming	13	inclined	8
steam	9	multitube	13	inclined plate	20
tail gas	10	quarter	1	inertial	21
Venturi	21				
		radial	2	lamella	20
scuffing	13	solidification	17	sand	8
scuffing resistance	14	tangential	2	steam	9, 13
scuff mark	14	transverse	2	top	8
scum	20	vat	13	septate fiber	2
scumming	19				
		sectional drive	13	septic	20
scutching	3	sectioning	14	sequential chlorination	10
seal	24	security paper	16	sequential velocity refiner	7
clearance	24	sediment	20	sequestering agent	10
dry-running	24	sedimentation	20	serial correlation	25
labyrinth	24				
		sedimentation basin	20	serpentine fabric	13
mechanical	24	sedimentation clarifier	20	serrated slice	13
o-ring	24	sedimentation thickener	20	serviceability	24
static	24	sediment concentration	20	service life	24
sealability	14	sediment volume	17	services lost time	13
seal assembly	24				
		seed fiber	3	sesquiterpene	6
seal box	12	seed flax	3	setback	17
seal bushing	24	seeding	20	set-off	19
seal chamber	12	seedling	1	set of rolls	13
sealed	18	seed tree cutting	1	set time	18
sealing strength	18				
		seizing	24	setting	18
seal leg	6	selective condensation	20	curl	7
seal tank	12	selective cutting	1	settleable solids	20
seal water	24	selective ion electrode	4	settling	20
seam	15	selective leaching	24	flocculent	20
clipper	15				
		selective wettability	19	free	20
felt	13	selectivity	8	zone	20
loop	15	self-loader	1	settling chamber	21
pin	15	self-pressurization	7	setup boxes	18
spiral	15	self-sizing	11, 14	sewage	20
warp loom	15				
		self-skinning roll	13	sewer	20
seasoned paper	14	semi-bleach pulp	10	combined	20
seasoning	11	semichemical mechanical pulp'g	7	main	20
steam	14	semichemical pulp	8	sanitary	20
seasoning (of wood)	1	semichemical pulping	8	shaded watermark	13
Secchi disc	20				

shadow marking	13	
shadows	19	
shaft	15, 24	
core	13	
shaft coating	17	
shaftless mounting	18	
shaftless winding	13	
shaft power	22	
shaft streaks	17	
shake	13	
shake-deflate baghouse	21	
shakedown operation	23	
shakeup steam	8	
shanker	13	
shape factor	11	
shape tolerance	13	
sharpening	7	
sharpening schedule	7	
sharpness	19	
shatter steam	9	
shaving	1	
shavings	12	
shear	1, 14	
cambium	1	
shear blocking	17	
shear plane strength	14	
shear thickening	17	
shear thinning	17	
shear wrinkles	13	
sheave	1, 24	
shed	15	
sheen	14	
sheet(s)	13, 14, 18	
air-laid	13	
bottom sided	14	
cut-size	18	
duplex	13	
filled	14	
flow	23	
folio-size	18	
free	14	
loaded	14	
senior-size	18	
simplex	13	
spongy	14	
square	14	
test	14	
top sided	14	
sheet calendering	18	
sheet consolidation	13	
sheet cooler	12	
sheeter	18	
duplex	18	
precision	18	
simplex	18	
sheet-fed press	19	
sheet flutter	13	
sheet following	13	
sheeting	18	
custom	18	

sheet release	13	
sheet roll	18	
sheet sealing	13	
sheet separation	13	
sheet shrinkage	13	
sheet splitter	14	
sheet stability	13	
sheet stealing	13	
sheet stratification	13	
sheet structure	13	
sheet takeoff	12	
sheet tension	13	
sheet transfer	13	
sheet wetting shower	13	
shelf life	17	
shell	9	
shell marking	13	
shellside	9	
Sheraton roll	13	
shim	1	
shiner	11	
shiners	14	
shive	11	
shive content	11	
shive count	11	
shive detector	12	
shivey pulp	11	
shock	3	
shock loading	20	
shock-pulse measurement	24	
shoe peg	1	
shooting	9	
short circulation	13	
short column test	14	
short dwell	17	
short dwell coater	17	
shortening (of fiber)	11	
short fiber	12	
short former	13	
short grain	18	
short ink	19	
short-rotation intens. culture	1	
short-sequence bleaching	10	
short-span tensile analysis	14	
short-span tensile curves	14	
short stock	12	
shortwood	1	
shortwood logging	1	
shower(s),		
air	13	
deluge	13	
flooded nip	13	
flooding	13	
formation	13	
knock-off	13	
lubricating	13	
needle	13	
purgeable	13	
sheet wetting	13	
steam	13	

washer	12	
wetting	13	
whistle	12	
weir	12	
showering	13	
face-side	13	
inside	13	
show-through	14	
shredded paper	16	
shredder	1, 12	
bark	1	
shredding,		
chip	1	
dry	12	
wet	12	
shrinkage	10, 12, 13	
free	11	
sheet	13	
shrink-sleeve press	13	
shutdown	13	
emergency	9, 23	
shute	15	
shute-faced fabric	15	
shute-runner	15	
shute-support fabric	15	
shut-in	8	
shuttle	15	
siccative	19	
side,		
back	13	
far	19	
felt	14	
front	13	
galvanized wire	14	
near	19	
printing	14	
right	18	
tending	13	
top	14	
wire	14	
side frame	7	
sidehill screen	12	
side loading	13	
side relief	8	
side run	13	
sieve tube	2	
sight glass	24	
sigmoid absorption curves	11	
signal	25	
signature	19	
significance test	25	
significant emission level	21	
silencer	24	
silica	5	
silica gel	10	
silicate	5	
silicating	18	
silicon carbide	7	
silk screen printing	19	

432

silo	1	pigment	17	slice gap	13
chip	1	reverse	5	slice geometry	13
silurian effect	13	self	11, 14	slice lip	13
silvichemicals	6	surface	13	slice mark	14
silviculture	1	top	14	slice nozzle	13
simple perforation	2				
		tub	13	slice opening	13
simple pit	2	vapor	13	slick	14
simplex sheet	13	sizing regression	14	slick finish	14
simplex sheeter	18	sizing test	14	slider bed	1
simulated watermark	14	ink flotation	14	sliding spreader	13
simulation	23	water immersion	14		
				slime	5
single coated	17	skating	13, 18	biological	20
single-drum boiler	9	skewed distribution	25	slime control	5
single face	18	skid	18	slime deposits	5
single facer	18	skidder	1	slime hole	14
fingerless	18	skidding	1		
		ground	1	slime spot	14
single finishing stack	13	skim	14	slimicide	5
single lined	14	skimming	20	sling psychrometer	13
single-line mill	23	skimming tank	20	slip	13, 14, 17
single-pass retention	13	skin	14	coating	17
single-phase circuit	22				
		skinning	13, 19	slippage	15, 18
single-sheet caliper	14	skipped suction	14	slippery	14
single-tier dryers	13	skips	17, 19	slipping	12
sinker log	1	skiver winder	18	slip plane	11
sinking time test	11	skiving	18	slip sorting	18
sintering (of size precipitate)	5				
		skyline carriage	1	slip test	14
sisal	3	skyline logging	1	slitter	13
site preparation	1	slab	1, 12	laser	13
SI units	23	slabbing	18	rotary	13
size	5	slabbing off	13	water jet	13
acid	5				
		slab-off losses	13	slitter band	13
acid-stable	5	slab press	12	slitter blade	13
alkaline	5	slack area	13, 15	slitter cuts	13
animal	5	slack draw	13	slitter-cutter	18
basic	18	slack edges	14	slitter dust	13
Bewoid	5				
		slack sized	14	slitter edge	18
fluorocarbon	5	slack start	14	slitter jump	13
neutral	5	slack tension	15	slitter rings	13
paste	5	slag	9	slitter runout	13
reactive	5	slagging properties	9	slitter table	13
rosin	5				
		slag screen	9	slitting	13
stock	18	slaked lime	9	slitting tolerance	18
synthetic	5	slaker	9	slit width	11
wax	5	slaking	9	sliver	1, 7
sized,		slash	1	slope	9
hard	14	ground	1		
				slope angle	1
slack	14	slash burning	1	sloshing	13
soft	14	slasher	1	slot	18
size precipitant	5	slashing	1	slot orifice coater	17
size press	13	S-layers	2	slotted plate	12
gate roll	17				
		sleazy	15	slotter	18
size press coater	17	sleek	20	sloughing	20
size specks	14	slenderness ratio	14	slow	11
sizing	13	slewing	1	slow beating	11
calender	13	slice	13	slowdown	13
degree of	14				
		auto	13	slowness	11
direct	5	nozzle	13	Schopper-Riegler	11
double	13	serrated	13	sludge	9, 20
engine	13	slice coefficient	13	activated	20
fugitive	14	slice edge bleed	13	biological	20
internal	13				

sludge *(cont)*		SO₂,		solid roll	13
bleach	10	aqueous	8	solids	9, 20
chemical	20	combined	8	dissolved	20
conditioned	20	free	8	fixed	20
dewatered	20	total	8	floatable	20
digested	20				
		soakiness	19	liquor	9
excess	20	soap,		nonsettleable	20
heavy	20	fatty acid	6	settleable	20
hydrous	20	resin acid	6	suspended	20
primary	20	tall oil	6	total	20
raw	20				
		soda ash	8	volatile	20
return	20	soda ash pulping	8	volatile organic	20
secondary	20	soda inventory	9	solids content	17
thickened	20	soda makeup	9	solids loading	20
treated	20	soda-oxygen pulping	8	solids retention time	20
sludge cake	20				
		soda pulping	8	solid state coating	17
sludge digestion	20	sodium aluminate	5	solid waste	20
sludge pit	20	sodium base liquor	8	solid waste disposal	20
sludge volume index	20	sodium borate	5	solubility	4
slug	9	sodium carbonate	8	alkali	11
slug hole	14				
		sodium chlorate	10	caustic	11
sluiceway	1	sodium chlorite	10	NaOH	8
sluicing	20	sodium hydrosulfide	8	soluble base	8
sluicing liquor	8	sodium hydroxide	8	soluble scale	9
slurring	19	sodium oxide	8	solute	4
dot	19				
		sodium silicate	5	solute exclusion technique	11
slurry	12	sodium sulfate	8	solution(s)	4
slurry filter	17	sodium sulfide	8	chlorine dioxide	10
slurry pigments	17	soft calendering	13	dampening	19
slush	12	soft cook	8	fountain	19
slusher	12				
		soft end	14	regenerant	20
slushing	12	softening	20	saturated	4
small log mill	1	thermal	7	standard	4
smashed blanket	19	water	20	tracer	20
smashed bulk	14	softening agent	5	viscose	4
smearing	19				
		soft fiber	3	solvation	5
smectite	5	soft fold	18	solvent	17
smelt	9	soft hardwoods	2	solvent-base ink	19
smelt bed	9	softness,		solvent bonding	13
smelt dissolving tank	9	bulk	14	solvent coating	17
smelt spout	9	surface	14		
				solvent extraction process	12
smelt/water explosion	9	softness (of paper)	14	solvent pulping	8
Smith needle	14	softness (of pulp)	11	Somerville screen	11
smog	21	soft process	13	sonic sheet tester	14
smoke	9	soft roll	14	soot	9
smoothing press	13				
		soft rot	2	soot blower	9
smoothing roll coating	17	soft sized	14	sorbed soda	12
smoothness	14	soft spot	14	sorbed water	11
optical	14	softwood	2	sorghum	3
printing	19	softwood pulp	12	sorption	20
smudging	19				
		sol	5	sorption cooking	8
snag	1	solenoid valve	24	sorting	1, 12, 18
snailing	14	soleplate	13	slip	18
snaking	13, 15	solid board	14	sort yard	1
snap	14, 19	solid density	1	sound	23
snapoff	13				
		solid fiber box	18	sounding (of a reel)	14
snapometer	14	solid fraction	14	sound wood	1
snap test	14	solidification section	17	source	21
snow	21	solid lubricants	24	point	21
snowflaking	19	solid print	19	source sampling	21
snowstorm	14				

sour-coated paper	17	rotational	7	spray coating	17
southern pine	1	wire	13	spray cooling	8
soy protein	17	speed-up	13	spray dyeing	13
spalling	9, 24	spent pulping liquor	8	sprayer	24
spanished embossing	17	spent sulfite liquor	8	spraying,	
spanishing	17	spherical digester	8	plasma	24
spar	1	spider	24	thermal	24
sparger	20	spill	20	spray nozzle	24
spear	13	spill collection system	20	spread coating	17
specialties,		spill pond	20	spreader,	
groundwood	16	spinning paper	16	chip	8
paperboard	16	spiral fabric	15	fan-type	13
roll	16	spiral heat exchanger	9	folding-type	18
specialty papers	16	spiral laid dandy roll	13	sliding	13
species	2	spiral seam	15	spreader bar	13
commercial	1	spiral thickening	2	spreader roll	13
wood	1	spiral winding	18	spreading	13
specifications	13, 25	spits	17	springback	11, 14
attribute	25	splash plate	9	spring roll	13
color	14	splice	13	springwood	2
roll	13	butt	18	spud	1
winder	13	defective	14	spun yarn	15
specific collection area	21	festoon	18	squared paper	18
specific edge loading	12	flying	18	squareness	18
specific energy	7, 9	lap	18	square sheet	14
net	12	splicing	13	squeeze	19
specific external surface	11	split coating	17	squeeze-out	19
specific filter loading	20	splitter	1	squeeze roll coater	17
specific filtration resistance	11	roll	13	squeeze rolls	13
specific gravity	23	sheet	14	squirts	13
specific loading	12	splitting	11, 19	stability	15
specific nip pressure	13	film	17	atmospheric	21
specific surface	11	split-top felt	13	base stock	17
internal	11	spoilage	19	brightness	10
specific tensile strength	14	spoiler bars	13	cross	15
specific volume	11	spongy sheet	14	dimensional	14
hydrodynamic	11	spontaneous combustion	1	fabric	15
specific volume curve	7	spool	13	foam	12
specific wood consumption	13	reel	13	hygro	14
specimen	14	spool starter	13	longitudinal	15
speckle	19	spore	5	relative	14
speckling	19	spot(s)	14	sheet	13
specks	14	alum	14	stabilization	5, 20
bark	14	backing roll	17	stabilization tank	9
binder	17	calender	14	stabilizer	5
rosin	14	dead	14	stack	9, 13
size	14	drag	14	breaker	13
spectrophotometer	14	foam	17	calender	13
spectrophotometric curve	14	greasy	14	single finishing	13
specular gloss	14	low	19	vent	9
				vomit	8
specular reflectance	14	pitch	14	stack dilution ratio	21
speed,		slime	14	stacked dryers	13
base	24	thin	14	stack effect	9
collapsing	13	soft	14	stack effluent	21
crawl	13	water	14		
		wax	14	stacker	1, 18
critical	13			stack gas	21
machine	13	spot coating	17	stacking	13, 18
paper machine	13	spot color	19	pick	15
peripheral	7	spot detector	18	stack test	21
rimming	13	spouting	13		

435

stage	10	
bleaching	10	
chlorination	10	
combination	10	
diffusion	10	
extraction	10	
neutralization	10	
ozonation	10	
staggered winding	14	
stain	2	
deckle	13	
Herzberg	11	
staining	2	
stainless steels	24	
stair-step cut	18	
stalactites	17	
stalk	3	
stand	1	
back	13	
defective	1	
mixed	1	
residual	1	
roll	19	
unwind	13	
standard(s),		
calibration	14	
cost	26	
effluent	20	
emission	20	
primary	14	
stream	20	
standard conditions	11, 21	
standard cost	26	
standard costing	26	
standard deviation	25	
standard environment	11	
standard error	25	
standard grammage	14	
standardization	4, 23	
standardized	14	
standard pulp	11	
standard solution	4	
standard test procedure	14	
stand density	1	
standpipe	24	
staple fiber	15	
stapling	13	
starch	5	
acetylated	5	
aldehyde	5	
ampholytic	5	
anionic	5	
cationic	5	
modified	5	
oxidized	5	
pearl	5	
preconverted	5	
pregelatinized	5	
thick-boiling	5	
thin boiling	5	

starch conversion	5	
starch derivatives	5	
starred roll	14	
starter	22	
startup	13	
startup costs	26	
starved	23	
starved joint	18	
static electricity	14	
static foam	12	
static friction	18	
static grounding	22	
static mixer	10	
static pressure	21	
static seal	24	
station,		
coating	17	
forming	13	
windup	13	
wrapping	18	
stationary firing	9	
stationary friction barker	1	
stationary syphon	13	
stationery	16	
statistic	25	
statistical analysis	25	
statistical inference	25	
statistical process control	25	
statistical quality control	25	
statistics	25	
stator	24	
status quo	23	
steady state	23	
steam	9	
backflow	7	
blow-through	7, 13	
dry	9	
flash	9	
live	9	
motive	13	
process	9	
purging	9	
saturated	9	
shakeup	8	
shatter	9	
suction	13	
superheated	9	
wet	9	
steam accumulator	9	
steam balance	9	
steam binding	9	
steam calendering	13	
steam cylinder	13	
steam demand	9	
steam distillation	20	
steam-distilled turpentine	6	
steam distribution	9	
steam drum	9	
steam drying	12	
steam economy	9, 13	

steam finished	14	
steam generating efficiency	9	
steam generating unit	9	
steam hammer	9	
steaming	8	
direct	8	
indirect	8	
two-stage	8	
steaming rate	9	
steaming tube	7	
steaming vessel	8	
steam-jet refrigeration	10	
steam joint	13	
steam-phase digester	8	
steam power	22	
steam recompression	13	
steam scrubber	9	
steam seasoning	14	
steam separator	9, 13	
cyclone	7	
steam shower	13	
steam stripping	20	
steam system,		
cascade	13	
thermocompressor	13	
steam tracing	24	
steam trap	9	
steam tubes	9	
steam washer	9	
stearate(s)	17	
aluminum	17	
ammonium	17	
steep brightening	10	
stem	1	
stem fiber	3	
step flow channel	13	
stereochemistry	4	
stereoscopy	11	
stereotype	19	
stereotype dry mat	16	
sterilization	20	
stethoscope	24	
stick	1	
stickies	12	
stickiness (fireside deposits)	9	
sticking of sheets	19	
sticky ash	9	
stiffening agent	18	
stiffness	14	
elastic	14	
fiber	11	
handling	14	
tensile	14	
ultrasonic	14	
stilbene	6	
stippling	18	
stock	12, 18, 19	
accepted	12	
base	17	
body	17	

stock *(cont)*
brown 8
center 13
cut 18
folder 16
greeting card 16

grey 12
growing 1
hard 12
high-density 12
hydrated 12

napkin 16
paper 12
pulper 12
short 12
sweetener 13

tag 16
thin 13
ticket 16
wet 11
wrapper 12

stock blending 12
stock cleaning 12
stock jams 13
stock jump 13
stock metering 13

stock preparation 12
stock preparation area 12
stock proportioning 13
stock pump 12
thick 12

stock size 18
stock wave 13
stock weights 18
stoichiometric mixture 9
stoker 9

traveling grate 9
stone 7
stone cell 2
stone groundwood 7
pressurized 7

stone sharpening 7
stone submergence 7
stopping reaction 4
storage,
buffer 12

bulk 1
cold 14
high-density 12
outside chip 1
pulp 12

storage acid 8
storage capacity 12
storied 2
stowage 1
stowage factor 1

straightening vanes 9
straight-through press 13
strain 14
built-in 14
dried-in 14

strained formation 14
strainer 8, 12
coating color 17
straining 12
strain gauge 24

straining rate 14
strand 15
strand number 15
strands 1
strapping 18

strategic planning 23
stratified batt 15
stratified jet 13
stratified web 13
stratified web forming 13

straw 3
cereal 3
flax 3
strawboard 16
streak(s) 14

applicator roll 17
blade 17
calender 14
coating 17
dye 14

shaft 17
wet 14, 17
streaming potential 5
streamline flow 13
stream standards 20

strength,
adhesion 18
biaxial 14
bleach liquor 10
bonding 11, 18

bursting 14
coloring 13
column 14
compression 14
creasing 14

delamination 14
dynamic 14
edgewise compression 14
fatigue 14
fiber 11

fiber network 11
flexing 14
folding 14
impact 14
interfiber bond 14

internal bond 14
intrinsic fiber 11
paper 14
rolling shear 14
sealing 18

shear plane 14
surface 14
tearing 14
tensile 14
torsion shear 14

wet 14
wet web 11
white liquor 8
z- 14
strength properties 14

stress 14
stress concentration 14
stress cracking 24
stress fatigue 24
stress relaxation 14

stress-strain curve 14
stress-strain properties 14
stretch 14
all-direction 14
damping 13

elastic 14
ultimate 14
stretch at break 14
stretch roll 13
striations 2, 17

strike-in 19
strike-through 17, 18, 19
stringiness 18
stringing 15
strings 13

stripes,
machine mark 13
tariff regulation 13
stripping 13, 19, 20
air 21

roller 19
steam 21
stripping column 20
stroboscope 24
strong black liquor 9

structural curl 14
structure 13
chemical 4
coating 17
felted 13

fiber 2
hydraulic 23
layered 13
microfibrillar 2
paper 13

pulpstone 7
roll 13
sheet 13
ultra- 2
structured pigment 17

stub roll 13
stuck web 14
studs 1
study estimate 26
stuff 13

stuff box 13
stuffer yarn 15
stuff gate 13
stuffing box 24
stump 1

stumpage	1	sulfonated chemi-mech. pulping	7	surface coloring	13
styrene-butadiene latex	17	sulfonation	8	surface condenser	9
subjective gloss	14	degree of	7	surface drive	13
subjective tests	14	sulfur	8	surface fatigue	24
sublethal toxicity	20	reducible	14	surface hardening	13
		total reduced	21		
sublimation	9, 19			surface loading	20
submergence,		sulfur bacteria	5	surface pH	14
drum	12	sulfur burner	8	surface properties	14
stone	7	sulfur dioxide	8	surface roughness factor	17
submersion coating	17	sulfuric acid	10	surface sizing	13
substance	14	sulfurous acid	8	surface softness	14
substance yield factor	12	sulfurous acid treatment	10	surface strength	14
substantivity	4	surfur-reducing bacteria	5	surface strength tester	14
substation	22	sulfur trioxide	8	surface tension	5
substitution reaction	4	sulky	1	surface void volume	17
substrate	17, 18	summerwood	2	surface water	20
printing	19	sump	20	surfacing	15
subtractive primary colors	19	Sunday drive	13	surfactant	5
suction box	13	sunn hemp	3	surge	23
dry	13	superabsorbents	5	surge tank	23
rotary	13				
		supercalender,		surging	8
suction box deckle	13	closed frame	13	survey,	
suction couch	13	double-finishing	13	aerial	1
suction dredge	20	open frame	13	drying system	13
suction forces,		supercalendering	13	microbiological	5
hydrodynamic	13	superficial flow	12	photographic	13
vacuum	13	super glazed finish	14	suspended solids	20
suction former	13	superheated steam	9	mixed liquor	20
suction head	24	superheater	9	suspension	17
net suction	14	pendent-tube	9	fiber	13
suction lift	24	superimposed profiles	14	suspension firing	9
suction line	24	supering	13	suspensoids	20
suction pickup	13	supernatant liquid	20	sustained yield	1
suction press	13	supernews	16	maximum	20
suction roll	13	supply air	13	swatch	18
suction roll former	13	supported sleeve	13	swatch book	18
suction roll noise	13	suppression	1	sweat dryer	13
suction roll strip	13	surface(s),		sweating	13
suction steam	13	curvilinear	12	sweetener stock	13
sugar	4	extended heat transfer	9	swell butted tree	1
sugar cane	3	fiber	11	swelling	5, 11
sulfamic acid	10	free	13	balloon	2
sulfate process	8	galvanized	14	degree of	11
sulfate pulp	8	grinding	7	swelling agent	4
sulfate-reducing bacteria	5	heating	9	swimming roll	13
sulfate turpentine	6	marble	14	swinging	1
sulfidation	8	specific	11	swinging load	9
sulfide	8	specific external	11	swing roll	13
sulfidity	8	surface activation	11	switch	22
sulfitation	8	surface active agent	5	sword hygrometer	14
sulfite process	8	surface activity	5	synergism	11
acid	8	surface aerator	20	synthesis	4
alkaline	8	surface analyzer	14	synthesized fiber	3
mono-	8	surface application	13	synthetic	5
multistage	8	surface area,		synthetic binders	17
neutral	8	active	13	synthetic dry-strength resins	5
two-stage	8	bonded fiber	11	synthetic filler	5
ultra high-yield	8	free fiber	11	synthetic latices	5
sulfite pulp	8	surface blowoff	9	synthetic lubricants	24
sulfonate content	7	surface charge	5	synthetic papermaking fiber	3

438

synthetic papers 14
    fiber-based 14
synthetic pulp 3
synthetic size 5
syphon 13

    rotating 13
    stationary 13
syphon shoe 13
system 23
systematic error 14

systematic sampling 25
system engineering 23
system retention 13
systems approach 23

T _____

table configuration 13
table harmonics 13
table roll 13
table roll baffle 13
tachometer 24

tack 18, 19
tackies 12
tackifier 18
tackle 1, 12
tack reducers 19

tactile properties 14
tag stock 16
tail 13
tail cutter 13
tail-end hook 19

tail gas 10
tail gas scrubber 10
tailings 12
    screen 12
tailrace 20

tainting 20
takeoff roll 12
take-up ratio 18
take-up roll 13
talc 5

tall oil 6
    acid-refined 6
    crude 6
    distilled 6
tall oil fatty acids 6

tall oil heads 6
tall oil pitch 6
tall oil precursors 6
tall oil rosin 6
tall oil skimmings 6

tall oil soap 6
tally 1
tandem roll stand 19
tandem thermomechanical pulp'g 7
tangential firing 9

tangential section 2
tank(s) 12
    blow 8
    continuous stirred 10
    detention 23

    dissolving 9
    draw-down 9
    dump 8
    filter 12
    flash 9

    foam 12
    holding 9
    level 8
    measuring 8
    radial-flow 20

    seal 12
    skimming 20
    smelt dissolving 9
    stabilization 9
    surge 23

tannins 6
tape paper 16
tapered inlet flowspreader 13
TAPPI opacity 14
tare weight 14

target plate 8
tariff regulation stripes 14
taxoid pit 2
T-bar support 13
tear index 14

tearing bond 18
tearing strength 14
tear outs 14
tear resistance,
    edge 14

    Elmendorf 14
    initial 14
    in-plane 14
    internal 14
technical audit 23

technical innovation 23
technical integration 23
technical papers 16
technical service 23
technical standards program 23

technological forecasting 23
technology 23
technology assessment 23
tee 24
telescoped core 14

telescoped roll 14
temperature,
    ignition 9
    liquidus 9
    time at 8

    time to 8
    wet bulb 13
temperature conditioning 19
temperature cycle 8
temperature-grad. calendering 13

tenacity 3
tender 14
tending side 13
tensile at fold 14
tensile energy absorption 14

tensile energy absorption index 14
tensile index 14
tensile stiffness 14
tensile strength 14
    specific 14

    wet 14
    zero-span 14
tensiometer 13
tension 13
    sheet 13

    slack 15
    surface 5
    web 13
    wound-in 13
tension burst 14

tension control 13
    winder 13
tension cycle 13
tension relaxation 13
tension sensing roll 17

tension wood 2
tension zone 18
teratogen 20
terminal conditions 10
terminal settling velocity 20

terpene alcohol 6
terpenes 6
tertiary 12
tertiary treatment 20
tertiary wall 2

test(s) 14
    abrasion 14
    accelerated 14
    accelerated aging 14
    acceptance 25

    aging 14
    burn out 17
    butyl carbitol 14
    chemical 14
    Cobb 14

    concora 14
    corrugating medium 14
    destructive 14
    drop 14, 18
    empirical 14

    end-use 14
    functional 14
    gap 14
    grease penetration 14
    heat curl 14

    helio- 19
    hydrostatic 9
    immersion 24
    incline impact 18
    ink penetration 14

test(s) *(cont)*
    ink rub resistance 19
    ink wipe 14
    jar 20
    kit 14
    microscopical 14

    NaOH solubility 8
    nondestructive 14
    oil penetration 14
    oil repellancy 14
    oil wicking 14

    optical 14
    paper 14
    pen and ink 14
    penescope 14
    performance 14

    pop 14
    runnability 14
    short column 14
    significance 25
    sinking time 11

    sizing 14
    slip 14
    snap 14
    stack 21
    subjective 14

    turpentine 14
    use 14
    vibration 18
    wildness 11
test accuracy 14

test determination 14
tester,
    air leak 14
    air resistance 14
    ballistic wet web 14

    Bristow 14
    chip 1
    dynamic puncture 14
    formation 14
    freeness 11

    hardness 13
    impulse 14
    linen 19
    liquid penetration 14
    Mullen 14

    pick 14
    resonance stiffness 14
    roughness 14
    surface strength 14
    torsion tear 14

    ultrasonic sheet 14
testing 14
    acoustical 14
    eddy current 24
    forced drape 14

    leak 24
    magnetic particle 24
    nondestructive 24
    proof 14
    radiographic 24

    round robin 14
    ultrasonic 24
test liner 16
test measurement 14
test method 14

test precision 14
test print 14
test result 14
test sensitivity 14
test sheet 14

test specimen 14
test train 21
test unit 14
textile plant fiber 3
text papers 16

texture 14
theodolite 24
theoretical air 9
theoretical commercial dryness 11
theoretical depreciation 26

theoretical production 13
thermal bonding 13
thermal coating 17
thermal conversion 5
thermal cycle 9

thermal cycling 9
thermal deactivation 9
thermal decomposition 4
thermal efficiency 9
thermal loading 9

thermal paper 16
thermal pollution 20
thermal power 22
thermal properties 14
thermal softening 7

thermal spraying 24
thermal vapor recompression 9
thermal watermarking 13
thermocompressor 13
thermocompressor steam sys 13

thermodynamics 22
    reaction 4
thermographic documentation 24
thermography 24
thermogrinding 7

thermomechanical chemi-pulp'g 7
thermomechanical pulping 7
    chemi- 7
    pressure/pressure 7
    tandem 7

thermophilic bacteria 5
thermoplanishing 13
thermoplastic 4
thermoplastic coating 17
thermoplastic laminating 18

thermo-refiner mech. pulping 7
thermosetting 4
thick black liquor 9
thick-boiling starch 5
thickened sludge 20

thickener 12, 20
    belt 12
    gravity 12
    roll-type 12
    sedimentation 20

thickening 12, 13
    helical 2
    shear 17
    spiral 2
thickening agent 17

thickening factor 12
thickening ratio 12
thickness 14
thickness calender 13
thick stock pump 12

thin 17
thin-boiling starch 5
thinning 1
    shear 17
thin papers 16

thin spots 14
thin stock 13
thiolignin 6
thiosulfate 8
third party maintenance 24

thixotropy 17
thrashing 3
thread,
    female 24
    male 24

threading 13
    air foil 13
    vacuum belt 13
three-phase circuit 22
threshold,

    lethal 20
    nuisance 21
    odor 21
throttling 24
through drying 13

throughput volume 20
thrust bearing 24
thrust load 24
thyristor 22
ticket stock 16

tickler refiner 12
tie layer 18
tie line 22
tier 18
tight area 15

tight draw 13
timber 1
timberland 1
timber rights 1
timbers 1

time,		
beating	12	
bleaching	10	
blend	12	
blow	8	
bond	18	
cooking	8	
detention	20	
drainage	11	
dryer dwell	17	
drying	18	
dwell	17	
flow-through	20	
impregnation	18	
lost	13	
open assembly	18	
retention	10	
set	18	
turn around	1	
up	23	
wetting	11	
time at temperature	8	
time series	25	
time to temperature	8	
timing valve	12	
tinctorial value	13	
tinny paper	14	
tinted	14	
tinted white	14	
tinting	19	
tissue(s)	2, 16	
carbonizing	16	
condenser	16	
facial	16	
flocking	16	
industrial	16	
interleaving	16	
lens	16	
sanitary	16	
separating	16	
toilet	16	
wrapping	16	
tissue machine	13	
titanium dioxide	5	
titration	4	
automatic	8	
potentiometric	4	
toe-in	13	
toilet tissue	16	
tolerance	14, 20	
cutting	18	
grammage	14	
impression	19	
shape	13	
slitting	18	
weight	14	
Tomlinson furnace	9	
tone	19	
continuous	19	
mass	19	

tone distortion	19	
toned paper	14	
tone value	14	
tongs	1	
tonne	23	
tooth	14	
top circulation system	8	
top colors	5	
top felt	13	
top liner	13	
top lip	13	
top log	1	
topochemical reaction	4	
topochemistry	4	
top paper	18	
topping	1, 13	
topping cycle	22	
top separator	8	
top side	14	
top sided sheet	14	
top sizing	14	
top-wire former	13	
torn-off paper	13	
torque	24	
differential	13	
torsion	14	
torsion tear tester	14	
torsion shear strength	14	
torula yeast	6	
torus	2	
total alkali	8	
totalizing belt scale	1	
total head	24	
total information system	23	
totally enclosed machine	24	
total organic carbon	20	
total organic chlorine	20	
total oxygen demand	20	
total reduced sulfur	21	
total solids	20	
total SO_2	8	
total titratable alkali	8	
tough check	16	
toughness	14	
fracture	14	
tour boss	13	
tow	3	
toweling	16	
tower	1, 8, 10	
acid	8	
bleaching	10	
cooling	20	
downflow	10	
fortifying	8	
upflow	10	
upflow-downflow	10	
tower packing	8	
towing	1	
toxicant	20	
toxicity	20	

acute	20	
chronic	20	
inhibitory	20	
sublethal	20	
toxicity equivalents	20	
toxicity level	20	
toxic waste	20	
trace	4	
tracer solutions	20	
trace substance	20	
trachea	2	
tracheid	2	
fiber	2	
ray	2	
vascular	2	
vasicentric	2	
tracing paper	16	
tracking	13	
railroad	17	
traction	13	
web	13	
trade name	23	
trade terminology	23	
trailing blade	17	
trailing blade coating	17	
trailing edge	13	
tram condition	7	
tramming	7	
tramp materials	12	
tramp metal	1	
transfer belt	13	
transfer felt	13	
transfer press	13	
transfer roll	17	
transfer roll coater	17	
transfer unwind	18	
transformer	22	
transformer/rectifier set	21	
transient state	23	
transit damage	14	
translucent	14	
transmission	22	
diffuse	14	
transmissometer	21	
transmittance	14	
transparency	14	
transparency ratio	14	
transparent ink	19	
transparentizing	18	
transport process	23	
transport velocity	21	
transversal flow press	13	
transverse direction	2	
transverse section	2	
trapping	19	
dry	19	
wet	19	
trash	20	
trash extractor	12	
trash rack	20	

travel	13
traveling grate stoker	9
traveling screen	20
traversing gauge	13
tray	13
saveall	13
tray column	21
tray water	13
treated sludge	20
tree(s)	1
bridge	7
broadleaf	2
deciduous	2
dominant	1
swell butted	1
tree combine	1
tree farm	1
tree farm license	1
tree harvesting machine	1
tree improvement,	
forest	1
genetic	1
tree-length logging	1
tribology	24
trichomes	3
trickling filter	20
trim	13
couch	13
maximum	13
trim allowance	1
trim chute	13
trim efficiency	13
trimmer	1, 18
bracket	18
trimming,	
edge	1
press	18
trimmings	13
edge	13
trim waste	18
trip	22
triple-layer fabric	15
triplex weave	15
tristimulus	14
tristimulus colorimeter	14
trolley	1
tropical hardwoods	1
tropolones	6
troubleshooting	24
troweling	17
truing	7
truck,	
clamp	18
fork-lift	18
trunk	1
trunnions	24
tub coloring	18
tube(s),	
boiler	9
branch	13

composite	9
diffuser	13
equalizing	9
fin	9
generating	9
preretention	10
sieve	2
steam	9
steaming	7
vortex	24
water	9
tube cooler	9
tube-in-shell heat exchanger	9
tube platen	9
tube settler	20
tubeside	9
tube-to-tube wall	9
tub sizing	13
tumble barking	1
tumblers	9
tunnel dryer	13
turbidity	20
turbine	22
axial flow	22
back pressure	22
condensing	22
extraction steam	22
gas	22
hydraulic	22
turbine agitator	24
turbine-generator	22
turboalternator	22
turbulence	13
atmospheric	21
intensity of	13
micro	13
scale of	13
turbulence generator	13
turbulence spectra	13
turbulent flow	13
turn	1
turn around time	1
turndown	23
turndown capability	23
turndown ratio	23
turning	7
turning point of steam	7
turning rod coating	17
turning roll	13
turning vanes	9
turnkey delivery	23
turnover	14
turntable	13
turn-up	13
turpentine	6
crude sulfate	6
destructively distilled	6
gum	6
refined sulfate	6
steam-distilled	6
sulfate	6

turpentine tapping	6
turpentine test	14
turret unwind	18
tuxy	3
tuxying process	3
twill	15
double	15
twinning	15
twin-wire former	13
twin-wire paper	14
twisting	11
two-blade coater	17
two-color printing	19
two-component wet-end system	13
two-drum winder	13
two-roll coater	17
two-sided coater	17
two-sidedness	14
two-stage steaming	8
two-stage sulfite process	8
two-temperature cooking	8
two-vessel digester	8
tylosis	2
tympan	19
typewriter paper	16
typography	19

U _____

ultimate biochem. oxy. demand	20
ultimate stretch	14
ultrafiltration	20
ultra high-yield sulfite proc.	8
ultra lightweight coated papers	16
ultrasonic sheet tester	14
ultrasonic stiffness	14
ultrasonic testing	24
ultrastructure	2
unaccounted for loss	9
unaccounted losses	13
unbeaten pulp	12
unbleached pulp	10
unburned combustible	9
uncalendered	14
uncertainty analysis	26
uncoated paper	14
uncoated weight	17
underburned lime	9
undercooked	8
undercut	1
undercutting	18
underfire air	9
underflow	6, 20
underliner	13

under-run 18
undersize chips 1
unglazed finish 14
uniflow vat 13
uniformity 11, 14

union 24
uniseriate ray 2
unit 1
  bone dry 1
unit cost 26

unitizing 18
unit load 18
unit loading rate 12
unit of product 25
unit operation 23

universal joint 24
universal testing machine 14
unloading 20
unoxidized black liquor 9
unsaponifiable matter 6

unsaponifiables 6
unsaturated compound 4
unscrambler 1
unsized paper 14
untrimmed 18

unwind,
  transfer 18
  turret 18
unwinding 13
unwind stand 13

upflow-downflow tower 10
upflow tower 10
up-milling 1
upright ray cell 2
upstream 23

uptake 13
up time 23
urea-formaldehyde resin 5
urena fiber 3
uronic acid 4

use tests (of paper) 14
utility air 24
utilization 23
utilizer 1

V —————————————

vacuum-assisted foil unit 13
vacuum belt threading 13
vacuum blower 13
vacuum box 13
vacuum breaker 20

vacuum capacity 13
vacuum coating 17
vacuum dryer 12
vacuum exhauster 13
vacuum pump 13
  liquid-ring 13

vacuum suction forces 13
vacuum system 13
vacuum washer 12
valence 4

value 14
  bulking 17
  calorific 9
  chelation 10
  critical 25

  dextrinizing 5
  fuel 9
  geometric mean 14
  heating 9
  mill net 26

  net present 26
  net realizable 26
  post color 11
  tinctorial 13
  tone 14

  water retention 11
  yield 17
value-added grades 16
value-added product 23
value analysis 26

value engineering 23
valve 12, 24
  automatic 24
  ball 24
  basis weight 13

  blow 8
  blowdown 13
  butterfly 24
  capping 8
  check 24

  circumferential 12
  composite 24
  diaphragm 24
  dump 24
  gate 24

  globe 24
  internal 12
  on-off 24
  plug 24
  pressure relief 24

  quick opening 24
  rotary 21
  safety 24
  solenoid 24
  timing 12

valveless filter 12
vanceometer 14
vanes,
  straightening 9
  turning 9

vanillin 6
vapor 21
  water 13
vapor absorption 13
vapor permeability 14

vapor phase pulping 8
vapor pressure 13
vapor recompression 9
  mechanical 9
  thermal 9

vapor sizing 13
vaporsphere 21
variability 25
variable,
  dummy 25

  independent 25
variable costs 26
variable crown roll 13
variable speed drive 24
variance 25, 26
  analysis of 25

variation(s) 25
  coefficient of 25
  coherent 14
  color 14

  cross-direction 14
  machine-direction 14
  random 14
  residual 14
variation of paper properties 14

varnish 17, 19
vascular bundle 3
vascular plant 2
vascular tracheid 2
vasicentric tracheid 2

vat 13
  combination 13
  counterflow 13
  dry 13
  filter 12
  uniflow 13

vat former 13
vat lined 14
vatman 13
vat section 13

V-board 16
V-drum chipper 1
vegetable fiber 3
vegetable hairs 3
vegetable parchment 16

vehicle 17, 19
veined paper 14
velin dandy roll 13
velocity,
  critical 13

  effective migration 21
  jet 13
  migration 21
  terminal settling 20
  transport 21

velocity forming 13
vellum 16
vellum finish 14
velvet finish papers 14
veneer 1

veneer core	1
vent	24
ventilation	13
hood	13
machine room	13
mechanical	13
pocket	13
vent stack	9
Venturi scrubber	21
vermiculite	5
vertical press	13
vessel	2, 24
annular	2
code	24
impregnation	8
non-code	24
reaction	10
steaming	8
vessel element	2
vessel element extension	2
vestured pit	2
vibration	24
vibration analysis	24
vibration isolation	24
vibration test	18
vibrator	1
vibratory screen	12
vinyl dispersions	17
virgin fiber	13
virgin forest	1
virgin pulp	8
viscoelastic material	14
viscometer	17
capillary	4
rotational	17
viscometry	4
viscose rayon fiber	3
viscose solution	4
viscosity	17
cellulose	4
cupriethylenediamine	4
intrinsic	4
viscosity modifier	17
viscosity of cellulose solut'ns	4
viscosity preservative	10
viscosity-reducing bleaching	10
visual efficiency	14
vitrified bond	7
void fraction	14
voids	14, 17
void volume	1, 17
void volume (of a felt)	15
volatile	4
volatile organic solids	21
volatile solids	20
volatility	4
voltage	22
volume,	
bulk	1
loose	1

pigment	17
relative sediment	17
sediment	17
specific	11
surface void	17
throughput	20
void	1, 17
vomit stack	8
vortex	13
vortex breaker	13
vortex cleaner	12
vortex finder	12
vortex tube	24
V-press	20
vulcanized fiber	4
vulcanizing paper	16

W _____

wad burning	13
wafers	1
waffling	19
wake effect	13
wake ratio	13
walking off	19
wall,	
cell	2
end	2
membrane	9
primary	2
secondary	2
tertiary	2
tube-to-tube	9
water	9
water tube	9
wall fraction	11
wallpaper base stock	16
warehousing	13
warm colors	14
warm-up period	13
warp	14, 15
flat	15
round	15
warp-faced fabric	15
warp loom seam	15
warp-runner	15
wart	2
warty layer	2
washboarding	18
wash coating	17
wash deinking	12
washer	12
bleach	10
chip	1
dregs	9
drum displacer	12
flat band	12
flat wire	12
horizontal belt	12

lime mud	9
mud	9
pressure	12
rotary pressure	12
rotary vacuum	12
steam	9
vacuum	12
washer filtrate	12
washer room	12
washer shower	12
washing	12, 19
brown stock	12
countercurrent	12
countercurrent bleach plt.	10
crude soap	6
diffusion	12
dilution/extraction	12
displacement	12
extraction	12
high-heat	12
water	9
washing aid	12
washing efficiency	12
wash liquor	12
excess	12
wash press	12
wash roll	13
wash up	13
waste	20
converter	18
core	18
hazardous	20
industrial	20
municipal	20
outside	18
paper	18
peel	18
solid	20
toxic	20
trim	18
white	12
waste acid	10
waste energy	22
waste heat	22
waste paper	12
post-consumer	12
reclaimed	12
waste paper grades	12
waste paper recovery rate	12
waste paper utilization rate	12
wastewater	20
clarified	20
raw	20
reclaimed	20
wastewater irrigation	20
wastewater treatment	20
advanced	20
biological	20
external	20
internal	20

wastewater treatment facilities 20
water,
    back 13
    boiler 9
    boiler feed- 9

    bound 2, 11
    brackish 20
    chlorine 10
    dilution 12
    free 2, 11

    fresh 13
    gland 24
    ground- 20
    imbibed 11
    makeup 9, 13

    marine 20
    potable 20
    process 20
    raw 20
    receiving 20

    seal 24
    sorbed 11
    surface 20
    tray 13
    white 13
    wire pit 13

water absorbency 11
water analysis 20
water balance 12
water-base coating 17

water-base ink 19
water bleed fastness 14
water box 13
water cellulose 4
water-color paper 16

water cook 8
water-cooled 24
watercourse 20
    artificial 20
water creping 13

water-damaged roll 14
water drum 9
waterfall wetting 17
water finish 14
water glass 5

water immersion sizing test 14
water-ink balance 19
water intake 20
water jet slitter 13
waterleaf paper 14

water lines 14
water-logged 13
waterlogged ink 19
watermark 13
    localized 14

    shaded 13
    simulated 14
watermarking,
    impress 13
    thermal 13

water of hydration 5
water pollution 20
water quality criteria 20
water repellency 14
water resistant paper 14

water retention agent 17
water retention capacity 15
water retention value 11
water sensitivity 14
watershed 20

water softening 20
water spot 14
water table 20
water treatment 20
    external 20
    internal 20

water treatment plant 20
water tube 9
water tube boiler 9
water tube wall 9

water usage 20
water vapor 13
water wall 9
water washing 9
waveline plates 12

wave plate 12
waviness 14
wax(es) 5
    microcrystalline 5
    petroleum 5

wax coating 17
waxed papers 16
wax emulsion 5
waxing,
    cold water 18

    dry 17
    hot 17
    opaque 17
    wet 17
waxing paper 16

wax pick 14
wax picking point 14
wax size 5
wax spots 14
weak black liquor 9

weak wash 9
wear 24
    adhesive 24
    drag 15
    fabric 15
    fabric edge 15

wear plate 1
wear resistance 14
weatherability 19
weather wrinkles 14
weave 15
    duplex 15
    plain 15
    planar 15
    triplex 15

weave construction 15
weaving 14, 15
web 13, 15
    fanning-in of 19
    fanning-out of 19

    stratified 13
    stuck 14
webbing 18
web compensator 19
web content chart 14

web cooler 12
web core loss 18
web handling 13
web instability 13
web lead 19

web offset press 19
web press 19
web saw 1
web separation 13
Webster-type former 13

web tension 13
web traction 13
web transfer 13
web turnbars 17
web wrinkles 13

wedge sampling 11
weft 15
weight(s) 19
    air dry 11
    basis 14

    coat 17
    heavy 14
    molecular 4
    oven-dry 11
    raw 17

    ream 18
    stock 18
    tare 14
    uncoated 17
weighted mean 25

weightometer 1
weight tolerance 14
weir 20
weir shower 12
weld 24

weld-associated corrosion 24
welded edges 19
weld overlay 24
welts 14
    moisture 14
    winder 14

wet angle 17
wet ashing 14
wet barking 1
wet beaten 12

wet-bottom precipitator 21
wet box 13
wet broke 13
wet bulb temperature 13
wet catch 21

wet combustion	9	whiskers	17	winder welts	14
wet converting	18	whistle shower	12	winder wrinkles	14
wet coverage	17	white,		winding	13, 22
wet cracking	9	Paris	17	combining	18
wet creping	13	satin	5	convolute	18
wet curl	14	tinted	14	loose	14
wet draw	13	zinc	5	machine	13
wet edges	14	white fiber	12	reprocess	18
wet electrostatic precipitator	21	white liquor	8	shaftless	13
wet end	13	clarified	9	spiral	18
				staggered	14
wet-end additives	13	oxidized	9		
wet-end balance	13	polished	9	winding drums	13
wet-end barring	13	raw	9	wind rose	21
wet-end chemistry	5	white liquor strength	8	window (of a forming fabric)	15
wet-end finish	14	whiteness	14	windup station	13
wet felt	13	whitening	19	winnowing	1
wet fiber compactability	11	fluorescent	5	winterization	24
wet fiber flexibility	11	optical	5	wipe ratio	17
wet fluor. mag. particle test.	24	white paper	19	wiping angle	17
wet laminating	18	white pigments	5	wire	13
wetlap machine	12	white pitch	12	backing	13
wetlap pulp	12	white rot	2	conveying	13
wet-lay nonwovens	16	white waste	12	face	12
wet machine	12	white water	13	forming	13
wetness	11	lean	13	wire change	13
		rich	13		
wet oxidation	9			wire cloth	12
wet pack	13	white water consistency profile	13	wire hole	14
wet picking	19	white water loop	13	wire life	13
wet pick resistance	14	white water system	13	wire life extender	13
wet printing process	19	whiting	5	wire loading	13
wet rolling	13	whole-tree chips	1	wire mark	14
wet rot	2	whole-tree logging	1	wire part	13
wet rub resistance	14	whole tree pulping	8	wire pit	13
wet shredding	12	wicking	14	wire pit water	13
wet soak paper	14	widening	13	wire retention	13
wet steam	9	wide-nip press	13	wire return rolls	13
wet stock	11	width (of a paper roll)	13	wire side	14
wet streaks	14, 17	wild formation	14	galvanized	14
wet strength	14	wildness test	11	wire speed	13
wet-strength broke	13	winch	1	wire turning roll	13
wet-strength paper	14	wind,		witherite	5
wet-strength resins	5	prevailing	21	with the grain	18
wet-strength retention	14	resultant	21	wood	1, 2
wettability	11, 14	windage	13	barked	1
selective	19	windbox	9	compression	2
wet tensile strength	14	wind direction	18	cord-	1
wetting	11, 13	winder	13	core	2
waterfall	17	bedroll-type	13	dead	1
wetting agent	5	center	13	decadent	1
wetting shower	13	combining	18	decayed	1
wetting time	11	converting	18	diffuse-porous	2
wet trapping	19	duplex	13	diseased	1
wet-up	13	nip-type	13	drift-	1
wet waxing	17	primary	13	early-	2
wet web adhesion	13	salvage	18	energy	1
wet web saturation	13	secondary	13	farmer	1
wet web strength	11	skiver	18	fuel	1
whales	13	two-drum	13	grinding of	7
whipper	13	winder specifications	13	hard-	2
whiskering	19	winder tension control	13	heart-	2

wood *(cont)*
    intermediate 2
    juvenile 2
    late- 2
    light- 1
    long- 1

    mature 2
    nonporous 2
    ply- 1
    porous 2
    pulp- 1

    reaction 2
    resinous 2
    ring-porous 2
    rough- 1
    round- 1

    sap- 2
    short- 1
    soft- 2
    sound 1
    spring- 2

    summer- 2
    tension 2
wood composition boards 1
wood-containing paper 14
wood density 2

wood flour 1
wood-free paper 14
woodlot 1
wood pile 1
wood pulp 8

wood quality 1
wood residue 8
wood residues 1
woodroom 1
wood rosin 6

wood rot 2
wood species 2
woodstave pipe 24
wood subdivisions 1
wood substance 1

wood yard 1
wood waste boiler 9
woof 15
working face 13, 20
worminess 14

worm roll 13
worms 14
wound-in tension 13
wove dandy roll 13
wove mold 12

wove paper 14
wrap(s) 13
    angle of 13
    bakers 16
    butchers 16

    blanket 19
    body 13
    capstan 13
    cylinder 13
    fruit 16

wrap around 13
wrap curl 18
wrapper stock 12
wrapping,
    corrugated 18
    roll 13

wrapping paper 16
wrapping station 18
wrapping tissue 16
wrap-up 13

wringer press 13
wrinkle(s) 14, 15
    calender 14
    charm-flex 17
    crepe 14

    cutter 18
    dryer 13
    hard 14
    shear 13
    weather 14

    web 13
    winder 14
writing paper 16

X _____

xanthate 4
xerographic bonds 16
xylan 4
xylary fibers 2
xylem 2
xylose 4

Y _____

Yankee cylinder 13
Yankee hood 13
Yankee machine 13
    combination 13

yard 1
    concentration 1
    log 1
    reload 1
    sort 1
    wood 1

yardage 13
yarder 1
    mobile tower 1
yarding 1
yarn 15

    spun 15
    stuffer 15
yellowing 14
yellowness 14
yellow pulp 12

yield 8
    bleaching 10
    color 13
    digester 8
    digester screened 8

    high- 8
    sustained 1
yield value 17
Young's modulus 14

Z _____

zeolite 20
zero-based budgeting 26
zero correlation 25
zero defects 25
zero discharge 20

zero-span tensile strength 14
zero steam velocity point 7
zeta potential 5
zinc sulfide 5
zinc white 5

zone,
    cooking 8
    dilution 10
    heating 8
    impregnation 8

    preheating 9
    tension 18
zone agitation 12
zone-control roll 13
zone settling 20

zoogleal film 20
z-strength 14